How to Market B

Over four editions, Alison Baverstock's *How to Market Books* has established itself as the industry standard text on marketing for the publishing industry, and the go-to reference guide for professionals and students alike.

With the publishing world changing like never before, and the marketing and selling of content venturing into uncharted technological territory, this much-needed new edition seeks to highlight the role of the marketer in this rapidly changing landscape.

The new edition is thoroughly updated and offers a radical reworking and reorganisation of the previous edition, suffusing the book with references to online and digital marketing. The book maintains the accessible and supportive style of previous editions but also now offers:

- a number of new case studies;
- detailed coverage of individual market segments;
- checklists and summaries of key points;
- several new chapters;
- a foreword by Michael J. Baker, Professor Emeritus of Marketing, Strathclyde University.

Alison Baverstock is Associate Professor in the Department of Journalism and Publishing at Kingston University, where she cofounded the MA Publishing in 2006, now with an international catchment area and reputation. She is a frequent commentator in the press and broadcast media on publishing and reading, a previous recipient of the Pandora Prize for Services to Publishing and a member of the Board of Management of the Society of Authors.

Endorsements for this edition

'Marketing is an increasingly crucial part of publishing – discoverability is the buzz word - and this updated version of Alison Baverstock's guide is essential reading for anyone involved in the business. It's lucid, practical, wide-ranging and especially good on the opportunities presented by digital and self-publishing.'

– Andrew Lownie, *literary agent*

'How to Market Books is a core text for our publishing degrees. Its combination of marketing theory, publishing knowledge, and practical advice, now thoroughly updated, is an immensely helpful resource to anyone setting out on a career in publishing. It's also a great place for current publishers to go to understand and improve their own marketing activities.'

– Professor Claire Squires, *Director of the Stirling Centre for International Publishing and Communication, University of Stirling, UK*

'*How to market books* is an easily readable, well-organized, comprehensive guide to marketing. It is an excellent resource for universities offering Publishing Studies and should be on every publisher's shelf. I wish I had written it!'

– Anne Converse Willkomm MFA, *Director of Graduate Publishing at Rosemont College, USA*

'This standard work on marketing for the publishing industry has proved invaluable to students of publishing and industry professionals alike. Taking you from the marketing mix to online marketing, this book tells you what you need to know.'

– Angus Phillips, *Director, Oxford International Centre for Publishing Studies, UK*

'This is a book that offers both an immense understanding of publishing and real practical value. It's the one indispensable handbook for every publishing marketing department, every day.'

– Susannah Bowen, *Head of Marketing, Higher Education/Library, Cengage Learning, Australia*

Endorsements for the previous editions

'There is a dearth of up-to-date information about the theory and practice of book marketing. Alison Baverstock has filled the gap admirably; her book should be required reading for the novice and will provide an informative guide for the experienced practitioner.'

– *The Bookseller*

'Over the years the book has attracted innumerable compliments for its common-sense and practical information: it has appeared on reading lists everywhere, on the shelves of libraries supporting study in the field, and in small firms and departments where publishing and bookselling take place for real... It does what it says on the tin – it offers a great deal of sensible and relevant information that readers really want and need.'

– *Library Review*

'This is excellent. The clarity of the whole thing is beyond praise – let alone the gargantuan task of compilation on such a comprehensive scale. Many congratulations. It deserves to become the "bible" of the publishing industry.'

– Professor Emrys Jones, *LSE*

'The most comprehensive and useful tome on book marketing available. It is an indispensible teaching tool and guide.'

– Gian Lombardo, *Publisher-in-Residence, Emerson College USA, and Director, Quale Press*

'I think this book will be of considerable interest to authors, as it brings together a good deal of information from different areas in the trade to which authors rarely have access. Most authors have contact only with their editor...and have no idea what goes on in the rest of the organisation.'

– Margaret Drabble, *author*

How to Market Books

Fifth edition

Alison Baverstock

Routledge
Taylor & Francis Group

LONDON AND NEW YORK

Fifth edition published 2015
by Routledge
2 Park Square, Milton Park, Abingdon, OX14 4RN

and by Routledge
711 Third Avenue, New York, NY 10017

Routledge is an imprint of the Taylor & Francis Group, an informa business

First edition published 1990 by Kogan Page
Fourth edition published 2008 by Kogan Page

British Library Cataloguing in Publication Data
A catalogue record for this book is available from the British Library

Library of Congress Cataloging in Publication Data
A catalog record for this book has been requested

ISBN13: 978-0-415-72746-4 (hbk)
ISBN13: 978-0-415-72758-7 (pbk)
ISBN13: 978-1-315-76183-1 (ebk)

Typeset in Galliard
by Taylor & Francis Books

Printed and bound in Great Britain by
TJ International Ltd, Padstow, Cornwall

For Harriet Clara Alice
who has lived with this book all her life

Contents

List of illustrations   xii
Author's foreword and acknowledgements   xiv
Foreword: Professor Emeritus Michael J. Baker,
University of Strathclyde, UK   xix

PART I
General principles and understanding   1

1   Marketing and marketing in publishing   3
    The meaning of marketing   5
    What marketing means in publishing   6
    Checklists for achieving good marketing   8
    Segmenting, targeting and positioning   13
    Branding   16
    Integrated marketing communications (IMC)   17
    Relationship marketing   18

2   What's for sale?   22
    Roles and situations in which content might be marketed   23
    Where the marketing and selling of publishing content goes on   34
    Who is involved in marketing?   36

3   Understanding the market: market research and other
    sources of market information   44
    Defining terms: market insight, insight hypothesis, market
        intelligence and market research   46
    Secondary and primary research   48
    How to commission market research   52
    Syndicated market research within the publishing industry   53
    Examples of how market research might get used in a
        publishing context   57

4   Profit, loss and accountability   61
Drawing up a budget   62
How a budget is divided up   62
How do you set a budget?   64
Sample costings for publishing products and services   68
When to spend a budget   72
How to monitor a budget   73
How to make a budget go further   74
Managing cash flow   78
*Securing sponsorship, partnerships and other methods of financial
    support   79*
Hanging on to a marketing budget   81

PART II
Putting this into practice   91

5   'The medium is the message'   93
*Important information before you start – to ensure your market
    can find you   94*
Different formats for marketing information   95
Advance information   96
A website entry   99
Jacket/cover copy   100
Catalogues   103
Leaflets and flyers   106
Posters, showcards and point of sale   109
Space advertising   109
Telesales campaigns   111
Radio, television and cinema advertising   112

6   How to write a marketing plan   113
Introduction   113
Coming up with a plan   114
What have we got to sell? Researching the product   115
Who is it for? Researching the market   118
What benefits does the product/service offer your market?   120
Initial situation analysis: where are we now?   120
Establishing objectives: what do we want to achieve?   123
Developing a strategy: how will we get there, in broad terms?   124
Formulating a plan: how will we get there, in detail?   124
Marketing basics   124
Developing marketing plans for individual titles   126
Allocating a budget: how much will it cost?   129
Communicating the plan to others   130
Motivating the implementation of the plan   131

Evaluating results   131
A final checklist for marketing plans   132

7 **Selling**   144
   Influences on individual buyer behaviour   146
   Selling to individuals   148
   Top tips for effective sales communication   150
   How selling works in a publishing context   152

8 **Direct marketing**   170
   Why the principles of direct marketing matter to publishers   171
   The essentials for a direct marketing campaign   172
   Plans   173
   The audience   174
   Offers   175
   The most appropriate medium for direct marketing   175
   Timing   176
   The copy platform   177
   Response devices   183
   Design services   188
   System of despatch   188
   Monitoring effectiveness   189
   Fulfilment services   191
   Telemarketing   193
   A final checklist for all forms of direct marketing   195

9 **Online marketing**   206
   Core principles for marketing online   208
   Specific advice for particular online media   215
   Websites   215
   Blogging   224
   Email   229
   Social media: Facebook   236
   LinkedIn   238
   Twitter   242
   Author involvement online   248

10 **Publicity and PR**   257
   The practicalities of dealing with the media   258
   The recipient – understanding journalists   260
   The role of the press release   263
   Offering an exclusive   268
   Review lists   269
   Literary editors   271
   Inspection copies   273

Author interviews 273
How to sell ideas to journalists by email and telephone 276

11 Working with authors and other vital partnerships　　283
Authors 283
How to work well with authors 287
Working with authors who have previously self-published 288
Working with other industry suppliers 292
Working with publishing colleagues 293
Working with individual freelance staff 295
Temporary staff on work placement or work experience 296

**12 Organising events, presentations and other opportunities
to share content**　　297
Ten top tips for preparing for events 297
Organisational meetings 300
Sales conferences 300
Promotional parties and title launches 302
Press conferences 305
Author tours, literary festivals and signing sessions 305
Exhibitions 311
Awards and literary prizes 311

13 Techniques for writing effective copy　　316
What is copywriting? 316
Six basic principles 318
Acronyms for copywriters 320
Further techniques for effective copywriting 324
Other ideas for attracting attention 334
Writing headlines 335
Writing copy for titles you do not understand 337
Disentangling long and difficult blurbs 337
Presenting and defending your copy 340

14 The layout and dissemination of marketing materials　　342
Design 342
What is good design? 343
How promotional text gets read 343
How to find a designer 344
How to work effectively with a designer 346
How a design job progresses 350
How to proofread text 351
Managing without a designer 352
Getting material printed 354
How to request an estimate from a printer 355

PART III
Specific advice for particular markets   359

15 **Approaching specific interest markets: the value and
   significance of the niche in publishing**   361
   Finding the general reader 363
   Marketing children's books 369
   Opportunities for children's publishers today 370
   Key difficulties for those marketing children's titles 374
   Marketing techniques for promoting children's titles 376
   Selling resources to public libraries 378
   How to send information to public libraries 380
   Public lending right 383
   Promoting to university academics 385
   Promoting textbooks to the academic market 389
   Summary books and study aids 391
   Research monographs 392
   Professional resources 392
   Selling to academic libraries 392
   Selling to educational markets 396
   How to reach the market 403
   Selling educational material to international markets 409
   Marketing to doctors and other healthcare professionals 410
   How to communicate effectively with doctors 411
   When is the best time to promote to doctors? 416
   Other opportunities for publishers in this area 417
   The role of medical librarians 421
   Selling to professional and industrial markets 422
   Important information for approaching professional markets 422
   Format of published and marketing material 425

   Glossary   429
   Appendix   449
   Bibliography   455
   Index   459

List of illustrations

Figures

2.1 The changing balance of income streams is reflected in table 2.1 and these two pie diagrams, which compare the different sources of income for BMJ in (a) 2007 and (b) 2013. Courtesy of BMJ   35

3.1 Discovery of books bought: volume, 2013. Data courtesy of Nielsen Book Services [trading as Nielsen BookData]. Layout and presentation courtesy of Nielsen Book Services [trading as Books & Consumers]   54

3.2 Purchase influences: volume, 2013. Data courtesy of Nielsen Book Services [trading as Nielsen BookData]. Layout and presentation courtesy of Nielsen Book Services [trading as Books & Consumers]   55

3.3 Buyer demographics: volume, 2013. Data courtesy of Nielsen Book Services [trading as Nielsen BookData]. Layout and presentation courtesy of Nielsen Book Services [trading as Books & Consumers]   55

3.4 Buyer weight of book purchase: volume, 2013. Data courtesy of Nielsen Book Services [trading as Nielsen BookData]. Layout and presentation courtesy of Nielsen Book Services [trading as Books & Consumers]   55

5.1 A sample academic flyer. Courtesy of Routledge/Taylor & Francis Group Limited   107

5.2 A dump-bin for Enid Blyton titles, shown both front- and side-on. Courtesy of Hachette Children's Publishing   110

6.1 Figure showing onion skin model of a product's benefits: core benefit, actual benefit, augmented benefit; adapted from Stokes and Lomax (2008: 221). Courtesy of Cengage   120

6.2 Figure showing how micro and macro fit together; adapted from Stokes and Lomax (2008: 38). Courtesy of Cengage   121

6.3 SWOT analysis diagram for a new fiction imprint   122

6.4 Cover for *Inside Book Publishing*, fifth edition. Courtesy of Routledge/Taylor & Francis Group Limited   133

7.1   Analytical thinking/practical thinking/relational thinking/
      experimental thinking diagram. Courtesy of Miradorus   149
8.1   Mailing results for a recent Reading Force marketing campaign.
      Courtesy of Reading Force   203
9.1   BookMachine website. Courtesy of BookMachine   217
9.2   Kingston University Publishing blog. Courtesy of Kingston
      University   226
9.3   Sample from Jessica Palmer's email newsletter. Courtesy of Jessica
      Palmer   235
9.4   CompletelyNovel Facebook page. Courtesy of CompletelyNovel 241
9.5   HarperCollins Game of Thrones tweet. Courtesy of HarperCollins 247
10.1 Diagram of how a press release can be effectively structured 265
10.2 Sample press release for *Mandela: My Prisoner, My Friend* by
      Christo Brand. Courtesy of John Blake/Midas PR   266
11.1 Picture of Kit Berry alongside her husband and fans at a book
      signing event in Glastonbury promoting the final Stonewylde book.
      Reproduced with kind permission of Kit Berry   292
13.1 Flyer for lawn-mowing service   323
13.2 *Winnie the Witch*'s cat Wilbur is sufficiently recognisable to be
      useful to his publisher OUP in various capacities, from featuring in
      marketing materials to becoming the star of new titles (he has now
      featured in a range of first concept board books). His creators are
      author Valerie Thomas and illustrator Korky Paul. Courtesy of
      Oxford University Press   334
13.3 Cornelia Parker, *Cold Dark Matter: An Exploded View*, 1991.
      Courtesy of the artist and Frith Street Gallery, London   338
15.1 The Society of Authors' old logo. Courtesy of the Society of
      Authors   369
15.2 The Society of Authors' new logo. Courtesy of the Society of
      Authors   369

Tables

2.1   The changing balance of income streams is reflected here and in
      figure 2.1, which compares the different sources of income for BMJ
      in 2007 and 2013. Courtesy of BMJ   34
4.1   Sample costings for publishing products and services   69
6.1   Table of marketing plan recommendations. Courtesy of Samantha
      Perkins   138

Author's foreword and acknowledgements

This book began in 1989, as a delegate handout for marketing courses being offered by the Publishing Training Centre at Book House in London, but quickly became a compendium of things I wished I had known when I began in the industry. I kept writing and soon had a contents list and several chapters of a book, which Kogan Page promptly agreed to publish. The deadline was provided by pregnancy and our daughter Harriet (named after Dorothy L. Sayers' heroine) timed her arrival perfectly. I completed the manuscript 4 days before she was born. As she arrived on a Friday, I framed – and hung on her wall – the front cover of the edition of *The Bookseller* that carried her date of birth (and there it stayed until adolescence meant all parental choices were reconsidered).

My guiding principle from the start was to include everything I would like to have known when I began work as a publisher; to set down a checklist of possible types of marketing activity that should be considered whatever the format or subject area of the list being promoted. In those days marketing staff were relatively new arrivals at the boardroom table (publishing houses had long had departments of Publicity and Sales, but not Marketing), and having spent a lot of time reinventing the wheel, finding out how to do things for which it turned out there were already established processes – just not generally known ones – it was pleasing to see it all set down in print. Given the enormous output of the publishing industry, it's been an ongoing irony that it has in general reflected so little on itself.

The launch of the book was timely, as it coincided with the wider establishment of Publishing Studies within universities. The book was quickly adopted by a range of such courses being offered within higher education, one of which I cofounded at Kingston University in 2006, with others now established throughout the world. Mind you, your work becoming a set book, and in the process achieving the status of a proper noun, means you are quoted in student essays and research projects – and therefore widely assumed to be dead.

The book went on to be widely translated – rights to 15 different language editions have been sold – and this new edition has been consciously written as an international guide. I am convinced that the same problems and issues face publishers wherever they are located.

I have updated the book at regular intervals (this is the fifth edition, sixth if you count a reprint with revisions in 1993) but probably more has happened in the past 5 years than in the previous 25, or some would say previous 250+. But at times of great change it's worth slowing down, isolating the theory behind practice and looking back for guidance on how previous generations solved problems – rather than just focusing on the dazzling range of options ahead.

For example, just because social media makes it possible to communicate within seconds, does not mean that we routinely should; there is a big difference between gaining 'attention' and 'approval', and communicating without thinking risks undermining your overall brand. I maintain that the principles of direct marketing remain a really solid basis for thinking about effective communication with a market in general, whether online or in person (think about the market and the problems or needs they have before you do anything; consider the brand you are trying to communicate and what you want them to do as a result of hearing from you; test your hunches before you commit to widespread rollout). Along similar lines, self-publishing is not necessarily a shortcut to the effective communication of content – the processes that exist for making content instantly available do not automatically ensure that it is easy to read. Self-publishing needs all the same stages as those required in the more conventional management of materials. If these are well handled, the outputs can be indistinguishable from those of the traditional industry, but much of the enthusiasm expressed for an unmediated route to readers reveals how poorly the value traditional publishers add to the process of making content available has been understood. If the outputs are to be replicated, and the reader's time valued, then similar systems need to be put in place, however they are resourced. An understanding of the value added by publishers, and how this is achieved, is vital if the industry is to avoid being sidelined as a useful, indeed admirable – but otherwise dispensable – process; managed by experts and studied in evening classes, perhaps like calligraphy.

Another interesting aspect of the publishing world today is the blurring of roles – the former distinct camps of agents, publishers, booksellers and authors, through whose sequential hands content travelled, are now variously combined. All are now actively involved in the publishing process; sometimes in combination, sometimes not. But whether or not a publishing journey is still mediated through all these stages, or takes place at its most direct (from author to reader), clear communication is vital. And when, as so often happens today, marketing copy is repeatedly forwarded from one group of stakeholders to the next, ensuring the words effectively represent the product or service at the centre of it all is of vital importance. Personally, when I have no other way of judging the accuracy of a claim that new content should have my attention, I generally rely on my speedy assessment of the literacy of the person writing the description – so long-established skills such as effective copywriting are still hugely important.

During my time in publishing, the industry has of course changed, and so has the significance of marketing – or perhaps the growing significance of marketing has been a key driver of change. Marketing has moved from being an area accepted slightly grudgingly, and definitely endowed with much less prestige than editorial, to becoming a central part of the publishing process – significantly today many chief executives of publishing companies come from a marketing background.

Along the way marketing has been variously redefined and reshaped, sometimes oversimplified and sometimes overcomplicated. It's also regularly inspired, providing the dynamic language of publishing's fast-developing future. As Charlie Redmayne, chief executive officer of HarperCollins UK, told the FutureBook Conference in November 2013:

> In a world where content is only discovered in two ways (by people looking for it or people recommending it), the core marketing skills can be reduced to just two: knowing how to manipulate search and understanding how to use social media.

But this beguilingly simple statement turned out to be based on a well-built scaffold of marketing theory and extensive practice.

> Of course the best way to get to grips with both search and social media is to look at the data: what do people search for? When? Which posts or tweets get the most likes or shares? What factors influence that?[1]

> Redmayne, and the conference as a whole, placed a huge emphasis on collecting and using customer data, whether as part of what marketing activity to undertake, when to target people or how to set prices. The idea was posed that prices too should be based on data and that *free* could be a realistic permanent model for some books/content, as part of building a customer base to whom you can then sell other content.[2]

Peel back the radical language and a series of strong marketing principles emerge: the importance of identifying and segmenting markets; studying their operation; understanding the external and internal influencing factors and hence establishing which marketing strategies are most likely to be successful; which combination of the promotional mix is likely to work and which positioning statement has most effect. And then how to build on this growing understanding with future planned activity.

I hope to follow a similar pattern: to build a firm structure based on an appreciation of marketing theory and practice, within an exploration of both societal and industrial context, which can then support the development of subsequent creative and speculative deconstruction; in the same way that those learning a musical instrument must learn the basics before they improvise.

Publishing has traditionally been rather averse to marketing theory, but with an increasing stream of those who have taken up Publishing Studies at a university entering the industry, who have in the process been required to engage with the principles of marketing, analysis and critical thinking, it's a sound place to begin. Innovation and radical thinking are not only firmly on the marketing agenda, they are also essential to the industry's future. If all we teach the next generation is how to replicate what has been done in the past, we are making it more difficult for them to approach the issues we are grappling with right now – and they will go on to face on their own.

I am delighted this book continues to fill a need. Its updating has relied heavily on various friends and colleagues who have kindly commented on sections. In particular I would like to thank Ishfaq Ahmad, David Aldulaimi, Wendy Allen, Fiona Allison, Deborah Anderson, Veronica Angel, Florence Ascoli, Peter Ashman, Laura Austin, Oscar Balla, Alberto Barraclough, Michael Bartlett, Jacqui Bass, Sarah Baxter, John Beale, Kit Berry, Carole Blake, Johnnie Boden, Steve Bohme, Elaine Boorman, Susannah Bowen, Susan Brent, Hugh Bulford, Graham Bulpitt, James Carey, Rowena Carey, Steve Carey, Irene Chalmers, Tom Chalmers, Jill Chapman, John Cheshire, Jane Cholmeley, Sheila Christie, Chris Chrystal, Christian Ciullo, Lisa Ciullo, Desmond Clarke, Genevieve Clarke, Chris Cleave, Mark Coker, Mike Coleman, Tracey Cooke, Wendy Cope, Debbie Cox, Sarah Crawford, Robert Creffield, Bill Crofts, Gill Cronin, Justine Crowe, Susan Curran, Susan Curtis-Kogakovic, Cathy Dale, Claire Daly, John Davey, Roy Davey, John Davies, Simone Davies, Eela Devani, Michael de Souza, Anne Dolamore, Nigel Dollin, Cathy Douglas, Philip Downer, John Downham, Margaret Drabble, Richard Duguid, Nancy Dull, David Dutton, Linda Ellery, James Ellor, Mike Esplen, Anna Faherty, Lorraine Fanin, Anne Fanning, Sue Farmer, Tim Farmiloe, Jon Finch, Frank Fishwick, Lindsay Fraser, Clare Freda, Margaret French, Martha Fumagalli, Anna Ganley, Alex Gibson, Philip Giorgi, Tim Godfray, Dave Golding, Hattie Gordon, Gillian Green, Stephen Hancocks, Holly Hardy, Lizzie Harper, Brian Harper-Lewis, Helen Hart, Per Henningsgaard, Jo Henry, Alan Hill, Jean Hindmarch, Caroline Hird, Talitha Hitchcock, Clare Hodder, Heather Holden-Brown, Steve Holland, Barbara Horn, Alastair Horne, Jo Howard-Brown, Kelly Howe, Robert Howells, Jeanette Hull, Matthew Hunt, Matthew Huntley, John and Kate Hybert, Louis Ingram, Amy Irvine, Ian Jacobs, Jan Jacobs, Liz James, Felicity Jenkins, Ram Jeyaratnam, Paula Johnson, Robert Johnson, Emrys Jones, Nicholas Jones, Paul Jones, Sue Jones, Irene Jordan, Lucy Juckes, Sarah Juckes, Simon Juden, Kavitasagary Karunasaagarar, Elizabeth Katay, Louise Kaye, Barrie Kempthorne, Jo Kennedy, Ruth Killick, Rob Langley, Clive Leatherdale, Tom Lee, Helen Leech, Anna Lewis, David Lindley, June Lines, Simon Littlewood, Tammy Livermore, Catherine Lockerbie, Katy Loffman, Wendy Lomax, Gian Lombardo, Dot Lubianska, Tory Lyne-Purkis, Simon McArt, Christine McAuley, Finbarr McCabe, James McCall, Jo McCrum, Ben McDaniel, Hamish McGibbon, Sheila McGlassen, Peter McKay, Robert McKay, Miranda McKearney, Ursula Mackenzie, Sally McKinnel, Sarah McNally, Hilary Mantel, Nicholas Masucci, Jane Mays, Alice Meadows, David Meerman Scott, John Merriman, Peter and Jean Milford, Sue Miller, Roger Millington, Godfrey M'Kandawire, Richard Mollet, Craig Mollison, Carol Monyios, Tony Mulliken, Katherine Naish, Mary Lou Nash, Victoria Nash, Mary Nettlefold, Kingsley Norton, Alice Noyes, Orna O'Brien, Pamela Oldfield, Chris Oliver, Ayo Onatade, Bob Osborne, Stephen Page, Ben Palmer, Jessica Palmer, Keith Palmer, John Park, James Parker, Madeleine Parkyn, Dharm Patel, Janette Paterson, Jeremy Paxman, John Peacock, Jane Pembroke, Samantha Perkins, Brian Perman, Anton Pfeiler, Jerome Phalippou, Angus Phillips, Chris Phillips, Kate Pool, Jane Potter, Jenny Powell, Alison Price, Joanna Prior, John Purefoy, Nicholas Purser, Margaret Radbourne, Sue Ramin, Deborah

Rea, Charlie Redmayne, Jon Reed, Sarah Rees Brennan, James Rennoldson, Kimberley Reynolds, Joel Rickett, Jennifer Rigby, Julian Rivers, David Roche, Dieter Roeschel, David Rogers, Joan Rutherford, Katie Sadler, Julia Sandford-Cooke, Helen Savill, Pippa Scoones, Gerald Scott, Allan Shanks, Mo Siewcharran, Zach Simmons, Barbara Singh, Susan Skipwith, Liz Small, Alan Smith, Dag Smith, Sarah Smyth, Nicola Solomon, Clare Somerville, Jane Spiers, Dominic Steinitz, Jackie Steinitz, Jillian Stewart, Andrew Sullivan, Laura Summers, Jane Tatam, Graham Taylor, Ian Taylor, David Teale, Mark Thwaite, Jonathan Tilston, Sara Tricker, Katherine Tozeland, Richard Tudor, Susan Turret, Jo van der Borgh, Sharan Wadhwani, Mark Waite, John Walsh, Philip Walters, David Walton, Hilary Wason, Judith Watts, Fay Weldon, Andrew Welham, Andrea Whiting, Laura Whitton, Louise Willder, Tom Williams, Howard Willows, Kate Wilson, John Winkler, Wendy Woodley, Mark Wray and Martin Wyn-Jones.

With this fifth edition the book moves to new publishers, joining the distinguished Publishing Studies list of Routledge, part of the Taylor & Francis Group, and particular thanks are due to Niall Kennedy, Eleanor Pike, Andrew Watts, Stacey Carter, Eric Rose, Michael King and Petra Bryce. I would, however, like to thank its previous guardians, Kogan Page, as well as my colleagues at Kingston University and my family who have been encouraging and patient throughout.

I would particularly like to thank Michael J. Baker, Professor Emeritus of Marketing at Strathclyde University who has written the foreword to this latest edition. Asking him to fulfil this role completed a very satisfying circle for me. The first edition of this book was written by a graduate of Mediaeval History and Fine Arts, whose understanding of marketing was based on extensive practice and (largely his) textbooks. As my alma mater at that time lacked a Department of Marketing, I boldly wrote to him at the University of Strathclyde, asking if he could recommend a colleague who might be willing to cast an eye over my material, to ensure I had not made any obvious errors. I can only admire the immense generosity with which he speedily wrote back, taking on the task himself and offering insightful feedback – and of course, in the process, affirmation. Given that I was not at the time working at a university, let alone his, this was unexpected – but entirely consistent with his determination to develop the discipline he has done so much to build. As you can imagine, I was delighted when he agreed to write the foreword to this edition.

Today the field of Publishing Studies is the new kid on the academic block, and I hope my approach to its development, as a valid way of enriching our understanding of processes and practice, can be similarly outward-looking and encouraging.

The final note of thanks should however go to my eldest son Alasdair for his proofreading and ironic commentary – along with a reminder that you really can start a sentence with 'and' (see Genesis chapter 2).

Notes

1 Charlie Redmayne, speaking at FutureBook Conference, 2013.
2 Anna Faherty, senior lecturer, MA Publishing, Kingston University, reporting on FutureBook Conference, 2013.

Foreword

Professor Emeritus Michael J. Baker, University of Strathclyde, UK

Strathclyde University was the first in Britain to offer a full range of degrees – undergraduate, postgraduate and doctoral – in the subject of Marketing, so recognising its status as an established and accepted academic discipline, enjoyed since the beginning of the twentieth century in the USA. As its founding professor, I needed to be thick-skinned to ignore the criticisms from others who doubted its introduction into the curriculum, but also evangelical to promote its claims for recognition. It was for this reason that I welcomed an approach from a graduate in Mediaeval History and Fine Arts for some advice on a proposed book for members of the publishing profession. Then, as now, this is a profession extensively populated by highly intelligent persons with literary rather than commercial interests and I was more than happy to offer some comments and advice on the proposal to help promote the cause. So, more than 20 years later, to be invited to write a brief introduction to a new fifth edition of this book is indeed a privilege.

For any book to remain continuously in print for such a long time is a testament to its real worth. For it to justify the preparation of a fifth edition is a clear indication that it addresses an important topic or issue undergoing rapid change and development, as evidenced by the addition of five completely new chapters compared with the previous fourth edition. As an author myself, currently in the process of putting the finishing touches to a new fifth edition of *Marketing Strategy and Management*, first published in 1985, I am very conscious of the changes that have occurred in the marketing discipline over this period and these have been incorporated into this new edition. More importantly, the potential impact of these changes has been adapted to meet the needs of the publishing profession.

In her introductory chapter, Alison is generous in acknowledging some of the original advice that I gave her. Specifically, she distilled my comments into four essential requirements for effective marketing:

1 Developing a customer orientation.
2 Taking a long perspective and proceeding logically.
3 Promoting organisational integration as a business philosophy.
4 Innovating and being flexible.

Today, in my view, these remain the essential principles that underpin successful marketing practice. However, explaining and elaborating these principles result in introductory marketing textbooks some of which are more than 1,000 pages long! While this may be appropriate for persons wishing to get an overview of the discipline as a whole, it lacks the focus that is required when seeking advice on how to proceed in a specific context or market. Indeed, one of the maxims of marketing is: 'Marketing problems are situation specific.' In other words, because exchange involves the interaction of two or more parties, it is fundamental that one begin by establishing what it is that they expect of each other. Only by doing so can one achieve the objective of 'creating and maintaining a mutually beneficial relationship', which happens to be my own definition of marketing that I still subscribe to more than 40 years after I first articulated it. It follows that whatever it is you wish to accomplish you must start with a clear understanding and definition of what it is that the other party to the exchange is looking for. Once you have this then you can decide whether you have the capability to satisfy this need in a way that will also be beneficial to yourself. In the case of publishing this requires acceptance of three vital propositions spelt out in the opening chapter, namely:

1 First, the publishing industry is a business, and if it is to survive it must either make a profit, or find funding from elsewhere.
2 Second, books (or any published content) compete for spending power against a whole range of products, not just other books.
3 Third, marketing is complex.

Provided that you accept the first two propositions, this book will help you to reduce the complexity by focusing on those aspects of marketing that are particularly important and relevant for publishers. More to the point, unlike many academics who mistake the use of complicated language for erudition, Dr Baverstock's prose is a model of clarity and easy to follow. The book's ability to engage the reader and hold their attention is amply confirmed by the many endorsements of it, its adoption as a 'set book' on specialist publishing courses, and the fact that it has been translated into 15 different languages. (If you are an author you should also read *Marketing Your Book* (2007), as should publishers, as this will give you considerable insight into the different perspectives of both the publishing profession and its principal suppliers.)

Early in my academic career, members of the Marketing Education Group (now the Academy of Marketing) charged me with the responsibility of organising a dedicated journal in which they might publish the findings of their research. Despite enjoying excellent relations with several major publishers, none of them felt this to be an attractive opportunity. In desperation the poacher turned gamekeeper and I set up a small publishing company of my own as a vehicle to publish the *Journal of Marketing Management*, which is now in its thirtieth year. Given its success, *JMM* requires the marketing, production and distribution expertise of a major publishing company and these are provided by Routledge. However,

Westburn still publishes three other journals and I look forward to using the insights and advice to be found in this book to ensure their future success in an increasingly competitive marketplace. So, in conclusion I can only reiterate the comment made by Martin Nield, then chief executive of Hodder & Stoughton, in his introduction to the previous edition: '[This book] should be required reading ... for anyone wishing to enter or understand publishing.' To which I would add 'and for anyone else who is interested in what is involved in getting published'.

Michael J. Baker
June 2014

Part I

General principles and understanding

1 Marketing and marketing in publishing

The meaning of marketing 5
What marketing means in publishing 6
Checklists for achieving good marketing 8
Segmenting, targeting and positioning 13
Branding 16
Integrated marketing communications 17
Relationship marketing 18

The relationship between the publishing industry and marketing has long been ambivalent. The industry's products and services can be isolated as 'public goods', supporting literacy and culture, but how that relationship is to be funded, if it is to continue, needs firm consideration. It is a frequent comment that today's publishing industry is driven by marketing; decisions about what to publish and the quality of content are subsumed into overriding concerns about whether or not material will sell. All stakeholders in the process – authors, agents, publishers, retailers and wholesalers – are looking for markets with a need for content and a corresponding ability either to arrange funding or pay, and for which resources can be developed, marketed and sold.

We will get into the detail of what marketing is and how it works (both generally and within publishing) shortly, but before going any further it's helpful to highlight three very important issues.

- First, the publishing industry is a business, and if it is to survive it must either make a profit, or find funding from elsewhere

Sir Stanley Unwin's famous comment that the first duty of a publisher is to remain solvent[1] is worth remembering in this context: if you publish material that is esteemed but does not sell, or sells but does not prompt a desire within the market to buy from you again in future, unless you have significant personal or external funding, you are unlikely to stay in business and hence be able to publish again in future. Successful publishing houses spread their risk by offering a range of materials, established and new, and for a range of markets, just as stockbrokers hedge their bets by diversifying their purchases across market sectors, enabling vulnerabilities in individual markets to be offset against each other.

While there are many good reasons for finalising content that do not involve its subsequent presentation and sale – family or organisational histories, personal reflections, picture books of holidays – this book is predicated on an understanding that the reader is motivated by a desire to market and sell material.

- Second, books (or any published content) compete for spending power against a whole range of products, not just other books

A manager may select an online consultancy service rather than an expensive reference work; a windsurfing enthusiast may find a short film on YouTube preferable to buying a book on the subject; a school principal may decide to commission a promotional film about the institution rather than spend money on publishers' teaching resources. And the amount of advertising competing for our attention and trying to direct our pattern of expenditure is enormous. By 2015 it is estimated that the total spend on advertising will be more than £20 billion in the UK, and US$600 billion worldwide.[2]

- Third, marketing is much more complicated than it looks

Marketing at its most effective appears simple: the slogan so appropriate that it is instantly memorable; the email that makes a product sound such a specific and personal match for individual needs that the recipient responds immediately. Making sweeping generalisations about how this is achieved is similarly popular – 'all you need is Facebook and a good headline' and the job is done. In reality this simplicity is not easily achieved; the marketing processes and the creation of effective marketing materials are much more complex. Effective marketing depends on a deep understanding of the chosen market and product, within the context of contemporary society and the available resources, and effective management of marketing tends to emerge through detailed research and planning rather than formulaic application of rules.

Whereas marketing may operate in an atmosphere of frenzy and participants may feel that simply by being busy they are fulfilling their goals, in practice the habit of planning marketing strategies – aims and objectives – is important to acquire. Drawing up a marketing plan acts as a mind-focusing exercise, encouraging clarity of thought and helping you prioritise. And, of course, carefully planned campaigns stand a very much better chance of achieving their goals. Remember too that effective marketing planning is vital in *acquiring* as well as selling published content. Agents or authors offering titles to prospective publishers will place considerable importance on suitor companies' various abilities to present (and deliver) coherent marketing plans.

Mike Markkula wrote his (marketing) principles in a one page paper titled: 'The Apple Marketing Philosophy' that stressed three points. The first was empathy, an intimate connection with the feelings of the customer: 'We will truly understand their needs better than any other company.' The second was focus: 'In order to do a good job of those things that we decide to do, we must eliminate all of the unimportant opportunities.' The third and equally important principle, awkwardly named, was impute. It emphasised that people form an opinion about a company or product based on the signals that it conveys. 'People DO judge a book by its cover', he wrote. We may have the best product, the highest quality, the most useful software etc.; if we present them in a slipshod manner, they will be perceived as slipshod; if we present them in a creative, professional manner, we will impute the desired qualities.[3]

The meaning of marketing[4]

Broadly defined, marketing is a social and managerial process by which individuals and organisations obtain what they need and want through creating and exchanging products and value with others.

(Kotler et al 2013: 5)

This is one of the shorter definitions of marketing in circulation. Some are based on a series of present participles ('informing', 'advertising', 'selling') that relate to stages or techniques, others use a range of nouns ('wants', 'demands', 'products', 'markets') and link them with a series of abstract nouns ('satisfaction', 'exchange', 'fulfilment'). Each marketing trailblazer has their own personal philosophy (and vocabulary to describe it). Even academics teaching and studying the subject cannot agree and a paper seeking to define the problem came up with more than 50 definitions.[5]

The reason for this diversity of meaning is that marketing is both a management philosophy and a function in an organisation. As a philosophy it insists that an organisation is focussed on the needs of customers. As a function, it includes activities which affect customers such as pricing, advertising, selling and market research.

(Stokes and Lomax 2008)

But boil down all the seminal texts and jargon and you are left with a relatively simple concept: marketing means effective selling; meeting customer needs profitably. So if marketing appears in your job title, it means you are involved with presenting and selling what your company produces. Whether or not you count the cash, you help prepare customers to part with their money and, in the longer term, to remain satisfied with the transaction – and hopefully return to buy again from you in future.

What marketing means in publishing

Marketing in publishing has a more recent history; in the past 30 years there has been a complete revolution. Thirty years ago some firms had only Publicity Departments – and no formal marketing responsibilities; marketing activity was generally product-orientated rather than market-orientated (commission products and then think about whom to sell them to rather than base commissioning decisions on what markets want and need). Today the marketing function is ubiquitous and of rising significance: publishing companies used to be run by editors; today they are largely run by marketers. There has also been an accompanying, and significant, cultural change, with an industry formerly characterised as one run by gentlemen opening up to the realities of business, including the social connotations of involvement in trade. The merits of this are debated. Some argue that high editorial standards are being sacrificed as firms spend ever-increasing amounts on pushing the product, irrespective of its merits. Others, that the money made from mass market titles and celebrity autobiographies has an important role to play in widening involvement in literacy and providing the profits that can be invested in new writing.

What you are up against

How many titles are published worldwide each year? This is a deceptively simple question with some very complicated answers.

If the latest Wilbur Smith gets translated into 50 languages, is that 50 titles or just one? If a book comes out as a hardback, then a trade paperback, then a B format paperback, then an A format paperback, each with a different ISBN, is that one title or two or four? What about the export edition or the airside edition (sold in duty-free bookshops at airports)? There are print-on-demand (POD) titles: some are new books, some are old books prevented from going out of print by going POD (with an old or new ISBN, depending on the status).[6] And then there are ebooks. An ebook may be available in ten different e-formats, but is that one book or ten – or is it none because it is available as a printed book and counted as that? What about novels disseminated as podcasts or as text messages straight to your mobile? Looking away from print, how should you count audiobooks, whether as downloads or physically formatted items?

Even if there is no consensus, a working total is useful. Nielsen Book estimates that there were 184,435 English language titles published in the UK in 2013 (a combined total of books published with an ISBN in printed format, ebooks and self-published ebooks).

Within the world as a whole, the total of English language titles published in 2013 rises to 1.8 million, of which 1.4 million were published in the US. And this is not counting the non-English-speaking world, of which China is the largest domestic market.

Also complicating the picture are the rapidly increasing number of titles being self-published, whether by the author or one of the self-publishing servicing companies that are growing in number. Those with an ISBN are counted in the figures above, but it is difficult to estimate the number of titles circulated without an ISBN but that nevertheless impact on the amount of reading material available to the public and competing for their attention – and which may make them more resistant to buying at full publisher price (or, if badly presented, more resistant to reading in general):

> Romance and literary fiction have helped drive the number of US books self-published in hard copy up to 234,931, an increase of 59% compared to 2011.
>
> Research by the book data company Bowker, which counts all the ISBN numbers issued to self-published works, suggests that electronic titles bring the total for US self-publishing up to 391,000. This figure – which does not include titles published without an ISBN and may include some electronic editions of books also published in hard copy – represents a 59% increase on 2011's total and compares with 301,642 produced in hard copy by traditional publishers in the US. No figures are available for the number of ebooks issued by traditional publishers in the US.[7]

In short, there are no available numbers – or, to put it another way, there are too many. Google your question and you get lots of interesting leads. One thing is universally accepted to be true: the number of books published (however you define it) increases every year.

An understanding of the breadth of the market should help you to guard against complacency. Having seen a forthcoming title on the publication schedule, it may feel very familiar to you – but there is no reason why the retailer or consumer should be equally knowledgeable. Cross-check your enthusiasm with an understanding of Maslow's hierarchy of needs[8] – using his scale that ranges from physiological to self-actualisation, just how important are these products? And if you want instantly convincing proof of how much material is jostling for the attention of potential purchasers, look online at the ranking numbers for titles in a category in which you also hope to launch material, or take a trip along to your nearest bookstore and examine the shelf on which the forthcoming title will hopefully sit, and in what company. The answer is usually 'lots'.

If you can get a local bookstore to take you on, a couple of days helping out will teach you a huge amount. Try to find out how many emails are received each day, or arrive when the post is being opened to see how much information a store receives in a single day; notice how much gets deleted or rejected, without even being looked at, as simply inappropriate. Even if you cannot work in one, acquire the habit of visiting – and buying from – bookstores at regular intervals. See how busy they are (particularly in the run-up to holiday or festival seasons); watch how customers peruse the stock (browse the top copy but take a fresh copy to the counter); listen to the scanty information they have about the titles they want. ('Do you have a book that was on the radio within the last month? I think the author was Joanne something.') Get used to the retail price of books (rather than always factoring in a publisher's discount, which distances you from what real customers pay), make comparisons with what other things cost – and so understand the choices consumers make, which may be more due to the consumer need that the book is fulfilling (relaxation, education, distraction) than perhaps the requirement to own another volume.

If you are a publisher, the aim of all this is to encourage you to stop viewing your list of titles as an interesting whole, united by its single publisher, and to see it rather as the consumer (whether individual or retailer) will see it, as a series of individual products. Your eventual customer will probably be more familiar with your authors' names than that of your publishing house or imprints. If you are an author or agent, this will hopefully help you appreciate that, while your title matters hugely to you, other options for reading time exist. For each title, rejection is the easiest option, and reasons for stocking and purchase need to be fully spelt out.

So where do you start in trying to develop coherent plans for your marketing? By thinking more closely about what marketing means, and how to achieve it. Happily the marketing world is able to offer a range of advice, including some snappy checklists.

Checklists for achieving good marketing

Here are two short summaries of what marketing is about. The first is a four-part definition of what marketing means in practice;[9] the second, a checklist for ensuring your marketing is on track:

Requirements of effective marketing

- **Developing a customer orientation** so that their needs, wants and values are prominent in your thinking; being market-orientated ('what do my customers need?') rather than product-orientated ('to whom can I sell this?'). Customer satisfaction is a vital organisational aim. Not only do happy customers act as a source of regular revenue (rather than to your competitors), they act as your ambassadors. They are also vastly cheaper to maintain than acquiring new ones. Estimates that it costs six to seven times more to acquire a new customer than to retain an existing one are widely accepted.[10]
- **Taking a long perspective and proceeding logically.** Marketing often suffers from an image problem; it can be viewed as a flurry of activity resulting in forcing unwanted goods on the unwilling. Allocating a huge marketing budget won't produce enormous sales the next day (it may even have the opposite effect: alienating your market by making you look cash rich and your products overpriced). Understanding markets and their needs, and the likely products they may require, takes detailed study and hence time. True marketing means planning what you want to achieve and how to do so, then implementing and monitoring it.
- **Promoting organisational integration as a business philosophy.** Marketing won't work if it's only seen as important by the marketing department or if it

attempts to work in isolation. The whole organisation needs to be involved and committed; ideas communicated and shared with colleagues, absorbed and passed on by them too, and the experience of the customer consequently seamless. Similarly, relationships are crucial in supporting marketing, both within and beyond the firm: with the market; with shareholders; with the next generation of customers – and potential employees. If the exchange of the product or service you are offering and what your customers are receiving is based on a relationship that is valuable to both parties, that relationship can grow in future.

- **Innovating and being flexible.** Markets and customers change all the time; their only abiding loyalty is to their own interests. Even bestselling products can become boring. If you want to stay ahead you have to think ahead.

The second useful checklist of ideas to ensure you stay on track has been credited to a variety of different gurus. The fact that it is so generally attributed perhaps shows its widespread adoption and relevance. Marketing is about offering:

- the right people;
- the right product;
- the right price;
- the right promotional approach;
- the right way;
- at the right time;
- in the right place.

Applying this checklist to publishing is a useful way to start thinking about how to plan your marketing.

The right people

For the marketing-orientated publishing company, the customer's needs should come before product or service development; products should grow out of an understanding of customer requirements. In exploring customer needs, a variety of different sources of information may be used: specialist knowledge from your authors and other content contributors; feedback from retailers and wholesalers including the sales pattern of related products and services; socio-economic data; website traffic and conversations from relevant forums, both on- and offline; relevant memberships and associations; general knowledge – talking to people and observing trends.

Whereas publishers' products often come from their own enthusiasms, and in the process of making such material available you may well find other people who feel as strongly as you do, for full exploitation of market opportunities it is vital that wider markets are explored, appreciated and their tastes and needs understood.

The right product

The right product (and for this also continuously understand service) is the one that customers want, or one that they will be prepared to want – and pay or secure funding for – once they have been informed of its existence. The manufacturer's initial concept should be refined until it meets this standard and, once established, undergo regular updates to ensure it remains relevant to market needs as they are developing. In addition to the particular format, and associated benefits presented, the product will include its brand image, packaging and after-sales service.

Applied to publishing, this means considering the best format (which is not necessarily a book – the market might find an app or magazine more useful than a single text, or prefer a combination of elements such as textbook, teachers' notes and supporting website). It can include changing the level at which the product is pitched, the cover, number of illustrations or price to meet the anticipated needs and preferences of the market. Although active involvement in this process may well occur only higher up in the publishing organisation, you should bear in mind that the author's first submission of text is not necessarily what will finally appear in published form (whatever medium is chosen). Appropriate and professional presentation to a specific market is a very important part of the publishing process, although one that content providers are not always inclined to acknowledge.

The right price

A product's price is integral to the offering made to the customer; it will be understood as part of the package, not something apart. There are a number of elements to be juggled to achieve the best outcome. The price is what the customer eventually pays, but it will be discounted to retailers and wholesalers who sell on the organisation's behalf, the discount allowing for the costs they incur during the selling process (premises, stocking, advertising and promotion, postage, discounting, etc.).

A starting point for establishing the retail price quoted to the customer is often to consider the costs of producing and delivering the product to the market, plus a percentage to allow for profit, but there may also be issues of lifestyle ('Does ownership enhance my image?') or timing ('I am an early adopter and like to have access before other people') for which the customer may be prepared to pay more. Customers who want a product tailored to their specific needs may be willing to pay a significantly enhanced fee direct to the producer in return for a bespoke service. And here it may be the convenience or discretion of direct supply that appeals, as much as the product itself.

Price is also often understood against a variety of other factors: what else is available; how great is the customer's need for the product; does it offer value for money; how reliable – long term – is the organisation doing the selling (and retailer reputation will be important here too)? Consider too the cost or value to the consumer of obtaining the product. So while one consumer may buy books online to reduce the associated costs (petrol, car parking, risk of a parking ticket) and to minimise out-of-stock issues, another may make a conscious decision to visit a bookshop and buy in person to spend some leisure time; to enjoy the physical pleasure of the environment, the company of other like-minded people and perhaps at the same time do some additional shopping in other stores nearby.

Within the international publishing industry, it is interesting to note how books currently cost very different amounts within different cultures, and whether in future worldwide sourcing will result in more uniform pricing.

The right promotional approach

Marketing information may be presented through a variety of different channels, from PR and sponsorship, through advertising and direct marketing, to the selection and management of appropriate distributors and effective sales management (all will be covered in more detail). Those responsible for marketing have to decide on the promotional approach most appropriate to both the market and product and achieve the best outcome within the marketing budget available. This is usually a matter of considering the options, and deciding where the associated budget can be spent to best effect.

Taking the selection of sales benefits a stage further, what offer in combination with your product is more likely to persuade the buyer to purchase? General advertising yields lots of examples: the free extra if an order is over a certain value; the complementary voucher that accompanies student bank accounts; the cast-iron guarantee of a refund if the customer is not completely satisfied. In general, it's better for organisational finances to give added value to the customer (giving them more of your product, which may be merchandise that is in any case spare) than to reduce the amount of income you receive (by giving a discount).

For some publishers, notably those catering for specific markets, in particular professions or educational institutions, methods of informing customers of new products may be well established, although it is important to remain alert to new methods of reaching markets (email alerts based on your previous purchases; blogs that are widely read; professional associations that now offer lively forums). General publishers, or those taking a speculative approach to new areas of content creation, may be forced to experiment from the outset, combining formal marketing avenues with social media campaigns, aiming to track which channels are particularly effective in reaching markets and then building the relationship.

The right way

This means the right creative strategy (style of copy, format, design, typography and so on) that allows the message to speak clearly to the market. Here selection is important, so rather than listing every possible sales benefit, concentrate on those that are most relevant to the market. For example, tyre manufacturers could stress a variety of different product benefits: competitive price, road-holding ability, value for money and longevity. They usually concentrate on a single one: safety.

So, when selling business information to companies, your tone probably needs to be clear, professional and centred on the potential competitive advantage you are offering. If writing copy for point-of-sale material to be used in children's book departments, the image chosen must both attract children and appeal to those who will make the buying decision.

The right time

The right time is the best time to be marketing. Advertising Christmas decorations in July, or 'beach reads' too long before the time when most people take their summer holidays may achieve some sales but will probably not produce the best possible results. Pharmaceutical companies producing drugs for seasonal illnesses frequently secure the best response if they time their marketing to doctors carefully, for example by circulating information on hay fever remedies when the pollen count is high.

For publishers it's particularly important to note that not all markets behave in the same way. The best time to contact teachers with information on an educational publishing programme is when they are thinking about how to spend their forthcoming budget or at the beginning of the new school year. If you send out information during the final weeks before the long holidays they will all be too busy to read your material. On the other hand, contacting university academics at the same time will frequently find them still at their desks and keen to make decisions about new titles for the year ahead, so that retailers have time to stock them for the start of the new academic year.

The right place

The right place is the most appropriate sales vehicle; the place where the largest number of your prospective customers will read your message and be able to buy what you have to offer. For example, in order to reach doctors you might decide on an email campaign, space advertising in a relevant publication or instructing a team of freelance representatives (reps) to take your product into medical centres. All three are different ways of reaching the same market. As part of the decision-making process you will have to consider ease of relationship management (are staff able/willing/equipped to sell your product range; have they sold books before; do they need special presentation and storage materials?); retailer image (will your market be confident to navigate their website or feel comfortable entering their premises?); management issues (can you agree on terms of supply and payment; how user-friendly are they to deal with?) and associated logistics (where are they located; can you make this work?)

You may also hear the above list referred to as the **marketing mix** – generally as product, price, promotion and place (all of which can be cross-referenced to the headings above) but this list expanded to include other Ps such as personnel/ people (those who retail your product become part of the customer experience), process (logistics, delivery, returns, guarantees, etc.), period of time (crucial in many areas of retailing) and physical evidence (what you can observe and learn from).

What is the difference between marketing, sales and promotion? Which role should be higher up the organisational hierarchy?

In that the aim of marketing is to produce sales, the separation of sales and marketing into separate roles is often seen as sleight of hand, particularly by those without an understanding of either function. 'Promotion' or 'promoting' are terms that are often used to mean marketing or selling and so further confusion arises.

In general, marketing staff research and recommend how a product or service should be presented to their customers; they segment the market, isolate groups worth targeting and recommend the approach or message most likely to prompt orders. Their sales colleagues target, ask for and take the orders, and in particular record outcomes so that future plans can be based on actual results. Within small organisations the two functions may be amalgamated into a single role. In larger organisations the roles are generally separate – but need to work closely together for maximum impact. Even if they are amalgamated, thinking of them as two functions is helpful; both need to be aware of the customer's alternative options – including spending nothing or buying something completely different.

Promotion (and promoting) are terms that get routinely used in the area of sales and marketing, but it is helpful to consider their more precise meaning in a marketing context, which is a strategically planned activity, temporarily negotiated, and with a specific aim in mind – for example to raise awareness, generate a short-term demand, get new customers to try a product, convert sales leads, encourage existing customers to buy more, get existing sales in more quickly or persuade them to pay in a more cost-effective manner. Thus a firm may organise a price promotion (e.g., a discount), a promotion to persuade the customer to buy more (e.g., multi-buy for an enhanced discount; buy two get one free) or use a promotion to establish a longer-term relationship (e.g., subscribe to our journal for a full year and receive a free pen).

You may also hear the **promotional mix** talked about. This generally refers to a range of different techniques – personal selling, social media, advertising, direct marketing, sales promotion and publicity. The promotional mix specifies how these are to be prioritised and costed within an overall marketing plan. Allocations of time, money and methods will be based on the nature of the market being approached, the goals of the organisation and the staff and money available, but in general there will be several constant requirements: to present information in order to enable the consumer to make a choice; to differentiate products and services in the consumer's mind; to increase demand.

Segmenting, targeting and positioning

In order to maximise the potential response from the market, and produce an income that supports further developments, it is important to concentrate marketing efforts and decide which parts of the potential market are most worth pursuing. For this purpose, markets are segmented into useful groups, targeted for their attractiveness and then communicated with by offering 'positioning' statements on a concentrated range of products and services designed to influence the thinking and behaviour of the customer.

Segmentation involves identifying different groups of potential customers who share similar needs and display similar characteristics. Segmenting a market makes sense in order to produce more manageable numbers and concentrate resources appropriately – and efficiently. Segmentation is an important strategic planning tool and promotes more precise definition of the market, enabling you to get to know both your customers and your competition better, to respond to developments within the market quickly and to test ideas before making them more widely available.

How to go about segmenting a market

You could begin by asking yourself some initial questions:

- Are there subgroups within your market with similar characteristics? For example, are they of similar age, gender or occupation?
- Is there information that will enable you to identify these segments (a) in existence and (b) available to you? If it is available but you are denied access and the cost of building it yourself is prohibitive, it may be wise to proceed no further.
- Is segmentation likely to be profitable? If you are to pursue them effectively, segments need to be measurable, identifiable, accessible and viable, and if the costs of building and achieving access are unlikely to be offset by resulting revenues, a detailed segmentation may not be a useful approach. Even if a sector is unlikely to yield a profit, you may find that someone else may pay for it as a philanthropic route. For example, many book promotion schemes to segments of society who are under-resourced with reading material or lack a reading habit have been developed in this way.

Case history in segmenting

A business publisher was approached by an organisation representing a group of professionals who were clearly identifiable, were confident of their expertise and specific role, and viewed their membership organisation as a valuable work and social forum. They did, however, have few specific resources published for their particular professional needs, and this contrasted with other markets with which the publisher was involved. The publishers decided to respond to an invitation to bid to publish the organisation's annual yearbook. They did so in order to explore the sector, thinking that this would give them the opportunity to create a range of bespoke resources for a market to which they would thereby gain direct access.

Once the yearbook contract had been won, and the working relationship progressed, it turned out that the professional organisation took another view. They saw the contract for the yearbook as an annual and discrete project, and would not counter any developmental activity with their membership that did not involve them too – and for this access they wanted significant up-front fees. As an organisation they had high institutional costs (expensive London premises), were cautious decision-makers – but they also significantly overestimated the profitability of the yearbook to the publisher. The result was that publisher commitment to the relationship was severely compromised and the publishing opportunity of creating content for an underdeveloped market segment not pursued.

Lessons

Given that the publisher's interest in the organisation was based on a range of future options for developing the market segment to which they would be gaining access, rather than the initial project in hand (the yearbook), the feasibility of these options should probably have been explored in more depth before proceeding. This could have been tackled on the basis of considering the wider aims for both organisations: in the case of the publisher, developing content for an established market; in the case of the professional organisation, to continue to be seen as being responsive to members' needs. Perhaps a lighter touch could then have been explored in order to limit risk; subsequent publishing would have offered the professional organisation the chance to present their brand to their membership, without significant investment costs, and this could have been achieved in return for a percentage of sales revenue – thus tying their remuneration to achieved results and limiting the publishers' risks.

The overall message is that a segment may be evident, under-utilised – and hence attractive. But if you can't access it without excessive cost, it may not be worth it. Relationships established in order to develop sectors that are mutually interesting need particular care and attention, bearing in mind the long-term aspirations of all stakeholders. An arrangement that only suits one of the parties will never be seen as fair or a good basis on which to build – and as a result all may lose out.

Factors to consider when segmenting a market

For those dealing with segments that are also mass markets, and hence generally equipped with correspondingly large budgets, there is a range of service organisations available to you, offering software that can analyse your database of customers and enable you to find other markets and prospects likely to be empathetic towards your product range. Bear in mind, however, that the more you seek to know about a segment, the more you may have to spend on acquiring the information.

In the life of the publishing executive, the opportunity to formally analyse a market segment may be rare, but spending some time considering the different reasons customers have for buying, and the ways in which they do so, may open your eyes to individual differences – and this can be done informally (and cheaply). For example, you can segment by:

- **geographic factors** (e.g., where are they? Rural or urban location; close to a bookshop or literary festival or not?);
- **demographic factors** (e.g., what age, sex or religion are they? Do they have any dependents? There are options for exploring their family circumstances, life choices, income, education, nationality.);
- **behaviouristic factors** (e.g., what do they do in their free time? What kind of organisations or groups do they belong and contribute to? What does their purchasing pattern tell you about how they like to buy? In what combinations do they tend to order; when; what kind of offers do they respond to; how often do they order – and when was the last time they did so? Are they spending their own or someone else's money?);
- **psychographic factors** (e.g., how do they feel about your product or where it is sold? What are the associated lifestyle and personality issues?).

Here general publishers are at a disadvantage, as selling through an intermediary (online or physical bookshop) means you have little direct customer contact and hence may miss this valuable information. Options for developing greater connectedness and building communities of customers with whom you remain in touch will be explored in Chapter 9.

The outcomes of such analysis may be various. At the very least you may gain some new angles for copywriting about a particular product – or in the process decide to invest in an additional experimental marketing campaign, making a specific pitch towards a hitherto neglected group. You might decide to concentrate resources in future on one particularly profitable segment, or to develop **differentiated marketing**, which involves developing different products and approaches for different sectors – bearing in mind that the associated logistics can be tricky. Alternatively you might find that even though you discover people use your product in different ways, for reasons of cost or ease of management, **undifferentiated marketing** (one product or approach for all segments) may still be the most effective response. These choices will be influenced by various factors from company resources, the product range to be offered and the organisational or their competitors' past experience.

Branding

The concept of a brand comes from a system for marking cattle with the owner's name, and this is a helpful way of thinking about how to confirm identity.

Brands today can be both powerful concepts and valuable assets; an organisation which can communicate a message that can reach beyond boundaries, get absorbed by others and projected onwards is a valuable asset to an organisation in a world packed with competing marketing messages and where getting heard is difficult.

Within publishing, while certain big brand publishing names exist (Elsevier, Penguin, Random House, HarperCollins, Pearson), your authors' names are probably better known than organisational brands, and some authors take branding a stage further by using different names for different kinds of book (Iain Banks and Iain M. Banks; Jean Plaidy and Victoria Holt; Joanna Trollope and Caroline Harvey).

But branding is not the preserve of large organisations alone. Maintaining a company ethic – and ensuring that potential customers understand it – is a particularly useful practice for independent and small presses to develop (think Faber & Faber in the UK or Coffee House Press in the US). Tell your customers a story and they may buy into it, feeling they have discovered something worth supporting. For example, you could consider telling them how you came to set up the firm, why you do what you do, what you did before (even better if you left a corporate lifestyle to publish what you care about). Quality of life and work–life balance are issues that have a wide resonance today, and describing how you came to find yours may bring both customers and long-term recommenders of what you are doing. Interestingly, this recommendation may start from the moment you first find an enthusiast. It used to be believed that a customer had to experience years of good service before they would start recommending you, but recent research has shown that, given the taste for the new in society, enthusiasts tend to pass on the name of their latest find immediately.[11] Consider how quickly you can start turning those who buy from you into advocates.

Integrated marketing communications (IMC)

An understanding of IMC is helpful in working towards the objectives of a marketing campaign. IMC promotes the coordinated use of different promotional methods and the application of consistent brand messaging across all the marketing channels used, whether through traditional or non-traditional means, off- or online.

> Brands are, at some level, just communities of interest and, with the internet, it's become so much easier to harness these communities to allow new connections to be formed. It's essential that externally facing departments work together co-dependently to ensure the right outcome and joined up thinking. It doesn't matter what the structure is, but to succeed in today's communication- and information-rich environment, departments must work together with the same outcomes in mind.
>
> Cathryn Sleight, marketing director at Unilever[12]

For organisations relying on a range of different supplier services (e.g., advertising agencies, branding agencies, direct marketing agencies, website services) harnessing all the outputs to benefit the commissioner, rather than allowing energy and spend to dissipate into services differentiating themselves from each other, is a challenge. The publishing industry's tendency to resource its own needs, and rely less on external help, has been a protection up to now, but as more firms use marketing services from external suppliers, and organisations increase the range of methods through which they share marketing messages, this needs vigilance.

Relationship marketing

New theories about marketing come and go, but **relationship marketing** is one that it is particularly helpful to explore: the promotion of customer satisfaction and hence retention, rather than focusing on shorter-term sales transactions. Rather than highlighting advertising messages or short-term promotional strategies, relationship marketing concentrates on the longer-term value of customer contact.

For publishers this is a sound strategy. Most customers only buy a single title once, and so persuading them of the value of your brand and general output can motivate them to be in longer-term relationships. In the case of educational or professional titles, working with customers to create longer-term satisfaction can be hugely profitable. The concept of relationship marketing has been much discussed in the marketing literature and press – and is now often referred to as CRM – or customer relationship management.

Concluding case study: Susan Curtis-Kogakovic of Istros Books – bringing the best of the Balkans to UK readers

The start-up small publisher specialising in literature in translation

The concept and objective of Istros Books dates from 2010, when I was still resident in Zagreb, Croatia. As a writer and book lover, I had made a lot of contacts in the region over my 6-year stay, and knew very well how woefully little of the literature ever made it to the UK market. With a desire to change that, but with very little experience of the publishing industry, I registered the company online and swiftly got down to the business of applying for funding.

As every publisher of translations knows, the translation itself is most often the most expensive part of the book. This is one of the reasons why so little of it is published on the UK market – that and our (miscalculated) idea that the English-speaking world gives us enough of a multicultural view. So one of the ways to cover the cost of an expensive translation is to apply for institutional funding; from ministries of culture, cultural organisations or the EU Culture Fund. I started with the latter, applying for four titles picked from Croatia, Montenegro and Bosnia, after first securing the services of experienced translators from Serbo-Croat to English. I also looked to other funding for my Romanian and Bulgarian titles, relying on the auspices of the Romanian Cultural Institute and the Elizabeth Kostova Foundation, respectively.

The foundation of a good publishing house is, of course, the quality of its writers, and in the case of Istros, also of its translators. However, this is only half the battle. Once I had relocated permanently back to London in the summer of 2011, the hardest part began: those slippery twins, marketing and PR! Although I had two titles ready for publication early in 2011, and had even found a designer and a printer by the autumn, they came out to a resounding silence. The truth of the matter is: if a tree falls in a wood and there is no one to hear, then it doesn't make a sound. If a book is published without any marketing input, then it does not exist on the market.

Istros' first step in the right direction came with the securing of a UK book distributor, in this case, Central Books, which has been providing this service for small publishers since 1939. Through them, it was also possible to reach out to book repping companies who represent small publishers on the UK market by their direct outreach activities and relationships with wholesalers and booksellers across the country. If a small publisher is to succeed on the open market, it needs to let book-buyers know about its titles and therefore needs the help of professionals. Before Istros Books was taken on by Signature Book Representation (UK), only a handful of books were being ordered from the distributor, whereas afterwards I had orders coming in from the wholesalers Bertrams and Gardeners, as well as individual bookshops nationwide. And each new title that we published was now accompanied by an Advance Information sheet and listed on all the necessary sites, so that it could be introduced to the buyer in good time. The reps also serve as a 'market voice' in that they quickly inform me if they think I am doing something wrong – from cover design to blurb description – emphasising the needs of the book-buyers and ultimately the customers. While I can get lost in the world of editing and funding applications, they keep me on track in terms of remembering the needs of the buyers.

A favourite question in marketing is – who is your target audience? Well, for Istros' titles, the focus comes under three umbrellas: those who hail from the region, or are connected to it through work or family; fans of literary translation; travellers to the region. Ironically for us, the groups are fairly airtight and there tends to be not that much exchange between them, so that even if a book gains an audience among translation enthusiasts, it would not be recommended to, or picked up by, people travelling to the country of the author.

In order to reach the first category, we maintain a strong relationship with UK-based cultural institutes and embassies, and often use their centrally sited London headquarters for launch events (e.g., the Romanian and Serbian embassies in the heart of Belgravia). For those who have a passion for literature in translation and writing from unusual places, we maintain links with people working and promoting in this area – the Free Word Centre, Literature Across Frontiers, PEN, European Literature Network, etc. The final group – those whose interest in the region stems from travel or holidaying – has been the most difficult to reach. Apart from the excellent policy of Daunt Books to shelf each title next to the travel books about the author's home country, the potential of these customers has not been tapped. One idea, which never came to fruition, was approaching travel and airline magazines from the different countries, in order to place an article or advert for the books. While some local distributors – like BuyBook in Bosnia – have taken it upon themselves to place Istros' titles at Sarajevo airport, others have not been responsive.

One of the main marketing questions for me was whether to focus on the writers as a group or as individuals? With the knowledge that most of my writers are endowed with names English people find unpronounceable – such as Koščec and Sršen – I decided on the former, hence my decision to group the 2013 titles as 'Best Balkan Books 2013'. As the Balkans has been viewed as a place of bloodshed and superstition for a long time, I see part of my job as to 'refine' this image rather than trying to achieve the impossible task of superseding it. We have a plethora of negative stereotypes to deal with, and we come at them obliquely. Marketing Balkan books is not the same as selling romantic novellas to 'ladies who lunch'; I go about it by drawing on the images of 'bad, bolshie Balkans', emphasising that we offer the edginess of subversive voices, along with an assurance of originality and authenticity. This originality has become a key part of our brand:

> Amongst our authors we have European prize-winners, polemic journalists turned crime writers and social philosophers turned poets. Uninhibited by Creative Writing courses and market forces, all our authors write out of passion and dedication to good stories, so you can always expect to find fresh and exciting writing at Istros Books.

In order to reach out to potential readers, Istros has relied heavily on the openness and dedication of a band of literary bloggers who are invested in literature in translation for the fresh voices and new perspectives it makes available. Our ongoing strategy is to forge relationships with such individuals – whether working on their own blog or as part of online magazines – and to strengthen relationships with them, as they are our main allies. While the handful of daily newspaper reviewers still in existence may be overloaded with the mainstream titles, independents still have the luxury of making their own choices and following their own tastes. We have to make stakeholders feel that they have discovered something unusual, rare and with attitude – whether they be reviewers, buyers or readers.

Susan Curtis-Kogakovic, Istros Books Ltd, www.istrosbooks.com

Notes

1 Clee, N. (2006) 'The last of the publishing mavericks', *The Times*, 6 May, p. 6.
2 WARC (2014) *UK Adspend to Hit £20bn+ in 2015*. Available at www.warc.com (accessed 21 May 2014). Clift, J. (2014) *Global advertising spend and economic outlook, 2014–2015*. Available at www.warc.com (accessed 21 May 2014).

3 Isaacson, W. (2011) *Steve Jobs*, New York: LittleBrown, pp. 71–2.
4 There is a more detailed examination of the meaning of marketing, supported by a full explanation of techniques for conducting a company audit and drawing up a detailed marketing plan, in Baverstock, A. (1993) *Are Books Different?*, London: Kogan Page.
5 Grönroos, C. (2006) 'On defining marketing: finding a new roadmap for marketing', *Marketing Theory*, 6(4): 395–417.
6 The Society of Authors has been keen to insist that there needs to be a 'meaningful level of sales' or rights should return to the author.
7 www.theguardian.com/books/2013/oct/11/self-publishing-boom-increase-diy-titles.
8 A theory proposed by Abraham Maslow in 'A Theory of Human Motivation', *Psychological Review*, 1943 and much quoted ever since.
9 I am indebted here to the work of, and correspondence with, Professor Michael Baker of Strathclyde University; David Stokes and Professor Wendy Lomax of Kingston Business School and authors of *Marketing: A Brief Introduction*.
10 This is widely attributed to Frederick F. Reichheld, founder of the loyalty research section at Bain & Company (no date), for example: www.brandingstrategyinsider.com/2013/02/18-customer-facts-marketers-cant-ignore.html.
11 Romaniuk, J., Nguyen, C. and East, R. (2011) 'The accuracy of self-reported probabilities of giving recommendations', *International Journal of Market Research*, 53(4): 507–22.
12 Quoted in Basini, J. (2011) *Why Should Anyone Buy From You?*, New Jersey: Prentice Hall, p. 114.

2 What's for sale?

Roles and situations in which content might be marketed 23
Where the marketing and selling of publishing content goes on 34
Who is involved in marketing? 36

How to Market Books was a working title for the first edition of this book, long before it became its official one, and in 1990 (the year of its first publication) it made perfect sense. Most of the publishers' content was presented in book form, and full consideration of how to market books was guidance that had not previously been available.

Titles often become stranded in time. So Carphone Warehouse is today a series of high street stores selling personal phones, a wide range of accessories and accompanying finance – far more than the location-specific communication devices offered in their title. Similarly, Kentucky Fried Chicken has more things on its menu than the title implies, and in the UK *Good Housekeeping* is a magazine for sophisticated women rather than one focused on household management. Sometimes organisations respond to this development by adapting their title to reflect the change in their priorities, maybe concentrating their brand into a single word or converting it into initials.

HTMB is now in its fifth edition, and how very much has changed in the meantime. Publishers have for a while now seen their role as 'content management' rather than simply book creation; some produce nothing printed at all. Even authors, long resistant to the 'content' word, are in general much clearer that if they want an external investor – whether publisher, bookseller or reader – they need to ensure their work is described in a way that attracts the eye and persuades the potential purchaser that it is a good use of both their time and money (and often the former is more significant than the latter).

So having explored what marketing is, we will now extend our thinking about marketing in publishing by considering the wide variety of formats and opportunities in which content may be made available for purchase, and everything you can sell beyond the book itself.

It's helpful to understand that a product is a flexible entity:

A product is anything that is capable of fulfilling customer needs. It is therefore not limited to physical objects, but includes intangible services, people, places and organisations.

(Stokes and Lomax 2008: 243)

Similarly effective publishing depends on meeting the needs of a series of different – and varied – interest groups. These can be isolated and selectively sold to, through a variety of different rights sales, each one approaching a different market sector, interest group or territory. For example, separate editions can be produced as co-editions or co-publications, digitised for e-publications, sold as extracts, for serial rights or adapted for audio, dramatisation and film, or for groups with particular needs such as large print or braille. Those managing rights sales on behalf of an author or publishing house like to acquire broadly and license narrowly, extracting the maximum amount of revenue from the project by selling it selectively, in each case working with the most appropriate partner. But beyond those managing rights, there will be further opportunities to make content available that may be developed by other colleagues and departments, e.g., Marketing, Editorial, Special Sales and Export.

This book seeks to promote entrepreneurial thinking and opportunity spotting, so after each potential opportunity for selling content, an opportunity for its wider marketing is suggested. Starting with the expected, we will move on to other products and services which might count as published content and which may be important in developing income streams for publishing organisations keen to pay attention to Unwin's advice, and remain solvent.

Roles and situations in which content might be marketed

Writing (often called content)

One of the really fundamental things that has changed about the publishing business in the past few years is the ability to communicate directly. Previously mediated by a range of different individuals and services, the supply chain can now be really simple – author to reader – via a website where they share their material or allow the reader to watch them writing and sign up to gain further direct access in future.

Content does not even have to be checked and original – it's possible to download material from Wikipedia and turn it into a book.

Opportunity: This is becoming a way of establishing and proving that a market exists for material that the publishing industry may decide to invest in or augment, e.g. by producing an edited or a luxury version. The challenge for those making the offer is to make it rise above the noise of everything else available.

The book (in general)

The basic codex has been around since Roman times; indeed Professor Michael Twyman of Reading University has identified it as a 'universal format', which once arrived at will change little. Modern marketing terminology builds on this understanding, offering 'vertical line extensions' of the basic product (new products in the same category, but at higher or lower prices).

Opportunity: In a digital age, the sheer persistence of a physical book can be celebrated. @scienceporn tweeted the following:[1]

Why not try a book?

- infinite battery life
- page always loads
- DRM free
- never loses your data
- immune to viruses
- compatible with all handsets/eyes
- vibration and drop resistant. Go ahead; throw that sucker against the wall.

Similarly, publishers are now making available enhanced line extensions that offer a range of different versions at the same time (e.g., electronic and printed text, audio material and musical score, launch party and branded party-bag – in issues that range from limited or signed delivered at special occasions to mass market, with prices that range widely).

Hardback

The hardback book is still the way high-profile titles with a correspondingly high level of anticipated sales are presented to the market before a cheaper mass market edition is made available. Even for titles with smaller anticipated sales, an initial hardback is often still produced on the grounds that serious purchasers (libraries, collectors) prefer a durable edition and that publishing in hardback format is the route to getting a title reviewed by the media.

Today the media will review new titles in paperback, but hardback editions are still used as a means of gaining an initial premium price for a product that will later be presented for mass market dissemination or for selling a title that has a specific and defined market willing to pay. Of late there have been explorations of the luxury hardback limited editions, signed stock – not necessarily by the author. For example, in 2011, Taschen released a retrospective of the work of photographer *Linda McCartney: Life in Photographs*. In addition to the standard hardback edition, there was a limited edition of 125 copies held in a clamshell box, each signed by her husband Sir Paul McCartney. Stock of the standard edition is still available; the limited edition sold out long ago. Another example is niche publishers in the US in the horror and thriller markets, who often produce an ebook edition and a high-quality limited edition hardback, with no paperback or ordinary trade hardback in between.

Opportunity: Hardback books make excellent gifts. If you want to achieve lasting memorability as a present giver, a hardback book with a personal inscription is an ideal solution. I recently heard of a bride who asked every wedding guest to give the happy couple a copy of their favourite book, with an inscription. This imaginative suggestion should be made more widely known. Should publishers be including their wares at wedding fairs, whether in person or via organisations promoting gift solutions?

Paperback

Paperbacks come in a variety of different formats, from those that replicate the page layout of the hardback, but with a soft cover, to cheap mass market editions on inferior paper. They are in general lighter and more disposable than the hardback.

Opportunity: It has often been assumed that people buy a title only once, although they may recommend it to others to read – and perhaps lend their own copy (frustrating if it is not returned). Publishers should encourage readers to buy more copies of those titles they love – to give away. Suggestions can be made creatively, for example parents buying copies of titles they already own, so that their children too can make a personal reading discovery. Few 14-year-old boys may want to know that their dad has already read *On the Road*, though.

Ebook

Ebooks offer electronic text, readable on a range of devices from specific ereaders to mobile phones and tablet computers. The extent to which material can be migrated between devices (should you be able to send a friend a copy, in the same way you can pass them a paperback?) is under discussion.

Opportunity: An ebook reader can hold vastly more material than you may ever be able to read, but this offers the users the personal comfort of having the content that matters most to them with them at all times; a reader's safety blanket, in your pocket. What could be suggested as material to carry around at all times?

App

An app is a computer programme that is designed to operate on smartphones, tablets and other mobile devices, usually available (some are free, others must be paid for) through the same distribution platforms associated with mobile devices. Apps are available for a range of leisure and professional uses from games and enhanced content delivery (e.g., a recording of a musical performance with additional text and related versions to enable the listener to compare) to processes for checking prices or transport connections.

Opportunity: Research has shown that more people are using their mobile devices to access apps than to access the internet, which means there are significant opportunities for the marketing of relevant products. For ideas on how one organisation is seizing the associated opportunities, see the interview with Tom Williams of Touch Press in Chapter 4.

Subscription

Publishers working with professional markets develop content services to which users subscribe, to receive online access to a service of continuously updated material. This can be on the basis of individual or group/organisational subscriptions (which allow multiple logins based on the number of anticipated users). The information provided by the publisher can be customised with the addition of examples and data relating to the host subscriber, perhaps making standard organisational wording or examples of cases dealt with available to all colleagues.

Subscription models are common in academic and business library sales, particularly of journals and digital publications. Such models are also used as a way of selling audiobooks and, increasingly, ebooks to individual readers. It can be highly profitable and offers the enticing prospect of customers who have committed to buying before the product has been finalised: money up front. It also has the appeal of fees being repeated monthly or annually, regardless of whether the content is actually read.

Opportunity: For professionals, learning to manage an information database within their specific sector can be a long process, but the first package used is often the one that is long stuck with (think how difficult it can be to adapt to alternative word-processing software). It follows that investing in making publishing packages available to students of the relevant professional discipline while they are learning, even if at a significant discount, is a long-term investment in their potential loyalty.

Similarly, observing how mail-order companies entice their customers to become more involved with them can yield many examples worth copying in subscription selling. Study the information they provide on delivery costs, 'recommend a friend' schemes and promotional gambits – you will find there is much to learn. Ignore the thought that those buying high-level resources are immune to marketing gambits – they are consumers too.

Translation rights

This is the most common type of right to be sold by English language publishers. If a book is successful, and has international appeal, foreign publishers will offer an advance and royalty to obtain an exclusive licence to publish the book in their own language.

Opportunity: These rights are marketed by the rights department through catalogues and rights guides, mailings and presentations at book fairs. Sometimes there may be the opportunity for the publishers of the book in a number of different languages and countries to work together on an international promotion.

Audiobook, radio, film and TV rights

There are a range of other rights to adapt the content that may be sold separately, together or in various bundles. All require effective presentation to producers and commissioning editors in the appropriate markets, resulting in the sale of rights. Because of the level of investment required in the production, these rights are always sold exclusively, on a fairly long-term licence.

Opportunity: A film or TV programme is the best marketing a book can have, and a mention on the radio is almost as effective. It gives plenty of opportunity for tie-in marketing and promotions. But don't forget local as well as national channels.

Permissions/anthology rights/short-term reprint licences

Author content may also be offered on a short-term licence, generally sold on a non-exclusive basis and restricted in various ways, e.g., by territory, format, term. The content will be cleared for a specific print run or 'lifetime of edition in all formats', which is the viable option for publishers with print and electronic formats to manage. This may permit inclusion in a combined product – say a textbook that takes relevant chapters from a variety of different works – or a temporary licensing agreement that permits publication for a short period of time.

Opportunity: Are there theatrical productions that would benefit from a chapter of an actor's biography for their programme? The use of an extract from another publisher's content could benefit both parties; offering the theatre ready-made and high-quality content, and at the same time increasing visibility for the full work within a captive audience, tempting them to buy the complete work. They too can benefit from high-quality content that already exists rather than having to start from scratch. Publishing companies creating apps are similarly likely to benefit from ready-made content that they can license.

Collective licensing

Collective licensing is used for small passages of content reproduced by institutions. Collective licensing organisations license schools, universities, local authorities, businesses and other groups of content users to photocopy or scan sections of content produced by the collective licensing organisation's members. In return those being licensed pay fees to the collective licensing organisation to distribute back to their members. Some now offer additional services such as managing permissions licensing on your behalf.

Opportunity: Some universities are now producing their own learning resource materials from a variety of different content providers, to match the course they deliver. Attractively formatted, they find such materials are popular with students. This may be an effective home for a chapter of a larger textbook, sold into a new format.

It's a good idea to ensure possibilities for this are made available to potential purchasers, for example by embedding links to collective licensing sites on your marketing materials or where your content appears on your own website, to encourage people to buy reuse permission. For example, see www.palgrave-journals.com/jors/journal/v65/n7/index.html where hitting 'request permission' takes you straight through to the copyright licensing website where you can purchase permission to reuse the article immediately in any number of ways.

Book club editions

Although this market has reduced significantly in recent years there are still organisations that make available a limited range of titles within a special format to their members. Many are reaching markets that would not otherwise have the opportunity to buy books presented during the working day, say to staff working on industrial estates or in staff rooms far from retail opportunities.

Opportunity: Could clubs offering home delivery of other kinds of merchandise (wine, food, tailoring) be persuaded to include a book in their offering? The advantage would be that the title presented to the audience would offer variety but not be competing with other books. In the same way, when ordering flowers there are a range of other products on offer from champagne to soft toys.

Special sales

These are titles sold outside normal trade channels, often at particularly high discounts of more than 60 per cent. Sometimes this may be through presenting titles to a 'non-traditional' retailer (i.e., with no previous history of selling published content) and so persuading them to take a risk on merchandise they do not usually carry; at other times it may be selling bulk stock to an outlet that accepts tighter associated terms and conditions, say stock may not be subsequently returned if it fails to sell (and the associated destocking required very quickly). The marketer may be required to present the titles for consideration on behalf of the publisher at a very early stage in their development. An attractive and instantly appealing cover will be of particular importance.

Opportunity: We have got used to seeing books in supermarkets, but where else might your customer be willing to spend? Perhaps there should be travel guides in firms offering travel advice or clinics offering pre-departure injections. And what about children's titles in preschools?

Own-brand editions

Content can be adapted for sale to particular markets, perhaps as gifts endorsed with a sponsor's logo or customised to match organisational branding, for example that of a supermarket; print runs can be from single copies, perhaps with a very special binding, to many thousands.

Opportunity: Many organisations are on the lookout for corporate gifts and a book may be a prestigious and popular choice. It's unlikely to be thrown away – even if not desired, it may end up in a second-hand bookshop and bought by someone else.

Remainder sales

Stock that does not sell within an anticipated period may be sold at a reduced price, and for no subsequent return to the publisher. These may find its way to remainder bookstores or special locations that sell reduced price titles (often heritage destinations and bargain bookshops on the high street).

Opportunity: When visiting leisure destinations at weekends, or during the holidays, a trip to the shop before returning home is common. Books work well in such locations, as shelving is already in place and they may be keen to stock such items. Unlike other consumables they may consider taking (special biscuits, confectionery), there are no sell-by dates to worry about on books.

Events

Many authors give readings and book signings, as well as making appearances at literary festivals. This gives readers and fans the opportunity to meet their literary heroes 'in the flesh', and in this internet age, they offer something tangible – and are growing in popularity (see Chapter 12).

Opportunity: Every graduation I have attended recently has offered the opportunity to purchase a copy of the associated video. Could filming be arranged for high-profile or particularly rare author events, with the royalty being spread between author and publisher?

Marketing initiatives

There may be opportunities to sell a product in new ways – whether format or pricing model – or in new combinations. A good example of this is young adult fiction made available to the adult market, either as is or with a new cover. Another is the repackaging of existing content (e.g., books for a specific market) with sets of questions that turn it from simply a book into a resource for continuing professional development (CPD).

Opportunity: Try to spot opportunities where a publishing product could enhance the business of a non-publishing organisation. For example, selling medical titles to pharmaceutical companies that can then be used as incentives to be presented to doctors. Or selling boxed sets of titles in a series that has now reached its conclusion, which may make presents or 'heritage' purchases for enthusiasts to buy for themselves. For information on how dental books were turned into CPD resources, see the case study in Chapter 15.

Marketing the publishing company

There are many instances in which staff responsible for marketing are presenting the publishing company to those who may be interested in working for it, writing for it or investing in it. Some publishers are very well known as brands in their own right, such as Faber & Faber, Dorling Kindersley and Penguin Books. The rise of self-publishing, and the resulting 'disintermediation' of the publisher has led to more questioning of the need for a publisher. This makes it more important than ever to publicise what publishers do, and the value they bring.

Opportunities exist in a wide variety of situations from the formal (presentations on publishing as a career choice at careers fairs or to groups of students) to informal (how you describe what you do to friends and family). Given strong latent interest within society in both writing (it has been suggested that the second most common new year's resolution is to write a book) and publishing ('Really? That must be fascinating.'), you will find that you are never off duty.

Marketing the author

Authors are brands, and often better known than their publishing houses – as asking your friends who publishes their favourite author may reveal. Marketers in publishing are regularly tasked with general marketing of the author rather than their work, and this may include anything from accompanying an author on a visit to a school or book signing to writing 'their' website for them. Sometimes event organisers can charge quite significant sums for the opportunity to meet an author, for example literary dinners that include a personally signed copy of an author's book.

Opportunity: The wide variety of literary festivals that are emerging create a lot of opportunities for content provision. It is often the publisher's role to locate opportunities, make the link and persuade those staging them that the author would appeal to their audience. Alternatively, consider hosting your own literary events from your offices or a local restaurant – it may be very helpful to all staff to see who your customers really are.

Press liaison

Making available, or extending, a story that has press appeal is often attempted by publishers – perhaps by offering content that relates to the general *Zeitgeist*: a story in progress or in response to news. You could respond by offering an author who can speak about the same issue or a publishing professional who can comment on the process.

Opportunity: Lionel Shriver, author of *We Need to Talk About Kevin*, found herself being regularly asked to appear on television and radio programmes to discuss children who kill, and eventually drew such contributions to a close. But each opportunity provided the chance to mention the associated book. What authors do you have who – from their personal or professional lives – could be useful spokespeople on particular issues?

Merchandising rights

Publisher content can be turned into a variety of different products from bedcovers and stationery to lunchboxes and clothing. Children's characters are particularly suitable for this, e.g., Peter Rabbit.

Opportunity: Publishers are still generally merchants of ink on paper, and the established format can, with relative ease, be adapted for wider sale. What items have you produced for internal use that might have a potential for external sale? Publishing houses often produce T-shirts and balloons for internal use, but these might have wider sales potential. Covers can be turned into postcards – and used instead of compliment slips – or adapted to decorate emails.

Advice on publishing

With so many people wanting to get published, and publishers employing people who have experience of how the processes work, publishing houses have turned to offering events and mentoring to writers. These range from one-off days to lengthy mentoring programmes. The market to which these are sold is enormous and authors signing up often optimistically interpret such events as assuming the publishers are looking for new talent.

Opportunity: Delivery has been largely in major cities, but online offering through distance learning could significantly increase the market able to purchase.

Widening literacy

There is a range of organisations involved in promoting wider literacy, encouraging children to read, adults to share, specific groups (e.g., boys, the workplace, the homeless, prisoners) to enjoy reading. Many of these initiatives use staff with experience of publishing to market the experience, opportunities for involvement and the need for funds.

Referring to comments made by Lawrence Lessig, the chief executive of Faber & Faber commented:

> It's interesting that in mediaeval times, Latin was the language of the educated, English the vernacular. Today I fear that video is the vernacular. It's not that books are becoming something for the elite – far from it in some ways – but that the power of video is there for all to see and making it part of digital books and the marketing of all our products is essential. We need to keep children reading.
>
> Stephen Page, chief executive, Faber & Faber[2]

Opportunity: Would your organisational output benefit from reader feedback? Children's publishers have experimented with getting individuals to review material and then listing those who participated in the credits at the back of the title – an excellent way of creating future sales from proud relatives, friends and schools.

And there is more. Later in this book we will explore how organisations use content to populate websites, apps and blogs as a marketing tool and how spotting what content could be used in a marketing sense plays an important role in product commissioning and development.

How what is for sale has changed – comments from Clare Hodder, associate director of rights, Palgrave Macmillan

When I first started my rights career more than 15 years ago, the rights we licensed were predominantly print-based subsidiary rights. At that time we did a lot of co-publishing with partners in the United States as well as translation, reprint and anthology and quotation rights. We also did the occasional book club and serial deal. The first academic ebook collection services were appearing around that time and, in those early days, sales to such vendors were commonly considered to be rights deals. As the ebook market evolved, the channels through which ebooks could be made available multiplied and publishers began to deliver their content in ebook-ready formats enabling publishers to make their ebooks available for sale directly as well as via third parties. With such changes the responsibility for such sales shifted from rights departments to sales departments – the sales becoming core to the publisher's business, rather than 'subsidiary'.

These days, when it comes to electronic content, it is hard to make a distinction between what counts as a core sale and what counts as a sub-licence, and the line between them is drawn differently by each publisher. Whilst translation and anthology and quotation rights are still a strong feature of what we do in the rights department, serial and book club sales are virtually non-existent, and we have consciously pulled back from co-publication and reprint licensing. Collective licensing revenues have grown significantly over the past few years as the range and extent of collective licensing globally has increased. We have also really grown digital licensing, finding opportunities to repurpose our content from selling information for marketing purposes to populating websites and apps. We have even had interest in licensing some of our jacket designs for use on iPad covers! What hasn't changed in all that time is the infinite variety of creative ways in which it is possible to license rights, or the buzz of clinching a great deal.

This section concludes with a case study on how a journals publisher is seeing the range and depth of their various income sources develop.

Case study:

What's for sale? Peter Ashman is publishing director of BMJ

BMJ is a wholly owned subsidiary of the British Medical Association (BMA), an association of 140,000 members.

BMJ (with a staff of 450) manages a portfolio of 60 journals with the broad overall identifying characteristic of helping doctors make decisions that improve outcomes for patients. The financial structures for these publications vary: some are owned by BMJ (e.g., their flagship journal *The British Medical Journal* and the *Journal of Medical Genetics*); some are co-owned (e.g., *Heart* and *Thorax*) and other titles are managed as 'contract publications' (e.g., *Journal of Family Planning and Reproductive Healthcare* and *Journal of the American Medical Infomatics Association*), which means they are produced on behalf of another organisation on the basis of a contract that comes up for regular renewal, the associated costs and income being variously apportioned – some clients are charged a publishing fee; in other cases the client and publisher share revenue, profit or a mixture of the two.

Although the range of organisations involved in this market is significant, the landscape is changing rapidly, presenting challenges for all serial publishers. Falling library budgets and the emergence of new ways to communicate – blogs, wikis, podcasts, networking sites, Twitter; as well as content being made available on mobile platforms – all reduce the market for both publications and print. Advertising revenues are also falling in general, in particular due to greater regulation of the pharmaceutical industry and limits on how much they are permitted to spend on promotion.

What is interesting in the context of this chapter is the shifting balance of income to BMJ. Some sources of income have a longstanding, such as institutional subscriptions that allow academic faculty members online access to journals subscribed to by the institution through their IP address. Copies of publications for individuals have also held up, against sector trends, but this is often because they are included within an overall subscription price. Some money comes in through job advertising, although in general job advertising is migrating online, and this yields around 20 per cent of the income from advertising in print. Other money comes in from industry advertising, as pharmaceutical companies use *The British Medical Journal* to advertise in, or place loose inserts – and there is also some use of these publications from a wider range of advertisers keen to reach doctors, e.g., charitable requests and holidays for a demographic with a relatively high income.

Another source of income is industry reprints – it's not uncommon for pharmaceutical companies to request reprints of BMJ material (which is copyright protected and so cannot simply be photocopied and circulated) – most usually research articles referring to particularly significant developments. This can be supplied to them for a variety of different marketing purposes (distribution via their reps, inclusion in promotional mailings) and results in income for the organisation. Although the material is available for controlled circulation electronically, most requests for reprints are for printed copies – this both controls access to the material and ensures its presentation is of a certain standard.

A relatively new, but growing, source of income is open access fees. Normally content for specialist journals is available only to subscribers, and remains behind subscription paywalls or access controls – on the grounds that subscribers are paying in order to remain up to date in their field. With some publications material may be made available after a prescribed period, say 2 years – but some never make material more widely available. In order to secure the immediate publication of particularly impactful research, authors may therefore opt – or be mandated by their funding organisations – to pay 'open access' fees up front, to cover the cost of making the piece ready for publication (peer reviewing, editing, production costs and so on), in which case the article is available via the web immediately to all.

Whatever the rationale for choosing open access, it has become an additional and important income stream to such publishers. Open access has at the same time also helpfully isolated the work (and costs) that a publisher has to carry out before content is ready for dissemination. Authors have been fond of implying that all a publisher does is 'press a few buttons'; the reality is much more labour-intensive – particularly in the case of high-quality journals that have a very high ratio of submissions to acceptance, but must pay for the review of all material they receive. Finally there is income generated from licensing and syndication fees, the charges for making information available to particular groups or other publications.

This changing balance of income streams is reflected in Table 2.1 and Figures 2.1 and 2.2, which compare the different sources of income for BMJ in 2007 and 2013.

Where the marketing and selling of publishing content goes on

Publishers have long benefitted from a range of retail outlets devoted primarily to their merchandise – bookshops – but of late, in addition to stocking books, such shops have often diversified into stocking a wider range of products, which require less physical management (unpacking, storing, getting rid of the packaging) and deliver higher profits (greetings cards being a notable example). Some have reduced the space for books by installing coffee shops, in the hope of becoming a 'destination store' for relaxation rather than just retailing. The extent to which publishers can provide their own display or 'point of sale' materials (promotional posters and bookmarks, single copy display holders for the point of purchase, dump-bins for multiple copies) has diminished, sometimes due to retailers' determination to offer customers a clutter-free environment, sometimes to management's decision to charge for marketing materials that are displayed.

Today the selling and stocking of titles aimed at a wide audience takes place through a variety of different mediators (retailers, off- and online, specialist and

Table 2.1 The changing balance of income streams is reflected here and in figure 2.1, which compares the different sources of income for BMJ in 2007 and 2013. Courtesy of BMJ

	% 2007	% 2013
Print subscriptions	45.5	15.9
Online subscriptions	25.7	49
Print ads	5.3	3.2
Online ads	0.4	0.8
Reprints	7.4	9.7
Licensing	11	10.8
Author fees	0	8.1
Other	4.7	2.5

(a)

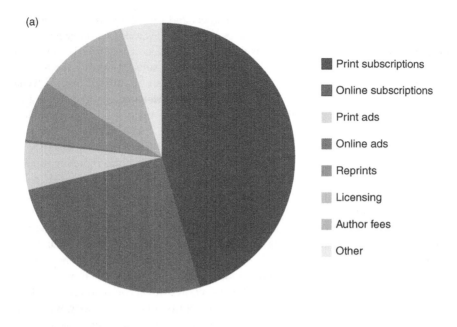

- Print subscriptions
- Online subscriptions
- Print ads
- Online ads
- Reprints
- Licensing
- Author fees
- Other

(b)

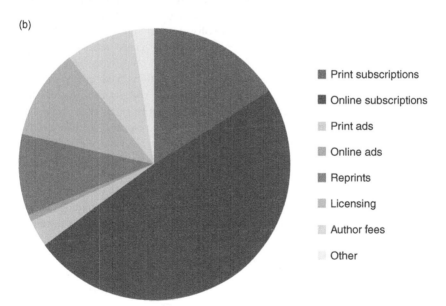

- Print subscriptions
- Online subscriptions
- Print ads
- Online ads
- Reprints
- Licensing
- Author fees
- Other

Figure 2.1 The changing balance of income streams is reflected in table 2.1 and these two pie diagrams, which compare the different sources of income for BMJ in (a) 2007 and (b) 2013. Courtesy of BMJ.

non-specialist in books; wholesalers; supermarkets and organisations who service the needs of particular markets, e.g., cruise ships or prisons; festivals and other temporary locations – see Chapter 7). Marketing is also increasingly conducted directly to the end user, for both personal and professional use, often by subscription or the lodging of a credit card with an online retailer so that orders can be fulfilled quickly. What is presented to the consumer at this point is heavily influenced by the words they use in their online search, and how closely they are matched by the product's metadata copy, which should have been search engine optimised (see Chapter 5).

There have been changes too in how publishers sell their wares to those they are hoping will display them for potential sale. Whereas individual representation to individual stores was the pattern, using a range of supporting printed materials, today materials can be presented online or via the telephone and a regular call can feel as personal. Large retail organisations may prefer to buy centrally, through their head office at the discretion of the nominated subject buyer, while smaller organisations may buy through a central consortium or still receive calls. A notable change has been in publishers pursuing direct relationships with readers, to gain the valuable additional information that can promote longer-term and profitable future contact.

Publishers who are developing and offering content to niche markets (e.g., business, professional, scientific, technical and medical publishers) have long worked to sell directly, but the sophistication of individual publisher information management systems has grown significantly in recent years. In part this was due to the decline of a list-broking or management sector, who increasingly found there was insufficient margin in the supply of customer data to make businesses sustainable, but also to the publishing industry's increasing tendency to manage their information themselves, investing in associated hardware, analytics software and staff. More extensive data protection legislation and in particular the insistence that customers opt in to receive information from organisations they wish to remain in touch with, raised the standards bar. A new breed of publishing services organisations have emerged that can manage all stages of a customer journey, either within the publishing company or branded as the publisher but outsourced. Today an entire series of customer communications can be managed automatically, as a direct response to their behaviour online (e.g., whether they browsed, bought, bought again or declined to renew). This saves time and labour costs – but also promotes organisational reputation, in the process building up information that can be invested in developing the relationship in future. Print and personal representation are still used by publishers working within these markets – for retention, renewals selling and relationship-building – but the culture here is fast becoming one of online accountability and rigorous testing.

Who is involved in marketing?

Ten years ago it was relatively easy to spot those with a sales or marketing function within a publishing house – they simply had 'sales' or 'marketing' in their job titles. These days there is a wealth of different job titles that match specific marketing functions which have emerged from 'web content manager' and 'community development manager' to 'special sales executive'.

It should also be stressed that those who were traditionally thought of as very firmly *not* in marketing may today find this is very much part of their brief. Thus commissioning editors have to find titles that the market will find appealing, production staff need to be acutely aware of a demand for higher design qualities within the market and hence the need to make their products as attractive and user-friendly as possible, distribution staff think about where potential customers may find it convenient to buy and HR staff need to be aware of the message sent out to the market (current and potential future employees) by the way both roles and the company as a whole are described. Ultimately, the need for effective marketing pervades all aspects of an organisation (see Chapter 1).

There may also be other individuals within the organisation who can market on your behalf if they understand the current priorities of the marketing department and the message being put across. These will include:

- senior management, when representing the organisation at a range of different opportunities from professional and industry representational to social;
- directors (executive and non-executive) and shareholders;
- rights sales people, who are looking for the key sales points for particular products, especially when attending book fairs and associated selling opportunities;
- those answering general enquiries including passing traffic and relationships with neighbouring businesses;
- those involved in social media, whether on a professional or social basis.

Concluding case study

How collaboration over marketing and selling works in practice: the relationship between editorial and marketing. An interview with Niall Kennedy and Eleanor Pike of Routledge (Taylor & Francis – Informa Group plc), an academic publishing house

Niall Kennedy is assistant editor for media and cultural studies at Routledge. He has an MA in English from Aberdeen University (his undergraduate degree) and an MA in Journalism from Brunel University (postgraduate degree). Prior to entering publishing, he had worked for nearly 5 years in bookselling (full-time at Borders bookshop in Oxford after university and part-time at Ottakars/Waterstones in Aberdeen while at university).

He has been at Routledge since January 2009 when he started as an editorial assistant on the theatre and performance list, moving on to be a senior editorial assistant on the literature list before becoming assistant editor for the media list.[3] As part of his job, he commissions book projects at various levels (A-level, undergraduate and postgraduate) in media, journalism, film, television, digital media, cultural studies, publishing, design, art and visual culture; and is both the primary point of contact for his authors and responsible for liaison with the marketing team.

Eleanor Pike is marketing executive within the media and arts team and markets both Routledge and Focal Press titles. She started her career marketing within the education sector after a degree in English Literature from the University of Sheffield. Having completed a Chartered Institute of Marketing Certificate she entered the publishing industry in October 2011, joining Routledge social sciences as marketing assistant. She transferred over to humanities marketing in 2012 and progressed in March 2013 to marketing executive, working on Focal Press and Routledge textbooks across the subject areas of media, communications and broadcast, theatre and performance. Overall, she is responsible for marketing more than 160 books annually, with particular emphasis on a front list of 50 core textbooks.

Niall is part of the team of 30 editorial staff, Eleanor part of the marketing team of 11. Editorial and marketing liaise and cooperate throughout the publishing process, on an individual basis, with those responsible for commissioning and marketing the same titles communicating regularly, such as at weekly publishing meetings and bimonthly media departmental meetings.

The first involvement between editorial and marketing is at the **title proposal stage** when a new publication is being considered for potential publication and material on likely content and presentation is submitted to internal and external review. The publishing meetings where titles are proposed run weekly and editorial members wishing to propose a new book project attend these with their respective marketing team members who comment on or query aspects of the proposal for the new book.

Although at this stage the initiative still lies with the editorial team, a key part of assessing the associated investment opportunity is a clear understanding of its associated market, an understanding of its particular needs and how well served they currently are and hence an appreciation of the new title's potential viability. According to Niall Kennedy:

> If it's a new edition, we will already be able to access where the previous edition has sold and have the details of courses on which it's been adopted. If the book project is not a new edition of a previously published title, we will have had a proposal for a new product written by the author and then assessed by peer reviewers prior to taking a decision on whether or not we want to proceed to propose the book to our editorial board.
>
> Author involvement in preparing a proposition for discussion is of key importance these days. They do not just give us a contents list for a new edition, rather we ask them to submit a proposal listing what they see as the potential market for their book (as well as competing titles within that market). We also ask peer reviewers for their thoughts in relation to this and feed back the information received to the potential authors to help them make their proposal stronger. The editorial department also do their own market research into educational and academic courses on which a book could potentially be used and try to estimate likely

course numbers wherever possible. We look at geographic sales patterns of previous editions or geographical sales of similar related titles we've already published. We consult our sales database for this information and discuss the viability of potential projects in different geographic markets with our marketing team and other members of editorial.

The blurb that is written at this stage is usually referred to as the **editorial description**. It's written by the title's editor and describes the key benefits for the marketing and sales team. Content is outlined but just as important are the product's unique characteristics: what is 'vital' or different. It's also us who draft the initial copy for seasonal catalogues, which are important for informing all markets who need to know a long time ahead: the sales force, agents, booksellers, wholesalers and library suppliers.

We have monthly briefing meetings with marketing colleagues about the title's specific benefits and their feedback is crucial. If they don't feel they will be able to promote the book to the right people or are sceptical about the market for it (e.g., it's already over-served, or very difficult to access), it's unlikely to get published. The 'yes' to a new title happens at the editorial board meeting. If there are no objections raised, we can go ahead and offer the author(s)/editor(s) a contract.

The **cover brief** is developed by editorial, often to match a series look but there is marketing input on these too. Designed jackets go on the online book jacket archive and the marketing team access them there. The cover is needed long before the title is finalised in order to illustrate marketing copy. At the same time a series of advance notices are developed for all the standard informing procedures sent out both internally and externally by Routledge. It is particularly important to ensure that the keywords used to describe the title convey those terms most likely to be identified by the market searching for relevant information (see search engine optimisation, Chapter 5). A seasonal catalogue is also produced quarterly, which is an advance listing of titles due to be published in 6 months' time. For example, the July, August and September 2015 seasonal listing is produced in January 2015.

Copy goes backwards and forwards between editorial and marketing, to ensure that detail is correct but also that the terminology used can be understood by the market and others making stocking or purchasing decisions who are not subject experts (e.g., librarians and retailers, whether online or physical). Information about books and related products is communicated automatically using a publishing management system (ONIX). ONIX for Books is a standard data format that is used to transmit information about books and related digital products between publishers, distributors, wholesalers and retailers in the book trade. The ONIX message is written in XML (eXtensible Markup Language) and is generally sent over the internet using FTP (file transfer protocol) or by email attachment.

Author information is vital in the preparation for making a decision about a forthcoming title, and once the title has been officially commissioned a second round of information will be sought – usually through an author marketing questionnaire that is sent to the author with their contract. Ironically this often asks for less detailed information and understanding of markets than the information they had to provide for an initial decision, but authors can be encouraged to fill them in more comprehensively. As part of this the author will be asked for an outline cover blurb and this is often very useful in helping to shape a revised version that is finalised by the editorial team before handing the project over to marketing. Niall explains:

> Once we have received the manuscript, liaison with the production team begins. Handing a project over for production is the culmination of a great deal of work between the author and the editorial staff. While it is by no means the end of that process or that working relationship on the book, it is a vital point for those working in editorial as the onus is now firmly on us to deliver the author's materials to production as quickly and efficiently as possible in the format that they need them, while making sure that they are all fit for publication. It is very important for the materials to be thoroughly checked (Does the book still meet with market requirements? Are all the elements that we have discussed with the author during the writing process in there? Do we have permission to include all material provided for the book?) and for intensifying the discussions with marketing colleagues about getting the book out to the right places and people on publication. Advance copies from the printer arrive just before official publication for both marketing and editorial and there is a mixture of delight that the final materials are in-house with us, relief that the one big aspect of the process has been completed, and excitement that work can now begin on the physical and digital versions of the product.

Eleanor Pike adds:

> For textbooks, there is a handover point at which the main responsibility moves from editorial to marketing and, although the editorial contact who commissioned the book is likely to remain a point of contact for the author, the marketing executive responsible will usually contact the author and seek their further collaboration. At this point the project costing is signed off and approved by marketing, editorial and managerial publishing directors. Marketing then issue the author with an author care pack, outlining the planned marketing activities and key contacts; this is typically followed by a detailed trawl through the author marketing questionnaire. There will be a variety of different media through which information on forthcoming titles can be shared and an

early job is to establish the targeting and communication of these various opportunities. Through author and editorial collaboration the marketing team will seek to establish:

- A key sentence summing up the book.
- A short description.
- Four or five key sales points that can be stressed in promotion.
- The primary subject areas (usually three) in which to categorise the book. These relate to how you would expect a bookshop or library to categorise a title and can help with its cross-referencing.
- The key market – define the primary market for which the book is meant (for textbooks this may be a specific course name or geographical territory).
- Segmentation and level of delivery – it's really important to be clear at which educational/academic level the title will mostly sell and whether there are any crossover areas. For example, 'background reading for final year undergraduates, but will sell mainly at Master's level' and 'essential reading for third year undergraduates and important background for Master's level students' could have very different potential sales paths.
- Research into competing titles.
- Whether there is any feedback or reviews from a previous edition; feedback on material circulated already. Might any of these be grown into a foreword?
- Information on individuals to whom it would be helpful to send a review copy of a title for review in a publication or inspection copy of a title for consideration for a course reading list.
- Information on associations and conferences that offer good opportunities to promote the title, perhaps on a general publisher stand or through advertising in the associated programme.
- Opportunities for e-marketing – author involvement on social media, opportunities for blogging.

Most large publishing houses approaching educational and academic markets have sales teams who visit schools and universities on a regular basis. Appropriate titles are presented to the sales teams at sales conferences or via sales broadcasts, in order to disseminate information (see Chapter 12) at least 4 months before publication; for titles to be published in January, February and March, the presentation to the sales team would be in September.

The process of wider dissemination of information is managed through integrated marketing communications; a consistent brand messaging across multiple marketing channels – brought together in a marketing plan. Eleanor explains:

> Given the high number of titles being managed at the same time, we have a minimum service level agreement for marketing activities for each text type, and activities are conducted based on the title's potential revenue. Some of these activities are carried out in cluster marketing

(several titles being marketed at the same time), others are attached to single titles for which we have high expectations. Marketing activities for internal and external stakeholders include both digital and offline marketing, from print materials (including anything from business cards to catalogues) to advertising (print and online, inserts, adverts, banner advertising and sponsorship) and working with online retailers. We also undertake targeted direct marketing to decision-makers such as lecturers and librarians in key subject areas (via email and print). Marketing also work closely with our global sales team to ensure they have the information and materials required to help sell our products effectively. Our sales teams work with a variety of channels to ensure our products reach the right markets across the globe, including wholesalers, online retailers, bookstores, libraries, institutes and lecturers.

We will undertake publicity plans too, sending out press releases to gain reviews in trade magazines, journals and blogs and encouraging authors to give talks, speak at conferences and sometimes take part in book launches, usually ones they organise themselves and for which we provide support. We send out inspection copies to markets where individual instructors need to try out a sample before deciding to adopt, give the leads provided to our sales team who follow them up and monitor the process to see whether the titles sent result in adoptions/the associated class sizes.

In the past five years we have seen a decrease in print campaigns and increase in online presence and content marketing. Presenting information online and promoting viral communication helps develop a sense of community and is vital in reaching out to our professional market. Digital marketing will include a variety of e-campaigns from newsletters and cluster campaigns to individual textbook announcements. We will aim to stimulate engagement and build brand awareness through social media, in particular Facebook, Twitter and LinkedIn. We have ongoing online catalogues that are updated constantly and for which links can be sent directly to the market encouraging them to purchase or seek an inspection copy. We also seek to present engaging material directly to the market by including information within content management systems (CMS) such as blogs and YouTube. Our website, www.routledge. com, is not just an ecommerce site, we also try to surround the material we offer with additional and interesting content that extends market involvement and hopefully moves readers towards adoption/purchase/ long-term commitment.

In terms of working out how successful campaigns have been there are a variety of metrics we report on in order to assess return on marketing investment. For example typical metrics include direct response rates, email open rates, email click-through rates, goal conversions (including the number of inspection copies ordered or recommendations to librarians) and a variety of sales figures.

Once the title has been officially handed over by the editorial team to marketing there is still regular liaison between the two. Monthly subject list meetings offer the opportunity to go over sales figures and key titles and on occasion there will be involvement from the journals team, with consideration for content being presented in other potential formats. Academic authors in particular need to be aware of opportunities to publish and share research that may result in a wider range of publications and may lead to the development of new formats; for example, combining several journal papers with a new introduction in a summative book that represents a significant development within a particular discipline. This could result in another publication to be itemised and might additionally serve to keep the author from straying to another publishing house.

There is daily dialogue between editorial and marketing about which titles should be sent to conferences (very important if the author is likely to be there too), about the compilation of area catalogues and print materials, about the value of sending out inspection copies to key individuals and about general author management. If both editorial and marketing are being contacted for free copies to send out to particular individuals and organisations then there is a danger of eroding the title's basic profit margin. Academic calling by editors and marketing on campuses to find out about course numbers, trends in the market, associated adoptions and any identifiable gaps in publisher provision are also important marketing opportunities: a chance to promote titles directly to their relevant markets and to gain the kind of market information that would not otherwise be available. As Niall comments:

> The idea for commissioning a new edition of *How to Market Books* with Routledge came out of a meeting I had with Alison to talk about the Publishing MA course she runs at Kingston University while I was campus calling. We discussed our publishing in this subject area and her thoughts on the competing titles for other publishers, and she told me there was the opportunity to do a new edition of the book with another publisher and that she'd be very pleased for the book to be published through Routledge given the strength of the collection of publishing titles we have built up. This led to further discussion and exploration of the market's appetite for a new edition by getting reviews from adopters of the book and key individuals in publishing teaching and training. I was then able to work with Alison on updates and changes to a new edition of the book before she began working on it.

Notes

1 21 June 2014.
2 13 June 2014, speaking at the TLC Conference, Publishing in the Digital Age.
3 Note the slight changes in the order of words within the job titles, which can have a seemingly disproportionate significance within the organisation.

3 Understanding the market

Market research and other sources of market information

Defining terms: market insight, insight hypothesis, market intelligence
   and market research 46
Secondary and primary research 48
How to commission market research 52
Syndicated market research within the publishing industry 53
Examples of how market research might get used in a publishing context 57

> Asked if he wanted to do market research, he said, 'No, because customers don't know what they want until we've shown them.'
>
> Steve Jobs quoted in the biography by Walter Isaacson[1]

The role of, and reliance on, market research within the publishing industry has been varied – and frequently at odds with its more widespread use. Within other industries, the commissioning of market research is a key stage in deciding which new products and services to initiate, which to develop and which to present within alternative market sectors. A few reasons for publishing's generally separate attitude to the usefulness of market research can be isolated.

First, the sheer number of products being launched and managed by the publishing industry has meant that individual market research for each product was seen as unaffordable. In terms of financial risk, publishing can be a relatively small-scale endeavour; the costs of commissioning and producing work from a new author can be low in comparison with new product development and launches in other industries, and with correspondingly low sales levels (a new novel was doing well if it achieved 1,500 sales) there was little prospect of the costs of wider market research being amortised over the longer term, through wider market penetration.

The high costs of externally commissioned market research also meant that within the general trade, what market research was commissioned was generally by genre or to look at a specific issue (e.g., response to covers, falling sales) over a range of titles, and for the *act of publishing* to be viewed as market research: for new initiatives experimented with, but planning and decision-making based on market responses to seeing the actual product.

To these reasons must be added the industry's strong belief in itself. There are undeniable difficulties in conveying, in snack-sized gobbets barely capable of drawing a sufficient response to be useful, a sense of a product demanding such high levels of involvement and commitment. The public is also unpredictable. Will they really buy what they say they want, or not buy what they don't currently understand? Sony apparently went ahead with the production of a handheld machine for playing an audio tape – what became the hugely successful Sony Walkman – even though market research said that a 'tape-recorder' with which you could not record would not be a success. Publishing is a creative industry and within this has emerged the role of publisher as seer, anticipating public taste and prompting customers to desire what is presented or described – in the same way that the manufacturers of greetings cards can draw an instant contemporary appeal from their customers that would arguably be destroyed if overanalysed.

Publishers have also tended to copy each other, to base decisions on what has been successful and their own reading preferences or those of their friends. The danger here is not including a sufficiently wide range of individuals or reading tastes within their consultation group. There have been prevailing assumptions about how the market thinks, how they will behave – and ignorance about other sectors of the market with whose tastes or lifestyle publishers are unfamiliar. Particularly prevalent have been assumptions about how much the individual brand means to the market or how well known the brand of the publishing house is to the reader, most being unaware of who publishes their favourite author.

The significance of self-publishing should be isolated here as it offers the author access to information about market preferences and requirements. In the past it has not been uncommon for authors to understand the market for whom they write, being part of it themselves, but to be met with uncertainty from those managing the publishing process; not understanding a market or a choice for spending time themselves, publishers were inclined to assume it did not exist. Self-publishing can yield excellent market research, offering authors the opportunity to road-test materials, acquire an audience and then approach an external investor with market demand and potential already established. The author who can outline a specific demographic or market for purchase, and a route through which to reach them, provide evidence of their willingness to purchase – both now and in the future – and enlist relevant product endorsements and marketing support, can be a sound investment for a publishing house.

From this introduction, it should be obvious that many previous assumptions about not commissioning market research may be self-fulfilling. Assuming low sales levels and therefore no wider market understanding may keep the organisation moving forward but requiring more and more product to sustain the same margins. Changes in retailing are also promoting change. Bookshops, as specialist retail outlets for the sale of predominantly books, are a wonderful resource for servicing a book-loving market, but reliance on them meant publishers were denied the direct feedback of those who bought their products. As the industry moves to a more market-focused future, with consumers increasingly seeking direct supply, techniques used by other industries are valuable and becoming more common. Market research is being used to isolate markets with unfulfilled needs, to consider how products could be augmented in order to achieve higher market penetration and to understand how marketing information and buying mechanisms are acted upon. It is also in authors' interests to understand how their work is perceived and purchased – and hence to understand the basics of market research. Many authors complain that 'the writing apprenticeship' – whereby gradually growing sales were tolerated in pursuit of longer-term success – is no longer available; authors must now achieve success from the outset of their writing careers.

Within specialist markets, such as academic textbooks or publishing for the needs of specific professional groups, large markets, tight timing and the risks of getting it wrong being correspondingly much higher, market research has been much more widely used. Publishers marketing to these customers, necessarily direct, are gaining more information about their buyers with which to refine both their product range and their understanding of the market – and hence are able to target them more effectively in future within the context of sustaining a long-term relationship. In such publishing companies increasing numbers of analysts and strategists are embedded in the marketing team, gathering data and interpreting it in order to promote good decision-making.

Whether or not you ever get the opportunity to commission recognisable market research, the aim of this chapter is to distil key information about associated processes and practice in order to prompt sensible and strategic thinking. In this sense, all publishers should be interested in market research.

Defining terms: market insight, insight hypothesis, market intelligence and market research

Market research does not have to be expensive or extensive to be useful and it's helpful if we begin by defining some useful related terms. Their common purpose is consistent: to improve market insight and test hypotheses in order to make better decisions.

Market insight

Market insight is an analysis of continuous or market data, a picture being built up over a period of time on the basis that markets are not consistent and do develop. This may come from an organisation's internal data (sales figures for the past 10 years), a wider picture of the specific industrial sector within which they operate (online sales for books are rising year-on-year) or the broader national or international economy (online sales for all kinds of products and services are rising, and are growing at a faster rate in specific territories).

Insight hypothesis

Insight hypothesis is thinking prompted by information. It may be gained by a simple observation that prompts intuition or the tracking of behaviour that deserves further investigation and may in the process yield understanding. Examples could vary from a straightforward observation (seven out of the ten people reading in my carriage this morning had a recent thriller with an eye-catching cover) to information provided by a company's distribution service (schools who buy from you direct often place one big order and then several more to 'top up' orders. As you offer free postage and packing, the cost of delivering the subsequent orders can come close to making them profitless). In both cases the insight gained offers a platform for further investigation through market research – perhaps experimentation with different cover formats to see which have most customer appeal, or in the case of schools to explore whether the trend spotted is common in all schools and if so whether those who place 'top-up' orders should be encouraged to consolidate their orders, perhaps by offering free postage only for orders of a certain size or providing a free returns service for material they order but do not subsequently use.

Insight hypothesis can be unpredictable in its arrival. But an organisation or individual who makes it clear they are keen to receive it, and will not blame the provider for potentially unwelcome tidings, is more likely to find it arrives.

Market intelligence

Market intelligence can be based on market data from a variety of sources secured in the pursuit of deeper and longer-term market understanding. It suggests a wider resourcing of information, often prompted by market insight but then supported through seeking information from a variety of sources – both formal and informal, and perhaps including some specially commissioned market research – in order to build up a detailed picture on which to base understanding, develop strategies and hence make good decisions.

Market research

Market research is just one of the methods of acquiring market understanding. But given that this is the more generally known term, it is worth exploration in more detail in order to consider how to structure a search for information.

> Market research is the means used by those who provide goods and services to keep themselves in touch with the needs and wants of those who buy and use those goods or services.
>
> Market Research Society

It implies ongoing vigilance and taking nothing for granted. Markets can grow bored with particular products, technology can lead to new developments, external events or fashion trends can mean new solutions or activities become more popular than those established; the role of market research is to help analyse information in order to make better decisions – primarily about the market and their needs, the product range and how it should be presented to best effect.

Market research is sometimes thought of as general information, but works best when defined as a specific research problem: a targeted question that specifies the information needed and understands the uses to which it will be put. This might be a need to know how consumers' tastes are developing within a particular market sector; what the key criteria are that customers use when making a buying decision; how an organisation's products or services compare in the minds of consumers with those of competitors; what impression products and services make on the market and why. It is important that market research is owned within an organisation, that someone wants to know the answer. Asking to know everything about everything would lead to muddle ('interesting, but so what?') and the information would be difficult to act upon. How that information is gained is dependent on a number of factors, but the process need not be expensive.

What kind of research problems should you identify?

There is no single answer; this will depend on what you most need to know in order to progress your business. For example:

- You might be looking for information on the decision-making process; types of buying behaviour or what influences what gets bought? This might be in the context of personal decision-making or within businesses, looking at the respective influencers of decisions, how buying processes work, how people feel afterwards and what might change the experience.
- You might be looking for how consumers find out about new products and services; how information is reaching them and how they assess it. Is their search for information active (seeking information) or passive (using what gets sent to them)? How aware are they of other solutions to their needs and how much do they really need a solution?
- You might be seeking more information on the characteristics of your buyer; their social (families, roles, status), personal (age, life-stage, occupation) or cultural (subculture, social class) characteristics; and how they respond to both stimuli you are able to control (the marketing mix you make available to them) and those which you are unable to control (the economic, technological, political and cultural circumstances that surround them).

In each case, the likely overall purpose of market research would be to implement what is learned by improving how operations work in future to maximise successful outcomes – whether through better describing the product or service in question by stressing to the market factors that are important to them, changing the method of service supply or altering your product insurance guarantees. Having defined the research problem, it is important to think about how information will be acquired. In general, it's helpful to think about secondary and primary research and then move on to consider useful analytical approaches.

Secondary and primary research

Secondary research

Secondary research, often called 'desk research', is 'data that has already been collected for purposes other than the problem at hand' (Malhotra and Birks

2007b). The advantages are that, once its existence is identified, it can be accessed and obtained relatively quickly, and given that it already exists, it may be relatively inexpensive – but these same advantages, and its lack of specificity to the problem in hand, can mean it is not fully relevant, or that it is inaccurate or out of date. Basing decisions on information assembled to meet someone else's research problem can lead to incorrect assumptions.

Secondary research may be found within the organisation itself (the records of the accounts department, information on the marketing department's previous campaigns, seasonal figures from the sales department or information from production suppliers) or from the wider information environment. For example, there may be government sources relating to the immediate administrative unit (county, state, region) as well as the country and wider organisational territories, such as information compiled by the EU or other specific areas of economic development. Such information may include census information, figures compiled to support legislative processes, family expenditure surveys, papers on economic trends and digests of statistics. Then there will be press coverage, perhaps based on academic research published in scholarly journals and republished for a particular readership (the bias of journalists presenting information for particular audiences always needs to be borne in mind).

Press features may be in reputable serious newspapers and associated websites, in specialist publications relating to the business market or the associated trade press, which reports on trends both within the industrial sector of interest to its market and the wider economy. There are online directories that seek to estimate a market size and activity (e.g., Dun & Bradstreet and Kompass), market analysis organisations that seek to classify the broader population by their buying behaviour (e.g., ACORN, MOSAIC) and subscription services that offer general information to their market, reporting on a series of specific markets (e.g., Mintel, Nielsen, Keynote, etc.). Professional and trade associations (e.g., Chartered Institute of Marketing, Chartered Institute of Information Professionals) may also issue bulletins on market size and scope, some of which may be more widely available as part of the industry information profile they present to the wider world, or available free to members but purchasable by others. All of which is relevant information to someone wanting to know about a particular market sector, but is not information targeted to their particular research question.

How do you establish the value of such material?

Information compiled to meet the needs of another organisation or sector may nevertheless have a strong value to other organisations, not least the significance of a market you are interested in already having been identified and explored. If you are going to base decision-making on such information then you need to think about a number of key factors, notably how up to date the information is you are reading:

- When was it published (bearing in mind that the research may well have been developed a considerable time before publication, available to subscribers only before being made more generally accessible)?

- How relevant is the information (for what purpose was it commissioned and by whom)?
- How accurate is it (what was the size of the sample and how were those who are reported on recruited; how many sources are quoted and is this a sufficient range to achieve a balanced view)?
- How was the research programme designed and to what end (and is there any associated bias that may result)?
- Who carried out the work (and do they have relevant experience)?

Primary research

Primary research is specifically collected for the purpose under investigation. It is original and thus belongs directly to the commissioning organisation. There are two main types of such information: qualitative and quantitative. Qualitative relies on in-depth interview and discussion and is asking for narrative feedback. Quantitative (the 'n' for numbers in the word is a handy way of remembering which is which) is designed to capture figures, and is most usually achieved through questionnaire surveys, experiments and observations that categorise behaviour into various prearranged sorts.

Qualitative research is often gained through in-depth interviews and group discussions. Overall it is more concerned with exploring concepts, perceptions, attitudes, opinions, needs, feelings and motivations than in acquiring numbers and may be especially useful when a subject area is sensitive or confidential or when it is difficult to get respondents together – for these reasons it is particularly used in business-to-business research.

Discussion groups (often called 'focus groups') or 'depths' (one-to-one interviews) may be assembled to reflect particular market segments and then asked to consider specified themes, the discussion being led by a trained moderator who works through a list of pre-agreed topics. Such groups can be very helpful in determining attitudes and behaviour, particularly when group members will 'spark' off each other and interaction results in a more engaged discussion than is likely through one-to-one interviews. Examples of methods used in qualitative research include projective techniques asking individuals to imagine how a product or service would behave in a particular context, a situation experienced by someone else or word association exercises, all of which (if skilfully handled) enable respondents to express subconscious thoughts or feelings without personal embarrassment or isolation.

Quantitative research is more often delivered impersonally, through questionnaires and surveys, experiments and observation. Surveys may be delivered in various ways (postal, telephone, face to face, through a central location – often called a 'hall test' – or via the web) and are based on gathering quantifiable information that can be subjected to statistically rigorous analysis. Although viewed as hard data, based on counting responses, quantitative research can be an effective way of gathering information on past and present experience, on awareness and attitudes and on likely future behaviour.

Questions may be structured (with the order and wording fixed, and perhaps a range of answers to choose between), unstructured (open-ended questions – that don't encourage the responder to say 'yes' or 'no' – and with a variable order) or a mixture of the two (e.g., a mixture of factual fixed-response and open-ended attitudinal questions) by asking respondents to grade their response to particular questions on a sliding scale and through offering boxes for additional comments. For material that needs longer-term consideration, 'in-home' placement might be considered, with consumers being given products to sample at home; this can work well for new product development (NPD) or product improvement, often with a self-completion questionnaire to guide the process.

How many people should you try to interview for effective market research?

Within reason (and cost constraints), as many as possible. Some markets may be more difficult to reach than others. Within a large population, to which access is straightforward, a random sample might be generated, perhaps as a percentage (or 'nth' selection) of the total available; a regional selection (e.g., everyone in a particular state) may not replicate a more widespread response. At other times there may be attempts to select quotas in order to secure a cross-section of the relevant population – age, gender and location, perhaps by using an external service to source the names. Sometimes quotas may be set for broader bands of the population (e.g., by gender, irrespective of age) if quotas are harder to fill. Alternatively, a questionnaire could be inserted within a publication reaching a target group, and so information sent to an entire population, within the associated constraints (do all market members read the publication; does this limit your response to those who (a) notice and (b) like completing questionnaires?).

How should you frame your questions?

In general, when preparing for both qualitative and quantitative research it is important that questions are clear, unambiguous and answerable within the delivery format – so avoid ambiguity, unfamiliar words, asking two questions in one and difficult or abstract concepts.

What you ask will depend on what you want to know – for example, what has been bought; customer loyalty; their sensitivity to marketing mix factors; how much they spend; how they spend their leisure time; their value structure. It is helpful if the overall thrust of the research is explained ('We are undertaking this survey because …') and different sections of the questionnaire are provided with a short introduction ('We are now moving on to ask you about …'). But beware the point at which your recipient feels you have taken too much of their time, or asked questions that feel invasive or inappropriate: they are likely to exit the questionnaire. There are books available on the subject (see glossary) and specialist services to publishers that have expertise in planning market research for publishing houses and understand their budgets. You can also manage the process yourself – perhaps through online questionnaires that offer analysis as part of the arrangement (see Survey Monkey and Qualtrix, both of which are available on subscription at reasonable prices).

How to commission market research

- Write a brief. There are key questions to answer. What is the most important issue to be addressed or the key objective of the research? How will the research be used? What specific questions need to be answered? Which form of market research is most appropriate – qualitative or quantitative? How will the feedback be required: for example, as a presentation for senior management, as a workshop for departmental staff, as an away day for training?
- What stimulus material can you offer to the research agencies as background to the organisation and the issues being explored (e.g., past promotional materials or book covers)?
- Draw up a short list of agencies (aim for two or three) who could potentially manage the project you have in mind, and that have the right kind of experience. Choice may be limited unless you are working in FMCG,[2] where there is generally more availability.
- Send the brief out to them, with a date by when their pitch must be received.
- When the submissions come in, assuming they have answered the brief, invite them in to make a presentation and talk in more detail at a face-to-face meeting.
- Make a decision on which agency to select. Negotiate over budget and timing. How fixed are your dates? Must it be completed by a particular time?
- The selected firm is informed and asked to develop their proposal and submit by a certain date.
- During the 'fieldwork', if the work is qualitative, the client should have the chance to observe. There should also be some update phone calls as the work progresses, especially if market research is new to the client, or if the agency has not worked for this client before.
- A presentation of findings is made, often called the 'debrief', to a prearranged group of people.

Post debrief there is administration to be completed to examine the process and how it worked. This will include:

- a check that the work met the brief;
- agreement on actions to be taken as a result of the research;
- the creation of some kind of summary document, easily accessed, as research debriefs can be quite detailed and difficult to use as ready reference. The summary should include a section on recommended/agreed actions;
- while the research agency can be involved in any of these stages, they may need to charge for their time, once the formal debrief is over.

Syndicated market research within the publishing industry

Another option is to use syndicated market research: a process whereby a variety of organisations club together to fund research in which all are interested. Examples include the measuring of television and film audiences within the longer-term demographic monitoring of large populations. On occasions it's possible for organisations involved to add (and usually fund) a question of specific relevance to them and for which the answer may come back to them alone.

Within the publishing industry, in the UK Nielsen[3] offers a variety of different mechanisms for monitoring information relevant to publishers. These include:

Consumer insight: Nielsen's Books and Consumers is an ongoing monitoring of book purchasing in the UK and US based on interviewing consumers about their book-buying behaviour. In the UK the survey is conducted via monthly online interviews with a nationally representative sample of book consumers aged 13–84. Each month the survey is taken by around 3,000 book-buyers who are asked up to 50 questions; the survey monitors around 36,000 buyers and around 80,000–90,000 book purchases a year. In addition to demographics, this dataset is enriched by further information on their media preferences, leisure activities and attitudes, locations of purchase as well as information on how they discover and choose the titles they buy. To get information about self-publishing ebooks that do not have ISBNs, Nielsen asks the respondent for information about the author, title and genre of their purchase and then use manual intervention (often by searching online retail sites) to identify the titles so that they can be reported correctly in the survey data.

Specific sector information: Nielsen also undertakes exploration of specific market sectors, e.g., children's books, cookery and gifting, usually on behalf of a syndicate of interested parties but sometimes on behalf of one specific company.

Retail analysis: Nielsen BookScan monitors weekly EPOS (electronic point of sale) information from books in ten territories through the book trade's unique identifiers (barcodes on the back of books that hold the title's ISBN; information captured when purchases are made). Nielsen BookScan collects title, price paid and ISBN, and that information is then run through the Nielsen database to add key metadata elements. The Nielsen BookScan service provides publishers with valuable information to aid their commissioning, sales, marketing and inventory management as well as inform their pricing decisions. Publishers can see their own sales and those of their competitors, depending on the type of service. Nielsen BookScan is a subscription service but also offers bespoke reports. The Nielsen BookScan data is also used by the media for the bestseller charts.

Analysis of digital sales: Nielsen PubTrack Digital monitors publishers' sales of ebooks; currently this service is available only in the US, but is due to be launched in the UK and Australia. Nielsen PubTrack Digital enables publishers, booksellers and libraries to gain an insight into the digital market.

Metadata and discovery services: Nielsen Book runs the ISBN Agency for UK and Ireland and therefore gathers information on the volume of books published in these territories. Nielsen Book also collects metadata for English language titles published worldwide and therefore has a unique view of print and digital book production; it is the leading provider of search and discovery services, via its Nielsen BookData range for booksellers and libraries around the world. The company provides a range of services for publishers large and small that enable buyers to discover their titles both in bricks and mortar and online outlets and through libraries.

Transactional services: Nielsen also provides a range of commerce services for publishers and distributors of all types, capabilities and locations. These include routing orders via its Nielsen TeleOrdering service from the buyer to the supplier to enable smaller, independent sellers to trade electronically to improve their customer service and order turnaround via its Nielsen BookNet service. The range of services includes EDI business messaging, outsourcing and consultancy for the larger organisations in the book supply chain.

This ongoing monitoring and information gathering, and the material's effective compilation, correlation and analysis, builds publishers' understanding of the market and its reasons for purchase, a sample of which is reproduced here by kind permission.

- Discovery of books bought: volume, 2013

Note: In exploring how purchasers discover the titles they buy, the differences between all books and ebooks are particularly interesting. Information on ebooks (whether traditionally or self-published) is likely to come through browsing, but also from online 'following', i.e., acquiring information that leads to purchase. It would seem that the more experimental the purchase, the more the purchaser comes to rely on their wider information resourcing. For self-publishing ebooks, site recommendations are particularly important; readers presumably build patterns of information sources that they trust.

All books	All ebooks	Self-pub ebooks
1. Read author/series	1. Read author/series	1. Browse online
2. Browse in shop	2. Browse online	2. Read author/series
3. Browse online	3. 'Follow'	3. Site recommend
4. Request	4. Bestseller list	4. 'Follow'
5. Read book before	5. Word of mouth	5. Advert/trailer

Figure 3.1 Discovery of books bought: volume, 2013. Data courtesy of Nielsen Book Services [trading as Nielsen BookData]. Layout and presentation courtesy of Nielsen Book Services [trading as Books & Consumers].

Figure 3.2 Purchase influences: volume, 2013. Data courtesy of Nielsen Book Services [trading as Nielsen BookData]. Layout and presentation courtesy of Nielsen Book Services [trading as Books & Consumers].

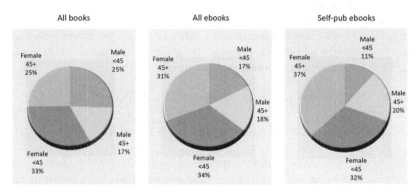

Figure 3.3 Buyer demographics: volume, 2013. Data courtesy of Nielsen Book Services [trading as Nielsen BookData]. Layout and presentation courtesy of Nielsen Book Services [trading as Books & Consumers].

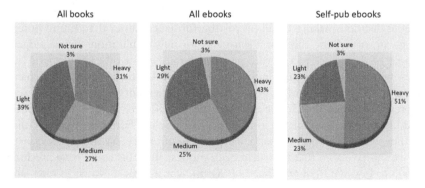

Figure 3.4 Buyer weight of book purchase: volume, 2013. Data courtesy of Nielsen Book Services [trading as Nielsen BookData]. Layout and presentation courtesy of Nielsen Book Services [trading as Books & Consumers].

- Purchase influences: volume, 2013 (see Figure 3.2)

Note: Observe the significance of price in prompting the purchase of self-published ebooks. The title blurb and the title's subject matter have more significance than author information.

For the book industry the importance of a title's 'gift appeal' disappears from the list of influencers for ebook purchase. This is significant for the publishing industry as a whole, which has benefitted greatly from the suitability of books as gifts. For an ebook to be given as a present, much more information and planning are needed about the intended recipient (do they own an ereader; which one; how do they exchange it if a duplicate is received; how do you personalise the gift – replicate or replace the experience of writing in the front?).

- Buyer demographics: volume, 2013 (see Figure 3.3)

Note: It has long been known that women buy more books than men, but the trend is amplified in the case of ebooks, and particularly self-published ebooks. Older readers (both male and female) buy more ebooks – perhaps because of the tendency of eyesight to fail with age, and the ability of the reader of an ebook to increase the font size on the device they are using.

- Buyer weight of book purchase: volume, 2013 (see Figure 3.4)

Note: Light (5 or fewer titles a year); medium (6–15 titles a year); heavy (16 or more a year).

Heavy book-buyers buy in all formats. This aligns with research (from Books & Consumers) that heavy book-buyers purchase from a variety of different locations, from traditional bookshops and supermarkets to online retailers and second-hand shops. The publishing industry cannot assume that its traditional customers will stick to purchasing through traditional providers.

Syndicated market research does, however, need to be interpreted carefully. It is never a total picture, and unsupported by wider investigations or thinking it can promote decision-making based on past performance rather than future potential. In the case of writers, this can mean ideas for new publications being judged on the basis of their track record with previous publishers or other publishers' lack of success with related materials – rather than the appeal of their material to a changing demographic for book-buyers – as well as the emergence of new market sectors not previously approached. For example, in the UK, Pete Ayrton of Serpent's Tail based his decision to publish Lionel Shriver on the old-fashioned principle that he liked her work. Had his company been able to afford access to her previous sales they would have seen that these had been modest, and this could have precluded a decision to buy *We Need to Talk About Kevin*, which went on to be an international bestseller and the basis of a highly successful film.

Other options for lower-cost market research include working with content collaborators, encouraging the trial of materials within classrooms, lecture halls and the workplace. This can both provide feedback on resources in the early stages of development but also act as marketing, embedding commitment to materials for longer-term adoption and sale.

Examples of how market research might get used in a publishing context

Research question: Do boys aged 8–12 find the subject matter of a planned new series of fiction interesting?

Encouraging specific groups to read can be difficult, and boys approaching their teenage years is one group that is often highlighted. New mechanisms for reaching the market need to be thought about as well as the first-hand appeal ('pick-ability') of materials.

Best methods of gaining market research

There are difficulties in reaching children and careful ethical management of the processes would be needed, involving permission from parents and carers. In addition, young children might not be able to convey their complex reactions through formal questionnaires. Basic secondary market research within the media accessed by the age group (games, magazines, television programmes, online materials) might provide an initial sense of whether this is interesting, followed by a series of focus groups within children of the right age group, under parental supervision. Once a design concept has been arrived at, exposing the market to new materials in the context of what else is available, under supervision and perhaps with parents watching through a two-way mirror, can be an effective way of assessing how attractive anticipated materials are to the market.

Research question: Is there a need for publisher-managed content within a specific professional market?

This is an issue of problem isolation and recognition and it would be interesting to explore the level of need or publisher reputation in being able to deliver. Observing group reaction to the product idea could reveal a 'slow dawning' or 'sudden impulse' response (both of which would be significant), and the extent of the need and the extent to which internal decision-makers would prioritise its fulfilment.

Best methods of gaining market research

Conducting a widespread quantitative questionnaire on market needs could provide significant detail but also reveal the opportunity to rival organisations; a gap might also be evident through close study of professional communications such as frequently asked questions in online forums or articles that appear on related subjects in the professional press. Conducting small focus groups might permit the publisher access to a group reaction to a product idea; how quickly does the market understand what is being offered; is this something that due to budgetary constraints and limited time may remain an unfulfilled need (and many do)?

Research question: Where do customers within a particular market sector get their information on publishing products and which information source do they rely upon most for guidance?

It would be interesting to explore whether their search for information is active (securing leaflets on relevant schemes, finding out what their colleagues have used before, searching online for cost comparisons) or passive (reading just the information that they already have or that which is sent to them). You could explore which sources are most influential, the optimum timing of marketing information and at what point they have too much information.

Best methods of gaining market research

This would depend on the size of the sample available. If it is possible to interview a large cohort of relevant people, this could be a quantitative survey yielding associated data, perhaps followed up by some focus groups to take the discussion further. If the issue is highly commercially sensitive, a few focus groups with key members of the market could work well.

Research question: How do buying decisions get made within a particular type of organisation?

It would be interesting to explore the structure of the organisation and how decisions get made. For example, how hierarchical is the organisation, how effective are internal communications and how collaborative are the decision-making processes?

Best methods of gaining market research

Within a business, this is likely to be commercially sensitive information and hence formal responses to an official questionnaire will be resisted. It might be possible to conduct a quantitative survey among members of a professional association if there were benefits to how that association understood their influence was perceived. Alternatively you might create focus groups within organisations you are thinking of working with, asking them how processes work. However you proceed, prior work will be needed to establish an outline to discuss and it will be particularly significant to explore the roles of the decision-making gatekeepers, who are the initiators, influencers, buyers, users and those placing the order, as well as the status of the products or services you are offering (are they fulfilling a need that is ongoing or just 'good to have')? Are there industry buying processes, perhaps through wholesalers or cooperative buying arrangements, that you need to know about?

Concluding case study

Given that the aim of market research is market understanding in order to secure a competitive advantage over rival organisations, it is usually confidential. The following case study has therefore been anonymised.

Market insight. The Indian office of an international publisher received an order for 30 copies of a British academic textbook. They held the titles in stock and were able to supply direct. The order was unexpected and prompted questions about whether this revealed likely future strong demand for the title. Were applications for such courses rising or new university courses being established in related areas?

Wider exploration and interpretation of the data revealed that the requirement for stock was not within India. The order had been passed on by the UK office, which monitored international allocations of stock. The university was seeking physical copies of a textbook in order to support a course that was delivered by distance learning but that began with a single week's residency. The course documentation, already advertised to all students, was a binder of information and a copy of the associated textbook, and it was hence very important that all students were presented with a complete resource pack of what had been promised on arrival. The title was out of print in the UK but the need for the physical materials to fulfil a pre-announced commitment to students meant that high delivery costs for timely arrival of the goods were tolerated.

Market intelligence was needed to broaden understanding, to find out more about the course being offered in the UK, and whether the trend was general. Are many universities now delivering content through distance learning, and is this reaching new demographics or just servicing the established markets for university education in new ways? At what academic level is this going on and do such courses lead to a qualification? Does this relate to wider governmental objectives about up-skilling the workforce? Is there financial support for retraining those who want to change their role or career? What about the resources to support these trends? What kinds are being used to support such courses: physical books; ebooks; short films; distance-learning software? A wide range of information might be explored and accessed from university websites, organisations that manage official application processes, government statistics about the numbers in full-time or part-time education; statistics on retraining and cross-checking this against longer-term commitments within the specific industries being serviced might come in useful. The relevant professional and sector media could also be accessed and interrogated (is this an issue they have covered; how often; does it attract comment and associated advertising?).

Market research could be considered to look into the specifics of market size and associated opportunities. Within the particular discipline for which the textbooks were sought, how many universities are offering low residency/distance learning; where and with what overlap for the areas for which the organisation publishes? This could be quantitative research through a survey of academics within a particular field.

Could other titles from the publisher's stable be incorporated within the overall package of information supplied to students and, if so, who should be contacted, what is their likely job title, what quantities might be appropriate; what terms and conditions would encourage the holding of stock? This might work best as qualitative research through focus groups with a few key individuals from the market meeting with the publisher.

Finally, what kind of demographic is opting for this distance learning and who is paying for it? Are there other groups who are benefitting from the process but who are not formally accounted for, e.g., is the course being offered to internal staff/a local audience as well as those who are paying from outside, and so the need for supporting resources might be greater than initially evident? This might be best answered through discreet qualitative interviews with course organisers to reveal actual, although unacknowledged, practice.

Notes

1 Isaacson, W. (2011) *Steve Jobs*, New York: LittleBrown.
2 Fast-moving consumer goods, e.g., groceries.
3 www.nielsenbook.co.uk.

4 Profit, loss and accountability

Drawing up a budget 62
How a budget is divided up 62
How do you set a budget? 64
Sample costings for publishing products and services 68
When to spend a budget 72
How to monitor a budget 73
How to make a budget go further 74
Managing cash flow 78
Securing sponsorship, partnerships and other methods of financial support 79
Hanging on to a marketing budget 81

Marketing costs money. Even if you concentrate on online marketing (Chapter 9) or publicity and PR (Chapter 10) you will incur costs: your time; the electricity and telephone bills. The long-term cost of free material given away for review, or feature that has a production cost (even if distributed online, material needs to be prepared for dissemination), also risks removing the recipients' need to purchase. While many of these activities will be paid for out of the general company over- heads, when it comes to drawing up a budget for the active marketing of a title, a much closer line of accountability needs to be created between effort and antici- pated rewards, and a firm decision must be taken on how much can be spent.

A glance at the title file of a forthcoming product should show you how many copies were expected to sell in the first year after publication, an estimation made when the title was first commissioned. The marketing budget will be designed to pro- duce these sales and so generate enough revenue to, first, pay for the direct outlay on the title (author advance or fee, development and promotion costs and so on); second, make a contribution to company overheads; and, third, produce a profit to invest in new publishing enterprises and (if relevant) remunerate shareholders.

These three considerations will be computed together as the eventual return on investment (ROI): how much the publisher invested in the project, and how much it got back. The period over which ROI is calculated, and eventually judged, will depend on the nature of the publishing project, its long-term sig- nificance to the organisation and the specific market being targeted. For example, projects that require customers to commit into the future, especially if paid up front with a commitment to a certain period of time (e.g., subscriptions to journals or online resources), may deliver much more in longer-term customer lifetime value and hence be financially accounted over longer periods of time.

Selling through retailers rather than direct to their customers has meant that in the past publishing firms have been distanced from accurately understanding the ROI for their products. This is changing. While some online retailers do not release information on buying patterns of customers, which remains proprietary information, publishers today are actively seeking to build up communities of purchasers themselves. New methods of marketing online allow them to measure the impact of their marketing on awareness and purchasing patterns – and in the process to understand the longevity and profitability of relationships with their customers.

Finally, one can speculate on how getting free or discounted materials impacts on publishers' attitude to price and what is value for money.

Drawing up a budget

A budget is a plan of activities expressed in money terms. Successful management of a budget means delivering, at an acceptable cost, all the elements detailed in the budget. It is not just a question of keeping expenditure within the prescribed limit irrespective of how many of the planned outcomes are achieved.

The budget assigned to the marketing department of a publishing house will be just one of a whole series of payments that senior managers have to allocate. Organisational overheads have to be provided for – both those attributable to specific departments (e.g., staff and freelance hours) and those from the company as a whole (e.g., audit fees, HR department costs and IT).

The amount allocated to the marketing budget (and to other departmental budgets) is usually based on a percentage of the organisation's (or section's) projected turnover for that year. What you can spend is dictated by what you will be receiving.

For each forthcoming product or service, the marketing manager will estimate market size and (based on previous experience, current market activity and the value originality or newness offered by the now item being announced) the percentage likely to buy. Anticipated future income from new titles is added to other sources of revenue such as rights sales for content (both in the original and in additional formats such as online or 'partial' publication), reprints and investment income. Projected turnover for the year ahead, and probably for the next three- or five-year period, is planned at high-level management meetings. Expectations are subsequently monitored against actual performance, usually on a monthly and annual basis. Comparisons are then made with previous years and long-term plans updated.

How a budget is divided up

The marketing budget is likely to be subsequently divided between several categories of expenditure. Four main categories exist, in decreasing order of importance:

- core marketing costs;
- plans for individual titles;
- budgets for 'smaller' titles;
- contingency.

Core marketing costs

These are the regular marketing activities that are essential to the selling cycles of the publishing industry. These include the marketing website, the production of catalogues and new title or stock lists (increasingly available in digital format only but therefore requiring ongoing updating throughout the year rather than timed production at specific intervals) and advance notices for each title planned. The total sum required for these items is usually deducted from the marketing budget before further allocations are made. These should only be cut as a very last resort.

Plans for individual titles

Once core costs have been taken out, the money is then generally divided between a variety of different publishing projects, each one of which is in effect a separate business. The manager calculates what it will cost to reach potential buyers, aiming to reach as many as possible with the budget allocated and deciding where the available resources will have the most impact.

New titles or series, or perhaps works that are already published but need actively promoting, should have specific amounts of money allocated to their marketing. The allocation is not always made exactly in proportion to the anticipated revenue: some markets may be easier or cheaper to reach than others, and need less extensive budgets.

If it is your responsibility to draw up these preliminary allocations, consider the options for reaching the market presented elsewhere in this book, decide on which titles or series the money could most usefully be spent, then look at the actual costs. How many people does it include and how many are you able to reach already? How many times do you need to 'touch' the customer before they will purchase? For example, will one series of book advertisements on the subway be enough to make them buy or must this be reinforced through social media and bookshops? Publishers used to have their relationships with their customers largely mediated through specialist retailers, but they are now moving towards systems that capture customer data so that the market can be contacted directly – and a community of interest built for the future sales. Those marketing specialist information to scientific, technical and professional audiences are further ahead here; they can estimate the size of their market accurately and, based on previous experience and the size of their subscriber list, appreciate their overall penetration levels. Consider what other products and services within the organisation can be marketed symbiotically to increase the possible size of an order – through the pooling of budgets and to present the customer with the breadth of what is on offer. It can be particularly hard to estimate anticipated sales for material that is destined for a 'general' market (see Chapter 15).

Budgets for 'smaller' titles

Next comes the allocation of money to titles needing (or receiving) smaller budgets. This may mean you will only be able to promote them actively if you pool the budget with that of other titles and do a shared promotion, e.g., several titles at the same time, or appeal to the same audience through a combination of cross-selling events, writing support and related boooks. This is not necessarily an unwelcome compromise. Boosting a range of related titles together encourages an awareness of your publishing house as a particular type of organisation, and may attract both new purchasers and new authors. In the same way, most editors have a responsibility for building a particular list. Cooperative promotions back up and give authority to your main title strategies, and can provide a useful push for the backlist titles included.

Contingency

Last of all may come a contingency amount to be used at the marketing department's discretion on any title or group of titles as good ideas come up, such as backing an author's initiatives or attending a relevant conference. It does not always reach the final budget: during the process of reconciling how much the marketing department would like to spend with how much is available, sacrifices are looked for. The contingency budget is often a casualty.

How the four areas of budgetary division are linked

The sum of these four areas of spending is usually based on (or at least compared with) the percentage of the firm's anticipated turnover, as discussed above. By drawing up a budget in this way the interdependence of all the titles in a list can be seen. If one title fails to achieve what it is budgeted to do, all the other titles in the list will have to work harder if the firm is to survive or profit margins are to be maintained.

Reasons for failure vary. An author may produce the manuscript late or produce a text that needs substantial and time-consuming reworking before it can be published; copyright clearance can take up to 6 months; production time may be longer than anticipated. Until a title is actually released for publication, recorded dues cannot be added to the sales figures. If this happens at a financial year end, sales will be lost from the year's figures.

If the manuscript cannot be remedied, the sales will be lost altogether – a serious situation if money has already been spent on promotion and the author advance is difficult to recover.

How do you set a budget?

If the overall marketing budget is based on a percentage of anticipated turnover (different amounts being allocated to various titles according to need and ease of reaching the market), what kind of percentages are we talking about? The question depends broadly on a judicious juggling of three considerations: the likely profit margin within the area of publishing in question; the associated development costs; the stage in the publishing lifecycle process. Finally there are a series of variable factors that influence the allocation of marketing budgets.

Considerations that arise from the likely profit margin within the area of publishing in question

There are established rough percentages spent on marketing within certain areas of publishing, and these are based largely on how the materials are sold, price levels, competitor activity and ease of reaching the market. For example:

Information resources for business and professional markets (whether online or in print) sell mainly at high prices (which reflect the costs of researching and continuously updating the content but also respond to competitor activity) direct to specialist markets, and little discount is given to the retail trade. Marketing budgets may be as high as 20 per cent of anticipated turnover, perhaps more to launch a major title in the first year after publication.

Prices within the **education market** servicing schools are generally low, with sales managed through educational wholesalers, and there will be less room for spending large amounts on marketing. Budgets will probably average 6–8 per cent of forecast turnover.

On **academic or highly specialised reference titles**, the prices may be high but the print run is very low (250–500) and so the percentage spent on marketing may be no more than 5 per cent – if that. The firm may rely on the author to implement marketing through their own networks and be effectively functioning as a packager, relying on the academic's need to be published (or that of the funder of their research).

Considerations arising from the associated development costs

Production costs are also referred to as 'origination' costs. These include editorial costs, artwork, paper, etc. Reprints after a title's initial print run has sold out can show healthier margins, once the basic origination (including editorial costs), permissions, illustrations and marketing costs have been paid for.

Publisher overheads generally include storage, despatch, representation and staff, as well as a contribution to general overheads, e.g., the costs of running head office. For printed titles, the amounts quoted in Table 4.1 depend on selling the entire print run. If stock is returned and has to be restocked, stored or pulped then this increases the publishers' overheads.

Publishing as an ebook from scratch, without a printed edition, is not (as is generally believed) necessarily vastly cheaper than producing a print title. The absence of print means that production costs are lower, sales management costs are significantly lower (with online retailers managing the selling) and the cost of *physical* distribution through wholesalers and bookshops is not needed. But the origination costs are very similar; many of the 'invisible' costs of publishing (structural and copy-editing, proofreading, creating an attractive cover and author remuneration) still need to be borne. It's often frustrating for publishers that effective publishing is often only evident when absent; a book that is well written and beautifully designed gives no clue as to the amount of work it has taken to get it to that state of affairs.

The marketing costs of ebooks may also be increased compared to those deployed to sell their printed counterparts, as there are some new ones to factor into the traditional mix, e.g., website management for author and publisher, managing social media, reformatting for different ebook readers.

Reformatting a product can further extend its reach within a niche market before it is made available in a mass market edition, or to meet the needs of a different mass market. For example, producing an ebook first, to test demand, and then producing a hardback and paperback; or producing a hardback and an ebook at the same time. Similarly sometimes a 'C format paperback' version (hardback edition size and type of paper, limp binding) will be produced in between the hardback and a mass market edition, in order to extend sales at a higher price.

But reformatting a print title as an ebook will always incur additional costs (it's not as simple – as is often assumed – as 'pressing a few buttons') and how much can be spent on marketing will depend on whether the fixed costs of origination are set against the print book or the ebook. In the UK, the Society of Authors calls for higher author royalties on unenhanced ebooks (versions of the existing print edition with no additional editorial changes) and this too impacts on the amount that can be spent on marketing.

The 'bundling' of formats may add incremental sales without necessarily damaging those within each category. For example, bundling a hardback with an ebook might make a very attractive proposition to a reader (one to display at home, one to have when on the move) and extend the income received, without necessarily diminishing the sales in either format (very few customers currently buy both).

Considerations arising from the relevant stage in the publishing lifecycle process

There may be a requirement to spend heavily on marketing at the time of publication in order to achieve an acceptable return on investment (ROI), because if sales do not take off well, the titles will flop in the long term, even if you subsequently alocate more budget. For example:

Information resources for business and professional markets (whether online, print or both) need large initial promotion budgets, perhaps for two or three years, until the sales strategy can become chiefly one of encouraging subscription renewals.

Within **educational publishing**, a major new series aimed at securing large-scale adoptions will need strong initial marketing momentum. Once the adoptions have been made and the scheme is being used in schools, less intensive selling will be needed.

When **promoting a new journal** it may be cost-effective to spend the whole of the first one or two years' individual subscription revenue on acquiring a subscriber. Once the subscription is recorded the subscriber should stay for a number of years and hence their lifetime value (generally computed to be around 7 years) will enable the venture to become profitable.

Launching a new author in a competitive market will require significant marketing investment. Some publishing houses spend early, to get a momentum going and build on this in future; others rely on the efforts of their authors in approaching the market and allow market forces to direct where to allocate future spending.

In general, the more the publishers have paid to acquire an author, the more they are likely to spend on marketing. In instances where it has been expensive to secure an author, and who need high-profile marketing campaigns to launch their transfer, it may only be after a second title that a publisher makes a profit, hence the popularity of two- or three-book deals.

Variable factors that influence the allocation of marketing budgets

Factors that can influence the economics of individual publishing projects, the amounts paid to authors and the financial health of the organisation as a whole – and hence impact on the size of associated marketing budgets – include:

The gap between commissioning of the work and delivery. The publisher is generally paying a variety of costs long before they have anything available to sell. Thus, in general, the quicker the publisher is able to move towards remuneration through sales, the better. Arrangements that involve paying commission on sales that are achieved (rather than anticipated) may enable greater risk-taking and a higher marketing spend.[1]

The terms on which titles are taken by retailers. The levels of discount given to different accounts will depend on various factors including the quantity taken, the terms on which the stock is provided (firm sale or sale and return) and the overall level of business between the two parties. Agreements that lock the two sides together (e.g., buying on firm sale, guaranteed featuring in marketing materials put out by the retailer) may result in a higher marketing spend.

Supermarkets get much bigger discounts in return for firm sale and high quantities, and often use the stock as 'loss leaders' to draw customers into their stores. This is generally paid for by increasing publisher marketing spend and reducing author royalties.[2]

Online retailers similarly get very high levels of discount. There is, however, ongoing concern about the accounting procedures of some and, in particular, arrangements for paying organisational taxation – and whether these are fair to the businesses they compete with.

The prices at which retailers sell the stock. In markets where there is no retail price maintenance (i.e., the price suggested by the publisher may be discounted by the retailer) the sums received may be much less than their official value. If the publisher has agreed to an additional discount on launch, in order to support initial marketing momentum, then increased sales may result. If, however, this does not result in significantly increased sales, the profits per title sold will be further reduced. The sums received by the author are generally based on receipts not the official value of stock.

Along similar lines, if the selling price cannot be guaranteed, marketing initiatives based on titles that will sell at full recommended retail price are particularly useful. For example, authors heading events and signing at literary festivals can add value to a product – and hence stock is usually sold for its full recommended retail price. Such opportunities may be worth backing with an additional marketing spend (or increased retail discount).

The level at which product prices are set. It's important to note that prices can be arrived at on the basis of market expectations as well as actual costs. For example, the higher cost of a hardback reflects aspects of production such as lower print runs and hence higher unit costs for each title printed, and a higher royalty rate, but also market perceptions of cost and expectations that a hardback title will be more expensive. Similarly, there may be a decision to 'skim' the market to fulfil all the demand for a high price before penetrating the market more deeply with a mass market version.

The availability of market research may also tempt publishers to spend more. Estimating the demand for new authors is always difficult. It follows that those who have demonstrated demand by self-publishing may be an attractive investment, particularly if in the process a new area of consumption has been identified and can be further developed in future with new material for the same audience.

Similarly, digital marketing and dissemination permit experimentation (and are often used to test or prove a market for which a subsequent print version could be considered). Digital marketing permits rapid experimentation with offers and free samples to build a market or establish a profile – or implement what has been observed. Often these 'loss leaders' do not generate a great deal of income for publisher or author but can be useful in building profile and readership, and their implementation through digital media means they can be established and taken down very quickly, to build on what is learned in the process (e.g., free for just 24 hours).

In some markets **sales or value added tax** is added to the merchandise being sold; sometimes there is VAT and sales tax on all products (perhaps at a different rate from the standard), in others just on ebooks and CDs. How this is managed is a further complication. Is it visible to the consumer (i.e., itemised on the receipt or invoice they pay)? Alternatively, is it absorbed within the margin of the publisher or the retailer – and if so, which? How tax is managed will impact on consumer perceptions of the value they receive and their tendency to purchase.

Sample costings for publishing products and services

Given all the specific circumstances and conditions listed above, there has been much discussion over whether the following figures should appear in this book at all. We eventually decided that they did have a role in helping to explain the *broad* structure of financing publishing. They are not designed to show that any one format or genre of publishing is intrinsically more profitable than any other, rather to isolate the variables that need to be taken into consideration when planning a marketing budget.

Table 4.1 Sample costings for publishing products and services

New general hardback title (print run 3,000)

	%	Amount	Balance
Published price			35.00
Less discount to retailers	40	14.00	21.00
Less production costs	15	5.25	15.75
Less royalties to author	10	3.50	12.25
Less marketing budget	10	3.50	8.75
Less publisher overheads	20	7.00	1.75
Potential profit on print run			5,250.00

Subsequent mass market paperback edition of the same title (print run 30,000)

	%	Amount	Balance
Published price			8.99
Less discount to retailers	55	4.94	4.05
Less production costs	8	0.72	3.33
Less royalties to author	6	0.54	2.79
Less marketing budget	10	0.89	1.90
Less publisher overheads	18	1.62	0.28
Potential profit on print run			8,400.00

Ebook version of the same title

	%	Amount	Balance
Published price			7.99*
Less discount to retailers	30	2.40	5.59
Less production costs	4	0.32	5.27
Less royalties to author	25	2.00	3.27
Less marketing budget	10	0.79	2.48
Less publisher overheads	20	1.60	0.88
Potential profit per title sold**			0.88

*Consideration of whether this is subject to VAT, and if so whether this is shouldered by publishers or retailers.
**No print run, so no limit here.

Ebook original

	%	Amount	Balance
Published price			7.99
Less discount to retailers	30	2.40	5.59
Less production costs	11	0.88	4.73
Less royalties to author	25	2.00	2.73
Less marketing budget	10	0.79	1.94
Less publisher overheads	20	1.60	0.34
Potential profit per title			0.34

Table 4.1 (Continued)

New academic textbook (heavily illustrated, print run 5,000, limp binding)

	%	Amount	Balance
Published price			29.99
Less discount to retailers	35	10.50	19.49
Less production costs	20	6.00	13.49
Less royalties to author	4	1.20	12.29
Less marketing budget	12	3.60	8.69
Less publisher overheads	20	6.00	2.69
Potential profit on print run			13,450.00

Academic monograph (no illustration, print run 500)

	%	Amount	Balance
Published price			45.00
Less discount to retailers	40	18.00	27.00
Less production costs	10	4.50	22.50
Less royalties to author	5	2.25	20.25
Less marketing budget	5	2.25	18.00
Less publisher overheads	20	9.00	9.00
Potential profit on print run			4,500.00

To summarise, publishing has a very complicated financial structure. Each title is in effect a separate business for which costs must be calculated and the marketing allowance is just one part of that equation – and cannot be seen in isolation. Jo McCrum, assistant chief executive of the Society of Authors comments:

> Bear in mind too that the retailer discounts can vary and be much higher than these examples. UK Amazon, book club and supermarket discounts are around 70 per cent on most trade titles. The 70 per cent Amazon takes from publishers' ebooks/books leaves 30 per cent to be split between publisher and author on a high-discount royalty basis. Sometimes special offers can apply on ebooks where the discounts can go towards 95 per cent. Wholesalers take 60 per cent of the cover price, so an authors' royalty at that point falls to a receipts basis and the share is therefore much smaller. Independent bookshops get the smallest discounts (35–40 per cent) but this means that author royalties received are calculated on the cover price, and hence more is received.
>
> Publishers will say that the level of discounts they have established with suppliers is confidential commercial information, so we cannot say with certainty what has been arranged. But from evaluating the number of copies sold (via royalty statements) and the monies actually coming in, it's not hard to work out that publishers are now forced to pay very high levels of commission on some titles, and authors – the original creators of what is being sold – are not getting a share that is either proportionate to their investment in the project or fair.

On titles that are self-published, Amazon takes a 30 per cent distributor's share and sends the remaining 70 per cent to the self-publishing author. It's ironic that authors who are self-republishing their out-of-print backlist titles are often getting better returns than they are on their front list titles from their publishers.

In the UK, losing the Net Book Agreement can now be seen as a disaster for the publishing industry, and a precursor of the ferocious discounting that is threatening to destroy it.

If it is thought essential to award a larger than average marketing budget, or indeed to assign more money to any of the routine costs of publishing (e.g., to pay the author a higher advance, give more discount to the book trade, or spend more on production) then either the unit sales must be greater to justify the increase or another variable must be altered. Options here include:

- selling the content in another way (e.g., in digital form);
- increasing the unit price (perhaps by producing a smaller number and building in exclusivity by numbering the print run or bundling the product with other items to make an augmented offer to the consumer for which more can be charged);
- lowering the quality of materials and hence the production costs;
- paying reduced royalties;
- looking for a co-publishing deal that makes production costs more favourable and eases cash flow.

But this needs to be managed against delivering the right message to the market. Spending too much might be counterproductive. For example, consider the fund-raising mailshots sent out by charities: they are usually printed on recycled paper, stressing an urgency and need that would be entirely defeated were full-colour brochures enclosed. But when it comes to their gift catalogues, they print in full colour to show the merchandise in its most advantageous light.

Some companies have tried to improve sales by substantially increasing their level of promotional expenditure, but if it costs proportionally more to achieve the resulting extra sales then the outcome can be financial ruin. Decisions to overspend on marketing may still be made, and sometimes the risks pay off, but it should not be forgotten that monitoring a budget is an essential part of drawing one up, and people can lose their jobs or firms go out of business for failing to implement what they have agreed.

Finally, it's worth noting too that even if you award identical marketing budgets to all your titles, some will always outperform the others – what Cory Doctorow has dubbed 'scratchcard publishing'.[3] If sales for one title disappoint and you have extra resources to spend, it is usually better to allocate the additional funds to titles that are doing well than try to recover the position of the poorer sellers: it's better to back the winners.

When to spend a budget

Once a basic marketing sum has been allocated, the next step is to budget for when it should be spent during the year. There are external constraints on you.

When the market wants to be told about new material

Promotion is usually a seasonal business; timings will vary according to the type of book being promoted and the market being approached. In markets where Christmas is a major holiday, roughly 40 per cent of the year's general sales in bookshops take place between the middle of October and 24 December. Most publishers for this market therefore time their main selling season so that the books are on the stockists' shelves ready to meet this bonanza. In the same way, educational publishers promote titles to the schools market at the times when teachers are considering how to spend their budgets, and academic publishers aim to reach their market when reading lists for students are being compiled.

When the titles themselves are scheduled

The production department will produce a list giving scheduled release (when stock goes out from the warehouse to the trade) and publication dates (when retailers can start selling). Promotion schedules should be planned around these dates; with some types of product, timing is particularly important. Printed year-books and directories must be promoted early because they age and get harder to sell as the new edition approaches. Books with seasonal covers (e.g., related to Christmas or summer weddings) need to be pitched early. Academic monographs too must be promoted ahead of publication: as much as 60 per cent of first-year sales can occur in the month of publication. If promotion plans have not been carried out and the dues recorded by the time of release, sales may never recover.

The need to promote early should be balanced against the risk of peaking too far ahead of publication date, with the danger that the effects will be lost. The fault may not be yours: the author may deliver the manuscript late; production can take longer than anticipated. And timings may need to be adjusted forwards too. Authors may share information on their forthcoming titles via social media before you anticipated this would happen, and you may find yourself facing sudden unexpected demand, long before scheduled publication; difficult if you have arranged production in a distant (but cost-effective) location and the costs of bringing the material back by air are extremely expensive.

Online sites offer the opportunity for customers to place pre-orders and this is a very useful way of generating initial momentum (guage how far in advance of publication to make them available, look at the terms and conditions and then consider prevailing market factors – too early an announcement may encourage competitor activity). All the pre-orders received are released on publication day, and thus the title's augmented first-day sales may be enough to raise it into the category of bestseller, with the accompanying attention.

Selling online also means that the variables of the marketing offer (price, costs for postage and packing, discounting) can be changed to fit in with marketing strategies. This permits the making of temporary offers, specific promotions to particular groups (e.g., offering the market a code that, when entered on a website, reveals the special price offered), and what is learned in the process can be fed into future campaigns.

When you have time to market them

Promotions that are not related to publication dates (for example relaunching old series or organising a thematic push for the backlist) can be scheduled for less busy periods in the calendar, but again market acceptability must be considered. Publishing is most often a seasonal business, and you cannot really avoid this. You must just accept that you will be busier at certain times of the year.

How to monitor a budget

Once the budget is established, stick to it – or only depart from it in a conscious fashion, with permission. In most houses once invoices have been passed by the person who commissioned the work (and it is generally that person who checks them against the quote), they are sent to the individual in the accounts department who deals with marketing expenditure (or in large organisations, a specific list/area of activity). A finance manager comments:

> In return, monthly reports are generally provided on spending levels, although reports can also be provided weekly, quarterly or annually, depending on the level of activity and the need. Generally speaking, we can produce reports the day after expenditure has been committed or spent on the finance system so, if we entered an invoice today, we could produce an up-to-date report tomorrow. It may be worth noting that we also report on variances against budget, so if one month your budget is £10,000 on staffing and resources and you only spend or commit £5,000 we would report a £5,000 variance which would then require an explanation such as timing or allocating of the budget to an alternative category.

How much financial reporting is provided directly to you will depend on your position within the organisation (whether or not you are a budget holder) and the scale of the funds for which you are responsible. Although more financial reporting may be available to you than you initially realise, it may still be worth keeping a running balance of how much you have spent (or committed but not yet billed) and what still remains from the title's budget.

It may be helpful to decide at the beginning of the year the percentages of the individual title budgets to be spent on online marketing, online support, print, design, copy, despatch and other key elements. That does not mean the proportions cannot be changed if specific scenarios occur. A marketing manager once spent a project's entire budget on a delegate place at a relevant conference because this brought with it a copy of the delegate list. She did not even attend.

When considering printed marketing materials, it's helpful to look at costs per thousand for leaflet production lists and mailing charges. Unit prices for print reduce as numbers increase, mailing lists and despatch charges in general do not (or not by very much). Harness your promotion expenditure to your marketing responses and you start to get very sophisticated market information. If you compare the costs of producing a catalogue (on- or offline) with the orders received directly from it (or perhaps received during the period over which it was being actively used for ordering) then you can compile a figure for orders per page and an accurate indication of how profitable your endeavours have been. This is easier for publishers promoting to markets that have limited purchasing options and hence where the results of their efforts can be isolated (e.g., professional publishing or STM), but accountability is a culture to be developed in any sector and is the way the rest of the retail trade is run (the key ratio is floor/promotional space to revenue).

How to make a budget go further

Affording effective marketing in publishing is tricky: the purchase prices in general are low, as are often the quantities in which books sell (15,000 units for a new paperback novel will generally afford it bestseller status). It follows that being awarded enough marketing budget to enable each title to reach its full potential is not always possible. At the same time, however, take comfort from the fact that there are more opportunities for the free coverage of books and their authors than any other product or service (see Chapter 10 on PR and free marketing). Try the following money-saving techniques:

Take personal responsibility for your budget

Take personal responsibility for your budget and you are more likely to be efficient in its use. So start by observing your own buying habits: what are the trigger points that make you part with your own money; how much information do you need to make a buying decision and what are the aspects of an organisation that make you comfortable/uncomfortable about buying from them?

Build a culture of accountability. Circulate the results from online campaigns; analyse the progress of each promotion; record sales figures before and after marketing efforts; make recommendations on how they could have been improved/why they were so good. There is often a reluctance within the industry to recording why marketing did or did not work – even if you decide not to share what you observe, keep a record for your own future instruction.

Watch what your competitors are doing, both publishing and non-publishing. Keeping a close eye on the publishing industry can be difficult, but one effective way of managing this is to give each member of staff in the marketing department a competitor to 'adopt'. They then become responsible for watching out for the competitor's marketing and plans. Pool the information at a meeting and you can have a very helpful overall survey of your market.

Learn from other industries by developing a general interest in advertising and marketing and not just confining your study of marketing materials to the messages put out by other publishers. Above all, be interested in your products and who buys them – and try to observe this in action.

Get your timing right

This is crucial, as was noted above. Timely handling of the standard in-house procedures for book promotion is particularly important. Ensure the title is listed on the website and in catalogues for the season in which it is due to be published. Be sure that the advance notice is ready to appear at the right time, containing up to date information.

Explore online marketing (see Chapter 9)

Although the same care must be taken in the preparation of information, the costs of informing a market online are much less than through sending out printed marketing materials. Ensure you have an effective website and *crucially* that you update it regularly to give those returning to it something new to look at – offer competitions, reduced price incentives for limited periods, free samples. Ensure this is linked to mechanisms for effective delivery, via a third party if you cannot arrange it yourself.

Benefit from viral marketing

Feed information on your titles to all possible carriers, association websites, those producing relevant newsletters and those active within enthuser-groups which might regard the information as useful to members or followers they attract.

If you find a specific community that is particularly interested, encourage them to be ambassadors for your project: to 'wear your books as a form of self-expression'[4] and communicate their enthusiasm through social media. Making sample material available to them free so they can run a competition or offer it as prizes may get them talking about it. Get them to endorse it for you and they may do even more. This is a particularly useful tactic for independent publishers, when you can build on a passion that unites you with the wider community who share your enthusiasm.

Spot mutually useful synergies

There may be mailings (online and print) going out that you could join if you asked; secondary markets may exist and prove highly profitable if you think of targeting them. Think laterally. Why not send all schools a catalogue request form in case they are interested in other areas for which you publish? There are certain well-known combinations of interest and profession (many academics seem to like opera, and lots of politicians seem to be interested in bird-watching); if you have products on your list likely to appeal, try them out.

Get better value for money for your spend on print

If you decide you do need a printed leaflet, don't spend too much on production. Instead of sophisticated design, concentrate your attention on effective copy and buying reasons that speak directly to the market (see Chapter 14). Remember that overcomplicated design can get in the way of effective communication.

Run-on costs (see Glossary) for leaflets are often very good value for money compared with the overall set-up costs for a job. Consider increasing the print run and then trying to circulate what you produce as widely as possible: through loose inserts in relevant journals; circulation at specialist meetings; insertion in delegates' bags at conferences; distribution to the author for their personal use and so on. If you are sending printed information to standard outlets (e.g., bookstores and libraries), use shared mailings rather than bearing all the despatch costs yourself. In surveys, most libraries, academics and schools say they don't care whether promotional material reaches them on its own or in company; it is the content that counts.

If commercial opportunities do not exist, then consider forming partnerships with non-competing firms to share costs (assuming the mailing list can be used in this way). Can you take exhibition space in partnership too? These methods may attract slightly lower levels of response than individual mailings, but the cost of sales will also be substantially reduced. You will be able to reach more people for less money.

If you prepare a central stock list or standard order form, run on extra copies and use in mailings, include in parcels or send to exhibitions. If you use a new book supplement in your catalogue (perhaps inserted in the centrefold) can this too be reprinted for use in mailings? If your catalogue is designed as a series of double-page spreads, could these be turned into leaflets later on? With this in mind, if you are working in more than one colour, ensure that anything you may want to delete later on (such as page numbers) appears in black only, which is the cheapest plate to change. Can full-colour material be reprinted for a second mailing in two colours rather than four?

Sometimes you may not need formal marketing materials at all. A sales letter with a coupon for return along the bottom can be a very efficient way of soliciting orders. (The opposite generally does not apply, by the way: brochures almost always need a letter to go with them.) Update your information not by reprinting but rather sending out accompanying photocopied pages of reviews or features that have appeared.

Use your authors

Author proactivity is often a highly effective route to the market and today author commitment to involvement in publicity is generally included in the contract (see Chapter 11 on working with authors). Have an early meeting with the authors of forthcoming books and discuss how you can work together to promote interest and sales.

Use free publicity to the maximum possible extent

The pursuit of free publicity should not replace your standard promotional tools; rather, it should back them up. But don't end up paying for advertising space if the magazine would have printed a feature with a little persuasion. Many magazines are willing to make 'reader offers' – an editorial mention in return for free copies to give out (because it helps them cement the loyalty of their readership). Nor should you offer to pay for a loose insert if your author is on the editorial board and could have arranged for it to be circulated for nothing.

To make maximum use of free publicity you need to exploit the link between what you are promoting and why people should be interested, and the background of the author may be more significant than their new title. Try to find media that serve the needs of specialist markets that are not routinely used by other publishers, and non-book outlets in retail, which can help your materials stand out. For example, find out about author's hobbies and interests and you may find a new avenue for promotion emerges, one where there is much less competition. Is your author interested in model railways or caravanning? Both have extensive associated publications with high circulations.

Negotiate as a matter of course

The publishing industry spends little on space advertising – it's one of the reasons why the survival of the book review pages is consistently threatened as they bring little revenue into media organisations. It follows that there is a general understanding that publishers are not cash-rich organisations and this can be used to your advantage. There is a standard publisher's discount of 10 per cent for booking advertising space. Sometimes more can be squeezed if you have not advertised with them before (a 'trial advertisement'), or the rate the medium quotes is too expensive for your budget. If you have the time, use it – the advertising sales representative will probably come back to you with a reduced price. Particularly good deals can be obtained just before a magazine goes to print – once it has gone to the printers the space has no value at all. If you go for a series of adverts you should get an additional discount, and likewise if you book a year's requirements in one go.

Do you have someone in the department who has previously worked in advertising sales? If so, ask them to handle negotiations for you, and you will almost certainly reduce your anticipated costs further still. Consider going on a negotiating skills course.

One final tip on dealing with discounted offers: decide where you want to advertise and then negotiate on price. If you allow yourself to get used to responding to the special offers available from magazines that you are less than committed to appearing in (i.e., they were not on your original media plan), your marketing becomes much less targeted and you run the risk of seriously overspending. Remember that space costs are only one part of the total outlay. Continually saying 'no' can be an exercise to find out just how much can be negotiated off the list price.

Managing cash flow

Effective management of cash flow is crucial to a business; an organisation may in theory have made many 'sales' but in practice received little remuneration. If a keen eye is not kept on the return of actual cash, the future of the organisation is threatened.

One way of reducing costs is to devolve distribution to a supplier. Distribution is labour-intensive and demands precision (customers want the materials they ordered, quickly and in perfect condition). Devolving it to a wholesaler or online retailer who can supply low-value small orders, leaving you to concentrate on creating product and associated demand, can be a cost-effective response leading to regular return of income.

The setting of terms (e.g., payment periods, the arrangements under which stock may be returned) with retailers is of crucial importance. Published products may be sent to trade outlets on a variety of different terms, some more beneficial to the publisher than others. Encouraging the trade to 'buy firm' rather than on 'sale or return' prevents unexpected returns that reduce sales and the overall profitability of particular titles.

If you are going to accept direct orders from individual customers, and benefit from the associated understanding of your market, provide every opportunity for those ordering to buy direct and pay early, and in the most cost-efficient way for you. Some credit cards charge a higher percentage of the sales invoice than others. To encourage them to buy direct you can try to promote the value of loyalty to something they believe in, reassuring them with a cast-iron guarantee of satisfaction or their money back. For example:

> We are an independent publishing house and would appreciate the chance to fulfil your order directly. Apart from ensuring that the book gets to you more quickly, this offers us an important benefit – the chance to make a sale – and hence to carry on producing the kind of titles we know you value.

Institutions such as schools, colleges and libraries will need an invoice to pay against, but can they be encouraged to pay sooner rather than later? State your credit terms on the website and again on the associated order form. For serial publications, directories and journals, offer customers the chance to complete a standing order. In return, offer to hold the price for a second year or perhaps give a discount.

The wording on company order forms does not have to be regarded as unchangeable (although you will need support and sign-off from colleagues if you intend to alter existing practices). Try to gain access to the metrics of any online ordering offered by your organisation and in particular the point at which non-completers gave up. Seemingly trivial amendments to the process could have a significant impact on completion rates. Is there anything in your auto-completion system that could mean a confirming email is picked up by a spam filter and hence not easily received by your customers? Study ordering mechanisms received as a consumer, and appropriate the best ideas. Experiment with different formats and styles, all with the intention of making yours as user-friendly and easy to understand as possible. Pay attention to the particular mechanisms that your market values – the chance to send a personal message with an item being sent to a third party; gift wrapping; gift receipts which do not reveal how much was spent – all of which can make the relationship with customers stronger.

Apply for all the free help you can get

Can your authors arrange for you to attend relevant meetings, run book exhibitions and make special offers to the membership? Does your firm belong to any professional associations from whose collected wisdom you can benefit? Find out about the special interest publishing groups that are part of your professional organisation, and get copies of the reports they publish; when you are more experienced it may be worth trying to attend or get yourself on to an associated committee. Read the professional press that your market reads (and the general press that covers it), and look out for helpful articles that improve your understanding of your customers. You will almost certainly spot useful quotes about market needs and key market issues that can be used in your promotional materials and perhaps spot marketing and promotion opportunities too.

Bulk sales

Are there any specific interest groups that offer the possibility for 'special sales': learned and professional societies and associations that may promote to their members? Deals you offer may enable them to represent themselves to their members as proactive and present better value to their membership for example, by securing relevant products or services at a discount.

Securing sponsorship, partnerships and other methods of financial support

Others may be willing to support your product development and marketing plans, given sufficient overlap between your respective aims. From experience, it's important to research their organisational objectives and meet them to establish their priorities and ethos. You may find that you offer a means of accessing or delivering a target group that they lacked the resources to achieve independently, or they find your mission aligns with their own whether from a business or altruistic point of view – either way, they may be amenable to making a financial contribution or supporting you in kind. For a successful relationship, the following guidelines may help:

- Try to establish relationships with personnel at a variety of levels within the organisation you are working with; then, should one employee leave, you are not then starting all over again.
- Keep track of their official information, which will have been the product of long discussion, to ensure a match between your respective aims and

outcomes. As with job applications, pay attention to the verbs they use and reflect them back.

- Your partner organisation may prefer the funding of a specific process or out-come, which they can both isolate and identify with, to a general contribution to overheads.
- Pay timely attention to the various mechanisms your partner organisation needs you to deliver – a short contribution for their regular published reports will almost certainly be required.
- Keep in touch at regular intervals: newsletters, phone calls, meetings in person.
- Acknowledge their involvement willingly and generously, and not just when you know they are present.

Other business models for funding

There are other new funding initiatives emerging to pay for publishing projects, several of which have been shown to work in other areas of industry such as the music business. For example, crowd-sourcing has been experimented with as a means of securing funding, offering enthusiasts the opportunity to invest in the publication of material they support – although ironically this looks back to subscription models of publishing used in the nineteenth century.

Other organisations are exploring how they can benefit from marketing mechanisms that are already established within particular groups. Using the old direct marketing principle that those who are happy to buy direct make better prospects than those who are professionally or temperamentally interested in the subject matter of your publishing, it may be more effective to pursue markets that enjoy online shopping, and look to sell them publishing products that you develop for them, than to build lists of book-buyers. For example, those loyal to particular clothing, food or home-ware catalogues might see books as a related brand extension, in the same way that they view bed linen, home-cured hams and gardening supplies. Associated marketing might be able to piggy-back on existing promotional plans, with the significant added advantage of being the only publishing material promoted – rather than in the context of a bookshop where there is so much choice. Potential partners may exist within the book market already for firms with a strong brand identity or particularly effective marketing mechanisms. For example, literary societies that publish special editions for their membership could provide an excellent basis on which to build the wider marketing of content. Similarly, investing in self-publishing companies could provide new revenue streams as well as the option of first access to titles and authors that demonstrate success.

One model publishers might be able to develop without an acquisition is freemium, the concept of providing some content for nothing while charging for other features. After all, with customers increasingly expecting free content, publishers need to create ways of still making a profit while giving content away. Major projects such as Pottermore and a 'Spotify for books'[5] might make freemium seem complicated and expensive to operate. Despite this, a simple successful model is already being used in China. Websites allow authors to upload stories that can be read for free;

once a work is read a number of times, the writer is labelled a 'VIP' and the site starts charging for their content. Payments are kept small so, as the UK lacks China's gigantic domestic market, British publishers would arguably either need to charge more or ensure any site could sell internationally.

Service provision between publishers is another growth area. While publishers have long distributed books on each other's behalf, the complexities of digital are providing further opportunities to sell services to smaller firms, with the likes of Faber Factory offering ebook distribution, marketing and account management. As Mike Shatzkin has explained, smaller publishers are incentivised to outsource 'parity functions', essential business functions that fail to differentiate the company from rivals.[6]

Hanging on to a marketing budget

Finally, although the marketing budget is just one of many financial responsibilities of the company, when times are difficult its reduction is often an easy way to reduce expenditure. How can you resist this tendency?

The best plan is to combat difficulties with information, so you know why titles are selling badly, and are making changes to market them more efficiently. Compare annual sales patterns year-on-year. Are any market changes responsible for the differences you see? If you are promoting through a number of key associates, did any perform particularly badly? By contacting new organisations you may be able to remedy the situation (although if you have had to market twice over to achieve your basic orders, the gross margin will still be reduced). Talk to the reps and customer services. Are products being returned because they do not meet the expectations of those to whom they were marketed? Is the offer unconvincing? Online sales patterns can tell you a great deal; the effect of changing variables (e.g., the price, the offer or the extensiveness of the guarantee) can be monitored very closely. Experiment with one variable at a time, so you can isolate the results.

If cuts are the only option, the key skill is knowing which elements to axe while doing the least possible damage to sales. Understanding the reasons that particular promotions have either failed or succeeded will help you decide what to avoid in future, and how to plan better for next year. The very last elements you should cut are the regular tools of the trade: the website, online catalogues and advance information sheets on which so much of the publishing sales cycle depends.

Case study

Crimson Cats:[7] How a small-scale endeavour, with a distinctive identity but low cost-base, can be both a highly effective and also personally satisfying commercial operation

Michael Bartlett was a BBC radio drama producer who commissioned and produced the afternoon plays on Radio 4 in the early 1980s. He was also a professional writer himself but while he was in control of commissioning other writers he did not feel it would be right to offer his work to the BBC. He enjoyed the editorial role very much but knew that rising higher in the BBC would mean taking on an administrative rather than a practical role, and this he did not want to do.

He left the BBC in 1988 in order to help a colleague set up a new commercial radio station in Guildford, with the agreed long-term aim of him then producing speech programmes for the channel. But once the station was established they found that achieving commercial funding for the kind of programmes he wanted to create was never going to be likely. He moved on, setting up a production company producing audio training materials for industry, first on cassette and later on CD. This initially proved lucrative, but when training materials began moving from hard copy on to the internet he found the motivation to produce yet another series on how to manage meetings or negotiate effectively increasingly hard to find.

He and his wife Dee Palmer (also a radio producer) decided to build on the skills they had in pursuit of something they both enjoyed doing. In 2005 they established an audiobook publishing company – Crimson Cats.

They avoided large set-up costs by using their existing expertise (spotting material likely to appeal; editing and developing scripts; recording and producing). They built on the recording equipment they already owned and establishing premises in a room they could soundproof in their new home in Norfolk. They used material that was either out of copyright, so close to being out of copyright or so long out of print that its publishers, often surprised to be approached, were willing to release rights in return for a share of the profits rather than requiring money up front.

The one ingredient they did not have at their disposal was the voices – professional actors whom they considered essential for a quality product. They got around this difficulty by coming up with a creative solution to paying them. Rather than paying agreed fees up front, they asked the actors to record without an initial payment in return for an enhanced royalty (15–20 per cent of the profit on sales, depending on the nature of the project and the size of the actor's involvement). To establish the total on which the percentages were worked out, only the direct costs of production (CD production, cases and the associated printing of jacket material) were counted before the artist's deduction was made. Michael commented:

> It's possible for any business to rack up all its overheads and so not have a profit to share with collaborators. We did not want to operate like this. All the actors we used had made a commitment to us, and having trusted us it was important that we delivered a fair return to them. Once we have paid for the CD duplication and printing and any specific copyright associated with that title (music for example), then the rest is the profit on which we calculate the royalty. We pay all other costs of

producing the recordings (website management, marketing, accountancy costs, etc.) ourselves. All our actors seem happy with the arrangement and have stayed with us.

After years in the broadcasting and audio production world they had many contacts, and judicious use of these enabled them to keep their costs low. Michael comments:

> We used all our broadcasting contacts to find a cost effective CD duplicator and printer (we use a company in Hull). We needed a graphic designer and that was someone (in Leeds) who we had worked with on commercial training projects for many years and had become friends, so he cut us a deal.
>
> Naming a new business is always a challenge and here again we used our network. We were looking for something a little offbeat and hence memorable and we came up with the idea of 'Sleepy Cats Audio Books'. We envisaged a logo of a sleeping cat – the epitome of relaxation. Then a friend pointed out that such a name would be a gift to hostile reviewers: 'Their audio books send you to sleep.' So we came away from that. We mentioned it to our designer and two days later the logo of the cat's silhouette arrived with the suggestion 'Crimson Cats'. It's not a name people forget easily which is a big advantage for a small company.

What to charge for the audiobooks was the subject of long discussions and research into other bestselling audiobook publishers. They eventually set their prices in line with the slightly smaller ones; organisations such as HarperCollins, Random Century and the BBC obviously have the benefit of scale. They had to consider the level of discount they could afford if they sold through bookshops. This is a tiny part of their sales but following reviews in the national press (which they have had for almost all titles) there was usually a small spate of bookshop enquiries. The bookshops have to make a profit too so there needed to be a discount for them. Sadly there are only two broadsheets left that publish audiobook reviews – the *Times* and the *Telegraph*. Sue Arnold of the *Guardian* was a great fan:

> For a tiny publishing outfit, two adults and a cat with a DIY recording studio in the basement of their Norfolk cottage, Crimson Cats produces some of the most sophisticated, original and genuinely interesting audios around.[8]

Postage and packing is paid by the customers so does not affect the unit price. Managing the process through their local post office has played a significant role in the local economy, as does the freelance help they employ when they are especially busy. They do a particularly healthy local trade in CDs for presents in the run-up to Christmas.

From the start they have specialised in unusual material: quirky taste and in particular material that cannot be sourced elsewhere; this is the only way they can gain an 'edge' over larger international publishers. Thus, while there are many recordings of *Three Men in a Boat*, Crimson Cats recorded Jerome K. Jerome's autobiography (*My Life and Times*). A recording of the death of Nelson, a reading of the graphic, eye-witness account of the surgeon on board the *Victory* similarly sold well (*Authentic Narrative of the Death of Lord Nelson*). And recordings of the early stories of Jane Austen (*The Beautifull Cassandra*[9]) and the letters, journals and stories of Katherine Mansfield (*Finding Katherine Mansfield*) have become strong sellers, mainly by making links with relevant societies – the Katherine Mansfield Society in Australia proved particularly good customers. If Michael and Dee are approached by writers with material they feel strongly about, and in the process spot something they think would appeal to a wide market, they use their editing skills to publish from scratch. This has led to success with one family's history of service in Afghanistan in the nineteenth and twentieth centuries, which resonates with involvement today (*My Grandads and Afghanistan*) and a collection of poetry and prose by women written during the First World War (*War Girls*).

Print on demand means they need to print only as much marketing and packaging material as they need – rather than seeking to anticipate (and store) their future requirements. Digital marketing enables them to keep in touch with their customers and let them know when a new release is out, and the internet allows worldwide sales, especially, but not exclusively, by MP3 downloads. And while the markets for some titles are highly specific, there is significant evidence that their customers enjoy browsing and buying across their whole list.

The business is now an established entity. They produce one or two new titles a year and servicing these and the existing back catalogue requires about two days a week of their time, an ongoing support for their wider lifestyle. They enjoy the process, find their customers relate to a small business whose taste and values they appreciate and that, by sticking to their instincts and spotting material that is new to the market, they have found a niche that is profitable. In short, they provide a perfect example of the business principles outlined in Chris Anderson's *The Long Tail* (Anderson 2009).

Case study

Selling apps: An interview with Tom Williams, marketing producer at Touch Press

Tom Williams took both an undergraduate degree in English and then a Master's in Modern Culture at UCL in London, researched and wrote a biography of Raymond Chandler,[10] moved into media journalism and then spent 5 years as a literary agent with PFD (Peters, Fraser and Dunlop a UK literary agency). He was always interested in the digital potential for content and was the first agent to sell an app on behalf of an author. He joined Touch Press in 2013 and is their marketing producer, working with a team of four others.

Touch Press produce apps for the Apple iPad. Launched at the same time as the tablet, their business model is thus only 4 years old. But the original team behind Touch Press were quick to spot the possibilities for content development through a new format, and when sample iPads were first made available to journalists, one of the pre-loaded sample apps was their *The Elements*.

The organisation produces apps in several broad fields of interest: science and technology (e.g., *The Elements, Journeys of Invention, Solar System, Incredible Numbers*), music (e.g., *Beethoven's 9th Symphony*, known within the organisation as *B9, The Liszt Sonata* and the forthcoming *Vivaldi's Four Seasons*) and literature (e.g., *Shakespeare's Sonnets* and a forthcoming app featuring Seamus Heaney's translations of *Aesop's Fables*).

Whereas early apps tended to be in effect interactive ebooks, textual content enriched with additional website links, today the app has shown its capacity to evolve into an experience that is both more complete and discrete, characteristically combining a central theme with additional material which intellectually engages the user in both its re-experience and re-evaluation. So the *B9* app allows the user to compare various recordings of the same work, to hear experts comment on stylistic and presentational differences and share their understanding of its history; an engrossing experience that enhances the user's understanding of the main content. So far apps for the adult market have tended to be in areas of non-fiction, although apps featuring children's stories have been developed with particular success by Nosy Crow.[11]

Within traditional publishing, marketing often comes late in the process, applied to a finished product to aid its wider dissemination rather than having been an integral part of its development from the outset. Tom's role at Touch Press involves him in product development from its earliest consideration. Ideas for apps can come from a variety of sources – colleagues' own enthusiasms (the sophisticated materials developed around music draw heavily on the passions of their staff), or established content-rich organisations seeking to work with them (e.g., publishers such as Faber & Faber and Profile). But organisations that approach them with ideas for apps are partnered not commissioned; all ideas are rigorously strategised about how they might best be developed, not just packaged.

As marketing producer, Tom sees himself as the customer advocate, looking at the development of apps and what features and processes the customer might want to see included; this is based on both empathy with the kind of people who buy their products and extensive feedback on how their customers use them. Selling through retail outlets has long distanced traditional publishers from their customers and denied them feedback on how they used or enjoyed the item taken home. But as apps can only be bought from a single source – the Apple App Store, and they are so far only available for this single device – Touch Press gain a clear understanding of who is buying and how frequently (they get daily sales figures). What is more, they are able to monitor usage data in great detail to see which sections are most explored, the time spent on each, and observe overall patterns of engagement.

Price is an important part of the marketing matrix and its digital presentation enables it to be experimented with and learned from – and for this to be quickly achieved. While traditional retailers understand pricing points, above or below which the customer's perception of value is affected, there are definite expectations for the purchasers of traditional publishing products of what books will roughly cost. Similarly, distinct 'sweet spots' are emerging for the selling of apps. For example, more will be sold at $4.99 than $3.99; more at $8.99 than $7.99. Interestingly offering material at a price of 'free' seems to change the relationship from one of transaction to one of technical involvement, and customers will often critically review material as 'work in progress' rather than simply appreciate receiving something for nothing. Mark Coker of Smashwords has confirmed the same experience for those offering ebooks free, whether as a pricing strategy or a limited special offer – 'customers are often harsher in their feedback on titles they have downloaded free than those they have paid for'.[12]

Initially Tom's team just announced the availability of new apps, largely online via YouTube and Twitter, offering links to longer blogs on websites. But having experimented with pre-releasing through the circulation of short promotional films, highlighting product usage and benefits (e.g., the *Beat Map* sound button that enables the listener to observe which parts of the orchestra are playing at any one time), they will continue this way. Smashwords too have confirmed the advantages of announcing ebooks as pre-orderable, and how pre-launch publicity can help build up market confidence and hence healthy initial sales figures on day one of official availability. Links to these promotional films are circulated via social media, and initial outline campaigns can be tested on a limited basis, and responses noted, before being rolled out more widely. They also offer free trials of their apps, a short extract so the market can experience what is on offer and make an informed choice about whether to proceed to purchase.

As regards the marketing messages, Tom's team develop – and test – specific vocabularies that suit each brand, refining messages, clarifying and developing tone, and once established these are kept specific to the products in question. This is not a new idea – in the 1960s John DeLorean noted that the various car models available from General Motors all had their own associated vocabularies[13] – but within the publishing industry it shows an unusual rigour. The long-term aim of refining the marketing messages, clarifying and developing their tone and effectiveness, is to build a lifetime value of the customer that is above the cost of managing the relationship in store (the retail price of the app less the discount to Apple on product plus the cost of servicing their account) and good judgements are made possible through the precise information on both how the marketing processes are working (pay-per-interaction and pay-per-view) and what is selling.

Purchasers of apps tend to be fairly affluent – because the device on which they are used is costly – and as a broad generalisation they are males and in the age range 25–45. The apps mainly get bought by the individuals who will use them, although a gift option is possible. There are limitations to the scheme as the potential donor has to know that the intended recipient has both an iPad and an iAccount. Touch Press's product range has strong relevance to students of all ages and discussions are taking place about direct supply to schools and colleges.

The titles get reviewed in the app press and the book pages of national media now also offer a review section for relevant apps. Both offer opportunities for associated press advertising.

Again, specific feedback from actual campaigns can direct future expenditure and Touch Press have found that advertising tends to work best in the location where the apps are sold, and where there is a linear route from reading about the apps to buying them; the consumer route from print advertising to online purchase has not been particularly successful. The online ordering facility includes a review section, although it is frustrating that customers tend to use this for offering feedback on functionality and glitches rather than submitting it via Touch Press's well-structured 'Customer Support' that comes as a standard part of app purchase.

Tom suspects that while awareness of different publishing companies and their various imprints is very strong within the traditional publishing industry, few outside it have much awareness of who publishes their favourite authors. Within app publishing, Touch Press promote themselves as creators of other apps their market may have heard of, or also own, and also through the brand names of those they partner with – e.g., Faber & Faber, Profile, The Science Museum, Deutsche Grammophon. They are trying to instil a sense of a Touch Press app as something special. They consistently build longevity into their products by insisting on highest quality – in graphics and resolution – so that when, as is inevitable, the platform hosting device changes, materials can be repurposed to fit.

The Elements was a book that became an app, *Incredible Numbers* and *Skulls* were both developed from apps into books and there are other possibilities for developing related product. But the organisation is conscious of the need to maintain the meaningfulness of their brand, adding value to content to make it something worth having. An app's particular facility in 'show not tell' offers advantages in making complex subjects comprehensible, and it is important to offer customers extension material that adds value to their overall understanding and experience – and can hence be monetised to ensure the organisation's sound development in future – rather than just because it is technically possible.

The biggest market for their apps is the US but Japan and China are catching up fast.

Translations have been created (16 different language editions exist for *The Elements*) but given that this is a product appealing to educated markets, and with a sophisticated multisensory nature, the potential remains for selling the original English edition to international markets. There is also scope for repurposing content for different groups, perhaps as specific and tailored experiences at much higher prices, in the same way that Nick Lovell suggests letting an organisation's biggest enthusiasts spend as much as they like on fuelling a profitable business.[14]

This sophistication of delivery does not however currently extend to being able to offer different pricing models for different geographical locations. Apple's agency model is a discount of 30 per cent and they require pricing within tight bands, and the application of the price established within all markets. It could be interesting to see regional variations explore different market thresholds.

Touch Press describe themselves as producing 'living books that define the future of publishing'. While their focused passion for content delivery in new ways and technological expertise are both undeniable, it's interesting to question whether in future such hubs of innovation within publishing will thrive best inside or outside the industry's official portals.

Maybe innovation works best when developed by independent partners to the industry rather than lodged inside traditional companies, within which innovators can become isolated, and perhaps overwhelmed by organisational history and cultural emphasis on how things were formerly done. Or has the range of organisations involved in publishing just changed? Other instances of innovative content development can be cited that have grown independently before coming back to reinvigorate the traditional industry, as the original fiction series created by Working Partners[15] for mainstream publishing houses has shown.

It would seem Touch Press also have much to teach the more established publishing industry about effective marketing. Their emphasis on its early involvement within the process of content delivery places the customer at the heart of the experience, a key principle of effective marketing. Their rigorous pursuit of consumer insight, based on a mixture of first-hand observation of the market and ongoing experimentation with isolatable variables, is worth much wider exploration. It offers the tempting prospect of cost-effective promotion to consumers about whom increasingly more becomes known.

In conclusion, within the general scope of a marketing role, it's possible to be involved in a variety of different selling situations. The key is identifying the nature of the customer, their needs and matching this with the right sort of information and buying opportunity – in order to move them towards purchase.

Concluding case study

Creating a sales proposition that others buy into

Born near Besançon in France, Jérôme Phalippou began working for the French Customs Agency and in this connection moved to Châtel, a mountain village in the Haute-Savoie region of France but close to the border with Switzerland. When the local customs post was due to close in 2009 he worked with Châtel's mayor, M. Rubin, to develop the building into a permanent information centre outlining the key role smuggling (and hence customs) played in the region before its economy became based on tourism. Working together, they accessed sufficient funding from central and regional governments to buy the building, placing on permanent display the touring exhibition Phalippou had built.

The wider aim of the project was to provide a sense of place and history for both locals and visitors. A cartoonist with a strong interest in local history, Phalippou was convinced there was a market for information in Châtel – from local people, those who come on vacation (winter and summer) and those who have invested in the area by buying holiday accommodation. Châtel has 23,000 tourist beds, with high occupancy and return rates, and mayor and artist were convinced that a book with high production standards would sell well. A grant of €15,000 was received from the central French government to cover the costs.

The text was written by a local doctor – whose first project was a book to mark the centenary of Châtel's church in 2008 (again underwritten by the Mairie). The doctor made the project known locally and asked for images and memories. These came flooding in, so much so that Phalippou, who was managing the layout, turned the anticipated volume into two – one on the history of Châtel, a second on the growth of the ski business. He was aiming for the feel of a family album, and when the project expanded he commissioned attractive protective slip cases for the two-volume set. All those who provided material received a written credit in the volume.

The twin book set sells for €50 through local gift shops, the tourist office, tourist information centres and the museum – all buy stock for €35 and the margin is their profit. The book adds diversity to the range of items stocked by gift shops (there are no other books on sale) and promotes Châtel as an attractive long-term destination, one to return to. The high production standards, in comparison with the small size of the resort, are very important to the mayor, who sees it as a branch of outreach just as important as a new ski lift.

The print run was 2,000 and so far more than half the print run has been sold at full price within a year, a significant number back to those whose material was included. The exhibition centre has had 8,000 visitors over the same period. It is hoped the centre will develop as an educational resource, with the possibility of updating it with information on what is smuggled today and comparisons between the penalties for those smuggling illegal drugs in the twenty-first century (long-term imprisonment; death) with those smuggling life essentials such as salt in the seventeenth century (2 years in the French Navy rowing galleys).

Conclusions

The cost of producing and marketing a book you want to develop may be underwritten by those who identify with your project and support its aims, for personal and professional reasons. Retailers and other locations without a history of selling your kind of merchandise may be willing to stock for similar reasons. Look for longer-term partnerships – significantly in France those holding mayoral office are, subject to re-election, allowed to remain in office for 6 years, and this permits the making of more sustained plans for development.

Notes

1 See the Crimson Cats case study at the end of this chapter.
2 Independent booksellers sometimes buy price-promoted stock from supermarkets as it is cheaper than ordering it from a publisher. Author royalties are based on receipts, so if stock is sold via a supermarket at a high discount, and then resold by an independent bookseller at full price, they gain in exposure and widened availability but generally not much in monetary terms.
3 TLC Publishing in the Digital Age conference, 13 June 2014, The Freeword Centre.
4 Mark Coker, Smashwords, seminar at Kingston University, 9 April 2014.
5 www.spotify.com, a digital music service.
6 Shatzkin, M. www.idealog.com/blog/full-service-pulishers-are-rethinking-what-they-can-offers/ quoted in McCall, J. (2014) 'Skunkworks? Freemium? Service with distinction?' *The Bookseller*, 16 April.
7 www.crimsoncats.co.uk.
8 *The Guardian Review*, 17 October 2009.
9 Incidentally, spelt that way to match Jane Austen's spelling.
10 Williams, T. (2012) *Raymond Chandler: A Mysterious Something in the Light: A Life*, London: Aurum Press.
11 www.nosycrow.com.
12 Mark Coker, Smashwords, seminar at Kingston University, 9 April 2014.
13 Wright, J.P. (1979) *On A Clear Day You Can See General Motors: John Z. DeLorean's Look Inside The Automotive Giant*, New York: Smithmark Publishers.
14 Lovell, N. (2013) *The Curve: From Freeloaders into Superfans: The Future of Business*, Harmondsworth: Penguin, www.nicholaslovell.com.
15 www.workingpartnersltd.co.uk.

Part II
Putting this into practice

5 'The medium is the message'[1]

Important information before you start – to ensure your market can find you 94
Different formats for marketing information 95
Advance information 96
A website entry 99
Jacket/cover copy 100
Catalogues 103
Leaflets and flyers 106
Posters, showcards and point-of-sale 109
Space advertising 109
Telesales campaigns 111
Radio, television and cinema advertising 112

One of the difficulties of promoting published content is that there are just so many other products competing for the market's attention. Other publishers' wares are one form of competition, but there are also all the other, non-book products and services that compete for the same leisure or professional spend. The publishing industry has long stood accused of promoting to 'readers' rather than 'customers' but this has arguably been a method of managing the communication of products that could literally appeal to anyone.

> Marketing communications flow from an organisation to its customers, potential customers and other groups who may influence its success. They involve many types of communications: some deliberate (e.g. advertising), others unplanned (e.g. personal recommendations). The communications may be supportive (e.g. personal selling) or critical (e.g. adverse press comments). In total, these communications form an overall impression, or image, which determines how people think about an organisation and how they may act in relation to its products.
> (Stokes and Lomax 2008: 286)

This chapter is intended to help you to understand the various means of marketing communication that have evolved for publishers to inform those they rely on to talk up, review, recommend or buy their titles. Once their various functions are understood, a decision can be made on how best to use them. Effective communications aim to establish a common understanding between sender and receiver, but this becomes more complicated as information is transferred and passed on through different channels. Of late publishers have tried to make such communication vehicles as multipurpose as possible so they can be used in a variety of different marketing situations (as the basis for web copy, as author handouts when giving talks, as loose inserts in relevant publications, as materials that can be used by booksellers). There are also new mechanisms for communicating directly with markets, mostly via social media, which make it possible to make specific pitches to appropriate groups of consumers, and these too will be explored. While the names of meetings and forms change from house to house, all seem to have similar procedures.

Important information before you start – to ensure your market can find you

Whatever the format of the information you present on the product or service you are offering, it is important that the words you use to describe it relate to the market whose needs you seek to fulfil. Pay particular attention to the buzz words or key terms that matter to the market and avoid in-house jargon that is not understood outside your organisation. Early product descriptions can become hallowed through familiarity, and you need to consider, from your earliest involvement, whether the vocabulary used sum up the priorities of the likely consumer.

Using terms within your copy that the market is likely to look for through online searches affects the visibility of your website or web page in the results of search engines and, in general, the higher ranked the information is on the search results page, the more visits you will get from search engine users. This process is search engine optimisation (SEO). In order to optimise website content, HTML and coding will need to be edited, to ensure that keywords are really visible and that barriers to the indexing operations of search engines are removed. It will also be helpful to increase the number of inbound links to your website.

This is not a computer programming manual, and more detailed advice on how SEO and search engines work can be sought from specialists. The general point for the marketer to understand is that your descriptions should be grounded in terms that the interested user may deploy during their online search for information. As examples of this in practice, novels might gain a much higher search engine ranking by being described as:

> A new romance set in Jane Austen's Bath.
> An epic romance in the tradition of *Gone with the Wind*.

than as

> A new novel set in the West Country in the early nineteenth century.
> A new romance set in Georgia in the nineteenth century.

The former descriptions would probably show up in searches for those looking for material related to things they had already enjoyed or locations they were connected to, within a genre and format that appealed to them. The latter examples are much less specific and therefore less likely to be found.

The writing of SEO-rich copy may feel both repetitive and externally focused; the latter point is particularly tricky as many writers are reluctant to see their work in a tradition established by others and prefer to appreciate their output as original. Both tendencies can be explained through their outcome, which is the promotion of access to, and hopefully interest in, their work. Author publicity forms (generally sent out for completion along with the contract to publish) now routinely ask for key terms relating to the work, which academic authors are already used to providing along with any journal submission.

Different formats for marketing information

Marketing information for the commissioning meeting

The decision on which titles to publish is taken at a formal meeting, attended by representatives of all departments (editorial, sales, marketing, production, rights, etc.) as well as senior managerial staff. For this meeting the commissioning editor will prepare an overview of all proposed titles, and this will include a market breakdown, an analysis of the competition and an estimate of sales. The marketing department will be asked to help with the preparation of this (although authors and agents are increasingly involved too).

While you may not hear the presentation of this information, you may well get involved in its preparation. Even if you have a hand in neither, it is vital that the information collected is passed to the marketing department, for use in the future. The commissioning meeting is a time when enthusiasm and optimism are flowing, and they need to be distilled for future use. As time goes on, competitors emerge, deadlines slip and the author may be inaccessible, busy on their next title – and publishers can start to wonder why they commissioned the title in the first place. So a look back to the initial rationale can be very helpful.

First announcement

The very first information the marketing department receives will probably be the initial in-house alerting form, usually sent by email, to say the product is definitely going to be published. This may be accompanied by a copy of the author's publicity form (requested from the author when their contract is signed but filled in to varying standards).

It is important to get this early information right, as the details submitted (metadata) at this stage will be stored on central industry and wider industry organisational or sector databases for retrieval and use in a variety of other guises, ranging from an advance notice to catalogue copy. In addition to paying attention to keywords, as noted above, pay particular attention to how the title is categorised, which could have a long-lasting impact on its visibility. The system of title classification within the international publishing industry as a whole is currently in a state of transition to Thema, an international system of classification that provides context for more specific information relating to an individual genre and permits the monitoring of subsequent title sales. For example, without context, titles on Java could find themselves listed under geography, travel or computing. Also be clear about the level at which content is aimed, for example a medical title for professionals that gets categorised as 'healthcare' (i.e., for the general population), risks not getting found by the designated market.

The short description or 'blurb' offered will probably have been written by the author or editor, perhaps a combination of the two. This initial mention of collaboration (and hint of compromise) should ring warning bells. Take note: the more you become familiar with copy you don't understand, the more you will come to assume you know what it means. So if your initial reaction is one of bafflement or confusion ('What is this about?' 'I thought it was about x, the current title is really misleading'), this will probably be the exact response of all other non-specialists – sales reps, general book retailers, information professionals and others who may consider ordering the title on someone else's behalf. It's similarly dangerous to assume that English will be every recipient's first language.

So get involved early. If you don't understand the blurb you are sent, or feel it is too wordy, lengthy or overly pretentious, attempt to unravel the meaning now rather than accepting that, at this stage, the information is still 'for in-house use only'. (There is no such thing: once a description is written you cannot control how it gets used.) Ask yourself whether you really understand the key features of the title. Are they lost in the description? Even for a highly technical title, the key selling points or reasons for commissioning should be instantly obvious. For example:

> *The Business of Digital Publishing* provides a good basic understanding of the business side of non-print publishing. It is divided into three sections; the first provides a technological context, the second part explores four key sectors of publishing and the sorts of products and business models that have developed in each and the third part looks at the key issues that digital publishing raises.
>
> Useful for students and professionals wanting to learn more, this key text covers the core components and formats of digital publishing, pricing and sales, selling rights, legal issues, financial changes and business models and looks in depth at professional, academic, schools and trade publishing for books and journals.
>
> Including case studies, questions and interactive exercises, this textbook will help anyone wanting to understand the history, current situation and issues for the future development of digital publishing.[2]

Advance information

Advance notices (ANs), advance title information (ATIs) or advance information sheets (AIs)

An advance notice is usually the first opportunity to alert both the firm and the wider market to the forthcoming publication of a new title. It is sent to bookstores (on- and offline), wholesalers, the company's reps and agents dealing with international markets, and any other parties interested in the firm's publishing programme. Ideally despatched 6 to 9 months ahead of publication (less in the case of 'perishable' titles), it needs to be with wholesalers and bookshops to allow time for the subscription of orders (i.e., the seeking of commitment to buy from key stockists). It should be sent further ahead if the information contained is to be catalogued and included in the recipients' own promotional material, or is the subject of a special publisher–retail promotion.

Because an advance notice is usually drafted by the editors it is often viewed as an editorial document, but its real task is to sell. A sample follows:

Travels in West Africa

Mary Kingsley

[COVER IMAGE]

Pub date: 29 January 2015
ISBN: 9780141439426
Price: £12.99
Series: Penguin Press Classic Non-Fiction
Subject: Travel
Format: 198mm x 129mm
Extent: 720 pages

A remarkable account by the pioneering woman explorer described by Rudyard Kipling as 'the bravest woman of all my knowledge'

THE PITCH

- Kingsley is one of the most important women explorers in history, and her book was a bestseller when first published in 1897
- Includes a fascinating introduction by Toby Green examining Victorian attitudes to Africa, plus explanatory notes by Lynnette Turner
- The book challenged Victorian attitudes to Africa and made important contributions to anthropology and botany. Today it's a key text for readers interested in empire, colonialism and women's history, as well as being a gripping and thrilling adventure story

THE BOOK

Until 1893, Mary Kingsley lived the typical life of a single Victorian woman, tending to sick relatives and keeping house for her brother. However, on the death of her parents, she made an extraordinary decision: with no prior knowledge of the region, she set out on a solo trip to West Africa. Her subsequent book, published in 1897, describes dangerous treks and deadly animals with enormous humour and verve, and has stood the test of time as a classic travel narrative by a woman whose sense of adventure and fascination with Africa transformed her whole life.

THE AUTHOR

Mary Kingsley was born in London in 1862. She lived the typical life of a single Victorian woman until 1893, when she embarked on a voyage to West Africa, followed by a second trip the following year. On returning home, she wrote *Travels in West Africa*, which was published in 1897. Kingsley made one final trip to Africa, enlisting as a volunteer nurse in South Africa during the Boer War. She died there in 1900 and was buried at sea. Lynnette Turner is Associate Dean of the Faculty of Arts and Sciences at Edge Hill University.

Toby Green is Lecturer in Lusophone African History and Culture at Kings College London. His book *The Rise of the Trans-Atlantic Slave Trade in Western Africa* appeared in 2011.

How to write an advance notice that people will read

The proposed text is usually sent to the marketing department before it is printed. If this is the first chance you have to take a detailed look at the proposed title copy, it is vital that you do so. Make sense of what you read, edit and amend, and submit your efforts for approval. Try to improve readability by shortening sentences or adding bullet points to highlight key features. If your efforts at simplifying are rejected on the grounds that the author is a specialist on the subject and they wrote the blurb you are attempting to unravel, gently remind critics that bookshops and reps receiving the information will not be specialists. Like you they should understand what they receive.

Relevant brevity is best. An advance notice serves to tell busy retail buyers why they should stock the title, and to provide the rep or agent with sales ammunition. Don't feel every inch of space has to be covered: densely packed copy is very off-putting.

Information that should be included in an advance notice:

- Author(s) or editor(s).
- Foreword? (Say by whom if this is already arranged).
- Title and subtitle (actual, not a working approximation).
- Format (actual dimensions, not in-house jargon) and binding or protective packaging (if special); word count and number of illustrations for e-options.
- ISBN (complete: include your publisher prefix, however well known you think your firm is).
- Extent (i.e., number of pages, number of words for an ebook and number of illustrations, colour or black and white).

- Imprint (i.e., which part of your company's organisation, e.g., Puffin is an imprint of Penguin).
- Whether part of a series (and if so, the ISSN).
- Publication date and price. Be realistic, not optimistic: publishers get a name for the accuracy of their predictions.
- Short blurb.
- Brief author information. Concentrate on why the author is qualified to write this title, and include a brief sales history of previous titles and editions if relevant. Where is the author based? (The rep for that area will want to persuade the local retail outlets to take stock.)
- Who is it for? *Briefly* outline the market.
- Key selling points. What is new about it? What needs does it meet? Why did your house decide to publish? Why should the retailer stock the title? Why is it better than the competition? (These are probably best set out as a series of bullet points.)
- Scope – i.e., broad description of what the book covers.
- Contents. If they are long and complicated, stress 'main features/papers' first.
- Key promotional highlights arranged so far. If you have already arranged for the title to be serialised in a major newspaper at the time of publication, say so. If it is a book with a strong regional flavour, say you will be targeting the local radio station. If the book is one of your lead titles for the season and so has a significant promotion budget, pass on the information. The recipient needs to get a sense of the expectations the publisher has for the title and the scale of associated marketing activities will help convey this.
- The availability of any point-of-sale material, e.g., if you are offering a dump-bin, state quantity, mix included, price and ISBN.
- The publisher's contact details: website, office address, telephone number and email address (of the sales department).

Some publishers put the title in bold or underline it, and then repeat as often as possible on the grounds that they are reinforcing the words in the reader's mind (the same technique used in radio advertising). The reader, on the other hand, will respond by recognising a familiar block of copy and moving quickly past. It may never get read. It's far better to use the space to explain why the material is being published.

A website entry

All publishing houses now have a website, but they often tend to be managed by different people from those in charge of printed marketing materials. In general, this is helpful: websites get read in a different way from printed materials. Care is needed, however, in managing the information that is loaded. Readers tend to have a much shorter span of attention when reading onscreen than on the page, so a lengthy advance notice or catalogue copy may be too much when presented online – some judicious editing will be needed before loading. Journalists often use websites for background information on titles they are thinking of featuring, so ensure what you offer on the website adds value to the other messages you put out – perhaps with an interview on the author or details of how you came to publish the title.

While there will be room for more information, hidden behind click-through buttons, you will have to manage carefully the order in which it is presented, through headlines, boxes with key features, lots of space and relevant access points to encourage browsers find out more. Try to organise your material in a logical manner. Putting the product specifications under 'how to order' may seem logical to you (because they both relate to the information that used to go at the end of catalogue entries), but the customer in a hurry might not think to look there. For more information, see Chapter 9 on online marketing.

Jacket/cover copy

The information on a cover is usually drafted by the editor in consultation with the author. What appears is very important: it often forms the basis of a decision to buy. If you watch how customers in a bookshop assess a new title, you will see that the typical sequence is to look at the front cover, turn to the back for basic information on the title, and if this looks sufficiently interesting, flick through the contents or read the first couple of pages. Pay particular attention to their stance while they are doing this. Holding a book in your hand, and then turning it over to read the back cover copy is not a comfortable position for the wrist to hold for a long period of time, particularly if at the same time they are trying to hold on to their other purchases and personal items. Resolve therefore to keep your copy short and enticing.

For a paperback book, cover copy generally falls into four areas: book title; cover 'shout/strap line', back cover blurb and author information. For a hardback title the information will generally be laid out on the wrap-around jacket – blurb on the inside front cover jacket-flap, author information on the back inside jacket-flap and there may be an endorsement on the back cover. Titles that are hardback-sized but without the jacket may be handled like a paperback.

Book title

You may have very little say in what a title is called, but if early acquaintance with the manuscript leads you to think that the title chosen does not represent the material to best advantage, may be misinterpreted (words change their meaning and can quickly become loaded terms) or will simply be missed by the market, then say so, perhaps targeting your message through someone able to make the point to those who control what appears.

Shout/strap line

Positioned on the front of the title, this will draw further attention. This is best handled as a summary of the feeling you get from reading the book, rather than as a quick outline of the content. Your best guide for writing effective shout lines is to begin a study of film posters. Thus rather than describing the details of a plot that featured an unknown creature attacking the staff of a spaceship, the poster for *Alien* read: 'In space no one can hear you scream'. Short shout lines work best (eight words is plenty) – try to be atmospheric and pithy. Alternatively you might decide to use a quotation from the review coverage, an endorsement (if you don't yet have any reviews) or a key statistic to show why this is important ('50,000 copies already sold'; 'A *New York Times* bestseller').

Back cover blurb

This should cover the essential sales points, while giving a sense of the type of title (but without giving away the plot, in the case of fiction):

- Why is it interesting?
- What is new/unique about the title?
- What it is about (briefly)?
- Who it is for?
- The scope.
- Any quotable extracts from reviews/experts
- Biographical details for the author.

The words you use should also give a flavour of the writing. So don't make a highly complicated title sound like an easy read for everyone, or a 'beach read' sound like a contender for a major literary prize. If someone has been misled by one of your cover blurbs before and felt let down by the contents, they may be wary of buying from your organisation again. As examples of this in practice, can you guess what kind of novels the following blurb extracts are taken from?[3]

1 Lantern slides, each one a vivid vignette, a bright glimpse of some significant moment.
2 It was going to be one of those days.
3 High-powered sexy, irreverent, hedonistic and perfectly content, Hildamay knows that if you don't love, you can't lose.
4 Successful young art critic SJ sets out to relate, in elegant periods, the history of his martyrdom.
5 He had nothing to recommend him but his smile, and she was surely too old, had too much common sense, to be beguiled by a smile.

---

1 Literary short stories. 'Each one' hints at short stories and the vocabulary at their literary nature.
2 Hard-boiled crime. A straightforward vocabulary indicating an action-based plot with little superfluous description.
3 Women's commercial fiction. The build-up of adjectives shows the humour and sets up the premise of a romance (she's so determined to avoid love, she is bound to find it).

4   Sophisticated humour. It is impossible to relate your own martyrdom and this initial confusion hints at complications to follow.
5   Historical romance. The historical setting is given away by the word 'beguiled' and the archaic phrasing.

Author information

The space available here will be limited so keep it relevant to the title in question rather than offering a potted authorial CV. You could mention the author's aim in writing it or their credentials for doing so (e.g., their previous well-known titles). A light touch is often effective. For example:

> Catherine O'Flynn was born and raised in Birmingham, the youngest of six children. Her parents ran a sweet-shop. She worked briefly in journalism, then at a series of shopping centres. She has also been a web editor, a post-woman and a mystery shopper.
>   Her first novel, *What Was Lost*, won the Costa First Novel Award and the Jelf Group First Novel Award, was shortlisted for the *Guardian* First Book Award, the South Bank Literature Award and the Commonwealth Writers' First Novel Prize, and was longlisted for the Orange Prize and Man Booker Prize.[4]

The empathetic first paragraph engages the reader's attention, the second shows why her writing is of note. In a second example, from an autobiography, the publisher makes deft use of a quotation from the book to give a flavour of what is inside:

> While at *Picture Post* she met Gavin Lyall – who went on to become the successful crime novelist. They had two sons and were married for forty-five years, until his death in 2003. She writes of becoming a widow: 'Marriage is the water in which you swim, the land you live in. You have to learn to live in another country in which you're an unwilling refugee.'[5]

Layout of text on the cover

Finally, do ensure that the cover copy is attractive and engaging to look at (bearing in mind that the reader is looking at this quickly). Ensure the text is easy to read – don't centre the text or fit it around 'cut-out' pictures so that the reader has to work hard to understand. Keep both sentences and paragraphs short and punchy. Similarly, use paragraphs of different lengths, quotations highlighted by the use of large inverted commas, a section of indented text to draw the eye in. Anything to avoid three justified paragraphs of identical size. Reversing the copy out of a solid colour makes it hard to read, reversing out of a picture is even harder (see also Chapter 14 on design).

How much of your jacket blurb will actually be read is debatable. Most readers will home in on the beginning and perhaps the end of the text, as Wendy Cope brilliantly captured in a blurb that appeared on the back cover of a promotional piece to advertise *Making Cocoa for Kingsley Amis*.[6]

> Brilliant, original, irreverent, lyrical, feminist, nostalgic, pastoral, anarchic, classical, plangent, candid, witty – these are all adjectives and some of them can truthfully be used to describe Wendy Cope's poems. Very few people bother to read the second sentence of a blurb. Or the third. Most of them skip to the end where it says something like this: a truly spectacular debut, an unmissable literary event.

Catalogues

The production of catalogues is one of the main regular activities of those marketing books. Successful management of their preparation and production is vitally important. Not only do they stimulate orders by presenting the firm's wares in an attractive light, they are part of the regular selling cycle that the trade is used to responding to and hence expects. Most firms still produce printed versions but the similar information can be offered as an ongoing and up to date resource on their website, an open shop window for a firm's wares, 24 hours a day.

Catalogues are important because they reflect (or arguably direct) the regular selling cycle of the type of list being promoted. How often they are produced depends on the type of list being promoted. Many general houses produce 6-monthly printed catalogues (usually autumn/winter and spring/summer) to fit in with their marketing cycles. The catalogue forms the basic document for presentation at the sales conference that precedes each new selling season. Mass market paperback houses may produce catalogues or stock lists every month, usually 3 months ahead of the month of publication. Educational, academic and reference publishers often produce a separate annual catalogue for each subject area in which they publish. In addition, most houses produce a yearly complete catalogue that lists title, author and bibliographical information for their entire list with a rolling and constantly updated version available on their website.

Catalogues are also a lasting form of promotion. An online catalogue is an authoritative and constant point of reference for those who want to know about an organisation's products and services. For printed catalogues, once the initial ordering has been done, there is a tendency not to throw away the physical object. For example, in bookshops catalogues continue to function as reference material for enquiries and specific requests, and in schools they act as the reference point for topping up stock levels.

The information needed for on- and offline formats is not however interchangeable without amendment, so resist assuming that text prepared for a printed catalogue can be loaded to form website copy. In general eyes get tired more quickly when viewing content online, or is it that attention span is shorter here? More visual variety is needed. The challenge is to keep the information 'sticky' and links need to reinforce the main site not redirect the reader's attention away. Ensure strong functionality of search mechanisms so that readers can punch in the details they have and find what they need. Metrics on site usability will tell you more about how it gets used, and this can be fed into its further development.

Whatever the final format, amassing title information and ensuring it is complete, checking publication and bibliographical details, rounding up illustrations, dealing with design and production – all involve a tremendous amount of detailed ongoing work.

The copy contained in a catalogue should vary according to the anticipated readership and use, with the marketing department adapting the basic title information as appropriate. To get ideas on how to present information clearly and attractively, study both the catalogues of your competitors and those of firms that have nothing to do with publishing (e.g., consumer goods sold by direct mail). The following tips may also help.

Space for major titles

Ensure that the allocation of space in your catalogues reflects the relative importance of your various publishing projects. It's reassuring for customers to know they are buying a successful product. A major scheme or series should stand out as such to the reader: reviews, illustrations and sample pages can all be added to impress. The same goes for backlist titles that are still widely used by the market. If the publisher gives them a poor allocation of space then the market may conclude they are scheduled for extinction. Catalogues selling consumer goods often repeat key items within the same edition, so however quickly the potential customer flicks through, the chances are they still note the products the firm really wishes to push.

As a guide to how much space to allow for different titles, try comparing sales figures (real or anticipated) with the available space. At the same time, do try to avoid a rigid space allocation, which is boring to the reader. For example, in printed catalogues the common practice of giving all the big titles a double page at the front of the catalogue, a page each in the middle to the midlist and then putting the 'also rans' as a series of small entries at the back carries a clear message about what is and what is not important.

What most interests the recipient will probably be what is new or revised, so make clear use of flags and headlines to attract attention. Similarly 'pull quotes' from reviews or satisfied customers can be engaging and interesting.

Ordering mechanisms

Include an ordering mechanism with each catalogue (reference to your website, order form, telephone number, postcard for obtaining an inspection copy), and monitor the response. Not all orders will come back directly to you, but if you take a note of the recorded sales before a catalogue goes out and a second reading a certain time after most orders have been received, you will have a reasonably accurate picture of how effective the material was. Some publishers compare space allocations with trackable orders (asking customers to quote a reference – 'the long number next to your address' – before taking the order), to produce an analysis of revenue per page. Such information over a number of seasons will enable you to assess the merits of different layouts and the effect they have on sales.

Offering a variety of different ordering mechanisms also gives useful feedback. Don't assume that the easiest method of ordering for you also meets the needs of your customers. How easy to use are the ordering mechanisms on your website? A quick question at the end of the ordering process – perhaps incentivised with free entry into a prize draw – can help you find out. You can test the benefits of order forms that are bound in as opposed to loose inserts or stiff order forms that fold out from the cover; those that require the customer to list titles selected against those that provide the information, requiring only a tick to purchase. Different methods of payment too can be tested against each other. For example, most institutions ordering in bulk will need to set up an account with you, but would asking them to send an order on their headed paper enable them to do so more quickly than requiring them to fill in a form, which needs countersigning and official approval? One final tip: have you noticed how consumer mailings often enclose two order forms with any catalogue? In so testable a medium it must be working. What other tricks can you learn from them?

Layout

The presentation of information within a catalogue should be clear. On each page or screen it should be instantly obvious which section is being referred to, perhaps by the use of 'running heads' showing section titles along the top (e.g., imprint and fiction/non-fiction). Educational publishers often use 'running heads' to indicate the age for which material is designed or the curricular subject area.

For printed materials, ensure there is both a table of contents (highlighting key new products with page references) and an index. For digital catalogues, ensure that the searches the customer wants to make are facilitated by the online management of information. These are vital for accessing information in a hurry.

Cover

Put photos of your product(s) on the front of your catalogue. It is far more interesting to the recipient than 'new autumn books from Dodd and Co'. Consumer mailers want you to start reading product information as soon as possible. If you don't use a product, try a really attractive and appropriate illustration. Educational publishers have been known to produce (in response to demand) posters for schools of popular catalogue covers.

For catalogues that will be used in one-to-one selling, for example by the rep visiting schools or bookshops, a light-coloured background on the front cover allows notes to be written, and noticed later on by the recipient.

For lists aimed at a particular vocational market (e.g., school books, ELT materials) a letter, perhaps from the editor, on the inside front cover of the catalogue can attract wide readership. It should always have a signature and look like a letter. Such a start to the catalogue can serve to introduce the list, attract attention to particular highlights and express an interest in the readers' ideas for publications.

Illustrations

Include as much illustration as possible. Covers are the first choice, particularly for a series. However prominently you write 'series' in the copy, the sight of a group of covers is more eye-catching and hence effective. If it's a series but not yet all the titles are available, offer a diagram that shows what is coming when.

Avoid featuring covers that are too subtle and 'designer' in appearance. What you see at full size will disappear when reproduced at postage-stamp size. Similarly, check that the titles on reduced covers are still legible. You can also use illustrations (always with a selling caption), sample pages, photographs (perhaps of the materials in action) and line drawings.

Academic catalogues

Full author affiliations and contents are vital. For which qualifications or academic level do the various titles prepare students? A mixture of different types of institution and author location always helps sell a title more widely. Can the authors also recruit endorsers for you?

Last-minute entries

One of the advantages of online materials is that they can always be updated. But for a printed catalogue, however well-posted your associated deadlines, last-minute copy on titles that simply must be included will always appear. Bear in mind that if you wait for every last correction you will never get to the market, and getting to the market when the market is expecting your information (and when your competitors' details will be there) is what really matters.

If your deadline has passed and the costs of remaking pages to include a particular important extra title are unjustified, try including the copy on a 'stop press postcard'. This can also function as an order form/inspection copy request card – and the author may welcome stock for handing out at speaking engagements.

Leaflets and flyers

Leaflets (often several pages or incorporating a fold) and flyers (often single sheets, printed on two sides) are simple printed marketing materials.

Figure 5.1 A sample academic flyer. Courtesy of Routledge/Taylor & Francis Group Limited. Note the addition of a special offer to the tittle's basic blurb from p. 96.

The information you provide, and the extent of detail offered, will depend on the intended purpose, but it's often a good idea to make these meet as many possible anticipated needs as you can. You can then add a letter to turn it into a mailshot, enclose in journals as a loose insert, send out with a press release to provide further title information, insert in parcels and give stock to the author for them to hand out at speaking events. Give details of how to order. If they are likely to be used in bookshops (say at author events) they should not include a discount for direct ordering. An alternative is to leave the order form space blank for bookshops to overprint or stamp with their name and address.

If you are producing a range of flyers for titles in a series, do make them look different – so it is clear to those only taking a cursory look that each one represents a different title. I once produced a range of slim leaflets advertising science titles. Each one was printed in black ink on yellow paper, one-third A4 size (about the cheapest printed format possible). The results were very eye-catching, but when attending a conference I noticed that delegates examining our stand, where they were laid out in separate piles, clearly assumed that they all advertised the same title. Thereafter I used a different colour stock for each leaflet.

Direct mailshots

See Chapter 8 on direct marketing.

Copy for emails, social media and other online marketing

See Chapter 9 on online marketing.

Press releases

See Chapter 10 on publicity and PR.

Presenters and brochures

Many trade publishing houses produce these for reps to use when presenting new titles to bookstore buyers, and in particular to impress their key accounts. Presenters often form substantial (four to six sides of card) glossy summaries of media and promotional plans, and anticipated spend for individual titles and their supporting backlist. Usually produced in full colour, they are often laminated or at least varnished.

When bookstore buyers are busy and reps have little time in which to attract their overstretched attention, such promotion pieces can play a key part in getting across quickly the importance of the title and its associated image. With luck, a corresponding commitment to take stock will follow.

Copy for these needs to be short and market-focused: you are trying to persuade the bookstore to stock rather than to tell them details of the plot. Thus information relevant to the bookstore should have priority (what promotional highlights have been arranged, how the author's previous title sold and so on).

Posters, showcards and point of sale

Posters are produced by publishers and distributed to bookstores to attract customers' attention to major titles, series or imprints at the place where they are available for purchase. The same themes may also be developed for use in street advertising ('adshells') and at transport locations (e.g., 'cross track' opposite railway platforms). The market's understanding should be instant, so such material should not be too copy-heavy or clever (eight words on a poster site is usually plenty). Sometimes posters are not even put up in stores that accept them, but they still serve to demonstrate to a retailer that a publisher is highlighting a major product, and so form an effective method of ensuring advance orders. The most attractive items may be put up in the staff room, or taken home, so it's a good idea to send stores a few copies rather than just one.

Dump-bins, which carry multiple copies of a key title, are often produced to encourage booksellers to take a large quantity of stock. These usually have a header that slots into the top of the box to attract attention. Use this space creatively. Avoid repeating the book title here, as it will feature on every cover beneath. The days of one-size-fits-all for dump-bins have gone. Several book-shop chains now refuse to take them altogether, on the grounds that they interrupt the shop's designed environment and they have their own material. You may be required to produce dump-bins to the exact space requirements of other outlets such as supermarkets – usually worth it if a large stock order results.

Other point-of-sale items may include give-away items such as balloons, bookmarks, badges, shelf wobblers and mobiles. Sometimes these prove so popular as branded items that they can become a product range in their own right, and of course this has the hugely valuable function of further promoting the list, while producing income.

Space advertising

Rich media advertising

Internet advertising can draw consumer attention through a dynamic mix of interactivity, animation and sound, for example allowing customers to watch a demonstration or feed in their data in order to receive a specific quotation. Now that broadband is more widely available, wider access to these opportunities is available. Such advertising is relatively cheap to establish and trackable, although technical possibilities need to be matched with their careful management.

Figure 5.2 A dump-bin for Enid Blyton titles, shown both front- and side-on. Courtesy of Hachette Children's Publishing.

See Chapter 9 on online marketing and Jon Reed's *Get Up to Speed with Online Marketing.*[7]

Classified advertising

Classified advertising is one of the cheapest methods of promotion. Copy is usually typeset by the publication in which it is to appear. With little space, no illustration and lots of similar advertisements to compete with, try to use the variables that are at your disposal to attract attention. Experiment with different type densities, capital and lower-case letters and highlight professional qualifications and official endorsements. Provide an incentive to do something now, such as look up the website or ring for a free catalogue.

For ideas on how to handle the medium well, consult the classified section of a magazine that is well known for its amusing and effective entries.

Semi-display ads

A step up from classified advertising, semi-display allows borders and illustrations. Don't take the permission to use reversed-out text too seriously, it is hard to read. Do allow plenty of white space around the advertisement – it serves to draw the eye in. Have a look through your local trade directories to see how effective – or otherwise – the use of a small advertising space can be.

Advertorials

Advertorials are advertisements that masquerade as editorial copy. In an editorially biased magazine or paper, advertising guru David Ogilvy reckoned six times as many people read the average editorial feature as the average advertisement.[8]

Use the same typeface, caption illustrations in the same way, and the same 'editorial' style as the rest of the publication. You may find that 'Advertisement' or 'Advertisement Feature' is printed by the magazine at the top of your space, but your message will gain in authority and readership and more people will remember it. For precisely these reasons some magazines do not allow advertorials. One word of caution: be careful that you don't end up paying for what the magazine would have printed free as a feature.

Along similar lines is 'sponsored editorial', whereby the customer takes advertising space in return for a commitment from the magazine to provide editorial coverage. Guest blogging on someone else's site has a similar effect. See Chapter 9.

For advice on promoting to specific interest markets, see Chapter 15.

Telesales campaigns

See Chapter 8 on direct marketing.

Radio, television and cinema advertising

Radio advertising

Listening to the radio creates a cosy empathy between audience and station, and this can work particularly well in the promotion of books. Tying the commercials up with promotional offers such as competitions can secure a lot of coverage at a very competitive price – the competition has to be trailed, run and then the winners announced – and all the while listeners are repeatedly tuning in. This may serve the interests of station managers; they are keen to keep their audience loyal, and they may be interested in a competition that serves to encourage the audience to return. The launch of new commercial radio stations has offered cheap opportunities to reach highly targeted groups of people.

Television and cinema advertising

The chance to work on these will occur rarely in the lives of most publishing marketers. When publishing houses can afford to mount television campaigns they usually assign them to specialised agencies. But small budgets can pay for regional television and radio advertising, and new channels may offer further opportunities.

If you are choosing between press and television as the best medium for a campaign, in general the less there is to explain about a product, the better suited it is to television. Cheaper, mass market products too work better on television; if customers are being asked to spend a lot of money they need a fuller explanation of benefits than is possible during an average-length advertisement. An alternative is to give a website or telephone number for further information at the end of the commercial.

Notes

1 McLuhan, M. (1964) *Understanding Media: The Extentions of Man*. Toronto: McGraw Hill Book Company Inc.
2 Hall, F. (2013) *The Business of Digital Pulishing*.
3 All written by writer and copywriter Cathy Douglas, reproduced by kind permission.
4 Cover blurb for *The News Where You Are*, Catherine O'Flynn (2010), London: Penguin.
5 Katharine Whitehorn (2007) *Selective memory*, London: Virago.
6 W. Cope (1986) *Making Cocoa for Kingsley Amis*, London: Faber & Faber.
7 Reed, J. (2013, 2nd edn) *Get up to Speed with Online Marketing*. London: Prentice Hall.
8 Ogilvy, D. (1983) *Ogilvy on Advertising*. London: Pan Books Ltd.

6   How to write a marketing plan

Introduction 113
Coming up with a plan 114
What have we got to sell? Researching the product 115
Who is it for? Researching the market 118
What benefits does the product/service offer your market? 120
Initial situation analysis: where are we now? 120
Establishing objectives: what do we want to achieve? 123
Developing a strategy: how will we get there, in broad terms? 124
Formulating a plan: how will we get there, in detail? 124
Marketing basics 124
Developing marketing plans for individual titles 126
Allocating a budget: how much will it cost? 129
Communicating the plan to others 130
Motivating the implementation of the plan 131
Evaluating results 131
A final checklist for marketing plans 132

> Marketing planning is a structured way of looking at the match between what
> an organisation has to offer and what the market needs.
>
> (Stokes and Lomax 2008)

Introduction

Preparing a marketing plan is a common activity within the publishing industry
and one on which many future developments may be based. Authors and agents
take close note of prospective publishers' ideas for marketing their work and, if
choosing between rival offers, the associated marketing plans will be closely scru-
tinised. Retailers being asked to invest in new product lines will want to know the
wider marketing planned by the publishers, in order to stimulate demand for
products they agree to stock or promote. Authors may in the past have been
resistant to talking about marketing, feeling their responsibility was for content
alone and preferring to leave the marketing to their publishers, but today the sheer
range of projects competing for the consumer's attention means that the author's
ability to outline the market they are writing for, and help communicate with it, is
a crucial part of a decision to invest in them. Unpublished authors seeking external

investment are well advised to prepare a marketing outline in order to help potential publishers and agents understand where consumers may be found, particularly if this is a new area for publishing. Finally writers planning to self-publish need to think about how best to allocate their efforts and the ability to develop a marketing plan is a sound basis for further activity, whether they assign the 'to do' list to themselves or others.

But before discussing how to go about formulating a marketing plan, it's worth stressing that while the thinking advised in this chapter can be used for plans of all levels of activity, from relatively straightforward organisation within the department to large-scale launches relying on external help, it is of little value if it is not subsequently implemented, or at least referred to. A marketing plan that sits in a drawer or on a computer is of little use. In this context it is helpful to think of a plan in three stages:

- Coming up with a plan.
- Communicating it to others.
- Motivating its implementation.

Most of the time and effort will go into the first stage, but the third one is the one that will probably need most effort and determination.

Coming up with a plan

As we considered in Chapter 1, marketing is usually centred on the goals and requirements of the customer, so thinking about the market and what they need or desire should be firmly developed before refining the kind of products and services to be offered. On a practical level, the publishing industry has long been accused of being product-orientated rather than market-orientated, tending to commission the product and *then* think about to whom it will sell, and the reasons for this have been explored within Chapter 3 on market research.[1] The user of this book, however, is more likely to be charged with the presentation of a specific product or service to a particular group of people, and this chapter is constructed accordingly.

Whatever your starting point, you need to be really clear about what your organisation is trying to achieve through marketing: to launch something new; raise the profile of an existing product; probe and eventually break into a new area of publishing? The best marketing is grounded in a clear understanding of the product or service in question, the target market and the wider situation in which you are operating. Only if you have this understanding will your copy be relevant and personal, and your marketing seen by those who need to read it in order to buy. Much research and thinking is needed before you decide on how best to allocate your efforts.

It can help to break down the planning into stages:

- What have we got to sell? Researching the product.
- Who is it for? Researching the market.
- Initial situation analysis: where are we now?

- Establishing objectives: what do we want to achieve?
- Developing a strategy: how will we get there, in broad terms?
- Formulating a plan: how will we get there, in detail?
- Allocating a budget: how much will it cost?

What have we got to sell? Researching the product

This means finding out all you can about the product or service you are to promote. Who is the author/provider of content: bestselling or unknown; always published by your house or new to the list; available at the time of publication for interviews or not; with other material in circulation? Look at the title. For example, *Confessions of a Celebrity Minder* will give you an idea of the content.

Is the content already available?

You will find that the delivery dates in contracts are not always kept by authors, and be wary of commencing work on a title if there is not yet a manuscript in-house. Even if the content is already with you, there will not be time to read every title for which you are responsible; the number of titles you have to look after will dictate the amount of time you are able to spend on each one. For example, a major new English scheme brought out by a primary education publisher should be examined in detail. If you have ten monographs a week to promote, looking closely at them all will be impossible and you will have to rely on what those commissioning the work have said about their reasons for doing so. Even if you don't have access to the manuscript, talk to your editorial contacts to gain more information. Not everything of relevance finds its way from one department to the other.

What are you saying about it in-house?

Most publishing houses have an evolutionary cycle of forms, altered product details passing on to second- and third-generation versions of the original. As you look through these you will acquire an understanding of the title and how it has developed. At one stage in the cycle (perhaps with the 'presentation' form or 'A' form, the name varies from publishing house to house) it will have been brought before a formal marketing/editorial meeting and approved. Some titles are made available as an ebook first and then a decision on subsequently printing a run of copies will depend on how well this sells. If there is to be a printed run from the outset, the anticipated totals for the first- and second-year sales will have been made. These are your targets.

What did you say about it last time?

If you are promoting a book that is already published, look at previous marketing materials. Find out from the customer services department what the sales and returns patterns have been. Ask the reps what the market thinks of your product and, in particular, what they call it. You may be surprised.

If it's the work of an author previously published by someone else, look at how they marketed it. Try to get copies of the promotion material they used. Was marketing one of the reasons the author decided to change houses? If so, what were their chief complaints?

Study the contents list

Ask yourself (or the editor) why the title was commissioned. What market needs does it satisfy? Are there any readers' reports in the file (reports on the manuscript before a decision to publish was taken)? There should also be an author's publicity form. The amount of time authors spend on compiling these varies, but a fully completed one can be an excellent source of information.

What does it cost?

Will the price attract (or rule out) any important markets? For example, academic libraries are more likely than individual lecturers to buy high-price monographs, but are there enough libraries in the market to make publication worthwhile? Corporate libraries may be able to afford the latest information, but can public libraries? By targeting your message to one market will you alienate another (and possibly larger) one?

Study the competition

Early in-house forms and the author's publicity form should list any major competitors to a forthcoming title, or say if a publishing project has been started to meet a major market opportunity. Bearing in mind that the competition may not just consist of other books, start gathering information on what your product competes with and how the alternatives are promoted. Book fairs are a good time to collect other publishers' information and catalogues. Consult their websites and see what they say, scan the relevant press for ads, and look at traffic on social media. You can pay a press agency to do this for you, but you will get a better general idea of the market, as well as early warning of any new competition, if you scan the relevant media yourself. Wherever possible register for electronic alerts with keywords to ease your search.

Look on retail websites and see rankings

Find out from your colleagues or boss whether any direct or teleselling has been done on this product or a related title in the past. As well as yielding orders you can gain a great deal of product information in the process. If the market is easily identified, try ringing a few prospects, or consult a directory for contact numbers. You will be surprised how many people find it flattering to have their opinion sought on the need for a new product. Librarians can be particularly helpful. See Chapter 8 for advice on telemarketing.

Ask the author

If there are still unanswered questions, ask the book's editor about contacting the author. Be prepared; ensure that you have read all the information the author provided about their work before you ring. It's irritating for an author to spend valuable time filling in a questionnaire only to be contacted by a marketing person who has clearly not read it. It may also be helpful to get the author to check your promotional copy. Similarly, the author may be able to help with testimonials or suggest individuals who might give the book a recommendation that you can quote in your marketing materials. The recommendation of one expert will be worth more than what you can think of to say.

Of course it can be daunting to ring an acknowledged expert on a subject you know little about. But just because you don't fully understand the subject matter of the product does not mean you are an inappropriate person to handle its marketing. Indeed, you may even do a better job if your understanding is incomplete, because you are forced to take nothing for granted, and to ask basic questions: who is it for, what does it do and so on. In many ways, this puts you closer to the target market and allows insights into how best to position your product.

By now the project should be starting to come alive. Start refining your thoughts by answering the following questions about the content you have to promote:

- What is it?
- What does it do?
- Who is it for?
- Who needs it and what benefits does it offer?
- Does it fulfil any human needs?
- What is new about it?
- Why is this product or service being produced?
- Is it topical?
- Does it meet a new or discovered need?
- What does it compete with?
- What does it replace?
- What are its advantages and benefits?
- How much does it cost? What value does this provide?
- Are there any guarantees of satisfaction?
- Are there any testimonials and quotes you can use?
- Why was this author or content creation team commissioned? What is special about them?
- How reliable are they and how qualified to deliver?
- How worthwhile is it for the customer to invest in a relationship? What else is on offer to develop the relationship?

Meeting human needs

Several copywriting gurus have outlined basic human needs in the belief that any piece of marketing copy should aim to appeal to at least one. For example, to make or save money, time or effort; to help your family; to impress, belong or emulate others; to self-improve or attract attention, gain a career advantage; feel pleasure or be part of the *Zeitgeist*.

A new online business package may offer the reader a valuable competitive edge and the chance to extend their invoiceable services – and hence make money; a new novel may offer a temporary escape from reality. Take this a stage further by making a list of selling points, the respective features and benefits of the product, and then put them in order. Successful marketing comes from making the message credible and comprehensible: there may be lots of benefits, but potential buyers need only one to be convinced – the important thing is knowing which one. If you include them then all you may only confuse. Hang on to your workings, as a list of product benefits may be helpful if you are later preparing to meet the author or have to write a press release at short notice.

Who is it for? Researching the market

Market research, whether formal or informal, should have been of fundamental importance to the commissioning and development of your company's products and services. You now have to find the groups of people who need what you have to offer before you think about how to persuade them to buy.

What is the market like?

What kind of people are they? Is the purchaser likely to be male or female; are there socio-economic indicators or area bias, and can these be related to the methods and media you choose? External help can be brought in here; for example, database and software companies can now offer very sophisticated socio-economic analysis of mailing lists. This is mostly done by postal or zip code analysis but can also draw on additional information such as the examination of house name or first name of householder.

Try to read publications the market has access to, both general interest and professional, and to meet some of the market. Can you go along to a professional meeting or annual conference? Once there, observe what goes on. Gathering this kind of information will help you to decide on the right promotional approach.

Questions to ask about the market

What needs does the market have? How will this product or service improve people's lives? How much will they benefit? How much do they want it or need it? – Who is the product for? Who will buy it? Who will benefit from it? Are they the same person?

These two sets of questions are not identical. Think of the advertising of children's toys on television at Christmas, designed to encourage children to ask for the products that parents and other adults will buy. Equally for academic publishers, new materials may be preferred and recommended by those running modules but while they add the titles to their reading lists, most of the buying will be done by students. The only organisational copies bought may be some stock for the library or learning resource centre, and this will depend on organisational policy – some purchase textbooks, others regard the central budget as there for spending on supplementary reading material, not core texts. Other questions to consider are:

- How big is the potential market? How does this compare with how many you plan to print? What percentage of the market do you have to sell to in order to make the project profitable? Will the ebook market extend your overall sales and help you get material more widely known or reduce the number of print copies purchased?
- Once you have established the primary market, ask yourself who else might need the product. Is there anyone who certainly won't buy it? (You can perhaps capitalise on this in your promotional information – 'Is $500 too much to spend on ensuring your children have the most up to date resources to support their homework?')

Segmenting, targeting and positioning

Marketing theory emphasises the importance of segmenting the market into different groups of people, and then targeting those most likely to purchase (or influence a purchasing decision). The marketing for a product can be segmented as follows in decreasing levels of interest. They are people who:

- can anticipate their need for a new product or service;
- have bought/used such a product or a related product before;
- need such a product now;
- used to but do so no longer;
- have never done so.

Your best strategy is to think carefully about what kinds of people are to be found within the first three categories (what other products have they bought; how much do they need what you have now?), investigate how to reach them (e.g., through your customer lists, social media activity and societies and memberships that reveal an affinity with what you are promoting) and then target them with a marketing approach. Once you have targeted them, and hopefully persuaded them to buy, you can then move on to trying to motivate them to enthuse about, or recommend, your product to others known to them. The power of positive word-of-mouth should not be underestimated.

What benefits does the product/service offer your market?

Core benefit, the fundamental reason for acquisition.

Actual benefits, key features the customer expects, e.g., features, attributes and design.

Augmented benefits, additional benefits that add value to the core benefits, e.g., guarantee and after-sales service. This can be presented in diagramatic form, see figure 6.1.

An example of this in practice: a pencil

- Core benefit: enables you to write and hence communicate.
- Actual benefit: colour of casing; softness; hardness of lead; with a rubber on the end; weight in the hand; brand and style.
- Augmented benefit: free case, guarantee, three for two offer.

Then consider a product's 'positioning'. This is the emotional relationship that the would-be consumer has with your product and your brand. It is *their* perception of what your product stands for, based on the impression created by the words you use, and the image you create through design and promotional format. This psychological positioning can be created by linking to existing consumer perceptions, e.g., 'the new Ian Rankin', 'the English Patricia Cornwall', 'the right wing John O'Farrell'.

Initial situation analysis: where are we now?

Marketing does not take place in a vacuum and in order to establish realistic and appropriate marketing plans, the wider environment must be considered. This can be broken down and analysed in various ways.

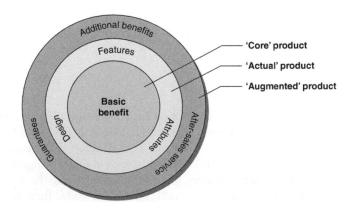

Figure 6.1 Figure showing onion skin model of a product's benefits: core benefit, actual benefit, augmented benefit; adapted from Stokes and Lomax (2008: 221).

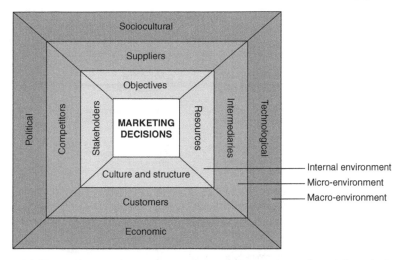

Figure 6.2 Figure showing how micro and macro fit together; adapted from Stokes and Lomax (2008: 38).

How an organisation (or individual) makes decisions is initially influenced by its own **internal environment**: its structure, objectives and resources. Next, its **micro-environment** consists of forces close to the organisation that affect its ability to serve its customers and over which it may have some influence. Examples may include the way in which it has conducted relationships in the past and hence the existence of latent goodwill, or strong established local relationships with retailers who have a long history of stocking and promoting merchandise.

The **macro- (or external) environment** involves larger societal forces that affect the whole of the micro-environment and over which an organisation or individual is very unlikely to be able to exercise influence. Macro-influences will include the wider business economy and events that affect all such as the weather or national sporting events that impact on the general mood.

Useful mnemonics exist for considering the forces at work. These include SWOT analysis and PESTLE, both of which are worth considering in more detail.

A SWOT analysis looks at the strengths, weaknesses, opportunities and threats of an organisational (or individual) position. Strengths and weaknesses are internal, specific to the individual; part of the past and present micro-environment. Opportunities and threats are external, deriving from outside circumstances; part of the present and future macro-environment. Figure 6.3 lays this out in a diagrammatic format for a new fiction imprint.

Bear in mind that the weaknesses of your marketing position may be beyond your control or inherited. For example, have potential customers previously had bad experience of your delivery methods or turnaround times? Is there resistance to your packaging, such as how easy is it to open/post/recycle and how

SWOT ANALYSIS

	Helpful to achieving the objective	Harmful to achieving the objective
Internal origin (attributes of the organization)	**STRENGTHS** (past/present) • Brand name (e.g., the authors or the titles) • Market share (perhaps defined by the genre) • USP of the new list (e.g., first titles to...)	**WEAKNESSES** (past/present) • Low levels of awareness (e.g., authors may not have a track record) • Lack of competitive advantage (e.g., many similar imprints already available)
External origin (attributes of the environment)	**OPPORTUNITIES** (present/future) • New markets (e.g., revealed by other authors' success) • New products (e.g., which reveals potentially big demand for related products) • Technology that enables online sampling	**THREATS** (present/future) • Competing uses for time and resources (e.g., non-reading use of leisure time) • Technology (e.g., ebooks, audio books, publisher backing the format that does not achieve wide acceptance) • Demographic change (e.g., aging population)

Figure 6.3 SWOT analysis diagram for a new fiction imprint.

environmentally friendly? How ethical, diverse or generally likeable is your organisation? What is its brand image? What holding organisation/bigger firm are you part of? Are there any hidden ownerships, dodgy products or previous alliances?

PESTLE is a similarly useful strategic framework for thinking in more detail about the external influences within the current environment and those most likely to influence. It stands for a series of forces that need to be considered. Namely:

- **Political factors** might include local and national governmental policies and in particular any international agreements that are either established or pending. Within publishing, countries featuring in the news may spark demand for associated backlist titles.
- **Economic factors** may lead to alterations in income, prices and savings – and hence the market's ability (or otherwise) to afford to buy. Overall market health and optimism may be affected by government policy on taxation, interest rates and national debt. Within publishing, the expansion of budget airlines and the development of airports as locations for shopping have boosted the number of customers available to airport bookshops, although the leasing of such outlets to chain stores means a more limited range of choice is being offered.
- **Social factors** may include changes in demographics (people living longer, certain diseases becoming more prevalent), changes in attitudes and lifestyles (new events to celebrate and rites of passage to mark) or cultural changes that affect us all (the hosting of the Olympics). Within publishing, the expansion of

book clubs, both ones you attend in person and hosted by the media, has provided significant marketing opportunities for publishers.

- **Technological factors** may include the new or cheaper availability of technology, making the processes of marketing, administration and distribution swifter or less reliant on humans. There may be advances in materials, production processes or alternatives available that impact on the final product or service delivered. Within publishing, the availability of ebooks has not so far had a significant impact on the sale of paperbacks. People are building up a stock of material for their ebook readers, as well as buying paperbacks, or are perhaps spending more time reading.
- **Legal factors** may include existing legislation, planned future legislation and an awareness of pressure groups and associated lobbies. For example, pollution control or product safety legislation could impact on production planning, and disability legislation on the operation of buildings. Associated lobbies for alternative courses of action are often looking for case studies, and businesses affected by relevant legislation can find themselves highlighted as a result. Within publishing, the maintenance/removal of retail price maintenance, and the development of libel and copyright laws all affect the development and dissemination of content.
- **Environmental factors** may include geographical location and associated population impact, climate and climate change. Publishers are finding their market is increasingly aware of how paper used for production has been sourced; ebooks are presented as a more environmentally friendly option.

Many of the factors an organisation has to consider may not be this discrete; for example, lobby groups may raise awareness of environmental issues, which are then addressed by law and have a wider impact within society. Customers' access to the internet may be influenced by both technology and environment and possibly by social factors (e.g., children lobbying for online access at home having got used to computers at school). But the isolation of these issues is a useful way of thinking in more detail about the wider environment for marketing plans.

Establishing objectives: what do we want to achieve?

Establishing objectives for marketing sounds deceptively simple (e.g., national media interest in a first novel; bestseller status by Christmas). The wiser approach is to think about where you want to be – or what you want to achieve – and then break it down into smaller quantifiable steps, ensuring that objectives are SMART (specific, measurable, achievable, realistic and time-related).

Establishing objectives that are too ambitious or within a time frame that is unrealistic will demotivate; on the other hand, setting objectives that feel realistic and also mutually stretching may encourage everyone forward, particularly if the stages are achieved and celebrated. So instead of national media interest, a more useful objective might be to obtain positive features in two women's magazines by the end of March.

Developing a strategy: how will we get there, in broad terms?

An organisational strategy is the long-term policy of an individual organisation accompanied by a broad understanding of how it can be implemented in order to be achievable. Marketing strategy can generally be divided into deciding where an organisation wants to concentrate its efforts, the segments that are most appealing, and then the process of targeting an approach to them through appropriate positioning of the organisation and its products to its market. It should include consideration of 'what business are we in?' (often presented as a mission statement), an awareness of priorities within that area and of the assumptions made, including that they may not be correct. This definition of the business we are in also defines the competition.[2]

Formulating a plan: how will we get there, in detail?

And so finally we come to what may be most recognisable as a plan; the practical implementation of strategy through decisions about how best and when to allocate resources to ensure objectives are met.

There may be different methods of doing the same thing – veterinary physicians, for example, may be reached by a mailshot sent to all veterinary practices, a space advertisement in a publication that is widely read by the group or a blog on a website they frequent. Increasingly social media is used to widen awareness; Twitter and Facebook are both influential and cheap. All are different methods of working towards the same goal, and the choices will depend on a range of factors from how often the market needs to hear from you in order to make a buying decision to the budget available.

Increasingly, a variety of overlapping methods of reaching the market are used, in a staged process. For example, for a high-priced product, with a strong anticipated sales level, there might be an initial email with a link to the organisational website, the subsequent despatch of a printed brochure and then a phone call to the customer to take an order (if the number and permission to call have been given). For mass market products the sequence might be a series of online messages with additional promotion via social media.

The plan will normally be a compilation of different marketing methods, based on understanding of how the market can best be approached.

Marketing basics

A good starting point for a marketing plan is to make a list of all the standard promotional boosts received by every product published by your organisation. Not only will compiling such a list give confidence, it will also be useful when you have to speak to authors or agents about promotion plans for a specific title. (Often these standard promotional processes are so familiar that they are easily forgotten.)

If the task of setting up these procedures is yours too, the following ideas will be helpful.

Entry into relevant databases for the publishing business

Nielsen[3] and Bowker[4] accept information on forthcoming published titles and then make it available to others who need to know. Take particular care in how you describe your product as allocating it to the wrong category (e.g., healthcare instead of medicine, which means it would be seen by the general public rather than medical professionals) can mean the intended market miss being informed. Pay attention to how the market for this product or service may construct an online search for related information and be sure to include key terminology in your description (this is called 'search engine optimisation', see Chapter 5).

A website entry

Once a title has been decided on, unless there are strategic reasons for keeping quiet (you do not wish to let your competitors know what you are doing), then information will usually be added to the organisation's website. This will include basic title and author details, an outline content, expected price and publication date.

An advance notice (AN) or advance title information (ATI)

This is usually in the form of a single sheet (sent by email and also available in printed format), includes all the basic title information and is sent out 6 to 9 months ahead of publication (see Chapter 5).

Inclusion in catalogues, seasonal lists and regular newsletters

Most general publishers produce two 6-monthly catalogues (spring and autumn); others produce a new titles list three times a year or even quarterly. Academic and educational firms usually produce a separate catalogue for each subject for which they publish. Catalogues generally appear 6 months before the books featured are due to be published, and are available in electronic and print format (although there are moves in some sectors to make them electronic only, see Chapter 5). Sections of the catalogue may be updated and emailed/mailed regularly.

Advertising

Are there any standard features in which all your firm's titles are listed? For example, are there standard space bookings for the export editions/on the websites of the trade or professional press?

Despatch of covers to major bookshops and libraries

Your production department can arrange for extra book jackets and covers to be printed. If you have these stamped on the back with price and publication date they can form useful display and promotional items.

'Silent salespeople'

This term was coined by Tim Farmiloe, former editorial director of Macmillan. There are a number of other destinations for your material, which take varying amounts of effort to reach, but may result in extra sales. These include sending information to:

- relevant websites and bloggers, who may write/enthuse about your product. Some of these sites get huge audiences. For ideas on which sites to use, start with your authors, who are often bloggers themselves (see Chapters 9 and 11);
- social media. All kinds of publishing houses, even the highly academic, are increasingly active on social media to create relationships with their customers and promote sales (see Chapter 9);
- governmental and other relevant organisations; for example the British Council promotes titles from UK publishers abroad;
- professional organisations and trade bodies. If, for instance, you are producing a title on writing, there are many organisations that would-be writers can join, and each has a list of useful published material on its website;
- web retailers such as Amazon and Play, particularly if you can encourage purchasers to use the mechanisms provided for reviewing what they have enjoyed. Many offer referral marketing ('People who bought this also bought');
- various retailers and wholesalers who produce their own catalogues;
- relevant associations and groups (many have websites that list recommended publications);
- appropriate media and press to stimulate features or the demand for review copies (see Chapter 10).

The marketing manager of one major academic publishing house found that 95 per cent of its sales were achieved through such intermediaries.

Developing marketing plans for individual titles

The checklist above can be applied to all marketing planning. To make your ideas specific to individual situations and products, a number of considerations need to be thought through before you start.

Marketing format

Deciding on whether to produce an email campaign, a cheap two-sided flyer or set up a bespoke website is often where many marketing action plans start. It's a much better idea to allow the decision on format to grow out of an understanding of the market and the product. For example, given absolute creative freedom to change format and words of an existing direct marketing piece you would be lucky to put up your response by more than 0.5 per cent. You'd probably be far better off reviewing the distribution of your materials, thinking through the product benefits in fuller detail or coming up with a new offer.

Nevertheless, armed with a marketing strategy to reach your customers, there is a lot of scope for lateral thinking on promotional format. Bear in mind that it is the slightly unexpected that secures attention. There are various ways to attract attention, such as different offers through email, different forms of social media, variously sized envelopes for mailshots, new sizes for space advertisements and so on (see Chapter 5).

Media planning

What are the best media through which to convey your promotional message? Should you use email, press advertising, posters, cinema, television and radio advertising, direct mail, display material, public relations, stunts, free samples? All are elements of the promotional mix, tools at your disposal.

Let's take press advertising as an example. Which magazines and journals does your target market read? Consult the author's publicity form and note where they suggest review copies should be sent. Talk to editorial and other marketing staff. Do you know any members of the market personally? If so, ask them what they think. Make a shortlist and look up the rates in a commercial directory or the magazine's advertising website. If they are within your budget, ring up and ask for sample copies as well as details of the readership profile (useful ammunition when the publication starts pestering you for a booking and you want a reason to say no).

Before you make the decision to pay for space, consider whether it could come free. Is there an associated website or chatroom? Could you start a discussion about the subject of your book? Alternatively, is the magazine looking for editorial copy? Might it run something on your product as a feature article, perhaps offering free copies for readers to write in for?

If you decide to advertise, how can this be incorporated within your wider marketing plans; for example, how can attention be directed to your advertising spend via social media; can copies of the publication be available to your reps for distribution to key accounts? Do you plan to take a single space or a series? If there is one magazine or paper that reaches your target market, you will probably get better results from taking a series of advertisements, perhaps featuring a different product benefit each time, rather than spreading the same message over several different magazines. If you go for a series of adverts you should get a discount.

Having decided which media you will use, study them. Can you get yourself added to the free circulation list? Look through the pages. Which adverts do you notice? Is this because of effective copy and design, or placing? Where is the best place to be? In general, go for right-hand side, and facing text, never facing another advertisement (most people skip past double-page ads). Can you get space next to the editorial, or another hot spot such as the crossword or announcements of births, marriages and deaths? Space on book review pages may be cheaper than on news pages, but by opting for the former, will you escape the notice of a large number of your potential buyers? If you are planning to quote your website, is the relevant information ready, waiting for those who go online to look for it?

Read the letters, and look at the job adverts – a close examination of these will tell you who is reading the magazine. If it is a weekly, is any advertiser writing topical copy? Does the lead time allow for this? Is it paid or controlled circulation? When you start writing you should be aiming your message at one individual reader. Can you picture them? This should be your aim, before you start writing to them.

What you say

The words used in a marketing campaign are often referred to (when combined with appropriate design) as the 'creative strategy'. The next chapters will provide ideas on how to make your approach relevant and effective, suggest new promotional themes and much more. For now I would just recommend that you nurture a general interest in all marketing copy. Don't confine your study to the publishing trade press alone. Start looking out for copywriting and design techniques that do and do not work, and think why in each case. Keep two files, one of ideas you like (and can copy), the other of mistakes to avoid – bearing in mind that mistakes can often be more instructive. It is daunting to realise how much marketing effort (and expenditure) goes entirely unnoticed. Get on as many mailing/emailing lists as possible to see how other firms are selling.

> I think good marketers see 'good copy' and 'effective images' everywhere and file them. You have to think deeply about the consumer and the best way to do this is to gauge your own response as a consumer and keep a record of what marketing really makes an impact.
>
> Laura Summers, BookMachine

In addition to making your approach interesting and eye-catching you also need to consider whether it is:

- interesting?
- persuasive?
- clear? Do they know what is being promoted and the associated benefits?
- believable?
- motivating? And in particular, do they know what to do next – and how to order?

Keep copies of every piece of promotional material you produce, on- or offline, along with a note of how it performed. This will help you to plan marketing strategies in the future, and save you repeating expensive mistakes. Reading through such a file from time to time also acts as a valuable lesson in objectivity.

You will quickly spot things you would like to change and, maybe in time, come to wonder if it really was you who wrote them!

Getting your timing right

When is the best time to promote to your market? Are there any key dates that must be observed – e.g., the start of the events that your products are being launched to commemorate, or the next academic year? When do you need your marketing materials to be ready by? Start working back through your diary, allocating time to all those involved such as designers and printers. See the sample schedule in Chapter 8 on direct marketing.

Planning too far ahead can be as bad as leaving too little time; it only allows everyone the chance to change their mind and the project to go stale. Responding and rising to the occasional need for marketing copy in a hurry is good practice, but in the long term this may block clear thought. Even if you are desperately short of time, try to let the copy sit overnight. What seems very amusing at 5.30pm may appear merely embarrassing at 9am the next day.

Allocating a budget: how much will it cost?

A budget considers the resources needed to achieve the plan: money, time, staff, etc. It should be related to the costs of reaching the market and the response needed in order to make this worthwhile. An estimated profit and loss for each campaign will usually be supplemented by consideration of the best possible/worst possible/most likely outcomes (Chapter 4 looks at costing marketing campaigns in more detail).

It's worth noting that the actual budget is deliberately quite low down the list in terms of planning order, simply because too early consideration can limit your thinking; there is often a separate way of reaching the market that costs less.

You also need to consider:

- How much will the market pay and how will they pay? If they are buying for the organisation they work for, how much can they spend on their own account without having to get a second signature to approve the purchase?
- At what point will you break even? How many do you need to sell to cover your (a) marketing costs and (b) your contribution to the organisational over-heads? You could do some break-even analysis by running 'what if' scenarios on spreadsheets.

Always be aware of the impression you are creating. Large promotion budgets do not necessarily lead to better sales – indeed, overly lavish material can directly contradict your sales message. For example, full-colour printed material to promote a product supposedly offering good value for money can lead the consumer to conclude that the price is unnecessarily high, pushed up by the cost of the sales message. On the other hand, when selling a high-price product through the mail, attractively produced promotion material, giving an impression of the quality of what is available and the beauty it will add to the customer's home, is probably essential. Look out for the advertisements for high-price 'collectable' volumes that show the products beautifully lit in prestigious surroundings and the enjoyment therefore available to those who own them.

Sometimes it may be advantageous to make your message look hurried and 'undesigned'. Stockbrokers who produce online 'tip sheets' deliberately go for a no-frills approach. If time has to be allowed for design and professional layout, the information is stale by the time it is received. Announcing an urgent meeting about an issue of local importance via a sophisticated leaflet would probably be counterproductive.

Communicating the plan to others

There will be those on whom you rely to execute a plan and those who need to know what you are doing in order to help the process

A common reason for plans failing is that insufficient resources have been allocated, and time and energy of colleagues are as important as money. Make a detailed list of the resources needed to implement your plans and discuss how these will be delivered before you start work – not at a crisis point. Draw up a timeline for who is responsible for what and when. Try to spot double bookings; the planned allocation of a part-time member of staff whereas in reality a maternity leave or leave of absence means the staff likely to be available will already be at full stretch. Try to consider early the various skill sets of the individuals involved and whether there are any gaps.

Whom to tell in-house

There is a range of other people you need to involve in what you are doing – and you will get the best effects if you consult them during the development of your plans rather than just inform them of what you have set up.

If you are going to fulfil the orders within your organisation,[5] your marketing materials should offer an option for direct supply and hence feature your website, email address and telephone numbers. Ensure these are ready before any marketing materials are finalised and consult those who will handle the orders. Whether your distribution is handled in-house or by a third-party organisation, passing all your planned promotions to a colleague in customer services will win you friends and expose you to the feedback they regularly get but seldom know how (or to whom) to pass on. Similarly, does the website manager, organisational receptionist and those staffing incoming calls know what you are offering? If you set up an 'out of office' on your computer, have you really briefed those nominated to speak on your behalf on what to say? If calls come through to your department, has everyone who might answer your phone been briefed? Persuading other people to answer your telephone or deal with your 'out of office' emails can be difficult. Try offering an incentive, such as a points systems resulting in chocolates or wine for every order taken in the department. Leave a basic list of prices or details of the current promotion for all to consult when you are not there.

If the magazine in which you are advertising offers a reader-reply scheme, do you have something ready to send out to those who respond? Colleagues making telesales calls need administrative back-up to ensure what they promise in calls is backed up in practice – with the despatch of samples and the execution of paperwork to support purchase. All these things – and more – need thinking through beforehand.

Does your organisation have any reps calling on retail outlets or head offices to discuss stocking? If your marketing plans are likely to result in increased customer demand, it is vital that they know. As a result they may be able to persuade retail outlets to take additional stock and hence produce more sales. Even if there is no other news than your plans are simply up to schedule, do send a copy of each forthcoming promotion piece to the reps. It is embarrassing if the customers they visit know more about marketing plans than they do.

Motivating the implementation of the plan

Seeing a plan through to fulfilment imposes the need for monitoring and measuring the outcomes: breaking it down into manageable chunks, allocating responsibility and noting progress against what was intended. The monitoring needs to be regular and rigorous, but need not necessarily be formal – perhaps just organising a check-up meeting among all those involved once a week, and then having an action list afterwards so everyone is clear on the priorities. With monitoring need to come controls – formal arrangements for who is commissioning spending and committing future relationships, but also alerting points at which triggers will indicate more extreme action is required. These systems are best established before a campaign is launched rather than halfway through.

If there are particular circumstances that mean a project should not be evaluated against normal organisational monitoring procedures, these need to be highlighted early. For example, a publishing house may be working with a major client who sees distribution of a key resource to the student market as a long-term investment, and is supporting this development by paying all the development costs. Such a project might result in few recordable sales, the normal measure of publisher effectiveness, and hence risks being read inappropriately by management not informed of the project's wider aims – or where the associated income would be recorded.

Evaluating results

Evaluation is also vital for plans to remain relevant, both for effectiveness of communication (how many people were reached, what was their level of subsequent recall of the messages circulated?) and effectiveness of progress towards organisational objectives (dissemination of brand; market penetration targets; sales;

budgetary objectives). Publishing is a notoriously optimistic industry and in the past can stand accused of having been unwilling to commit resources and time to evaluate campaigns, being in general too busy getting on with the next one. Part of monitoring a plan should be an ongoing referring back to objectives and hence feeding what was learned into the next campaign. Remember to use both internal and external sources of information, and to rely on a range of opinions, not just your own.

A final checklist for marketing plans

1 What are you trying to achieve and by when? What are the management expectations for this product/campaign? These are vital bits of information that will shape everything you do.
2 What is the product and how does it work/compete/improve with other solutions?
3 Who is it for? What are its key benefits to the market?
4 What is the organisation doing already? What standard promotional processes will take place, that you can benefit from, to get this product better known?
5 How, in addition, can you reach the market? Make a list of all possible vehicles including those you could not possibly afford (because you may be able to think of other means to achieve the same thing).
6 What budget is available? Is there any possible overlap with other titles, which means that budgets can be pooled and wider marketing gained for the backlist?
7 Which parts of the communication mix will you use? What other mechanisms do you have at your disposal (such as free and negotiated publicity)?
8 What can the author/content supplier do? Who else can you encourage to be an ambassador/enthuser?
9 What are the key dates and can these be formulated into a schedule? What must you have done by when?
10 Who must you inform about what you are up to, for both pragmatic and political reasons? Those you are relying on to handle resulting orders (customer services) as well as those dealing with feedback or even possible flack (PR staff) need to know what to expect, and you should always keep your line manager informed.

Case study

A marketing plan for the 5th edition of Inside Book Publishing *by Giles Clark and Angus Phillips, by Samantha Perkins*[6]

Publication date: 30 June 2014
HB: 978-0-415-53716-2
PB: 978-0-415-53717-9

Figure 6.4 Cover for *Inside Book Publishing*, fifth edition. Courtesy of Routledge/ Taylor & Francis Group Limited.

HB: 978-0-415-53716-2
PB: 978-0-415 53719-9
RRP: £75.00, £24.99
Size: 246x174mm
Extent: 350pp
Initial print run: 2,000

The definitive text for all who need to learn about the publishing industry.

Publishing Training Centre

Primary market: Publishing Studies and Media Studies students.
Secondary markets: other newcomers to the industry, authors, publishers.

About the book

> *Inside Book Publishing* is the classic introduction to the book publishing industry and has established itself as the bestselling textbook, becoming a staple of publishing courses and a manual for the profession for more than two decades ... The book provides excellent overviews of the main publishing process, including commissioning, product development, production, marketing, sales and distribution (from the AN).
>
> The website, www.insidebookpublishing.com, supports the book by providing up-to-date and relevant content, as well as offering research and news on the publishing industry.

Updates (from the AN):

> The 5th edition has been updated to respond to the rapid changes in the market place and contemporary technology.

- Now more global in its references and scope. While based on the UK model, updates including international case studies and a globally relevant introduction make the book more suitable for international markets.
- The book explores new tensions and trends, including the rapid growth of ebook self-publishing and purchasing, and the breaking down of conventional models in the supply chain. And there is a greater coverage of digital and digital business models.
- The internet is now viewed as the primary channel to market for 5th edition.
- The book has been completely rewritten, particularly the marketing chapter.
- Abstracts have been added to chapters.
- New illustrations have been added.

About the stable it comes from

Part of the Routledge List – a range of high-quality resources for this market

Inside Magazine Publishing, *Turning the Page*, *How to Market Books* (Dec 2014), *Inside Journals Publishing* (Jan 2015), i.e., part of a strong list with an identifiable brand within a specific and developing discipline of Publishing Studies.

Competing titles

The Professionals' Guide to Publishing, Davies & Balkwill (Kogan Page)
Routledge's book is more clearly aimed at those taking a qualification in
publishing and offers much more detail, particularly in digital publishing
(from the AN).

The authors

Very strong team; one publisher and one academic – hence covering both
markets.

Giles Clark: co-publishing adviser at the Open University and very well
connected within publishing.

Angus Phillips: former publisher with OUP, now director, Oxford
International Centre for Publishing Studies. Former chair of Association for
Publishing Education and well connected in industry and academia.

Target market

Publishing and media students (UG and PG levels)
Size: 2.5 million UG and PG students in UK in (2011–12)[7]
UG students make up 77 per cent and PG 23 per cent[8]

The cohort of those studying publishing has tripled in size to 1,370 students in 2011–12, almost half of whom are postgraduates.[9]

Age range: 18–24 = 61.7 per cent
24–29 = 12.1 per cent
30+ = 26.2 per cent[10]

Spending habits:

- Outgoings have increased, but social spending is down since 2012.[11]
- Spend £22 per month on books,[12] up £2 from 2012.[13]
- Four in five worry about money.[14]
- Students are brand loyal.[15]
- While the majority of the UK's undergraduate students are now using
  ebooks, none are yet relying on them as a primary source of information.
  Print continues its hold as a key resource for at least two-thirds of students.[16]
- 88 per cent of undergraduates still use printed books and lecturer handouts ... 48 per cent of students using printed books obtain them mainly
  from the library – more than double the amount buying them new or
  second-hand.[17]

There is little information on the spending habits of postgraduate students,
but anecdotally they are inclined to spend more heavily on resources to

support their course, particularly if they are using postgraduate education as a route to a career change.

Science and technology students

Skillset reports that 36 per cent of publishers believe that the biggest challenge facing the industry is a 'lack of relevant skills within emerging workforce'.[18] Publishers are increasingly looking for candidates with backgrounds that aren't in arts and literature: 'The industry's continuous digital progression has increased the need to recruit individuals with a much more diversified set of skills.'[19] While journal and academic publishers are increasingly interested in students with a background in science, the industry as a whole has a skills gap for technology and business-minded students.

In 2013, 47 per cent of graduates were working in non-graduate positions,[20] with 13 per cent unemployed.[21]

Many students take a topic that interests them but don't necessarily want to follow normal career paths for that topic, or change their minds. While others may find it difficult to find a job in their discipline with decreasing funding and stretched budgets.

Working in publishing offers graduates the opportunity to work with their specialist subject, just in a different industry.

Other potential users

These could include:

- those who want a career change (currently more likely with recent redundancy/job loss);
- those moving into the industry from other creative industries (e.g., coders, app developers);
- graduates who do not want to do a Master's/PhD;
- those without graduate training, although most publishers now require degree-level education.

Many of these are likely to go on a publishing training course. It is also likely that they would consult a career adviser, recruitment agencies and relevant websites/blogs for advice on how to get into the industry.

Self-publishers/authors

Digital developments have led to authors being increasingly involved in the publishing process as social media, author websites and blogs have made the author's brand and platform more important than ever as they are now in direct contact with their readers everywhere. 'Self-published titles have grown by nearly 60% in 2012, and in 2013 it showed no signs of slowing.'[22] These authors are increasingly 'working hard to educate themselves like never before'.[23] Phillips reported good feedback about the book from self-publishers.

Publishers/lecturers

The combination of new updates and its position as *the* publishing textbook will be appealing to established publishers who want to keep up to date with what their new recruits know. For the same reasons this will also be of use to lecturers in other creative or technological industries as: 'More and more publishers are outsourcing to freelancers for help with editing, proofreading, illustrating, indexing and graphic design.'[24]

Market reach

- Publishing and other mentioned students can be targeted directly through lecturers who can recommend the title or put/keep it on their reading lists.
- Booksellers.
- Relevant newspapers and magazines.
- Websites and blogs for authors, self-publishers, publishers, careers advisors and recruitment agencies.

Current trends and affecting factors

- Reduced marketing budgets because of the recession and industry changes.
- Library funding cuts.
- Ebooks.
- Phillips reported that Waterstones keener on non-fiction as less affected by ebook sales.
- The recession will likely affect company and customer spending for the next few years.
- The rise of self-publishing.

Rights and international

'Around a third of UK Publishers' sales are exports' (Clark and Phillips 2014: 9).

Routledge have 'a dedicated international sales team', with offices in Europe, Singapore, India and China. This should be exploited as much as possible.

Korean translation and edition for China this year.

Target the CIVETS (Columbia, Indonesia, Vietnam, Egypt, Turkey and South Africa).[25]

Recommendations

The following recommendations aim to provide maximum market reach at as low a cost as possible:

Table 6.1 Table of marketing plan recommendations. Courtesy of Samantha Perkins

Recommendation	Market(s) targeted	Resources needed	When	Cost	Measurability
Angus to email the course leaders he knows – contact those that he doesn't already know. Send review copies. Ask the Publishing Training Centre to publicise the new edition as this will also benefit the sales of their online course 'Understanding Book Publishing', which is based on this title.*	Publishing students (university and training courses)	Review copies E-promotional material	On publication	37 review copies	Confirm whether or not the book is on the reading list and estimate amount of students who bought it
Email careers advisors at universities and specific companies giving useful information (to engage them), e.g., current trends in publishing recruitment (see above) and explain benefits that the book will have for those interested in publishing.	Other university students and newcomers to the industry	Carefully selected contacts for optimum sales/ recommendations Review copies E- and print promotional material	On publication	cc50 review copies cc500 cards	Contact after six months to gauge interest in publishing/ the book
Encourage author talks at conferences/bookshop events.	Publishers, publishing students, self-publishers and authors	Research and book events Print promotional material Travel expenses	Staggered over first year of publication	Low	Gauge interest at events and get feedback where possible

Table 6.1 (continued)

Recommendation	Market(s) targeted	Resources needed	When	Cost	Measurability
Email recruitment agencies, e.g., Inspired Selection and suggest they recommend to those that apply/enquire but aren't yet experienced enough.	Newcomers	Persuasive email E-promotional material	On publication	Low	Contact every six months to guage interest in the book
Target broadsheet newspaper(s) with a targeted press release – a likely article topic would be the popularity of self-publishing.	Self-publishers and authors (depending on article angle) Publishing students	Persuasive press release	Contact four weeks before we want the article(s) published	Low	Record and analyse sales for a minimum of four weeks after publication
Contact relevant magazines, e.g., *Publishing Talk* (which targets self-publishers also), *Bookseller, Publishers Weekly* as well as a variety of book-related websites and blogs for an article/interview.	Publishers, publishing students, self-publishers and authors	Persuasive press release	Contact ASAP for October article aimed at students and six months before any publishing/self-publishing related events	Low	As above
Use Routledge's social media sites to share any publicity received, optimise this visibility by connecting with as many relevant people/accounts – particularly in growing markets.	All target markets should be directed here	Ongoing maintenance	Ongoing	Low	Measure interest with tools like hootsuite

Table 6.1 (continued)

Recommendation	Market(s) targeted	Resources needed	When	Cost	Measurability
Redesign the website and make it more functional. This may be out of budget, but turning the website into a real community for publishing students (and the other markets) will lead to a lot more publicity and encourage increased sales in the long term.	All target markets should be directed to here	Web developer Maintenance by those at Routledge that manage their other companion websites**	As soon as possible, but in time for course beginning in Sep/Oct	High for development Low-medium for long-term maintenance	Analyse site use
Use guest bloggers from publishing courses as well as Routledge staff.					
Publish some of the new abstracts for the chapters to directly encourage sales and enhance discoverability online.	Target all markets	Some copywriting	From pub date onwards	Low	Measure click-throughs and sharing via social media
Guest speak at or sponsor one or two relevant events, e.g., SYP who attract students and newcomers to publishing, BookMachine, and Byte the Book, which is aimed at both authors and publishers.	Publishing students, self-publishers, authors	Promotional material Publicity Drinks/events budget	October	Low-medium	Use a hashtag for the nights and get feedback from the host.
Offer a discount on the book and encourage social media publicity.					

Table 6.1 (continued)

Recommendation	Market(s) targeted	Resources needed	When	Cost	Measurability
Encourage Waterstones (and other booksellers) to display and promote to authors and self-publishers also.	Self-publishers and authors	Arrange meetings/ email	In line with events throughout the year	Low	Monitor sale as get feedback
Include in a variety of e-campaigns, e.g., newsletters or cluster campaigns targeted at the different markets.	All markets	E-promotional material	In line with events and publications throughout the year	Low	Monitor click-throughs and sales
When the above-listed titles in the Routledge list are published the opportunity to publicise this title should be taken whenever possible. Discuss with other authors about promoting each other's titles on Twitter.					

*'Understanding Book Publishing', Publishing Training Centre, www.train4publishing.co.uk/courses/online-training/understanding-book-publishing (accessed 20 April 2014).
**Textbook Companion Websites. Routledge, www.routledge.com/books/textbooks/companion_websites/ (accessed 20 April 2014).

Additional notes

- All communication with channels to market should be individually targeted and persuasively written.
- Should encourage others to write reviews (e.g., Amazon) or publicise with social media whenever possible.
- Really push the idea of it being core/foundation text for publishing to attract students (and others) who are on increasingly tight budgets.
- Discuss marketing plan with the rights department and adapt the recommendations to international markets.

Notes

1 A complete discussion of these can be found in Baverstock (1993).
2 For further exploration of this area see Michael E. Porter's five forces model of competition (1980, *Competitive Strategy: Techniques for Analyzing Industries and Competitors*, New York: Macmillan) and discussion since.
3 www.nielsen.co.uk.
4 www.bowker.com.
5 See page 192, 'Postage and packing' for guidance in this area.
6 MA Publishing 2013–14; this was submitted as an assignment within the 'marketing' module, for which she received a distinction. @sam_publishing.
7 'Patterns and Trends in UK Higher Education' (Universities UK: London, 2013), www.universitiesuk.ac.uk/highereducation/Documents/2013/PatternsAnd TrendsinUKHigherEducation2013.pdf (accessed 20 April 2014), p. 5.
8 Ibid.
9 Matthew, D. (2014) 'Analysis: the subjects favoured and forsaken by students over 15 years', *Times Higher Education*, www.timeshighereducation.co.uk/features/ analysis-the-subjects-favoured-and-forsaken-by-students-over-15-years/2010435. fullarticle (accessed 20 April 2014).
10 'Patterns and Trends in UK Higher Education', p.13
11 Ibid.
12 Butler, J. (2013) 'Student Money Survey 2013', www.savethestudent.org/ money/student-money-survey-2013-results.html#2 (accessed 20 April 2014).
13 Butler, J. (2012) 'What do students spend their money on?' www.savethestudent. org/money/student-budgeting/what-do-students-spend-their-money-on.html (accessed 20 April 2014).
14 Butler, 'Student Money Survey 2013'.
15 The Beans Group (2012) 'Student Spending Report', http://tbg.beanscdn.co. uk/ems/reports/reports/000/000/012/original/student-spending-report.pdf? 1355871237 (accessed 20 April 2014), p. 7.
16 Bowker (2012) 'British university students still crave print, says new BML study', www.bookmarketing.co.uk/uploads/documents/pr_bml_bowker_student_survey_ v1_YA68F.pdf (accessed 20 April 2014), p. 1.
17 Ibid.
18 Creative Skillset (2013) 'Industry panel results: future skills survey', http://creative skillset.org/assets/0000/6529/Industry_Panel_results_Future_skills_survey.pdf (accessed 20 April 2014), p. 10.
19 Signorelli-Chaplin, K. (2013) 'What skills do publishers need?', The Publishers Association, www.publishers.org.uk/index.php?option=com_content&view=article &id=2415:byte-the-book-event-23rd-january-2013-what-skills-do-publishers-need- &catid=499:general&Itemid=1608 (accessed 20 April 2014).

20 Office for National Statistics (2013) 'Graduates in the UK Labour Market 2013', www.ons.gov.uk/ons/dcp171776_337841.pdf (accessed 20 April 2014), p. 13.
21 Ibid., p. 5.
22 Palmer, A. (2014) 'A look ahead to self-publishing in 2014', *Publishers Weekly*, www.publishersweekly.com/pw/by-topic/authors/pw-select/article/60783-pw-select-january-2014-a-look-ahead-to-self-publishing-in-2014.html (accessed 20 April 2014).
23 Ibid.
24 Wood, F. (2011) 'The best books on publishing', *The Bookseller*, www.thebookseller.com/feature/best-books-publishing.html (accessed 20 April 2014).
25 CIVETS, Investopedia, www.investopedia.com/terms/c/civets.asp (accessed 20th April 2014).

7   Selling

Influences on individual buyer behaviour 146
Selling to individuals 148
Top tips for effective sales communication 150
How selling works in a publishing context 152

You might expect this chapter to get straight down to business by offering you a series of techniques likely to result in sales. We will turn to this, but my aim is first to promote a longer-term view. If you begin your sales campaign by considering the needs of the buyer, their buying history, current circumstances and how much they understand about both organisation and product, it is more likely that your approach can be relevant, specific, personal – and therefore also heard.

Selling is often understood as a simple process: the offering of goods in exchange for satisfaction; the fulfilling of needs. As a skill it was surely quickly acquired when early man bartered food for tools. Today, however, how the sales role is described is both culturally and organisationally specific; in some cultures, trouble is taken to hide the essentially transactional nature of selling, referring to those in sales as 'representatives' or involved with some aspect of 'communications', with an accompanying implication that information rather than money is changing hands.

Within the publishing industry, the existence of specific retail outlets that managed the sale of books to customers (bookshops) meant that distance was established in the selling process. In many markets this was supported by the existence of retail price maintenance, which meant books could not be sold for less than their net price.[1] Publishers sold to third parties, wholesalers and retail buyers, not to the end user, and direct selling to the customer was frowned upon. This was combined with a professional, and frankly class-based reticence about involvement in the selling process and money actually changing hands. The marketing function emerged to provide sufficient information to prompt a buying decision, the assumption being that the market knew what they were looking for and would find it through advertising copy on the jacket or in catalogue materials sent to the retailer.

But since the demise of retail price maintenance in many markets and the rise of new selling mechanisms, many of which are online, consumers have become much more aware of their own best interests. Searching for information and purchasing online has accustomed consumers to being specific about their needs and careful in their use of vocabulary in searches, hence the importance of publishers ensuring the copy for their products meets the requirements of search engine optimisation (see Chapter 5). Consumers increasingly want to be an active part of the buying process rather than simply purchasing what is offered and experience of this has empowered them to take part in the evaluation of information, to hunt for the best deal, to cut out middle people whose involvement raises prices without adding value to what is on sale. And this now suits publishers, who want to develop rather than delegate these buying relationships, so that *they* (rather than the retailers and wholesalers) gain the valuable marketing information that can be secured at the same time, and build longer-term relationships.

Direct selling has also been influenced by the policies of local government, where the level of parking charges and rises in high street rental and rates have often reduced the ability of independent shops to operate, and hence the quality and variety of the local shopping experience available to the consumer – who may henceforth choose to drive to out-of-town shopping centres or malls, or buy online. New shopping services offered direct can make available a wider and enhanced range of delivery options that feel personal to the consumer (e.g., evening delivery to home addresses when those ordering are more likely to be in; extended options for returning what is not needed through a much wider range of collection points; free delivery both to and from the consumer; significantly extended guarantees of satisfaction). Some of these are organised through existing retail outlets such as 'click and collect' through high street stores, which allows the customer to place an order online, but have it delivered to a local store which reduces delivery charges and congestion and encourages the customer to buy something else while they are collecting their order.

These changes have led those managing the sales of publishing products to adapt their selling processes and priorities too. There have been significant changes in how publishers sell their wares to those they are hoping will stock, display and promote them for potential sale. Unless the shop is particularly important, individual representation to individual stores, using a range of supporting printed materials, is much less common. Today materials can be presented online or via the telephone – and a regular voice call or email can still feel personal. Large organisations may prefer to buy centrally, through their head office at the discretion of the nominated subject buyer, smaller organisations may buy through a central consortia or a professional/representative organisation. Terms and conditions will be part of the arrangements, and these will include a variety of isolatable variables, including the terms on which material is supplied (firm sale or can it be returned; who pays for carriage; how long is the payment period?). The growing familiarity with online shopping has also reduced its associated perceived risks, and this too benefits publishers – for example, fiction titles (especially ebooks) are generally low in cost and individual customers can be willing to try a small-scale purchase on the grounds that the price was minimal should it not prove what is wanted.

Influences on individual buyer behaviour

Given the centrality of the customer to the marketing process, we have looked in detail already (in Chapters 2 and 3) at the various influences that may be impacting on their readiness to hear a sales message and their willingness to absorb it. These may range from influences close to home, within the micro-environment (e.g., personal change or institutional reorganisation that impacts on their willingness to buy; reduction in personal income or departmental budget) to those within the wider external or macro-environment (e.g., decline in the economy or a forthcoming general election). The salesperson's ability to affect these may vary; in the first instance it may be possible to effect a short-term change, say by lowering prices or offering longer-term credit options, in the latter to empathise and make a note to keep in touch to contact again once the situation changes or perhaps improves.

Then there are a range of new influences on timing that stem from online retailing. The digital lifecycle moves faster and is more malleable. It's possible to organise short-term pricing and special offers to stimulate interest and to measure the results within particular markets or on specific populations, feeding back observations into subsequent campaigns.

These complexities will be apparent depending on the nature of the item being purchased, whether it is a straightforward repurchasing of standardised items or services that are already listed (arranging the delivery of basic utilities; office supplies such as paper or the photocopier), a modified purchase that offers the opportunity to reconsider how the product or service is delivered (computer servicing for a family that allows for various people wanting access with varying levels of skill; contracts with designers which anticipate a move away from print to web-based delivery) to a completely new purchase, to meet new situations that must be costed and secured from a very basic starting point (organising a funeral for the first time; arranging space for the establishment of a hub for online delivery, when the existing warehouse has always been located next to the organisation).

There are likely to be significant differences in how the organisation behaves when buying compared with the individual. Kotler et al's (2013) model for buying behaviour within business is divided into three stages – consideration of the wider environment at the beginning, the buying decision-making process of the specific organisation in the middle, impacting on the buyer's responses at the end. How this works in practice will vary between organisations, but there are likely to be more people involved in the purchasing, and each of these will have different responses to the various stimuli within both the organisation and the environment, some based on their role (production may have different technical requirements to those of colleagues in distribution), their experience to date (ordering key components long distance was not a success last time) as well as their personal responses (perhaps a preference to buy from organisations selling ethically sourced products). It is also likely that selling to organisations will involve working with professional buyers, those who have been trained to manage the process of purchase and are hence effective negotiators. The requirement to work with a range of different individuals and departments within the organisation will mean that negotiation and the decision-making process are likely to be both more complex and more formal.

There are also many potential influences on buyer behaviour to consider, from those within the wider business environment (are the banks willing to lend to us? If we hold off changing our supplier now, can we buy better when the technology has improved in a year's time?) to those that operate within the individual organisation (what is our policy on how many suppliers to accept; long term are we trying to reduce our reliance on too few suppliers and create more purchasing options?). Within this mix must be considered interpersonal influences such as status of the individuals, their relative seniority and their tendency to be influenced by each other (e.g., do they automatically reject the recommendations of colleagues from other departments or those from lower levels of seniority?) as well as the responses of the individual to this situation (do they fit in with the suggestions put forward by colleagues, persist in making recommendations for change or decide to move on, taking their purchasing recommendations to a competitor?), all of which can impact on organisational purchasing patterns.

Within an organisation, the different stages of making a decision may be represented through a series of involved individuals – the gatekeeper who allows (or blocks) access to the selling process, the initiator who begins the search, the influencers who shape the process, the individual who decides, the buyer who places the order and the users who work with what is decided upon. In some organisations these roles will be established clearly, with associated job titles, in others they may be less apparent, and the salesperson may be forced to try to work out the politics of purchasing and who best to approach and in what order; hence a hunt for the manager with the authority and need for purchase.

Example of individual roles within a buying situation

The sale of materials to schools gives a good example of the complicated nature of organisational purchasing patterns. Teachers are generally highly collaborative when considering material for use in class – what is chosen will be used by a range of colleagues in curriculum delivery and once a purchasing decision has been made, another choice will not be affordable for a considerable period of time. While precise operation will vary according to institution and associated personalities, in general the following roles can be identified. The gatekeeper is often the school administrator, or receptionist, who can block or permit the entry of marketing information and providers into the organisation. This may be by relatively simple means such as deciding (or not) to circulate marketing information and passing on information on callers. The initiator of a suggested purchase may be a teacher who has moved from another school and used different materials, or is tired of the existing ones. Influencers will be other teachers involved in delivering the curriculum, other staff who have experience of installing new materials and the suggested provider or those with a specific interest or responsibility, for example the school's (appointed/self-appointed) IT coordinator who is interested in the extent to which materials receive publisher support and online updates. The individual who decides may be the head of section (generally the head teacher in schools for younger children; the head of the curriculum area in schools for older children). The person who places the order may be the finance manager or the school administrator. At each stage in the process of considering, deciding and ordering, the process may be influenced by a range of different factors from the previous purchasing decisions to personal relationships (and cooperativeness) between individuals.

Selling to individuals

Having explored the background to sales, it's time to think about how to communicate with those who will make decisions about the products and services you have to offer. This is perhaps best thought of in terms of the relationship that is built up with individuals.

Building long-term relationships with customers

By sales development consultants www.miradorus.com

Looking at sales purely in terms of totals achieved risks creating a series of 'here today, gone tomorrow' relationships. So rather than looking at one-off sales, how can we really make a connection with customers? How can we spot the personality type we are dealing with and look towards a longer-term relationship? Perhaps it's best to begin by understanding that we really do have a say in the outcome of the sales process.

Let's consider for a moment what happens when we meet someone for the first time. Before we begin to discuss business with them, they need to feel safe and trust us as quickly as possible. According to Dr Michael Solomon of New York University, we assess a new person within the first 7 seconds of contact, and we make decisions about 11 different aspects of that person, including their credibility, level of sophistication and personal values.

This process of information gathering takes place against a backdrop of general assumptions about what a 'salesperson' looks like, probably based on a bad experience with an overbearing salesperson who had their 'patter' and was not going to stop talking until every word of the script had been delivered. In short, there are various factors working against effective communication within a sales situation.

There are other pressures on the person delivering a sales message:

- Buyers will only engage in sales activities if *they* want to and if they can see that doing so will deliver results – no matter how much *you* talk at them!
- People will generally only do business with people they like and trust.

So how can we at least increase our chances of being trusted and liked? To actually close that first sale we need to develop a relationship with the potential buyer. The initial investment of time and effort to do this should be on the basis that it will form the foundations of a longer-term relationship, one where multiple sales and referrals may well take place over a period of time.

When we are selling something, whether product or service, we have to consider what we are selling and why we need to do so. We then need to look at our potential customer in a similar manner by understanding their needs and therefore what value the solution we are offering (or selling) represents to them. The way in which we do this will determine just how effective the relationship can be from this point on.

The quickest way to create rapport and establish our credibility is to treat our potential customers in a way that we would like to be treated. Put another way, we need to understand how our customers prefer to think so we can interact using their language and their style. This will ensure that we do business with them in the way they prefer, not the way we prefer.

Science tells us we give off clues to our preferences all the time, so as salespeople we need to understand and apply what those are in order to increase our chances of success. We would recommend starting with an objective and easy to understand approach such as Herrmann International's Whole Brain Thinking® Model. This brain-based model has established that there are four distinct thinking preferences (see Figure 7.1) and that we all have a strong preference for at least one of the quadrants.

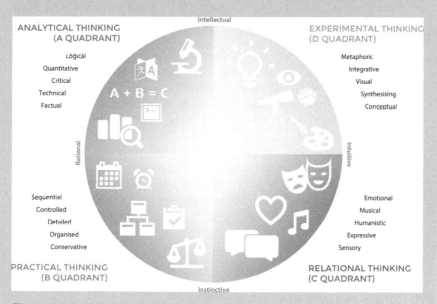

Figure 7.1 Analytical thinking/practical thinking/relational thinking/experimental thinking diagram. Courtesy of Miradorus.

The global database of more than 3 million individuals who have completed the Herrmann Brain Dominance Instrument (HBDI survey) demonstrates that more than 90 per cent of the population have multiple thinking preferences, which means they are likely to give off multiple clues.

So just how do you translate personal thinking preferences into something that helps you engage, build a relationship and gain the trust of a potential buyer? If you are unfamiliar with your customers then you will need to ensure your approach appeals to all four thinking preferences; once you know them better then you can target their preferences more accurately. Whatever your starting point, some preparation and practice will be required prior to any initial interaction.

- Customers with a left, blue (A) quadrant preference are looking for a brief, precise, clear and well-articulated sales pitch. Be sure to have your facts and figures to hand; and if you don't know the answer, be honest and say so!
- Customers who have a left, green (B) quadrant preference will want to experience a step-by-step sales process that minimises potential risks associated with buying from you and your organisation. If you try to push these people into a quick decision, or introduce any last-minute surprises, then you are unlikely to see them for dust!
- Right, red (C) quadrant preference customers may well only be talking to you because someone referred you. If they do not feel comfortable with you, their body language will make that obvious and you will see them physically pull back to put space between you and them. Once this happens it is time to start the rapport-building process again, if you want them to do business with you.
- Customers with a preference in the right, yellow (D) quadrant are looking for something new and innovative. They want just a high-level overview, so try to avoid detail and data if you want to retain their interest. Don't be surprised if they lose their train of thought mid-sentence, they may well have thought of yet another good idea!

Enjoy practising clue-spotting with family, friends and customers – remember very few people are 'single' minded, most people have a combination of multiple quadrants so taking a 'Whole Brain Approach' is your best tactic. And as you begin to become skilled at stretching your arguments into other people's preferences, just take a moment to notice how much easier the sales process has become.

Top tips for effective sales communication

1 **Understand that sales communication is not just about talking.** Communication is a two-way process that involves listening, picking up clues that tell you

why the customer might need the product in question, how they might use it – and who else they might be buying it for. Buying reasons may vary and the customer's focus may be different from your own. A good adage is that you have two ears and one mouth, and they should be used in the same proportion.

2 **Focus on the buyer and how they will use and benefit from your product or service rather than seeing sales as the initial entry point to an organisation.** The role of the sales person can be integrated within the organisation at a variety of levels from someone you see on a regular basis (but don't really engage with) or someone who can be relied upon to provide a quotation and estimation of delivery times (often against which to judge other estimates) to someone who is a trusted adviser and can recommend particular solutions for specific organisational needs. Sellers who understand a business's needs and the forces that drive them are in a better position to communicate solutions and promote a longer-term business relationship. It follows that understanding what the customer wants and why they are buying is likely to lead to more embedded and sustained relationships.

3 **Look for the right person to receive, and hopefully act on, your message.** Within an organisation, this may be a manager with the authority and need for the product or service you have to offer; within a family there may be a range of key individuals who influence the buying decision. You need to consider whose needs are paramount but whose perspectives must also be accommodated – or just shown respect.

4 **Maintain the relationship.** Longer-term commitment to maintaining a sales relationship, through acting as a business consultant or wise adviser, can both promote activity in the short term and yield much more prolonged longer-term results.

5 **Promote the ability to deliver an effective and succinct summary** (a 'pitch') that is relevant to the selling situation in hand. Get to the point while remaining alert to recognise buying signals. But how do you ensure this remains fresh and relevant? Jenny Powell of Miradorus comments:

> Once you have gained an understanding of the customer's needs, and the drivers for those needs, then you will be in a position to make sound recommendations at a business level. As you communicate what products and services you can provide, you will need to edit the information you present to include only those that are relevant to the customer's needs. This will ensure that your pitch is always customer specific and never generic. Consider how to deliver this in a way that also takes into account the customer's thinking preference(s).

6 **Close the deal by asking for the order.** Without it, you are simply providing information, not selling. But how can you spot that the customer is ready to order? Sue Farmer of Miradorus comments:

> When the customer seems confident in what you've recommended, then it will be time to decide together how to proceed. Sometimes it is obvious when

to close the meeting and ask for the order and the customer will take that step for you. At other times you may have to look for less observable signs of acceptance. Words, tone and body language may all give clues that the customer is ready to buy or move forward in the sale process, and you need to consider how to do this in a way that respects their individual thinking preference(s).

How selling works in a publishing context

Kotler et al's (2013) theoretical model of buyer behaviour concentrates on a series of logical stages from problem recognition and information search to information evaluation, decision and post-purchase thinking, all within a context of marketing and other stimuli that may affect buyer thinking. While this has a strong relevance to decision-making over publishing products, and what goes on within organisations making buying decisions that affect many people (e.g., deciding which reading scheme to use within schools or which online information service to support a legal firm), in reality the purchasing of reading material is often subject to much less considered influences, and frequently whims – books are regularly an impulse purchase.

Reading material for leisure is seldom a life essential, and the 'need' may be fulfilled in other ways, perhaps through buying published items from other suppliers but also through the purchase of alternative discretionary items (e.g., chocolate, drinks, lottery tickets). The purchasing of reading material can also take a lot of time in comparison with other personal spends (observe the wide range of what is available and wonder where to start, look at the cover designs and see what draws your eye, read the cover blurb of titles that attract you, read the first few paragraphs of the book to see if you find the style appealing) and it may be that other, more simply branded, purchases offer a more straightforward route to satisfaction (e.g., buy a magazine that you know from habit will appeal to your taste). Publishers try to make the decision-making process simple by presenting markets with category clues – women's commercial fiction will have a distinct cover look that separates it from crime fiction – but it is still often the case that choosing a book can take considerably longer than other types of leisure purchase.

Within the book business in particular there may also be time-specific influences on buying decisions. Seasonality is very important, particularly the run-up to Christmas, the return to school and the start of the academic year within universities and colleges. Other traditions are emerging too – from the promotion of book-giving to mark Mother's Day to the Easter promotion of crime literature within Scandinavian countries. Literary prizes have a big impact as well, and stock of the winning title for certain major annual awards will need stickering with the associated announcement and quickly rolling out through shops eager to benefit from the accompanying media interest. Books also make effective materials for celebrating key events, and much associated commemorative publishing goes on.

All this makes it complicated – and expensive – to develop sales pitches specifically relevant to each market. Publishers are generally selling to niche markets, but generally at mass market prices, and this does not yield a lot of income for tailoring specific sales pitches to a series of small customer groups. They often have to hope that their copy and promotions will work across markets, through the variety of market segments they hope are listening. This chapter will therefore now consider four particular markets: home sales, export sales, rights sales and sales direct to consumers, and offer advice on how the selling may best be achieved in each case. It will conclude with a case study of how one publisher juggles these various requirements in practice.

Selling to the home market

Retail outlets specialising in books

Whereas sale of publisher stock to individual bookshops used to be coordinated by publishers' reps visiting stores, today sales are more usually handled centrally with a key accounts manager visiting a chain's head office, stock delivered to a central organisational warehouse and then rolled out to the individual stores – with local managers retaining a much reduced (or even no) flexibility to order additional stock for the particular needs and tastes of the local markets. Decisions about what to stock will be based on fit for the retailer brand, their audiences and stores, and those doing the buying cannot be assumed to be reading enthusiasts. They will want to know the level of 'publisher support' (read marketing spend and discount available) before committing to significant stockholding.

Larger independent bookshops may receive calls in person, or order by telephone or online. Authors may also seek to encourage their local bookshop to take stock of their work, particularly if this ties in with local events that are being organised.

A difficulty for publishers today is that the number of titles taken by traditional book trade is, in general, significantly reduced. Publishers used to set their print runs according to the number that had been subscribed (or committed to) by book-sellers, but lower quantities being ordered can mean this is often a dispiritingly low basis on which to proceed, and may underestimate how many may be needed if other title alerting mechanisms take off, e.g., coverage via social media. While reprints can be arranged swiftly, or very swiftly in the case of 'print on demand', the risk of how many to produce rests with the publisher.

Many traditional book retailers have also diversified their stocking policy, and now take a wider range of products which require less physical management (unpacking, storing, getting rid of the packaging) and deliver higher profits (greetings cards being a notable example). Some have reduced the space for books by installing coffee shops, in the hope of becoming a 'destination store' (or 'third space'[2]) for relaxation and meeting people rather than just retailing.

The extent to which publishers can provide their own display or 'point of sale' materials (promotional posters and bookmarks and single copy display holders for the point of purchase, dump-bins for multiple copies) has diminished, sometimes due to retailers' determination to offer customers a clutter-free environment, sometimes to management's decision to charge for marketing materials that are displayed.

Online retailers

Publishers submit information on their titles for listing as part of what is available from online retailers – based on an understanding that online stockholding is limitless because items listed need not be physically held, simply available for despatch by the original producer whenever a customer orders. Publishers also target buyers within the head office of the online retailer about the holding of physical stock for titles likely to be particularly popular. Publisher materials can be included within a range of online sites, not just book specialists. Particular care needs to be taken in product descriptions supplied to online retailers, as the lack of a physical copy of the work (even with 'search inside' available) if it is wrongly categorised it may result in not showing up in online searches undertaken by the consumer.

Libraries

Libraries may buy direct from publishers, and also view (either online or in person) the collections put together by specialist retailers dealing with this market (see Chapter 15).

Other third-party organisations that sell books

There are a range of other wholesalers and consortia dealing with particular types of institutions (e.g., specialist libraries, the Armed Forces or prisons) and whose needs are serviced as 'approved suppliers' through regular presentation and stock management and delivery, often with particular additional requirements (protective covering of titles and insertion of the mechanics for servicing loans). Publishers work to get their materials listed within the viewing collections presented to buyers or seek to target those who present potential stock items to them.

Temporary festivals

There is now a range of short-term (sometimes dubbed 'pop up') festivals (e.g., literary, science, thinking, or book-specific, e.g., crime fiction or romance). Some festival shops are contracted out (with or without an associated fee) to local booksellers – or a chain who will come and set up a store – and publishers who wish to see their materials stocked have to communicate directly with them. Other festivals organise their own shops. Negotiations and stocking decisions will probably be influenced by how flexible the organisation is – can you deliver quickly if demand outstrips what was anticipated? Will you take back stock that does not sell?

Heritage organisations

Historic houses, castles and other heritage sites open to the public usually have a shop on site, in addition to a café. Stocking decisions will vary – some shops are managed centrally, others are private concerns.

Leisure outlets

Other leisure outlets such as sports centres, theatres and arts centres may similarly have a retail outlet. Stocking can be at the individual manager's discretion, or may be a policy decision by the local authority or other overseer.

Supermarkets and department stores

Most supermarkets now have an aisle or two for books and stationery – and this is often seen as a more leisurely browsing zone, particularly welcoming for those accompanying active shoppers who can be persuaded to lurk here and buy. Stocking is usually arranged through their central buying facility, direct to head office with decisions made centrally and stock rolled out to individual stores.

Some large department stores have a books department, which stock a limited range of goods on the grounds that they can predict the type of titles their customers may wish to buy. Some of them are amalgamating the online and offline services, with the customers able to have items delivered to a store rather than their home address.

Selling to the export market

Export sales departments look after the sale of content to customers and partners outside of the home market. What is sold may vary – from printed books to the licensing of content within specific markets – but while there may be variations from the basic product for particular markets (e.g., an export trade paperback rather than home market hardback), in general the content will not have been otherwise customised through translation or the significant amendment of content. It follows that export sales operate within markets where the standard home edition is acceptable: territories where the same language is spoken, is widely understood or is acceptable within certain segments (e.g., business or academia). In that they extend the possibilities for sale of the standard content, export sales have the potential to significantly expand an initial sales estimate and make publishing projects viable. Another factor in their favour is that the return rates within export sales can be lower than those for the home market. Retailers stocking books are entitled (according to the terms on which sales are made) to return unsold stock within certain time periods, but in practice the return rates from export sales tend to be significantly lower, perhaps due to the unwieldy associated processes – or increased and longer-term levels of commitment to stock ordered from territories for which local retailers are convinced there is demand.

While the potential for export sales may be significant, some caution is also needed. The population figures for certain markets may seem to offer a tempting prospect but it is important to understand that not all in a market may be interested. For example, for publishers selling in English to a country with a large population, there will be people who speak the language but not all of them may be able or willing to read for pleasure in English, or want to access professional information in that language.

While publishing companies often operate federally, with different imprints developing material of different genres for various markets, export sales are often organised centrally within the organisation, with all titles being presented to external markets from a consistent source – the export sales department. Smaller publishers may contract out their presentation within export markets to agencies who act on their behalf, often larger publishers or consortia of publishers working together. In between exist all sorts of different arrangements, with agencies generally remunerated within the specific markets they service through a commission on the sales they make, and variously supported with the provision of marketing materials. Arrangements with agencies often depend on the ease and experience of contacting and selling within individual export territories as well as short- and long-term market conditions – anything from political instability to local cultural issues (e.g., willingness to buy direct from particular territories; established and valued relationships with existing agencies).

Publishers sign contracts gaining a range of rights for the titles they develop and territories into which they can sell them. Some are 'open markets', where the same content can be sold by a competing publisher (for the English language this is usually a publisher on the opposite side of the Atlantic Ocean and generally includes Europe, Asia, Latin America, the Caribbean, Middle East and Africa), and some are 'closed markets', so whoever owns the rights for that territory will be the only permitted retailer in the area (for UK publishers this usually includes Ireland, South Africa, India, Australia and New Zealand and any other UK commonwealth territories; for US publishers the closed markets usually include Canada, Puerto Rico, the Philippines and Guam). But today previous arrangements and understandings are circumnavigated by online selling, which often ignores international boundaries. For example, it is currently more expensive to order a book from www.amazon.com in the US than to order the UK edition from www.amazon.co.uk. However, with amazon.com offering free shipping to some countries, it may be cheaper to buy books from them than from local shops – although the other consideration may be the waiting time before the item is supplied.

This is not necessarily disadvantageous – servicing individual bookshop accounts in distant territories may be expensive, and it may be more effective to rely on an online partner in a different territory to supply directly to individuals, and hope word-of-mouth within the market promotes wider interest until a local retailer sees sufficient demand in order to stock for sale.

Some territories are visited by export sales staff from the home base, at regular intervals, often around book fairs, or they attend the sales conferences organised to brief local importation and distribution partners on new titles. Customers may be kept informed in between visits by the despatch of marketing information. But it's expensive to keep someone on the road, particularly for long-distance destinations; in the longer term more sustainable methods of representation may be sought. This may include the establishment of a sales office within a particular territory – and it's becoming common for UK publishers to establish offices in Dubai or Hong Kong, from where it may also be possible to source local production opportunities. Other solutions have been to manage key cities across geographical boundaries from a central point (e.g., London, Paris and Brussels may be serviced from the UK via the excellent rail connections).

The benefits of contracting out export sales are lower overheads – someone else manages the day-to-day presentation to the local market – but there may be an associated loss of control. The marketing messages being passed on may drift from the original and agreed central thrust, and while this is often pragmatically done in order to benefit from local knowledge and market conditions, the information on which messages have worked and why may not make its way back to the publisher, who does not therefore learn in the process. The home organisation is also gaining little knowledge of the market being sold to, information with which to refine future marketing processes. There can be conflicts of interest in being sold by one of your competitors, who may present their materials for the same market before yours, or use early information on titles being commissioned to refine their marketing pitch or development plans for future titles of their own.

The book trade has traditionally been very catalogue-driven, and while some publishers still produce printed materials to present their wares to export markets, many have found that the high costs of delivery, and the uncertainty of keeping delivery data updated, means that they are moving to online supply. Printed materials are also out of date as soon as they are created. Marketing materials to support sale to customers may be designed in the home market and then despatched for local customisation in the export territory, or created from scratch in the local market. Such information on forthcoming titles is provided long ahead, and may include mock-ups of anticipated materials, such as press campaigns and poster sites at railway stations. This is usually to give a sense of the publisher's expectations for particular titles – and hence anticipated spend on consumer marketing – in the hope that the export market will seek to match.

Export stock that needs to be returned may be variously managed, often depending on how trusted the customer is and how difficult to reach. The publisher may be satisfied by confirmation that titles for return have been destroyed, or they may require proof that titles are no longer saleable (by returning the cover or the title page). For expensive products, the publisher may require their return for restocking and resale, and hence return in a saleable condition. Carriage is generally paid for by the customer, as is the return of stock no longer required, but these may be points of negotiation in particularly competitive situations.

Case study

Interview with Simon McArt, export sales manager, Little, Brown Book Group, a Hachette UK company

I really enjoy my job which is to manage the sale and marketing of Little, Brown titles to customers in territories outside the UK. These customers include individual bookshops, national chains, online retailers, local wholesalers and exclusive national importers and distributors. We may manage the relationships directly, work through offices we establish in specific territories or contract part of, or the entire function, in particular territories to sales agencies (sometimes other publishers) who work on our behalf. Our department – which reports to the head of sales and marketing – has colleagues who cover the whole world; how often they travel depends on the ease (and cost) of reaching the territories for which they are responsible. My specific responsibilities are Ireland, Africa, the Middle East, North, Central and South America and East, South and Southeast Asia. I love the variety – travelling to interesting places, and meeting a wide range of our partners, with many of whom I have built relationships over a long period of time. In several cases I have got to know both them and their customers so well that they will listen to my recommendations for which of our forthcoming titles and backlist will work for them.

We operate a long way ahead of UK publication dates, often up to seven to eight months, and I am thus securing orders for stock that is not yet published – and in some cases not even in production. We also keep them up to date on the availability of our backlist, which is particularly important for titles in English. As an example, two of our bestselling titles in China are both more than 20 years old, and both have been made into successful films – *The Thorn Birds* and *84 Charing Cross Road*. I undertake long-distance sales trips to Africa and India a couple of times a year, usually around key events such as book fairs or forthcoming sales conferences. The challenge on such occasions is maintaining energy levels. I generally have between 100 and 300 titles to present and little time in which to explain their individual benefits. I have to spot the most relevant sales messages for each individual I talk to, all the while remaining alert for signals that they would like me to stop talking and are ready to place an order. Different customers take different amounts of time.

Trying to secure sales is always highly competitive but the competition is various and can be helpfully segmented. In closed markets (where we alone have the rights to sell the UK edition of a particular title) we are facing competition from other publishers and their wares, in some markets we may be competing with firms to which we have sold rights for a local language edition of the same title, and in open markets we may be competing with a US publisher to whom we have sold rights for them to produce an edition for their market too. Sometimes the US publisher may be our own sister company, which has access to many of the same titles we do.

While this may sound a difficult starting point, we have a strong offering. In markets where we face other publishers' stock we have on our side the editorial merit and sheer saleability of our titles, which have good covers and have been formatted with export requirements in mind (and so often sport supporting cover quotes from an international range of individuals and institutions). In markets where we are competing with very similar products from other publishers, or even our own sister organisation, we can compete on ease of supply and the effectiveness and continuity of our working relationships. UK publishing houses tend to produce small print runs (3,000 at a time is common), which means that we can supply (and resupply) stock very quickly. For some titles we also print stock worldwide, so delivery may be achieved from a printer close to them. While price is often a key bargaining point, there are other factors that affect customers' decisions to give us business, notably the consistency of service we offer: 'We have stock in our warehouse right now, which could be delivered to you by the end of the week. If you buy elsewhere you will have to wait until larger organisations have placed their orders.' Other factors may be our reliability (titles are published, and hence available, when we said they would be) and our sector knowledge (we can recommend stock for business start-ups, specific business development opportunities or to meet particular market needs). You may also be able to draw on your longer-term commitment to them as customers: 'I was the first person to tell you about this title'; 'I am here right now, asking for your order, having taken the trouble to visit you.'

We need to remain alert to different market preferences and understand that buying reasons may vary across cultures, often rooted in the cultural value placed on books and indicated by the prices at which they retail (how expensive is a book in relation to the local purchase of a cup of coffee?). For example, in the US it's common for those buying books for their homes to prefer hardback titles and larger format editions, often with luxury production details such as coloured or ragged end pages and more heavily designed covers, e.g., incorporating 'cut-outs'. Understanding these preferences will influence the order in which you present new stock and the highlights to which you draw attention. You also need to remember which titles have worked well in the past in specific markets, and it may be sensible to build on this rather than pushing new materials. Effective selling demands a good memory for detail and an ability to apply it selectively.

What we take with us on long sales trips has changed. We used to depart with huge bags of covers and other sample printed materials. While some publishers still use printed marketing information, and we may still produce highlight sheets for key events such as book fairs and conferences, we now base our presentations entirely on online materials, which means that up to date details can be presented to buyers from a portable screen. Those we cannot visit, we send online sales information, which is updated frequently and despatched with ease. We find regular despatch of relevant information keeps all relationships warm.

Export selling is a very price-driven market, but rather than just thinking about how much can be charged, it is important to keep up to date on a range of economic factors that influence both your ability to sell effectively and a market's willingness to buy. You need to understand how international exchange rates work – and fluctuate – and the particular conditions and current state of the market economies you are visiting. You need to know how you will be paid, the relevant local currency and dealing periods. Certain payment and banking routines will exist within particular territories (e.g., stock in Lebanon is usually paid for in US dollars so the customer will be carrying a risk of the currency fluctuations between the US dollar and the pound sterling). There are certain trade routes that are well established, and where competition to secure business will ensure low rates for transportation, others where there is no established trading route and direct supply from the nearest supply point may be much more expensive than supply direct from the home base. You need to know roughly how long transportation of stock will take – is it possible by road (two to three days) as in Europe or must it be delivered by boat to markets such as South Africa or Australia (at least a month, maybe much longer)? While it is the buyer who pays for transport of stock in export markets, remaining alert to what they will have to pay and how long they will have to wait are key parts of securing business.

There are other difficulties to watch out for that may make securing sales unprofitable in the long run; in particular, payment periods may make selling complicated, or benefit one party more than another. For example, an organisation that places an order does not have to pay immediately (120 days' credit is common) but might have an automatic entitlement to a refund should they return the stock ordered. So if they order, then take up their immediate right of return, the sum will be refunded before it has been paid for – and the cash flow of the publisher is affected. Similarly difficulties in the political stability of an area may impact on its principal source of income (tourism or manufacturing) and hence willingness to stock non-essential items such as books. While purchasing patterns are low/non-existent and visits unlikely to be cost-effective, it will probably still be worth maintaining the relationship through servicing online with information and stock. Other short-term difficulties over particular items of stock may arise, perhaps due to local cultural sensitivities towards particular titles, but if activity within a market is based on a licence to operate, and this is revoked, it may be very difficult to reacquire. Care over offering the most appropriate titles in the first place may be sensible.

Finally, it's also worth mentioning that the role of selling in my job is not restricted to the information I offer to customers – I am also often on the receiving end of product pitches. Editors who are preparing to present materials to colleagues for potential investment need 'buy in' from their sales colleagues; they must convince them of the merit of what they are planning in order to secure support at the crucial forthcoming meetings. Export sales can play a key part in 'bulking out' the overall anticipated sales figures for a particular title and hence making it a viable proposition so our support is significant. It's worth noting that different sales information will be needed by different groups, and in each case it will be appreciated if the details are delivered through engagement of the listener's attention rather than simply telling. For example, a publisher pitching to an editorial or company meeting may stress the key significance of the author, their anticipated sales and potential long-term value to the organisation; a sales presentation to the reps who will henceforth offer the title to retail outlets may concentrate far more on associated story-telling on which retailers can base hand-selling in future. Copy that gives a flavour of what is on offer, by offering books with 'parents' (e.g., 'John Grisham meets Bernard Cornwell') or that refers to films covering similar areas, may also work – even if those listening have not seen the film they may still understand that this is an area of mass market interest. Long pitches can make people switch off. The circulation of proof copies of forthcoming manuscripts can get word-of-mouth going and can build on initial enthusiasm to create viral campaign – but this has to be judged against the risks of information leaking to competitors too soon.

Rights sales

Colleagues involved in 'rights' are taking content and managing its development, with other collaborators, for additional markets. This may be managed by a publisher who is working on behalf of an author they represent, or their agent (literary or otherwise), and may be variously achieved – through selling all rights to one publishing partner for further exploitation or through establishing relationships with a wide variety of third parties with whom arrangements are either already in place or whom they may seek to get to know. The outcomes can be varied: editions in other languages; versions for specific interest groups (pocket editions, luxury editions, editions branded for particular selling outlets such as supermarkets or memberships); particular formats (a serial in a newspaper, an audio book edition or a braille edition); content for inclusion in a mobile app or to populate an online database – or even just reusing small parts of the content in other works, which is generally referred to as permissions.

A key requirement of the rights role is to find the right customers to sell to, and suggestions may come through your past customers, wider research (web-based or in person at book fairs, from perusing catalogues, following up leads provided by authors or by potential collaborators finding you). Information on the content available can be offered through a variety of means, from catalogues and specific rights guides to email campaigns and website information. But throughout the process of making information available, it is important to have effective skills in sales presentation (making a relevant pitch to the right organisation) and sales management (ensuring that the rights being sought are indeed available; considering whether the licence being sold will adversely affect organisational sales and managing the process through to completion – and afterwards).

Whatever the organisational structure, or anticipated outcomes, the role of the rights manager is likely to include:

- understanding the nature of the material available: the specific content on offer, its appeal, provenance, value, potential and wider applicability;
- establishing contacts with organisations or individuals likely to appreciate the content and making judgements about who can effectively and appropriately exploit it for their particular market.

- building trust so that offers will be taken seriously
- maintaining such links in between business arrangements so that they can be rekindled when relevant new material becomes available
- presenting the material in its most attractive light, varying the presentation according to the market/potential collaborator being approached
- making decisions about who would make the best collaborator and negotiator likely to achieve a mutually satisfactory conclusion; considering this within the longer-term best interests of all parties
- managing and communicating the detail of the arrangements
- monitoring outcomes to ensure all parties are satisfied.

Rights staff negotiate the terms under which material is licensed, for example whether the arrangement is exclusive/non-exclusive; the format; the territories in which it is to be available; the languages; the 'term' of the agreement (for how long) and the associated 'financial consideration' (for how much money), and then draft and exchange contracts that confirm what has been agreed. How the money gets accepted can be similarly complicated. Payment may be through royalties but it needs to be decided whether these are to be based on list price or net receipts and the length of the accounting period (annual or semi-annual?). If there is to be an advance, will it be 100 per cent on signature or perhaps 50 per cent on signing and 50 per cent on signature? Alternatively a one-off fee may be agreed, with a fixed print run or sales limits, and again the payment periods and term of licence need to be agreed. There may be provision for some material to be available gratis, perhaps for charitable or author reuse, but again this must be specified. A key part of the rights role is also ensuring that monetary arrangements are stuck to, and in addition to invoicing there will be cycles of chasing payment, chasing and checking the licensor's finished item, ensuring royalties are accounted regularly, renewing an agreement on expiry/re-licence elsewhere and reporting back on what has been achieved.

One of the particular satisfactions of a rights role is the promotion of a stronger commercial relationship between content providers and their publisher. Securing an author's wider availability in other markets and formats strengthens the relationship between them and their publisher or agent and builds for the future. Success in this can also bring promotion for the rights manager, more involvement in decisions over what gets commissioned or sought as well as what subsequently gets sold. The role can also feel very creative.

Case study

Interview with a rights manager of a major publishing house

Rights is a particularly pleasant form of selling. We are offering content to collaborators – in my case mostly other publishing houses in Europe – but rather than a straight sale, we are marketing the opportunity to make this project their own; to share in how an author is presented within their local market and partner in their reputational development; to co-create. We are also looking to the longer term, offering a collaborating publisher ownership and the chance to work with us in future, and this may involve sharing marketing materials, media campaigns and other involvements that promote the best interests of all parties. In the process some very long-term collaborations can be established.

It can also get quite competitive. We work in a team, each of us managing the same content but for different territories or formats, and if one colleague is having a lot of interest in the work, and you are having less immediate response, it can be helpful to compare marketing approaches – and the different stresses being made in the marketing pitch. The editors brief us on what they have bought and we have regular meetings at which we discuss how we will present material. Through sharing our proposals they become stronger – although they always still need tailoring for the particular markets we approach.

Rights staff have to look outside the organisation and must have a wide economic awareness, an understanding of the economic circumstances of the markets or areas they are approaching. They may have to present material that is not to their own particular reading taste, and must be guided by its commercial value to other markets.

It's also important for them to appreciate – and probably further explain – that the process of selling co-ownership may compromise how material is presented in the author's home market. Chosen collaborators will present material onward as they see fit, and this may differ from how individual authors feel their material would be most effectively displayed. It may be in an author's best interests to understand that once they have made their work available, how it is interpreted will not be their exclusive preserve. Even if they don't like the cover or illustrations selected by collaborators, they may still be encouraged to take refuge in the wider availability of their work.

Whatever their precise role, rights staff need effective presentation skills, detailed market knowledge, and then sufficient tact and diplomacy to explain the outcomes to those impacted.

Selling directly to the customer

Sales of publisher materials used to be routinely channelled through intermediaries – bookshops, wholesalers, specialist agencies dealing with particular markets. Today, however, there is a search for direct relationships – and the market information and long-term selling potential that comes from building communities loyal to the publisher. For more information, and guidance on how this can be best effected in various markets, see Chapter 15, but here is a case study on selling to a customer with a specific interest.

Case study

*Marketing and selling antiquarian and facsimile books:
an interview with Dieter Roeschel (author of various titles
on facsimiles) and Anton Pfeiler, owner of
Fachbuchhandlung für Faksimiles (bookseller of antiquarian
and facsimile titles), Germany*

Antiquarian and rare books are old editions, those that are no longer in print and hence routinely on sale. The range of what is available to acquire is thus limited by what is on the market – or may become accessible in future. 'Antiquarian' usually refers to titles printed before 1900, 'rare' generally means scarce; for example, titles that had very low print runs (poetry being a common example).

Facsimile books are reproductions of titles, usually those that are extremely precious, and ownership hence allows collectors access to volumes in the same way that the originals were owned; in private. They are produced when owners of precious manuscripts offer specialist publishers access to photograph what they hold and a limited edition is produced for sale. The subsequent financial value of what is produced is at least partly dependent on whether or not the owner plans (or subsequently decides) to offer a new access in future; weighing up financial gain against the inevitable associated damage that production processes bring to the fragile manuscript. So for collectors, whereas the number of copies of antiquarian books is necessarily finite, the position with facsimile editions may be less certain.

All the same marketing and selling skills are required as with new titles, but in the case of antiquarian and facsimile editions it is particularly important to know your market and what they collect, to build a relationship of trust based on the dealer's scholarship and market awareness, hence guaranteeing the authenticity or rarity of what is being purchased. Longer term, few things are a completely sure investment – and books are as subject to the vagaries of market forces and wider economy as other collectibles – but associated interests can form the basis of very long-term relationships between dealers and their customers.

Booksellers dealing in antiquarian and facsimile books place a lot of emphasis on knowing the customers, maintaining relationships with them and conveying the quality of what is on offer – usually through high-quality printed catalogues and leaflets, although younger generations may view material online, particularly if a quick decision is needed. As book collectors age, it is also pragmatic for dealers to promote interest among younger generations, particularly those likely to inherit – and hence perhaps develop – a family collection. Advice on how to understand their collections (expert commentary in books or articles in magazines or journals), how to store and look after titles, may be particularly valued. It is also possible to sell a range of supporting products to the same market – fabric 'book worms' that hold pages open, materials for storing out of direct sunlight and gloves for their management. Such items are not always necessary but their associated processes can be part of the joy of owning.

Longer term, prices for books generally depend on the demand for a given title, the number of copies available (low print runs are particularly attractive), the role they played in the author's developing reputation and their condition. Higher prices may be paid by those collecting particular early editions or titles of a specific provenance (who owned them previously or perhaps their status as part of a particular institutional library).

A related development within traditional publishing has been republishing (whether in print or digitally) titles that now form part of the 'rare books collections' that all libraries either host or share with a range of related institutions. Making available scholarly work of particular significance in this way can have a particular appeal to information professionals, offering them the chance to make a range of works accessible again but without damaging the originals. Such materials are best presented on the grounds of enhancing a collection, raising its profile and prestige, and making a complete range of information available again.

In conclusion to this chapter, publishers have to sell to various groups and individuals, with different messages and terms that vary according to different circumstances. In the process they have to manage a complicated series of relationships. We therefore end with an example of how this works in practice.

Concluding case study: how a small independent publisher manages selling across various audiences

Background information on the organisation

Grub Street is an award-winning small, niche independent publisher, publishing within two distinct areas: cookery and military aviation history. Anne Dolamore (cookery) runs the business with her partner John Davies (aviation).

Within cookery, their aim is to publish the very best in contemporary and classic food writing and they were delighted to be voted International Publisher of the Year at the World Cookbook Awards in 2000.

> A number of our cookbooks have won prizes over the years. Most recently, these have included the highly acclaimed *Ice Creams, Sorbets and Gelati* by Caroline and Robin Weir, voted Cookbook of the Year by the Guild of Food Writers in 2011. *The Complete Robuchon*, by the influential chef Joel Robuchon, was awarded Best Translation at the Gourmand Awards in 2010.

Anne first got interested in food writing through the columns of Jane Grigson and firmly believes that the text is the part of cookery books that really matters. This bucks the trend in an age where celebrity cookbooks are all the rage, and are often created to match individual celebrity brands rather than through any understanding of food. Grub Street rather include photos where they feel they are required, not regarding the cookbook as a single entity, where one size fits all: 'There are books that don't need photographs and some that do, there are cookbook-buyers some of whom always want pictures and some who never do. It is a question of tailoring the concept and format of the book to the perceived customers' requirements.' Across the company they publish 30–35 titles, so about 15 for each side of the list. Their backlist (across both) is now almost 200 titles.

> What distinguishes Grub Street books is not just their alluring recipes, but their authoritative tone. Many authors, argues Dolamore, only have one great cookery book in them. Other publishers will urge authors on to superfluous follow-up books, making them flit from rustic Italian to barbecues with dizzying speed. Dolamore does the opposite, encouraging writers to cover one subject definitively and passionately, and then stop. This is good for the author and their reputation, because Grub Street books stay in print much longer than other cookery books. Occasionally established food writers will come to her and say, 'What do you think I should write about?' to which she replies, rather formidably, 'If you ask me that, you're never going to get on my list.' Once you have a Grub Street book on your shelf, you are unlikely ever to part with it.
>
> Bee Wilson[3]

She also feels that one of the secrets of their success is being able to judge moods, where interests are going and being there when it has got to that point when a book will sell. They managed this with *The Essential Olive Oil Companion*, which they packaged for Macmillan in 1988. When the original publishers put the title out of print they got the rights themselves and republished in 1999. The initially modest sales started to rise and the book was available from Grub Street when everybody finally woke up and wanted to read about olive oil. The upshot of this success has been that if anybody needs an authority on olive oil, they wheel Anne out.[4]

Managing the selling process: communicating with the market through the food press

Grub Street's books have always been supported and well reviewed by food journalists, of which there are many, but the specific foodie press is currently experiencing a lot of competition. One of the best-known UK magazines in this area – *Food Illustrated* – was acquired by upmarket supermarket Waitrose and is now contract-published monthly for them. There are now also many supplements to national newspapers, such as *Observer Food Monthly*, the *Life and Style: Cook* section of the Saturday *Guardian* and similar sections in other newspapers. So while the specific foodie press is under pressure, interest in reading about cookery is now much more mainstream – and of course this provides opportunities for coverage of Grub Street titles. They do almost all the press liaison in-house, mainly because they personally know the journalists involved.

How you convert review coverage into sales is however more problematic. Readers would complain that they could not find the books they read about in their local bookshop and they had to be specially ordered.

Sales to book retailers

Selling to stockists is still important, and Anne arranges to see buyers from all the major firms, both off- and online, at regular intervals. The market is however dominated by the glossy television tie-ins and Grub Street reps can find it difficult to convince retail buyers to stock their titles, especially as their titles often have no pictures.

Selling directly to customers

Given that their brand attracts such strong recognition and loyalty, it's now possible to sell directly to consumers – using a combination of PR and online selling through Amazon, Hive and BOL. Delivery is managed through their distributor and more profitable as direct sales are usually at full price.

PR continues to be important, and Anne's personal authenticity works well on- and offline. She is personally committed to food and wine and spent 4 years on the Committee of the Guild of Food Writers and 2 as chair. She was a trustee of Sustain, an organisation that campaigns for food and farming, and now mentors students of MA Food and Culture at Oxford Brookes University. To her, food is more than just publishing, it is a way of life and she believes that people should be eating better and be able to cook. She publishes from the heart and says 'If I wasn't prepared to go out and buy the book myself, why am I doing this?'

Selling through bloggers

Particularly important now are relationships with bloggers who write about food, and can be relied upon to give honest and passionate advice about relevant books. Writing and maintaining a blog is a lot of work (see Chapter 9) so they don't run one themselves, rather they liaise with those whose passion for food is as strong as their own. Anne seeks to understand the bloggers' preferences and provide them with review copies and background information so they can write their own story – pushing and overdirecting them is not a good way to manage these relationships, and feedback from bloggers has been that they relish (and find somewhat unusual) being treated in this respectful way.

Rights sales

Selling translation rights used to be a source of income but it's getting harder all the time, with more associated activity on the aviation side of the list than cookery these days. Anne remarks:

> That's because non-English language markets are now producing some very beautiful cookery books of their own and the English language domination of that market no longer exists. To the extent that these days I'm often buying English language rights to foreign cookbooks. This year for example I have two books coming translated from Danish and one from French. We also look into ebooks and have about 80 titles available in this format.

Cookery does not sell particularly well as an ebook – the stains on the page are part of the lived experience of working through the recipes – but aviation does.

Selling themselves to and through authors

Both partners take great care of their authors and the relationship clearly works both ways. As Anne comments: 'They revere the Grub Street list so much for its reputation they have no desire to go elsewhere. In fact on both sides of the list we often acquire authors because of their experiences at other publishers!' They try to encourage their authors to help with the marketing of their titles, and to use social media – but don't force them to. Some of the aviation authors are particularly effective here.

Resulting sales figures

The numbers sold can vary enormously, from a few thousand to tens of thousands; some of their bestsellers can reach 60,000–75,000 over a number of years. Anne says:

> Because we are a backlist publisher, keeping books in print is what we believe is most important to us and our authors. One of our bestselling titles was first published in 1988, has never been out of print until now and that's because we are about to issue a revised and updated edition. We will continue to reprint books as long as there are sales, and short-run digital printing means we can cost effectively reprint little and often. We have not so far used POD because we feel the quality of the books

produced is still below the production standards we want for books carrying the Grub Street logo.

Looking ahead, their formula works and Anne will stick to restricting her output: 'I want to be able to pick a book and say I am proud of this. I don't want to do 24 books, where 12 are excellent and 12 are just filling in slots.' She is firmly against 'reinventing the wheel'. 'If the best book has been done on a subject, why do another one? That is why I like reissuing books. Leave it be and try to find something new.'

www.grubstreet.co.uk @grub_street

Notes

1 In the UK, this was the Net Book Agreement, no longer defended after 1995. Resale price maintenance still exists in other markets, e.g., most of continental Europe.
2 After home and work, this is a location to head for on a routine basis, often to meet people, e.g., a gym, favourite café or pub.
3 *Sunday Telegraph*, 23 January 2005.
4 www.goodwebguide.co.uk.

8 Direct marketing

Why the principles of direct marketing matter to publishers 171
The essentials for a direct marketing campaign 172
Plans 173
The audience 174
Offers 175
The most appropriate medium for direct marketing 175
Timing 176
The copy platform 177
Response devices 183
Design services 188
System of despatch 188
Monitoring effectiveness 189
Fulfilment services 191
Telemarketing 193
A final checklist for all forms of direct marketing 195

Even if you are in a hurry to get on and learn about online marketing, please read this chapter first. It contains advice on how we arrived at the position of being able to communicate directly – and principles we should never forget when doing so.

Direct marketing means selling or promoting straight to the customer, without the intervention of an intermediary such as a retailer, wholesaler or sales agent. This may take place through a variety of different media (e.g., email, post, telephone, parties). What turns an advertising campaign into a direct marketing campaign is the inclusion of a mechanism for responding directly to the organisation advertising. Thus a party where a new range of cosmetics are shown or a catalogue distributed door to door both become direct marketing operations if an order form is made available or a website address is available for related orders, perhaps with an offer included for responses within a certain time period.

This probably sounds very obvious. Of course any form of marketing material should tell the customer how to order. For large parts of the publishing industry, however, and the general trade in particular, direct communication with its customers is both relatively recent and has been hard won. The existence of a range of specialist retailers – bookshops – while offering an automatic and welcoming destination for their products also had the side-effect of tending to distance general publishers from their customers. They were discouraged from fulfilling orders themselves and as a result often knew relatively little about who bought from them.

But physical bookshops could not be expected to stock all the industry's output. It was difficult to persuade retailers to stock titles aimed at professional markets, or those of very high price, as this involved tying up large amounts of capital on stock for which there was an uncertain demand. Direct selling to customers for specialist and professional titles therefore emerged, grew in sophistication, and the associated expertise and in particular information management techniques are now pollinating the rest of the industry. General publishers are making up for lost time, still keen to get their materials into bookshops and other relevant retailers, but also to build a relationship with those who appreciate their products – and will buy from them in future.

Why the principles of direct marketing matter to publishers

The precision of thinking and clarity of instruction required for effective direct marketing are valuable disciplines for any form of marketing, and can play a key part in setting the standards for an organisation's overall marketing activities.

Today direct marketing is being used through a variety of different media and in new ways, often in combination. Integrating your message across multiple media can be a very effective way of establishing sequential customer relationship management (CRM): an initial email to arouse interest; a printed brochure on request; a follow-up telephone call to solicit an order. Direct marketing is also now highly significant within mass market retailing. Loyalty cards operated by supermarkets are a vast direct marketing exercise to support their brands aimed at their core market, and find out more about their shopping habits and aspirations. Political parties are using direct marketing to make specific pitches to groups they wish to influence.

For publishers, the high costs of postage and low overall response rates have often meant that direct mail is too expensive for lead generation, but it still has a significant role to play in customer retention and renewals, in buying situations where a niche market can be clearly identified, or where collaboration must take place before a decision is made (e.g., the educational and professional markets). Direct marketing using a combination of media, e.g., email, telemarketing and print, is an effective way of remaining in touch with the customer and building a long-term relationship. Selecting which is the best media to use comes down to knowing the audience and using the most cost-effective channels to reach them. And all the associated thinking is a very good start to marketing online.

The essentials for a direct marketing campaign

One of the most significant characteristics of effective direct marketers is that they are well organised. This is a marketing medium that requires attention to detail more than huge dollops of creativity. But before any associated marketing activity is planned there are a variety of factors to be taken into consideration, and you will find your objectives easier to achieve if these things are thought about before you begin planning your campaigns, rather than as you are doing them. You will need:

- a plan;
- an audience;
- an offer;
- a decision on the most appropriate medium;
- a decision on timing;
- a copy platform;
- a response device;
- design services;
- a system of despatch;
- a method of monitoring effectiveness;
- fulfilment services.

We will look at each of these essential elements in more detail, and mostly in relation to printed material – and then with a short section on telemarketing; both practices illustrated through a relevant case study.

Why print is still significant

Once organisations could routinely communicate online with their customers, many assumed this would signal the end of printed direct marketing materials (direct mail and flyers). Not so. As data handling has become more efficient and market niches more precise, mailers can store and access sufficient information to deliver really effective and specific campaigns. And the huge increase in email means that many people delete 'junk mail' (or 'spam' as it is termed) without reading it carefully, if at all. An effective printed piece can still grab attention, as it is physically in front of them. Yory Wurmser, director of marketing and media insights at the UK's Direct Marketing Association (DMA) recently quoted an average 4.4 per cent response rate for direct mail compared with email's average response rate of 0.12 per cent.[1]

Print is still a useful medium for direct marketing when:

- you can be really precise about whom you want to get to and how to reach them;
- you have a long or complex message to convey;
- you have evidence that the market wants to be talked to this way;
- the financial rewards of contacting them are sufficient to make it worthwhile;
- the product you are promoting is impressive, and carries a status and weight that is best relayed through print;

- the product or service needs to be discussed before a commitment is made – this may be more easily achieved with a printed format that people can share than by providing an online reference;
- the product or service is best promoted *without* an implication that targeting has been used, and a personally addressed email or letter would be threatening or intrusive (e.g., the promotion of locally available funeral and dating services via unaddressed leaflets delivered door to door).

Also, given that one of the reasons for considering the principles of direct marketing is to think fully about the implications of the relationship being developed, rather than to communicate as quickly as possible, it makes sense to consider how this works in a slower medium.

Plans

All successful campaigns begin with a plan. What is your objective? Do you want a direct response or to spread information about your products? If the latter, will orders come back from other sources? Deciding what your objective is then dictates how you will measure the success of your activity. Are you seeking value of resulting sales or the number of responses? Not all successful campaigns need to generate sales.

Direct marketing can be usefully divided into two types: direct response and direct promotion. *Direct response* marketing invites a direct response back from the customer, so emails or mailshots advertising particular titles might ask for orders to be returned to the publisher. *Direct promotion* marketing is more concerned with spreading information about products, which may be variously fulfilled. The promotional message is still sent to the customer, but while the response may indeed be returned directly, it may also be fulfilled elsewhere, through the websites or shops of other organisations. Small publishing houses who promote to their customers, but are keen to avoid managing a despatch service themselves and hence content to rely on the services of third-party retailers to fulfil the resulting orders, are executing a system of direct promotion.

You need to understand both what has been achieved so far within your organisation and what is expected of you in future. A good starting point is to explore both the expectations and budget for the products in question. Try to find out the answers to the following questions:

- What are the anticipated sales for this product/service?
- Are there any existing or pre-orders? And if so from where?
- Are there any internal constraints (e.g., the requirement to sell a certain quantity by a particular date)?
- Are there any other backlist titles can you sell on the back of this campaign?
- What kind of people benefit from the product? Who/where are they?
- Are they the same people who do the ordering? Whom should you target?
- When is the best time to market?

- Does the customer need to see the product before making a decision to buy (i.e., must it be available on approval or with a firm guarantee)?
- What is new/excellent/noteworthy about the product?
- What is the history of the organisation selling similar products directly in the past: are there list successes worth repeating, or failures worth avoiding?
- Where is the product available from and by when?

The audience

> You need to think at the earliest stage about the likely audience you wish to approach and how they can be found. There has been a tendency for those considering direct marketing to think in terms of lists of possible customers, but a list is just the contact details of those who can be reached (and may not even include all those you would like to be in touch with). We prefer the term 'audience', which includes their profile and background information about who they are, how they behave and how you should talk to them. A detailed understanding of audience is invaluable at the creative development stage, and knowing detailed information about your current and potential customers allows you to project this onto external list sources, using like to find like.
>
> Alison Blake, digital and direct marketing strategist[2]

The audience to which your marketing material is sent matters more than any other single component of a direct marketing campaign, because unless information is sent to the right people, it stands no chance of achieving a successful outcome. An understanding of audience should thus form the basis of all the elements of your campaign, from the media through which you will communicate to the tone of voice deployed in the copy.

Lists of customers are increasingly developed and maintained by publishers, with information that comes back from the market ('undeliverables') being used to update the database, usually auto-updating in the case of online marketing. You need to meet with those managing your data and ask them what they can tell you about your customers. You may also be working with external organisations such as professional associations or membership organisations, in which case you need to ask about whom you are approaching, and what their motivations and buying criteria are. For example:

- Where do they work?
- What organisations do they belong to?
- What are they interested in?
- What have they bought in the past?
- How often do they buy and how much do they spend?
- How does the approval staircase work?
- What does experience tell us about how they like to be treated?

There are also data owners and list brokers who can advise on, or suggest access to, commercially available lists for rental or leasing in a format of your choice. Today they also offer a range of additional services that enable the marketer to forward copy for dissemination, with them managing everything from design and despatch of personalised emails and to bespoke direct mail campaigns with individually customised materials.

Offers

Consumers today are used to getting added value in every purchase, through price promotion or perhaps the aura of exclusivity that early ownership brings. How effectively you communicate the benefits of purchase to your market will have a big effect on how willing they are to order or remain your customers.

You need an understanding of what will motivate your target customer to buy/recommend/ask for your product. It may be just your product, and the prestige endowed by early ownership or the solution it offers to a longstanding problem, or it may be the added value you are able to include (free carriage, strong guarantee, money off for an order placed before a certain date, additional free gift).

Thinking of an offer to consumers is an important stage in a direct marketing campaign, because focusing on how to attract attention generates excitement and enthusiasm. And once you have thought of a benefit to offer, it helps you write the copy. Another option is to make a choice of offers, so the recipient gets involved in deciding which one to take, and moves further along the route towards response. One final point on offers: in general try to offer added value rather than discounts. The perceived benefit of giving an additional book for orders over a certain price point may be greater to the customer than the actual cost to you. Offering a discount, on the other hand, has a direct impact on your overall profitability, and may create expectations for something similar in the future.

The most appropriate medium for direct marketing

You have a wide variety of different media for reaching your customers by direct marketing. These include:

- email;
- postal mail;
- telephone (both incoming and outgoing calls);
- website;
- social media (e.g., Facebook, Twitter, Pinterest, YouTube, LinkedIn, etc.);
- door-drop (house-to-house delivery);
- 'off the page' advertising (space advertising in a magazine or newspaper with the response 'off' the page back to the organisation that placed it);
- online advertising;
- poster sites (e.g., in the street or transport advertising such as in bus shelters, train stations and beside escalators);
- television and radio advertising;

- text messaging (SMS);
- catalogues;
- parties for direct selling;
- clubs (some with rules, offering special arrangements to members, others just called 'club' to promote identity);
- conferences;
- 'reader get reader' promotions: incentives to individuals to recruit other potentially interested parties.

Your selection should be based on the type of customers you are talking to, the product or service you are promoting, what you want them to do and how long it may take them to reach a decision. For example, a high-price item may need expensive marketing materials and supporting evidence to be sent through the post (e.g. testimonials), posting reviews and discussions on social and business forums such as LinkedIn with a follow-up e-marketing campaign and a visit by a rep to take the order; a low-cost product may be best promoted through emails or text messages – encouraging orders through a website. Charting previous customer journeys will help you make sensible decisions.

Timing

You need to think about when your potential customers are most likely to be responsive to your marketing approach, as well as when you can best handle the work involved – and what else your organisation is sending out to the same market, to avoid over-communication.

How to plan a schedule for direct marketing

Work backwards from the date you want your message to arrive with your prospects. If you are going to complicate your approach by including a 'sell by' date, or the market has a key deadline looming (e.g., the end of the school term), you must be very accurate. It is easy to allow slippage but it can be fatal to a campaign's success.

For a postal mailing, the schedule could look like this:

Response device in the mail	1 week
Time prospect needs to consider the offer and respond	5 weeks[3]
Best time to arrive	1 September
Time in the post, by most cost-effective means	1 week
Stuffing the mailshot	1 week
Printing	2 weeks
Circulation of final proofs, passing for press, ordering lists	1 week
Design and layout, corrections	2 weeks
Copy approved and passed to designer, visual prepared and circulated	2 weeks
Finalising copy	1 week

Copy presented, discussed and circulated	1 week
Time for writing copy	2 weeks
Drawing up schedule, briefing suppliers, requesting estimates, sourcing lists, setting up monitoring procedures for mailing response	2 weeks

Working back and allowing a little extra time, you should start thinking about the mailing at least three months before you want it to arrive.

Of course mailings can be accomplished much more quickly. An email campaign can be decided upon and effected within the space of an afternoon – but the sequential thinking about all the different stages still needs to be thought through. How will the customer respond? When is the best time to inform them? When you are ready to send may not overlap precisely with when they are most ready to receive.

Don't forget to factor in how long it will take you to organise. Dr Dominic Steinitz has this formula for working out how long any online project will take: make your first estimate, multiply it by two and then add a unit. Thus if you think it will take, say, 2 hours it will probably take you 4 days. If you estimate 3 weeks it could be 6 months and so on. In my experience this is very accurate.

The copy platform

Direct marketing is above all a writer's medium. Whether you have to write the copy yourself or commission it from freelances, it really matters. There is no eye-contact, no body language to coerce the recipient into purchase and so the words, and accompanying images, are hugely important.

> In the digital era, a picture is also worth 1,000 words. Facebook, Twitter and Pinterest all work better through images and the suitability of images for promotion will depend on the nature of the item you are promoting. Does it have graphic content or does it lead to the imagination of content? Strong images with strong calls to action work best. The exception is in email where writing an effective subject line in 50 characters or less is a skill in itself.
>
> Alison Blake

If the copywriting and image sourcing fall to you, begin by thinking (about the market and how best to present the product or service to them) rather than just writing. If you think as you write you will find it takes longer, and is more muddled. You need to think about how the words you use can persuade the market to take the next step you have intended. An outline of your overall strategy, with the impression you are trying to create, can grow into draft headlines and the basic message you plan to communicate.

If you are commissioning the words from a freelance copywriter, you will need to provide information on how the product or service benefits the anticipated audience. Can your copywriter also have access to all the various in-house forms and so gain an idea of the evolution of the project (on a confidential basis, of course)? Don't forget to pass on all the background information that you take for granted, such as details of rival products. An effective copywriter will write for a specific format (they may well suggest an alternative to your original idea) and provide you with a rough layout indicating what goes where for the designer. For further guidance, see Chapter 13 on copywriting.

Information to put in a direct marketing promotional piece

The best way to learn about how to put together a direct marketing piece is to become a direct marketing user – if you are going to use direct marketing in a professional capacity you need to see how others are doing the same. Through this process you will start to notice that most direct marketing consists of four components (even if they are part of the same physical thing). In direct mail, for example, there is almost always:

- an outer envelope to get the information to the recipient – usually with a message on it;
- an accompanying letter, to introduce the contents of the package, the product being sold and the offer. This could be from the organisation or you could consider presenting it as a 'lift letter' from someone the market respects, an endorsement that can provide the credibility to help convince the audience (or you could have two letters);
- a brochure or leaflet, to explain in further detail;
- a reply device or order form.

In some mailshots these components may be amalgamated, for example into a long sales letter that has an ordering coupon along the bottom. Similarly, in an off the page advertisement, all the component parts must necessarily be part of a single space. An email or telemarketing call will be structured in a similar way. But even the simplest direct marketing format will combine the features of the four items listed above:

- a headline with an offer or key benefit;
- an introduction;
- an explanation;
- a means of ordering.

How to make each component as effective as possible

Your task in putting together a direct marketing campaign is to ensure your package is compelling to read and motivates the customer's journey to whatever stage you anticipate next. All the advice in Chapters 5 and 13 on techniques for preparing successful copy will be relevant here too, but the following hints are specific to direct marketing. Although they are based on a physical mailing, the principles discussed can be extended to other marketing formats.

The envelope

The aim here is to ensure the package gets opened – and the subject line on an email works in the same way. If you can't get your audience sufficiently interested to open either, your campaign is doomed.

The envelope must give the return address for undeliverable items – and if you are paying to have it overprinted with this, you may as well include a sales message too. It is sometimes claimed that for direct mail going to people at work the outer envelope is less important because the post is often opened by an assistant. Even so, many people flick through their in-tray first, and something that looks different may be pulled out and opened, or if the envelope is sufficiently intriguing it may get passed on with the contents. Bear in mind what else the reader will be receiving at the same time (how much, how interesting?) and the time of day it will be opened. Most working people open mail sent to their home address in the evening. Some suggestions:

- Provide a 'teaser': start a sentence that sounds interesting, but don't finish … (e.g., 'How spending £100 now will help your organisation save thousands more … ').
- Say something controversial (but not so alienating that people are repelled).
- Print on both sides of the envelope, so whichever way up it lands there is something to look at.
- Make the envelope an unusual shape or colour.
- Add a quick checklist on the back for recipients to either request more information or have themselves deleted from your list.

The return address can be either your company or your mailing house, as long as the information is batched up and passed to the list provider.

If your budget won't stretch to overprinted envelopes, a cheaper solution is to have a message that sits on your office franking machine and is reproduced every time an envelope is stamped. The cost is small and the technique works well for simple slogans:

- Out now
- *Who's Who* 167th edition
- 33,000 biographies
- From A&C Black

Ask the person who looks after your company's outgoing mail about having one produced.

The accompanying letter

The sales letter is the one essential component for a direct marketing package, research having consistently shown that packages with a letter pull more response than those without. Sometimes you can dispense with the brochure altogether, just send an effective letter and a suitable means of ordering.

Why is this? A letter is a highly personal form of communication. Watch how you react to the next mailing piece you receive. If the sender is not immediately apparent, you look for explanation. The almost universal reaction is to extract the letter, turn it over and look for the signature and company name at the foot of the second page.

- Your copy will work best if it is personal. Picture an individual recipient. What do they look like; what do they wear; what are their interests?
- Make your tone conversational and personal, not stilted. Be reasonable and logical. Over-claiming can discredit your sales message. If you can, make your copy topical and newsy, fascinating to read. Check for readability by reading the text aloud.
- Keep your sentences short so the copy reads well. For the same reason, avoid very long paragraphs (around six lines is fine). Don't use too many adjectives or complicated verbs; they slow the reader down.
- Start with a headline stating the main benefit: what the product will do for the recipient, how much prestige they will gain or time/effort/money they will save by purchase/subscription.
- Begin the main text with a short sentence to attract attention, or a question (that doesn't invite a quick 'no').
- Introduce the offer, and explain the benefits, rather than features. Repeat the message (in different words) to be sure your key points come across – not everyone will read from start to finish.
- Use bullet points for the main selling themes; these can always be expanded in the main brochure. Numbering the selling points can be effective, but don't use too many (three is often considered optimum).
- Underline key benefits for extra emphasis. Blue underlining apparently improves the response still more (although do not overuse this technique). You can also use the second colour for your signature at the bottom of the letter.
- Provide enough information for the reader to make an immediate decision about what to do. Describe in clear detail how to order.
- Mention all the other items in the mailing. Provide a shortcut to the order form for those who have already made up their minds to buy and do not need to read the brochure.
- The final paragraph too needs to be strong, to urge a positive reaction to the product and your offer, and to provide the motivation to fill in the order form straight away.
- Another very important part of the letter is the PS (apparently the second most widely read part of the letter after the headline). Think of a really important reason for buying and put it there.

- Don't make assumptions or use jargon, even when mailing past customers. You will almost certainly get it wrong and may sound patronising.
- Long copy usually outsells short copy provided it is being read by the right person, is relevant and interesting. However, if your letter is designed to create leads for the sales force, don't make it so long and detailed that the recipient has no need to see a rep.
- A two-page A4 letter (the standard length) should break at the page end in mid-sentence on something interesting.
- Layout is important: make it look like a letter. Resist the temptation to try out layout gimmicks. Don't use anything other than a plausible computer typeface. Ensure your finished copy looks varied. Make the paragraphs different lengths, give subheadings, allow plenty of space to attract the reader's eye.
- Never say that someone will follow up the letter with a phone call: it's a turn-off.

The addressee

Database management makes a range of personalised mailshots possible, but if price rules this out or the list has not been used for a while and may be out of date, business-to-business direct marketing may be better addressed to a job title (e.g., 'Dear HR Manager') rather than a named individual. Past customers might have moved on, and the mailshot will then make sense to the new incumbent. Consider how you can make a specific greeting to the job title you are approaching, for example 'Dear Senior Partner' is perhaps better than 'Dear Sir or Madam'. Think about what greetings you find patronising: 'Dear Decision-Maker' may fall into this category. Try testing to see whether increasing the precision of the greeting improves the response.

The signatory

This should be the person the recipient would expect to sign. This is not typically the chairman of a multinational or managing director of a publishing house, although that person's name might go on an optional extra item in the mailing such as a 'lift letter'. In academic and educational publishing it's sometimes thought letters signed by the relevant editor are met with more respect. Don't be afraid to adapt your job title if it's not appropriate. For example, in my first job in publishing, arts academics often responded poorly to 'product manager' on my business card. Science academics were generally less concerned and those teaching Business Studies viewed it positively.

One final point. A letter is a very personal communication. Although you should try to avoid offending sensitivities, don't worry unduly if you get a few angry letters protesting about the content. As copywriting expert Roger Millington commented, if you don't get a couple of cross letters per campaign, no one is reading your material. If you get them, notice your response (you probably feel rather uncomfortable). That's part of the power of direct marketing.

The brochure

The brochure generally develops the product benefits. The sales points will be those covered in the letter, but explained in different words and ways so that the information seems fresh and interesting.

- You have more room in the brochure to explain your product and answer questions that, were recipients examining the item personally, they could answer for themselves.
- Give precise and believable information, not vague puffery.
- Again, stress the benefits to the recipient, not the key features from an internal perspective.

Checklist for writing brochure copy

Those reading marketing materials generally have fragmented attention, and it's helpful to offer information in a variety of different formats – straightforward text, details in boxes, captions for all illustrations. When writing copy for direct mail brochures I have a standard list of questions I seek to answer. Often some of this information may go into 'summary boxes' or be delivered as a series of questions and answers.

- What are the key benefits of the product to the market?
- Who is the product for? You can give a list of professions or job titles.
- How can it be used? Give examples applying to the recipient's everyday work.
- Who is the author? What are their relevant qualifications, experience, appointments and previous publications, national and international? If possible, include an author photograph but ensure it is captioned (a well-known name is not the same thing as a well-known face, and captions get read before body copy).
- What interesting facts are included? General, interesting information in a brochure tends to get read.
- What is the scope, i.e., breadth of coverage?
- What are the main contents or main revised sections for a new edition?
- What does it replace?
- Who has reviewed the title and in what?
- Third-party opinion is influential. Can you provide testimonials or quotes? If not, might someone be persuaded to offer one?
- What does it look like? A photograph of the book cover is useful. If it is not yet available, get your designer to make up a dummy. This is as interesting to direct mail purchasers as it is to browsers in bookshops. If the title is expensive and has an impressive format or long extent, ensure the book is shot from the side, spine upright to show the value for money it represents and the prestige it gives to owners. If the product is digital, and a print version

exists, a shot could show how many book inches [i.e. book thickness/extent of pages] or titles it replaces (as well as the need to store them).

- What is in it? Offer a substitute for the bookshop browser's flick-through. Choose pages to reproduce that show the book to its best advantage. Use arrows with captions to make sales points. If you reproduce illustrations from the book, they too must have captions.
- When is the title due to be published? What are the publication details? Give the extent, number of illustrations, number of entries, date available and so on.
- Who else should see the information when the recipient has finished with it? When mailing institutions, try printing 'route instructions' on the top of the brochure to suggest that it be forwarded to the librarian, the head of department and so on.
- A high-price product might be better justified by describing it as not a book, but a volume, indispensable reference, source, file or library. All sound more expensive.

Response devices

The response device is your point of sale. It must:

- stand out;
- be easy to use;
- invite response, however the intended audience will find it most convenient to respond.

Remember the overall level of response will always be in inverse proportion to the level of commitment required, so you must make ordering as trouble-free for the customer as possible. If you can supply goods on approval, do so. If not, ensure there is a complete guarantee of satisfaction, such as a money-back offer, restated on the order form. If you cannot accept large orders from institutions without payment in full or a credit check, explain how this helps protect them as well as you.

It's sound advice to spend time reading ordering information from those who manage the process well. For example, insurance proposal forms and the annual tax return are excellent examples of clarity. Both provide reversed-out white space for anything the customer has to complete; you can see at a glance whether all the required information has been given. If working online you can make questions compulsory (although this may deter response, and site metrics will show you at what point people gave up).

Format of the response device

You may decide to drive traffic to your website for orders. But if you are dealing with a market that does not necessarily have online access, you need to consider how they will place an order. Will they prefer to ring up and speak to someone or to fill in an order form and return it in an envelope?

In general, and if you go for print, separate order forms attract a higher response than integral ones that have to be detached from the brochure or letter. You have various options. Some order forms are complete sheets of paper with arrows marking where they can be folded to turn them into mailable items ('self-mailers'). Others leave it to responders to provide the envelope, perhaps offering a freepost address so they don't have to pay for the stamp. The cheapest format for separate order forms is probably a reply postcard with blank spaces for the customer to complete on one side and a freepost address back to the publisher on the other, but if you ask for complex or personal information (e.g., credit card details) you must send an envelope as well.

In a brochure with an integral order form (i.e., it's part of your brochure), probably the first thing to be laid out should be the coupon. Never cramp the coupon to make room for all your brochure copy; rather cut the copy. As for how to detach it, perforated forms tend to do better than ones that require a pair of scissors, but again the extra finishing costs more. If you cannot afford perforations, show a pair of scissors and print a dotted line where the cut should be made. Don't put product information on the back of the order form – most people like to keep a record of what they have ordered until it arrives.

If your direct marketing is part of a printed advertisement then the order form should preferably be the bottom right-hand edge of a right-hand page so that it can be accessed with the minimum of disruption to the text (most people prefer not to cut up a publication). If your advertisement backs on to another ad, do ensure that the order form or coupon does not back on to another coupon (if a magazine does this to you, ask for a refund). For similar reasons, never produce a cleverly shaped coupon that is time-consuming to clip, or one that is in an awkward place to cut out.

Be aware of the number of people reading the magazine or journal in which your advertisement will appear; it may have a far wider circulation than just the original subscriber or purchaser. So if you are providing a tear-off card or coupon for response, ensure that your address and number for telephone orders appear elsewhere on the advertisement. It can happen that people cut out an order form to send, and then find the address is not provided on it, but is back in the advertisement, in the magazine – wherever that is. Similarly, invitations that do not carry the full details or location or the person to reply to – and necessitate a further hunt – are irritating.

Consider too human responses to what is received – or what is commonly referred to as 'the fiddle factor'.

We won a DMA[4] Gold award once for an insert for British Telecom where the insert card was L shaped and the response device was the perforated shorter edge. People were happy to tear off the shorter edge to make the card neater, in the same way they are reluctant to cut into a square sheet.

Alison Blake

Always fill out your own order form before finalising the layout – this will help you to understand how easy (or not) it is to fit the required information in the space you provide. Be sure to ring all the telephone numbers quoted before you pass for press, just to make sure they are what they say they are.[5] Similarly, try out your online ordering information before it is finalised and consider whether you find it easy to use and how you would like the process to be managed. Does the tone of voice feel appropriate? Personally I use online ordering a lot for buying presents – and so am benefitting from someone else organising delivery. But I am always keen to know how I can personalise what is sent; add a special message, have the item gift wrapped, etc. I don't like having to hunt – or ask for – this information.

Information gathering

Direct marketing works on the basis of gaining permission to continue a relationship, and so your response device can be a useful way of gathering information/ checking the details you already hold, within the context of prevailing legislation. How much detail should you seek? Asking for too much information may offend recipients or dissuade them from completing the form. Again, fill it out yourself and consider how you feel. Do you feel you are being asked to populate their customer database with information you would rather not share? As an example, I recently tried to give feedback on good customer service in a store and the resulting online form posed so many additional questions I was tempted to give up.

Other tips for making response devices work harder

- An order form should be a mini version of the advertisement, restating all the main selling points. Start with the chief one: 'Yes, I would like my family to have access to the new *Children's Encyclopaedia.*'
- The less small print, the better. 'Offer subject to our standard terms and conditions, available on request' covers most eventualities.
- Free draws for swift responders attract replies. If you try this on a regular mailing to the same list, be sure to announce who won: it boosts credibility and creates a club atmosphere.
- Try a pre-publication offer or, for projects that are even further from completion, a 'pioneer supporter' price: this can work particularly well for expensive multi-volume sets that take years to come to fruition, and helps to subsidise your development costs.
- Involve the reader on the response device. Some physical mailing pieces ask the recipient to stick peel-off labels or yes/no stickers on the form. Increasing customer participation boosts response levels.
- Repeat the offer and contact details (including website, phone number and email enquiry line) of the publisher on the order form. If it gets detached from

the main part of the information package, people will still have sufficient information to enable them to order.

- Offer the option of a standing order for titles that are part of a series. Stress that an invoice will be sent each year before renewal so it is possible to opt out but this will ensure their sequence of volumes is uninterrupted.
- For titles that are being price-promoted, put the non-discounted and discounted prices side by side, with a line through the former to attract attention to a bargain.
- Spell out clearly what you want the recipient to do with the order form – e.g., 'insert in the envelope supplied, put in the post (no stamp needed)' – or 'click here to order'.
- Repeat the main benefits on the order form, the terms of the offer and the guarantee of satisfaction.
- How much commitment do you require? If not much, make a benefit of it.
- List the various ways you accept payment. Choice involves readers in selecting and moves them towards purchase.
- Ask for all contact details to be printed LARGE, particularly the phone numbers. Assume all your customers are long-sighted and in a hurry.
- Offer recipients something else in case they don't want the main offer.
- Ask them to recommend a friend who might also like information.
- Include an envelope so the recipient does not have to hunt for one. Use freepost or business reply for offers to consumers. For business-to-business mail it does not make much difference.
- Put a time limit on the offer.
- Offer a free gift for a prompt response. Your warehouse is probably full of suitable items – just ensure it does not increase the band for return postage, and so push up your costs more than the anticipated additional response.
- Keep the shape simple – no complicated cut-outs, however pretty they look. You may have seen coupons in the shape of maps or telephones but I bet not many get returned.
- Give email addresses, telephone hotlines and ensure the numbers are really large and put little diagrammatic symbols next to them to attract attention, so customers can find the numbers in a hurry and don't ring the wrong one by accident. Again, assume that all respondents are long-sighted and in a hurry.
- Name your product on the order form and show a picture of it if you have room.
- Test payment up front versus approval.
- For credit card ordering, be sure to ask whether the card name and address being used are the same as for the person ordering. Provide a box for writing the additional information if necessary.
- Test third-person copy against second person ('readers have found' rather than 'you will find', which may be a little too close for comfort if the product is of a sensitive nature), and vice versa.
- Test putting all the facts (ISBN, extent, etc.) against minimal facts.

- Use rushing words to encourage the reader to act immediately – 'hurry', 'express', 'now'.
- Personalise the order form by pre-addressing, i.e., printing all the recipient's details on the order form. If this is too labour-intensive, or expensive, put the address on the order form and use a window envelope so it shows through for posting.
- Test integral coupons against separate coupons.
- Test charging postage and packing against giving it free, or make it conditional on the size of the order. Similarly, test offering free insurance for larger purchases.
- Add extra tick boxes: for a catalogue, or to hear about future titles in the same field so that customers keep in touch with you even if they do not want to order now.
- Try different colour order forms, or use spot colour on an integral one.
- Include a second order form.
- Stick real postage stamps on the reply device and ensure they are visible through the window of the envelope before it is opened: this increases the reader's perceived value of your mailing package.
- If you accept cheques, make it clear to whom they should be made payable.
- Code the order form so you can see which list gave you the customer.

Other items you could consider including in your mailings

- A postcard with the address and numbers, writ large, of your website and telephone enquiry line – for them to keep in a useful place (but do tell them that's what it's for and where to put it – e.g., 'Put this card on your notice-board to ensure you can find us when you need us').
- An extra order form. Once customers have ordered they will have the opportunity to buy again. Code it so you can see the response it generates.
- A 'lift' letter from a supporter or existing user, or perhaps a colleague.
- A checklist of all the related titles/resources you publish.
- A 'recommendation to purchase' form for recipients working in institutions (academic and business) to pass to the information manager or librarian. Many new academic and company library purchases are the result of recommendations by colleagues.
- Another letter, perhaps a 'lift letter' from a satisfied customer or a (famous) admirer of the product, or a 'publisher's letter', say from your firm's managing director or the book's editor. Such a letter need not come from someone famous, just someone plausible. For example, when contacting schools the ideal candidate is a head teacher or subject adviser working with children of similar ages. Charities use this technique in fundraising mailing pieces, for example, enclosing letters from field workers describing the value of their work.
- A sheet of quotations from published reviews of the title you are promoting.
- A news sheet on an existing product. Even bestselling titles can become boring to the market. How about a news sheet describing developments

being made by the editorial team, a quiz or competition, a 'questions and answers' sheet covering the issues you most regularly get asked about or a case study, offering information on how the material is being used by some buyers?

- Instead of offering a discount or stressing value on the order form, try a 'money-off coupon' for customers to enclose with their order. Again, it involves readers and adds value to the package. Put 'offer limited to one voucher per household' on the coupon and you further increase its apparent value.
- A reply envelope for the return of the order form.
- Information from another company that sells non-competing products to the same market, and subsidises your marketing costs (provided your list can be used in this way).
- Forthcoming related product information.

Design services

Attractive and appropriate design makes your message appealing to the market. This means thinking about the look and feel of what you are planning. Your market will make instant decisions about what to do with your marketing piece, without rationalising why, other than being aware that they have a choice over whether or not to invest time in reading it.

Research has shown that when looking at marketing material, reading habits are seldom linear; people do not move logically through the content. Rather they dart around, allowing their eye to be grabbed as it will. Your design layout should anticipate this and provide lots of interesting locations in which they can graze for information.

Provide a complete brief on what you are trying to achieve and the ideas you have had so far before the designer starts work. For further advice on dealing with designers, see Chapter 14.

System of despatch

This determines how your material gets to the market. It needs planning rigorously, and with accurate time allocated to each stage of the process, working back from the date you want your material to reach the customer. Whether you are using an external supplier, colleagues in another department or your firm's warehouse, do give them plenty of notice of your schedule.

Mailing houses and bureaux can handle the despatch of bulk mailings, and have specialised equipment to handle the insertion of complicated combinations. Machine insertion (as opposed to manual) means the costs go down. Remember too that they are experts and see many more campaigns (and hence many more mistakes) than you could ever do. Learn from them. Discussing your proposed marketing materials with a mailing house before they are printed may save you money. For example, folding a rectangular leaflet on the short side rather than the long may result in it being hand- rather than machine-stuffed (more expensive), but will probably make little difference to the overall impact. If you provide the mailing house with details of the format and paper weight of all your planned items (i.e., long before final proof-stage), staff will be able to work out the overall weight and hence mailing cost, and perhaps suggest amendments that would reduce the financial outlay. Similarly, using a cheaper envelope could bring you within a lower weight band for mailing and save money.

Put all your instructions in writing, making it absolutely clear what goes where. In the case of a mailing piece, make up a sample and physically send it to those handling despatch. Deliver slightly more of each item than you are expecting will be despatched, as loading items on to machines always results in some spoilage. Try to anticipate potential problems. For example, what should the mailing house do if it runs out of stock of any of the components? A letter or order form can be photocopied, but what about the brochure? Will the size of mailing entitle you to a discount on postage? Can the mailing house organise the discounts for you? Do you need a freepost licence or to set up a postage paid impression (so your envelopes do not need stamps)? Sort out all these details now rather than hold up the printing of your material while you wait for a licence number.

Monitoring effectiveness

You need a system that will monitor how effective your marketing has been and help you to take appropriate action. This needs to be based on the kind of information you want to capture and the uses to be made of it in your future marketing and publishing decisions.

Testing

Direct marketing is a very testable medium – and an opportunity to learn from past projects and improve each campaign before you commit significant resources. All large-scale mailers test the market before they commit themselves to extensive campaigns, by mailing a selection of addresses from all the lists they are considering.

Don't confuse yourself by testing too many variables at the same time, rather test the issues that are likely to have the greatest effect on your response rates, and hence:

- the list;
- the offer;
- timing;
- format;
- method of response.

Don't forget to include a 'control' in your test, which should be your standard format marketing package. Use this as a benchmark against which to test different elements and then select the best-performing combination for your next activity.

A 10 per cent test is recommended for a statistically viable outcome although this is not always possible. As regards choosing test names when producing the list you could code for – and then trial – an 'nth' selection from those you plan to circulate, perhaps every fifth or tenth name. The entire list being approached needs to be recorded before the nth selection is made, otherwise there need be only one change to the master list between your trial and your actual mailing, and you will end up mailing some people twice.

If your budget does not permit large-scale test mailings:

- Compare like with almost like. What is the track record of your company's promotion of related products to similar markets? Does this give you any useful hints about the audience and what kind of materials might work best?
- Try testing at the time of mailing. Send two different sales letters/emails to two halves of the same mailing list, or try different subsidiary titles on the order form to see which produces the most orders.
- Change the cheap elements in your direct marketing packages, e.g., the printed letter (usually a single colour) rather than a full-colour brochure.

How to work out whether your direct marketing is successful

Go back to your plan and consider the objectives you sought.

If you were seeking orders, and a substantial proportion will come through other retailers rather than direct (e.g., online sales through the internet retailers), examine sales figures before and after a promotion, and compare the total with the original estimates of market size and possible penetration (usually made when a title is commissioned). Other outcomes could be improved customer responsiveness, inspection copy requests or the improved year-on-year sales figures. You probably also need to consider your efforts in the context of customer lifetime value (see Glossary) rather than a specific campaign. Many campaigns should not be measured on their initial results but on how many subsequent orders they generate over a given time period.

To establish the cost-effectiveness of a specific campaign you need to work out your response rate.

$$\text{Response rate} = \frac{\text{number of replies} \times 100}{\text{number mailed}}$$

No guarantee of what to expect can be made, and your criteria will depend on product specifications. If it is high-priced you could make money even with a very low response rate.

More important than the response rate is the cost per order, i.e., how much it is costing you to secure orders.

$$\frac{\text{Cost per order} = \text{costs of each mailshot} \times \text{number mailed}}{\text{number of orders received}}$$

Your costs of mailing will include all the various elements of the campaign: data management/list rental, printing and design costs, copywriting if you have to pay for it, despatch and postage. A quick comparison of your cost per order and the selling price of the product will show whether your mailing is heading for profit or loss.

For more specific information on profitability you need to establish the contribution per sale for each title sold. To calculate this as well as production costs for the titles promoted you need to know your company's policy on the allocation of overhead and other costs: your department's share of everything from bad debts and warehousing to staffing and photocopying costs. A quick way of doing this is to establish a production and overhead cost for the main item you are selling (say 50 per cent of the sales price of the key product featured). This enables you to calculate the break-even response rate: the minimum quantity your campaign must sell before it starts to justify the costs of the promotion and make money. The equation for working this out is as follows:

$$\frac{\text{cost of each mailshot} \times \text{number mailed}}{\text{cost of production for main title}}$$

If responders order more than one product, or become long-term subscribers, your total costs will be a smaller proportion of total revenues generated, and the economics of the campaign improved.

Fulfilment services

Before any promotional information goes out, fulfilment services need to be in place to support the marketing offers you have made so that customers who order can receive a prompt service. So the warehouse that will send out your products needs to have systems for locating, selecting and packaging items, and the customer information lines you offer (email, telephone or both) need to be ready before you make them available.

The fulfilment service needs to know all the things you know, but will not know them unless you tell them. For example:

- What is the offer and how long does it last for?
- What is your policy on orders that arrive after the deadline – will you still honour the offer?
- How much is being charged for delivery?
- What guarantees are provided and what is the policy on accepting returns from dissatisfied customers?
- The format of the promotion piece and the mailing date.
- When are orders likely to arrive?

Bear in mind that the more you involve staff, the more enthusiastic they are likely to be, particularly if they are geographically distant from the main offices. Asking those who will handle the orders to comment on your marketing pieces, before they are finalised, is a very good move.

Coding an order form

Ordering devices need to be coded so that when orders come back you can identify where they came from. Printers can add codes to order forms through 'scratch coding' (stopping the machines to amend the code) or split runs. Order forms can also be coded in specific places, with more detailed codes and reference words, even with sequential numbers, but with each additional specification the costs rise.

A key part of establishing codes for order forms is ensuring that they are captured when orders are processed. If orders are coming into telesales operation, you will need to provide guidance on how this should be managed. What is said should sound beneficial to the customer rather than your organisation. For example, 'Can you give me the long number at the top right hand of your order form so I can be sure we have all your details if we need to get back to you?' may sound friendlier than 'What's your customer number?'

Postage and packing

This is a standard customer charge for most direct marketing, and your customers will not be surprised to see it (although that may not stop them resenting it, or seeking to avoid paying). Postage and packing can become one of your marketing variables, to be experimented with in the hope of making your material more attractive.

Can you describe this more enticingly? Visit the people who pack up your parcels, watch what they do and consider how the service can be made to sound as if it offers additional value to the customer. 'Careful postage and packaging' sounds better than 'p&p'. 'Courier despatch' sounds faster than 'delivery'. 'Shipping' sounds international. Signing for a delivery can be annoying because customers have to be present to receive it, but it protects both parties' interests should a parcel go astray. Describe the precious commodity they have ordered as such and you increase both its value and the pleasure with which it will be received.

Think too about relating the additional cost for carriage to the cost of going to place the order in person: the petrol, the search for a parking space, the hassle, the time, the threat of a parking ticket. Suggest they order online or by phone, and they could be doing something else within minutes.

If you are a small business and cannot afford to offer free carriage, explain why. For example:

> *Why do we charge for postage?*
> We seek to keep our overheads as low as possible, and to offer our customers the best possible value for money. At the same time, we are a small

business and costs that we cannot control eat into the sustainability of what we do in the future. We are always pleased to see customers who want to collect their goods from our offices, but for those of you who are not able to travel, rest assured that the postage charge we make covers the cost of getting your goods to you in a condition we consider vital to ensure their protection, nothing more.

What to do with the returns

All direct marketing campaigns produce returns, because the messages go to individuals who are essentially unpredictable. However well the list is kept, people on it will have moved, changed jobs or died. The important thing is to ensure the changes that produced the returns are noted. You should get a credit if the returns total more than 5 per cent of the list you rented, otherwise you will simply have contributed to cleaning the list. Firms renting email data generally use undeliverables to auto-update their database.

Telemarketing

Telemarketing remains a popular medium, both for creating sales and following up other direct marketing initiatives. Selling over the phone is the natural extension of the personal contact for which direct marketing strives, but by talking directly to the market much more comprehensive feedback can be obtained. It can be useful both inbound (for the placing of orders and customer enquiries) and outbound (for teleselling, renewals chasing and promoting good customer relations).

Examples of telemarketing usage within publishing

- Market research

Telemarketing is an effective way to test customer reaction to new products and ideas; to identify new market sectors and measure market attitudes; to find out who within an organisation should be targeted with sales information and how large their budget is; to test a price, offer or incentive.

- As part of a direct marketing campaign

Telemarketing is an excellent way to update information held, to 'qualify' (establish real interest from) sales leads generated, to follow up a mailing piece and thus increase the response rate, and to carry out post-campaign research and analysis.

- To generate sales opportunities for reps

Telemarketing can be used to canvass sales leads and set appointments. This reduces the need for cold calls, establishes the prospect's interest in the company's products before the call is made and improves the effectiveness of the sales team.

- To build customer relations

Telemarketing is a very good way to handle potential or actual problems such as customer enquiries or complaints, and to reactivate old contacts.

Who should do the ringing?

Successful telemarketing is a skill. It requires a combination of product knowledge and an ability to communicate on the telephone. The caller has to build a relationship with the prospect, while noting information passed on (whether directly or indirectly), preparing the next question and keeping the conversation going.

Whereas publishing staff may have all the requisite product knowledge, creating the time and the inclination to carry out telemarketing in-house can be difficult. To find a freelance or employee, you could advertise in the local paper or on your website. Provide a telephone number for those interested to ring you for more information, so you will hear them in action. Bureaux look for staff in the same way: the telephone manner should be confident and friendly and the voice clear.

If you recruit salespeople to work in-house, you must provide the administrative back-up they need. Each call they make may require some follow-up: a confirmation of order by email or a letter to accompany a brochure that was requested. These are hot leads and must be dealt with straight away; they must never be allowed to sit at the bottom of an overworked (and perhaps resentful) administrative assistant's in-box for three or four days.

A dedicated telemarketing agency probably offers the best way to test the water. Having briefed them on your product, market and competitors, you benefit from their expertise on how best to target and time the approach. They are responsible for training the people who will work on your account, in both product knowledge and selling skills. Most agencies offer a basic package including the creation of a 'framework for calls' (never a 'script') based on a thorough understanding of product benefits, an initial number of telephone contracts and a report on the results, paying staff according to the number of calls made and the time taken, with an incentive bonus scheme based on commission. After this the client may decide to drop the campaign, make changes or carry on.

Planning a telemarketing campaign

Give detailed consideration to the objectives of the campaign, and how far they are measurable by telemarketing. Establish a framework for calls. It should act as a basis for questions rather than a script to be read. For this you need to consider which of the selling benefits are most relevant to the target market, whether a special offer is appropriate, how customers can pay, what further information is available should a prospect ask for more details, and how the information obtained should be recorded for future use. If the product being sold is complicated it should be demonstrated to the people making the calls; if it is portable there should be one in the telesales office.

As well as the framework for the call, you need to provide your telesales people with the relevant information to deal with possible objections or questions. This is probably best stored on a series of screen prompts or cards that the person making the call can refer to quickly.

A final checklist for all forms of direct marketing

- Is the copy really strong on product benefits and reasons to buy?
- Have I made it clear what I want the customer to do?
- Would I buy from me? Is the copy strong enough?
- If you are writing about something you do not understand, has the copy been checked by an expert such as the editor or the author?
- Have you called the product by the same title, with the same capitalisation, each time?
- Have you used the title too often (boring)?
- Is it clear what the basic price is and how much should be added for postage and packing, etc.? If carriage is included in the price quoted, have you made it clear this is a benefit?
- Is it clear how to order and by when?
- Are the publisher's name, address, telephone, email and website details on all the elements of what is sent? If the order needs to be sent somewhere else, is it clear which address is which, and would it be better to offer just one address to avoid confusion?
- Are the contact details large enough to find and read in a rush?
- What does the customer do if he or she is unclear about some aspect of your product? Are you offering a telephone number for enquiries? Is it working? Try it now.
- Have you included an option for capturing non-buying prospects?
- Triple-check the final proofs for press for consistency, grammatical errors, etc. Publishers are expected to get these things right! Last-minute changes are very expensive.
- How is your marketing piece to be followed up: by your reps, by re mailing, with telemarketing, etc.?
- If you offer a slot for those who do not want to order now saying 'Please send me further information on ... ' have you sorted out what you are going to send?
- Have you told everyone who needs to know, from customer services to those who may answer your phone or out-of-office email response?
- Is your address on the outer envelope so that undelivered shots can be returned?

Concluding case study: Reading Force, www.readingforce. org.uk

Building a database to communicate more effectively with a market, information on a sample direct mailing campaign and consideration of how this could be extended through telemarketing

Reading Force is an initiative that encourages Forces families to communicate more effectively, particularly at times of stress, through shared reading. Military families face a range of pressures not experienced by the wider population, such as frequent moving of house (and associated changing of schools, disrupted friendships), long absences of partners due to training, deployment and active service – and associated worry throughout. Developed by an Army wife, the scheme is based on the principle that when families are under stress it can be hard to talk about what is really going on – and due to all the moving, wider family and friends are often physically distant. Families are therefore encouraged to set up a reading group, choose a book together, read it – and then pool their feedback in a special scrapbook they receive, which can be kept as a memento. These can be returned to Reading Force for comment, a certificate of participation, a book prize and entry into a competition, or just kept by the family. They are always returned to the entrants by 'recorded delivery' post to ensure safe arrival.

Encouraging families to share books, and talk about what they have read, is an effective way of living through a difficult time, often offering the opportunity to 'project' worries on to characters or situations in a story, and in the process pulling everyone together. The idea is based on principles developed within other community reading and reader development schemes and has been shown to be very effective in the 4 years that it has been running. The scheme is for families of all ages and compositions and participation is free.

Hattie Gordon, Director of Communication and Projects for Reading Force comments:

> Our starting point was Aldershot, home of the British Army, where with support and small grants from both the local council (Rushmoor Borough Council) and the area authority (Hampshire County Council) we piloted an initial scheme. We contacted all the local schools, set up a steering group (which consisted of everyone who responded), and worked with them to develop a scrapbook that they then distributed to local Services families through the schools and libraries. In addition to this support from school head teachers and librarians, we made many visits to local playgroups and youth groups to talk about the scheme, and also worked with welfare officers supporting the families and the local HIVES (information centres on all military bases). After the

scrapbooks were submitted to the competition, prizes were presented to families at a storytelling day at the local community centre. But while it was all a success, and we received a grant from the MOD to extend the scheme over a wider region, we were very aware that so far success had relied heavily on personal communication, and if it was to spread wider it would need much more formal marketing, and this time through non-personal means.

Ideally we wanted to communicate with Services families directly, but the problem was locating them. We discovered that no reliable and complete data is kept on Service families – their constant mobility makes keeping track of them difficult and no organisation knows exactly how many there are.

In our second year we planned to make the initiative available through four counties, following the same distribution model as the pilot, reaching families through schools, and running for 6 months over the summer. We worked with an educational marketing company but despite their highly sophisticated, multilayered information database, which offered a wealth of additional information to their users (e.g., which Maths or English scheme a school was using), the key data we needed on whether or not they had Services children within the school was not something that had been hitherto requested – and hence was neither recorded nor available to us.

We emailed head teachers in schools in areas we thought likely to have Services children through the educational marketing company, but after a poor response became very aware of how much email schools are receiving – and therefore that not all of it is being read. We felt we needed to make a personal link with an individual member of staff who would take responsibility for the wider sharing of our message.

During this period we were joined by Elaine Boorman as director of marketing and development and together we did some analysis of our second-year response. This highlighted that, while the mass mailing to all schools across the four counties had been achieved at relatively low cost, it had proved ineffective. Clearly we needed to adopt a more targeted approach and this led to a complete review of our marketing plan. We divided our markets into:

- service families;
- routes to reaching them (e.g., schools and welfare units);
- potential supporters who could refer our project to those interested;
- the media

and then sought to build up contacts and more rigorous information in each case.

Elaine comments:

Relevant data was, and still is, hard to find. Lists of Service personnel (or the location of their housing) are not available to outside agencies, and we found we needed to communicate through a range of different methods to build awareness and reach families. Our challenge was how could we start targeting our messages effectively with a lack of appropriate data? The Directorate Children and Young People (DCYP, part of the Ministry of Defence) was set up in 2010 to manage professional and practical support and safeguarding for Services families and had the compilation of data high on its agenda, but by the launch of Reading Force their own list was still in its infancy. A database of schools, compiled by Service Children in State Schools (SCISS, which is part of the MOD's Children's Education Advisory Service) is the nearest thing to a ready-made means of contacting Services families via schools but is not available to external agencies. It is also incomplete as schools are 'entirely self-nominating'[6] and it does not in any case include private schools, which large number of Services children attend through assisted places at boarding school.

With this lack of relevant data we had no choice but to build our own database from the ground up, which has been challenging and time-consuming but well worth the investment; the data we've compiled is invaluable in allowing us to target our efforts, resources and messages to much greater effect.

We started by sourcing the information handbooks that garrisons distribute to families and we were able to identify the schools they listed.

We then tried to establish a 'Reading Force Ambassador' in each school to whom we could send information and materials to distribute. While most schools with Service pupils allocate a specific responsibility for their care to an individual member of staff, finding out who it was proved to be quite a challenge. We now have on our list of useful contacts the following: 'Nurture Teaching Assistant', 'Parent Support Adviser', 'Literacy Leader', 'Services Support Manager', 'Home Link Support Worker', 'Pastoral Support Manager' and 'Service Pupils' Champion'.

Wherever we work with partners to promote the personal delivery of materials (e.g., working through BookStart coordinators or service welfare departments) we see stronger engagement with the scheme. Service welfare units within garrisons are a direct route for us to families but establishing a list of personal contacts has proved difficult as we have found that this is a specific responsibility that changes all the time (Services personnel tend to get 'posted' at least once every two years, often more regularly). A generic 'Families Officer' will work for postal mail, but email addresses are much harder to locate, partly because individuals change but also because of the immense complexity of the construction of email addresses within the Forces.

Working through Services units also risks making us reliant on Service personnel passing the information on and from the outset we have been keen to avoid implying that Reading Force is an extension of the Service person's employment and in any sense an official or monitored process. Post rooms in Services units often have a waste basket, and items for communication with families are often found deposited here. We found that Service families were quite resistant to what was often perceived as 'organisational bureaucracy', as well as being labelled as 'Forces families' and thus seen as part of an indistinguishable mass rather than as individuals. There is also the issue of how to reach families with a Services link who are not either formally part or geographically close to the unit they are involved with, for example, families of Reserve Forces, or children of parents who are divorced or separated and do not live with the Services person. All this makes it even more important for us to communicate directly with families.

We have achieved this by encouraging Service families to register with us directly by offering an incentive of a free book. As they generally keep the same email address when they move house, this has provided a much more sustainable method of keeping contact. We now have a number of families who have taken part each year, bringing in new friends and wider family members to share and encouraging others to join in the scheme.

We also found it effective to build links with the Services charities, of which there are many, with other organisations active in this area such as the Service Children's Support Network[7] and with the media, both Services-related and general. As the profile of the military varies in the media, according to what is topical, so projects to support their unusual lifestyle become more significant to other people – and news spreads. It was a great boon getting funding from the Armed Forces Covenant Libor Fund, which redirected fines from financial services firms towards Services charities, and this has given us the money to extend to a scheme that is now nationally available.

Our database is continually being updated and is fully categorised according to our target markets, enabling us to make our communications more relevant. We send out regular e-newsletters, varying them according to the target group. With families we share information on how other people have used their scrapbooks or experienced the scheme as well as news of who has won prizes – all with the aim of boosting longer-term involvement. We keep teachers up to date with the social and educational benefits of our scheme; funders and our trustees get additional specific information relating to their contribution. What keeps us going is the positive feedback we consistently get from those involved – and we now have a wealth of lovely quotations from Service families who have taken part and found the scheme very beneficial:

'Next time Daddy deploys we are going to choose a book and repeat this process, we are sure it will help give us something to talk and focus on, as well as counting down the days.'

'I enjoyed being able to share a book with my family even though I wasn't at home. It really made me feel included and I enjoyed hearing [on the phone] Annabelle reading a very tricky book.'

'When we received our Reading Force scrapbook we thought it was a great opportunity to get together as a family and share a book. Annabelle was very excited about it and we spread it out over a few weekends when Daddy was working away and he joined in using face-time which made it really special.'

'Today I listened to Isla Jane read me her book on the phone as I am in Diego Garcia in the Far East working away with the Royal Marines and I have never heard anything so sweet in my life.'

'We read together every night and we like to talk about what we read. It was nice to be able to involve Nan and Auntie Mary too – they don't normally read the same books as us. It gave us extra things to talk about with them on the phone.'

Looking ahead, we want to invest in a more sophisticated marketing database to capture and leverage even more data for integrated marketing activities. For example we want to be able to cross-reference the book titles families choose to share (useful information for maintaining our relationships with publishers), capture more complex data on the age-groups involved (do we need a different communication style/varied materials for different age groups?) and analyse the high quantity of data on levels of involvement that we are gathering (in order to further refine the scheme).

There are also certain synergies that are emerging from the project that may make it more valuable within society as a whole, and that we need to formally track. For example, it has been reported back that the scheme has a real role to play in helping Service families through difficulties that are more widely experienced within society, such as divorce, single-parenthood or long-term illness. Rushmoor Borough Council spotted early that the scheme could be highly relevant for children in care, or those with a parent in prison, as it provides a long-term means of keeping in touch. Those working with young offenders have spotted benefits in the scheme in that, because it encourages 'projection' (discussion of difficulties through attributing them to third parties), it may be a pathway to therapies that require self-analysis and consideration of both personal responsibilities and the consequences of actions.

In conclusion, as the scheme has spread we have become convinced that the key to effective delivery, and to Service families understanding and appreciating the benefits on offer, is to communicate with a variety of different agencies – and to keep careful records of their involvement with us to date. We also want to be able to communicate more effectively, and more regularly, with the Service families taking part, and a more sophisticated database, with more options for automated communication, would enable the despatch of messages to our audience, at specific stages on their journey with Reading Force. This would help us keep the excitement going ('Did you receive your free book?' 'How are you getting on with your scrapbook?' 'How are you enjoying the book?') and further encourage those taking part to both share the scheme with their family and let us know how they are getting on (by contributing their feedback to our website). The more touch-points we have with those who take part, and the more our communication becomes two-way, the more motivated they are to continue with the project and refer it to others – and reap the associated benefits. How this is to be resourced is our ongoing main priority.

Mailing a sample resource pack to schools and other organisations to encourage registration to Reading Force; to spread awareness of the scheme and promote participation in the first competition of 2014

SMART objectives:

1 To achieve a minimum 10 per cent registration response of the total mailed. Registration to be by printed form returned via Freepost envelope, or online via the website.
2 20,000 scrapbooks to be ordered/despatched via registered schools/ organisations.

Plan: To mail an introductory letter and guide booklet, a registration form and Freepost envelope plus a sample scrapbook, leaflet and stickers (a resource pack) to schools and other organisations both new to Reading Force and previously involved.

Lists:

1 Reading Force's own database of schools and organisations.
2 Primary schools in HIVE postcode areas (commercial list).

Offer:

1 A free resource pack for organisations (scrapbooks, leaflets, stickers, for distributing to Service children, posters and a guide booklet).
2 The materials for distributing to Service families encouraged families to sign up and receive a free book – and to enter the associated competition.

Decision on the most appropriate medium: direct mail to ensure they see the high quality of the materials.

Decision on timing: November, when new initiatives are prioritised for the new term – offering a choice of delivery of materials in December or January.

Copy platform: encouraging, affirmative – non-corporate. Stress how easy it is for schools/organisations to get involved; fun for families. Ensure it is understood that there is no cost to those taking part.

Design services: locally secured, brief was to reflect: free, fun and easy for schools/organisations to sign up; child friendly scrapbooks; parent friendly leaflets.

Fulfilment/system of despatch: mailing materials organised by Reading Force. Fulfilment through an educational mailing service.

Method of monitoring effectiveness: evaluating responses direct to Reading Force (post and online form on website) from schools/organisations; despatch of materials requested. Evaluating families requesting free books (having received materials distributed by schools/organisations). Returns used to update the mailing list.

See Figure 8.1 for the results.

Associated telemarketing

Associated telemarketing backs up the campaign and helps us reach schools that have been identified within an area containing Services housing, and sent information packages, but that have not yet participated in the scheme. No cold calling is done. Calls are only made to schools/other organisations who have been previously mailed but have not yet taken part. So the call would be developed through sharing *some* of the information, depending on the response of the person being called.

It is important to establish early on in the conversation whether or not the person receiving the call is interested; one outline conversation does not fit all situations and not all the relevant information should be offered. Hattie Gordon comments:

> Just last week I spoke with a Service family supporter in a school (new to the job) who said she was finding it hard to find initiatives for Service children and she was so pleased to have come across RF online. And so we progressed to taking their details and sending a pack of materials very quickly.

Type of contact	No. mailed	No. registrations	% response
Schools – mailing samples	2,500	253	10%
Organisations – mailing samples	375	48	13%
	2,875	301	12%
Schools – third-party email (CEAS/SCISS schools)	2,200	24	1%
Referral/word-of-mouth		57	
		382	

Breakdown of registrations from mailing

Types of school/org

Pre-schools	28	
Primary	264	
Secondary	42	
HIVES	23	
Service Welfare Units	12	
Library	9	
Agency	3	
Community group	1	
	382	New to RF/ Not taken part before = 88%
Online registrations	298	
Printed form returned	79	
Phone	5	
	382	20,599 Scrapbooks ordered

Chosen delivery time for scrapbooks:

December	73	2,933
January	260	14,110
Feb/Mar	34	2,068
Apr+	15	1,488
	382	20,599

Figure 8.1 Mailing results for a recent Reading Force marketing campaign. Courtesy of Reading Force. CEAS = Children's Education Advisory Service, a tri-service organisation funded by the MoD. SCISS = Services Children In State Schools.

Examples of conversations around Reading Force

RF: (after saying name) I am ringing from Reading Force, a shared reading scheme for Forces families, in order to:

- ask if you have anyone within the school with a specific responsibility for looking after Forces families within your school;
- check to see whether you have received the Reading Force letter and samples we sent you;
- check you are aware/understand the benefits of Reading Force.

Possible response: We don't have any Services children in our school.

RF: That may be the case right now, but it may be that a Forces child will join the school in future and it would be good to have the material on hand.

You are close to the xxx units/Forces based in your neighbourhood.

We have discovered through running the scheme that schools often have the children of Reservists in their school, or those who are closely linked to a Forces member but perhaps do not live with them. For example, there may be children from Forces families whose parents are separated or divorced and while they are no longer living on a daily basis with the Services person, they feel a difficult combination of strong concern but isolation. Having their identity as a Services child confirmed, by taking part in RF, can be really important to them.

Plus as all children who take part receive a free book, it would be good to ensure any children you have who are entitled to one do get it.

We would like each Services family to know that this is an opportunity and resource available to them, whether or not they choose to take part.

Action: If details given of person with responsibility for Forces children within the school, note name and spelling. If they do not have anyone with a specific responsibility for Forces families, is there someone whose general responsibility it would fall under? It's helpful to suggest who that might be, e.g., pastoral or welfare officer.

When talking to those who sound unfamiliar, or who have not previously heard of the scheme, describe again:

RF: Reading Force is a shared reading scheme for Forces families. Use over 4 years has shown that it encourages families to remain in touch when facing difficulties and has been much enjoyed by those who have taken part.

Possible response: We have enough schemes to administer without adding to the workload of our hard-pressed staff.

RF: Of course we understand that schools are under pressure, but this is an unusual scheme that targets a group of children who often slip under the radar. Services families have particular needs and this scheme has been designed especially for them.

We would like each Services family to know that this is an opportunity and resource available to them, whether or not they choose to take part.

The scheme promotes family literacy, we hope that it supports the aims and work of the school rather than being a distraction. All children who take part receive a free book, and we have found that this can be a real motivator in encouraging them to read for pleasure.

Possible response: This would not appeal to our Services children.

RF: Of course you know your children very well, but we have now been working on this scheme for 4 years and have a lot of evidence that children really enjoy reading with their families – particularly when times are stressful. We would love you to see a sample of the materials to see how motivating they are.

We have a leaflet showing how schools have got involved and why they have found it helpful – and this includes feedback from families who have taken part. And there is also extensive feedback on our website. Can we send a copy to you for you to share with your colleagues?

Possible response: In our experience Services families tend to be private and prefer to deal with these things on their own.

RF: Coping with the absence of a key family member is a difficult situation, and we know that Services families find different ways of managing this. But the scheme was developed by a Services wife with long experience of managing separations, and one of the benefits experienced by schools using the scheme is that through Reading Force Services children often find other Service children in their school – and form bonds.

We would like each Services family to know that this is an opportunity and resource available to them, whether or not they choose to take part.

Notes

1 www.dmnews.com/dma-direct-mail-response-rates-beat-digital/article/245780.
2 www.addagency.co.uk.
3 This will vary according to the market and the approval staircase involved. In general, teachers being contacted through their school would need more time than individuals being reached at home.
4 www.dma.org.uk (Direct Marketing Association).
5 I once ran a competition in a magazine going to direct marketing professionals asking people to name their worst direct marketing disaster. Someone had, by mistake, printed the telephone number of the local police station on their order form. A bad case of wasting police time.
6 SCISS Handbook.
7 www.servicechildrensupportnetwork.co.uk.

9   Online marketing

Core principles for marketing online 208
Specific advice for particular online media 215
Websites 215
Blogging 224
Email 229
Social media: Facebook 236
LinkedIn 238
Twitter 242
Author involvement online 248

This chapter covers marketing online: the creation of an online presence or digital identity in order to prompt interest and sales. We will look at strategy and marketing effectiveness rather than the mechanics of how to establish and support associated systems, as these are beyond the scope of this book and are well covered elsewhere (notably in Reed 2013).

The establishment of a presence online is often talked about as establishing a 'platform' and each different method of communicating online can be similarly described. If we are going to use this terminology, then the initial image of the diving board – or jumping-off point – provides a helpful visual metaphor. There are various different ways of communicating online – for example, through websites, the effective use of email, blogs and social networking – and these can be thought of as the range of diving boards, at different heights, all leading into a single pool of water. Given the extent of the internet's reach, and the possibilities for messages spreading, this is perhaps best thought of as an infinity pool; but wherever they are in the water, the splash created by others can affect everyone else. For organisations active online, the aim is generally to have all the various entry points and associated activities reinforcing, rather than detracting from, each other – and all benefitting from the associated wider ripples.

Having an online presence is increasingly important, as access to online information is sought by those considering any form of involvement with your organisation and its products. Whether they are thinking about buying from you, working for you, inviting you or an author to an event, they will check out your organisational presence online before taking the relationship any further.

The advantages of online marketing are many. In theory it's an effective and good value way of reaching a worldwide audience, 24 hours a day, 365 days a year, with live information on your product and service range – and keeping the names and contact details of those who want to hear from you again. You have the opportunity to acquire big data and ongoing market research, your observations of their interests and habits online, and more individual feedback on how customers respond to marketing campaigns and ideas for new content.

There are other, more subtle advantages to promoting online. When well handled, online marketing feels personal and can build trust; given that people prefer to do business with people they know, online marketing enables you to spread information on what kind of organisation you are. It also offers the ability to start a conversation with your customers, to manage and develop a two-way communication and create confidence, offering a place where your customers can return, feel listened to and reassured. In the process communities of interdependence are built.

When an organisation is active online, it's difficult to tell their physical size from the extent of their social media presence.[1] Smaller organisations can be particularly well placed to compete, with fewer levels of management to work through to get approval and less reliance on external suppliers whose various presentations and language have to be patrolled in order to ensure a joined-up approach. When difficult situations arise, online presentation through a website can offer an opportunity to make an effective presentation, without being interrupted. In short, there are many reasons why online marketing is now rightly established as a firm part of most organisations' official strategy – not least because it is increasingly how customers like to buy.

But it's not as simple as this may sound. There are associated challenges in being able to interrogate and use the data you gain and qualitative feedback obtained in the process can be hard to store and action. Beware too of overestimating the cost advantages as, although you don't have to pay for print, paper or physical despatch, in practice employing an online team with real experience and giving them proper tools, such as good analytic tools and training, isn't necessarily cheap.

Longer term, however, the possibilities are huge. With recent improvements in technology and the wide availability of superfast wireless broadband, content can be downloaded very quickly. At the same time, the enormous amount of information available, and hence choices on offer, means that customers increasingly feel time-pressured, and have less space to consider marketing messages (which is why brand awareness needs to be promoted less through organisational information and more through consumer buy-in, interesting conversations and contributions from experts). As a society we seem to want ever quicker access to ideas, and images are a particularly effective shortcut to attracting our attention. Smartphones have been the primary access point to the internet for a while now, and as customers read on the move they also update their Twitter and Facebook statuses at the same time. 'Hand-selling' in retail outlets is being replaced by social engagement via personal online communication.

The wider implications of this for marketers are significant. Online activity is demonstrating a shift from 'push' to 'pull' marketing, as rather than presenting wares to those potentially interested (so-called 'megaphone marketing') organisations seeking to make available engaging, interesting, valuable content that attracts their customers' attention draw them nearer and involve them in a conversation. It's also becoming increasingly mainstream; 'online marketing' and 'marketing' are becoming the same thing and together they should be viewed as part of overall marketing, not as separate areas of activity.

In this chapter we will begin with some general principles for online marketing, and then move to thinking about how to get the best out of specific online media – primarily those used by publishers and their customers.

Core principles for marketing online

Making information available online can be achieved within minutes. But doing so effectively and pragmatically takes planning, practice and dedication; as Leonardo da Vinci is often assumed to have said 'simplicity is the ultimate sophistication'. Remember too that this is not the first time that new technology has expanded the options open to the communicator. The invention of printing with moveable type was accompanied by a similar need for thought before action:

> When the last treason act was made, no one could circulate their words in a printed book or bill, because printed books were not thought of. He [Thomas Cromwell] feels a moment of jealousy towards the dead, to those who served kings in slower times than these; nowadays the products of some bought or poisoned brain can be disseminated through Europe in a month.
>
> Hilary Mantel, *Wolf Hall* 2009

Those already involved with social media in a personal capacity will have an initial understanding of how to go about being active online – posting holiday photos on Facebook is marketing your lifestyle to your friends and taking part in an online discussion about an issue you care about is virtual networking – and you could start by thinking about the different motivations, behaviours and profile characteristics that lie behind these various forms of activity (sharing/informing/communicating/boasting). But while being active online in a professional context is a natural next step, it's vital to achieve an appropriate tone and to offer information commensurate with your business aims.

1   Online activity needs to be strategic not random

Just because marketing online can be achieved more quickly than through other methods, and its usage permits the enticing prospect of saving money on the physical costs of other forms of marketing (notably print and postage), it needs just us much careful consideration. Arguably it needs more, as the outcomes can be much more widely spread, with enduring consequences and a potentially damaged reputation.

Online marketing activity needs to be strategic and pragmatic, based on the same criteria that should underpin any marketing campaign. It should fit with overall organisational objectives, different target audiences and their media consumption in order to build a brand presence and not be guilt-driven or prompted by an awareness that others are involved and so you should be too. Sending out a few random tweets or setting up a blog you don't have time to service is not an online marketing policy.

Nor is online marketing a standardised process or set of techniques, rather it is changing all the time. If you are going to get involved, it is important to be up to date with how it is being more generally used – there are fashions and trends to learn from, and the community you are trying to reach will be influenced by what else they are observing.

The key issue is brand management; publishers aren't often brands, but books and authors are. As a publisher with lots of different products and services on offer you may need to spread various forms of information relating to different aims, but it's really important to think about where you direct each campaign and to what end. For example, does divergent use of different social media around the same brand cause confusion (and hence prove counterproductive) – and might too much free content give the market enough information to take part in an associated discussion and hence reduce their need to buy the product or service being promoted? There is a big difference between gaining attention and approval, and the organisation's overall marketing aims and branding need to be considered before online activity is undertaken.

2   How to establish a strategy for online marketing

Effective online marketing requires a logical sequence of planning: identifying your customers, considering your objectives, thinking about how you can communicate with them most effectively, integrating your activities with non-virtual methods to ensure a joined-up approach and then measuring the outcomes of your activity.

- **Begin with your customers.** What are their difficulties right now and what are they looking for? What is the nature of their relationship with you, and how could it be improved? Ensure that when they search for the product or service you offer, they can find you. You need to be sure that you have researched the keywords that ensure your product/service be found and that these are embedded in the HTML of all pages of your website and used in all your online communication, on an ongoing basis. Without keyword focus, no one will find you. So think about what keywords your competitors are using to achieve ranking and try to build a mixture of frequently searched-for and less frequently searched for terms (so that you show up in obvious searches but also extend your reach).
- **Consider what you will try to achieve.** You might decide that you will target a specific group online with a view to increasing the size of the community of customers involved and boost their levels of engagement, to build an author profile to get online pre-orders established, to have a 'retweet and follow' campaign to boost your presence – or to build a relationship with a key retailer.
- **By when.** Once you have established your strategic goal for the audience intended, try to establish some timed markers (e.g., what do you hope to have achieved

within the next month, 3 months or year). These should be SMART objectives (see Chapter 6) that the organisation is capable of working towards.

- **Think about where to find your market.** Where do your customers spend time online and how can you create a conversation with them through their customer journey that will lead long term to a sustained relationship and sales? Think about what the customer cares about and the best way of tapping into their lifestyle in order to plan all the different touch-points in the customer's contact with you and how they fit together.

- **And then where best to concentrate your efforts.** You don't need to engage in every form of social media available. Rather research and learn about the makeup of the audience that populates each social network so you can work out where you should focus (e.g., professional publishers may be active on LinkedIn whereas self-published writers may congregate more often on Facebook or Twitter). Match the information you have to make a strategic selection, using a combination of content tools (e.g., websites and blogs) and outreach tools (e.g., Twitter, LinkedIn, Pinterest and Instagram), optimising the messages to each individual social network rather than doing a cut and paste and assuming the same content can be delivered through a variety of forums.

- **Think about the resources you need.** Your strategic selection should be linked to an appreciation of the resources needed to maintain what is established, and a determination to be consistent in effecting what you have established.

- **Decide who is doing what.** There needs to be a policy on who is updating social media, how often and what level of information is shared – to ensure maintenance of the organisational brand and that those involved know what each person is doing. The burden of managing your online presence can be shared out between colleagues in a logical schedule; tasks can be broken down and teams deployed. Offers and other marketing approaches need to be coordinated and sequenced so that the customer hears from the organisation in a logical manner; it's irritating to receive different alerts from the same organisation with contradictory promotions. Sharing the workload through multi-author logins allows several people to update and schedule messages ahead; encouraging others to comment on your online activity or volunteer a guest blog can extend your reach. Similarly, by aggregating your activity – linking your various involvements or sites so they update each other automatically – you gain added impact. This means you need to allocate less time but retain control of what is said about your brand. Although it is possible to delegate such communication to freelance or virtual support, the key to effective communication online is authenticity, and this is best managed by those really involved.

- **Strategise your starting point.** Rather than committing fully, you can similarly strategise your start in online marketing, perhaps by experimenting as a guest, blogging on a website belonging to someone else before establishing your own, or deciding to establish a presence on Twitter and observe before taking part yourself, in the process allowing confidence to grow.

- **Involvement in online marketing needs to be part of your marketing outreach rather than being seen purely as a method of selling.** Earlier chapters of this book discussed the meaning of marketing in some detail. It's generally a multistaged process that boosts the visibility of your business, reaches out to potential clients, pulls prospects in towards a relationship that prompts sales, and hopefully repeat business. In the case of the publishing industry, marketing often has to work through many intermediaries before the buying point is reached. Marketing online, and in particular social media, offers you the tempting prospect of direct contact with your customers, and it can be equally tempting to take a shortcut through the stages and ask for the order straight away. Slow down. Marketing online needs to be managed with care, used to build your brand, reputation and relationship – rather than immediately ask for money.

> Stop talking about your products and services. People don't care about products and services; they care about themselves.
>
> David Meerman Scott, marketing and sales strategist and the bestselling author of *The New Rules of Marketing and PR*[2]

There is a range of different social media available to you and it is used in different ways, and while nearly all businesses are using social media to sell things, the tone of voice used on each medium needs to be slightly different. Thus while a more direct approach may be acceptable on email and Skype, in phone calls and in face-to-face meetings, a more subtle approach will be needed on Twitter, LinkedIn and Facebook. Knowing which tone to use in which medium is best achieved by knowing your community.

3 Build a strategy for long-term involvement

Although using social media for marketing can be one of the quickest means of getting a message out to your potential market, it works best when managed with long-term interests in mind. So build a sustained relationship that seeks to convey your understanding of the potential customer's possible desire or difficulty, and what you as an organisation or individual can do to help or provide the next step. Clients want to be involved with you because you can solve their problems. It might be that you have products they want to buy, or they're a self-publisher who needs some guidance or you have particular skills that they need. Whatever the reason, online marketing offers you the possibility of a low-cost long-term relationship as you work together towards achieving mutual satisfaction.

4 Build a culture of precision

Lord Leverhulme's famous comment about 'Half the money I spend on marketing is wasted, the trouble is I don't know which half' is potentially overturned by online marketing, as the metrics gained in the process can provide a precise indication of what is working and what is not.

There are opportunities to experiment: with different offers, copy and design approaches, times of despatch – to see which produce the most beneficial outcomes for the goals you initially set (e.g., sales, click-throughs to a website or referrals to other people). You can also make use of general information about online media to give you a competitive advantage:

> According to research by sumall.com, each network has a different optimal time during which posts receive their highest engagement. For Twitter it's 1–3pm, Facebook 1–4pm, Google+ 9–11am, Pinterest 8–11pm, and Instagram 5–6pm. Reasons for these optimal times could be everything from the work day slowing down in the afternoon, to checking your phone before bed.[3]

But while there are many possibilities, there are also real associated challenges that come with them. For example, rewriting information for each social medium, for each author and each book, can lead to the need to manage countless bits of content and numerous campaigns, and managing this across various staff involved can be tricky.

Along similar lines, there are huge constraints on both the completeness of the statistics available and their full and effective interpretation. Getting exact online statistics and metrics is very difficult, and in general one tends to build a picture through combined feedback: from unique users and looking at how they explored the site, the 'bounce rate' of those who clicked through to the website but went no further, and some related social statistics that together build a picture of what is going on. Skill is required in interpreting the information that is held and deciding what to do next. For example, increasing a Twitter following overnight does not necessarily bring more customers, and certain information will not be available (you may know how many 'click-throughs' you get, but not how many order from the organisation arranging fulfilment – which will need cross-checking with reorder rates and stock levels). Analysing data and making precise recommendations on the outcomes requires time and analytic skills, and there is a deficit of both within large parts of the industry. Third-party software (e.g., Bitly[4] and Hootsuite[5]) can be of considerable help.

5   Make it two-way

Be authentic and genuine; create a two-way relationship. Effective marketing online relies on effective communicating and sharing, not pretending to be something you are not.

Conversations where people say the same thing repeatedly get boring. So, despite all the software that helps you post the same content everywhere, offer different information in different places, so the potential customer engages with you more deeply – rather than thinking that they have read this before and are switching off. Brands that push the same content across Facebook, LinkedIn and Twitter do not create a genuine dialogue and consequently find it difficult to create rapport online.

Forward links likely to be useful to your market, even if they did not originate with you. Others will appreciate your generosity and do likewise when you offer content worth sharing. Everything should, however, pass the 'so what' test; in other words, what benefits will your customers gain from the service/relationship/

information you are offering? Value can be variously quantified, for example by making your customers feel they are valued, or the receivers of privileged information, by expressing empathy for the difficult market conditions they are experiencing, or by including them in a story you think they might appreciate:

> It's not about how many people are following you or how many people you follow. It's about helping and solving people's challenges and offering useful insights without necessarily asking for anything back.
>
> Matthew Hunt[6]

Encourage people to remain in touch. Having taken the trouble to find people online, it makes sense to keep in touch with them and there a variety of options for encouraging them to do so. You could encourage them to:

- sign up for an email newsletter (saying how often you will send one and perhaps the benefits of them doing so – ensuring they are up to date with your research, hearing about new offers);
- visit a website;
- read a sample of your material;
- look at your Pinterest selection;
- become a fan on Facebook or follow you on Twitter;
- buy something from you or trial a subscription;
- enter a competition;
- ask a question or make a comment, receive an answer and use this information.

Make the sign-up simple, encourage potential customers to get involved with your material through trial or a free sample – asking too many questions will put them off. Pareto's Law[7] about 80 per cent of business coming from 20 per cent of customers is relevant here; aim for 80 per cent of your communication to be information they value and 20 per cent commercial offerings.

6 How to ensure your online marketing is joined up

You need to control access over who is using social media on behalf of your organisation. Things can go viral for the wrong reasons and attract unpleasant 'trolling' where individuals protected by anonymity use online media to criticise or abuse points of view they disagree with. Some other advice on effective online marketing campaigns follows.

Some key elements of good online marketing campaigns

Writer and online strategist Mark Thwaite – Head of Online at Quercus Books, and founder and managing editor of www.ReadySteadyBook.com – offers the following advice. You can find him on Twitter @readysteadybook.

There are some key elements of all good (online) marketing campaigns. What are they? A useful acronym is: **COPE**. How will you cope with a good campaign and how will you get it right ... ?

Coherence: a good marketing plan – online or offline, online *and* offline – is always *coherent*. These days, there is no discrete online and offline marketing – or there certainly shouldn't be: you always need both aspects for a good, rounded plan. For sure, different ratios, different mixes of those elements will be needed for different campaigns. But *all* campaigns will need *both* elements. What is particularly important is for the offline and the online elements to *cohere* properly (to join up), *and* to make sense: e.g., if you've got a #hashtag to use, have you checked it is viable? Not previously in use by something you wouldn't want to associate your brand/product with? Have you printed the (correct) #hashtag/website address/Facebook link on all your associated offline materials? Online and offline solutions each have their own strengths, each need to be used properly and combined – you need to know your tools, and know the right tool for the job; you need to know your platforms and where your audience/consumers hang out; you need to know your consumers/ (potential) community and what approaches do and no not fit with them. Some online tools are easily trackable and provide great analytics, some do not. It is good to have an idea of what success looks like, and how it can be tracked and measured. Some tools are good for that and some are not.

Objectives: a good marketing plan knows how to specify success. It has clear and measurable (and realistically achievable) goals. For this to happen you need to know your market and know your product. And you need to know how to measure success. What does success look like? More followers for your author? More pre-orders on Amazon? How will you measure that success and – crucially – show how your campaign has made (some of) that happen?

Planning: a good marketing plan is well planned. What is your strategy? How are you going to achieve your goals? What are your timelines? Are they realistic? Can you really source all the materials you need, co-opt other team members, get the kind of content written for exactly when you need it? Use natural advantages: know your team members' skill sets; does your author/brand/product already have a good online/offline presence? Do your research.

Execution: no point having a great plan if you can't implement it. And for your campaign to be successful you're going to need great material: eye-catching; appropriate; clever; funny; relevant; irreverent ... Perhaps you could crowd-source (some of) it for further buy-in? Perhaps you'll have the chance to test (some of) it with a focus group of some kind. Perhaps you'll have been able to work with a retail/brand partner or with a community to extend the reach/make more relevant/more authentic?

And execution goes through and beyond the end of the campaign. Part of the campaign must include the autopsy of that same campaign. A campaign isn't over until you've learned all the lessons it can teach you.

Specific advice for particular online media

We will start with content media (websites, blogs and email) and then move on to other online forums. Bear in mind that the best effects will be achieved where these overlap and work together.

Websites

A website is an (if not *the*) most essential marketing tool for your business. First, it gives credibility by showing you exist, offering an initial port of call for anyone with an interest in your organisation, at any time of day. It is a shop window that is always open and anyone thinking of involving themselves with an organisation tends to head for their website first. In addition to often functioning as the hub of your wider involvement with online marketing – your blog, Twitter presence, activity on Facebook, etc. – it should also offer a route for customers responding to offline communications to engage more with your organisation.

The options for what kind of website to establish are varied. You could set up a largely static website that functions as an online organisational brochure, available 24 hours a day. Alternatively it could be more informal and interactive by operating a blog (short for weblog), which can be updated with regular posts. Or you could have a fully functioning ecommerce site that takes payments, with links to online selling mechanisms such as PayPal, eBay and Amazon. And of course there are many stages in between.

For publishers, given the huge amount of products and services being offered, it is important to think about your target audience and what kind of website is needed. For example, it may not be necessary to have one for each author or each book, but rather to organise by imprint or launch date. You need to think about what your audience needs to know and hence wants your website to do, in the context of what other online content/activity is going to be most useful at the level of individual products.

How websites get created is varied. You might decide to construct it yourself, or to use a web designer – website design is also increasingly offered by graphic designers. Whatever route gets taken towards creation, some thinking will need to be done about what kind of website is needed, by when and what you need it to do for you. Drawing up the specifications of what you are looking for will act as a mind-focusing exercise, perhaps encouraging you to start creating your own – or making it clear to you that it's a task beyond you and external support is needed. Bear in mind that this is not a one-stop process, like the creation of a printed catalogue that is finished when passed for press and will be used until a new version is created. A website is always a work in progress, with new information being added to refresh and update it, information from how customers use it being used to inform how it is developed in future.

Elements to be considered before planning a website

- **Choose and register a domain name.** It's a good idea to secure a domain name for your planned website, particularly if it is a word that is key to your ethos, subject matter or ambitions. If you are not yet ready to create a website, a domain name, once secured, can be used to host your email, although you may find customers start looking for the associated website. There are various companies selling domain names and web hosting, and it makes life easier if you get the two from the same place.
- **What do you want your website to do for you?** How complex do you want it to be? Will it be a simple outline brochure, a blog to connect with your customers or a fully functioning ecommerce site? Or will it be a combination of these things? A static website can have links to a blog and an ecommerce site that make the customer/reader feel they're still on the same site, when in fact they've gone somewhere else.
- **What kind of budget are you willing to allocate?**
- **Are there any time constraints on you?** Do you want your website to be up and running by a particular date? Is this reasonable or achievable?
- **Who is your target audience?** What do you know of it and can you be sure that you are right? If you understand its values, buying signals, gender and age you might be able to create something specific – without hopefully alienating other types of enquirer. Are you selling business to business or to consumers? If both, who is more important to you, both now and in the future?
- **How are you going to direct people to your website?** Off- and online routes need to be considered, and how a synergistic approach can be created.
- **What kind of look and feel are you after?** How do you want your customers and enquirers to feel about your organisation and its brand? Can you gather some physical brochures and named sites that create the sort of look you seek? What colour palette and typeface do you find attractive and best represent the effects you are trying to create?
- **What do you want people to do having seen your website?** What is the main call to action? This will affect how the site is structured.
- **What pictures do you have available?** What images will you use to illustrate your website and are these already available to you? Do you have the right to use them or is permission needed?

What information to offer on a website

A website consists of a range of pages that interconnect and enable the user to navigate with ease. It can be helpful to think of it as a series of curtains on a stage,

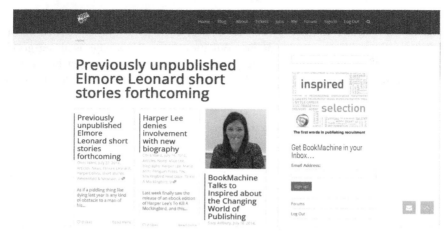

Figure 9.1 BookMachine website. Courtesy of BookMachine.

as each one rises, there is a link to more information behind. Many options exist, but visitors to your site will inevitably use their previous experience of navigating websites to understand how yours works. So there will be expectations in the market to find most of the following:

- Home page

This is the landing page for all those who arrive on your site – and is therefore very important. It is a permanently open doorway. It should make an initial impression on the visitor, and one that illustrates how you want your organisation to be seen. Many customers will get no further, so the homepage should provide both a clear sense of what else is available on the site and information on what has changed since the last visit.

- Your story/About us/Who we are and what we do

This is your opportunity to share information on the organisation, its history and your vision; customers are in general interested in these things. A helpful starting point is to think of this page as a permanently available opportunity for journalists to find out about how you started and what you seek to do. This is a great place to offer information about your inspiration and ethos, particularly when this is as yet unsupported by any physical experience of the customer.

- Contact us/Get in touch

Providing you are willing to accept and deal with customer enquiries (and not all websites are set up to do this, which of course carries a strong message) potential customers need an opportunity to find out more. You can put contact information (email, location and telephone) at the foot of each page but given that most websites offer a direct route to finding out more, a separate page is also a good idea. If spam is a problem, it's helpful to offer those who want to get in touch a contact form rather than an email address, and to make sure you use a 'captcha' to ensure responses are from genuine individuals rather than computers. If you put up an unprotected email address you can end up being inundated with spam – and as spammers steal your email address and use it to spam others, you can then find yourself blocked.

This is also a good place to put frequently asked questions (and the associated answers) and to share information on who works for the organisation. This can move the burden of thinking about who should answer a query on to the customer, in the process encouraging a greater degree of familiarity with how your organisation is structured.

Staff profiles can be displayed here, with individual contact details and a photograph. Some organisations then offer 'day in the life of' information for a sample range of staff – so that those who are looking at the website in order to decide whether they might like to work there, or with an interview coming up, can learn more.

- Information on your products, services and what you offer

You could offer a summary page, with links to more detailed information elsewhere, and perhaps a call to action 'Order now' for those who wish to place an order straight away.

- Search facility

A search facility is useful for customers who want a specific detail from you – say to find out when a particular author is appearing at a literary festival without the bother of having to work their way through the entire programme.

- A shop

Where items get bought and paid for and where offers made elsewhere are fulfilled. Maybe incentivised so the customer buys direct rather than hunting for information on your site and paying elsewhere.

- Feedback/What our customers say about us

A section offering feedback from customers may be reassuring to new arrivals who have not ordered from you before. Press coverage might be made available here too, or on a separate page, perhaps along with copies of your most recent organisational press releases.

- Latest news/Find out what's going on section

If you have not put this on your homepage, you could have a separate page that offers updates on activities – perhaps a copy of your most recent newsletter or access to your blog.

- Free materials

Many websites engage the interest of their potential customers, and impress them with the quality of the service/advice/product range on offer, by making available content that can be downloaded or accessed free. Publishers have a wealth of material that could benefit their customers – information on new titles, sample chapters from existing materials, interviews with authors, question and answer sessions on how to get published. The key skill is to provide sufficient free content so that customers engage with your organisation and get a flavour of what they would pay for should they decide to get further involved, without giving them so much that there is no need to monetise the relationship.

- Legal information

When establishing and maintaining websites there are specific (and often regional) legalities that need to be attended to. If you decide to have a page devoted to this, it's also a good place to make it clear, and offer reassurance regarding, how you will use the customer information you acquire.

Finding out how your website is working

Web analytics help you measure the effectiveness of your website. This service is available from various suppliers and you sign up for an account, receive codes to add to specific locations within your site, and in return get access to statistics on site usage. Using an analytics service is likely to involve the use of 'cookies' and, if you are based in the EU, you will need to gain consent for this from your site visitors.

In addition to building a website, it is vital to have a strategy for driving traffic to it. Users access search engines to find the information they seek, and the decision-making algorithms that decide which web pages are recommended first are based on the relevance and authority of the content they find. How can you affect the ranking of your site? A site's relevance is based on the vocabulary used within it, hence the importance of search engine optimisation, which can be used to influence how closely your vocabulary aligns with key terminology in the sector in which you are operating. You can also improve your positioning by using paid word placements (e.g., using Google or AdWords) or attracting inbound links to your site, by commenting on other people's blogs, offering guest blogs and contributing within chat rooms – linking the content you provide back to your own home base online.

Case study

The central role played by our website in promoting what we do, by Laura Summers of BookMachine[8]

BookMachine is an event organisation and online hub for the publishing community, formed by a group of publishing professionals keen to keep in touch as they progressed in their careers and navigated through various publishing houses. At the time, there was a lack of informal, affordable gatherings in London for publishers to meet and learn from others. Book-Machine quickly filled that gap and built a network of face-to-face events in a number of cities, with London, Oxford, Barcelona and New York hosting the largest crowds.

Publishers use the BookMachine website to find jobs, read about latest events and catch up on publishing news and opinion. There are a number of marketing techniques employed by the BookMachine team on both a periodic and a frequent basis, to drive readership of the site.

We have developed a mix of offline and online marketing strategies, all with little or no budget. Our regular events act as offline PR and promotion for our burgeoning digital platform; hundreds of publishing professionals attend them and then head back to the office the following day to spread the word.

Marketing a brand or an idea requires consistency. Research shows that people need to see a message at least seven times[9] before taking action or even recognising a brand. In an online world where we are bombarded with messages on every screen, a constant and frequent delivery of a message is much more effective than just one blast of content.

We have learned that keeping communication short, and make sure it is regular, works best. Potential buyers will decide to take action or to buy at a time that suits them; the aim of marketing is to be right in front of them when they do require your services.

Without Twitter, BookMachine would never have happened. From the outset, Twitter has been an invaluable tool for promoting our events and driving traffic to the BookMachine website and more than 50 per cent of our new website traffic is sourced from here.

Twitter has worked for us in part because the publishing industry has an active and vocal Twitter community. We have tried Pinterest, which can work well for sites with very visual content to share, but as we have lacked such content this has never become a primary generator of traffic for us. For a business-to-consumer (B2C) sale, then Facebook might be the best social media channel to use.

Our advice is to pick one or two online channels and use them well. If you are working for a large publisher, someone can be dedicated to each of the social media channels and, providing they are coordinating their efforts, this can work effectively. In a small company you need to use your time wisely, and dedicating yourself to growing your customer base on one platform is more effective than using all platforms ineffectively. Track where most of your website traffic comes from, and as soon as you find a winning formula then stick with it.

How people will engage with social media in the future is unclear. Over recent months Facebook have made changes to the way brands can promote themselves on the platform, and now companies need to pay to reach even their own fans. Twitter is likely to follow this trend, as investors demand higher returns. This is one of the reasons that BookMachine also built BookMachine.me. This is the team's own platform, which not only enables us to keep in touch with the audience directly, but will also ride any seismic changes in social media trends. This strategy is particularly relevant in a community-based business, but even for a B2C product it's always useful to have a back-up plan and to cultivate a direct relationship with your customers.

One of the best tools for gathering data and growing traffic to your site is also one of the most tried and tested: email. Everyone has an email address, and needs it as a starting point to all communication online. There are certain demographics that are less email responsive than others, but by getting permission to use someone's email address you have a big chance of being able to continue communicating with them. An individual makes a bigger commitment in giving their email address to an organisation than following a brand on social media, so respect that and make sure the communication is as personalised and relevant as you are able to achieve.

The website is the centre of most marketing decisions. By analysing the data from traffic-measuring services such as Google Analytics and Mixpanel, insights can be gained into what people are interested in and how best to focus. For example, a recent blog post on XML tips gathered one of the highest traffic volumes yet on BookMachine. It led the team to understand that digital training is of top priority and we are using that knowledge to influence new content on BookMachine.

Most importantly the website needs to feel right for your audience. This might mean researching your competitors and getting a sense of what the marketplace is used to. From there a design and format can be established that resonate with your target market, or this can be used as a starting point to make sure that your brand stands out among the competition.

Establishing the credibility of your site is also important. Poor loading times and out of date design won't inspire even the most enthusiastic customer. Most users will stay on a web page for just 10–20 seconds unless there is a compelling reason for them to hang around.

Finally, we have worked hard to ensure that the BookMachine website is mobile-optimised. With mobile devices driving 30 per cent of website traffic,[10] it is important to always consider how prospective customers will access the site on the go.

Case study

The integration of online and offline in effective selling: an interview with Philip Downer, MD of Calliope Gifts, Dorking and Alton, UK

Philip Downer began his career as a sales assistant with music retailer Our Price in 1980. He progressed into store and regional management and finally into board-level positions, staying with the firm as it moved from being a feisty independent to a division of the much larger predominantly stationery retailer WH Smith. He spent 2 years in the US (1994–6) working with the Waterstones brand, competing head-on with local book retailers such as Barnes & Noble and Borders. He returned to the UK and then from 1997 to 2009 was involved in a reverse development, setting up and developing the Borders brand of book retailing in the UK. In order to have an immediate critical mass in the market, rather than build from scratch, Borders began by purchasing the UK chain Books Etc., and Downer worked for them as operations director, managing director and later CEO, until Borders closed in the UK in 2009. In short, he has a lot of experience in retailing books.

After Borders closed he did some consultancy within the trade but found the combination of offering advice and seeing some of it implemented was less satisfying if you were not also involved in the longer-term management of the outcomes. With a former Borders colleague, Andy Adamson, who had long experience of logistics, inventory systems and managing supplier relationships, he planned a return to retailing on a much more local level. Together they aimed to offer a new kind of store on the high street that could draw on their vast shared experience and offer what they had observed to be the most profitable parts of the Borders experience (stock for children and the cross-selling of related merchandise under a single roof – notably music, stationery and refreshments) but for which they would be responsible.

There are three guiding principles behind Calliope Gifts,[11] established in the market towns of Dorking (2013) and Alton (2014). First, that it should be an attractive environment where people want to spend time – although market research shows that gifts are predominantly bought by women, many gift shops feel overtly feminine environments and they wanted the full range of their customers to feel comfortable. Second, customers should be able to find, or be helped towards, a gift for anyone: men, women, children – and for the full range of 'special occasions'. Third, they wanted to use their shared experience of retailing and offer the kind of product range that is disappearing from the high street: books, music and the many other items required to service an ongoing human need – to buy presents for other people, and particularly those we love. Stock is broadly themed and changes all the time, being moved around and supplemented with new additions and stock lines so regular visitors have new things to look at. They try hard not to replicate what else is available locally – they don't want to get involved in price wars – so they don't sell the books that are available in WH Smith and have different suppliers for lines such as jewellery and scarves. They do, however, feel very loyal to the community they are part of, see themselves as contributing to the attractiveness of the local retail environment and get involved with its management by local government.

Their website is an extension of their service, complementing what is available in store as a 24-hours-a-day shop window. Significantly it requires little additional management time or space. Every stock item that comes into the shop is loaded on to the inventory database, photographed and given a few words of descriptive copy and this then serves as both a stock-holding guide for the shop and website copy. Customer orders placed online are packed in the shop, giving those in store something else to do when business is slow, and then taken along to the local post office – 'I bet that's what Amazon did when they started'. Philip Downer continues:

> We ask customers if they want to go on our mailing list when they are in the shop and then anyone who orders online gets added too, having ticked the 'opt in' box. We have approached local groups and made relevant special offers, and this is an area ripe for development. I then do an email newsletter every couple of weeks, more often towards Christmas, making special offers and inviting them to call in – perhaps to our second store in Alton now. I have a particular tone of voice when writing these communications which is upbeat and enthusiastic – which is partly a reflection of the customer base but also how I feel. I want to create an environment where they think a spare 15 minutes could be pleasantly spent in our shop.
>
> We get to know our customers well – they're in their 'family years' but this can be from their mid-20s to their mid-60s, with opportunities to buy presents occurring throughout that period, from presents for their children to those bought for the new grandchildren of their friends. They are intelligent, aware of the world and like good design – but are also busy and have lots to think about.
>
> People like to buy locally and feel a connection with a shop and it's interesting that we are seeing quite a lot of 'reverse show-rooming'. Show-rooming is the practice of looking in local shops and then buying online, but we are regularly finding instances of the process working the other way for us. Customers browse our website on their tablet at home, often while doing something else such as watching television or eating, and then come in to see what we have in person before making a choice – enabling them to do a quality check or see the actual size before committing themselves, and perhaps buying a card and wrapping paper at the same time.
>
> Retailing is about understanding the local market and getting the detail right. There is a thrill in seeing merchandise you have chosen for

your customers come into the store, putting it in the window straight-away, and then seeing the first person come in and buy – and commenting on their choice. I get satisfaction from the immediacy of the process. The combination of strategic and operational processes at the same time feels purposeful as we seek to understand our customers, meet their needs and develop the relationship.

Gloomy predictions are consistently made about the future of the high street, and it's likely we will see the further automation of 'functional shopping' – with groceries and items that are heavy to carry home helpfully delivered to the door. But people are social creatures and like to get out, mingle and meet with others as the continued rise of coffee shops has shown. And as they are short of time, a retailer who understands their needs and can present a relevant selection of stock for them to browse and choose between is able to offer a really valuable service. We feel up-beat and positive about our new venture, and the recent award of the prestigious 'Best newcomer' by the trade magazine *Progressive Gift and Home* has confirmed our confidence.

Blogging

'Blog' is short for a weblog, an online diary that allows the regular posting of contributions. For example you could offer interesting and timely comment on current issues, suggest solutions to problems that are generally perceived, offer a list of top tips within a particular area, share more information about how you came to set up your business or the story behind the product and service range you offer. If you provide the opportunity for readers to comment on your blog, and then give feedback on what they say, you further increase engagement.

Running a blog can be an excellent way to demonstrate your expertise within a particular sector, increase your visibility on the web and your position in online rankings. Not only does a blog create more pages to be indexed, if you use plenty of keywords relating to your business area, focus each blog on a single topic or relevance, make links to others involved in the area, and drive traffic towards it through mentioning it on other platforms (e.g., Twitter and Facebook) you will prompt more links and hence a spurt in your influence online.

The mechanics for establishing a blog are fairly straightforward. If you already own some web space and have your own domain name, a blog can be hosted on your own server. If you don't yet have a domain, there are platforms such as Blogger and WordPress that offer different 'template' options that can be linked to your website. You can start off with a hosted blog and then pay to upgrade your account, so that your domain name can be used once that is up and running.

If you are thinking of establishing a blog, bear in mind that it's much easier to start one than keep it going. So before you begin, it's a good idea to read as many as possible, consider how much maintenance they require and what kind of response they get, before proceeding. You need to think about:

- What could a blog do for you (attract interest and attention, give you a means of sharing content, demonstrate your expertise within a specific market)?
- What's going on in your specific area of expertise or in the markets you want to communicate with? Blogs are in a state of constant change, and you do need to remain up to date in how the medium is being used (short/long contributions? Short blogging via Tumblr?).
- What ground rules you will set for its operation? How often you will blog, how long your contributions will be – they need not be extensive – what kind of information you will offer, will you allow other people to take part?
- How much time can you devote to this? Bear in mind that blogs can be short and also created in batches for subsequent delivery (you can program a series of sequential contributions). So instead of writing long pieces, consider dividing them into a series of useful comments.
- How personal should it be? Keep in mind that once information is out there, it's there.

Top tips for writing an effective blog

- **A blog is a conversation not a lecture**, don't use it to hector, rather explain your thinking processes and chat around your area of expertise.
- **Decide who is going to write the blog(s).** Internal or external contributions? Who else might be asked for endorsement or occasional contributions? Who is going to check for consistency or manage the loading?
- **Have a sample reader** in your mind as you write – talk to them as you go.
- **Take your time.** Identify the issues you cover and handle them one at a time – giving your readers something to come back for. Don't use all your material in the first column you write.
- **Allow yourself to build trust**, show expertise.
- **Connect with what your market finds interesting and feed back when they respond.** Look at the statistics to see what keeps people reading – and where they go next.
- **Create connections** with other related sites and individuals and build the associated community. Comment on other people's blogs and involve people in yours; consider organising a blog tour. By creating networking opportunities for all you encourage readers to help you reach a wider market.
- **When a blog (a website) is set up, whichever platform you are using (Blogger, WordPress, Tumblr, etc.) sets up a feed for you**, so readers can opt to be alerted when new additions are made. Ensure your responses (and responses to responses) keep the conversation going.
- **Include plenty of keywords** relating to your business.
- **Be topical**, offer advice on how to do something. Offer fresh content or an innovative interpretation of information that is widely available.
- **Integrate with your other social media**, e.g., drive links to your blog from Twitter.

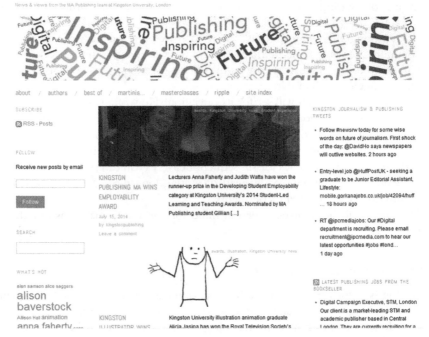

Figure 9.2 Kingston University Publishing blog. Courtesy of Kingston University.

Case study

The role of a blogger

Ayo Onatade has a day job working as an administrator within the British Courts of Justice. Her second life is as a blogger, writing about thrillers and crime fiction. The website is http://shotsmag.co.uk and the blog is at wwwshotsmagcouk.blogspot.co.uk.

She started neither website nor blog herself. The website began as a magazine, set up by crime fiction enthusiast Mike Stotter and it ran in this format from June 1994 until January 2001, was briefly an e-zine until autumn 2004, when it became a fully fledged website. The blog started in 2007. Through her own love of the genre she met Mike and was persuaded to write initially for the magazine and then for the blog as well, and gradually ended up writing so much of the content for the blog that those previously managing it suggested she take over. The Shots website and blog belongs to the Shots collective, of which Mike is the overall editor, but he is fully consulted and all feel involved.

The expectations from the audience are high. The blog gets over 10,049 hits a month (December 2013; 410,601 in its lifetime) but readers will only keep coming back if there is interesting new material to read, and Ayo contributes at least three new posts a week. To give her something to write about she has to keep up to date with news from the sector (who has been signed up, who has a new book coming out, who has won which prize) as well as finding time to read the crime titles publishers send her for review. The scale of this endeavour may be judged by the fact that she has now persuaded her postman to deliver all the packages from publishers at the weekend rather than during the week, when they will not fit through the letterbox. Most weeks this amounts to at least ten packages and Royal Mail now sends a van on a Saturday.

But while her influence is high, and growing, this is a role for which she is not paid. Arguably this is the significance of her position: she is free to say what she does and does not like and her readers appreciate her honesty and follow her suggestions. They tend to buy the titles she recommends and avoid those she feels do not work and her influence on the market is huge. She is currently chair of the CWA Short Story Dagger judging panel.

The books that are sent to bloggers and reviewers are theirs to keep, and some use this as a handy income stream, selling them on to second-hand bookshops – even sometimes before publication day. This, however, is not encouraged. Ayo gives away titles she has no room for – to family, friends, colleagues at work, local libraries and schools as well as to other enthusiasts – including her postman.

How to work well with a blogger

Read their blog. *Before* **you get in touch with them.** Starting your email with 'I love reading your blog and find it so interesting' and then sending them material that is not relevant/they have shown they dislike shows that you are starting your relationship by lying. Unlikely to be well received.

- **Respect their influence.** They are communicating directly and authoritatively with your market in a way that, as a producer with something to sell, you will never be believed. The history of selling books through retailers has meant that publishers have long been isolated from their purchasers. Although they are now building up mechanisms for direct communication (websites offering reading group support materials and guidance on reading journeys, email alerts and direct buying mechanisms) the unbiased blogger who understands and respects the time of readers in search of recommendations and offers third-party endorsement, will be more believable. With the decline of book reviews in the broadsheets, the knowledge of the genre blogger is becoming even more important to authors and publishers.

- **Respect their time.** Understand that however much commitment they put into this role, it is generally not their day job. Be realistic in what you send them. Ayo tends to hear from publishers by email (with an occasional DM on Twitter) rather than phone calls – which she cannot take during the day (and does not have time to return). Along similar lines, Ayo is regularly contacted by (often first-time) authors who want feedback on their work. With generosity she tends to give it, but it should be noted that this is an assessment by a sector expert on the merits of the writing, not a longer-term tutoring opportunity! Longer-term correspondence is not invited.

- **Understand that most do this job for love**, because they like being at the centre of things and knowing what is being published and they have been involved in the genre for a long time. They like the feedback they receive from readers and authors, the sense of heavy involvement with a community they are part of – and the accompanying sense of worth that comes from being listened to and value placed on their judgement. Acknowledging this passion-funded expertise, rather than marvelling at how much time it must all take, is a good start.

- **Let them get to know your organisation and its plans.** Involve them in treats, parties, meetings with authors, new commissioning decisions (e.g., send the latest catalogue promptly) and 'cover reveals' (the first availability of the jacket image for a new title). Provide new information each time you are in touch with them, not just repeated rehashing of the jacket blurb. For bloggers who are particularly important to your list, consider offering an 'exclusive' – perhaps access to an author or information that you won't be making generally available, or signed copies of books that they can use for competitions. Bloggers get satisfaction from making their blog the 'go to' destination, so anything that helps them maintain this position is likely to boost your relationship.

- **Understand that bloggers tend to communicate.** Whereas rivalry among authors can be intense, the atmosphere within the crime-writing community is remarkably mutually supportive – one author commented that they had no need to stick the dagger in each other as they could do this to their characters. The same feeling apparently applies to the associated blogging community, and those writing for other crime fiction sites communicate with Ayo and meet at the events they get asked to. They read each other's posts and will comment on their various reactions. Some authors handily capitalise on this wider information network by offering to guest blog or to do a blog tour, but offering various sites the same information in the hope it will be posted widely is not a good idea. Ayo insists that while she welcomes guest contributions (500 words for a blog; 1,000 for a website contribution), they must be original and not about to be posted elsewhere.

Email

When marketing became increasingly common through social networking, many thought that email would be killed off. But email marketing is still very important. There are several reasons why it works particularly well for marketing in business.

First, you own the data. Social networks are hosted on third-party sites and this means that, should your social media platform be withdrawn or fail, you could suddenly lose your carefully constructed connectedness. This does happen, both through technological failures and litigation; for example, when an individual leaves employment a discussion often arises about whether their Twitter following is their property or that of their employer. Your email responders have, however, given you permission to communicate with you in future and the information on how to contact them belongs to you.

Second, email is an effective means of direct marketing and a more appropriate sales channel than social media – which people generally feel is for recreation and talking about themselves. While you still need to take care over how your message is presented, and the constant repeating of 'buy from me' messages can get tedious, in general those who have provided their email addresses expect, at least on occasion, to be sold to in this way.

Third, email ensures deliverability and gives you the associated data. Not everyone uses a social networking site, and those who do are not necessarily active all day, every day. Email collection is generally much more frequent (and part of the working day) and all emails require action on the recipient's part. You also get to find out how long they read it for and whether they clicked on any links. Whether the response is to delete on sight or engage with the content, emails sit in the recipient's inbox until they decide what to do with them. Being spotted on Facebook or Twitter is harder. Unless an individual is specifically copied in (for example by naming them within a tweet, e.g., @alisonbav) or they are looking out for items with a particular #hashtag, there is a danger that comments will be missed and then disappear down an individual's timeline.

Finally there are the inbuilt advantages of the medium. Email is a relatively straight-forward medium to use, which enables the user to monitor the relationship created in a structured way. It's quick and convenient for the recipient to respond to; quicker than a physical mailing piece, and non-intrusive (unlike telemarketing). It also offers much lower costs of delivery than other direct marketing methods (although this needs to be compared with responsiveness; as the number of emails sent rises, a common customer response is to delete incoming marketing messages). Bear in mind however that it can be expensive – even 'freemium' services can become costly in terms of time, support and the associated training required for effective management.

How to gather an audience for your email

- **Don't use your own email account to send out a mass mailing.** It takes only a low percentage of people to classify your mail as 'junk' to risk the suspension of your account.

- **Rather use a professional email service provider (or ESP).** This not only enables you to comply with the law, it also offers supporting statistical analysis. Multi-emailing facility software packages offer a contact database as a storage solution for collecting email addresses and maintaining lists. This allows you to mail lots of people individually at the same time (without the entire circulation list appearing at the top of the message).
- **Build your own list.** It is possible to buy or rent lists of email addresses but organisations that rent data often insist on managing the mail-out for you, so you don't see the number of generic emails (e.g., 'sales@' as opposed to individuals) or the number of 'goneaways' received after it has gone out, and in the process appreciate how up to date (or not) it is. Those who come back to you direct can be asked to sign up to your newsletter. Increasingly publishing companies are growing their own lists. Email is permission-based marketing, not spam, and it's a good idea to build lists of people who want to hear from you.
- **Create a sign-up form** – a standard feature of all email marketing services – and put this on your website or blog: 'Sign up to our newsletter.' Encourage people to do this before they look at anything else on your site and provide an example of what they will receive if they do – a link to the last newsletter you sent out. You can also incentivise sign-up by offering free items or early access to new material.
- **Ask in person**, as part of your overall communications strategy. So whether you are communicating on- or offline, emailing them or accepting a business card, ask if you can add them to your newsletter.
- **Use social networks to gather names** by promoting the chance to join your mailing list on the forums you use. Tweet a link to your newsletter or mention it on Facebook.

Deciding on the objectives of your email campaign

What are you trying to do – provide news, build a relationship, prompt a more considered change of attitudes, promote trial usage or achieve sales? Probably the most common form of email marketing is a regular newsletter to all those on an email list, but you can also use the process to carry out market research, make specific offers, announce news and offer them case studies of how products and services have worked with other customers.

Make your email campaigns opportunities to learn

Always send yourself a test email before you send to your entire list to ensure your message looks as you intended, the links work and there are no obvious errors. Spelling and grammatical errors can destroy your credibility and are very damaging if you are making claims for the excellence of your content (essential for publishers). Then (unless your timing is particularly crucial, e.g., you are responding to news events) leave it overnight before finally despatching to ensure you have a double-check on the tone of voice deployed. What seems pleasingly ironic in the early evening may sound smug – or incomprehensible – the next morning. You don't know at what time of day your recipients are going to open your mail – or in what mood.

Post-despatch, ESP services offer the metrics of your campaigns, so you can see how many people opened what you sent and how long they spent perusing its constituent parts. In this way you can find out more about your customers and how they respond to your communications. In the same way that some stand-up comedians record audience reactions and how long applause or laughter lasts, you can learn from the first-hand response to the message you sent – and improve your future performance. Along similar lines, follow good direct marketing practice and change the variables to see which combination produces the best results, however you have defined them (e.g., most clicks through to the website, most orders, most new followers on Twitter). You could also experiment by sending out messages on different days of the week and different times (Friday afternoon is said to be a particularly good time as people wind down for the weekend). Direct marketers using the mail often keep very specific records, even noting the weather or news agenda when their mailshots were both despatched and received.

How to write an enticing email

Begin by thinking about the recipient rather than the act of writing. Consider whether they will read it and, if so, in what order, and what you are hoping they will do next. Think how you can use the space to develop the relationship rather than just announce that something is available.

An effective email should be targeted to the appropriate audience, be short and entice a reply. The goal should be to start or develop a relationship with a recipient that can be sustained through mutually beneficial activity (e.g., sales, feedback on products and services that enables their improvement, recommendation to other potential purchasers).

- **Send it from and to a real person** – rather than a generic title (sales@ etc.). It is far more likely to get opened if it seems like a real approach from a genuine individual rather than a department.
- **The subject line is vital** – this is what recipients see before they decide on whether to open the accompanying email. Ensure it is short (definitely no more than 55 characters) and interesting or it may get deleted on sight. ESPs will allow you to do a split test on subject lines used in campaigns, so you can see which one produced the best results.
- Your ESP should take care of the **formatting of your message**, and ensure the text can be read comfortably. But in general keep the information short, in manageable chunks of different lengths.
- **Aim for visual variety** – it is the space in a document that draws people in, not the words – so have paragraphs of different lengths and use some typographic colour (bold, underlining, etc.) to draw attention to key parts of your message.

- **Offer a single – or very limited number of – call(s) to action** to suggest they do something – sign up for a newsletter, visit your website, download a sample.
- **Think about what you have to offer them that could further develop the relationship** – an exclusive offer, a sample chapter, author information, a press release or early announcement of an event, the opportunity to ask a question. If these are posted on your website, they may browse to learn more about you. In general it's best not to include attachments.
- **Ensure 'unsubscribe' information is clear** – to reduce accusations of spam.
- **Put all your contact information in a footer** so that you can be both found and meet statutory requirements. In the UK, for example, businesses are required to include their registered address and number on websites and emails as well as on their printed stationery. This information can also be reassuring to individuals who are often more protective of their email address than their terrestrial one. For example, you can cover who the message is meant for and the use to which you plan to put the data by saying: 'We will keep your details on file to keep you up to date with our publishing programme but will never pass your email address on to a third party.'
- **Use your signature block** as another place to offer interesting information. In the same way that the PS is a highly noted place on a sales letter (see Chapter 8 on direct marketing), people often move to the bottom of an email to see who has sent it. Play with the information you present: provide links to your website or online coverage, add colour – and change it on a regular basis so it continues to be seen. We generally don't read information if we think we have read it before, and if you never change your signature block regular recipients will become used to its formatting – and continue not to read it.
- **Bury links to other sites within your text rather than spelling out the full website address** – or use abbreviation sites such as www.bitly.com, which allow you a shortened format. Don't include too many external links – you want to keep your customers focused on your message and the outcome you had intended.

Case study

How to use email to promote yourself: Jessica Palmer, cover artist

Jessica Palmer is an artist and illustrator who works with paper to design intricate paper cuts, collages and paper sculptures. Her artwork is used on book and record covers, in design and decoration, on websites, in magazines and even as wearable art jewellery. She does not have a specialised background in marketing, so using email for marketing has been a voyage of exploration and discovery. Jessica says:

> My use of email evolved over time, as did the development strategy for my career as an artist and illustrator. In the early stages, I used email to target

individual publishers and other potential art buyers, drawing email addresses from websites, from meetings and personal recommendations. While this had some success, the process of identifying individuals and relevant organisations and then finding their contact details was time-consuming.

So next I bought into a company called Bikini Lists[12] that provides a mass-mailing mechanism for visual artists to reach a much greater volume – potentially thousands – of publishers, PR companies, design companies and similar across the world. The key to maximising the value of this facility is the follow-up after the bulk mailing. In practice, a relatively small proportion (in my experience 10–20 per cent) of recipients will open the initial mailing and an even smaller proportion (5–10 per cent) will then click on the link to my website. The important thing is to then make direct contact with these 'clickers' – ideally by phoning them. Your portfolio is online these days so it's harder to offer to bring it in to show them. However, it is the case that you make yourself more memorable if you have personal contact, even if it is by telephone, and it gives you an opportunity to try to discover upcoming opportunities.

Alongside the Bikini List approach to emailing the corporate contacts I also maintain my own private mailing list from my business. I started to develop this list as a consequence of my first Open Studio when, over the course of one weekend, we received several hundred visitors. Many of these people were asking to be kept informed about future events and any workshops I would be running. So I noted down email addresses from everyone who was willing to share. Since then I have added to this list the email addresses offered by people coming to each event I lead, along with those obtained from other contacts. I'm now at a point where, within the space of a couple of years, I have around a thousand named individuals on my list.

I promise everyone that I won't inundate them with emails and the main way that I use the list is by issuing a monthly Art Newsletter. Normally this focuses on three main items, for example if my work is being displayed in a forthcoming exhibition or event, or news of upcoming workshops. Just occasionally I may augment this with an additional in-month mailing, for example to remind people a few days before the start of an Open Studio.

In terms of process, my husband Keith and I work as a team to produce these newsletters. We agree between us the items that should be covered in each issue and I then draw together a first draft, using a Toddle[13] template. Toddle is an email marketing tool for non-geeks. Keith then goes through the draft in the mode of a subscriber. Sometimes this results in quite a few changes – not least in the early days when I was more burdened by a sense of not 'being worthy' and would, in his view, understate what I was doing!

Our overall aim is to keep the initial information as brief and chatty as possible, so we provide buttons to click through to the full detail (for example, the booking details for workshops). The frequent cry I hear from potential clients is 'If only I had known about you doing this or that!' so I try to tell myself that I am providing a useful source of information rather than an irritating piece of marketing. Our recipe is to design something with eye appeal, several images and minimal text. The feedback I receive about these newsletters is invariably positive and I get, at most, a handful of 'unsubscribe' requests each month.

This DIY approach has been a useful introduction to the business of online marketing. However, it has been pretty laborious in that we have to load up segments of our mailing list one at a time as blind copies to a series of emails to circulate the newsletter. It also means that it takes several days to get each newsletter out to my complete mailing list because of the daily limits imposed by our email provider (Outlook). I'm therefore thinking about using a mass mailing system such as MailChimp[14] in the future to streamline the process.

Looking more broadly, as you begin to market yourself, you start to understand that you are becoming a brand. You have to think of your professional self impersonally as a separate entity from your private self. This means finding pictures of yourself to represent not just what you do but also what you are like, always trying to select the best images of your work. This is not necessarily easy and requires careful thought about the impression you want to present to the world. One of the hardest things to do is to exercise a critical eye and choose only your best work for display.

The more information products you offer up to public scrutiny, the more you begin to realise that they must also be of the best possible quality you can muster. For instance, I work with paper in much of my art work. Therefore, the leaflet that I have designed to tell people something about what I do – commissions, design and illustration, workshops and events – needs to be on extremely good paper with a fine texture. It seems an obvious thing on reflection but is an important detail in the marketing mix.

Once you embark on email marketing you become aware that you are nothing without an extremely good website. This is especially crucial in a visual field like mine. I need to be able to feel proud of it and unashamed to promote it widely. It took us a long time and a lot of trial and error to find a way to do this that was both affordable and beautiful. The site is like a garden. It must be constantly tended and added to and refreshed. It must work fluidly and smoothly, and be simple to navigate. But it is worth all the time, effort and money as it is my shop window to the world. It is also the destination that we send people to from our leaflets, emails and mailshots. It's our opportunity to show the range of my work and my ultimate marketing tool to generate the next great job!

Jessica Palmer can be found at www.jessicapalmerart.com. You can subscribe to her monthly art newsletter by emailing palmerk@outlook.com or by going to http://jessicapalmerart.com/wordpress/index.php/contact-me/.

ETHAN JOHNS

MAY
07 WESTON SUPER MARE LOVES CAFÉ
08 EXETER PHOENIX
09 BRIGHTON THE GREAT ESCAPE
12 MANCHESTER CASTLE
14 BALLATER THE DEESIDE INN
15 INVERNESS IRONWORKS
16 STORNOWAY WOODLANDS CENTRE
17 ULLAPOOL THE CEILIDH PLACE

18 FORT WILLIAM WATERCOLOUR
19 IONA THE LIBRARY
20 TOBERMORY, MULL AN TOBAR
22 EDINBURGH VOODOO ROOMS
23 STOCKTON THE GEORGIAN THEATRE
26 CAMBRIDGE PORTLAND ARMS
27 LEICESTER COOKIE JAR
28 LEEDS OPORTO
29 LONDON KINGS PLACE

TICKETS: KILILIVE.COM / SEETICKETS.COM

/ETHANJOHNSMUSIC   ETHANJOHNS.COM   /ETHANJOHNSMUSIC

ETHAN'S NEW ALBUM THE RECKONING AVAILABLE MAY 7TH

A KILIMANJARO & FRIENDS PRESENTATION BY ARRANGEMENT WITH ATC LIVE   POSTER ILLUSTRATION JESSICAPALMERART.COM

The Reckoning by Ethan Johns

Multi instrumentalist and singer songwriter Ethan Johns has commissioned Jessica to design his new album cover, upcoming tour poster and sleeve note illustrations.

For a free 3 song download from The Reckoning - a tale in music and poems of two brothers set in 1860s Devon and America - click on the link below.

Read more

Figure 9.3 Sample from Jessica Palmer's email newsletter. Courtesy of Jessica Palmer.

Social media: Facebook

Facebook is the biggest social networking opportunity. Material is organised into timelines where participants post photographs, messages and updates on what they are doing. It's a closed network, meaning that individual friend requests must be approved before people can interact and it's possible to set up additional specific groups for private discussions or events.

Although Facebook began as a social network it is now also one of the most widely used online marketing tools for business, simply because it is so large, and its age profile is also rising. With such a significant number of members, you can find specific communities likely to be interested in your particular passions.

For those new to Facebook, begin by creating a profile. Write it in a friendly way, and include a mention of your business and your website. Include photographs and consider customising your page with illustrations or a background photograph. You can then use other online marketing and social media (e.g., blogging, email or Twitter) to drive traffic to your Facebook page.

You can measure your results by the number of 'likes' you receive, the number of friends or fans you have and the extent to which others talk about your content (those who have created a story about it) as well as through your weekly total reach.

The best advice is to post regularly, remember to respond promptly to the comments you receive back, include photographs as often as possible and avoid direct appeals – posts requesting comments or likes will not get much traction. But users also need to remain aware of how this online format is developing, and how best to manage associated communication as a result.

Case study

How a publishing house run by a university uses Facebook as part of its outreach, and how that use has changed over time: Ooligan Press, assistant professor Per Henningsgaard, Portland State University

Ooligan Press[15] is a publishing house staffed by students enrolled in the Master's degree in Book Publishing at Portland State University, US. Publishing three books a year and selling them in bookstores across the nation as well as online, Ooligan Press provides a hands-on experience that is not replicated in any other Master's degree in the US. Students participate in every step of the publishing process – from manuscript acquisition to editing, from design and production to marketing and sales – with guidance and supervision provided by expert faculty staff. Students take lessons from the classroom and apply them to real-world publishing challenges, resulting in numerous award-winning and bestselling books that span every genre. Participation in Ooligan Press is required of all students in the Master's degree in Book Publishing.

Like most publishing houses that publish books for the general trade, Ooligan Press has an active social media presence: Facebook, Twitter, Pinterest, Instagram, Tumblr, Google+, LinkedIn, YouTube and Goodreads. At the start of each academic year, one student is appointed to manage all of these social media properties. For a student who hopes to graduate with a Master's degree in Book Publishing, and go on to work in the marketing department of a publishing house, this experience is invaluable. Notably, the student is not responsible for creating all the content for these social media properties (although the student will do a fair bit of this, as well) but rather managing and coordinating the creation of content by individuals across the publishing house. It is important that the student appointed to this position maintains open lines of communication with others in the publishing house so that updates are not overlooked. It is also important that this person enforces a consistent tone across all updates. Fortunately, however, it is not required that Ooligan Press coordinates this tone with the university and departmental branding since this would be a cumbersome task.

In 2009, 8 years after the founding of Ooligan Press, its first Facebook account was established. A couple of years later, Facebook added a new type of page that allowed users to subscribe to public postings by another user and follow them without needing to add them as a friend. Consequently, Ooligan Press, like most other businesses at the time, made the shift from a Facebook profile to a Facebook page. There were two key benefits driving this shift. First, there is a limit to the number of friends users are allowed on a Facebook profile, but there is no limit on a Facebook page. Second, Facebook pages offer analytics so that users can see statistics on the success of individual status updates.

For the first few years during which Ooligan Press used Facebook, it was the lynchpin of Ooligan Press's social media marketing efforts. Facebook is, of course, the most popular social media property, so it only makes sense that Ooligan Press devoted a significant amount of time and energy to this forum. Since 2013, however, Facebook has implemented various measures designed to encourage businesses with Facebook pages to pay for their outreach. It used to be that if someone chose to 'follow' Ooligan Press on Facebook, then they would receive all of Ooligan Press's status updates. But now individuals who choose to 'follow' Ooligan Press receive only a small number of Ooligan Press's status updates. In other words, the organic reach of a business's Facebook status updates has been significantly reduced. Only if a particular status update begins to attract attention in the form of likes, comments and shares, will that status update begin to appear in the news feeds of a larger number of individuals who chose to 'follow' the business on Facebook. Alternatively, businesses are encouraged to 'boost your post' by paying so that more people will see it in their news feeds.

For these reasons, the effectiveness of Facebook as a marketing tool for Ooligan Press has become more limited over time. Beginning in 2013, Ooligan Press has focused on developing its presence in other social media properties. Nonetheless, Facebook remains a valuable part of Ooligan Press's overall marketing strategy. In particular, Ooligan Press has found that status updates highlighting the extraordinary accomplishments of an individual (whether an author or a staff member) continue to attract large numbers of likes, comments and shares, thus increasing their overall reach. Event announcements, on the other hand, seem to have a very small reach. Ooligan Press also uses Facebook as a forum for driving traffic to other sites, including the Ooligan Press blog and the social media properties of Ooligan Press authors. Despite its limitations, Facebook still merits one or two status updates each and every day.

LinkedIn

LinkedIn is the world's largest professional social network, and it works as if you are handing out your business card in cyberspace. Again this is a closed network that users learn to navigate. You can leave specific content for those who look for you – or use your home page, profile, network and interests to try to drive those interested to your information.

LinkedIn has an older demographic profile than Facebook, and this makes it a useful forum for those looking for business connectedness. The language you use should be matched accordingly. It's a good place to present yourself as an expert or promote your business – and also works for recruitment. Again you can create a LinkedIn group to service a particular need or event.

Top tips for LinkedIn

- Connect with everyone you come across professionally – you never know how useful they will be.
- If you are contacted by unfamiliar people and asked to connect, look to see if there is an overlap between their contacts and yours. Bear in mind that there are people you 'know' on social media that you have never physically met, and this may be sufficient recommendation.
- Research different companies to find out which are a good fit for the services and products you offer and the markets you approach.
- Start and join groups and conversations; when you answer a question or share expertise, you are building your reputation as an expert or thought leader. Participate strategically in your client area, e.g., science groups for science editors; construction or sustainability groups for those specialising in the built environment.
- Work your network: you may be closely connected to some key decision-makers.

- Consider **premium membership** if you're going to use it a lot. LinkedIn has some very powerful tools like InMail (which allows you to send an internal LinkedIn email to anyone on the site, for a price) and other features that are available if you upgrade. Depending on the amount of communication and access that you want to have on LinkedIn, these memberships can be good value for money.

Case study

Using Facebook, LinkedIn and Twitter as part of an integrated social media campaign to promote CompletelyNovel, a publishing and reading community, by Sarah Juckes of CompletelyNovel www.completelynovel.com

The nature of self-publishing means that indie authors can often feel as if they are 'going it alone'. Although CompletelyNovel exists primarily as a publishing platform, we wanted to ensure that authors had a space where they felt like they had people on their side. As a result, there is a strong focus on community on CompletelyNovel, and much of our time is spent engaging with new and existing customers on a more personal level. Facebook plays a significant part in this: it offers a nice way for us to connect with users by sharing things we think will be interesting to them more generally as writers and readers, alongside our offers and updates.

It's fair to say that our engagement on Facebook has stepped up considerably in the last year. Prior to that we did have a presence, but were much quieter. Our increase in activity has tied in with a shift in Facebook's strategy towards a larger presence for brands and sharing external content. We felt this gave us a better opportunity to contribute with content that fitted in with the Facebook environment, rather than risk people seeing it as an unwelcome intrusion into a space they felt was reserved for family and friends.

As a small, fairly new company, we have also made use of Facebook's feature to 'watch' other pages to compare our progress with that of our competitors. By doing this for a range of pages with a similar target audience to our own, we hope to be able to pinpoint what type of post and schedule works best to increase engagement.

We have a very active Twitter account. Twitter is fantastic for alerting potential new customers to CompletelyNovel, but not necessarily to convert them to becoming a user. We therefore regularly link to Facebook from Twitter in the hope of generating new 'likes'. By encouraging our customers to 'like' our Facebook page, we hope to be able to communicate with them on a more personal level.

With this in mind, our tone on Facebook is usually much more informal than with, say, our LinkedIn page. On LinkedIn we are targeting either potential or existing partners, or perhaps customers who are interested in producing professional books for their business. On Facebook, we are sharing images or links relating to writing – some targeted to motivate entrepreneurial indie authors, others capturing the 'romance' of writing, others just for fun (because we are strong believers that publishing should be enjoyable!). We also regularly link to CompletelyNovel articles and keep users up to date with what we are up to. We almost always encourage people to act on the post with a call to action, to encourage engagement.

In the past, we've found the following posts have generated the most engagement:

- Adding photos from The One Big Book Launch event, where ten authors launched their book on the same night. The authors involved shared these images with family and friends, and we got plenty of likes as a result. Each photo was also linked to CompletelyNovel, to capitalise on any conversions as a result.
- A 'limited time offer' that we pinned to the top of our Facebook page to maximise conversions. This was a good way to maximise the engagement of a post that was important for converting 'likes', to CompletelyNovel users, without 'spamming' the news feed of existing customers.
- Announcing partnerships with established firms. Our recent collaboration with Greene & Heaton literary agency received a great deal of interest from existing and potential customers. Customers recognised the brand of Greene & Heaton and were more likely to engage as a result.
- Sharing fun pictures on the theme of writing or books. These are important to build up a level of engagement with our network, so they are also aware of our 'conversion' posts later on. They are often light or funny – the kind of thing you would share with friends.

As a general rule, we always post with either a link or an image, as these posts are physically larger onscreen and more likely to be engaged with. We also add text to accompany each of these posts. We've found the following three-tier format works well for this text:

> hook;
> summary;
> call to action.

For example:

> BREAKING NEWS!
> We are very pleased to announce our collaboration with Greene & Heaton literary agency.
> Read the full announcement below! #selfpublishing #agents?

Figure 9.4 CompletelyNovel Facebook page. Courtesy of CompletelyNovel.

We've found that Facebook doesn't always work the way we are expecting it to, and so much of what we post is trial and error. For example, we created a #WednesdayBookSnack hashtag, mirroring the campaign run by the Tate art gallery, where they shared an image of a painting that provided a weather forecast for the week. We shared an image of a book cover every Wednesday that included or featured food, asking users to share what books they are snacking on that week. Despite sharing popular books from across publishing, these posts received few impressions or engagement, and it was discontinued.

Although it was a neat idea, on reflection we thought it was perhaps a little too far removed from the core interest of writing for our followers. And although people like to contribute, our call to action may have demanded a little more thought than most users are willing to put in when they are just scanning through their newsfeed.

By pinpointing the posts that don't do so well and thinking about why this might be, we can continue refining a Facebook marketing strategy that maximises engagement and conversions from 'like' to 'customer'.

Twitter

Twitter allows the sharing of news and status updates in an ever-updating timeline. It offers an excellent medium for sharing links, which makes it an effective outreach tool for most forms of social media content, especially blogs.

Twitter works well for businesses because it can reach niche audiences who are interested in what you have to say; it creates an online community. It also allows you to show your personality; in the case of the publishing industry, many of the most interesting accounts are from individuals working for specific houses rather than the official house Twitter account.

Getting involved in Twitter allows you to build a strategic connectedness with a wide range of people – including the highly influential. In terms of the message you deliver, Twitter requires it to be succinct (only 140 characters) but memorable, and as more and more content is available, a picture or a link to another piece of information can be effective.

Twitter accounts are easily set up at http.//twitter.com. Choose a username with care so people can find you easily, and the addition of a profile picture is very important (those without them have little credibility). The 160-character biography that has to be provided can include links, hashtags and @usernames. You can also customise your design to convey colours that match your branding or display a background image. Hashtags are clickable keywords and adding them to your tweet means the line can be found by all those following. Twitter will record your interactions and allow you to see whenever anyone includes your @username, retweets or favourites your tweets, or begins to follow you. You also have a status page ('Me'), which offers your biography and your last few tweets. Bear in mind, however, that Twitter is a very public medium, all your previous tweets will be visible to anyone who follows you – as are your responses. You can 'direct message' those you follow who also follow you, but security is not complete. Prosecutions have occurred over the sharing of inappropriate information.

What to tweet:

- News;
- Opinions;
- Funny stories;
- Links you think others will find interesting;
- A daily tip;
- A link to your blog where new content is available;
- Links to competitions.

Top tips for making effective business use of Twitter

- Be part of the community; offer free help and advice; share useful links and others will do this for you. Remember to respond to @mentions.

- Be authentic and accessible: people engage with people they like. Don't auto-DM every new follower or schedule tweets in an obvious way. Be polite and informal but be yourself.
- Include a #hashtag theme in your tweet to make your ideas visible to all those following the relevant thread (although there is some discussion currently about removing hashtags).
- Upload pictures and make links with other web content you want to share. Twitter has become very visual over the past year, and is learning a lot in this respect from Pinterest.
- Practise strategic following. Follow people in your industry, people who use certain keywords in their biography, or even people who follow the people you follow. Some of these will follow you back. If they retweet you, it will introduce you to their followers.

In terms of how successful you are on Twitter, the number of followers is an obvious start, as well as notifications which tell you who has retweeted or favourited any of your content. You can also use metrics available to refine how you communicate further. For example, you can use www.twocation.com to find out where your followers are geographically, and this may give you indications as to what time zone you should be tweeting in (to find your followers awake) and in what currency to invoice. Look at your links (via Bitly) and look up your ranking.

Case study

Use of Twitter by an academic publishing house: Alastair Horne, social media and communities manager, Cambridge University Press

In the English language teaching (ELT) department of Cambridge University Press, the social media team is responsible for running the publisher's global social media accounts, and also works with the organisation's many local branches, offering support, guidance and content for the accounts they run in their own markets.

The Cambridge team views social media as a means of building a long-term relationship with their audience that goes far beyond marketing to include market research and customer support, with the ultimate aim of becoming part of that community's lives: it's about getting to know the audience (mostly teachers) better, establishing and maintaining a sense of trust in the Cambridge brand, and finding out what that audience wants and needs. Cambridge does this primarily by providing free content daily through its various social channels, from webinars with well-respected authors and educators, and thought-provoking blogposts, to excerpts from its many textbooks and guides to methodology.

Cambridge divides its social activity between third-party social platforms – principally Facebook and Twitter – and its own platforms, including Cambridge English Teacher, a professional development community for teachers, with its own blog and series of webinars. Third-party platforms offer considerable advantages – most notably that they already exist, and so don't require building at great expense; and as people already have accounts, they don't need to be persuaded to join up. However, they also make publishers heavily dependent on other businesses for their ability to reach their audience, which can create its own problems. Like most brands, Cambridge has seen a marked decline in its Facebook views over the past six months as Facebook increasingly encourages companies to pay for promoted posts to reach their fans. Increasingly, therefore, social media activity is focused on directing the audience towards platforms where interaction is not mediated through third parties: Cambridge's website, blog and webinar series.

Twitter plays an important part in Cambridge's social media activity. New blogposts and forthcoming webinars, for instance, are promoted regularly with tweets scheduled for different times of day to reach different audiences, and highlighting different aspects of the content, to interest different types of people. Customer queries are answered as swiftly as possible, and passed on where appropriate to the customer services department or relevant editor.

One of the most popular features of Cambridge's use of Twitter has been its live tweeting of events including webinars and conferences, offering those unable to attend in person an opportunity to keep up with what they're missing. These 140 character summaries of key points from talks are often among Cambridge's most retweeted and favourited tweets, and lead to a noticeable rise in followers.

In addition to sharing its own content, Cambridge also adds value to its Twitter feed by curating the best ELT content it finds online, and particularly from the accounts it follows back. Making sure to credit these discoveries to the original finders is not only best practice, but also emphasises that the relationship between the Press and its audience works both ways.

Like Facebook, Twitter is increasingly seeking to persuade companies to pay for premium access to potential customers, with options including promoted tweets and Twitter cards, and a recent Cambridge campaign around the launch of a new mobile app for Cambridge's bestselling self-study title *English Grammar in Use* marked the team's first use of these options. Timed to coincide with a two-day price promotion, the tweets targeted mobile users, pointing them towards a page that would send them to Apple's App Store, if they were using an Apple device. Android users were sent to a page where they could register their interest for that version of the app, to be launched a month later. The campaign not only prompted thousands of app purchases, but also saw the Press's Twitter account gain nearly 1,500 followers in 48 hours, an increase of almost 20 per cent.

Although Cambridge carefully monitors analytics to measure the success of posts and campaigns, not everything is easily explicable. Last year, the team took over responsibility for the publisher's Cambridge Dictionaries Online accounts, and immediately saw follower numbers rise on the Dictionaries' Facebook page from 60,000 to more than 1.5 million in under a year. Very little had changed when the team took over the account – most posts still comprised a 'Word of the Day' for students keen to extend their vocabulary, with an example sentence and link to an extended definition on the Dictionaries site. The page had simply hit critical mass in terms of its popularity, with each new follower increasing the likelihood of further followers signing up.

Case study

Using Twitter for a major marketing campaign: Katie Sadler of HarperCollins

Katie Sadler is digital marketing manager for Voyager (HarperCollins' science fiction list). She recently ran a second campaign for George R.R. Martin's fantasy epic *A Song of Ice and Fire* series (1996 onwards) published to coincide with its televised version as *Game of Thrones*. Twitter described it as 'the most engaging campaign they had ever seen', quoting an exceptionally high engagement rate of 18 per cent. How did she and her team do it?

We publish the five books (split into seven volumes) on which the *Game of Thrones* television series is based. So our market is anyone who loves *Game of Thrones* but has not yet read the books (or wants to recommend or share them with others). We know, both from our market research and from following conversations on Twitter, that the depth of characterisation and plots offered by the books really enhance an appreciation of the television series. Fans who have read the books tend to get quite irritated with those who lack this wider understanding of what is going on.

It's hard to generalise about the market, but the research carried out by our in-house consumer insight team has told us that viewers tend to be 25–30+ in age, and the audience for fantasy fiction is more weighted towards females than males.

This is the second year we have run a marketing campaign around the series. Last year we used a combination of Facebook, Google advertisements and Twitter, but this year we are running exclusively on Twitter, as we found this produced by far the best levels of engagement.

In the US, *Game of Thrones* airs on a Sunday night and so we both benefit from the energy created around the programme there, and feed this into the marketing that surrounds its airing in the UK the next evening. For example, we watch what's going on Twitter in the US, see what are the main quotes to emerge from each programme, and then commission a series of Tweet 'quote images' that show the quote in full, who said it and from which book it comes. These are then tweeted to the UK audience in the run-up to the Monday evening, shown during it, and then while the debate is going on afterwards. Given that the images are essentially pictures of text, in a designed and branded format that viewers find easy to spot, they enable us to share far more content than can be delivered in the 140 characters officially allowed – and because they take up more space in the Twitter timeline and are branded, they are easy to spot and hence are both responded to and retweeted. Conversations follow.

Conversation is also the way many fans respond to the series. As one fan commented:

[My friends and I] talk about it constantly, face to face, but also via WhatsApp – mostly after the programme has finished. I started off watching the series but am now catching up with the books, and my friends have all read them.

A big fan of the show herself, Katie manages the message content herself, as she is concerned that the quality of all the associated communications should reflect the epic nature of the books.

HarperCollins has several imprint Twitter accounts – another is Harper Impulse for their romance list – and this does enable a consistent voice and relationship with the audience to be developed. If you are tweeting about a range of titles, from children's books to gory horror titles it would be difficult to build consistent conversations.

But the despatch of her tweets, as well as the design and despatch of the 'quote images', are managed by the social media marketing and technology PR agency 33 Seconds, who also organise a digital spend to support the tweeting. Payment covers the tweeting of the 'quote images' to anyone who is currently following #gameofthrones or anyone who has used that hashtag in the past week. The campaign began a couple of weeks before the programmes went out and will continue until a week after it finishes, and offers a very directed spend reaching a market that is highly engaged.

The HarperCollins publicity team support their efforts by blogging on the main *Game of Thrones* website (www.westeros.org) from which smaller fan sites tend to take information, so one blog can cascade into a much larger

HarperVoyagerUK
@HarperVoyagerUK

If things carry on like this, there won't be anyone left in Westeros! Check out the first of our 3 #GoT infographics.

↩ Reply 🗑 Delete ★ Favorite ••• More

Figure 9.5 HarperCollins Game of Thrones tweet. Courtesy of HarperCollins.

online presence. Many enthusiasts buy in a linear fashion, moving from blog to online purchase, but the titles also sell well through conventional book-stores, and particularly well in airports. Associated sales figures won't be available until after the campaign finishes, but the company is certainly well satisfied with the results. Katie again:

> Considering the television series is in its fourth year, and the programmes are based on the first seven books, we are very happy with the sales.

And as the author's productivity shows no sign of slowing down (there are two more series titles in the pipeline) and as devotees his work tend to share their enthusiasm with great passion, future demand looks very healthy.

Author involvement online

Given the complexities of involvement online, some publishing houses manage the online presence of their authors, creating web pages for them within the organisational site and even organising social media involvement on their behalf. There are, however, many writers who now incorporate online activity within their creative process, and are active in online marketing – and involvement in these areas is increasingly significant in the commissioning decisions made by publishers.

All the opportunities itemised above apply to author marketing in the same way as they do to publishers, but it's worth isolating the particular risks and consequences of author involvement – and considering the most appropriate ways and times in which to be active to the cumulative benefit of work to be made available.

Having a presence online, and in particular using social media, can allow a writer to share information with their audience, to talk without being interrupted, to warm up for writing, to try out new ideas and get feedback – often very quickly. Having a blog can help writers avoid what is often suspected to be the over-mediation, assumptions or even elitism of the traditional industry, and offer the opportunity to gain a sense of the wider community potentially interested in their work.

But as the artist Jane Watt said: 'Just because the medium of a blog is acces-sible, unmediated and immediate, doesn't mean it is an easy thing to write.'[16] Writers need to take care with presentation, bearing in mind that writing material is a different skill from editing it, and the responsibility for what ultimately appears lies with the contributor:

> My website has an inbuilt fault that all websites have; it is edited only by me. I have always been at my best as a writer when I was edited by someone else.

Newspapers do that. Newspaper editors have this awkward habit of asking you what you mean, checking up to see whether you have got it right and they bring the whole force of the publication to bear on helping you to be better.

Clive James, writer and broadcaster speaking on Radio 4[17]

In addition to demanding support from a different bit of your brain (the ability to edit and create are quite different skills) – or perhaps the involvement of someone else in helping you finalise what appears – there are wider associated dangers. Blogging can result in sharing work at the *wrong* stage in writing development, airing ideas before you are ready to receive feedback or the associated product for sale is ready for distribution. It can also drain the energy from the writing you want to make available in the longer term; the activity is not only unpaid, it also risks reducing the audience's need to buy an associated product – the market may feel they know enough about you already. Blogging can also be *too* quick (the law still applies to what you write online) and as the writer is in sole charge, 'unmediated' can mean 'incomprehensible', inadvisable or illegal.

Why it might be a good idea to spend less time on social media

Not everyone sees being active online as a permanent and useful requirement. Disengaging from screens and forcing the brain to make its own synaptic links can yield great creativity and writers have often found physical activity to be a key part of their creative process. In the acknowledgements for her most recent novel, *NW*, author Zadie Smith paid credit to two internet applications that allow individuals to block online access other than at controlled and pre-agreed times and hence 'creating the time' in which to write.[18]

Sitting at a computer may not promote creativity. It's known that walking stimulates creative values and promotes cognitive function. Researchers at Stanford University have been conducting experiments that confirm the differences between those who walk versus those who sit, showing that the former are definitely more creative. And there are options other than online ones for gaining stimulus – author Carol Shields talked about how much she enjoyed being part of a 'Literary Theory Group' that met regularly for lunch. They never discussed what was in their title but found it an excellent stimulus for their shared writing goals – and a lot of fun. Alternatively you could encourage others to blog about your work or review the work online, or contribute to other edited formats such as newsletters and house journals.

I conclude this section with an interview with a writer who has decided to limit the time he spends online in order to promote his creative process, re-engaging at a time when messages can be usefully spread in promotion of a product to which his publishers and he commit together. In a world sated with online information and opportunities to share, and where publishers need to think about their role in supporting material that is both esteemed worthy and will last, it's a useful model for consideration.

Case study

An interview with author Chris Cleave

Chris Cleave is a writer. His debut novel *Incendiary* won the Somerset Maugham Award. His second, the Costa-shortlisted *The Other Hand* (known as *Little Bee* in the USA and Canada) was a *Sunday Times* bestseller and a *New York Times* #1 bestseller, with 3 million copies in print. His third, *Gold*, was a global bestseller and his new novel is due out in 2014.

An early adopter of social media, he initially maintained that while his publisher promoted his novels, his presence online was to keep the relationship with his readers going in between books. He established and managed a thoughtful website from which he ran a regular blog, sent engaged replies to those who emailed him about his work and was active on Twitter. The past year has seen a complete change. While he dropped out of Facebook a while ago, over the past 12 months he has completely ceased using other social media: the Twitter account has been dormant; the website untended; emails batched and responded to – but often long after receipt.

The result? A new book of which he is by his own admission 'pretty proud' that has taken him a year to write (a third of the time taken to write the previous one); a tighter writing style that more often feels 'right first time'; a strong awareness that his approach to writing feels more focused; a personal life that feels calmer and happy. This interview explores how this happened, and why other writers too might decide to spend less time and energy on social media.

By his own admission, Chris had always been an 'accommodating author', willing to support his publishers through engaging with readers and taking part in planned activities. For each book he went on a series of long promotional tours (the last book resulted cumulatively in 9 months away), the rigours of the schedule permitting no down or writing time. His publishers similarly encouraged his habit of replying to readers and maintaining a general presence through social media.

Facebook was the first thing to go. He had experimented but eventually found that 'if you get a measure of success it's very difficult to post anything you care about without it attracting stalking responses'. Increasingly he found he couldn't use Facebook for its intended purpose – that of having an extended circle of friends – and having to separate himself from the person he presented, by only posting contributions that were devoid of any material he genuinely cared about, seemed false.

He did, however, continue to update his website each day with his location and a brief summary of activity ('Today I am writing'), adding short journalistic pieces as blogs for wider comment. Plans to offer space to guest bloggers were never activated due to shortage of time and it became too easy for involvement with the website to promote the erosion of his writing time, 'allowing friends to become part of the working day'.

Twitter he got on well with. 'The medium promotes short pithy expression and this initially aligns well with the role of the writer; you can be yourself. But there is a big difference between crafting 140 characters and 100,000 words for a novel', and the drain of energy and attention for the former did not improve the latter. In any case he was not sure in the long term that it was needed. 'My readers don't need to hear from me daily, what they want is the best book I can produce when it is ready.'

Overall, as these various commitments online grew, he was finding his time consistently under pressure; the personal administration of life plus maintaining the constant commitment that social media required was draining both his energy and time for writing. With his long-term preference for only taking on what he can do really well, he felt spread too thinly. Increasingly he wanted to push at the limits of his writing, to be free to imagine and develop characters, and that heavy involvement in social media was not helping him to get better. He came to the conclusion that 'it's the writer's job to do the best possible work they can', and that social media was a blockage.

The growing realisation that something had to give to make room for him to produce his best work he could was translated into action from a hotel bedroom in San Francisco. 'I could not drop my commitment to my writing, my family or my publisher, so something had to go.' The response was radical. He physically disabled the Wi-Fi on his laptop, restoring a more appropriate hierarchy of control, with technology supporting his writing rather than barking instructions. He also gave up alcohol, obsessive exercise and mindfully began to rework himself to be better able to address the very difficult task of crafting fine writing.

It's perhaps not insignificant that this repurposing was accompanied by his fortieth birthday – and an awareness that writing was as important to him now as when he started. Now, however, it was time to be the best writer he could be, not just as good as possible, and taking control of his time meant the best part of the day could be preserved for writing.

The website remains as a space for reactivation in future, for the promoting part of the writing life he accepts still exists, and to which he will return to support the efforts of his publishers when the time is right. Given that it already has an associated community, it can also be offered in future as a space for guest blogging, to help nascent writers whose work he appreciates, and he admires other writers who find the time to do that. He has not blogged during the period of writing his latest book but the construct remains for use later on – particularly valuable now that he no longer works as a journalist.

Wider involvement online he avoids. He used to be a regular contributor to Goodreads, but stopped participating after it was bought by Amazon, finding an ethical difficulty in a corporation buying a community – an 'intellectual land-grab'.

Looking wider, he questions the ethos of social media as it 'promotes an inevitable regression towards the mean'. The process of submitting both self and ideas to an internet consensus is not thought-provoking; rather it is 'dissipating energy and preventing non-canonical thought in a profound way'.

Challenging the traditional notion that the internet is broadening to the mind, he suspects it rather closes it down, blocking the writer's ability to think new thoughts, 'submitting yourself to a low level consensus; the highly opinionated views of others on fragments of work or passing ideas that in no way represent the whole person or work that is being developed'. He claims that the writer who wants to be producing work worth reading needs to concentrate 'not on the high-frequency, low-intensity communication, but rather on low-frequency, high-intensity work'. He wants to be free to push his work in whatever direction he feels appropriate, to make it as weird as he chooses it to be and available when he feels it is ready, unencumbered by group opinions on what he should write next from the community active on social media, which is not – in any case – his entire readership. He feels the writer has to be a solitary individual, a lone wolf, engaging with the collective when the book is ready for wider sharing, but the decision on when at their sole disposal.

He remains convinced that thought needs to be deeply developed and no longer has the desire to be involved in short and intense dialogues during the working day. He also questions the honesty of social media that encourages the appearance of friendship to many; the promotion of a false loyalty, when it is impossible to be a friend to everyone. He feels he can contribute more honestly by plying his trade, writing and producing the best work he can.

He has stopped doing many of the things that had become expected of him: accepting every interview offered; offering pithy quotes to journalists who require an urgent range of opinions; blogging about his life and work; the 'low level administration that could take all day if you let it'. Rather he thought carefully about how other writers had put themselves in a position whereby they could develop their craft and make proper time for their writing. 'It's a problem for writers that we are embedded in civilian life' and you need to find a method of getting away to concentrate on the writing: 'If you were trying to climb an 8,000-foot mountain without oxygen people would understand that you couldn't carry additional baggage.'

Email he remains alert to, noting when the tone of voice changes from polite alerts to urgent reminders with consequences, but in general he now batches it up for block responses rather than feeling he must respond immediately. Each day he gets about 100 emails that divide into spam, things that need routine responses and can be dealt with quickly and emails that require engaged feedback. He found those contacting him quickly got used to the changed situation and now know that he will respond, just not with as rapid a reply as they may originally have expected.

He questions the way publishing houses have begun to measure the success of their marketing operations. Judging their contribution through metrics such as the extent to which they are successful in persuading authors like him to participate in social media and to extend author/publisher branding promotes short-term attention rather than necessarily enhancing long-term appreciation for a writer's work.

Finally he questioned the idea of 'the writing career', rather viewing each book as a separate entity prompted by particular circumstances and created by an individual during a specific period of time. But while resisting the notion of his own writing career, the rededication to his craft feels similarly single-minded. His routine is now to rise early for a couple of hours' writing, to manage five to six hours once his three children have gone to school and then to finish around 3pm for a restorative potter – in preparation for the following day.

Henceforth he affirms the solitude of the writer and wants to avoid collective comment. He rejects the bullying consensus of new media, 'the forces that weigh you down rather than liberate you to think and write', and seeks to concentrate on developing a dialogue with readers in a different way – 'through a beautiful novel that is as good as it can be' rather than sharing random thoughts on Twitter. From now on he (and his longstanding agents, Peter Straus and Jennifer Joel) will decide whether his work is any good or not, and when it is ready for sharing.

In short, Cleave is using a ruthless re-examination of his allocation of time as an opportunity to make himself into the best writer he can be – and at the same time to consciously pursue a more thoughtful and honest way of living. From our long and fascinating discussion, I would say there is strong evidence that this is working.

Concluding case study

The future of online marketing, by Jon Reed

Jon Reed writes about and teaches social media marketing. He is the author of *Get Up to Speed with Online Marketing* (www.getuptospeed.biz) and runs the blog Publishing Talk (www.publishingtalk.eu). He previously worked in publishing for 10 years, including as publishing director for McGraw-Hill.

> We've come a long way in a short space of time. When I started in publishing (20 years ago, at Routledge, the publishers of this book), the internet was new and many of us didn't even have email. Now online marketing is a routine part of any marketing strategy – and social media has become the way we do that. Social media as we know it has only been around since 2006 – the year Facebook opened to the public,

Google bought YouTube, and Twitter launched. These services are now a part of daily life for many people. All media is becoming social, and all our social lives are becoming mediated, on the go, with Instagramed selfies and a running commentary on Twitter. The trends that led to this explosion in social media – in both technology and culture – look set to continue.

The global online population is now around two billion people – and more than half of them are on Facebook. Twitter is catching up fast.[19] More people will come online in the coming years, as online access becomes seen more as an essential utility than a technological luxury. These people will join the global conversations taking place on social media. More people, more users – more readers.

The way people access the internet is also changing. Outside the US and UK, 60 per cent of internet access is now mostly mobile.[20] Widespread use of smartphones has led not only to wider internet access but is a major driver of the adoption of social media, as we post status updates and images on the go using apps.

Hand-in-hand with mobile access to social media is the growth of the visual web, facilitated by speedy connections and a camera in every pocket. Now that we can take decent quality pictures from our phones and upload the images to Facebook, Twitter and Instagram with a few taps, we're doing so. It is notable that two of the most successful newer platforms – Instagram (2010) and Pinterest (2011) – are visual tools. There's a lot of noise to cut through online, and images help you to stand out – including on the more established platforms Facebook and Twitter, where images are now far more prominent than they once were.

Pinterest has quickly become the most successful social bookmarking site because it is a visual one. Used by writers to create mood boards, and publishers to create themed promotions, is it is a virtual pin-board that promotes a visual lifestyle that others want to 're-pin' on to their own boards. It is used particularly well by Penguin Books, for example (www.pinterest.com/penguinbooksusa). But even if you don't want to use Pinterest, you can benefit from it simply by including images on your web pages and blog posts. Images make it possible for people to 'pin' your content on their own boards, which others can click through from, like and share. And it's not all glossy lifestyle images: if you publish academic texts, infographics created around your content are popular and pinnable.

Video is also becoming easier, thanks to smartphones and cheap handheld video cameras. Short, six-second looping videos are shared on Vine,[21] and up to 15-second ones on Instagram.[22] While you currently still need a higher-end video camera, and to learn to use video editing software, if you want to create anything professional-looking, these barriers will continue to reduce.

We will see more hashtag campaigns, as these now apply not only to Twitter but across social networks, including Facebook, Google+, Pinterest and Instagram. At the time of writing, HarperCollins is running a month-long campaign (throughout June 2014) to promote its new imprint Borough Press, with the hashtag #bookaday.[23] With a different nominated theme each day, my Twitter and Instagram timelines are filling up with pictures of my friends' favourite books, from 'Best bargain' to 'One with a blue cover' to 'The one I always give as a gift'.

The growth in social media is not just due to technology: it is also about culture. Today we trust 'people like me' rather than companies and institutions. Just as a cover quote is worth more than a publisher's blurb, word-of-mouth peer recommendations are more powerful than anything you could say yourself. The advent of social media is a revolution in the way content is produced, shared and consumed. Bottom-up rather than top-down, in the laptops of the many rather than the printing presses of the few, and inextricably bound up with the future of publishing. The growing reach of social media has coincided with the boom in digital publishing and, more recently, self-publishing – the biggest trend in publishing to date. This heady mix of digitisation, democratisation and disintermediation cannot be ignored.

I've seen publishing from all sides: as a print book publisher, as an author with a traditional publishing house, and as a digital self-published author. The future of online marketing is bright, visual, mobile – and growing. But it is also open to authors as well as publishers. And the online tools available to them are not just marketing tools but self-publishing tools too.

Publishers therefore need to think carefully about where they can add value to the process. This can include help with social media, from setting up author blogs and websites, help with the more challenging forms of content creation such as video, or social media training.

Social media is mainstream and part of your readers' daily lives. But it's not just about which tools you use: it's how you use them. Coming up with smart, imaginative marketing campaigns that engage your target audience and make them want to share your content is just as important. Connecting with readers where they are already spending their time is how the successful marketing campaigns of the future will be built.

Notes

1 Hence insistence in many organisations that before setting up an arrangement to do business in future, a physical relationship must be established between the potential partners – to check they are capable of delivering what is advertised online.

2 Blog at www.webinknow.com. The associated book – *The New Rules of Marketing and PR: How to Use Social Media, Online Video, Mobile Applications, Blogs,*

News Releases, and Viral Marketing to Reach Buyers Directly – has a clever title. Itemising the variety of different methods of communicating online means it is likely to score highly in SEO and be picked up in a variety of customer word searches.

3 Evan Le Page, http://blog.hootsuite.com/social-media-tips-to-enhance-your-content-marketing.

4 www.bitly.com.

5 www.hootsuite.com.

6 www.PoweredBySearch.com.

7 The principle is named after the Italian economist who pointed out in 1806 that in Italy, 80 per cent of the land was owned by 20 per cent of the population and developed the principle further. Today this is also known as the 80–20 rule, or law of the vital few, on the basis that roughly 80 per cent of effects come from 20 per cent of causes.

8 www.bookmachine.co.uk.

9 www.tutorialspoint.com/management_concepts/the_rule_of_seven.htm.

10 http://marketingland.com/mobile-devices-generate-30-pct-traffic-15-pct-e-sales-75498.

11 www.calliopegifts.co.uk.

12 www.bikinilists.com.

13 www.toddle.com.

14 www.mailchimp.com.

15 http://ooligan.pdx.edu.

16 *Projects Unedited* www.a-n.co.uk/artists_talking.

17 BBC Radio 4, *Heresy*, 2009.

18 www.dailymail.co.uk/news/article-2196718/Zadie-Smith-pays-tribute-software-BLOCKS-internet-sites-allowing-write-new-book-distractions.html#ixzz35iGy6MHJ.

19 www.statisticbrain.com/twitter-statistics.

20 http://marketingland.com/outside-us-60-percent-internet-access-mostly-mobile-74498.

21 http://vine.co/

22 http://instagram.com

23 www.boroughpress.co.uk/blog/bookaday.

10 Publicity and PR

The practicalities of dealing with the media 258
The recipient – understanding journalists 260
The role of the press release 263
Offering an exclusive 268
Review lists 269
Literary editors 271
Inspection copies 273
Author interviews 273
How to sell ideas to journalists by email and telephone 276

Features and reviews of books in the media are one of the most influential ways of promoting purchase. Coverage is important to almost every kind of reader, from academics noting reviews in a journal they respect to general readers in a bookshop (on- or offline) turning to the back cover to see which newspapers or columnists have endorsed it. For some material it is not even important that the coverage is favourable; negative coverage can do tremendous things for sales.

Coverage in the media is often dubbed 'free advertising'. But even if you set no value on your own time, done well it takes an immense amount of time and effort. This chapter is devoted to telling you how to go about it.

Opportunities for media coverage go far wider than their traditional location on the book review pages. As well as the traditional section-heads (home and foreign news, features), other specialist sections are growing too (cookery, travel, family, gardening, home) – and these are echoed in opportunities in broadcast media too.

The internet has also vastly increased the possibilities for both specific and mass market coverage, in as many specific fields as there is publishing output – and each community is likely to have its own specific forum(s), whether on- or offline, official or independent.

In all these locations, presented as editorial content (rather than as an advertisement), you have the chance to inform and re-orientate popular debate, or simply to spread information by word-of-mouth. Similarly, getting authors on to 'talk shows' or news programmes as an expert can make a tremendous difference to their public image and interest in their material. When coverage is harnessed (as it always should be) to information on the associated product or service available for purchase, you should achieve the real aim: larger sales.

The practicalities of dealing with the media

Who liaises with the media?

The large general publishing houses usually have a team of specialist press officers or publicists that liaises with the media on behalf of a variety of lists. There are also specialist press and PR agencies and it's common for large campaigns to be contracted out to them. In smaller houses, this is a job that generally falls to the marketing department.

What you need to succeed in dealing with the media

The personal attributes for dealing with the media are an effective combination of determination, charm and originality. This needs to be supported by knowledge and belief in the range of products being promoted (whether it's a physical entity or access to an individual, the need for an assured presentation is essential) and an ability to summarise a complex argument in a couple of sentences, a skill that can be particularly hard for publicists working for academic or technical publishers. An ability to think on your feet is also important, so that an alternative idea or scenario can be put forward if the first suggestion is rejected. Creativity and imagination are vital in order for the ideas to feel fresh and innovative. Finally, a good memory is a big asset – for particular journalistic and author preferences or what has worked well or gone wrong before.

When to start pursuing coverage

The best time for thinking about media coverage is early in a title's development. Radio and TV series are commissioned at least a year in advance, and the lead time is often longer for television. Literary festivals start planning some 6 months in advance. Magazines, newspaper features pages, radio magazine programmes work around 2 to 4 months in advance. Author tours, competitions, entry for literary prizes and other publicity-promoting initiatives are also best thought about well in advance as they take a lot of planning. Social media by contrast usually needs to be planned early but implemented late as those who pick up on something online tend to want it to be available immediately – it can however work well for longer-term teaser campaigns, to build up demand and pre-orders – see Chapter 9.

If you are liaising with authors you will have their long-term commitments to consider too; the author publicity form should have alerted them to what kind of involvement may be needed. Of course having written a book does not necessarily make them fluent speakers, but it does generally mark them out as experts of some kind. Whereas in the past authors may have preferred to leave it to their publishers to organise publicity, working through an established range of publications and broadcast channels, a process of media fragmentation[1] has made it much harder to predict where an audience is likely to be spending time. Today authors generally understand that their help is vital in getting their work better known – and a requirement to contribute to marketing their work is increasingly included within their contract.

Whom to contact

Planning press coverage is easiest if you have an existing network of media contacts with whom you are in touch on a regular basis. It is a good idea to make a list of all the publications and programmes likely to be significant to your list, and to find out the name of the features, news or production editor. Ring up and introduce yourself, confirm that they are the right person to send information to, and check the address and spelling of their name. Ask if you can meet the most important contacts – suggest you treat them to a coffee or lunch: it will be easier selling ideas if your face is already known. PR specialist Ruth Killick[2] comments:

> I can't overestimate the importance of personal contacts. Journalists get literally hundreds of emails a day. Why are they going to bother opening yours? You can send out dozens of pitch emails (and feel comforted that you've 'done something') but on their own it probably won't generate much (unless you have a star author or are yourself someone the journalist already knows and trusts). Don't be shy of getting on the phone! It's amazing how many publicists don't.

Your list of contacts might include:

- national daily newspapers;
- national Sunday newspapers;
- local and regional newspapers;
- specialist newspapers (e.g., the religious or educational press);
- free-sheets (from city newspapers distributed at transport hubs to pickups within specified locations);
- national monthly consumer magazines;
- news weeklies;
- special interest magazines;
- B2B (business-to-business publications, including professional journals);
- contract magazines (magazines produced on behalf of an organisation, e.g., titles for supermarket customers bearing the organisational brand);
- society and membership journals, often free with a subscription;
- alternative press (e.g., independent titles, often produced by pressure groups or lobbyists, generally working on low resources towards a collective goal);
- national and local radio;
- national and local TV;
- digital and online publications (all the sub categorisations listed above apply here too);
- blogs (ditto).

Details of formally published titles can be found in databases and media publications. For online publications, society membership magazines and blogs it may be a case of discovering relevant media opportunities through online searches. For each publication, however, there will almost certainly be an associated website where more information can be found, including details of whom they consider to be their audience. You can learn a lot about them from the way in which they write about themselves. You may also be able to see back issues, which will give you a sense of their scope and format.

If you are starting completely from scratch, or are particularly short of time, one way to get information out to the press is to subscribe to the services of a media agency. For an annual subscription you will receive access to a website that lists all the press names you might need. You can then get in touch whenever you want to send out a press release – you won't own the list, but you can access it whenever you want. Although this will give you a pleasingly large number of destinations for your press releases, in the long run it's a good idea to develop your own list of personal contacts to whom you can send information you know will be of interest – and then follow up with a phone call.

Don't just pursue contacts in the media that you read or watch yourself – and don't let your own reading prejudices get in the way. Try to get into the habit of buying a variety of different papers to see the kind of opportunities for coverage that they offer; watch and listen to broadcast programmes of all kinds; pick a theme about which you know relatively little and search online for information. What you observe may surprise you. For example, mass market newspapers have more regular book-buyers among their readers than the 'quality' press, simply because their circulations are bigger – and they are also often quite inventive in how they run a book story. The Richard & Judy[3] promotion in the UK showed that, contrary to many assumptions, the viewers of chat shows are big book-buyers.

Remember to send copies of your press information to the news agencies (e.g., Reuters and the Press Agency) – they may feed it to many different regional papers. The local papers or radio station in an author's hometown will almost certainly want to do a feature too.

Whatever system you decide on for the management of your lists (in-house or out-of-house) do keep a basic point of reference available and ready to refer to at all times. Be very methodical about recording ideas that particular contacts have responded well or badly to in the past, their particular interests, days off, deadline days, the best times to contact and so on.

The recipient – understanding journalists

> You have to remember that there are two kinds of people, those who do things and the drones who carp about what has been done. Those I interview tend to be doers. Journalists are drones.
>
> Jeremy Paxman, journalist[4]

If you are going to get coverage for published content, it is almost certain that the ideas presented will be mediated – most usually by a journalist. The journalist(s) to whom material is either given, or passed on, will make a range of decisions from whether it merits coverage at all to how the story is presented, so it's worth spending some time thinking about how best to communicate with them as a species. Here is Joanna Prior, a publisher who had a brief sojourn at *The Sunday Telegraph*, before returning to publishing as publicity director at Penguin, commenting on the experience:

> It is the most cut-throat, uncaring and tough environment I can imagine. Teamwork is not something they are into. Journalists like the mystique, [to give the impression] that when they are being rude on the phone it's because there is something very important happening.

Now she understands press deadlines. 'We expect far too much of journalists – we expect them to read our books', she says. Now she knows that pressure of work means that they will not read anything on spec. She knows that pitches should be made in the morning when journalists are able to listen, and not panicking about the day's stories. Her experience has made her more aware of editors' priorities. 'One revelation was how uninterested they are in their readers. They care about numbers, they care about circulation.'[5]

This was written about working at the extreme end of the profession, on a prestigious magazine supplement with a large readership and in a hugely competitive market. But although journalists may be operating under a variety of different pressure levels, in a range of different roles, there are several issues that can be extracted from this:

- **Journalists will see those contacting them in the hope of coverage as PRs rather than publishers.** This is not a compliment. Associate professor Beth Brewster[6] comments: 'Journalists are irritated by those who relentlessly pursue them with the same idea, over and over again. They are immune to the "charms" of the PR, whom they see as a regrettable necessity rather than a friend.'
- **Journalists operate in an atmosphere of constant busyness.** They can come over as abrasive if not rude – or just otherwise engaged (eating or typing while on the phone are both common).
- **Journalists want special treatment.** They like things made particular to their format/needs and for the material you present to be available to them exclusively. In return, if a stronger story comes along, they will change their minds about featuring yours – or have the decision made for them by their bosses. Ruth Killick: 'Journalists don't see it as their job to promote your product. It's up to you to make it attractive to them.'
- **Journalists expect you to know their format and market really well,** as well as what they have recently covered. Even if their publication is not mainstream or their programme on at a time of day when a working person could not be expected to catch it, they will expect you to know. So ensure you are familiar

with the audience they approach and their viewing figures *before* you get in touch. Beth Brewster comments: 'What journalists hate is PRs approaching them with ideas that would never run in their publication. Journalism is a carefully targeted product with a very specific readership.'

- **Journalists see their role as keeping their readers or viewers interested** and hence continuing to buy or remain tuned in to their particular format. It follows that their job is not (as is widely assumed) to tell their readership the latest news, but to tell it from the viewpoint of their particular readership, to find stories that reinforce their readers' and viewers' sense of valuing the publication or programme and feeling part of the associated community.
- **Journalists specialise.** There are editors, programmers, writers of features/news/leaders/comment pieces – and many more roles. All want to be fed information on stories according to their particular speciality based on what you know they have covered in the past. So a weekly columnist, a gossip columnist and a leader writer will have very different requirements. Having written the information for them, in a format they will find easy to absorb, the risk is that they then present the finished piece with *their* byline at the bottom, failing to mention the product or service being promoted, and which provided the starting point for the story you sent them.
- **Journalists are ambitious.** They want to see the story they present highlighted in the eventual format, so the more ways in which you can help them do this, the better (offer a list of interesting anecdotes; an effective and as yet unused quotation from someone relevant; an eye-grabbing photograph opportunity; a short quiz).

So it follows that they want relevant stories with:

- **Emotion.** Beth Brewster: 'Journalism is about what makes people tick'; a story that attracts empathy from the readership in question. As famous newspaper editor John Junor said: 'An ounce of emotion is worth a ton of fact.'
- **Absorbability.** An author or their publisher can probably think of many reasons why their work is fascinating, but these will have to be condensed into a pithy format before they are passed on to a journalist. Remember the information you offer will have to be re-communicated many times – to section/programme heads, producers, editors and others. It will survive best if it is slimmed down to its essentials.
- **Examples and quotes.** If you are telling them a story, they will need examples of how this works in practice – because readers and viewers find it easier to engage with an issue if there are accompanying (and preferably photogenic) examples. They will need empathetic individuals who can be quoted (or are available to talk), statistics that can be absorbed easily (fractions or percentages are easier to hear than numbers).
- **Relevance for their readers and viewers.** You need to think about who their readers are, what they want to know and how you can assist the journalist or publication in giving them what they want.

How to please a journalist, by Beth Brewster

- Offer well-placed, and preferably exclusive, story ideas that fit their audience.
- Suggest interesting ideas for coverage (the chance to meet a relevant interviewee somewhere unusual; access to a building or point of view that is not generally available).
- Make yourself into the expert – do the research for them, go the extra mile.
- Join the conversation – via social media, tweet links to their pieces (not just about your products) showing that you are interested in their opinion and will work with them to extend the coverage they offer.
- Thank them afterwards. It's a simple courtesy.

How to irritate a journalist:

- Offer them a story as an exclusive that you have pitched to other people at the same time. They will not trust you again. If you are offering a story as an exclusive, do so to one medium at a time, giving a deadline for an expression of interest and waiting to hear back before offering it again.
- Offer a story with no sources (finding their own, with nothing to go on, is harder work).
- Supply quotes that aren't attributable (so can't be used; they then have to find their own) or quotes from people who are not available for interview (cannot be checked, or built upon to ensure their story is different from the line other journalists are taking).
- Press releases that are sent out by someone who then goes away on holiday (so the story cannot be followed up). For this reason, give the names of two people who are able to provide more information on the story, and give their mobile numbers so they can be called out of hours.
- No contact phone number (can't follow up on the story).
- Undated press release (so you don't know how old it is).
- Ring at the wrong time. The best time for catching them at their desk seems to be after about 10.30am until about 12.45pm, then from about 2.45pm until 4.30pm (although not in the afternoon for daily papers). It isn't that those are the only times they work, just that those times provide the best opportunities of catching them at their desks and willing to talk to you.

The role of the press release

A campaign for coverage usually starts with the sending of a press release to a list of journalists, often tailored to the specific needs of the recipient. This is often followed by telephone calls to try to secure definite features or other promises of coverage.

The press release will probably go out as an email attachment, but you will need printed copies to go out with review copies of books and to hand out as and when you meet relevant people. Never assume that just because you have sent a journalist a piece of information once, they will either remember or hang on to it. Journalists are inundated and as it is you who want something from them (coverage), the onus is on you to give them what they need in order to be able to write about your title – even if you have sent it to them before.

If you are charged with preparing a press release, what should it say? The most important point is that a press release should contain news. It is far more likely to be the news value or topicality of the subject matter that appeals to the journalist, rather than the fact that another book has been written. News is like infection, it should get passed on quickly.

Don't devalue the impact of your press releases by producing them too often or sending them to the wrong homes. If you send information 'just in case', journalists will almost certainly take a similarly marginal view. The danger is that they may then devalue what you send in future. Don't feel you have to justify your role by sending out press releases to as many possible homes as possible. A targeted, bespoke pitch to a publication central to your market may be worth far more than a scattergun approach.

How to write a press release

A press release should tempt the recipient to want to know more, but provide sufficient coherent information for inclusion should they decide to use it straight away.

Press releases get read (and often used) from the top downwards, so the information needs to be presented in a similar order. Sub-editors, especially those on regional papers or local radio, may have gaps to fill and be looking for copy. If your information is succinct and sufficiently interesting it may get used whole (in which case it will be cut from the bottom upwards).

The first couple of paragraphs of the release should tell the basic story (who, what, where, why and when?). Follow the initial explanation with an expansion of your arguments, illustrated with examples from what you are promoting. Tell enough of the story to make the journalist want to know more, but not so much that there is no angle left to discover.

- Consider organisational fit. Will the message you are sending detract from or add impact to the overall brand you seek to create, whether you are a publisher, an author or from another stakeholder within the industry?
- Aim for pithy and interesting – and a maximum two pages. One is even better.
- Cover the basics: date of publication, author information, publisher and contact details (at least two people should be available to provide more information and give their phone numbers – mobile and landlines – and email addresses). Ensure the date includes year of publication in case the book gets put to one side for use later. Correct information saves the journalist time and makes it more likely that your material will be used. If they have to stop and make a call they may not bother.

- Keep language simple and avoid jargon. Use short sentences and avoid hackneyed adjectives: 'leading', 'unique', 'world-beating'. Keep tenses consistent: past, present or future. Check spelling and grammar – recipients really do care.
- Provide a list – ten things you did not know about. Offering information in a variety of formats (headline, body copy, list of bullet points, photograph and interesting caption) can help the journalist extend the coverage they get.
- Offer a list of questions and answers to give people an idea of what's in the book, or a crib sheet for radio interviewers who won't have time to prepare. Any additional material sent with a press release can make the whole package more useful to the recipient.
- Find out when the 'copy day' is (i.e., when publication is sent to press or the decision about programme content made) and target material accordingly (to arrive just before it). For example, for a Sunday paper, Friday is a very good day for news material to arrive. Other sections of the paper may have gone to press by then, so features need to be negotiated much further ahead.
- As with all promotional formats, the conventional can bore, whereas the attitudinal sound-bite or quirky approach may attract attention.
- Adding an embargo date to your release means every journalist has the same chance to prepare the story before publication; no one should print the information before that date and 'scoop' their rivals (very important if you have sold serial rights). The release (or the date) risks being ignored for precisely the same reasons.

How to write an effective headline

The biggest mistake publishers make here is to assume the book title is the headline, and then to start the body copy by saying how pleased they are to be publishing it. Think again. Consider the news contained in the story, ask a question, extract a

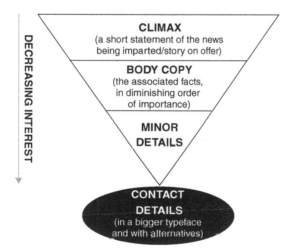

Figure 10.1 Diagram of how a press release can be effectively structured.

JOHN BLAKE

The true story of one of the most unlikely friendships to come out of apartheid South Africa

MANDELA
My Prisoner, My Friend

By Christo Brand

John Blake Publishers
Hardback £17.99
3rd March 2014

Christo Brand is in the UK and available for interview from 27th – 6th February

Author event & book signing at Waterstone's Piccadilly on March 3rd at 7pm

Christo was just 18 and Nelson Mandela 60 when Christo was first appointed as Mandela's prison guard on Robben Island. Their friendship began from this unlikely point through acts of small kindness on both sides, continuing when Mandela was moved to a prison in Cape Town, where Christo and Mandela would play hours of ping pong together in secret and Christo would be sent on missions to buy Mandela's favourite hair cream, Christo taught Mandela Afrikaans to help his political career and also brought in planters and seeds so that Mandela could start his own garden.

When Mandela cooked with food he had grown himself in prison he would share it with Christo and when Mandela was ill Christo would be the one to take him to the hospital. Christo also broke all the rules by smuggling Mandela's granddaughter into prison so Mandela could hold her in his arms, he also knew of the mental anguish Mandela went through in being separated from his family, as it was Christo's job to read and censor each and every letter sent to or received by Mandela on Robben Island.

Then when Mandela's prison sentence was relaxed and he started to meet with government officials and dignitaries, Christo accompanied him on each of these visits, seeing first-hand how the country he lived in was beginning to take a new direction. When Mandela was freed he arranged for Christo to have a job in parliament. At state meetings, if Christo was there, Mandela would introduce Christo to each and every delegate as a friend and a great man. Christo was one of only a very few white people to be invited to Mandela's private funeral and continues to be a great friend of the Mandela family

In his book, *Long Walk to Freedom*, Mandela wrote that during his time in prison the most important person in any prisoner's life was not the Minister of Justice, not the Commissioner of Prisons, not even the head of prison, but the warder in one's section and Christo was that warder.

The story that Christo has to tell is one that no one has heard about. It is the story of what it was like day to day for Mandela to be in prison, how he got through it, and how his time in prison helped him to change the world.

For further information please contact Tory Lyne-Pirkis at Midas PR
tory.lyne-pirkis@midaspr.co.uk / 020 7361 7860

10 - 14 Old Court Place, Kensington, London, W8 4PL Tel: +44 (0)20 7361 7860 Fax: +44 (0)20 7938 1268
E mail: info@midaspr.co.uk www.midaspr.co.uk

Figure 10.2 Sample press release for *Mandela: My Prisoner, My Friend* by Christo Brand. Courtesy of John Blake/Midas PR.

stimulating example of the point you are making. Talk about the story, not the organisation. So, for example, to launch a new book on typefaces, rather than:

PROFILE BOOKS IS DELIGHTED TO ANNOUNCE PUBLICATION OF A NEW BOOK ABOUT FONTS

try instead:

What do the Beach Boys have in common with easyJet and Ikea?

or:

Comic Sans not your type? How we learned to lighten up.[7]

Supporting quotes

All journalists want quotes to support the story they write, so it's helpful if you provide them, enabling them to reinforce their argument without having to go look for further amplification (useful if they are in a hurry). What they don't want is to feel that every angle of the story you are offering has already been explored. So if you include quotes:

- give the name of the source (it's good practice for journalists to attribute all sources, so if you don't tell them they will have to spend time finding out);
- don't provide too many;
- remember that an interesting quote from the author can be effective, prompting the journalist to suggest an interview.

If you are absolutely sure where you want your information to appear, tailor your approach to an individual medium. Ring and discuss the prospect of a 'special' and 'exclusive' feature with your editorial or production contact, offering sole access if they move quickly. Such a call may also establish how a particular format wants information presented, and suggest the angle from which your title will be considered. The easier it is for a paper's staff to assimilate your material, the more likely it is to be used. Make reference to what else they have done recently, to extend a story that appealed to their readership in the first place.

In addition to getting editorial coverage, there are also lots of opportunities for getting images used. And don't forget that the trade press in particular likes to receive relevant pictures.

> ## Top ten tips for getting images into the trade press, from *The Bookseller*
>
> - Make the images interesting. Four people lined up with drinks in their hands is not interesting. Editors of the trade press do not want their pages to look like wallpaper!

- Send them in at the right time. Unsurprisingly, the main seasons for launching books are when most images get sent to the trade press. So be imaginative about when you send them in. In January, Easter and the summer holidays journalists are often actively searching for images, so you stand a good chance of being included if you approach then.
- Send the image in the right format. About 70 per cent of the images received cannot be used because the resolution is too low. Use at least 300 dpi.
- Close-ups are more interesting than long shots, unless the building is particularly significant (and if so, say why).
- Say who is in the image – and be specific. Don't assume the magazine knows who the marketing director is, however well-known he or she is within your company. Ensure all names are spelt right – if it is wrong, it's the journalist who gets the blame.
- Submit a caption too. The publication may or may not use it, but it gives a starting point on how to write about the image sent. Avoid in-jokes that only you understand.
- Be exclusive. Don't send the same image to competitors without telling them (in which case it probably won't get included). If you are sending it just to one publication, say it is exclusive, and it is much more likely to be featured.
- The trade press likes images that reflect the whole trade, so if you can line up your author with a bookseller, or member of the publisher's staff, that is great. They like to reflect all jobs, so don't assume an image has to be of the great and good within your organisation – it's good to have pictures of the more junior staff too.
- They would love more images of promotional highlights, 'screen grabs' or stills from television advertising or features. This is an excellent way to extend the coverage you have already paid for – but not often thought of by publicists.
- By all means let them know an image is coming, or check to see they have got it, but don't keep contacting them. The high quality of the stories and images you send should speak for themselves.

Offering an exclusive

Rather than sending out a uniform press release it often pays to make a specific pitch to those journalists you particularly wish to take up the story. Whether or not you get coverage is often due to not just the interesting nature of the story you present but the surrounding package of ideas you offer. You are trying to tempt journalists to cover your story to the exclusion of all the others they have competing for their attention, so do be imaginative! For example, could you offer a specific journalist an interview in an interesting place featured in a forthcoming title (with afternoon tea or cocktails?) or a tour around a building/along a beach important to the plot of a novel? Many authors do not want to be interviewed in their own homes (too revealing), so offering a third-party venue might suit all parties – and can become part of the piece they eventually write.

Suggest ideas that sound appealing – locations, people, vehicles – perhaps in unusual combinations. Features do not have to be written by the paper in question. If you can arrange for an author to write an article for a particular magazine, he or she may receive a fee[8] and the book a valuable push (publication details should be mentioned at the end of the piece). Similarly, can you persuade the educational press to accept an article by a teacher on how your new reading scheme works in practice, or one by a mother for the parenting press on how her son, through using it, has at last learned to read? Often the personal stamp on this kind of feature gives it more authority and makes it more interesting to readers, who in these two examples would consist mostly of other teachers and other parents.

Review lists

You will be required to put together a review list for almost every title published by your organisation as having a title reviewed for its peer community or natural readership is of great importance; reviews can be quoted in subsequent editions and marketing materials. Sending titles to publications that offer to review them within your market sounds simple, but the process takes organisation and patience. National dailies may be able to offer a relatively quick turnaround from receipt of book to appearance of review, but in academic journals it can take months, during which the author is impatiently waiting to see the title featured.

How to compile a review list

Many marketing departments already have an established review list, either in print or as a shared digital resource. It may be a fairly extensive document divided into different subject areas or perhaps consist of a series of different screens or sheets, each one listing specialised media in specific areas. The fact that this list is readily available should make you suspicious. Magazines and broadcast media change their readership and formats extremely quickly these days: new ones are launched, old ones go out of business; a media agency reckoned that each month there are more than 2,000 changes to its contacts directory.

A ready format means it has been around for a long time and probably no one has got around to updating it. Use it as the basis for your review list and you will end up opting for journal and magazine titles because they sound right not because of what they currently are. Worst of all, ticking a list and sending it off for central despatch deprives you of the chance to add a personal message, and unless your mailing list is very up to date, address it to the relevant review editors by job title. Media agencies specialising in publishing insist on sending out the books themselves, for precisely this reason.

When considering where to send materials for review, search the book's title file for suggestions; locate the author's publicity form; have a think. Look through media directories. Use your wider contacts: do you have any friends or friends-of-friends who work or are interested in the relevant area? If so find out which publications they read and which are most influential. Ask the title's editor. Keep an ongoing reference point for review editors you have worked with in the past and those who represent journals that are important to you – and update it as you go along.

If this throws up potential media where you have no contact, ring up and find out who the review editor is. Introduce yourself. Mention the title in question and ask if the publication would be interested in reviewing it. Better still, if it is a journal likely to be useful to your area of responsibility in the future, suggest you meet up. You can use the opportunity to guide the review editor through your company's publishing programme for the next 6 months, and perhaps offer them page proofs of forthcoming titles before other journals as a 'scoop'. Ask about the reviewing policy (time taken, where to send, the kind of books they like to see, etc.). Note it all down.

Then, prompted by the information you have secured, remain in touch. Tell review editors about the books you want to send; suggest how they could feature them; gently remind them they have not yet reviewed what you last sent. Such contacts often enable you to speed up coverage: can the book be sent directly to the reviewer, to the editor at home or to a new feature writer?

When not to give books away

If you have a limited number of copies available for review (and, if the print run is low, giving away five more than you need can make the whole project uneconomic), send out a press release to the journals you think may feature the title and ask the various review editors to contact you if they would like a copy. The national papers, however, won't respond to this kind of approach – they expect to be sent the book.

Similarly, bear in mind that today it isn't just the marketing department and magazine staff who know the meaning of the term 'review copy': you will receive many requests for free copies of the titles you are responsible for promoting. Don't erode your basic market.

What to send out with review copies

It is essential that review copies do not go out unannounced. It is surprising how many publishers forget to enclose a 'review slip' giving title and author details, ISBN, publication date (including year) and recommended price (which is not always shown on the jacket). Provide a name, address (email and physical) and telephone number from where more information can be obtained and to where copies of any review should be sent.

In addition, send any other information you think may secure the interest of review editors: a press release, a copy of the book's promotional leaflet if you have it already, photograph of the author (not for use – there should be a version available digitally if they want it – just to whet their appetite and make them think the author looks interesting), a copy of an illustration from the book, reviews of a previous book by the same author, 'puffs' from others, and a handwritten note from you saying why you think coverage of this title will appeal to their readership. In fact, send anything that might encourage them to select for review the title that you sent, in preference to all the others received the same morning.

Sending out very expensive/desirable titles for review

What happens to all these books once they have been considered for review? In general those doing the reviewing regard the books as a perk. They are usually sold on to specialist bookshops; the prices paid depend on how recent they are. A difficulty arises here for the publisher of very desirable or expensive books: to decide whether requests for review copies are genuine. Send out a large pile of books to a comprehensive list and you will still get calls from editors on the list to say that they have not yet received their copy.

One solution adopted by a fine art publisher was to send out review copies by special delivery/taxi and ask for a receipt from each magazine before handing the book over. Publishers of very expensive (e.g., encyclopaedias) or confidential (e.g., long-awaited works from highly prized authors) may hold a viewing day for journalists to attend in a hotel, or send out review copies with an invoice that they cancel once the set is returned. Alternatively, they may offer to sell the work at a trade discount to the reviewer. When the final *Harry Potter* book was due to come out, in order to avoid information leaking, early reviewers were invited to see the early finished copies in the publishers' offices – but they had to sign confidentiality agreements that they would not release information about the title before an agreed date.

Literary editors

Literary editors form a subsection of journalists, but one that is particularly important to publishers. It's they who control access to the book review pages and their tastes and specific foible are therefore much pored over. It's ironic therefore that the book sections within much of the media have started to look a little beleaguered of late; they attract little associated advertising revenue, and have therefore been increasingly under pressure – with some high-profile literary editors being made redundant.

In addition to spotting interesting titles to feature or review in their pages, literary editors may also provide access to other journalists; they tend to get personal satisfaction from seeing book features on pages other than the literary section. Paula Johnson, previously literary editor of the *Mail on Sunday*, told me that every Friday she would put together a list of book-based snippets that might be useful to other journalists on the paper – perhaps the news editors or the gardening correspondent. With this list she would send copies of all the relevant press releases sent in by publishing houses. So even if you do decide to send your review copy and press release to the news or sports desk, it is often worth sending one to the literary editor too.

Top tips for putting together press releases for literary editors:

- Do you really need a press release? Would an email or phone call to a key contact work best, particularly if you want to make them an exclusive offer (e.g., you have taken on a new author or an existing author has been chosen as a judge for a major literary prize – and you want to offer the chance to talk to them)? This may spark them into asking your author to write or review something, giving valuable pre-publicity.
- Bear in mind the environment in which your material will be received. A literary editor on a prestigious newspaper will get 40 to 70 book packages a week, into an office already overflowing with other titles, press releases and people. Titles are generally shelved by the month in which they are scheduled for publication, but additional piles of books soon build up wherever there is floor space. It follows that clearly laid out information that is easy to digest is best.
- Put the press releases inside the book you are sending so they don't get separated on opening.
- Get the name of the literary editor you are sending it to right – they do notice misspellings or if you are sending it to their predecessor. Neither is appreciated.
- It's absolutely unforgivable to send a literary editor material containing grammatical errors.
- Be sure to mark paperback originals as such; they will be given special treatment as they have not been reviewed as hardbacks. If you fail to make this clear they are likely to appear in the 'new in paperback' feature with much less space accorded.
- Don't put copy that is on the book jacket in the press release that accompanies it. Literary editors consider this an insult to their intelligence.
- Think carefully before sending free gifts to attract attention to your title (lavish cakes delivered in a taxi with the book; burn cream in the package to show the title enclosed is 'too hot to handle'). When asked, literary editors often say that the book should stand on its own merit and that they therefore take a dim view of 'bribes' or additional enclosures. But if no one else is doing this, an occasional stylish package with intriguing contents may find itself written about on the diary pages. Tony Mulliken, chairman of Midas PR, commented that they will sometimes use intriguing packaging to draw attention to a title – wrapping, ribbons, boxes and shiny bags. Parcels that are a particular pleasure to open may stick in the mind.
- If you are to follow up a press release with a telephone call, ensure your timing is right and that you have a real reason for calling. So send out copies 4 to 6 weeks before publication and phone up when the copy should just have landed on the review editor's desk. When making a call, you can begin by checking it has reached them. Most will respond by saying they will look at what has been sent, and this is your opportunity to say why they should feature the title or author. Ensure you have a reason for their interest before you make the call – maybe they reviewed the author's last book or they are a supporter of literature in translation. Whatever you do, don't give the impression you are

'ringing round' – which feels inappropriately unspecific to both their medium and role.

- Don't ring and remind literary editors if they haven't yet covered a book – most hate it! Rather, find a reason for contacting them again. For example, you might be able to follow up a press release on the grounds that you have some new information that was not made available when you first contacted them – perhaps the author has been nominated for a prize or the story they highlight is in the news for another reason. But again the pitch should be specific and the approach respectful, enhancing the overlap between the title/author you are suggesting and the readers whose interests they represent, rather than chasing them.

Inspection copies

The recommended reading lists produced by academics and teachers feature only the briefest of details (author, date, title, edition and publisher) but inclusion is vital. Most educational publishers offer 'inspection copies' for this market, sending unconditional free copies to particularly influential figures. Be sure to keep the market informed on the availability of new editions as not all recommended reading lists are fully up to date. See Chapter 15 for further information.

Author interviews

As well as considering setting up interviews in newspapers and magazines, would your author come over well on radio, television or perhaps through hosting a forum on a website? Are there specific programmes that would be interested in recording their point of view? Local radio stations offer lots of opportunities for coverage. If the author is unavailable, could you do the interview yourself? Alternatively, offer a different author from your list for interview and you may still secure coverage for your house's titles ('switch selling').

If you set up interviews, be meticulous in confirming all the details to everyone concerned, even if you are planning to accompany the author. Write down the name of the programme and interviewer, and where the author should be and when. Suggest they listen or read the medium for a few days beforehand so they understand the presenter's style. Brief the author on the programme's reaction to the press release you sent. This may give hints of the type of question to be asked. When it's all over, if it went well, consider sending a postcard or email of thanks to the relevant journalist or producer, or even a small memento (you have a warehouse full of suitable items). You may want to be in touch again.

Other opportunities for getting authors interviewed may arise when they do not have a new book out, but when a story relating to their work is in circulation and the media is looking for a relevant spokesperson to interview or gain an associated quote. An author may be immensely knowledgeable about a particular area, but need help in learning to speak to the media. If you are charged with helping an author prepare, the following guidance may be helpful – and hopefully ensure they get asked again:

- **They have been asked for an interview because they are an expert – so they need to come across accordingly.** Authors generally sound authoritative in print but can be inclined to self-deprecation in person; there is some research to be done on whether authors generally typify the stereotype of big ego, low self-esteem. The author being prepared for the media needs to be reminded that people will tend to take you at your own estimation and just before an interview is not the time for a crisis of confidence. If a commercial publisher has paid to publish your work they have invested in you and believe in you. Encourage them to take support from this.
- **Encourage them to summarise their contribution to the debate**; this does not imply they are 'dumbing down', rather ensuring that they can be understood as widely as possible. Get this right and they will really see their ideas spread.
- **Encourage them to practise responding to questions** without their notes in front of them; an interview will have more impact if what is said is spoken to an individual than read out. Those interviewing will be very resistant to allowing speakers into the studio with sheaves of notes.
- **Encourage them to contribute interesting accompanying personal information** that makes them sound interesting.

Writing interesting author information

Most authors think their book is the most interesting thing they have to offer to the media; the media is often just as (if not more) interested in who wrote it. They will want to know why a particular author is worth featuring and so it's helpful if you run through this with the author before writing a press release. Encourage them to share human details. These need not be invasive, but help create a rounded sense of the individual in question, and may help prompt a more empathetic interview. Nor need the information they provide be directly relevant to the title in question. The following questions from Tony Mulliken of Midas PR may help you get started:

- What is interesting about you? What have you done that would interest our readers and viewers?
- Where do you live and who lives nearby?
- What about your family – size, age and location? Any interesting relationships?
- Who are you friendly or unfriendly with?
- Any unusual hobbies or pets?
- Any odd experiences or jobs in the past?
- Who have you met who is famous?
- What have you done that would interest me?
- Why do readers need to know about your research?
- Why should they care?
- What new angle can I bring to an existing story?

Authors do, however, need to bear in mind that stories they release without sufficient thought may remain in circulation long after they wish they had not mentioned them. There is a big difference between attention and approval and while short-term attention may deliver headlines, it may not support their longer-term ambitions to be taken seriously. See the interview with Kit Berry in Chapter 11.

Coaching an author to speak effectively on radio and television

How you or your author prepare for a presentation on the air will depend on the attitude of the interviewer: whether it is likely to be 'hard' (typical for prime-time current affairs slots) or 'soft' (like the majority of local radio interviewers). Think carefully about your aim(s) when accepting an interview. Authors who are not experienced may find it easier to start with a soft interview.

Politicians react to a hard interviewer by 'spring-boarding', using each question as a possible launch pad for conveying what they have decided are the essential points to get across ('I'm glad you asked me that, but of course we must not lose sight of the really important issue, which is … '). The 'hard' interviewer resists tangents and puts forward difficult questions that demand real answers. A 'soft' interviewer will allow the interviewee to shape the discussion, guiding or prompting with questions to ensure an interesting programme, or to change the subject (about 4 minutes per topic is considered sufficient to satisfy the attention span of the audience for popular radio).

If you are doing the interview yourself, immerse yourself in all the information you can find and practise answering questions in your head on the way there. Don't over-rehearse; you will sound wooden and unconvincing. If it helps, take along a postcard with three or four prompt words to remind you of the key points you want to get across, and perhaps a couple of important statistics to refer to, but certainly no more than that. Lots of notes will confuse you and produce 'rustle' – and many presenters will not allow them on to the set or into the studio. In any case, talking from memory enables you to concentrate fully on the questions being asked. Talking of key statistics, remember that figures are hard to absorb at first hearing. Don't use too many. Alternatively, can you restate them as fractions? Whatever you do, don't read out prepared statements; not only does this sound very impersonal, if it is information in your press release then the interviewer will probably have used it to introduce you.

Live interviews need not be daunting. The knowledge that it is for real (not for editing later) can help you to marshal your thoughts. It is easy to forget how many million listeners there are when you are actually talking to just one.

Programmes like to match up contrasting points of view and you may be invited along to take part in a discussion; sometimes you are warned of this, sometimes not – and the first time you meet the opposing viewpoint may be in the studio. It's important that the best discussion takes place on the programme, not in the green room – the audience does not know what you said to each other there so don't assume this is part of what they know already. Ruth Killick again:

> I always encourage authors to ensure they have some really good stories to give colour to an interview. Also to remember that if you're asked a question, don't answer it concisely (as you probably would in a normal conversation). 'How was your trip to India?' 'Lovely thanks, especially Delhi' might be a good answer to a friend but an interviewer asking you about your book on India will expect something more along the lines of 'a real eye-opener actually; I had no idea that people still went to Ashrams in such huge numbers. When I was researching my book (and try to mention the title) I talked to this fascinating Yogi who … ' A question is an opportunity to tell a story.

Dealing with authors who don't see achieving publicity as a career positive

There is not always a complete overlap between the author's reasons for writing and their publisher's requirement for the resulting product to sell. Within the academic community in particular, it's very difficult for material to achieve both academic and popular recognition and it's not uncommon for authors of highly academic works to be relatively resistant to cooperating over the more widespread dissemination of their work. If this is a difficult issue for you, an argument that is gaining ground, and governmental support, is of academics displaying the wider impact of their work within society – material that allows the academic, and their university, to engage with the public and have a positive effect within society. You could also quote Alain de Botton, the champion of public engagement:

> *What are you proudest of achieving?*
> We live in a world that's divided between academics and the general public. On the one hand, you've got people saying culture is getting dumbed down. On the other you have people saying you have to do lowest common denominator stuff. I'm trying to build a bridge between what's serious and what's popular. I'm proud to have made a programme about Schopenhauer that got 2 million viewers. I like to think of how I can use unconventional means to get sensible ideas across.
> *Are you bothered by the negative reviews you've received?*
> I'm frustrated by the monstrous snobbery of certain academics that surrounds conveying serious ideas to the wider public. I'm trying to do something like Brian Cox is doing with physics – which is to transmit ideas.[9]

How to sell ideas to journalists by email and telephone

How successful you are in setting up the kind of coverage suggested in this chapter will depend on the kind of titles you look after and the way you target and present information on them. But equally important will be your own personal contribution: how persuasive you are when suggesting ideas to journalists and following up by talking to them on the telephone. Here is some basic advice on how to sell ideas by email and over the phone.

Begin by trying to put yourself in the right frame of mind; you are contacting them to offer something that should be interesting and that (if you are in touch with the right person) is both relevant and useful to them in their role. You are the interpreter or negotiator, with assets at your disposal, not just someone interrupting their day. If it helps, think of yourself as playing a role, one in which you are going to professionally represent your organisation; offer access to interesting material they do not yet know about and talk knowledgably to the person you reach.

How to write a persuasive email to a journalist

- Write the title line last. It's so vital you should come back to it – but in the meantime delete whatever is sitting in that space at the moment, just in case you forget to change it later. Keep it compelling and concise.
- Think about the tone of voice you will use. You have no eye-contact to soften what you say, and need to match the level of formality to the relationship you have with the recipient or product you are promoting and organisation you are part of. Achieving a flow of information that they absorb rather than question is much harder than it looks.
- Get to the point – what do you want the recipient to do as a result of receiving your email? Begin with what you have to offer and what outcome you are seeking. Cut out the long introduction that warms them up to the subject – they need to know quickly why you are getting in touch: 'Your readers are clearly concerned about global warming and in his new book Dr Fred Blogs offers proof that the situation is much worse than previously thought. We are offering an exclusive interview when he is in the US next month.'
- Include space. Most writers concentrate on the words, but space is the part of any document that pulls in the reader's eye. It follows that including space in your text, through bullet points, indenting paragraphs (ensuring your paragraphs are of different lengths so that the text does not look 'blocked') and other space management devices will make what you send more readable – and hence likely to be more easily absorbed.
- 'To make your arguments "digestible", break them into small "chunks", and present each point with a similar format and sentence structure.'[10] For example, an interview with Dr Blogs would enable you to:

1 Build on your recent coverage of this issue.
2 Allow your readers to put their own questions to him.
3 Redirect the debate to what surveys have consistently shown most people are concerned about – and politicians do not seem to understand.

- Give specific proof of your case, in a way it can be heard – fractions, percentages, nth selections ('one in ten people think'). If you have to use large numbers try to use words ('a million' not '1,000,000') or restate them figuratively ('the population of Texas').

- Provide a quote that confirms what you say – so your case is widened and it's clear the message should be taken seriously.
- Conclusion. At the end of the email, restate the conclusion in a way that provides the recipient with the next logical step. Keep it simple and specific; it should be a benefit to both parties, not just confirm that a book is about to be available.
- *Now* write the subject line. This matters hugely, which is why it's best drafted last – once you have worked out what you are asking for and what evidence you can offer in support of your request.

> Ideally, a subject line should accomplish two important tasks: (1) interest the recipient enough so that the email gets opened and read, and (2) imply the conclusion that you want the recipient to accept. In most cases, the best way to accomplish both tasks is to encapsulate a benefit (or benefits) that will result from the decision that you'd like the recipient to make.[11]

For example:

> 'What your readers don't yet know about global warming'
> 'Why the deadline for running out of fossil fuels is closer than we think'
> 'Children's author denies suspicion that no one reads any more'
> 'An explosive book!' (a title about volcanoes)
> 'Simon Singh launches Simpsons book in Springfield (Wales)' (a new title on the long-running television series)

How to make an effective phone call to a journalist

If you are unused to ringing journalists, whether to propose ideas for coverage or follow up a press release you have already sent, making the call can be daunting. So here is some advice on how to approach the task.

Most workplace offices are open-plan these days, so it's likely you will be trying to concentrate in the midst of other noise – and that your colleagues will be able to hear what you have to say. All the more reason for taking what you have to do seriously.

Before you start, make sure you have to hand:

- Notes on what you plan to say, so you don't forget anything – but it's vital to make this a directed conversation rather than the delivery of a monologue.
- A short pitch. How can you describe this title/author/opportunity most effectively? This is often referred to as an 'elevator pitch'.
- A clear idea of what you can offer (an author interview with rough dates when they might be available, a visit to a school to see a major new scheme in

progress with times that might be possible, a new angle on an existing news story that your new title permits).

- The right information. If you are following up a press release be sure to have a copy of what was initially circulated – highlight the important points that you think will most interest them. Many of those you call will say they have either not received or can no longer find it. In which case you will need to send it again – and to do this straight away so that the new copy of your release is received while your conversation is still in their minds.
- An alternative proposition. So that if they say no to your initial idea, but seem disposed to talk further (or even ask you what else is coming up), think about what else you have that might interest them. 'Switch selling' is when you replace one idea with another, to ensure you still get the sale.

And here are some top tips for making the calls:

- Start with a list of people to call. Somehow it's easier to break the inertia if you are working your way down a list. Whatever you do, however, don't give the impression that this is what you're doing!
- Think about the best time of day for finding your contact at their desk. Ask for them by name. If you find an answerphone in place, leave your name, *briefly* state the issue you are ringing about, and say you will call back. Remember to do so.
- If the correspondent you want to speak to is not available, and someone else answers their phone, find out if they work together – in which case you could deliver your pitch with someone who is more likely to influence a decision over coverage than you are.
- If an assistant answers your call, and you cannot be put through to the person you intended, be polite. They are getting dozens of calls like yours, so even if you have been repeatedly fobbed off, stay bright and courteous. If they suggest that the journalist you are seeking will return your call, don't expect it will happen; it probably never will. You are the salesperson and the journalist will expect you to ring back with your story.
- If you get through straight away, don't be put off by the abrupt manner in which some journalists answer the phone ('Yes? What is it?'). Concentrate on the job in hand and speak (rather than read) to the person you are calling.
- Say who you are (first name is fine), the organisation you represent and why you are calling – which is to give them early or exclusive access to an author or to tell them about a newsworthy issue – and not because the firm you work for is publishing a new book.
- Ask if now is a convenient time to have a *quick* word with them (because you know they are busy). If it is not a good time for them you will generally be offered a time to call back. The journalist you call may be in the middle of writing something, and just launching into delivery of your message can be irritating.
- Make it relevant to the person you are calling. Involve them. If the format has covered the author before, jog the journalist's memory about the story that

appeared last time, and say how this one builds on it or differs. If you are talking about a well-known author then provide some little-known details to perk up interest. Mention other familiar instances in the media of the issue your story highlights.

- Make this a two-way process. Listen. Ensure you are being heard by putting your points across clearly and using open-ended questions that invite a reply ('Do you remember Mary Robbins? Would your readers be interested in hearing about why she decided on this topic? How does that idea sound?').

- Don't talk too fast or be afraid to hesitate. If you listen to some of the best radio interviewers you will hear they repeatedly rephrase their questions, and use 'um' and 'ah' to ease the impact of hard-hitting ones. It is all designed to involve interviewees, and coax them into answering responsively. Think of yourself in the same position: you are trying to persuade the journalist to take interest, but with no eye-contact or body language at your disposal, your voice has to do it all.

- Try not to be too complicated. Use words that are readily understood and that you won't stumble over. Keep listening to what they say in response.

- Don't overwhelm the listener with information. A brief description of the story on offer followed by two or three good reasons why the journal you are ringing should cover it is plenty. And listen.

- Note down what was said immediately after the call (you may think you will remember, but soon will not be sure which call or contact was which).

- They will very often say they'll think about it or talk to their editor. In which case you could ask when a good time to call back is. Then get in touch with useful information at a later date, perhaps an update on progress or a related story.

- If an interview or visit is promised, confirm everything by email, ringing the contact numbers you were given (just to make sure they are correct) the day before to make a final check on the arrangements. Make friends with the secretary or production assistant who is more likely to spot double bookings.

- Don't forget to let your reps know about forthcoming coverage; anything that is likely to increase demand can encourage retailers to take more stock. Let the trade press know. Tell your colleagues: it's motivating to know that your authors are being featured in the media, and they may get the chance to talk this up further.

- Track the coverage you get. Scan the papers to which you circulated the press releases for what subsequently appears, or employ an agency to do this for you. Stick a copy of each item of coverage in the title file so it can be incorporated in publicity or used on the jacket of a new edition.

Don't give up

Getting a journalist to come along to hear at first-hand the story you are pushing is not the end of the matter: you then have to hope that the promised feature appears. Someone may accept your call, turn up to talk to your author and then come back with supplementary questions – but this can serve only to increase your anxiety as the days go by before the story finally turns up in print or on screen.

It's so frustrating when, as often happens, your carefully nurtured feature is squeezed out at the last minute by something much more up to date, with the added annoyance of having to start all over again with a now rather dated story. Or having offered a scoop, you are turned down at the last minute when it is too late to fix up an alternative.

If, after much effort to set something up, a journalist calls you to let you know they can't run an idea, recognise that they called because they felt committed to the idea or to you. They did not have to. So acknowledge the effort they made: 'That's a shame but I do appreciate your letting me know/telling me why.' Don't sulk, even if you feel like doing so!

It is worth remembering that you would have scant respect for a medium that featured everything it was offered. In dealing with the press, a very large part of your success will depend on the skills you develop in matching your expectations to journalists' ability to deliver. Like so many other parts of marketing, it can be both utterly frustrating and absolutely exhilarating.

A final piece of advice from Ruth Killick:

> Keep on pitching. Whatever success I've had in this business has been because I don't give up. If you're in a hole with no coverage for a book there are two alternatives: do more research (who else has written on this area that I could contact?) or get out more pitches. Go back with helpful information: 'I know you're thinking about that feature on Vanessa Able's journey around India in a tata nano[12] – you might have seen this news story that shows how utterly unsafe it was. Perhaps she could write something on "my love affair with the little car that was just too cheap"?' (This got me a 'Comment is Free' piece in *The Guardian*.) I often think I've had 'hits' because I've kept on going while most publicists have given up.
>
> Finally, do pat yourself on the back when you do get a yes! In our office we have a bell we ring when we get a hit. It started as a joke but now 'ring that bell' is an office slogan!

Notes

1 i.e., many new forms of media.
2 Ruth Killick Publicity, www.catbrook.co.uk.
3 In 2004, the Richard & Judy Book Club, along with the Richard & Judy Summer Read, was responsible for a revolution in the nation's reading habits that still remains a literary phenomenon. The Richard & Judy Book Club titles have sold in excess of 10 million copies and generated more than £60 million in book sales. Its featured titles are known to increase sales by as much as 3,000 per cent overnight, and it has turned at least eight authors into multimillionaires. The Richard & Judy Book Club continues today exclusively with WH Smith. Their first set of book club titles, which launched in June 2010, broke all records with *Sister* by Rosamund Lupton making Number 1 in the paperback chart and becoming the fastest-selling title by a debut author in WH Smith's 200-year history. All 8 of their titles

went into the top 12 paperbacks in their first week of sales with close to a million copies sold overall; www.richardandjudy.co.uk.

4 Speaking on *Saturday Live!* BBC Radio 4, 31 May 2014.

5 Interview with Danuta Kean, www.guardian.com, 1 March 1999.

6 Head of department, Journalism and Publishing, Kingston University.

7 Garfield (2010). Text from press release by Ruth Killick, adapted by Beth Brewster.

8 The question of fees is increasingly tricky. It's worth having this conversation with your author. Some authors will on principle not write something without a fee, even if they have a book to promote, while many newspapers expect to get it for nothing in return for a book plug.

9 Alain de Botton, *My Rules for Atheists are Based on Virtues*, http://metro.co.uk/2013/02/13/alain-de-botton-my-ten-commandments-for-atheists-3446357.

10 www.inc.com/geoffrey-james/how-to-write-a-convincing-email.html.

11 Ibid.

12 A very small but fuel efficient car.

11 Working with authors and other vital partnerships

Authors 283
How to work well with authors 287
Working with authors who have previously self-published 288
Working with other industry suppliers 292
Working with publishing colleagues 293
Working with individual freelance staff 295
Temporary staff on work placement or work experience 296

The publishing industry has a long tradition of relying on key external suppliers, most notably from authors who provide their content to the industry but are not full-time employees. This chapter, new for this edition, will help those marketing books to understand how it feels to be an author – and show how you can harness their energy and expertise to promote the effective sale of the products you have created together. We will then consider how other relationships with service providers can help in the effective marketing of publishing content.

Authors

One of the remarkable developments over the past few years has been the rise of author involvement in marketing. Publishers increasingly rely on their authors to help them promote projects to which they have jointly committed – and the extent of their online connectedness may play a big part in decisions over whom to commission. Significantly there is also increasing author marketing activity without the involvement of the traditional industry; building a following through self-publishing, and in the process demonstrating demand for a particular writer's work, has become an important new way for publishers to discover content in which they decide to invest.

How authors feel about publishers

How an individual author feels about their publishing house is likely to depend very strongly on their path to getting published. Authors who have self-published in order to test demand for their material, or been recruited by publishing houses on the basis of their successful self-publishing, are likely to be vastly more informed about the publishing process and hence more keen on involvement as their work progresses. Far from self-publishing meaning working alone, recent research has shown that self-publishers have often recruited a series of publishing services to help them manage their path to publication, and this brings a strong understanding of the stages, timings and costs involved. This chapter will begin by considering how best to work with authors who are new to the publishing process, and then think about the best way of developing relationships with those who already have some practical experience of how the process works.

The marketing department's relationship with authors

The author's first contact within a publishing house is generally with their commissioning editor, the person who signs them up to write and liaises with them thereafter. If your house is taking part in a bidding process to secure a new author (or to retain the services of one who is considering moving to a different publishing house), the marketing department will get involved in preparing a marketing outline, including ideas on where the market is and how to reach it, and you may (or may not) be involved in its formal presentation. If the author has already been commissioned, the marketing department's role will be the same but slightly lower key; again you will be required to estimate the size of the market or predict the type of marketing campaign most likely to be successful, and to show how you would put it into practice for the most cost-effective (read cheapest) budget, linking the title with any others on your list that make cross-promotions possible. But for most new marketing staff, authors appear first as names, listed next to their anticipated titles, on schedules of forthcoming publications and in catalogues.

This is how many authors would prefer to remain. While all now accept that their publishers will require them to assist in the marketing of their books, with specific clauses included in the contracts they sign, there is no reason why those who can string words together on the page should be able to do so when interviewed by journalists. What bestselling author Margaret Drabble has referred to as the 'travelling circus' that today surrounds publication – the requirements to talk the book up in media interviews be witty on the air and go to literary festivals and enthuse – are now part of the experience of being published, and not all authors welcome this.

Important things for publishers to understand about authors

- Most authors have (and need) a strong ego

The very act of writing requires a strong ego – how else could they prioritise their time so the writing gets done, and then assume that what they have to say should be read by others? The process of trying to get published is beset by difficulties, and the easiest option is always to give up. For the would-be published writer, there is rejection at every stage of the process – from submitting their precious work to houses and agents who turn it down (often forcefully and, they suspect, without really engaging with it), to the editing process (seeing their work corrected can feel like being back at school), to the production (difficult if they hate the cover but are told it will sell well), to the review process in the press (those allocated space to develop an argument may barely refer to the title they were commissioned to review, or use the opportunity to score points) to the huge unpredictability of the internet (where an individual's right to comment can mean unrepresentative and hurtful opinions are publicly aired). What keeps the author going through this process are self-belief and determination. Publishers, who, let us not forget, are dealing with the successful arrivals – those who have got through this torturous process – may view these same personality characteristics as bloody-mindedness or self-obsession. The reality is that authors simply require some of both these commodities in order to get published.

Ironically, however, while authors can appear to have impenetrable egos, most of them have a very soft underbelly and are easily hurt; many can recite wounding reviews word for word or recall casual feedback with a backdated emphasis that has turned an off-the-cuff remark into a deliberate barb. So don't assume that authors fully inhabit the resilient exterior they present; many are all the while steeling themselves to be assertive on behalf of the titles they have created. And whatever you do, never imply that the creation of a book has been easy, or give the impression, as so many authors feel deep-down about publishers, that you would do the writing as well, if only you had the time.

- Authors are often socially isolated

Publishers work in busy offices; the marketing department tends to be particularly frenetic with phones going, people calling in and a general atmosphere of buzz. The author is most usually at home, on their own. Writing is in general isolating, lonely and fattening (all that unrestricted access to the biscuit tin). It follows that if you promise to ring on a particular day, or at a particular time, they will be expecting the call, indeed they may put off really getting on with their writing until you have talked, which can make it even more frustrating if the promised contact does not take place. So don't say 'ten o'clock' unless you mean it.

Second, as authors do not work in offices and have the chance to chat, their social skills may be a little rusty; you may need to warm them up rather than use the same efficient tone you use when dealing with other suppliers. On occasion they may call you, but from their point of view, it's intimidating to call a busy office where you sense that you are struggling to hold the attention of the person on the other end of the phone; you can hear other phones going, and you sense that perhaps the general rush means they would like to be off the phone and on to something else as quickly as possible. Publishing seems like a mightily pally world to an author; publishers are one big pool of people who move around quickly and all know each other – it's off-putting and intimidating.

- They are over-concerned with their own work

It's easy for the marketing department to typecast authors as selfish creatures. You have lots of competing priorities; they have just one – their own work. Unless you have been allocated to a big-selling author (unlikely on your first publishing job) you probably have many titles to market at the same time.

Manage their expectations. Whenever there is any contact they will dwell on what was said and how it was said long after you have put the phone down or sent that email. Take care with how you communicate. Don't give them a false impression of likely media interest or possible sales. If expectations are unmatched, the relationship will be soured. As well as telling them what you can't afford to do for their book, be sure to pass on the details of what is possible – notably all the standard processes the book will receive on its path to publication (see Chapters 5 and 6 for more details) – and what they can do to assist.

- Authors worry

It's not uncommon for those marketing titles to have little understanding of their subject matter; and the more specialised the title, the more likely this is. There are many more arts than sciences graduates working in the industry, and given the importance of scientific, technical and medical publishing to the industry, there is bound to be a disparity between the number of people needed to work on such highly technical subjects and the quantity of qualified staff available. This is not necessarily a problem, provided the marketer is willing to be interested in the potential purchaser, engage with the need for the product and the benefits the user will receive from purchase.

If you find yourself in this position, be sure to read the information on which a decision to publish was based: the commissioning form (the name will vary from house to house but the purpose will be the same) that describes the designated market and the product's benefits. And do this *before* you have any contact with the author. If you make it clear that you have little understanding of their key discipline, but were not even sufficiently motivated to do some basic research, they are bound to feel anxious.

- They will probably underestimate your role

While there are exceptions, in general, authors tend to underplay the role of the publisher in bringing their work to market; there's a commonly stated (and very annoying to publishers) view among authors that all they have to do is 'press a few buttons' and out comes a book. In fact the role of the publisher in presenting work to the public, shaping the voice, managing the text to ensure meaning shines through, arranging an attractive cover and launching at the best time is all part of a highly skilled business. Low-quality self-publishing operations have shown how effective management of content is most apparent when missing. Encourage your authors to have a sense of how many people are involved in the presentation of their work.

- They probably earn less than their publishers

On hearing that his son had had a book commissioned, the father of Alan Sillitoe[1] commented: 'You'll never have to work again.' How wrong he was. Bestselling writers apart, writing in general is not well paid. Surveys have repeatedly shown that, in general, most authors earn less than the recommended minimum wage for their writing. They produce the raw material, those selling it get better remunerated. It's hardly a situation designed to improve a relationship.

How to work well with authors

- Educate them

Traditionally, authors have known little about the publishing process and, ironically, the better the process has been managed, the less inclined they have been to enquire – effective publishing is often most evident when absent. Today how much they know about the process is changing, as those who have experimented with self-publishing appreciate just how much is involved. Helping them understand all the silent processes (reviewing and rejecting content, editing, managing production processes) that lead to the rightness of a product may encourage stronger collaboration.

- Encourage them to get in touch with you at the right time in the production cycle

A list of key contacts given to you on publication day is far too late; you need information a good 6 to 9 months ahead and preferably when the manuscript is handed over. The starting point should be the author publicity form, which you should make clear is a key marketing platform. As a marketer I have seen many sloppily filled in, with inadequate information ('IRA, Boston 2015?' instead of the full name, dates and details of the organisers for a key conference) and arrogant responses to key questions ('I have already told your editorial director – ask them'). Explain that you are busy and they really do need to take the time to fill this in properly, and not assume that you have time to fill in gaps. You could tactfully say that you will be relying on colleagues and not everyone will be fully familiar with the initials they take for granted, so spelling them out in full is really helpful.

- Encourage them to consolidate their requests/suggestions/contacts

Ask them to send them in, and in digital format (so they can be forwarded), not just ring up, at sporadic intervals, as and when they think of them.

- Enlist their help

Are they connected on social media and could they blog effectively in the lead-up to publication? Could they arrange to speak to a local group that would be interested in the subject of their book and either tie up with a local bookseller or distribute leaflets that prompt a discount for a direct order? Whom do they know who could endorse the book? What organisations do they belong to which could either make a special offer to fellow members or endorse through an organisational newsletter?

- Give them feedback

Find out what in-house procedures there are for keeping authors up to date on what has been achieved. Are they sent copies of their reviews (consolidated, every now and again); a copy of their new book as soon as the advances come through? It's surprising how many long-term relationships with authors are soured by comparatively minor incidents. Keeping in touch with them through an occasional phone call, a Christmas card or an email is usually far more appreciated than publishers realise.

- Support their marketing efforts

Many publishing houses now supply authors with a basic website (a page or two on the organisational site), advance information sheets and leaflets and even training in social media to help them promote their work. Ask if they are members of societies that would circulate a flyer on a forthcoming book with its journal. Support their efforts to offer talks, preferably including a copy of the book in the price paid by the audience. Authors who have titles with several publishing houses might like a leaflet to list all their books, to use when they are speaking. You could pay a proportion towards production, much cheaper than paying for the entire piece yourself. Most authors have websites, so have yours link with theirs (which will increase the ranking for both of you).

Working with authors who have previously self-published

Authors who have self-published have already been through all the stages of manuscript preparation and dissemination. They may be moving into the confines of a traditional publishing house because they have decided they would rather write than publish, having discovered in the process that publishing is far more labour-intensive than they had realised.

A successful relationship can be built if their knowledge is both appreciated and built upon. Arrange a meeting to talk about their understanding of the market, the face-to-face responses they have received from readers. Build on their online connectedness to develop your own. Reinforce each other's efforts, particularly significant given that their effective self-publishing was the reason they were commissioned.

Case study

Working with publishers after a self-publishing start: an interview with author Kit Berry

Kit Berry is the author of the five-book Stonewylde series (www.stonewylde. com). She is not particularly keen on labels but her work could probably fit within the overarching brackets of magical realism/romance/the healing power of nature/environmental awareness. Perhaps more significantly, she also fits into the growing category of successful self-published authors now acquired by a traditional agent and publisher – and who, having managed the various processes herself, does not want to be marginalised from expressing her qualified opinions.

Setting up a website for the Stonewylde series was the first thing I organised, as soon as I'd published the first book. My new partner, an IT expert, created a really interesting website with a contact facility. This enabled readers to get in touch with me, which they did with great enthusiasm. From this early interaction, my partner built a thriving social network for Stonewylde fans.

From the outset I sought to make links with organisations that wanted talks, as a means of bringing my work to new readers. I am a former English teacher, and know that schools are always looking for authors who understand the National Curriculum, learning outcomes and class involvement. My series of books is suitable for young adults and I enjoy speaking to and working with students. School visits are paid, with expenses too, so this was a source of income that allowed me to keep writing. I also offered talks to adult groups within a reasonable travelling distance – Women's Institutes, Townswomen's Guilds, Probus, U3A, libraries – anywhere that would have me. I have been invited several times to the Netherlands and the work has brought other invitations from overseas.

I found that people were interested not only in my books, but also in my personal story. Many people want to write, and they also like to hear of a real romance with a happy ending. As a divorced mother of three, I had worked full time as a teacher, juggling the marking of exam papers for additional income. It was frankly very hard going. I had always longed to be a writer and finally plucked up the courage to make the change after a mesmerising experience with a hare in some woods. Writing the books led to an increase in my confidence and then, after many years of being single, to meeting a new man – the IT expert whom I subsequently married. There are a lot of middle-aged women looking for a change in their lives, and I have consistently found they relate well to the story I tell. I am encouraged that people have taken comfort from my transformation, and some have used it as motivation to get started on their own life changes.

Sometimes I would get a fee, sometimes just expenses, but the chance to talk to a group of people always prompted book sales and, if they liked the work, word-of-mouth publicity. Whenever I attended an event I aimed to dress the part; a lesson I learned early on is that to the audience, an author is someone rather special, so it is important that one's appearance reflects this.

Magazine interviews were another very positive form of marketing in the early days, and I would seek to be interviewed by any magazine with a relevant readership. My story fitted particularly well with magazines aimed at mid-life/career women who like reading about stories of change and new love. I always insisted on holding a copy of my first book in the photographs, as this was the whole point of the exercise.

As another potential market, I became involved in the mind, body and spirit (MBS) circuit of festivals and exhibitions. These events can attract really large audiences, and people are often prepared to spend considerable amounts of money, for example, on tarot readings, palmistry and psychic healing. I refined a talk that focused on the healing power of nature, one of the themes in my Stonewylde series. I then encouraged the audience to buy my first book and try the techniques themselves, and this proved really successful in building sales and finding new readers. One of the advantages of writing a series of books is that people will go on to buy the others if they have enjoyed the first one.

The online social network that my partner had created early on was an excellent way of keeping people interested and engaged. We joke that we should have started a dating agency too, because four different couples, now happily living together, met through our Stonewylde network. Nowadays Facebook and Twitter dominate the social media, and we have switched our efforts to these platforms. It's important to maintain a constant presence; I find that my readers are keen to share their love of Stonewylde, which creates an ever-growing market for the books. Everyone today understands the need to promote themselves online, although constantly plugging your books is a sure way of putting people off. In my early days I did quite a lot of this, and now cringe at the thought of it. You must be a little more subtle.

I believe it is very important to maintain your author persona online, and not inadvertently mix personal and professional identities. Readers love to think they are gaining an insight into one's personal life, but of course this must be carefully managed. I used my personal story to add interest to my talks and magazine interviews, but I would never share private information or feelings with any audience, online or in person. I have seen writers get into a mess by mixing their professional and their personal lives on Facebook and other social media. When anyone can ask to be your 'friend' online, it is important to remember that most of these followers are not your friends. If you have children, it is even more important to keep family life private. For instance, on Facebook I would post a picture of my dog looking adorable, but I would never dream of posting pictures of a family celebration. Even if you are OK with strangers seeing your personal photos and events, family members or friends may object to your thousands of followers seeing all.

One way round this dilemma is to write under a pen-name. Long before I started writing, a famous author told me that she wished she'd used a pseudonym from the outset, because now it was too late. Every time she used her debit card in the supermarket or garage, her identity would be revealed and she would be asked for an autograph. I remembered this advice, and consequently I keep my author name and profile separate from my real, personal one. Privacy cannot be reclaimed once it has gone; think big and assume you will be famous one day! Nobody wants to be stalked, so best keep private stuff that way. If you use social media as a business tool, remember the old maxim about never mixing business with pleasure.

Right from the start my partner and I consciously built up a mailing list, asking people who visited the website if they wanted to stay in touch, and then sending out newsletters at regular intervals. Anyone who emailed me to give feedback on my work, or to ask questions, was similarly added to the list. This created a community to whom we could later launch each new book, offering reduced prices for advance orders and building anticipation and excitement for the next title.

Being signed by a literary agent and then the work being sold to Orion was wonderful. I assumed that henceforth I would just get on with the writing, leaving the professional marketing and PR to the publishers. But having been responsible for it for so long, and observed what worked and what did not, it's hard to switch off. I know my own market better than the publishers do, and I gain real energy from continuing to meet and interact with my readers. Everything I learned as a self-published author I still put to good use. Once one's book is out, the publishers move on to marketing their next new book by their next author. But I know how important it is to maintain the marketing impetus, as there is a wide and untapped audience out there. So as long as the books are in print, my marketing will continue.

I kept back the merchandising rights when I signed the publishing deal, as we do well out of associated T-shirts, bags, posters and stationery. I produce bookmarks and badges as giveaways to reinforce the name. We have put a lot of effort into building Stonewylde as a brand, and want to ensure that we maintain its integrity. Before I sold my series to Orion, I trademarked the name and logo of Stonewylde. Having such a unique name has really been invaluable, and I was anxious that nobody would use the name I had invented, nor exploit my loyal readers in any way with shoddy goods. Although registering a name as a trademark is expensive, I'm very glad I did it. I've already had one run-in with a company in the USA who were using it – and who have now ceased doing so. I would advise writers to buy any domain names they think they may need in future right now. I bought 'Stone-wylde' and 'Kit Berry' before I'd even started writing the books, and I'm so glad that I did. I have now started writing a new book very different to my previous work. I hope, using my mailing list and social media platforms, to bring my existing audience along with me. And it will be a challenge to build up a whole new audience as well, among readers who enjoy historical fiction. To reflect these new horizons, we have created an additional website, www.kitberry.com.

Figure 11.1 Picture of Kit Berry alongside her husband and fans at a book signing event in Glastonbury promoting the final Stonewylde book. Reproduced with kind permission of Kit Berry.

Working with other industry suppliers

In addition to authors, the publishing industry has always relied on a wide range of other service providers, and in the course of a publishing career you will find yourself dealing with freelances or organisations offering copywriting, ghost writing, design, illustration, print – as well as a range of consultants and agencies responsible for particular aspects of your service provision, e.g., web marketing consistancies, analysts and marketing agencies. Specific advice on how to work with them and several case studies are already included within this book under the relevant chapters. As regards general advice for working with suppliers, there are a few additional things to mention.

- **Ensure they have access to the same information that you do** – and you may assume they know. So if the organisational mission has been redrafted or repurposed, or the house style redesigned, they need to know. There is a real danger that you will assume they are as familiar as you, particularly if they used to work for the organisation and are now operating freelance.

- **It's important to remember that they are working for the organisation**, and should enhance the organisational brand and aims of the specific campaign. This becomes potentially difficult if you are relying on several different agencies to deliver different aspects of your marketing; there is a vital need for central coordination to ensure compatibility of the outcomes of those working on your behalf.

- **Ensure they feel appreciated.** Even if, as they will assume, their work is subsumed into the overall organisational communication machine, the part they played needs to be isolated and noted by those who commissioned it. Specific and informed praise will be more motivating than a general 'well done' – and rather than resulting in raised bills in future (as is commonly assumed, and a frequent reason for not providing feedback) it may result in even better value for your budget. Just as significant, they may be more inclined to help you out in the next short-term emergency that arises.

Working with publishing colleagues

A short description of how publishing organisations work is useful background information for those trying to implement effective marketing. In the rest of the world, business organisations are often hierarchical, with levels of management and accompanying responsibility, title and salary; policy is decided on at a senior level and filtered down through staff communication systems – although there are regular initiatives to create more employee responsibility and a sense of belonging.

Publishing houses tend not to be organised this way. Whereas there will still be a senior management team, and associated levels of responsibility, the management of publishing products and services tends to depend on a series of deals at job-function level. Thus a title cannot get out on time and to budget unless staff in various departments cooperate: editorial must make sure the manuscript is ready for production, production staff must source the dissemination and delivery capabilities so that once the words are ready the processes are not held up: the design department must create cover artwork that key retailers have agreed will sell the title, the marketing staff must prepare outline plans and the sales team persuade retailers to take stock. And all these functions must be going on simultaneously, thus a high degree of coordination and cooperation is required.

At the same time, publishers are not natural bureaucrats, and there is a tendency to keep information in the department where it originated rather than share it with colleagues. Authors often comment that information sent to their editorial contact, but that also is relevant to other departments such as rights or marketing, tends not to get passed on; they attend meetings or speak to staff who ought to know about things they do not. They often conclude that rather than sending one email and assuming the content will be passed on to all who need to know (as in the case of dealing with a bank) they must do the circulating themselves. In a world where ordering direct means that all the details of your relationship with a company tend to be recorded onscreen, for whoever handles the contact next, publishing can seem old-fashioned and frustrating.

Off-site staff

There may well be other parts of your publishing house that are not physically in the same place as your office, or other independent organisations with which you are required to deal as part of your job. For example, you may have your own warehouse, or contract this function out to an independent organisation; similarly customer services staff may be part of your firm (although often sited in a separate location) or your firm may contract this service to a third party. The sales force may be salaried by your organisation, or you may be part of a group that jointly funds and benefits from the services of a firm offering such a service to various small publishing houses.

Good marketing relies on effective communication and, in general, the more you consult and involve those working with you, the more they will feel inclined to do a good job for you. Too often however, an 'us' and 'them' spirit evolves when those who are not in head office or not full-time employees feel isolated, if not alienated from the main organisation.

Ways in which you can improve the relationship

- Go and see them

It sounds obvious, but it's surprising how often publishers have never been to see staff on whom they rely on a daily basis. Find out where they operate from and ask for a tour around the facilities. Record the names of those you deal with on a regular basis (and note their individual email addresses rather than their generic ones) so that you are able to chat with them as well as give instructions. This will be appreciated.

- Find out how their jobs work

Ask them to talk you through the process they take in fulfilling their function; this may give you additional ideas for things you could ask them to do – or new ways to describe the service they deliver. For example, when taking an order over the telephone, could an onscreen prompt encourage them to offer something else at the same time? How do they feel about marketing special offers and are there any that have brought in responses particularly quickly? If they are handling accounts other than yours (and many agencies are) are there useful things you could learn from what other firms are doing? Watch how items are packed for despatch and consider how the process could be effectively described. Considering blogging or tweeting about your experiences – describing a machine in action or a process that is hidden from the general public can be interesting.

- Find out what commonly goes wrong

This may be what customers routinely misunderstand or complain about. Too often this first-hand feedback from the market is never captured, either because the person taking the call does not think it will be relevant further up in the organisation, or does not know to whom it would also be relevant.

- Involve them in the development of your marketing campaigns and associated materials

It's a very common complaint that customer services staff feel compromised by the information the marketing department send out. For example, the first they hear of a special offer is when a customer rings up to claim it, and their initial denial compromises their relationship over the phone. Then there are all the basic errors that creep through (wrong postage and packing details, incorrect telephone number) that mean the customer is in a bad mood by the time they finally get through to the person who can accept an order, as well as one-off marketing offerings that do not fit with their ongoing procedures (e.g., they can't send material out on approval without a credit check).

So consult them, send them a proof or a draft web page for the offer you are thinking of making, encourage them to comment on your order forms so they feel involved. They are also very good at spotting mistakes or likely problems so, in addition to improving communication, you will also almost certainly avert potential problems.

- Encourage them to talk up your organisation

Send them free materials, include them, ask them to things. A reference publishing house I know always invites someone from their warehouse to every press event they organise – and tasks someone to look after them and ensure they meet other people. This is such good – and cheap – PR and is worth a huge amount in increased cooperation. Make them feel you are all part of the same team; share successes and lessons learned with them. And if things go particularly well, remember to say thank you, preferably written and specific – a precise response will mean much more than a general 'well done'.

Working with individual freelance staff

The publishing industry has always relied on freelance staff to help get the work done, and in a variety of different capacities. While this is useful for both parties – staff who have opted to go freelance due to personal or family circumstances, or a chosen change in lifestyle, will appreciate the chance to go on working, and in the process their experience and expertise are retained, without the expensive overhead of a full-time salary – you need to work hard to ensure they still feel included and valued.

Ways in which you can develop the relationship with freelance staff

- All the advice above on involving and including relevant staff applies, but in double measure. Those working off-site, or for other organisations but on contract, at least have each other. Freelances tend to work alone.
- Pay them quickly. Even the slowest paying of internal finance departments can usually ensure quicker terms for small accounts. Long-term payment issues create difficulties when you want something done in a hurry. My father was fond of saying 'short accounts make long friendships'.
- Give credit for what they contribute. Freelances like to be appreciated, particularly if they once held a very senior position within the industry and are reliant on much less regular work. For example, those who have left work to have a baby will quickly realise that the rest of the world patronises and marginalises pregnant women; so if their former employer suddenly sees them in a different light too, it can be a very dispiriting experience.
- Remember that freelance staff may have contacts with a wide variety of other publishing houses and so have a better overall grasp of trends within the industry than you are able to acquire from your full-time desk job. You could have some excellent market research available to you, if only you think to ask for it. Similarly, benefit from their connectedness. If they are active on social media, find out if they would talk up your titles too.

Temporary staff on work placement or work experience

Students today have to be extremely conscious of how they present themselves. Schools give classes on how to write a CV or a personal statement for a university application form, as well as how to present themselves for interview. They are encouraged to gain as much work experience as possible, and getting a placement in a publishing company is a great start towards a full-time job in the industry. There will also be those enrolled for courses of Publishing Studies at universities who seek placements as a route into the industry; there is a well-established route from successful placement to employment by the same organisation.

If you are put in charge of placement students doing work experience, do try to ensure what they experience is a real job, not a series of all the awful jobs you do not have time to do. Try to explain the context in which the job fits and why it is important. Think how you would like to be treated, rather than continuing with any in-house tradition of ignoring the intern (even if that was your own experience). Longer term, interns are likely to become industry colleagues, so it is worth taking the trouble.

Note

1 Author of *Saturday Night, Sunday Morning* (1958).

12 Organising events, presentations and other opportunities to share content

Ten top tips for preparing for events 297
Organisational meetings 300
Sales conferences 300
Promotional parties and title launches 302
Press conferences 305
Author tours, literary festivals and signing sessions 305
Exhibitions 311
Awards and literary prizes 311

Publishing is a collaborative endeavour, and it often happens that material has to be assembled to convince others – whether organisational colleagues via a meeting to consider a range of options for investment or members of an external audience that may be prepared to buy. Whatever the nature of the event being prepared for, some common rules may be identified.

Ten top tips for preparing for events

1 Understand the audience

Who, where, when? How many, how interested, currently how positively inclined towards you or your organisation? What would they rather be doing and what comes next on the programme?

2 Understand the wider context

What kind of event is this, and what else is going on – both within the organisation and within the wider world? For example, a meeting held in the context of sustained sales growth or decline may be more or less inclined to invest in new ventures; a talk at a new festival may appreciate a different type of presentation than one that has been long established. References to organisational experiences, culture and local detail, and how this replicates a national or international pattern, may be particularly appreciated.

3   How much time is available to you?

Let's dwell early on the importance of not taking more time than has been allocated to you. While this may sometimes be tolerated (within the context of a meeting, where an important related discussion arises) or not (within the context of a tight programme where to run over would delay the start of the next event) it will nearly always be resented. Running over shows a lack of respect for the audience's time, a lack of consideration for other speakers and an inability to manage material within the period allocated.

4   What do you want your audience to understand – and do – afterwards?

A presentation is not the opportunity to tell those listening everything you know about a particular product, service or idea. This can be gathered afterwards, prompted by handouts and developed through other opportunities to share. Rather it's the chance to present tempting details, to encourage your audience to want to know more, and preferably buy the book. So concentrate on thinking about your key message.

5   How can you best get the message across?

What core and additional resources do you need to enable your audience to *hear* as well as *listen*? These could range from sharing delivery among several speakers and commissioning supporting cartoons to themed dressing up or offering samples of what is being talked about – or small takeaway gifts. Whether your presentation is to two colleagues within a publishing house, or a vast audience of potential readers for a new book, take care. All will be people who value words, ideas and their effective presentation. You do not have to be word-perfect but it is important to be prepared, to have thought about what you want to say, and for your ideas to be in order.

6   What to say

Provide yourself with a list of key points to mention and practise talking around them. Talking from memory, while engaging eye-contact, is much more persuasive than reading from a script. Even worse is reading aloud from documentation that they too have in front of them. Speak slowly, particularly at the beginning. You don't have to be word-perfect; this may encourage you to speak too quickly. Hesitations and occasional repetitions help to get the message across. Practise and time yourself.

Some presentations are group affairs with teams of people involved. Not every member of a group needs to be part of their delivery team to feel they have participated, and too many contributors can detract from the idea or product being presented. Again, consider how you can best encourage the audience to hear. Practise and time yourself.

7   The use of slides for presentations

Presenting your ideas on sequential slides can look branded and professional, but if they all look alike it may be impossible for the audience to distinguish one from another.

Too much text on the screen also inhibits listening. In a study of how the medium works, Professor John Sweller of the University of New South Wales commented:

> It is not effective to speak the same words that are written, because it is putting too much load on the mind and decreases your ability to understand what is being presented … It is difficult to process information if it is coming in the written and spoken format at the same time.[1]

Screen presentations work best as support to the verbal presentation, with images that confirm the ideas being presented, and the offering of key word summaries, not as a doubling up of content.

8   Involve the audience

Make eye-contact, not just with those you know are sympathetic – allow your gaze to move around the room so everyone feels included in what you say. Ask questions and share associated anecdotes; vary your tone and pace.

9   Deal effectively with feedback

Presenting ideas for the engaged attention of others is an important part of growing a project and helping your ideas develop. The point at which you promote debate and gather ideas is, however, generally at the disposal of the speaker – so say whether you would like to make a short presentation and then receive questions, or whether you are happy to be interrupted if what you say is not understood.

There will also be feedback that moves towards a less productive outcome and you need to be prepared to deal with objections. If the question is surprising, restate it. Confirming your understanding of what is being asked may serve to get the audience on your side and buy a little time. While being prepared to deal with objections shows your own commitment to a project or idea, it may detract from the purpose of the event – or how the rest of the audience want the time to be managed. If there is a danger of spending too much time on this, and getting behind schedule, suggest you discuss further difficulties in a separate meeting.

10 Think about what to wear

However the audience is constructed, there will be more of them than there are of you. It follows that their attention will be focused on you, so how you present yourself, and in particular what you choose to wear, are both important. If possible, try to stand to present – it gives you authority – but ensure your shoes support this. Resist the temptation to fiddle with your clothing or hair. Breathe deeply before you start and remember to smile. The questions at the end are part of the presentation, allowing you to respond more specifically to their enquiries and showing that your audience has been listening – so do try to maintain the confidence from your presentation.

Having offered general advice to those presenting, in any context, here is some more specific advice for particular occasions.

Organisational meetings

The business of publishing is regularly conducted through meetings at which all functions are represented, whether this is on a departmental or organisational level. For example, meetings of the editorial department generally present new publishing ideas to all colleagues; later in the decision-making chain other publishing functions (sales, production, marketing, editorial, rights, etc.) will be present at meetings which discuss product streams and overall direction.

Sharing ideas in this way enables their precise description, to gather feedback from others and in the process to both refine and improve them. Although this may mean that an initial concept may move away from its original thrust, it may be a more effective and more generally owned solution that emerges. Airing a forthcoming project before a critical but home audience can be immensely useful in helping you develop your thoughts and marketing approach – or not, as such presentations also offer the opportunity for 'paralysis through analysis'. It's usually a good idea to brief the person who will be chairing the meeting about particularly important agenda items.

Sales conferences

Most publishing houses brief their key selling staff – representatives who call on shops, deal with key accounts or represent the house in other ways – at regular sales conferences. New titles are presented, feedback on previous promotions sought, information on company news passed on and team-building promoted.

When they are held depends on the kind of list being promoted. Educational publishing houses may hold one in the school holidays before the start of each term, or perhaps one before the autumn selling cycle, and another in the spring. A general publishing house will usually tie the conferences into the major selling and catalogue seasons: one mid-year to launch the Christmas list, another around the turn of the year for the season ahead.

At first the role of junior members of staff will probably be to put together the documentation for these events, and you may not even get the chance to attend. If you can manage to get an invitation, there is much you can learn for when it's your turn to present, from your reactions to spending the majority of the day listening and the presentational style of those you hear.

If the organisation of a sales conference falls to you, here is guidance.

- Keep in mind the real purpose at all times

While a sales conference offers a valuable opportunity for marketing and editorial staff to get together, and everyone enjoys a day out of the office, the real function is to brief those who sell on your behalf. These occasions give them the chance to tap the brains of those who commissioned and authorised the material they will try to sell over the next few months – and to find out all they can about them.

- Consider who should be there and for which parts of the programme

It may be pertinent to invite the organisational head to give a motivational or overview presentation at the beginning or end of the day, but consider whether their presence throughout may inhibit reps from asking the questions they need to get answered. Very large groups can jeopardise both the presenter's ease of delivery and the audience's willingness to respond out loud.

If political necessities mean the entire hierarchy is assembled for the formal presentation, consider organising an informal session afterwards for questions. Alternatively, can you divide into two smaller groups (perhaps home and export staff) and present different subjects in different locations at the same time? This is harder work for the staff presenting titles, but worth the effort if improved recall results.

- Provide materials to accompany presentations and promote recall

Even though presentations can be downloaded, or covers made available online, your audience is likely to remember more if they can make notes and find them again afterwards, and a physical representation of material that will have a physical presence is similarly important. Provide the delegates with a folder containing copies of advance notices, leaflets and covers for all the titles to be presented at the conference along with other relevant information (copies of news stories showing the currency of the material, comparisons with the competition). They can then make notes on these as they listen. If speakers are presenting by PowerPoint (see p. 299) you can make a copy of their slides for the file. While it's tempting to distribute hot-off-the-press promotional materials as you speak, wait until you have finished unless you want all present to participate in a live proofreading exercise.

- Have a session chair for each section of the programme

This is to ensure variety, draw attention to particular key points, keep to time and provide a second voice. Encourage them to restart the programme promptly after breaks. Running late is a big attention-blocker.

- Produce a varied programme

What other contributions could be used to extend the experience – a guest speaker, a quiz, a sporting activity? Consider asking an author along to talk about a 'big book' or to make a short reading. Brief them very carefully; this is a star appearance to motivate those who will sell the associated work, not a lecture. What the reps really want are anecdotes with which they can enthuse the retail buyers: 'As David Beckham told me ...'

• Organising the space

You may inherit a room layout used by everyone else, but try to consider its best arrangement: as a conventional boardroom (with everyone sitting around in a circle, behind tables), 'café style' (various tables with chairs around each) or as an audience (chairs in rows)? Sitting without desks between speakers and the audience can mean people feel more obliged to take part and ask questions, but also reduces their ability to make notes.

• What equipment do you need?

Should there be a lectern at the front for speakers, or is there then a risk that they will hide behind it and feel isolated from the audience? Encourage speakers (if they feel sufficiently confident) to stand close to the audience, and to move around. If there is no lectern, there does need to be somewhere for speakers to put their notes and a glass of water. Any venue that offers conference facilities should have all the equipment you need, but a preliminary visit is essential.

Promotional parties and title launches

The publisher marketing technique that most debut authors have heard of is the launch party. It's also now probably the rarest form of author promotion.

The theory was that a promotional party or book launch would prompt media interest and coverage and hence lead to more sales. Today the exigencies of time and budget, and a desire for greater accountability over costs, mean they are much rarer. But a party still may be organised as a celebration, to boost the company name, as a cumulative effort – perhaps to encourage publisher brand awareness of all authors published within the past 6 months – or to keep a particular author or agent happy.

Launch parties can also be organised on a variety of different scales, and a home-based gathering, with food you have produced yourself, a group of interested people invited and a journalist from the local paper along to report can be as effective as a larger gathering in a city centre – and vastly cheaper. Authors organising their own party may be able to ask their publisher for a contribution towards the costs.

Top tips for organising effective parties and title launches

When to hold them

Match the day you choose to those you are hoping will attend. Journalists working on Sunday papers do not work on a Monday and Tuesday is a little early in the week for them to be interested – the story may be stale by the weekend. Fridays are best avoided as they may clash with religious observations and the start of the weekend. As regards timing, after work is convenient, say from 6–8pm, on the assumption that people will be going elsewhere to eat. Alternatively, try breakfast or lunchtime. Those attending will expect some form of refreshment.

Whom to invite

Ask enough of the author's friends and relations to make them feel comfortable and prevent the room from looking empty. Ask all the relevant journalists and 'media people' you want to cover the title. Consider who else is interested in the title's subject matter; politicians, captains of industry, television personalities can all be invited. If there are well-known names who can't be there, but are fully committed to the subject, ask them if they can provide a message of support that you can read out – or to give a presentation by Skype.

Send out the invitations three to four weeks ahead, accompanied by a press release giving more information on the title being launched. Provide your name and email address and telephone number for RSVPs and make it clear where the event is being held. All the information needed should be on the email or card – so delete the address beneath your email signature or letterhead if this is different.

Make a list of all those invited and possibly still expected, in alphabetical order by surname. On the day sit by the entrance and ask the names of all who arrive, tick them off and hand out pre-prepared name badges (if appropriate). If possible get someone experienced to stand next to you so you don't ask the company chair for their name. All members of the home team should carry a badge saying who they are; it has the added advantage of deterring them from talking to one another.

If you are inviting a VIP or main guest, the event may have to be organised around their diary, and when they can be available. Find out in advance what they like to drink and if there are any limitations on their diet. On the day, ensure someone is ready to receive and host them for the rest of the evening. 'Big name' or not, they may still be nervous.

Book a photographer to take pictures of (preferably recognisable) guests enjoying themselves. Brief them on the combinations of people you want recorded. You can circulate the results afterwards to members of the press who failed to turn up, and still secure coverage in the media. Try offering an image to one medium as a scoop first, in return for a guarantee that it will be featured in a prominent place. Newspapers are much more aware of the artistic and intrinsic merits of the camera than they used to be. No longer do all photographs have to appear as illustrations to the text; a good photograph and caption can form a feature on their own. Photographs can also be used to generate a buzz, both during and after the event, via social media (see Chapter 9).

When to expect the guests

If you put 6.30pm on the invitation, most will arrive around 7pm and stay (depending on how good the party is) for about an hour. You can influence how long they stay by the timing of the welcome speeches: most will wait until they are over.

What to provide

Make the drinks as simple as possible. In general, more white than red wine will be drunk, and many will ask for soft drinks: the commonest mistake is not to provide enough. Guests are usually given a drink as they come through the door into the reception; thereafter glasses are most easily replenished by waiters or staff walking around with bottles and topping up; offering to top up glasses can be an effective way of moving around the room. If you decide to provide more exotic drinks (e.g., cocktails or spirits) have them ready-mixed on trays; waiters can circulate and offer to exchange empty for full glasses.

For early evening receptions, organisers generally lay on simple 'cocktail party' nibbles. Include vegetarian selections. Most people prefer to help themselves from passing trays rather than have to make their way to a single delivery point and load a plate – which they then have to juggle with a glass while risking looking greedy. For lunchtime launches, something more substantial may be needed, but choose dishes that can be eaten with a fork, standing up.

If it's a sit-down meal, provide a seating plan and place cards, but put the names on both sides of the card so they can be read by those across the table. Consider moving guests between courses (every other person moves two places to their left) so they have the opportunity to meet a variety of those present.

Speeches

After the party has been in full swing for about half an hour, someone should thank everyone for coming and the author(s) for providing the occasion for the party, welcome any key guests and reporters and make a few pleasant remarks. The author may want to reply – or ask someone else to do so, on their behalf. You may find some resistance to formal speeches, but it is very important to concentrate people's minds on why they are there, to provide a focal point to the event. However, do ensure that the speeches are neither too long nor too numerous.

What to have to hand

Even though you have already sent out press releases with the invitations, keep a pile of printed materials to hand. There will almost certainly be journalists who want to go away and write up the story up straight away but have lost or not yet located the necessary information. Copies of what is being promoted should be on display. They are very likely to be removed by guests (a traditional perk), so if the material is valuable then the number available needs to be carefully controlled.

What to do afterwards

Follow up journalists who did not attend and offer them a photograph and a story. Try to ensure those who said they would feature the title do so, but do this through helpful reminding ('Is there any other information you need?') rather than scolding ('I can't believe you have let me down. How could you?'). Something more newsworthy may genuinely have pushed your story out, despite their best intentions, and you will almost certainly want to work with them again.

When circulating a photograph, always send it with an effective caption: it can make the difference between the shot being featured and being ignored. Ensure you repeat the caption on the accompanying press release as a reminder to the people assembling the pages that there is one available. See Chapter 10 for advice on getting images into the trade press.

Did the venue provide all it said it would; did all go smoothly? If not, negotiate.

Press conferences

A press conference calls together representatives of the relevant media to impart a story or version of events. They should only be called if you have definite news to announce. If you call a press conference and there is no news story then you will make journalists wary of accepting your invitation the next time you ask them.

You will need someone to chair the event: to coordinate questions and ensure that all the news points are raised. The book's editor or author may be the ideal person. Alternatively, consider asking someone with related interests who is a 'name' in their own right. If chairing your press conference links the person's name with a cause they support, or their personal ambitions, they may do a particularly good job for you.

Press conferences don't have to be physical. There are lots of possibilities for organising media interest online (see Chapter 10).

Author tours, literary festivals and signing sessions

Promotional tours during which popular or newsworthy authors gave a series of talks, or signed copies of new titles, were once a familiar promotional gambit.

They also took a huge amount of organisation. While these may still be organised for particularly important titles, or newsworthy authors, the large number of literary and other local festivals that now exist offer similar opportunities to publishers, but with someone else doing the organising. The scale of this activity is both wide and spreading. Carl Wilkinson writing in *The Financial Times* commented:

> just over 30 years ago, in 1983, when the Edinburgh International Book Festival was launched, it was one of only three. Today, according to www. literaryfestivals.co.uk, a website that tries to keep up with them all, there are more than 350 in Britain alone and a further 100 in Australia and New Zealand. Not to mention others in Gibraltar, Colombia, India, Spain, Kenya ... [2]

There is an increasing public appetite for meeting their favourite writers, or simply those whose point of view they are interested to hear, and as many festivals are either hosted or serviced by local booksellers, they draw more people into bookshops and can prompt significant sales. Festivals tend to be the one remaining location where stock is not discounted and stock signed by the author is generally not subsequently returned to the publisher for credit. Win-win.

Part of festival management will be to manage associated marketing and publicity, but there is much that supporting publishers and contributing authors can do to assist, through social media and other opportunities. Some festivals seek financial support from publishers, asking them to take advertising space in the programme. If the event is being coordinated by publisher and bookshop, it is common practice for the publisher to share the cost of some preliminary space advertising in local papers and to jointly build associated social media activity.

Whether you are making contact with a festival to try to get your author(s) on to the programme or confirming details of arrangements already established by someone else within your organisation, it helps to be prepared.

Ten top tips for effective publisher collaboration with literary and other festivals

1   Find out about the festival before you make contact. Read previous programmes and study their website. You will discover that most were started by local activists who feel strongly about where they live, had observed festivals elsewhere and wanted to offer something similar to their neighbourhood for like-minds to enjoy. Find out about their ethos, motivations and history and ensure your early discussions are infused with this. Be particularly clear about how long they have been going – if you imply a long-established festival is part of their more recent expansion, you will offend.

2   Find out the names of the programme managers and make a tailored submission to their festival by email. This may prompt a telephone discussion if your ideas look sufficiently interesting. However much thought you put into this, and however complete the information you provide, the festival will want to own the event – so it will help if you are flexible and willing to listen to their suggestions and improvements rather than defend your outline at all costs.

The outline you send should be based on the kind of event they like to host (as you read their programmes look out for 'returners' who seem to get asked back every year): local details that make it particularly relevant to them (local history, vegetation, politics), their wider ambitions (to be more inclusive in the range of people they attract or more self-sustaining) or forthcoming anniversaries. Then offer a range of appropriate, relevant events – offering a selection means they can make a choice, but whatever they select, your house and authors hopefully remain on the programme.

3   Contact the festival management in plenty of time. Most are planning next year's events almost as soon as the current year's programme is over. Do so with one specific outline rather than repeated requests for a meeting.

4   Understand the context. They are juggling many different publishing houses and authors, not yours alone. If what you are offering is big enough, or sufficiently attractive to their audience, they may move events to fit – but other publishers and authors will be inconvenienced in the process. And vice versa.

5   Once a programme item has been agreed, be meticulous in confirming all the details. What kind of event has been agreed on (talk, participation in a panel, discussion?). Sort out the money early, to avoid confusion or resentment later. In general, if an author's name is appearing on the ticket, and the paying public are being charged for the opportunity to listen, then as the main content provider they should be remunerated:

> There is no such thing as a literary festival without authors in it. It's the one component that a literary festival can't lack.
>
> Guy Walters, author, interviewed by Carl Wilkinson[3]

But there are significant associated costs – a week may take a whole year to organise, the weather is unreliable and ultimately it is the festival that is taking the risk:

> The only people who make money from these festivals are the caterers.
>
> Jeremy Lee[4]

Some festivals offer presents rather than fees to offset the significant costs of mounting such events, sometimes authors agree to do a guest appearance for nothing as investment in getting themselves better known. Establish who is paying for expenses. Some festivals do, others ask supporting publishers to pick up the tab. If a contributor is registered for VAT or sales tax then this must be added to the fee they receive, not deducted from what is offered (which is illegal).

6   Many festivals prefer to work with traditional publishers who handle a range of authors, as this cuts down on administration. Individual authors can put themselves forward, and this can work particularly well for locals, but it may be a good idea to suggest an entire event, with several presenters and a relevant chair. Make it clear you are professional and easy to deal with.

7   Respond quickly to their requests for marketing and publicity support – quotations, photographs, checking of copy. This is a chance to have someone else market your author or publishing house for you. Build on their efforts, retweeting and blogging about your involvement. Add details of your involvement in it to your own website.

8   Note the specific venue and find out who is managing arrangements there. A centrally managed festival may be working with a number of different venues. Find out the names and mobile numbers of the key staff on site.

9   Festivals are often organised in conjunction with a supporting retailer, and some retailers will be charged for the opportunity to sell books. The range of titles they stock is a commercial decision, so the more flexible you are able to be about its provision (sale or return, redelivery timings) the more inclined to stock your material they may be. Establish the name of the supporting retailer and liaise directly. Mistakes can happen (stock unordered or that fails to arrive, insufficient quantity requested) and while it's a good idea to take

some with you on the day just in case of emergencies, it is perhaps best kept to one side, or in the car boot, until it's evident whether or not it is needed.

Be aware that the bookseller managing stock for sale at the festival may not be the same one who runs the high street bookshop around the corner, even if they sport the same logo. And this may have caused some local resentment about a non-local retailer, or head office, swooping in and selling to customers with whom they are uninvolved for the rest of the year. Ensure you are dealing with the right manager before you complain about non or insufficient stocking.

10   Some authors will appreciate or require being accompanied by a representative of their publishing house, others will be happy to go alone. Whatever arrangement you come to, a phone call or text message afterwards, to find out how it went, is generally appreciated.

Case study

Interview with Sarah Smyth, artistic director of the Times Cheltenham Literature Festival

While it's almost never too early to contact us, we appreciate it if the first approach is made by email – which means we can consider your suggestions in the context of the festival as a whole, and the other submissions we have received – and then follow up with a telephone call if appropriate. We are looking for a well-worded submission that shows some understanding of the *Times* Cheltenham Literature Festival, the kind of event that works well, and flexibility in how we might work together in delivery.

It's always more attractive if the author(s) being proposed are flexible about the kind of event they would like to be part of (e.g., presentation, interview, panel discussion) and over the dates when they are available.

Managing a programme is an immensely complicated process, and it's helpful if those submitting ideas have some appreciation of this. Being pragmatic, it's a good idea to establish the cut-off date for the programme – the date by which the full programme must be decided – in order to get the information out to the audience. Throughout the planning process, we may have several dates out on offer to speakers we particularly want to secure, and be waiting to hear back from them – and so 3 months before the cut-off date, literally no options to offer other contributors. But once we have heard back from key speakers, options may emerge that were not previously available – and so an email two to three weeks before the cut-off date may yield a positive response. The day before the cut-off date is far too late.

Another issue to bear in mind in connection with timing is that for us the festival starts well before the first event. So if there are changes to be communicated (there has been huge and controversial press interest in this author) or particular issues to bear in mind (the speaker has broken her leg and will have difficulty getting up stairs) do try to let us know as soon as possible – rather than just before the event. We may need to inform others (change a hotel booking; ensure the bookseller knows about potentially increased demand) and so the sooner we know, the sooner this process can be implemented.

While Cheltenham is a festival of international scope, we particularly appreciate programme suggestions that offer some specific value to Cheltenham. So, for example, a talk on castles would go down well if mention was made of its relevance to Sudeley Castle and Berkeley Castle, which are our nearest. Or is the author willing to show specific materials to the audience, before, during or after the talk? We appreciate visual material that can be used in event promotion – photographs they have not released before, or items from their personal archive that they are willing to share. For example Jung Chang, author of *Wild Swans*, brought along her grandmother's tiny shoes, for which her feet had been broken and bound. An author of a book on gardening brought along a series of samples in pots with which to illustrate her talk and which the audience could examine afterwards. Our press team appreciate quirky stories that are likely to attract press attention and circulation on social media in the short term, and in the longer term promote the range of fascinating content on offer to audiences at the *Times* Cheltenham Literature Festival.

Ten top tips for preparing authors for an appearance at a literary festival or tour event

1 An enquiry about availability is not the same thing as a booking to appear. Festival managers may express interest in a title and ask if the author is available, but they will be going through the same process with many other authors, publishers and agents before the various options are distilled into the final programme. Just because the author was excited to be asked, and immediately noted the dates in their diary, does not mean they have an automatic place on the programme. Indeed the more difficult they become, the less likely the organisers may be to include them – or work with their publishing house or agent in future.

2 If booked, confirm all arrangements clearly, make a note of key mobile numbers and read the briefing notes carefully. Be clear about what kind of event has been arranged, the specific contribution required, and for how long. Find out who else is taking part, who is going to chair the event, and do some research into how they tend to contribute – for example, are they inclined to be supportive, seek controversy or score points? Send the chair a copy of the book and provide a few interesting briefing notes with which to introduce the author – not just a reworking of the jacket copy. Mention any specific local connections. Sending the other participants a copy of the book may be appreciated too.

3 Encourage the author to understand the specific context of the festival in question and to make effective preparation – rather than delivering the same

speech offered the last time they did an event. Have they ever been to the locality before? If so, make sure they mention it.

Guide them on the kind of audience to expect as regional variations can be marked. In general, if a reader has paid to see a particular author, they are keen for that author to do well – and will tolerate hesitations that indicate a writer is present rather than a talker. But do provide a warning that audiences at literary festivals can sometimes convey a strong ownership towards a title in which they have invested both time and money. They should not be surprised if questions feel invasive bordering on impertinent – 'Why did you let the main character do that?'; 'Your understanding of today's mental health patient is quite wrong.'

4   Leave in plenty of time to ensure arrival without worrying the management – most will specify how soon before an event to arrive and offer a location for refreshment and relaxation. Ask them to arrive in time to absorb the atmosphere. If possible encourage them to attend another event at the festival – and ensure they make reference to it. Or have them mention what they wish they had been able to see. Conveying a wider sense of the festival rather than assuming it's all about them will generally be appreciated. If short of time, suggest they buy the local paper or talk to the taxi driver or person sitting next to them on the bus.

5   Remind that audiences are seeing all speakers in the context of the other events they attend and are inclined to sympathise with those who are not being treated fairly; for example, during two-author events when the first speaker encroaches into time that should be at the disposal of the second speaker, looks bored during the other contributions, or dominates during question time.

6   A programme manager comments: 'There is nothing that will sell a book less than authors continually announcing that their title is available from the bookstall after the event. The audience knows that. They are at a literary festival.'

This is really important. The more they mention the availability of their book, the less people may feel inclined to buy it. Let the chair do the talking up for them. Just before an event, maybe at the sound check, is a good time to let the chair know if anything has changed – maybe the title of the book or the addition of a foreword.

7   Grand, idiosyncratic or newsworthy behaviour may appeal to the audience – or it may repel. As Andrew Franklin, founder publisher of Profile, commented to the AGM of the Society of Authors, 'if your books sell, you can be as difficult as you like'. But be aware that what is communicated will not stay within the confines of the event – not only will the press develop stories based on controversial content, the audience may be live tweeting.

8   Signing stock. Some authors insist they will only sign copies of their new books – this is often resented by loyal readers who, while bringing along a less than pristine title for signature, are identifying themselves as long-standing fans. Others offer enhanced personalisation through the addition of ink-stamping or drawings, which may be particularly appreciated.

9   Warn them that some people in the queue will ask for only a signature, rather than a dedication. This may be because they are planning that the purchase

will be a gift, or perhaps is destined for more commercial reuse – books signed by the author and resold online generally attract higher prices. You might take the view that a book sold is helpful, however it is later distributed; some festivals limit the number of titles an individual may buy for signing if queues are likely to be long.

10   Thanking the organisers is always a good idea – preferably in person before departure. It is particularly appreciated if all involved are included – so if a specific driver, stock manager or member of the event support team has been helpful, do mention them by name. Letters or cards of thanks afterwards are similarly appreciated. Juggling so many contributors and their retinues is much harder than it looks.

Exhibitions

Some firms instruct reps or have mobile exhibition teams who will provide everything needed if you inform them in good time of the nature of the exhibition and the stock required.

If you have to mount the display yourself, find out what will be available on site (screens, tables, chairs, platforms and so on) and from what time the exhibition room is available for assembly. Take enough additional promotional material to make your stand look interesting (posters, showcards and so on). A large cover for the table looks professional – a few yards of crease-resistant polyester may suffice and, whatever your organisational livery, if it is black it won't start to look grubby. All those who are to help run the stand need a name badge to identify them as part of the company.

Never underestimate how many people you need to help run an exhibition stand. Organise a rota with several taking stints rather than relying on one person.

Business cards are treasure troves of relevant information – far more detail than you could write down in the short time generally available at fairs. People respond well to having their business card received with respect and interest, so when handed one, consciously read it before adding it to those already received. In some cultures, it is polite to receive a card with two hands. Once they have moved on, either write relevant information on the back of the card or staple it to a larger card on which you write additional notes (using card because the firmness means it is easier to write on).

You should have stock of your brochures and catalogues ready to hand out, but you want to ensure that they re-emerge from the ubiquitous exhibition carrier bag handed out to visitors as they enter. Can you mark the products you discussed with a highlighter pen? Staple your own business card to the front of the brochure to make recall more likely.

Awards and literary prizes

Literary prizes and awards are hugely important, offering a market overwhelmed with choice a convenient and topical selection. Winners of key prizes are featured on the news pages (not in the book section) of the national press and they can offer both shortlisted and winning titles the promise of substantial extra sales. The publication of many novels is scheduled in order to ensure work is eligible for consideration for particular prizes.

If one of your titles is a frontrunner for a forthcoming prize you will be required to put together a plan of action to support and sustain media interest, and further capitalise on it if the book wins. For example, you may have to produce (overnight) stickers to go on book jackets for circulation to booksellers saying 'Winner of X' and prepare attractive point-of-sale material for retail use. Trade organisations issue lists of which prizes are run and when and how to enter titles.

Choosing a venue for events and presentations

Whatever kind of event you are organising, a location is a starting point. Here is some associated guidance.

1   Start with the obvious

Give yourself a scaffold on which to build ideas and expectations. An online search into possible options will probably give you a shortlist of hotels and other locations with conference facilities and often isolate a point of contact – a conference or events manager. Enquire about conference packages, the 'delegate daily rate' and juggle this with how many you estimate will be attending.

2   Consider more imaginative locations

Other locations may occur to you, perhaps the contacts of the author or organisation, and if they are particularly relevant to the service, product or purpose of the event they may be worth further investigation. Working with a venue unused to organising events may ensure yours feels fresh and original but you may be able to rely on them less. Early consideration of the location and associated transport/parking is vital – beautiful but remote could be difficult if everyone is relying on the same taxi to collect them from the nearest station.

3   The price

Look at the overall price for hire, delegate rates and any other additional costs (do they charge for internet access, do they insist you take overnight accommodation too?). Overall, is what is on offer reasonably priced? Negotiate with the venue's manager about the room rate for the day(s) and other options for refreshments ('Do you have anything simpler?'). The printed price list and sample menus should never be accepted as absolute, particularly if the venue or time of year is not busy and the opportunity helps get their venue more widely known.

4   Ask about programmes of work

Find out about building renovation programmes in advance; they tend to be noisy and not to run to schedule. So if you are assured they will be over by the time you arrive, have it confirmed in writing. Is there air-conditioning; how loud is it? If not, will opening the windows make it impossible to hear the speakers over the roar of passing traffic?

5   Record the names of those responsible

Find out the name and mobile number of the operations manager whose responsibility it is to check that everything is working and get familiar with the practicalities (how do you dull the lights during presentations, is there a light for the speaker?).

In general, launch parties fell out of favour because they were expensive to organise and uncertain in outcome. Much more common is becoming the organisation of events that boost the relationship between consumers and publishers and which extend the range of publisher content for sale: from what is purchased to be read to what is listened to, or otherwise experienced.

Concluding case study

Bloomsbury Publishing, *The Writers' & Artists' Yearbook* and the Bloomsbury Institute

Bloomsbury have been proactive in organising events to engage with the reading public. They organise a series of events to tie in with the *Writers' & Artists' Yearbook* and launched the Bloomsbury Institute in January 2011, a new programme for the public held at their offices in Bedford Square.

Associated events divide broadly into two types: 'how to' and experiential, with some overlap in the middle. 'How to' events may include months of one-to-one tutoring, whole days on the processes of publishing, or short seminars offering guidance on specific issues. Experiential events may include book groups that include a copy of the book and an opportunity to meet the author or debates about key trends within publishing, reading and the extension of literacy. The overlap between the two tends to be those who want to hear about how work came to be spotted or commissioned – and are gleaning hints about how their own might be developed. They want to hear how the editor for a particular title found the author or book; find out about their particular writing process; interact with them on the meaning and observe how best to present to those they are hoping will invest in their writing.

Eela Devani, digital development director of Bloomsbury, comments:

> From research among authors I became aware of the stages the writer goes through in crafting their manuscript: starting out with their first concept; crafting their work; reviewing and finalising the manuscript; trying to stimulate external interest from agents and publishers. Taking our basis as the cumulative expertise and experience contained within the *Writers' and Artists' Yearbook* we now offer a range of events, both online and in person, that support the writer's journey and offer advice that is both inspiring and practical, with plenty of opportunities to hear first-hand how techniques have worked or experiences felt for others approaching the same challenges. This is finding an interested audience and proving successful – making a significant financial contribution and promoting our brands within core markets.

Claire Daly is manager of the Bloomsbury Institute and works with James Rennoldson in organising the *Writers' & Artists'* events for the public. These range from literary salons and debates on a topical issue to the regular hosting of the Bloomsbury Book Club, for which the charge includes a hardback copy of the book and the chance to attend an event with the author, usually in conversation with the title's editor. Claire says:

> I try to organise the kind of event I would like to attend myself, and take huge care with how we describe what is on offer. When we plan *Writers' & Artists'* events, James and I send the copy backwards and forwards between us many times, and we involve others to help improve it too. In the process we are linking with people who previously only knew the names of our authors and reminding them that these titles are published by Bloomsbury.

Information for both markets – which are relatively separate – must be enticing, clear and error-free; the anticipated standards and usefulness of the event and a decision on whether or not to attend will be based on the sur-rounding copy. Once the programme has been established, however, online marketing offers the opportunity to present customers with information directly, and this can be further shared through social media. If it's possible, hosting events at the organisational headquarters keeps costs down, although there may be some additional unanticipated costs (the temporary employment of security guards to guard against theft; expert removal people to dismantle, move and later reassemble the boardroom). Writers are remunerated for their involvement but also appreciate the associated pro-motion of their work and the guaranteed sale of stock. Staff attend in return for a day off in lieu during the week; journalists and academics contributing to debates are paid. All participating may be willing to provide additional content of interest to the market – for the website or by writing a blog – and on the day, live tweeting of what is happening can spread enthusiasm, creating awareness among those present of the uniqueness of what is on offer and reaching out to those who may come next time.

Timing for such events needs to be carefully considered. Avoid periods when your key contributors are too busy (the build-up and timing for major book fairs if you are hoping agents will attend) and times when the market is likely to be away (over Christmas and other key holidays). But there are also good synergies to incorporate – the start of the new year or a long holiday period is when so many budding writers decide to embark on their writing resolutions, or encourage 'living the dream' by tying your events in with the announcements for major prizes.

Looking wider, this is a significant trend within publishing, part of a closer relationship between publishers and their readers that boosts awareness of – and confidence in – the publisher brand, helps make buyers aware of who publishes their favourite authors and encourages them to try other titles from the same stable. It also offers access to changing patterns of consumer spending. De-cluttering and a wider desire for high quality experiences mean that such opportunities access the treat, gift and personal investment market for which there are higher expectations of cost.

In the longer term, such programmes may affirm publisher brand and build relationships with those who may have work worth future publisher investment. In the shorter term, they can make a useful contribution to organisational finances and help fund the launch of new writing.

For more information see www.writersandartists.co.uk and www.bloomsburyinstitute.com.

Notes

1 www.smh.com.au/news/technology/powerpoint-presentations-a-disaster/2007/04/03/1175366240499.html.
2 www.ft.com/cms/s/2/1ed23824-e687-11e3-9a20-00144fcabdc0.html#ixzz33SlMqodS.
3 www.ft.com/cms/s/2/1ed23824-e687-11e3-9a20-00144feabdc0.html?utm_content=buffer2458e&utm_medium=social&utm_source=twitter.com&utm_campaign=buffer#axzz33NenBYKx.
4 Ibid. Jeremy Lee runs www.JLA.co.uk, an agency for speakers.

13 Techniques for writing effective copy

What is copywriting? 316
Six basic principles 318
Acronyms for copywriters 320
Further techniques for effective copywriting 324
Other ideas for attracting attention 334
Writing headlines 335
Writing copy for titles you do not understand 337
Disentangling long and difficult blurbs 337
Presenting and defending your copy 340

Writing copy for publishing products and services is a common requirement in the early stages of a publishing career, and you might have expected a chapter on how to write effective copy to consist of a long list of top tips for attracting attention through words. If you are required to write copy for products and don't know where to start, or if you want to improve your writing techniques, this chapter will indeed provide guidance – but it will start by encouraging you to think in detail about the task before you, and all the associated stakeholders. Effective copywriting is a much more sophisticated endeavour than the publisher just offering news on what the customer might like to buy.

What is copywriting?

Promotional copywriting means selling through words, however they are presented: printed leaflet; website; T-shirt. A copywriter's key purpose is to put across a believable promise to the right audience and in the process to prompt awareness, interest, purchase and loyalty.

The copywriter's role is essentially a silent one; you are the customer-advocate who can appreciate all the various benefits of a product but then select the message likely to speak most effectively to the market. And although the role demands a huge facility with language, and may have been sought as part of a long-term plan to get published, all that technical ability with words needs to be deployed on behalf of the product or service being presented. A copywriter's key objective is to get customers to respond, buy and enthuse to others – not to show you have a novel in you.

Being a promotional copywriter can be both a political and an unappreciated role. Political because it is your job to produce the slightly unexpected – and then persuade your colleagues of the validity of the approach taken. Customers tend not to read messages that feel familiar, and having done the research it is therefore often the role of the copywriter to surprise. This is not always well received among those who commissioned or created the products being written about, and the copywriter will have to think carefully about not only their copy platform but also how to persuade their colleagues of its likely efficacy. There will always be a temptation to write the kind of copy you know will achieve a swift path of acceptance by colleagues; but copy without a frisson of excitement can feel bland and dull to the rest of the world.

Well managed, the words that explain a product or service can seem self-evident, and their creation assumed to be facile; it's common to assume that a short message has taken a correspondingly short time to write. Similarly, successful copy, deployed to persuade a market and demonstrably doing just that, can be seen as evidence of the author's ability to manipulate. Being 'good with words' is not always seen as a compliment.

Rules for copywriters

The first rule for would-be copywriters is that there are very few rules. The practice of laying down rules for writing would probably result in stilted and formulaic copy. Nor is past skill at literary criticism any guarantee of success. You may have thought a degree in English Literature or a high A-level grade in the subject an excellent grounding for copywriting, but many such qualified candidates find the linguistic freedom off-putting.

Suddenly you have an immense amount of freedom: to start sentences with 'and' or 'but'; to use dashes rather than colons and semi-colons; to miss out the verb in a phrase altogether if the message is clear without it; to ignore the paring skills acquired through note-taking and repeat your basic message again and again, each time in slightly different words. All become techniques at your disposal in the wider aim of attracting attention to the product you are promoting.

Along with a consciousness of your own writing style, out must go your partiality for particular products. Ironically it can be very difficult to write about something for which you have a great passion, as whatever you draft does not seem praise enough. The copywriter's job is to do an effective sales job for whatever they are promoting, even if they personally think it is not worth reading. It is your job to put yourself into the frame of mind of would-be readers, and to think what they might look for from the product, to develop empathy with the market.

Given that publishing attracts more arts than science graduates, marketing staff often find themselves working on scientific and technical products of which they have no understanding. While this may feel daunting, in my experience people often do a *better* job writing about something with which they are unfamiliar, as they are forced to ask a series of questions: who is it for, what does it do, how does the customer benefit?

This chapter will begin with six basic principles and then continue with ad hoc suggestions – this is in the hope that prompting an appreciation of good copy can prompt its effective emulation.

Six basic principles

1   Think in detail about the market and the product before you start working out what to say

The best copywriting starts with thinking rather than writing. However tempting it is to get started, and however many other priorities you have competing for your time, if you do the thinking as you write, what you produce will be more muddled, and it will take you longer.

So before you start, immerse yourself in an understanding of the market you are writing to and the product you are writing about. Why do people need it? How does it compete on price with the competition? How will people pay for it? What other options do they have (not necessarily book-related)? Can you picture a member of the market? Your copy is far more likely to be effective if it is personal. Summon up an image of a typical member of the market and then explain to that person one to one.

Now think about what you are hoping they will do as a result of receiving the message you plan to send – for example, to ask for a brochure, go online to look at your website or order immediately? How much do they already know about your organisation or author and the product on offer and what information do they need to persuade them to move to the next stage? There is often a difference between the information they want and what you want to ensure they understand; they may be considering your product for an entirely different range of reasons from those you assume.

You will find it easier to get on to other people's wavelengths on a regular basis if you start varying your own absorption habits. So don't just read the same newspaper or news website, watch or listen to the same news programmes every day (it will simply confirm your impression that everyone is as reasonable as you are). Read different ones, tabloid and broadsheet, commercial and public service, and see how different media report the same stories. Similarly, try to widen the opinions you hear. You can probably guess the opinions of your close friends and family, but how about those outside your immediate circle? The most useful asset for any would-be copywriter is a strong curiosity.

> From the axe-wielding serial killer through the pious grandma to the neurotic mother, never a truer word spoken than: 'To think like someone else, you have to remember that they don't think they're wrong'.
>
> Claire Simpkin, letter in *Guardian Weekend* magazine,
> 19 February 2011

2 Ensure your market can find you

Ensure that the information you present on the product or service you are offering relates to the market whose needs you seek to fulfil. Pay particular attention to the buzz words or key terms that matter to the market and avoid in-house jargon that is not understood outside your organisation. Early product descriptions can become hallowed through familiarity, and you need to get back to basics and consider whether these terms (which were perhaps also initially unfamiliar to colleagues) really do sum up the priorities of the likely consumer (see the section on search engine optimisation in Chapter 5).

3 Avoid grammatical howlers

Copywriters are free to break the rules of more standardised language only if they know what they are – and those promoting managed content need to be particularly careful that their sales messages are error-free.

Check your work carefully for mistakes such as the combination of singular verbs and plural subjects, misspellings and, in particular, avoid the split infinitive (see Glossary). This is not because it is wrong, but because most people believe it to be so. The split infinitive will attract the attention of many who ignore far more casual uses of the English language; they will stop reading your message and start congratulating themselves on catching you out. Their conclusions will be that if a publisher can't get such a basic grammatical point right its material must be unreadable. Watch out, too, for the confusion of similar words with different meanings, such as 'accept' and 'except', 'principle' and 'principal', 'affect' and 'effect'.

4 Avoid assumptions

Make no assumptions about the market you are writing to. You will offend part of it when (not if) you get it wrong. Do not write to the business community as 'Dear Sir' or assume all nurses and primary school teachers are female. If writing 'him or her' feels clunky, it is now acceptable to use plural pronouns (e.g., 'they', 'their', 'them') with singular subjects (e.g., 'anyone'). Pay particular attention to the photographs you use to illustrate your words and ensure they are representative of the market you are approaching.

5 Avoid the predictable

Do not write exactly what the market expects: we do not bother to read an advertisement if from a cursory look we already know (or can guess) the content. This does not mean that you have to compensate by tending towards obscurity or outrageousness, just that to be interesting – and therefore get read – copywriting needs to be slightly unexpected. As an example, if asked to write advertising copy, look at the space available to you and consider how other people have used it – would offering significantly fewer words and more space attract greater attention? Along similar lines, build on ideas that are familiar to the market in new ways – clichés and well-known quotations can be very useful for attracting an initial attention that you then redirect.

6   Never forget that the market has a choice

The assignments you wrote at school or university had to be read in order to be given a mark. Not so with copy: the market has plenty of other options and will only read what you send if it is interesting and relevant. As advertising creative director Andrew Sullivan commented: 'The only people waiting to see your next ad are you, your client and your Mum.'

How to learn more about effective copywriting

There are books and distance-learning courses available but your principal option is to learn on the job, from other people you work with or for and from the wider world of advertising. Teach yourself by gaining access to all the promotional material you can. Watch what your competitors are producing, and compare it with the past and current efforts of your own publishing house. Build an awareness of what makes for good and bad advertising. Learn to recognise good copy and formats that get frequently repeated, in particular those that are used in direct response advertising: they must work.

Although there are no rules for writing copy, there are some useful acronyms for thinking about what you write. These perhaps work better as mantras to keep in your head, or as a readily available method of judging what you have written. Slavishly working through them, letter by letter, is more likely to result in predictable copy.

Acronyms for copywriters

Acronyms are words formed from the initial letters of other words, for example NATO, SWALK (sealed with a loving kiss) and the more recent TLI (three-letter initials). The publishing industry seems to embrace the use of initials with particular enthusiasm: each house has developed its own terms.

AID(C)A

AIDA is one of the best-known copywriting acronyms, and has been around for over 100 years.[1] Originally it served as a structure for writing direct mail letters, but it works equally well as a guide to writing emails, press advertisements, leaflets, telemarketing frameworks and other promotional formats. It was recently updated with the addition of a 'C', and so now stands for attract, interest, desire, conviction, action.

Attract

What is it about an advertisement or piece of promotional material that first attracts the reader's eye? It may be the subject line on an email, a stunning photograph, an attractive layout, a message on the envelope of a mailshot, a personalised name and address at the start of a sales letter, a headline or slogan on a space advertisement or billboard. Whatever it is, if you start thinking about the process of attracting attention and start noticing what grabs yours, you are well on the way to writing successful copy yourself.

Interest

Once you have secured the reader's attention, your next task is to keep it: advertising guru David Ogilvy reckoned five times as many people read the headline as the text beneath. You must develop the copy in such a way that the reader stays with you, absorbing the sales message as he or she goes.

Explain the benefits of the product; use subheadings to assist readers who want to 'skim' before they read in detail. Talk logically through the sales points in a tone that is friendly without being either condescending or patronising.

Desire

As you stimulate interest, create a desire to own or benefit from the product you are describing. Be enthusiastic: it's worth having! Will the reader be one of the first to benefit from this new kind of information source? Are stocks limited? Is there a pre-publication offer so that the reader will save money if the order is placed before a particular date? Has it already taken the United States by storm? Provide all the reasons you can to create the desire to purchase.

Conviction

Provide proof: testimonials; review quotes; how long it took to develop and trial the material now about to be published; the current sales trends; your cast-iron guarantee that shows your company's great confidence.

Action

Finally, direct the reader to take the action necessary to secure the product you have described. What is the publication date and where is it available? If you take direct orders, make it easy to do so: offer freepost, the chance to order by telephone or online, in both cases paying by credit card. Restate the comforting guarantee: your security procedures; if the buyer is not completely satisfied there is a full refund.

FAB

This stands for features, advantages and benefits: a useful checklist to ensure that your copy is relevant and interesting to the market. Many copywriters get no further than listing features. These need to be converted into what really interests the reader – benefits. Here are two examples, one from general advertising, the other from publishing:

> New Snibbo toothpaste contains newly researched ingredient XPZ2 (feature);
> which reaches the plaque that covers your teeth, even in hard to reach places (advantage);
> which means you and your family need fewer fillings (benefit).

> This new Maths course has been extensively piloted in schools to ensure it meets the needs of a wide range of abilities (feature);
> which means the whole class can be using the same material at the same time (advantage);
> which means you get more time to concentrate on individual needs (benefit).

The same principle was also neatly summed up as 'sell the sizzle, not the sausage'.

Publishers are rather prone to describe how their systems work: how particular products came to be developed or how they are available for inspection ('We are delighted to announce … '). The market is more likely to be interested in the benefits *they* will accrue rather than the process of development. So think about the benefits available, or how else people might spend their time. For example, consider the advertisement in Figure 13.1.[2] Rather than just offering a mown lawn, the writer makes an imaginative leap to talk about what else the happy recipient of the service could be doing with their time. This is easily replicable within publishing. Sometimes I read books because they are what other people are talking about, or because I feel I ought to, but more often it's because of the way I want to feel: relaxed, excited or involved. When reading stories to children, it's the shared time, the cuddle that is important, and when reading the same story again and again (which is what very small children like), the language is particularly vital. These are issues I find rarely mentioned in publisher marketing.

USP

The search for a unique selling proposition for every product was at its height in America in the 1950s. A USP is what makes a product different from everything else on the market; if one was not immediately apparent it had to be invented. Here are some examples of a USP providing an identity for products that may be similar to others on the market:

> Minstrels: The chocolates that melt in your mouth, not in your hand.[3]
> Ronseal: It does exactly what it says on the tin.
> Esso: Put a tiger in your tank.

Today the practice is no longer obligatory. Some products are deliberately very similar to their competitors (known as the 'me too' market) and are best promoted on the basis of similarity, value for money or simply how strongly people

AVAILABLE SHORTLY

BY

BPM Grass Cutting Services

A superior grass cutting service
at an affordable price.
Save yourself all the hassle.
Just think of all the things you could do
with your family instead!!!

Yes I will cut all your grass for only £7.50, and leave your lawn in a neat & tidy state.

No more hard day's at the office followed by a hard couple of hours struggling with that five a side pitch out the back.

Let me do all the graft while you count out a mere £7.50 in freshly minted coins of the Realm.

Please annotate your preference below:

☐   Yes please, come and save me from the tortures of mowing the lawn (as I can't afford any goats)

☐   No thanks, I find gardening hard graft and a bit of a pain, but it'll save me £7.50

Name

Address

I WILL COLLECT THESE FLYERS IN THE NEXT COUPLE OF DAYS. MANY THANKS FOR YOUR RESPONSE. Ben McDaniel.

Figure 13.1 Flyer for lawn-mowing service.

feel about a product. John Hegarty of advertising agency Bartle, Bogle and Hegarty commented:

> Advertising has moved from the USP to the ESP, or emotional selling proposition. Product quality differences are far less, because technology has moved forwards so much. So today it's a matter of how you feel about a brand.
>
> (quoted in the *Sunday Times*, 18 April 1999)

Nevertheless, if your early product investigations make you aware that the title you are promoting is unique (new to the market, a completely new look at the subject, new format, etc.), make the most of it.

WIIFM?

Everyone reading promotional material or responding to advertising has this question in mind, and if the question is satisfactorily answered they will keep reading, right to the end. The message is: what's in it for me?

KISS

Explain yourself clearly. Don't be overcomplicated or verbose. In other words: keep it simple, stupid!

Further techniques for effective copywriting

The information that follows are offered as spurs to good thinking rather than step-by-step guidance. Interpret these ideas in the context of the product being promoted, the market being approached and the space available.

Write clearly and logically

Once you have established all the sales benefits of the product you are promoting, rank them and use them in order: one idea per sentence, one theme per paragraph. Use short sentences. David Ogilvy reckoned that the first sentence of advertisement body copy (the text that follows the headline) should contain no more than 11 words. Thereafter ensure sentence length is varied to avoid monotony. Use words from everyday speech (demotic language), and don't use long phrases where single words would do. For example:

> Use 'most' instead of 'a great deal of'.
> Use 'respected' instead of 'widely acclaimed'.
> Use 'consider' instead of 'take into consideration'.

Writer Georges Simenon (the creator of the detective Maigret) deliberately stuck to a vocabulary of just 2,000 words so that his books could be understood by everyone. Dr Seuss' famous book for children *Green Eggs and Ham* has just 50 words, and yet is never dull.

Use short words (often Saxon in origin) rather than long ones (often from Latin). For example:

> 'news' or 'facts', not 'information';
> 'find' not 'discover';
> 'show' not 'demonstrate';
> 'now' not 'immediately'.

On the other hand, the occasional use of long words can attract attention, particularly if they are surrounded by monosyllabic terms that throw them into further relief. Prince Charles' use of 'carbuncle' at a speech to the Royal Institute of British Architects was well chosen. Positioned among short familiar words it had an added bite: 'what is proposed is a monstrous carbuncle on the face of a much-loved friend'. If he had instead described 'a monstrous carbuncle on the frontage of an elegant and familiar early nineteenth-century building in Greek Revivalist style in a much-visited central London attraction', the words would have received much less emphasis.

Similarly, the linking of apparently contradictory terms (oxymorons) can be most effective. For example:

Dangerously romantic
Ridiculously bloodthirsty

Try to use vivid words, rather than stale ones:

Vivid	Stale
hate	dislike
adore	love
cash	money

Use active verbs, not passive. For example: 'You can see' not 'It can be seen … '
Better still, use an imperative:

See how …
Watch!

The present tense implies action, for example:

'Research shows' not 'Research has shown … '
'The author talks to … ' not 'The author was interviewed'

Steer clear of overused words. I am grateful to bookseller Justine Crow (www.booksellercrow.co.uk) for the following list of words that make her yawn. They appear in order of frequency:

unique ('almost unique' is even worse and makes no sense)

major	moving
timely	exciting
a must	heart-rending
outstanding	hilarious
exceptional	invaluable
revolutionary	essential

brilliant	remarkable
eye-catching	compelling
absolutely fabulous	original
unputdownable	wicked (in particular of children's books)

author at the height of their powers
and nothing is quite what it seems ...
nothing will ever be the same again ...
left holding the baby, literally
this book is bound to be a success
more frightening than anyone could have imagined in their worst nightmares

So as not to be negative, here are words from recent campaigns that did catch her eye and got her reading the rest of the copy:

high-rolling	enrapturing
twizzling	engrossing
exuberant	vital
banal	frisky
bizarre	striking
abrasive	inestimable
eye-washing	incomparable
delirious	

Justine commented, 'I believe the secret of good copy is enjoyment. If I, as a buyer, find that I am relishing what I read, I will enjoy actually selling the product and buy more from you.'

You should also avoid publishing-ese – words that mean different things to those involved with books from the rest of the population. For example, the heavily overused 'accessible' means to the rest of the world that you don't have to stand on a stepladder to reach it. Similarly, avoid using in-house jargon and production specifications – most of the population cannot recognise a 'C format paperback'.

Get to the point. Avoid long, flowing sentences of introduction. Home straight in on the main benefits to the reader. When dealing with complex subjects with which they are not wholly familiar, many copywriters use the first paragraph to work their way into the subject, to demonstrate their understanding. Readers are not interested – get on with what is in it for them. It is remarkable how often simply deleting the first paragraph will improve the readability of copy.

Don't be clever or pompous, even when you are writing to an audience that is either or both. Imagine you were explaining the benefits to a prospect face to face: you would be concentrating on the product, not your presentational style. Many people assume that when writing to academics or high-powered business people they should produce a suitably lofty tone. Avoid this. It slows the reader down and impedes access to benefits. What is more, if you are not expert in the subject, you may get the jargon wrong or sound patronising.

Don't drone on about your organisation. The average reader could not care less; it is the specific product that has attracted their attention. If there is information that is relevant to the product give it, but spare the reader the rest of the potted company history – or refer them to your website to read more. The following is plenty:

> This new 20-volume work comes from the publishers of the respected *Everyperson Encyclopaedia*, and was researched and written with the same accuracy and attention to detail.

Avoid flowing passages of purple prose, even if you are particularly pleased with them. Indeed, your own admiration for sections of your work should be your guide to what needs deleting. If it stands out to you as a particularly good use of words it will probably strike the reader in the same way, and slow down their reading flow. Or as author G.K. Chesterton put it, 'Murder your babies'.

Cut down on your sentence length

Long sentences are tiring on the eyes, and the market has plenty of other things to do. Cut down your sentence length and you make your message easier to read.

Here is an example of publishing copy:

> An introductory survey of the history and the principles and practice of citizenship, based on the premise that the current conditions and debates about citizenship cannot be fully understood without a knowledge of the historical background.

By amalgamating the ideas, and dividing the content into two sentences, you make the message easier to absorb:

> Citizenship is impossible to understand without a grasp of its historical background. Here is a complete introductory survey of its principles and practice.

Tell a story, talk to the reader, adopt a tone of sweet reason

This is best achieved by completing the research on the product, noting down the main sales points and then writing from memory. By doing this you explain the benefits to yourself as you write, and your copy is more likely to be convincing.

Overcome any objections the reader may think of while reading, perhaps by using question and answer panels, for example:

> Why is this new biography needed?
> Who will use this manual?

While controversy may raise interest, it's not a good idea to be confrontational in copy, or to provide material for readers to argue with. The result will be that they stop reading altogether, either to analyse their reaction in more detail or through sheer annoyance. Your sales message is wasted.

Let the copy flow. Use linking phrases so that the text reads fluently. Copywriter Roger Millington calls these phrases 'buckets and chains':

And of course ...	For example ...
At the same time ...	This includes ...
Not to mention ...	In addition ...
Did you realise ...	On the other hand ...
After all ...	Finally, I must mention ...
Just as important ...	Two final points ...

Make your copy personal. This means using 'you' rather than 'one' or 'they', and relating the examples you use to the interests of the reader. For example, instead of:

One-third of the population will develop cancer at some time in their lives; for 20 per cent of the population it will eventually be terminal.

try:

One in three people get cancer; one in five die from it.

or:

You have a one in three chance of getting cancer, and a one in five chance of dying from it.

Quote actual people rather than statistics. For example, instead of:

20,000 copies sold

try:

20,000 art lovers have already bought this book.

Keep editing

Write long and then cut back to the essentials. Are there still words that are not really necessary to the sense and that you could manage without? Delete extra adverbs and adjectives: they slow the reader down. Avoid the language of property sales: a bland and predictable prose, where one adjective is never used where two can be squeezed in (a practice that seems to be spreading with alarming rapidity). For example:

this perfect and handy ground-floor apartment
a convenient and well-positioned house
a useful and timely book

You don't need both. One, three or none might attract more interest.

Structure the layout of benefits and selling points

Don't oversell. Guard against providing more selling points than the reader needs to reach a buying decision. One or two may be plenty. Your final copy doesn't need to make use of everything you have thought of: use too many selling arguments and the market can feel bullied.

If you are writing longer copy, don't end the page or column with a full stop. Make the text 'run over' so that the reader is encouraged to continue. Writers of mailshots often save the biggest benefit for the end of the sales letter, perhaps putting it in the PS (regarded as one of the most highly read parts of the letter). There will be hints that this big benefit is coming for those who read from the start, to encourage them to keep going.

Using space to draw the reader in

If you walk along a street of terraced houses with no front gardens you will find your eye is automatically attracted to the first gap, perhaps a side street or a house set back from the road. Look at a page of text and the effect is the same: see how your eye is sucked into the spaces.

There is another reason. Most of us are short of time, and faced with a page of text (even if we have written it) we 'skim read', homing in on the features we find most interesting. Use this information to attract your readers to the most important parts of your message.

For the same reason, think carefully before asking for text to be set 'justified' (with both right and left margins vertically aligned). Use a ragged right-hand margin to attract the reader's eye into white space. Aim for visual variety. Ensure your paragraphs and sentences are of varied lengths. Short sentences attract attention: try this technique at the beginning or end of paragraphs. It works.

Use bullet points (heavy dots at the beginning of each line) for a list of short selling points. Beware of over-bulleting just because you can think of a large number of benefits to highlight: the text can end up looking riddled and the effect of sharpening the reader's attention is lost. The magic number is three; five or six is the maximum you should ever use. However many you use, ensure they are different shapes – a long list of identically shaped short lines tends not to feel inviting.

Subheadings attract attention to your main selling points. Each one can be fully explained in the paragraph that follows.

Try indenting paragraphs for extra emphasis, using both the right hand of the page and the left for maximum effect.

Number your paragraphs. Use underlines and CAPITAL LETTERS (sparingly though). Print important text **in bold** or in a different typeface. Your software will allow you to produce a variety of wonderful effects, but do be careful that your finished text doesn't resemble a sampler designed to show the machine's capabilities rather than advertising copy. If you put text in a box, try putting a tint behind the box, or reverse the text out (that is, making it paler than the background, but use this technique sparingly as it is harder to read).

Many readers who cannot be bothered to read a lot of text will have their attention caught by illustrations. So ensure every picture has a caption, and that the captions pass on the main sales benefits. Tables and bar charts divide up the copy and, armed with captions, reinforce your message.

Give facts, not opinions. Qualify every statement you make. If you don't, doubt may creep into the reader's mind as to the validity of your arguments. So instead of:

> widely used in major companies

say where (with permission):

> in extensive use at Astra Zeneca and BP
>
> This prize-winning book ...
> Winner of the 2015 Belling prize for scientific research
>
> This new work is based on extensive research.
> These two volumes are the result of over 20 years' research in the Wedgwood family archives, the British Museum and other sources. Publication marks the first time that the subject has been explored in such detail and the information is invaluable to any serious collector.

Review quotations are more valuable to the reader than your opinion, but when deciding which ones to use, choose those from journals best known to the market, even if the comments are slightly less complimentary than those that appeared in less well-known journals.

Getting other people to write your copy – by securing testimonials

Given the huge amount of published material available, the value of a relevant endorsement can be immense. Testimonials work because they are generally seen as objective; the publisher or content provider is expected to write marketing copy, and the opinion of someone the market respects can be really helpful in isolating material likely to appeal to them too. Information that comes from a third party also has authority – advertising guru David Ogilvy (1983) claimed that if you put the headline in quotation marks you increase recall by 25 per cent – and in the midst of a wealth of competing attractions can help the reader make a quick and relevant choice.

The process can add value in any area of publishing, from highly specific materials aimed at professional audiences to mass market fiction. Securing a testimonial can be particularly valuable before publication, when there are no reviews to quote.

Top tips on asking for endorsements

- Pick the right person. Think about market segments, which ones you are most seeking to appeal to, and how the person you want to involve will be appreciated by them. Brainstorm with colleagues and produce a list of those you might ask. It's awkward to ask someone and then realise you could have made a better choice with a bit more prior thought.
- Involve your author or series editor. They may well have better links than you to people who would endorse a product. And if they will manage the process for you, you can get on with something else.
- Remember what is in it for them as well as what is in it for you. While you are seeking an endorsement for a particular title, there will be advantages to the person being asked: the pleasure of their opinion being sought (there were presumably other options); increased profile; association with a product they like. Phrase your request carefully, setting it in this wider context, rather than just sending off a request with an associated deadline.
- The person asked to endorse a title does not need to be famous, just relevant. For example, in the case of a book I co-wrote on parenting teenagers, there were three endorsements on the cover, one from the UK Children's Laureate Jacqueline Wilson (very famous), a second from the local director of education (name unknown outside the area, but showing the book has a strong educational pedigree) and a third from an Oxfordshire teacher and mother (showing the book has value to ordinary people and is not of the 'celebrity' variety). This balance worked well, and I hope gave a flavour of what is inside.[4]
- Apply no pressure. The person being asked for an endorsement must be free to decline without incurring long-term resentment from publisher or author. If they do not respond, while you can discreetly check to ensure the information reached them, never hound.
- If they ask to look at the manuscript before making a decision (entirely sensible on their part) ask in what format they would like to receive it. If they ask for a printed copy, send one. Even though you could send an email and an attachment the same day, they may be less technologically adept, or simply prefer to read in a printed format and should not have to bear the cost of printing it out.
- On occasion, the person being asked for an endorsement may be happy to oblige but short of time – and hence ask you to draft something for them to sign. Use this opportunity carefully – it should sound like the person

whose name will appear at the bottom, not like a publicity department press release. This is not a time to rehash the book's back cover copy.

Don't make the reader sound stupid

You probably don't realise that this new research has been published.

That is not a good line to take: it sounds patronising and may alienate, particularly if the reader is aware. How about:

Market research showed us that many people did not realise that this new research was available. I am therefore writing …

This shifts the blame from the reader to the publisher.

Using the negative

There is no clear advice here. The use of the negative can certainly confuse your message. You risk your reader missing the negative or associating the negative with your product. So, instead of:

If you do not find this title essential to your everyday work we will refund your money.

you could consider:

You will find yourself consulting this title every working day or we will refund your money.

Avoiding the negative can also offer more creative ways in which to link to your potential customer. Consider the following (written about negative thinking):

Often we create prisons for ourselves by thinking and talking in certain ways. Just shifting the way we use words can be enough to let us out. Say you've been trying to give up smoking but each time end up going back to the habit. It would be easy to describe this as 'I can't stop smoking', 'I always fail' and so on. If you did that, it would probably evoke despondent thoughts about your inability to give up, and that would be unlikely to prompt further attempts to quit. If instead you changed the description to not succeeding so far, there might be some room left for reflection about what went wrong and how to make it work next time.

Antonia Macaro[5]

The copywriter seeking to outline the benefits of self-help titles could find this advice very useful.

Negative thoughts can, however, be used to attract attention, particularly at a time when the prevailing tone of copy written about competing items for sale is positive. For example, by looking at a publishing product as an experience rather than seeking to outline its particular features you may create fresh things to say and a fresh emotional connection with your market. So instead of:

> Makes an ideal Christmas present.

how about:

> Dreading Christmas? This book guarantees you some quality time alone during the festive period.

Using humour

Avoid humour unless you are a very good writer. As copywriter Claude Hopkins said: 'No one buys from a clown.'

Repeat yourself

Someone once spelt out the basic theory of writing a direct mail sales letter, and the practice can be extended to many other promotional formats where there is space to develop an argument, such as brochures and press releases:

- Tell them what you are going to tell them.
- Then tell them.
- Then tell them what you have just told them.

Although it makes sense to repeat yourself, do so in different words each time. Don't be boring. Probably the dullest start to any advertisement is to repeat either the title of the book or the headline. Equally boring are:

> This new book/title is ...
> We are thrilled to announce publication of ...

It may be more impactful to start in the middle of a sentence. For example:

> Brings a whole new perspective to ...
> Offers readers a completely new experience ...

Get used to using a thesaurus

The most difficult word to find a synonym for is 'book'. Try the following: new edition, title, report, work, text, study alternatively you can qualify the book as a casebook, sourcebook or reference book. In some circumstances, describing a title as a book may sound insufficiently expensive or well researched, in which case you could try volume, compendium, dossier, resource or other alternatives.

Other ideas for attracting attention

See Chapter 8 on direct marketing for top tips in writing headlines and managing the ordering process.

Feature the author

Are they controversial, newsworthy, interesting in their own right? Allow the new book to be promoted on the back of the name; to the media the personality is often more interesting than the fact that they have written a book.

Invent/use a character to use in the promotion

Several school publishers have lifted characters from their software programmes and illustrated schemes to enliven their promotion material. This can be particularly effective in communicating with the nostalgia market (often parents spotting titles they enjoyed as children).

Figure 13.2 Winnie the Witch's cat Wilbur is sufficiently recognisable to be useful to his publisher OUP in various capacities, from featuring in marketing materials to becoming the star of new titles (he has now featured in a range of first concept board books). His creators are author Valerie Thomas and illustrator Korky Paul. Courtesy of Oxford University Press.

Offer a firm guarantee

It shows complete confidence in your product and can compensate for asking for money up front. Challenge the reader. Are you offering the best value for money, a fantastic read or your money back? You'll be surprised how very few people claim refunds; far more will be impressed by your immense certainty that your product is excellent.

Learn from how other organisations offer guarantees, and consider turning problems you have observed into elegant restatements of your organisational policy. Consider the following stylish but firm text from UK clothing retailer Boden, presented on their website and in printed brochures:

> What's your returns policy?
>
> We operate a no-quibble returns policy and if you return an item within 3 months of receipt, we'll give you back the amount you paid for the item (see postage and packing cost terms) or offer an exchange, whichever you prefer, no questions asked.
>
> After this period, until the first anniversary of your order arriving, you can still return anything that does not meet your naturally high quality expectations (things like wear and tear are included, though garments that have been mauled by pets, drawn on by nephews, worn while decorating, and so forth, don't qualify).
>
> So if you're not happy, we will give your account credit for the amount you paid for that item. Almost all of you are lovely people and will see this as us being helpful and confident about how well made our clothes are, but there will be a few rotten apples who might look on this as an opportunity to refresh their wardrobe for free each season (you know who you are).
>
> Anyone repeatedly trying to do this will get spotted, and a dim view will be taken, probably resulting in us parting company. When returning goods which you bought using a discount or offer, we will adjust the refund accordingly if you fall below the discount/offer threshold, as that discount or offer will no longer apply. Should anything spring a fault in the first 6 months, we will, of course, give you your money back.
>
> If you are a pathological chancer and simply can't help yourself, we recommend trying it on with our competitors instead.

Writing headlines

When looking at the email inbox, the subject lines get a lot of attention. Ironically they may get none from the person sending it (who perhaps just uses what is already there, potentially very out of date). Similarly, when looking at an advertisement or promotional feature, most readers instinctively look at the headline first. Whatever the format, a good headline can grasp the reader's attention and set the tone for an interesting advertisement.

Yet still many publishers' advertisements start with information that is interesting to themselves rather than their customers. 'New from Snodgrass and Wilkins' is accurate, and may even be interesting if the firm has a world-renowned geography list and the feature appears in the *Geography Teachers' Review*. Remembering that the market has a choice, let's try to be more imaginative – in order to secure greater attention.

- It may sound obvious, but the headline should go at the top of the page or space. Flick through any recent newspapers or magazines and you will see how your eye is attracted to the bold headline, wherever it appears. If it is sited in the middle of the page, and is sufficiently interesting for you to carry on with the rest of the text, you will find yourself reading what is immediately beneath the heading, even if that point is halfway through the explanatory copy.
- Advertisements attract attention if the copy or look of the material is personal and relevant. So if you are writing for a specific market, name it:

  Calling all mothers!
  Important information for all Maths teachers.

- Target benefits to the audience as specifically as possible. Which of the following headlines would be of most interest to Sally Brown, new promotions assistant at Harcourt?

  How all promotions departments can work more effectively.
  How all new promotions assistants can do their jobs better.
  Promoting books? How you can do *your* job better.

- Don't be ambiguous or clever. Blind headlines (which can only be understood once the rest of the copy has been read) are best avoided. If the meaning is only semi-apparent, most readers won't bother to investigate further.
- One of the most reliable techniques for starting a headline is to ask a question:

  Why? What? Where? How? Who? When?
  How will this book save you time and money?
  Why is everyone talking about this new novel?

- Start your headline by saying something controversial (preferably something that stimulates debate rather than causes an outright denial and the reader to stop!).
- Feature a strange word.
- Use catchwords that are instantly interesting: now, free, introducing, announcing, secret, magic, mother, unique, money off, save, sale, offer closes, guarantee, bargain. What areas of general interest does your material excite? Agency creative director Alastair Crompton (1987) listed the following: animals; babies; cars; disasters; entertainment; fashion; holidays; money; royalty; sex; sport; war; weddings. Think how closely this list follows the chief headline interests of the tabloid press.

- Include a promise, for instance: 'A completely new kind of DIY manual: satisfaction or your money back.'
- Feature news or a new way of using the product you are promoting:

Why each year over 100,000 new businesses fail.

Writing copy for titles you do not understand

Having to write copy for a product you don't understand, or for a market you don't relate to, is very common in publishing. Few people end up marketing work that would be their first choice of reading material; you may even do a better job if you are required to think about market needs and content delivery, rather than just enthusing about how much it appeals to you.

If you are in this position, first be assured that you don't have to develop a special way of writing. Publisher information is best presented as simply as possible, so avoid long sentences, paragraphs and complicated syntax. While it's tempting to reproduce lengthy and highly complex information drafted by the author or book's editor, assuming that once it reaches the right market it will be understood, remember that your title information will also be read by a range of other people who are not subject specialists: booksellers, reps, librarians and those standing in for academics on leave of absence or maternity leave – and that English may not be the recipient's first language.

Consider what the market needs to know about the title you are promoting, perhaps the treatment of a subject, the currency of the content and the names of those involved. The following are likely:

- list of contents;
- brief summary of the main features;
- detailed description of the contents;
- designated readership and level;
- information on the author;
- extracts from review coverage;
- sample pages;
- photograph of the cover or the author.

The last item may surprise, but well-managed information will generally win admirers (and possibly new authors). You spend a long time in the company of the author of a textbook; it's only natural curiosity to want to know what they look like. Bibliographical information must be correct, and accurate, not optimistic. Ensure you cover the following: author; series (if any); publication date; illustrations; format(s); publisher; extent; ISBN or ISSN; size.

Disentangling long and difficult blurbs

If the first information you receive on a forthcoming title is a long and complicated blurb, and written by the title's editor or author, the temptation to reproduce it whole rather than try to simplify it can be enormous, particularly if you have no inkling of the subject matter and are short of time. Remember that most academics can tell by looking at the title and contents whether or not a product is relevant to them, so a detailed list of the contents is always preferable to a long description.

The danger is, the more you become familiar with the difficult blurb, the more you will come to think you know what it means too. Your first reaction is the one to hang on to. Remember there will be many other non-specialists who need to understand the key selling benefits too.

Where to start? I'm fond of using the analogy of conceptual artist Cornelia Parker blowing up a garden shed. She then measured the distances to which the pieces fell, threaded each one on to chicken wire and hung them in a corresponding pattern from the ceiling of the Tate Gallery in London (*Cold Dark Matter*, 1991; see Figure 13.3). In the centre there were lots of tiny pieces, but around the edge of the room were all the major chunks (roof, walls, door, window frame). It was still recognisably a garden shed, but this time one with energy. Do the same with the text facing you; instead of simply providing a product description (which risks being boring), think again. Rather than editing it (which simply produces something more complex and even less flowing, a bit like a poor translation), blow it up. Read it slowly, looking out for all the main ideas. Try dividing up long sentences, lifting out the main features and highlighting them as bullet points. Divide up long paragraphs so the copy looks more readable. Explain to the editor (or author) what you are trying to do and ask them to check your results.

Figure 13.3 Cornelia Parker, *Cold Dark Matter: An Exploded View*, 1991. Courtesy of the artist and Frith Street Gallery, London.

Avoid starting your copy with a general sentence or paragraph ('We are delighted to publish this new summary of key developments in nuclear physics, which has been thoroughly updated since its previous incarnation'): generalities are usually more concerned with demonstrating your understanding of the subject matter than with the market's need to know. If it helps you to get started then by all means write one, but delete it once you have finished; your arguments should hold water without it. Try to answer the following questions:

- If it is a new edition, what has changed since the previous one? Can you quantify change in percentage terms? Do you have factual information on the number of items in the index and the number of chapters completely rewritten?
- If it is a textbook, what course is it for? For what level of students?
- Who has reviewed or endorsed it, and in what publication? Your own opinion will carry far less weight than that of the academic's peer group.
- Who is it by? Include qualifications, current position, special areas of research that are relevant to the subject and book.
- Have you made it clear whether the book is a collection of the writings of several authors or an entirely new title? Make sure you distinguish conference proceedings as just that.
- How does the recipient get in touch with the publisher? Is there a website or reply mechanism for requesting inspection copies, an email address or telephone number for ordering?
- How will the recipient who wants to order pay for the title? Is an institutional sale more likely than one to an individual? If so, how can you facilitate payment?
- What payment facilities and what guarantees do you need to offer?
- Is your copy too 'hard sell'? It is a practice best avoided: it will not be convincing and probably makes the recipient suspicious.

Remove bland and unconvincing words ('prestigious', 'unique' and 'completely comprehensive') unless you can make them specific to the product. Expand on product characteristics that are relevant rather than bunching them together. For example, the following sentence was written about an updated textbook on communications:

> It is written in a clear and accessible style by well-known authors who have used a new streamlined organisation and a fresh teaching style.

There are four ideas in this sentence:

- clear writing style;
- well-known authors;
- reorganised content;
- offering a fresh teaching style.

By running the points into each other, as part of the same sentence, the copywriter has ensured none of them really gets noticed. Instead, you could home in on the more important one, and talk about it in more detail:

> This is a famous textbook, but while you may be familiar with the name, the new edition has a completely fresh feel to it.

Alternatively, present the different ideas as bullet points (as noted above).

Academic jargon is more problematic. There will be certain words that you have to include to show that the book deals with current issues; check the list provided by the author in the author publicity form. As a final check, always have the editor, or author, check what you produce.

Presenting and defending your copy

The urge to alter someone else's copy must be one of the hardest temptations to resist. Faced with almost any piece of text, one can always think of a better way of wording it. As part of the management process, copy shown for approval tends to mean copy changed (otherwise there is no evidence of managerial input). So how can you deal with this difficult problem? Here are some suggestions.

- Try to influence how others will read your copy. Send your copy with a covering email or note on your research into the product and market; explain *why* you have written it the way you have. If the recipient understands that what has been drafted is the result of detailed thought, they may be less inclined to change it. The points need to be written down, however, not just said (people will be busy reading and may not listen). If time permits, send it before you despatch the copy – and ask for confirmation of receipt.
- Keep the approval committee as small as possible. The more people you send it to the more changes you get, and if you make them all then the flow of your argument will be ruined.
- If you give a deadline by which changes must be received, never chase those who have not replied.
- Remember that few people keep a copy of their corrections!

Often changes cancel each other out; you cannot make everyone's and still have a piece of copy that hangs together. Novelist Fay Weldon, formerly an advertising copywriter herself, described a very effective technique for dealing with corrections based on this. She would research, write and circulate the copy and then wait for the corrections. When they came back, she would include all of them, and then re-circulate. When the recipients responded with horror, she would re-circulate the original, which this time would meet with unanimous approval.

If you have persistent difficulties with a manager being negative about copy you provide, try these ideas:

- Are you being over-resistant? Are they right? Can you suggest a team discussion (or departmental in the case of particularly important projects) about the tone of voice you are trying to create, and how you want to come across (this is 'positioning'). Do you have a house style manual that talks about core values of the organisation; are there sample materials from other firms that are admired so you could discuss how you could all work towards them? Promoting a shared understanding of the goals, and being part of the debate, is vastly preferable to a constant awareness that nothing is ever right.

- Gently remind the person that if comments are always negative, it is demotivating to staff. Ask whether, as well as putting red lines through things they do not like, they could also use ticks or boxes to indicate what they do like. This will boost confidence; most of us respond better to encouragement than constant evidence of our failings.

- You could tactfully point out that providing this level of corrections would take a long time, and that you want to work together towards improved performance, to make better use of everyone's time.

- Hang on to how it feels to be corrected. Being objective about your own work, and precise about your own reactions, will help you when you come to commission copy from freelances and in-house staff.

Notes

1 It was first formalised by St. Elmo Lewis in 1898 and published in 1925 in the *Journal of Applied Psychology* by Edward Strong.
2 This was put through my door more than 20 years ago and yet it still feels fresh and lively. Sadly the distributor never came back (probably snapped up by an advertising agency) but if you can help me pay credit to the copywriter, do contact my publishers so we can get in touch. Swindon area.
3 I am proud to say this was written by my Uncle Bill, husband of my father's sister when he worked in advertising. Not a blood relation, but still a source of great pride.
4 Hines, G. and Baverstock, A. (2005) *Whatever! A Down to Earth Guide to Parenting Teenagers*, London: Piatkus.
5 'Should we mind our language?', *FT Magazine*, 8–9 March 2014.

14 The layout and dissemination of marketing materials

Design 342
What is good design? 343
How promotional text gets read 343
How to find a designer 344
How to work effectively with a designer 346
How a design job progresses 350
How to proofread text 351
Managing without a designer 352
Getting material printed 354
How to request an estimate from a printer 355

Design

Once copy has been written it needs to be presented in a suitable way for wider dissemination. This usually involves the services of a designer. You may have an in-house design department that will work for you. The advantages are speed and accessibility – you can go from draft copy to onscreen approval of the final image in one afternoon. Alternatively, it may be left to you to commission the work out-of-house, by using either a firm of designers or one of the local freelances that serve your company.

Whereas at one time every publishing house had its own in-house design department, today many are finding it more cost-effective to recruit such services out-of-house when they are needed rather than pay for them all the time. Publishing tends to be a very seasonal industry, which results in some equally frenetic promotional cycles. A firm may require the services of several designers one month, but only a month later have very little for them to do. Standard promotional items (web pages, catalogues, advance notices) are often managed by in-house staff. But the assumption that effectively laid out information can be produced by those without proper training on the equipment they are using is usually a mistake.

Whoever you decide to use, do remember that the brief is yours. You may not have a design qualification, but nor will the market, and your common-sense ability to distinguish between what is easy to read and what is not is just as relevant. Remember the story about the emperor's new clothes – it was the little boy in the procession, with no training in court etiquette, who pointed out that the king was not wearing anything.

What is good design?

In the context of the preparation of marketing information, effective design encourages the designated market to read and absorb the sales message and act on the recommendation to buy. Good design should stimulate without swamping, and be implicit rather than explicit. Kate Hybert of Hybert Design comments: 'A well-designed piece looks as if it was really simple to lay out, like it always had to go that way.' If readers start admiring decorative borders that frame text, will they remember to return to reading the list of product benefits?

Prepare yourself to recognise good design. Start scanning both the publications you are likely to advertise in and the general media for advertisements, and assess their impact. Observe your own habits as you surf the web – what kind of pages are hard to read and why? Read Ernst Gombrich's *The Story of Art* (1995) and David Ogilvy's *Ogilvy on Advertising* (1983). Visit art galleries, ask to look through designers' portfolios or your company's promotional archives, read relevant magazines such as *Creative Review* and *Design Week*, and let your awareness of design grow. This is not a one-off exercise, but must become a habit – it is important to try to keep up to date. Design is as volatile as clothing and car styles – fashions change and design styles can look just as outdated as last season's fad.

How promotional text gets read

The designer needs copy. As the person who either wrote it or commissioned it, you will probably do a final check before you pass it on. You will start to read at the top of the page and work your way methodically through, looking out for spelling mistakes or verbs that have been used too often. (You may well miss some: it is very difficult to proofread your own work, particularly onscreen.)

If, on the other hand, you can imagine yourself coming upon the text cold, or perhaps seeing it for the first time in its final form as an advertisement, you will realise that your reading habits are in reality much more haphazard. Uninvolved readers wait for their attention to be attracted, allow their eyes to flit around the page looking for something of interest and certainly do not feel duty-bound to read everything that is provided. They may look at the headline or picture, and perhaps at the caption. Their eye may be drawn in by quotation marks – someone else's opinion is much more interesting to them than the view of the advertiser. If their interest is stimulated they may look to the bottom right-hand corner or the back of a brochure to see who is advertising. Only then will motivated readers start on the main text (or body copy). The vast majority will not get that far. If people are reading on a screen then their boredom threshold may be even lower. Today we all seem to want ever-quicker access to information; if we are not engaged we move on, and quickly. Advertising material has to work hard to draw a response.

The message is clear. You cannot take your readers' interest for granted, and so must use all the means at your disposal to encourage them to get involved: through the words you use, the illustrations you provide and the design layout that unites them.

For most publications there is also a style and order in which the articles and features are read. Awareness of this can help you present your sales information in the position or way most likely to ensure it gets noticed. Start observing your own reading habits.

So how do we read? In search of a quick review of what a magazine includes, many people flick through from the back forwards, so the inside back cover is a very hot spot for would-be advertisers. Similarly, it is common to start reading a newspaper with a speedy trawl through the pages, allowing your attention to be grabbed by particular headlines. Some people pause to read the articles beneath, others return to them later after having scanned specific sections of the paper where they habitually find items of interest: the gossip column, the obituaries, crossword or the letters page. Many papers provide a series of 'news in brief' paragraphs on the inside front pages, allowing readers to quickly grasp the essentials of the stories on offer that day. Page references indicate the more detailed articles within. All these make good locations to try to place your material, as either a paid-for advertisement or a publicity feature.

Mailshots are read in a particular way too. Chapter 8 on direct marketing gives further information on this, but in general the letter gets read first, with the headline, the signature and PS being the most highly noted parts. Look at the next one you receive and you will see how the senders have anticipated your reading habits.

A brochure or mailshot is an edited presentation, a distillation of what the marketer wants the potential customer to know and a direction of their reading energy. When it comes to reading onscreen, the individual is often in a much less stable environment, fuelled by adrenalin and an awareness that – given that all possible content is in front of them – they need to take action in order to start somewhere and find a route to what they need to know, with other options for the use of time consistently beckoning. The web designer needs to present stimulation and clarity, to hold the potential customer's attention while offering them sufficient visual variety and useful information to maintain their interest. It's a difficult balancing act.

How to find a designer

If there is an in-house design department then the choice of whom to use is largely made for you, although if there is a particular designer there whose work you like, try to steer it that person's way (which can be difficult if the studio manager has other ideas).

Finding freelance designers or local firms can involve more legwork, but in most towns where there is a demand for design you will find local services available. Ask your colleagues and printers that you use for recommendations and look on local trade and freelance websites.

It is important to bear in mind what you are really looking for and what level of services you require. An individual freelance designer may long have provided a flexible, reliable source of design expertise to your organisation, producing a range of advertisements and flyers – and with low overheads be able to offer a very competitive price. For the creation of high-profile point-of-sale material or highly illustrated catalogues by a specific deadline you may find you come under managerial pressure to commission a larger design group, to ensure that there will be additional staff to work on your job should a crisis strike.

In reality, what you want to ensure is that whomever you instruct feels a responsibility for managing the whole job through to completion. While having a larger group involved will certainly add to the associated costs, it will not necessarily lead to greater efficiency – indeed it can mean the dilution of that vital sense of ownership. In recent years, due to difficult economic conditions, many large design groups have come under intense pressure and an alternative option is emerging, of teams of individuals (some of whom were made redundant by larger groups) who work together in networks of related professional expertise (e.g., graphic designers, web designers, illustrators, printers and other production specialists). Although not located under a single roof, such networks are tied together through a deep understanding of each other's capabilities, talents and reliability under pressure, and can be the basis of very effective partnerships.

A designer does not have to be local to be the basis of a good relationship – indeed the formality of instructing a designer you can't physically see can help the process of clarifying what it is you are looking for. It is, however, helpful if your designer and printer can be reasonably geographically close for the signing off of proofs before production (but as designers generally have printers with whom they enjoy a good working relationship, and vice versa, finding one collaborator will generally lead you to other service providers).

You should certainly ask to see the portfolio of previous work of any designer you consider using. Look to see if the designer has done similar work to what you need. Why not ask in-house designers to show you their portfolios too, as a guide to the kind of projects they have worked on in the past?

Once you have found a couple of designers whose work you like and who respond well to a brief, hang on to them. While it may not be prudent to rely solely on one designer – you need to ensure you have other options – it's not a good idea to spread work too widely. Give those who work for you a decent amount of business so that they have a real incentive to please you.

To get an idea of the prices designers charge, pass on printed copies of a couple of previous jobs and ask for an estimate of what they would charge for preparing something similar. Check their estimate against what you actually paid. If they are far too expensive, it may be best to discreetly tell them so and use someone else rather than become a routine haggler. You may get a special price once but if you are consistently beating suppliers down below what they feel is a fair price you will earn resentment, and they will be less inclined to help you when you need a favour, for example a job that needs doing in a real hurry.

You may call in a new designer to discuss a potential project, but if you end up asking for their rough design ideas make it clear whether, if what is submitted is acceptable, they will get the job, or whether there are other candidates.

Alternatively, agree a rejection fee of, say, 10 per cent of the fee. Most creative people understand that would-be clients like to brainstorm, and you have to spark – but taking someone's ideas without recompense arouses long-term resentment.

Time is likely to be an important factor. Ask for an estimate of how long the job is likely to take and when you can expect a first visual. Most freelances live with the difficulty of juggling a variety of different jobs (it is impossible to predict what will arrive when, and dangerous to say no).

How to work effectively with a designer

Architects say the more their clients tell them about their lifestyle the better the job they can do. It works the same way with designers. Remember when commissioning design that good designers will not only try to meet your project objectives but also take pride in what they do, so the more you can involve them and communicate what you are trying to achieve, the better.

The best design results are always obtained by clients who have a clear idea of what they want and can express it effectively, providing as much information as possible about the project at the beginning of the job. This is crucial. Designers are experts in finding visual solutions to problems, but you should be aware that once they have come up with one, it can be very difficult for them to see the project in another way. It follows that if you are specific about what you are trying to achieve at the outset, without being over-formulaic, you will harness the designer's talent in a more effective way. The other benefit of taking the time to fully explain your thinking is that your bills will be lower. Thinking things through in order to explain them to a third party clarifies your own mind – and in the long run, the more you change your mind, the more the costs go up.

How to brief a designer

Writing a design brief is difficult. You need to provide a structure within which the designer's creative juices can start to flow, not a straitjacket to inhibit the good ideas that you alone would not think of. If you are too prescriptive, designers may respond with just what you ask for, denying you access to their professional expertise.

So while it is tempting, and saves time (in the short term), never just pass on the copy for a job and assume the designer knows as much as you do. It is your role to formally brief them. And even though you set up a meeting to discuss your plans with a designer, never rely on a word-of-mouth briefing alone as sufficient information. You both need something to refer to afterwards. After all, think how different people can report entirely different opinions on the same conversation – we tend to hear what we want to hear! And if with insufficient information, or simply the wrong take on what is needed, the designer does set off down a false path, it's not just time and money that are wasted – motivation is also substantially reduced.

A four-stage guide to briefing a designer

1 Describe the market you are talking to

Who are they, what kind of people are receiving what you send in what kind of circumstances? You can generalise to give a flavour of a market: for example, teachers tend to open their mail in the busy staff or faculty room. In general they have to consult each other before making a buying decision; they are natural collaborators.

If you can, pass on other information aimed at this market, such as copies of their professional journal, a website reference for a site much used by the market, or a feature from a newspaper that describes the market you are talking to.

2 Describe the product or service you are promoting

What benefits does it offer the market? How does it work (briefly) and what is its pedigree? How soon will the market notice a difference if they do buy what you offer?

3 Outline how you want the recipient to feel about your organisation and the product or service you are selling

In marketing terms, this is 'positioning'. You are establishing a relationship between your product or service and the market you are talking to, and this is done through the image you present as well as the words you use. For example, do you want your market to see your offering as a prestige product that gives status, or as practical and good value for money?

4 Indicate what you want recipients to do as a result of seeing your information

Should they rush to fill in an order form or reach for the telephone to place an order, grasp the keypad to consult your website, or resolve to discuss a decision with the others likely to be involved?

Once you have established brief and succinct answers to these four questions in your head, put them in writing for the designer, either as an email or on a single sheet of paper, no more. This is hard – it's much more difficult to write something short and succinct than to send people a copy of your marketing plan.

Supporting information needed by the designer

Once you have established the tone of what you want, the designer also needs some more specific information in order to do a good job.

- Your house style

Many publishing houses have prescribed design choices, such as which typeface or background colours to choose, and all have a logo. Others take this further and have drawn up standard borders for all sizes of advertisement in print and onscreen. While such rules save time and ensure consistency, marketing attracts attention by looking interesting and often slightly unexpected, so if everything looks identical it may not get noticed. This is part of a wider debate. For now, your designer needs to know the rules, and with what rigour they are policed.

- The copy you are providing

Indicate how much copy there is, and which are the really important sections. You can indicate this in the text, but it is worth emphasising too, by adding supporting notes. Ensure it is correct, as all subsequent typographical changes will be charged to you.

- What kind of promotional piece you have in mind

Try not to be closed to suggestions – the designer may come up with a better idea than you. If you have to stick to a prearranged format, include precise details (size and extent), and provide a sample of what you want if you have one.

- What you are going to do with the material

If it is to be mailed, the overall size and weight must be considered in relation to postage bands. If the paper is to be very lightweight (to make posting as cheap as possible), the design will have to be planned accordingly to reduce the 'show-through' of printing ink. Similarly, if you are planning a space advertisement in a magazine, as well as a sample of the magazine you need to provide the mechanical details (trimmed page size, size of margins, extent of bleed and 'safe text' area). These details will be given to you by the publication concerned. If you are booking the same advertisement into several publications, do not assume they all require it in the same format or size.

- The budget you have for design

It is perhaps best to indicate the ballpark rather than the exact figure. Provide for a supporting contingency.

- What supporting work is required

You must make it clear whether you want the designer to handle the production (e.g., print, packaging, loading on the website) for you as well, and if so the details of what you want and have a budget for.

● The illustrations

You may need to commission special photographs (pack shots, point-of-sale shots, perhaps studio sets and so on). These can be arranged by the designer, or you may have your own (in-house) photographer to organise. Do bear in mind, however, that the arrangement, proportion and colour of the illustrations will be an important part of the design of the promotion piece, so if you plan to use existing illustrations then your designer needs to know before starting work. The captions for illustrations provide an excellent spot for passing on key parts of your sales message. Reproducing covers also gives those reading your advertisements the chance to recognise your products in the shops.

● When you want the finished job by

Never just say 'as soon as possible'. Look through your diary and note down a specific date for both parties to work towards. Doing this makes it clear you are well organised, and your job is consequently less likely to be left until last. Be sure to pass on any vital dates, such as the final acceptance date for delivery of loose inserts that you have booked with a magazine.

The designer's viewpoint

A designer comments:

> What kind of clients end up paying more than they should? Obviously this is a difficult thing to talk about – a client is a client after all – but in general problems often arise if there is no written brief. And then there are:
>
> - Clients who don't know what they want until they see it.
> - Clients who know exactly what they want but can't communicate it to the designer.
> - Clients who require visual after visual until we extract a brief from them, with both sides getting increasingly frustrated in the process.
> - Committees. Committees are often difficult to deal with. We may deal with one person within an organisation, but that person may need approval from several others who may not be in agreement with the requirement for the job (or even whether it needs doing at all), let alone how it is to be handled. The result is often the compilation of several design ideas with a dilution of the original concept, just to get the job out, with very little sense of satisfaction.
> - Clients who pass back lots of amendments individually rather than collating them and passing back one set. It is very time-consuming to do amendments, and it follows that the more sets arrive back, the higher the costs will be. Don't forget too that lots of sets of amendments can cause confusion and a greater risk that the job will have errors.

Another designer, Jo Kennedy,[1] is similarly frustrated by lots of different sets of amendments:

> From a designer's perspective, it's lovely to receive clearly set out amendments. If it's a long document being amended by lots of people, one final drawing together of the changes by a single individual with whom we can communicate directly is so appreciated. Our favourite method for receiving amendments is to have them listed in order, according to page number, paragraph number and then finally the line where the amendment needs to be made. It also makes a lot of sense for any overall design changes, which could affect the whole layout of the amendments to follow, to be listed at the top of the document under a 'Generic changes throughout' heading. The worst situation is receiving a complete Word file again and the client apologising because they have made the changes throughout, but haven't made a note of what or where they are. Luckily that does not happen very often.

How a design job progresses

Definitions for commonly used terms and abbreviations are included in the Glossary at the end of this book.

Should you ask for alternative designs for a single job, bearing in mind that this will use more of the designer's time? You may prefer all the effort to be channelled into thinking of one presentational idea that really meets the brief, rather than two, in which most of the design time has centred on making them different from each other. On the other hand, if you need designs to be approved by a meeting or outside body, more than one alternative may be advisable. Bear in mind that two or three choices presented to a meeting will nearly always result in a decision (whether a straight choice or combination of bits from different versions). This is a useful technique when dealing with difficult committees.

Using your brief on what kind of job it is, the designer will do a lot of thinking, make a few key decisions and then start work, providing you with a visual to show what the finished job will look like. This will display format and design layout, the colours, the position of headings and so on.

Once you have approved the overall concept, the designer will proceed. If you subsequently decide to change the layout, the amount of copy or any other element of the design, the additional resulting costs will be your responsibility.

You will then receive a proof of your job for you to check, and usually this will be onscreen. Never rely on proofreading onscreen, even if what you are checking is for a website. Print it out and check it carefully. Changes are expensive because they are time-consuming. To lay out a piece of text may take 10 minutes; to go back into it and locate precise errors in specific lines may take just as long.

You may have to circulate proofs in-house, and this may be a source of further expense. It is a common failing to be unable to take copy seriously until it has been laid out, and most people to whom you show the proof will feel they have not taken part (or 'managed' you) unless they correct something.

How can you avoid the large correction bills that result from late changes?

- Establish who needs to see what and at what stage before you start work, so you don't end up circulating all the various stages of a job to everyone who could possibly be interested.
- If you have to circulate a visual, make sure you attach a note of what you are trying to achieve and why, so that everyone understands how the piece has been put together (and you have a chance to influence how they view it). Ask all those to whom you circulate it to respond with their comments by a certain date. Never chase.
- If several sets of corrections are expected back from your colleagues before a job can proceed, amalgamate them before you pass them back to the designer. If they cancel each other out, consider which route to take.
- For jobs that have been changed heavily, circulate a note of the extra costs that resulted: this should get the message across!
- People may write all over proofs but seldom seem to keep a copy of their changes.

Finally do remember the power of saying thank you. If you are pleased with a job then tell your suppliers. I suspect that many clients fail to do so because they assume that if customers show they are very satisfied, the bills will go up in future. The opposite may be the case. There is nothing more rewarding than providing a service that is appreciated, and if your working relationship is flourishing, your creative bills may well go down.

How to proofread text

Don't assume this is easy. It's a job that needs your full concentration, and there are courses (including by distance learning[2]) available to teach you how best to do it.

It's very difficult to read for sense and to read for typographical errors at the same time. Try the following sequence:

- Read from a printout, not onscreen.
- Look at the headings and subheadings (it is very easy for mistakes here not to be noticed, especially if all the words are in capital letters).
- Read the whole text against what you provided (always keep a copy of what you gave the designer).
- Examine the individual words that make up the text, keeping an eye out for awkward word breaks, spelling mistakes and additional words (e.g., 'Paris in the the spring') and words that are proper words but the wrong ones (e.g., not/now, it/if).
- Errors that are easy to miss include a narrow letter missing (e.g., 'signifcance') and an extra letter (e.g., 'billling' or 'acccountancy').

- Beware of skimming over long or familiar words; an error may be lurking there.
- Read for sense.
- Check the author's name. Twice.
- For direct marketing pieces, ring all the telephone numbers quoted and try sending an email to the address given. Consult the website to make sure it is a valid address. Double-check the postcode for return mail to be sure that it has not been changed. If you are offering instructions on how to find somewhere, check that the postal address and the postcode for satellite navigation to the location are the same (often they are not).

When checking the final proof, look out for the following:

- If you have not seen the job since passing on your corrections, check that they have all been made.
- Check the position of headings.
- Where copy is split between columns (bottom of one/top of the next) check that the breaks are sensible. Try to avoid splitting dates, numbers, proper names and so on.
- Is there any awkward spacing? Too much of a gap at the end of one page, too little space on another? Should elements be rearranged slightly to make the whole thing easier to read?
- Circulate copies only to those who need to see them, making it clear they are for information rather than alteration!

If the design is for a printed item, once the proofs have been approved the designer will proceed to create finished artwork, usually a PDF proof, which the printer will need in order to print. It follows that any late corrections, received once the artwork has been made, will be extremely expensive.

Managing without a designer

It is not always necessary to use the services of a designer. For product information that stresses new information, hot-off-the-press or value for money, an overtly designed format could be entirely inappropriate. (The most obvious example is market research – the more you 'package' your promotional material and the report itself, the less it will sell, and the lower your price will have to be.) If you decide to go ahead on your own, there are a few things to keep in mind.

Draw attention to what is important

Assume that all your prospects have poor eyesight, and make your information easy to read. Cut down on special effects that detract from the main message. Make it easy for readers to home in on the essential sales benefits of the product you are advertising.

Ensure the headings and subheadings are clear. Put a box around particularly important text or have it printed in a different typeface or colour. Do make sure, however, that the colour is really legible. Bright colours are difficult to read; most people find 'muddy' colours much easier on the eye.

Put the main heading at the top of the brochure or advertising space, not half-way through the body copy: as noted earlier, a headline in the middle of an advertisement encourages the reader to carry on reading halfway through the sales information!

Offer visual variety

Ensure the presentation is visually varied without being jarring. A good designer will use 'typographic colour' (special effects such as the emphasising of subheadings, underlining, bold text, etc.) but without overusing it. A great mass of flat-looking text is suitable for the page of a novel but not for advertising copy.

Use the space you have effectively, bearing in mind how the reader will respond

- However much you feel you must say to promote your product, avoid over-filling the space. A format that looks confused or 'heavy work' will put the reader off. Use bullet points, vary your paragraph lengths and don't ask for text to be justified.
- If your advertisement is appearing in a larger space (for example, on a news-paper page), pictures work better on the outside edges of the space, rather than disappearing into the centre gutter. For both advertisements and feature articles, headlines on the right-hand side of the page tend to be more eye-catching than those on the left.
- Readers do not have to absorb every word of what you say. Allow them to assimilate blocks of copy by scanning the headings. Make the words you use recognisable at a glance by setting in a 'serif' typeface (easier to read); limited use of italics can also be effective. Eye camera studies have shown that column widths in excess of 80 characters are more difficult to read.
- When booking advertising space, routinely ask for a right-hand page rather than a left, and always for a space facing text rather than another advertisement. Most readers flick past double-page spreads of advertising. Tell the person handling the layout what you have booked, and provide them with a sample of the publication.
- Find out what is going next to you, and in particular what is going beneath. There is a natural tendency for the eye to move down the page; if there is a small feature (whether advertising or editorial) beneath the space you book, it may well draw attention away from your copy. If you are placing a direct response advertisement, put the coupon where it is easiest to cut out, and ensure that it does not back on to another such coupon.

How many colours to use

The costs of full-colour printing have fallen greatly in recent years, but if it is still beyond your budget, you don't need to pay for full-colour materials to make your promotions stand out. Consider the use of 'spot colour' in newspapers that are predominantly black and white. A good designer can make a two-colour job look extremely attractive, but it requires skill. You may also decide to use fewer colours to make your material look as if it has been cheaply produced, and is therefore more cost-effective. Political parties often produce their materials in just one or two colours to look more cost-conscious.

Design techniques to avoid

- Don't use upper case (CAPITAL) letters too much. They are hard to read and prevent words from being recognised at a glance. For this reason don't put headlines in capitals.
- Don't make the lettering too large: 50cm is the normal reading distance for a magazine or newspaper; if your lettering is poster-size, it will be illegible.
- Don't put extensive amounts of copy at an angle – it's very difficult to read. (On the other hand a 'flash' across the corner of an advert can be a very effective way of attracting attention.)
- Don't reverse out too much text, it is very hard on the eyes (although for limited amounts of text this can be a very effective way of attracting attention).
- Don't place text over an illustration unless the picture is truly 'faded back' behind the words. (Even then it doesn't always work.)

Getting material printed

Most printers receive artwork from designers in digital format, the most common being a high-resolution PDF proof. Commissioning printing and finishing may be the responsibility of a departmental print buyer or designer, or it may fall to you. Production of a reasonable job is likely to depend on three factors: your ability to match the job to the appropriate process, a supplier who can produce the goods on time, and a competitive price. Coming up with the right combination is more likely if you understand what is involved, although in addition to technical information, you also need to be able to ask specific management questions. For example, is the printer who is offering to do a job for you in fact planning to subcontract it to someone else?

There are a variety of different printing methods. None is superior to all the others; all have different benefits for different applications. The two most commonly used for jobs originating in the marketing department are lithography (litho) and screen printing, but you may also find letterpress, photogravure or flexography being used, according to the requirements of the job. Digital printing is getting better all the time, and offers the facility to introduce personalisation and variable data into materials, which is likely to become the norm in the future.

For smaller items, such as flyers, mini-brochures and folders, digital printing is usually cheaper for print runs under 400 copies. Litho printing is more cost-effective when the print run is significantly larger than this.

Finishing includes all the processes that turn the printed sheets into the finished product required, for example, varnishing, embossing, laminating, collating, folding, binding, die-cutting, assembly and packing. It's unlikely that a single printing house will offer everything you need, so it's quite common for printers to subcontract on your behalf. If it is you that is doing the arranging, and print and finishing are being placed separately, it is vital to ensure the two suppliers communicate to ensure the right inks and materials are used.

The entire job, in all its specific detail, must be confirmed to the printer in writing. Nigel Dollin of John Dollin Printing Services Ltd comments:

> This is something that customers, for whatever reason, are reluctant to do and quite often will say 'as per our conversation' or 'as per estimate number'. It is wrong to assume that the supplier knows what you want as the only person who knows this is the person placing the order. Insist on receiving back a confirmation of the order.

Finally, you must ensure that the printed materials arrive where needed, by the required date, by the most appropriate delivery method and in a satisfactory condition. Printers can handle the last two processes for you, but your own warehouse or office may have established contacts with carriers, especially to your regular customers, and therefore be able to offer a better service.

It's important that file copies are delivered to you prior to the main consignment so that any problems can be dealt with before the bulk of your print run reaches its destination. Apart from allowing you to make your own check on quality, you will need them for your records and for any early despatch, e.g., to authors (getting stock back from the warehouse after delivery can take a disproportionate amount of effort!). Be sure to send copies immediately to those you are relying on to carry out whatever marketing initiatives you have set up. It's a particularly good idea to send copies to the firm's reps and your customer service staff: they will be dealing with the response!

How to request an estimate from a printer

Buy or subscribe to a guide to printing prices to use as a basic reference for what you should be paying for printing. Two or three quotations should precede any sizeable job. Ask for samples of the paper the printer will be using, and remember to ask about recycled and environmentally friendly materials. Whereas 'repro' work was previously generally handled by the printer, these days it is more likely to be managed by the designer, who will create a PDF proof that is ready for printing – and in turn receive a print proof to check before a job is passed for press. The printer will need the following information from you in order to be able to estimate (they may provide you with a form to fill in).

In addition to a description of the component parts of the job, they will need to know:

- their size and shape;
- how many printing colours;
- how many different versions;
- the size and number of the type of material you want to produce (e.g., brochure or letter, and if the whole package needs to be under a specific weight for mailing);
- how many copies;
- when the finished job is required by;
- what type of proof you require (PDF, match print, digital or wet proof – see below);
- who is going to check the printer's proof, and where they are located;
- where to deliver and what special packaging is needed;
- any additional requirements, e.g., coding order forms, numbering, collating, laminating, saddle stitching;
- the job reference number you would like to be used in any correspondence.

However specific your instructions, the resulting estimate will probably be marked subject to sight of artwork.

If you have a sample of the kind or quality of material you are seeking to produce, do pass it on. It will give the printer a clear idea of your expectations of quality, presentation and so on. Alternatively, ask to see printed samples of a similar kind of work that the firm has handled before. If the quantity required is likely to change (e.g., the export department has not yet let you know how many copies it needs), ask for a run-on (r/o) price, say for 10,000 and 1,000 run-on. Or ask for a series of quotes: 1,000, 2,000, 3,000 and 10,000. This saves you from continuously ringing the printer for further information. Run-on prices may be surprising as it generally doesn't cost a proportional amount more to have a couple of hundred or even a couple of thousand additional copies made, which may be useful. On the other hand, setting up ('prepping' and then 'washing up' afterwards) a litho machine again to reprint items you have run out of will be much more expensive. Set-up costs for digital printing are much lower.

Remember that mailing houses generally ask for an over-delivery of all the stock they are sending out, to allow for 'spoilage' (stock damaged during processing, e.g., when setting up the machine run, which will inevitably happen). Many publishing houses also have internal distribution lists for all marketing materials produced, to ensure everyone is informed, and associated stock is often removed from deliveries the moment they arrive in the organisational warehouse. This may further deplete the total amount of printed material available for you to use.

Which estimate should you accept?

Price should not be the only consideration on which you award a particular project. You should also consider reliability, service and the likely quality of the finished product. Some publishing houses negotiate contract prices for jobs that occur frequently, but these need to be reviewed regularly to ensure competitive rates are being maintained. Other houses cease to bother requesting quotations from habitual contacts. This is usually a mistake.

A good guide to working out whether a new firm is going to be easy to deal with is to ask about its quality accreditation and how its working procedures operate. Does it have a complaints procedure? If asking questions like these arouses hostility, you may not be in the right hands. Remember to ask for the names of those you will need to be in touch with – just in case your key contact turns out to be on holiday when your job is going through.

Paul Jones, account manager of Impress Print Services Ltd,[3] comments:

> Also assess the print company's willingness to visit you to discuss the job, or to show you first-hand around their premises. Don't let them hide behind technical jargon, and feel free to ask for explanations. This may be to do with environmental credentials of a paper stock, a type of finish or a type of fold. For slightly more complex jobs, and if time allows, an unprinted finished dummy can be a good indicator that both sides know and understand how the finished job should look.
>
> If there are various elements to be printed at the same time, as part of the same job, it is always advisable to try to keep as much with one printer as possible, as this will reduce managerial input and help ensure uniform quality. If price makes you keen to look elsewhere, mention your desire to keep everything 'under one roof' as spreading elements between different suppliers can become both stressful for you and a series of very small accounts for those instructed. Using a single supplier helps the coordination of timings, and quality control within one production team.

Organising a proof

Asking a designer to check a printed proof before a job is passed for press can avoid many difficulties. In general, the higher the specification you choose for the digital proof (and hence the more it costs), the closer what you see will be to the finished job.

There are various different types of proof to choose between:

- **PDF proof:** an acronym for portable document format; a digital proof created using Adobe Acrobat. This is currently by far the most common way to sign off proofs.
- **Digital proof:** a proof from the digital press produced prior to printing digitally.
- **Match print:** an ink jet proofing method using the same file that will create plates for data integrity. This is cheaper and less time-consuming than a wet proof. It shows a good colour match for full colour CMYK[4] print work.
- **Wet proof:** created using the plates and inks for the final print run. This is the most accurate way of proofing – but also the most expensive and often therefore impractical.

A compromise may be to view the job on the press, at the printer's premises, and to do the 'sign off' there.

Problems after delivery

But what if you are just not happy with the final job? Your immediate concern should be the source of the mistake, and if it is the printer's, what the firm will do to put it right. If you think the material is usable, but below your (demonstrable) commercial standard, a discount should result; if it is not usable then the printer should reprint at no cost to you. The two bargaining positions will be the printer's view of the job as 'commercially acceptable' (they will not want to reprint) and your concern for the reputation of your company (you will not want to send out substandard material, even if it is costing you next to nothing). Be very wary of becoming known as a discount merchant and one who accepts poor quality or mistakes.

To avoid the situation arising in the future, you need to decide whether the mistake was due to:

- The printer's incompetence – if so, don't use them again.
- Bad luck. If the firm agrees to put it right you can try it again, but watch out for possible cost recovery from it on the next job (charging you more than the going rate to make up for money lost last time).
- The development of too casual a relationship between yourself and the printer, for example, failure to put instructions in writing or to make specific require-ments clear. You can remedy this. For example, when you have sent a formal instruction to a printer, always look for a written order acknowledgement with evidence that specific timeframes and deadlines, quantities and split deliveries have been understood.

You have one sympathetic ally in the company who will be able to advise: the production director. There may also be an advisory service run by a professional print buying association that you can consult.

Notes

1 www.us2design.co.uk.
2 www.train4publishing.co.uk.
3 www.impressprint.co.uk.
4 CMYK means the four inks generally used in colour printing: cyan, magenta, yellow and key (black).

Part III

Specific advice for particular markets

15 Approaching specific interest markets

The value and significance of the niche in publishing

Finding the general reader 363
Marketing children's books 369
Opportunities for children's publishers today 370
Key difficulties for those marketing children's titles 374
Marketing techniques for promoting children's titles 376
Selling resources to public libraries 378
How to send information to public libraries 380
Public lending right 383
Promoting to university academics 385
Promoting textbooks to the academic market 389
Summary books and study aids 391
Research monographs 392
Professional resources 392
Selling to academic libraries 392
Selling to educational markets 396
How to reach the market 403
Selling educational material to international markets 409
Marketing to doctors and other healthcare professionals 410
How to communicate effectively with doctors 411
When is the best time to promote to doctors? 416
Other opportunities for publishers in this area 417
The role of medical librarians 421
Selling to professional and industrial markets 422
Important information for approaching professional markets 422
Format of published and marketing material 425

All definitions of marketing agree on the importance of the customer, and in order to approach them in an appropriate manner – to be able to identify the products, services, offers and marketing messages that are most likely to appeal to them – it's vital to understand who they are. This chapter therefore offers a more detailed exploration of several markets that are particularly important to publishers.

For those working in some areas of publishing, without a specific background or understanding of the market, this may initially feel difficult. We will therefore begin with a few general principles before moving on to examine some particular markets in more detail.

- **Begin with an enquiring mind.** Whatever your level of understanding, and however specific the area you are now approaching (e.g., medicine, dentistry, engineering), you need to begin with curiosity. All marketers need to be fascinated by their customers: the range of products they buy; how they choose; how and why they need them and through what means they pay. It's your job to be interested and involved rather than think how unusual or odd they are.
- **Find out all you can about them.** Read the publications and blogs they read and examine the websites they frequent. If they have meetings, national or regional, try to attend one; observe them in action and watch how they behave. Look out for general trends: how do they speak to each other; what do they wear; can you generalise about their demographics; how diverse are they? Even if the subject of professional interest is completely new to you, what tone of voice is used in the correspondence or vacancies sections of the forums they use?
- **Approach with caution.** Observe rather than speak; store away information to fuel your understanding of the group you are required to work with and note key words in order to reflect them back later on. Bear in mind that, lacking information to the contrary, the market will probably assume you care as much about their profession/specific interest as they do. Say little until you feel you can contribute without letting the side down:

  > Better to remain silent and be thought a fool than to speak and to remove all doubt.[1]

- **Feel confident.** You bring objectivity. Lack of experience, provided it is managed in an appropriate way, can lead you to ask the right questions about products and services and how they benefit the market, avoiding the peril of assumption that may have fuelled past approaches and led to lost sales. There is a real danger that the reasons the publisher or author gave when planning to offer a product or service may not be the same as those relied on by the market when deciding whether or not to purchase. Your insight in exploring such gaps may be really valuable.

Case study

The Writers' and Artists' Yearbook (Bloomsbury) has been published annually since 1907. It offers a compendium of names and contact information for those wanting to get published or sell their work, and a range of relevant articles from key figures in this field. It is also a book that gets widely used within publishing houses, the names and address sections providing a valuable, and regularly updated, address book for anyone wanting to contact the media or find new professional contacts. Publishers, however, tend not to read the articles – being fully involved in the profession, they do not need to read about how to find an agent, or how authors can best manage their marketing. Year-on-year the book has expanded in size and, in order to keep it to a manageable length, the publishers were considering which parts of the book could be trimmed. Before doing so, they commissioned some market research into how the book was used.

A questionnaire was included in all titles sent out from the publishers' warehouse and lodged with booksellers willing to cooperate, and who could be persuaded that this was not an attempt to get people to order directly. The conclusion was that the main market (writers) liked to read the articles and did so long before they got around to using the contact information in order to target those who might help them get published. In other words, the main reason the publishers found the book useful was not the same as that of the market.

Finding the general reader

When approaching specific professional markets, it's relatively easy to understand your audience – you locate the relevant professional journal or forum, observe what's going on and start building your knowledge. More general markets are much more difficult to understand – members could be anywhere.

The advance information produced by publishing houses often lists the target market as the 'general reader' or sometimes their more cultivated counterpart, the 'educated general reader'. To start with, it's a very unspecific term, and the segmentation of markets into smaller, more manageable groups through demographic analysis or lifestyle stages may include general readers in every category. How can we be more precise?

This book will be available worldwide, so providing specific and local guidance to markets close to every reader is impossible. It's therefore important to emphasise the value of keeping track of what is going on in society as a whole, of remaining observant. You need to remain alert to a variety of different viewpoints, and the number of people they represent; to move beyond your own comfort zones and assumptions.

It's important to consult a variety of websites and blogs; to read a range of different newspapers and magazines; to watch and listen to a variety of television and radio stations – and above all to listen to people talk about the concerns they have. Watching soap operas or observing which major films are coming out (and which ones are successes) are effective ways of keeping track of current trends in society and learning to interpret them. Growing older can help too – provided we are stimulated by change rather than resistant to it – our ability to spot what's going on around us, and newly emerging markets, becomes more acute as a wider range of things happen to us. So remain alert to what is going on in your life, and in those around you, how the experiences feel and what opportunities you spot for presenting published content in the process. As generalisations, and to get you started, here are a few current trends:

- Shortage of time. Time famine is established worldwide, and various forms of rage are now itemised as proof of how much we hate waiting ('road rage', 'trolley rage' and now 'car park rage'). To get more done in the time available we multitask, often with several screens in front of us at the same time: texting while talking and surfing the web while chatting online. This does not mean that everything has to be achievable super-quickly, but if you are going to ask for an audience's time, make it sound like an experience they can justify, both to themselves and their wider circle of influencers/responsibilities.
- Desire for better experiences – in friendships, relationships, conversation – often fuelled by a belief that these are our right. A desire for deeper, more fulfilling encounters often seems to be accompanied by restlessness; a greater desire for things to be better, yet a reduced tendency to work at them to make them so – or blaming/suing others if we are less than fully satisfied.
- Optimism. There is a big appetite for stories that distract, lift and show a positive spin on life, hence the many popular formats through which celebrities can announce their relationship/baby/marriage/new life after divorce with lavish pictures and supportive text.
- Curiosity. We like to read about ourselves – or those we can assume represent us – in publications that highlight the oddities of everyday life; disasters that have befallen people, how it feels to live through a situation or dilemma we may later face too.
- Competitiveness. This is now imbued into all levels of society, from stories of children being given additional academic tuition to help them pass exams earlier and earlier into their lives to beauticians offering better outcomes through a variety of procedures. Advantage is purchasable and reading about it expands the understanding of options.
- Brands. As society becomes increasingly international, there is increasing demand for badges that signify specific attributes (style, money, membership) and work across national and cultural frontiers.
- Respect. The internet coaxes the individual into relationships, offering us attention, understanding and an idea that our individual needs will be met. This spills over into how we expect to be treated in our daily lives and fuels intolerance and resentment if we feel we are not being treated as we should be. Our decision to move on if we don't like the prevailing tone of voice can be instant (think how speedily we leave websites that get it wrong) and young people are often quick to claim that they have been patronised.
- Concern about the environment. This is growing very fast, steered by environmentalists, encouraged/blocked by politicians and championed by children, who are putting pressure on the generations above them.

All these trends create opportunities for promoting and selling products and services, and published products can be strong beneficiaries. But marketing messages need to be made specific and relevant to anticipated audiences, so it's important to think through the market characteristics and the benefits *they* are likely to be looking for from the product or service you are developing and where it might be convenient to buy. There will usually be many options. So, for example, a home subscription to an online encyclopaedia could offer:

- A reliable and constantly available support for your children's homework, answering questions you cannot (shortage of time).
- An authoritative research tool to ensure you are able to quote reliable information to those who may look to you for a professional opinion (competitiveness).
- A fascinating distraction (optimism, curiosity).
- To mark the owner's home as a place that values quality (brand).
- Ease of access. Installation of the product has not required trees to be cut down, delivery lorries to pollute while offloading, or new storage solutions (concern for the environment).

The messages you choose will depend on the markets you are approaching, how big they are and how busy; how much extraneous noise you have to rise above in order to be heard. You need to consider the vast range of alternative distractions on offer that were not (or not widely) available 10 years ago. For example, people spend time and money on the internet, talking to others, information seeking and in online games, and the customisation that is now available for viewing and listening means they can make a personal timetable rather than be forced to rely on the broadcaster's schedule. In response, remind them how reading feels: the one-to-one personal engagement with a mind they admire or story that engrosses them.

In addition to remaining alert to customers' interests and buying habits, it's a good idea to build their appreciation of what you offer, to understand your brand. Tell your customers a story and they may buy into it, feeling they have discovered something worth supporting. Tell them how you came to establish the firm, say what you did before; even better if you left a corporate lifestyle to publish or sell what you care about as quality of life and work–life balance are issues that many can relate to. The stories you share may spread quickly – it used to be believed that customers required years of good service before they would start recommending a supplier, but recent research[2] has shown that there is a strong taste for the new and enthusiasts tend to pass on the name of their latest find immediately. How quickly can you start turning those who buy from you into advocates?

Top tips for turning your organisational brand into a community that other people want to belong to

- Share your vision for your organisation and its future; describe how you came to set the company up and what motivates you to do what you do. Tell the story.
- Have a visitors' book on your website to allow people to record their thoughts (most people like to see their name quoted and may make the link further available through social media).

- Similarly, host a blog or chatroom on your website to create a sense of community; encourage (mediated?) feedback and post news and replies to show that you respond.
- Encourage enthusiastic correspondents to add their comments to Amazon and other book review sites.
- Where relevant, offer reading copies of new books for book groups.
- Make occasional offers of free copies, run competitions and prize draws either through your mailings or on your website.
- Offer proof copies to selected people to encourage them to 'talk you up'.
- Most publishers send out manuscripts for review before committing to print. Widen this to form a reviewing community and enc0ourage feedback. Then print the names of those involved in a special section within the book. Not only will this spread ownership, if the reviewers are children this can prompt lots of additional sales in schools and among grandparents, parents and other encouragers.
- Offer branded goods that relate to your products, such as T-shirts or associated stationery (postcards, posters). You can test the market with a single item, and if there is positive feedback, produce more. This was how Penguin's highly successful T-shirts of 'paperback originals' were born. Initially produced for distribution to sales representatives at the seasonal briefing conference, they were found to have a far wider appeal and are now successfully sold through bookshops. The product range has been expanded to include deckchairs and mugs.
- Produce information sheets, whether web-based or printed for specific needs – for example, for book groups; guides to terminology or key place names for saga/fantasy addicts; bookmarks and window stickers for distribution through reps and shops.

Case study

How an organisation can enhance its image with an effective brand: the Society of Authors' new branding, 2013

The Society of Authors[3] is a trade union for professional authors with more than 9,000 members, writing in all areas. It advises members on rights, fees or any other professional query. It also provides training, lobbies for authors' rights and administers a wide range of grants and prizes such as the Authors' Foundation, one of the few bodies making grants to help with works in progress for established writers. It acts as literary representative of the estates of a number of distinguished writers including George Bernard Shaw, Virginia Woolf, Philip Larkin, E.M. Forster, Rosamond Lehmann, Walter de la Mare, John Masefield and Compton Mackenzie. The society's influence is widely noted within the publishing world and beyond – the organisation has more than 17,000 followers on Twitter.

To mark the arrival of Nicola Solomon, their new chief executive, the Society of Authors changed the text colour on their standard letterhead from blue to green. This was both an effective (and extremely low-cost) way of marking the end of an era, but also outlined a longer-term future ambition. From the outset Nicola, a former partner at a high-profile legal firm, was keen to standardise the society's communications, make them fresh and accessible to ensure that both their membership and the wider range of those who could similarly benefit understood the range of services and expertise on offer. There was also determination to reach out to potential younger members and encourage them to join – and to acknowledge the wider range of situations in which writers are writing and needing support. Finally she was keen to affirm the organisation as a whole, which was started in 1884. Early supporters included George Bernard Shaw, John Galsworthy, Thomas Hardy, H.G. Wells, J.M. Barrie, John Masefield, E.M. Forster and A.P. Herbert, to name but a few. The first president was Lord Alfred Tennyson and George Bernard Shaw said of the new organisation: 'We all, eminent and obscure alike need the Authors' Society. We all owe it a share of our time, our means, our influence.'

While the initial task was to produce a new organisational brand, in the longer term this was to be far more than just a rebranding exercise. Nicola was clear that this was the launch pad for an exercise in appreciating the range of the organisation's activities and understanding them as a coherent whole, and developing and promoting a wider understanding of its usefulness. She was keen to ensure a greater harmony in communication: in typefaces, presentation and tone of voice; this not to diminish individual contributions but to ensure that the membership is conscious of the organisation and that staff benefit from all the opportunities to absorb information from each other. Her only stipulation was that she wanted the brand eventually selected to be text and not image-based, having had experience of how images tend to attract and then polarise opinions.

The starting point was to find a firm with expertise in organising branding and through talking to other relevant organisations that had been through a similar experience, they found Brandguild.[4] This was a specialist branding agency that had previously worked with organisations of a comparable size and ethic – and whose quotation for the work involved came within the agreed budget of £10,000.

Brandguild were appointed and began by doing some research among the members of the Society of Authors. Those chosen for interview by the society were from a variety of ages and writing genres, and Brandguild also talked to others who regularly interact with the organisation (publishers, agents, retailers) and those who could belong but don't yet. They were asked about how they saw the organisation, what it was good at and not so good at – and what they called it. Interestingly whereas staff tend to refer to the organisation as 'The Society', members generally call it 'Society of Authors' or 'S of A'.

The next stage was for Brandguild to facilitate a 'creative day' for all staff, and in the process to find out from those who are most aware of the services offered by the organisation how they feel it is currently understood and appreciated. A temporary member of staff was brought in to look after the telephones and all staff were asked to spend time thinking about the personality of the Society and how best to project that outside the organisation. All staff were asked to come along having thought about what kind of character the society had, and to illustrate this through the choice of a familiar character.

This produced some interesting answers. Jeeves was mentioned several times (very well connected, highly competent, but discreet and in the background), as was the coherent, articulate but essentially shy Clark Kent (rather than his alter ego, Superman). Many staff articulated frustration at the Society's tendency to hide its light under a bushel. Later in the day, the words used to describe the organisation were similarly considered – in order to best convey the values and expertise of the organisation to an external audience. They spent time looking at colours and typefaces, and how these worked in a variety of different platforms.

Online communication manager Anna Ganley comments:

> Brandguild then presented their feedback. They talked about their research into the role of the society, its audiences (actual and potential) and discussed how the organisational brand could best be expressed in personality, words and colours. Focusing on the strategic aims of the process prevented it from just being an exercise in everyone commenting on their favourite colours. There were reference points to build on; the long-established connection between blue ink and writing, and the printing colours that worked well with blue. We wanted to have different versions of the same brand for each of the society's subgroups – and enjoyed thinking about sensible links. Blue and gold for awards information seemed particularly appropriate.

As a result of the creative day and wider research, three designs were presented to staff and discussed by the board of management. One emerged as the favourite early on, and once officially confirmed as the choice, Brandguild were given the go-ahead.

Ironically, the final stages took almost as long as the initial ones, when much bigger decisions had been made. There were serifs and decorative scrolls to play with, and Pantone lists to move up and down in search of the perfect combination. Some issues also emerged at the last minute (were they 'The Society of Authors' or 'Society of Authors'?) but also at a late stage a very useful set of monograph 'crops' emerged, ideal for presentational use on certificates.

Nicola Solomon comments:

> When it was ready we just started using it. Some have expressed surprise that we did not go for a formal launch of the new design. But we felt this process had been about us as an outward-facing organisation, and

so having decided on how we wanted to present ourselves we should just get on and do so. Fundamentally the new brand is there to show we are fresher and better but does not signify a change of direction. And we have had only positive feedback. Right now it is being rolled out across all the information we send out, as materials are used up we reprint or represent with the new branding in place – and this has shown us once again just what a wealth of information we offer our members.

Was it all worth it? Resoundingly yes. The rebranding has been positively responded to by staff, members and those we seek to influence. Overall it represents a positive – and very busy – future for the society.

The Society
of Authors

Figure 15.1 The Society of Authors' old logo. Courtesy of the Society of Authors.

Figure 15.2 The Society of Authors' new logo. Courtesy of the Society of Authors.

Marketing children's books

Most general publishing houses have a children's division and, although pioneering work was done (in particular by Kaye Webb, founder of Puffin, and Sebastian Walker, founder of Walker Books), until comparatively recently they were often seen as subsidiary activity to the development of the firm's main list. Advances and royalties on children's titles were based on lower-selling prices and so were worth less in cash terms to authors and illustrators. Children's authors attending events got less for their appearance than those writing titles for adults. The books received smaller promotion budgets and shares of company attention.

Today the area is vastly more active, and this is happening worldwide. The quality of children's books is better than ever and they are reaching the market through an increasing variety of outlets. Children are also buying books for themselves, often through school bookselling operations. Within the children's market in general, it is notable that sales are robust and have been relatively stable for the past 10 years, holding their own in a market where sales of adult titles have been declining. There has also been a slower encroachment of digital media on the physical market here, with digital products accounting for around 11 per cent of sales in both the UK and US.

Opportunities for children's publishers today

- Polarisation of the marketplace, with the emergence and dominance of key brands and authors in bestseller lists

In 2005, market research company Mintel reported: 'The *Harry Potter* series has become something of a crossover, popular with both children and adults, as has *The Curious Incident of the Dog in the Night-time*. This could perhaps mark the creation of a new genre of books, appealing to all ages.'[5] 'Crossover titles' subsequently entered the publishing industry's vocabulary and has led to separate editions of the same book being jacketed differently for various age groups. For example, books by J.K. Rowling and Philip Pullman, originally created for children, became media properties and were increasingly read by adults. This heralded the emergence of the young adult (YA) market, with authors such as Suzanne Collins and Stephenie Meyer becoming huge successes; as they became media-driven phenomena they were increasingly and enthusiastically read by adults, and now dominate in the bestseller lists. The specific vocabulary of these mass market titles has become part of popular culture – pub quizzes and crossword puzzles require you to know the meaning of 'muggle', 'alethiometer' and 'vampire romance' – and they consequently get read by all generations.

Other opportunities have emerged for big sales. Humorous titles aimed at younger markets such as *The Diary of Wimpy Kid* series and books by David Walliams were seized upon by schools and literacy champions as material that encouraged wider participation in reading and have become hugely popular. The rise of online gaming, and its spin-offs as book-related products (e.g., Minecraft), and the rise of character and brand licensing (often related to content that has nostalgia for parents, e.g., Lego and *Star Wars*) have proved very significant in this sector.

- New formats for children's publishing

Children today are digital natives, born into a world where time online is part of their daily lives – and if they do not gain access at home, they learn to use computers at school. Through this, new opportunities for accessing and sharing content have emerged, and the dictionary definition of the term 'passback' has widened from its use on the football pitch to include the handing back of a mobile phone or tablet computer to children in the back of a car to keep them quiet. New computer formats (e.g., the tablet) have led to new delivery mechanisms for content sharing within children's literature which are encouraging children to read and involve themselves in the stories they access. Many (but not all) of these opportunities are being developed by traditional publishers, with their understanding of content development and marketing, to home and international customers and agents. As Kate Wilson, founder of Nosy Crow[6] (children's books and apps) commented:

> We make innovative, multimedia, highly interactive apps for tablets, smartphones and other touchscreen devices. These apps are not existing books

squashed onto screens, but instead are specially created to take advantage of the devices to tell stories and provide information to children in new and engaging ways. We don't want reading to be the most boring thing a child can do on a touchscreen.

We know it's subjective, but Nosy Crow wants to be proud of everything that we publish and make. We want to be sure that it meets the need of a reader (or emerging reader), and meets that need as well as it possibly can. That means great illustration, great design, great audio, great video, great animation and really great writing. We go out of our way to find these things from new and established talents.

- New selling locations to reach the mass market

Supermarkets experimented (through Walker Books) with own-brand books in the 1980s, although the novelty of being able to buy children's reading material where you bought other essentials was quickly overtaken as supermarkets turned to selling branded blockbuster titles as 'loss leaders' to draw shoppers in store. But the ongoing needs of the gifting market, which remains consistently buoyant for products for children, have promoted an expansion of other places to buy and helped lift children's books to be rated alongside toys and computer games as a first-class profit opportunity.

Today most large centres of population are ringed by out-of-town super-markets and superstores where people with small children are likely to shop and, crucially, find it more convenient to buy books. As well as selling books through supermarkets, books also sell well through superstores selling child-related merchandise, and can benefit from being displayed alongside non-book child-related products such as toys and prams. Through these outlets, books are being sold to a much wider group of people, as many of the customers are probably not regular bookshop browsers. Purchases are often made on impulse, and there is huge demand for high-profile media-related properties of the kind publishers can offer, with a price offer or associated discount being a key part of the consumer expectation.

Leisure and food venues are another key opportunity for publishers to work in partnership with organisations who are approaching compatible audiences but with non-competing products. Partnerships are beneficial both ways: publishers reach many non-regular book-buyers, but the merchandise they make available may confer brand benefits on the host organisation. Major publishing houses spend a lot of time trying to establish and maintain such sharing, for example with books being included in branded children's meals and as part of the customer value proposition for 'day out' venues.

Another new arena is the sampling of books through non-retail outlets, and in particular the workplace selling of books, which has expanded dramatically in recent years. Firms involved in this (notably The Book People[7] in the UK) buy large quantities of a limited range of stock, display the products in staff space and collect orders at the end of the week. Children's titles can work very well here;

backlist titles can drive subsequent demand for the front list, in particular with nostalgia titles that are familiar to parents. Similarly books on sport for boys, reference titles linked to the school curriculum and reading packs that offer value for money are all popular. Retailers can demand huge discounts but they are reaching customers who do not frequent bookshops (and hence are expanding the market), they buy firm (no stock gets returned) and their orders can often make a print project financially viable.

Packaging is vital for these locations. Books often become more attractive when marketed in combination with toys and clothing, as a branded item appealing to a child with specific interests. Packaging that adds value to the product is particularly important: for example in warehouse clubs, catalogues and cash and carries, shoppers tend to be looking for a higher price and bulkier looking purchase (this is particularly important if the item is to be given as a present, as customers appreciate a large box to wrap). For some outlets the publisher may produce own-brand items; packages that consist of 'books plus' may become part of the store's gift or hobby range rather than book range. What is more because they are aimed at gifters rather than book-buyers, they target new audiences – and hence may be stocked in greater depth, particularly during peak times in the seasonal gifting market.

The traditional book trade has reacted in varied ways. In general the children's department is easier to find than it used to be, and children's titles are now part of the major promotions at the front of the store. Some major bookselling chains have experimented with dedicated children's shops, but the combination of excessive rents for high street sites and low-price products is a difficult one, and many casualties have occurred. Even shops that were once thriving concerns, functioning as centres of advice and encouragement on reading, with welcoming premises and detailed knowledge of their stock are now threatened, and the closure of the Lion and Unicorn Bookshop in south London in 2013 – the first children's store ever to win the prestigious title of Independent Bookseller of the Year – was dispiriting. As head of membership services at the BA Meryl Halls commented, this would 'leave a huge hole in the specialist children's bookselling sector, and in the visibility of children's books on the high street, and in schools'. Halls added: 'The closure highlights the torrid pressures on high-street booksellers, and retailers generally – a massive rent increase can put a once-thriving business over the edge of viability, and taken together with business-rate pressure, the combination can all too often be fatal.' She also called on local and national government to 'look at the health of our high streets with increasing seriousness if we are not to see a continuing diminution in the vitality, diversity and creativity on our high streets – bookshops being a key indicator of the health of our local retail communities'.

Other retailers have nurtured special markets. The organisation of school book fairs and school book clubs is an area of strong competition and activity. There is some special publishing for this market, in the form of book and activity kits. But with growing market assumptions about buying online being a norm, and consumers often using bookshops as showrooms where they examine what they will later purchase from home, it can be very difficult to compete.

- Character licensing arrangements

With the wide availability of films for children, online and via networks, and the marketing efforts of the Disney Corporation, there has been considerable growth in demand for 'character' images created for a book or film to adorn a wide variety of specially designed merchandise – from nightdresses and bedroom slippers to rucksacks and school lunchboxes. With their backlist of character titles, publishers are well placed to take advantage of this opportunity.

Superstore purchasers shop thematically, following the child's interests; they may not be looking for anything as specific as a book or cutlery set, but a Pooh Bear or Thomas the Tank Engine item and books can benefit enormously from the creation of 'retail theatre' through cross-merchandising, displaying books in an accessible position alongside related merchandise. Event publishing and seasonal opportunities are of increasing importance, tying in with periods of raised consumer footfall such as Mothers' Day, Christmas and other key gifting periods. Some stores take this a stage further by launching specific boutiques within stores for certain characters that have a strong affinity with their own market.

- Educational upheaval and parental anxiety

Changes in the educational environment have created an opportunity for children's publishers, in both new resources for schools and to support parental anxiety. For example, there is now a considerable market for resources to practise for tests and assessments as well as resources for reading and project-based homework. There are also opportunities for publishers arising from events and anniversaries, e.g., World War One, the Olympics, happenings within the Royal Family and annual events such as the birthday of Martin Luther King or Shakespeare. Major publishing houses employ reps to call on schools and sell both educational and reading resources, usually basing rewards on commission.

- Opportunities to meet authors

Book events, festivals and other opportunities to meet authors through special appearances are of growing importance for book-buying. The rise in literary festivals has been a notable trend worldwide, and each of them now generally has its own associated children's programme that often holds some of the most highly attended events – and at which huge numbers of titles can be sold. British author Jacqueline Wilson holds the record for the longest book signing – more than 8 hours (incidentally without a comfort break). Children want to meet their favourite authors, and these opportunities have become hugely profitable.

In some instances, where children's books are the product of team writing, a range of different authors may be despatched to talk on behalf of the writing team. Along similar lines, for non-technical authors – or those disinclined to participate in marketing – it may be the publisher who maintains a website, updates it with new information and replies to letters from children.

In addition to live events, there are opportunities to connect through social media and to live stream author events in real time. Authors can therefore connect with fans without going on time-consuming or costly tours, and digital assets of author events are created in the process.

- The long tail for children's titles

The marketing manager for a children's list will also spend a good deal of time and money promoting the backlist, not just new highlights. Whereas a new general hardback fiction title will have its heaviest sales period in the months following publication, with another boost when a paperback or ebook appears, children's titles can take a much longer time to get established – and then go on selling for much longer than adult titles. Where titles last between generations, there can also be a significant nostalgia market, with parents buying books by authors they enjoyed, or about similar subjects – some of which never go out of date, but may be presented in new combinations (e.g., fairy stories, tractors, dinosaurs, teddy bears).

Key difficulties for those marketing children's titles

- Marketing is often through intermediaries

While school book fairs and book tokens and vouchers offer the chance for children to choose first-hand, there is a key difficulty for children's publishers in that the marketer often has to convince a middle market. Booksellers and wholesalers have to be persuaded to stock titles, and parents, relatives, teachers and librarians to buy on behalf of the children they represent. Even those promotions that are sent straight to children (e.g., school book club leaflets) rely on teachers to organise and parents to pay. A high percentage of book purchases are paid for by adults; parents but also 'graunties' (grandparents/aunts and uncles/closely involved adults). In demographic terms, the spread of adults buying for children is very wide, making the targeting of marketing very difficult. For example, many titles are bought by adults who are not responsible for children or by much older generations, and their preferences have to be borne in mind.

Each year publishers produce catalogues and leaflets detailing their new and existing titles. In addition they prepare a range of promotional material for display in shops, schools and libraries: posters, leaflets, balloons and so on. This must be attractive both to the adult (so it gets put up) and to the children who will see it. Appealing to 'the child in us all' is not as easy as it sounds. Children today are sophisticated and acutely conscious of being patronised. They can be persuaded that a book is not for them by a quick glance at the cover (particularly important when they are doing the buying through an online bookshop and that is *all* they see).

Children's language also changes all the time, and while they will not expect to see the current hot terminology on the back of book covers, they can be very disparaging about words that sound out of date, and hence inclined to damn the product through association. Publishers do not need to talk like teenagers (they could not do it anyway) but they do need to have a sixth sense to spot terms that will date.

Just to illustrate this, here are the current terms used by three 14-year-old boys in specific locations in Bath (UK), Melbourne (Australia) and Portland, Oregon (US). I say specific locations, because 10 miles down the road they would probably be different.

	Bath	*Melbourne*	*Portland*
good	sound	good	sweet
very good	bless	great	raw
cool	safe	swag	gnarly
attractive	peng	hot	hot
bad	peak	bad	bummer

This illustration is not designed to pass comment on their vocabulary, but to illustrate how rich, temporary and localised it is.

- Children's publishing is probably the most price-sensitive area of the book trade

Economies of scale are vital where high development costs on mass market novelty formats necessitate high print runs and hence volume deals. Mostly this is done using a schedule of discounts, rising according to the quantity bought. At the same time, costs must be kept as low as possible, and most authors are remunerated on the basis of net receipts rather than published price.

Children's books are highly price-responsive. There is a symbiotic relationship between retail price and volume in the mass market; adding an extra 10 per cent to a title can ruin its chances of success. Shoppers in out-of-town superstores are particularly price-sensitive. People are often looking to spend a specific amount of money, and given that there is so much choice, will allow the pre-set budget to be the main criterion for decision-making. When pricing new materials publishers need to benchmark their prices not only against competing books but also against non-book products (e.g., toys, stationery and gift items) that jostle for the same leisure spend. Money off can be a significant marketing gambit at certain times of year (e.g., Christmas), but in general low retail prices mean there is less margin to play with.

Finally, children themselves are very price-conscious. Youth today has more disposable income – working parents who are not at home tend to compensate with bigger allowances – but with this has come an increased consumer confidence. They are used to shopping around and an awareness that books in particular can always be found somewhere cheaper was ironically fostered while they were still at school, by teachers encouraging them to read. For many UK children, their first experience of market economics was at primary school when they learned that the new *Harry Potter* was available and that it was cheapest at a particular supermarket.

Marketing techniques for promoting children's titles

The new selling locations have necessitated a switch in marketing techniques. Instead of concentrating their energies on pursuing every possible opportunity for free coverage (how children's books used to be marketed), publishers have had to become increasingly aggressive to maintain these opportunities, which are under threat from both adult books and a variety of other merchandise with potentially higher stock turns and profits.

Attractive printed material is still a mainstay of children's marketing: something that will make an impression on the book-buyer and provide a taste of the quality of the product. Posters and other free material for schools and libraries may directly impress an author brand on pupils with long-lasting consequences. For other markets where value for money is important, cheaply produced materials give a quick impression that there is plenty of choice, limited price special offers, or deals so that purchases above a certain price attract free carriage, can all encourage a quick response.

The creation of interesting websites where children can find out more about their favourite characters is also very important. Children feel a character or title is more real if they can access information online to back it up. Such websites need to be sophisticated, interactive and regularly updated – publishers are marketing here to the most net-savvy generation. Similarly, non-fiction titles that offer checked web links can be welcomed by parents. Books have been through extensive processes of checking and so are more reliable than the web, but 'listing 1,000 checked websites' on the front of a reference title makes it look more appealing and up to date to the children they are buying for, and is reassuring and time-saving for parents (they don't have to check the sites themselves).

Generating free publicity

Children's publishers often complain of the paucity of review space devoted to their books, although blockbusters such as *Harry Potter* have broken the mould, with reviews commissioned from children who stayed up all night reading the new book appearing on the news pages (the experience handily enhancing their CVs at the same time). However hotly editors protest their independence from advertising, it is true that children's publishers in general spend little on space in anything other than trade magazines, and that is usually concentrated in the run-up to relevant book fairs. But as the area becomes more profitable, and they advertise more, there will be more editorial features on children's books.

Opportunities for free coverage may include:

- **Social media.** Children are not officially allowed to be on Facebook until they are 13 or Twitter if they are under 10, and data protection and online security issues impact on signing up for online fan sites without parental approval, but social media can certainly be used to reach their parents. The blogosphere is particularly important in creating pre-launch buzz and social media can offer opportunities for giveaways, samplers, exclusive content, allowing authors to connect with the fan base in a direct way. Mentions on sites frequented by the parents, blogs and tweets can all drive traffic to relevant websites for more information, or ordering mechanisms for those who decide they want instant gratification.

Social media platforms cross international boundaries, and it is helpful to benefit from access to global digital content. The noise created around new products when launched in other markets can be helpful, as can an attempt to ensure consistency in packaging across markets in order to benefit; sharing digital assets such as authors interviews and book trailers. For ideas on how to work with a blogger, see Chapter 9.

- **Organising promotional links with websites, magazines and newspapers** read by parents and children, for example, features that 'review' new titles, articles on key authors, and sponsoring competitions which feature the book as prize and hence promote word-of-mouth. Magazines aimed at children are often particularly keen on featuring extracts from forthcoming titles that appeal to their core audience.

- **Producing free branded material for information carriers** such as posters, bookmarks, balloons, height charts, party packs, 'make and do' samplers. All of these offer longevity and thus may go on promoting the associated titles long after distribution.

- **Arranging author tours**, usually to a specific region for three to four days at a time: handling bookings from schools and libraries; liaising with the local press; arranging for copies of the relevant books for signing sessions.

- **Organising the firm's material for national and international book trade events** and working with agencies involved with inclusion and the promotion of literacy. In the UK, events such as National Children's Book Week,[8] World Book Day[9] and the Reading Agency's Summer Reading Challenge[10] encourage reading stamina, and generally operate through a combination of online activity and an accompanying press campaign to raise awareness and the despatch of physical materials to encourage the organisation of reading-related events in schools and libraries. Along similar lines, working with agencies such as the National Literacy Trust,[11] Reading is Fundamental[12] and other inclusion organisations that promote literacy.

- **Supporting specific local initiatives:** perhaps supplying local booksellers with marketing material for a promotion they have organised or arranging for a character in costume to pay a special visit to a school.

- **Sponsorship of events relevant to the market.** It's common for primary schools to have dressing up days, and book-based themes are popular (e.g., come as your favourite character).

- **Entry of titles for literary prizes.** The resulting media coverage brings the winning titles to the attention of a wider public, as well as promoting reading and books in general.

Book fairs, exhibitions and conferences

At book fairs the major trade players gather for the sale of rights and to display their wares. The trade press lists attendees, and this provides a useful summary of the main houses involved in children's books. Notable events include the Bologna Book Fair and the Shanghai Children's Book Fair. Other international book fairs around the world have specific exhibition space for children's publishers, and many publishers have an exhibitions team that can be despatched to mount displays at teachers' and librarians' conferences, teachers' centres, schools, local fairs and other events. Local sensitivities and laws will have to be borne in mind when deciding which titles to present, and which may need rewriting for local markets (e.g., alcohol is available to 18-year-olds in the UK; in the US the age limit is 21).

Exporting children's books

Gaining an export deal for a children's title, or series of titles, is often the way to make the process profitable, and if material can be translated and exported, there is the opportunity to raise valuable revenue from co-editions, rights and royalties. A series of co-edition deals, secured at the right time, can be the key to successful publishing of a children's title, allowing the publisher to extend the initial distribution and keep the price down. The more expensive the format, the more important this becomes, so it's especially vital in colour books. Some publishing houses have set up arrangements with indigenous publishing organisations in their formerly traditional markets, to buy export editions or co-publish for the home market bearing in mind particular market sensitivities and catering for distinct market tastes and trends. For more information on exporting, see Chapter 7.

Selling resources to public libraries

The words 'and libraries' often appear on the marketing plans for new titles, but it is worth thinking about why libraries should be a key part of all marketing planning. In the past publishers have known relatively little about the public library world; there are very few job moves between the two professions, and publishers have tended to take library sales for granted. It's also worth understanding the role of the public librarian, which is far wider than just lending books.

Librarians offer the markets they serve access to content in a variety of different formats and delivery methods. But their prime function is access, not recommendation; their loyalty is to the markets they serve, not to any particular format or publishing house. While the vast majority of the stock they buy is still focused on popular leisure reading, increasingly they are interested in stock that supports the wider needs of their communities. For example they buy stock to support public health initiatives, basic literacy, job hunting and up-skilling, community development, equalities and non-English speakers. They also work with broadcasting campaigns and charitable partners such as the Reading Agency and the Royal National Institute for the Blind to reach new audiences, and work in partnership with publishers to raise awareness of key titles.

Sue Jones, former Hertfordshire librarian and now working for the Reading Agency comments:

> Library support for the huge rise of reading groups in the UK is a good example of how libraries support community initiatives. Local groups will probably support local authors, and although libraries may be unable to buy stock on spec, local advocacy may lead to creating a demand that they will try to meet. I think requests from reading groups are increasingly driving purchases – libraries frequently get multiple sets of new choices if they think that other groups will be interested. Hertfordshire Libraries lists what other groups are reading on their website and in their e-newsletters. Libraries also regularly run their own mini reading festivals and collaborate in organising local writing competitions. So authors who would like to promote to a local audience are well advised to request an opportunity to speak.

Librarians will tell you their regular users are skewed towards those who are at home for at least part of the day: the retired, the unemployed and mothers with small children. However, some very interesting groups are spending more time in libraries. In the United Kingdom, the National Centre for Research in Children's Literature has revealed that children from ethnic minorities, and in particular girls, make much more use of local and school libraries and there are new community initiatives to keep libraries open, or open new resources, through volunteering and book donations.[13]

Rather than just seeking leisure reading, today many of their customers are using libraries in new ways: local businesses as a wide-ranging resource for market information, job seekers who access the internet for job vacancies and updating their CVs, local and family historians for the specialist services available. Libraries also play a significant role in countering the digital divide by helping people to get online. All these activities result in active use of the library's resources but record no corresponding loans.

In the UK, adult loans are down but children's borrowing is rising. The decline in adult loans may be for various reasons. The reduction in library opening hours, cuts in the book purchasing funds and reorganisations of how the money is both allocated and administered can impact on the attractiveness of the stock available – and readers lose interest if fewer titles by their favourite authors appear on the shelves and the stock starts to look worn. Purchasing budgets for libraries increasingly have to cover information access through methods other than title purchase, and the costs of libraries offering technology and entertainment through internet access, audio and downloads all depletes the book purchasing funds. It is also significant that opportunities to purchase publishers' output have expanded, both online and through accessible prime retail sites (supermarkets, garage forecourts, garden centres and so on), and this has arguably increased the public's willingness to buy rather than borrow – and do something else rather than read.

How to send information to public libraries

Public library purchasing has undergone a radical change in recent years, moving away from the former model, which enabled individual library authorities to select and purchase their stock from their choice of supplier. Libraries are now locked into consortium arrangements whereby the library authorities to which they belong provide detailed demographic profiles of the areas they cover and these are matched by centralised library suppliers, with publishers pitching to get their titles included in the selections that are presented to libraries. This is partly due to reduced budgets, but also to central governmental plans for the cost-efficiency of national purchasing models (which cut down on administrative costs, increase the size of the resulting orders and ensure best prices – and hence value for money).

What librarians decide to stock is based on the information they receive and their wider understanding of what is available. Organisations that sell resources to libraries edit the range available and offer a selection, and most librarians rely heavily on this filtering service. As one commented:

> We generally treat unsolicited approaches badly – partly because there's a wealth of poor-quality material out there and partly because of lack of time. We prefer to get approaches through our aggregators first, and from the purchasing consortia or from other trusted agencies.

This is supplemented by their own awareness of the wider range of material available, but lack of time means this is usually a personal commitment rather than a job requirement.

Librarians read the professional and trade press to gain information on what is being launched; they also respond to their users' requests for specific resources. They acquire information on what their regulars want to read or use through experience and constant handling, checking and updating of the stock, but they also have local agendas to meet, such as widening access and outcomes for learning and skills, health and well-being and community cohesion. Most librarians retain a particular interest in searching for, and purchasing, locally available material likely to be of interest to the increasing numbers of people researching their family history.

When targeting librarians via their purchasing consortia, through their official publications and via forums they access, bear in mind that the profession is highly collaborative, in that decisions on what to buy are taken in consultation with colleagues. But it's vital to note that while decisions are discussed, most of the subsequent buying is done online. Thus while librarians may look at a synopsis and the cover, they don't get the chance to read a few paragraphs, or to handle a publication, before deciding whether or not it should be stocked. The information publishers provide is thus vital in creating the right kind of buying information for each title, and organisational reputation as a firm that maintains standards of a particular kind (whether good or bad) will support the decision-making. Memories of failed promises can live a very long time.

Information to emphasise to librarians

Librarians are information management experts so it is vital to ensure that information sent to them is well managed: fully navigable, logically presented and accurate, backed up by the appropriate bibliographical details. Other information that may be particularly relevant to the library market includes:

- **Which courses or educational stages your title is relevant to:** in particular, if your products relate to project or course work for specific educational stages. For example, local children's libraries in one area are well stocked with reference books on Spain for 10- to 11-year-olds because a local head teacher sets a project on the country for the final year of junior school.
- **Any significant overlaps between subject areas.** This may enable them to pull money from several allocations. The wider the spread of interest groups they serve, and that you meet, the more likely your resources are to be purchased. Cross-curricular, interdisciplinary areas are particularly attractive.
- **Feedback from readers.** If titles have attracted demonstrable evidence of popularity, perhaps through online sampling or reader feedback, this could be important evidence to offer.
- **Author availability.** Authors who do events in public libraries, and support the ethos of free availability of reading matter within the communities, fit the library ethic and are an asset to librarians.
- **Products that offer librarians the chance to enhance the prestige of their collection.** Librarians identify with the collection they look after and products that enrich the collection as a whole, and enhance the resources available to their users, are attractive.
- **Librarians often have to order at the last minute** or risk losing their budget for the year ahead, so information that might make them choose your content in a hurry is valuable. An appropriate high-price product takes less time to order and enhances the range of resources available to the reader in one go.
- **Production details.** Librarians are looking for resources that will last and are consequently keen to hear about appropriate product specifications – search engine usability, acid-free paper, sewn rather than glued bindings and so on.
- **Good covers matter enormously.** Librarians play an important role in tempting people to read and titles are often displayed face out, rather than spine on.

Case study

How libraries and publishers can work together to greater effect: an interview with Helen Leech, virtual library services manager, Surrey County Library Services

In a climate of financial cutbacks in public spending, with the value of libraries and their usefulness being questioned and many librarians facing budgetary cuts or closure, the response from librarians has been robust. Many have established new initiatives to promote awareness and cooperation, to expand and change working practices, to reach out to the wider public and stress the value they offer.

There are now many libraries run by volunteers. The model tends to be that of 'Community Partnered Libraries' where the council provides the resources (including the premises and their upkeep) but the local community provide the staffing. Other solutions include 'Community Links', which generally means making collections of books available in village halls and other premises, the community providing all resources and staffing and the library service providing the books.

> We are becoming more community-focused, meaning a number of things: we're moving away from being a take-it-or-leave-it service with minimal engagement, and we're broadening our range of services and actively working with community groups. For example, Surrey Library Service runs a support service for domestic abuse survivors, for which we won an award, and just this morning one of our staff sent me a list of the things we do and the partners we work with for each 'protected characteristic' within the Equalities Act, and it's remarkable. We are moving from supporting leisure reading, which is certainly a declining market, towards services supporting local agendas, working with a range of local partners.

As to how libraries and publishers can work together in future:

> The key message from the Society of Chief Librarians is that public libraries are keen to work with publishers. We're part of the same ecosystem; we have the same passion for books and reading, the same desire to lead the reader to the right work, a lot of the same issues in terms of the challenges of a hugely changing market. It would be to the benefit of both sides to work more closely: libraries can offer access to a very large market; publishers can offer experience and content.
>
> In terms of what we bring to the relationship, publishers are interested in our huge audience. Even though loans are falling, the number of those using the libraries is still huge. In Surrey one person in six (200,000 people out of a population of 1.1 million) has used the library in the past year. In addition to those who use the library premises, we have a large community outreach through our newsletters and online services.
>
> Libraries offer a huge showroom window for publishers' works and given that a large part of our remit is reader development,[14] this too offers big opportunities for publishers. At a time when high street bookshops are closing, we're introducing readers to new authors and encouraging people to broaden their reading habits. These days we are also much more involved in promoting titles to our readership than we

used to be, and very aware of the power of the cover to attract. Like booksellers, we now put a lot of our stock face-on and expect the book to sell itself. There are also simpler book recommendation schemes operating within libraries such as the recommendations of our very knowledgeable staff, our 'just returned' trolley (which is where many of our visitors head first on reaching the library) and the book recommendation schemes we run, which encourage people to move outside their reading comfort zones.

Many reading and some writing groups are also run under the auspices of libraries. Within Surrey alone we support more than 700 such groups in a variety of ways: drawing up and circulating lists of suggested titles; providing loan stock of multiple copies of the same book; promoting and hosting some of the groups within libraries. We also send out a regular newsletter to 120,000 readers in the area. There are associated opportunities for publishers to gain 'focus group' feedback on jacket design and format, and for the test marketing of new materials, subject areas and authors.

We are very interested in the communication possibilities around books as a way of extending involvement. For example the Reading Agency's Digital Skills programme has been encouraging libraries and publishers to work together and one of the things we've found really helpful is the promotional materials that publishers can provide – not just the traditional posters-and-bookmarks, but now the online reviews, ratings, recommendations, graphics, 'who-else-writes-like' forums, blogs, and other things that help us to generate interest and discussion. We take a much more retail-, business-like approach to books these days and, like every other part of the book trade, we're far more likely to promote a particular author when we've got the materials and it's quick and easy.

We also offer market data on reading patterns. Although this is in its infancy, it is an area of growing interest and one that could be capable of growth to enable more precise targeting of information. Speaking on behalf of Surrey, we collect information on library-user postcodes and age, but this has significant opportunities for development. Potentially we could identify pockets of gardeners in Lingfield and Chinese people in Woking and we could possibly tell you what they are reading. Demographic analysis is an area we need to develop, bearing in mind data protection restrictions, but there's a huge opportunity to work with and learn from publishers.

Public lending right

Most territories now have some form of recompense payment to authors for loans of print books (and there is hot discussion over the inclusion of ebooks). The principle of the legislation is simple. Authors earn their living through the royalties on books sold; those sold to libraries may have many readers but only produce one sale and royalty payment; the schemes act as compensation for these 'lost' royalties. The funding comes from the public purse and arrangements for distribution vary from country to country.

Such schemes have revealed interesting borrowing patterns, which do not always tie in with sales patterns through bookshops – and perhaps there are titles it is logical to borrow rather than buy. The feedback provided is used extensively in public libraries. This includes subject breakdowns, lists of 'classic' authors and comparisons of local, regional and national trends.

Finally, don't forget that in the same way that public library services are working with local community volunteers to ensure continued access to reading material, there are also library facilities that originate within the wider community that meet similar needs. Book-rich environments are often seen as relaxation zones that enhance community living, and each one offers the chance to promote reading and publishers' wares.

Case study

Betty's Reading Room, Orkney, Scotland[15]

Craig Mollison and Jane Spiers, a couple now living on Orkney, created a library there in memory of Betty Prictor, a close friend and book lover who died unexpectedly. Craig, Jane and Betty were at university together in London, all went into teaching and had regularly spent holidays on Orkney, all planning to live there in the longer term. When Betty died before this could be achieved, Craig and Jane were keen to create a positive memorial that would also benefit the community as a whole. As Betty was an avid reader, they hit on the idea of a reading room in her memory – and her books are now part of the collection that is named after her.

The starting point was the shell of a derelict bothy[16] in Tingwall, donated by a local farmer. This they refurbished and decorated, with help from the local community, to create an attractive environment for relaxation and reading. The building is heated by a wood-burning stove, lit by gas lamps and it is kept open at all times. Craig or Jane pop in at least once a day, not least to light the stove in winter, but otherwise it operates entirely on trust. The visitors' book shows that it has become a popular dropping in place – one wrote that the experience of stepping inside 'gladdens the heart'. It's also become a haven for those waiting for the boat from the Orkney mainland off to the isles, who would otherwise have to wait outside in their cars in the cold and dark – and is now also firmly on the Orkney tourist trail.

The stock comes from their own books and those of Betty, donations, gifts and swaps – readers are welcome to take a book and leave one of their own in its place. They provide attractive bookplates that can be stuck into the front of titles that are taken, and ask that once finished, they are passed on to other readers. Craig and Jane appreciate the random nature of book discovery and so the books are placed on the shelves in a serendipitous order. One librarian used the visitors' book to comment that she found this frustrating – she longed to submit them to the Dewey classification. The only titles they keep to one side are children's books, which they place in a separate corner.

The room is used by several book groups and reading circles and has also been used in poetry festivals, The Orkney Story Festival and for musical evenings. It's now a valuable community resource, firmly on the tourist trail – and word seems to be spreading. Craig and Jane are sure that Betty would be absolutely delighted.

Promoting to university academics

There have been huge changes within universities in recent years. If you are tasked with promoting to this market, it is important that you understand what has happened.

A huge increase in student numbers

There is a worldwide move towards mass education at higher level (its 'massification'). Targets are various, but based on evidence of university attendance as a long-term investment in an individual's future, the intention is to have a much higher proportion of the population which has benefitted from a university education.

Changes to funding models

The vastly increased numbers mean that older funding mechanisms have had to change. Various models for this have emerged. In some countries, large numbers of students are subsidised through commensurate rises in taxes, although governmental funding often leads to tighter control of student numbers and fierce competition for places. In other countries, students are forced to pay either a proportion or the full cost of their education (its 'marketisation').

Governments that rely on those benefitting from a higher education to pay for the privilege can generally accept more students, and there is thus a wider market for potential publisher resources, but this tends to be accompanied by less time for reading and less money available for book-buying. In general, funding works through a system of student loans, which recipients start repaying once their post-graduation income reaches a particular level. But this means that many students are holding down part-time (or even full-time) jobs to pay the fees, and there is consequently little money around for buying resources.

Paying for learning has arguably always prompted an assumption that with the contract comes some transfer of responsibility. As schoolmaster Bartle Massey commented in *Adam Bede*:[17]

You think knowledge is to be got cheap – you'll come and pay Bartle Massey sixpence a week, and he'll make you clever at figures without your taking any trouble. But knowledge isn't to be got with paying sixpence, let me tell you ... So never come to me again, if you can't show that you've been working with your own heads, instead of thinking that you can pay for mine to work for you.

There are signs today that with the changed responsibility for funding higher education has come a changed attitude of students. They are tempted to see themselves as consumers of – rather than participants in – the learning on offer. Naomi Klein (2000) commented in *No Logo*:

Many professors speak of the slow encroachment of the mall mentality, arguing that the more campuses act and look like malls, the more students behave like consumers. They tell stories of students filling out their course-evaluation forms with all the smug self-righteousness of a tourist responding to a customer-satisfaction form at a large hotel chain ... students slip into class slurping grande lattes, chat in the back and slip out. They're cruising, shopping, disengaged.

Academics who mark their work regularly report that students subsequently lobby for an increase in the percentage awarded, significantly not on the grounds that a specific piece of work deserves a higher mark, but that their overall average requires it. The new ubiquity of access to information online has also been accompanied by a blurring of awareness as to whom it belongs, and the technology that permits access also enables the precise monitoring of its use – universities now generally require the online submission of work and its automatic assessment for originality. Plagiarism can be spotted and the penalties for this and other forms of academic misconduct (cheating in exams, getting other people to write your work for you) are severe.

Sometimes casual student behaviour conflicts with wider marketing forces. While for the lecturer it's irritating to find students texting while in class, if they are instead live tweeting – which has the potential to spread enthusiasm for courses and draw in new students – then attitudes may differ.

A changed model of how education is delivered

The increase in student numbers has not, in general, been matched by a commensurate increase in staffing or facility improvements, and overall the character of the teaching experience has changed. Everyone is short of time. The pressure on academics to research and publish as well as teach has increased significantly. Some of the burden of classes has been moved on to research assistants, PhD students and part-time lecturers. Students are taught in larger classes and seminars, there is more use of group assignments (promoting collaboration and the development of presentation skills but also requiring less individual marking) and there has been a marked reduction in the former closeness of academic–student relationships.

Some would argue that this motivates students to become independent learners, others that higher education is fast becoming a process of transferring information.

In general, publishers have been reluctant to give up the textbook model, which has long yielded profits and that parents (who understand from their own time in education that books support learning) have often been willing to underwrite (sometimes through online access to their own book purchasing mechanisms). Rich profits have been made by publishers offering the single textbook that supports a popular course. But the textbook model is now being reviewed for the online generation. Students are becoming increasingly unwilling to buy print editions when they become out of date so quickly. In some disciplines new editions appear annually, with few changes apparent, but an insistence that the new edition be purchased.

There is increasing demand for publishers to deliver *content* rather than a single format, with the availability of additional supporting materials (e.g., website and downloads) playing a key part in deciding which resources to adopt – even if they subsequently get little used.[18] A publishing house is much more likely to sell content if it can make the bibliographic details and print-on-demand facility available, quickly and in standard electronic formats. Some publishers are developing standard 'content cartridge' models so that core content to support students can be loaded into the online learning tools used in universities.

Information managers are working with academic staff to build electronic profiles based on their interests, and they want to work with publishers and other suppliers to access information about new titles through these profiling processes. Instead of course reading lists, which students lack the time or inclination to consult, course administrators may now put together course packs that pick and choose from the various materials available, and provide all the supporting material in one handy source. But the huge class sizes mean that libraries cannot possibly hold enough copies of supporting resources in print form, and hence they are looking to publishers to provide them with 'granular access': e-content licensing opportunities so they can secure the bits they want, much as happens with online journals and databases. All are becoming intolerant of time-wasting in the ordering process.

The pressure to gain access to the resources they need will only grow, and information managers are meanwhile dealing with students and staff who demand instant gratification for the resources they need to support learning. All expect Amazon-style delivery, and electronic access wherever possible. Significant too is the internationalisation of higher education. Most universities have an international presence and these students, who pay higher fees, want electronic access to learning resources, not to know that there are ten copies in the library, wherever that is. Senior information adviser, business[19] Margaret French comments:

> Undergraduates tend to expect both print copies and ebooks to be available. The increasing availability of ebooks is not the solution we thought it would be. This is because the pricing of popular (i.e., core) ebooks can be extortionate. For example, 100 accesses to an ebook can cost up to triple the price of a print copy and with large numbers of students on some modules, 100 accesses does not last very long.

A change in the role of the academic

In order to win promotion academics must publish their research, and juggle how it is made available (via 'open access', which costs more at the time of publication, or available only to the subscribers of the journals in which it is published). External assessment processes review institutional research output and high-scoring institutions win increased funding as centres of excellence. This has led to the emergence of a premier league of universities, with strong research departments, which are thus well placed to win further research funding.

Whereas at one time academics had job security for life, today this is increasingly fragile. Many new appointments are made on the basis of a rolling contract that must be reviewed, sometimes annually. If the university (or a particular course) is not paying its way, then staff can be transferred to another department or laid off. Research assistants and research fellows seldom have any job security at all, and no identifiable career path. Over the past few years there has been a strong trend towards the 'casualisation' of the academic workforce and regular reports say that academics' standard of living has declined in relation to comparable professions. Politicians may say that education is a priority, but they usually mean basic skills such as reading and writing, not university teaching.

There has been a significant growth in the requirement to bring income into universities, perhaps through carrying out research for industry and other parties willing to pay. Academics often get no personal share of this external revenue (although part of it reverts to their department or school and they can often use a proportion in pursuit of their own research interests). Over the same period, administrative demands on staff have grown substantially, often through governmental increases in workload, for example teaching quality assessment and research assessment exercises to establish how much is going on and of what quality.

An increased pressure to retain students

Universities are expensive places to run, and there is a real pressure to both recruit students and retain them once they have enrolled, particularly international students who bring even higher levels of fees.

A reduction in the value of the first degree

Another consequence of the wider availability of higher education is the need to stand out within the employment market. One response is the growing popularity of a higher degree, the MA or MSc, which many students (and their parents/supporters) are opting to fund, to try to differentiate applications in the workplace. Many of these are profession-specific (e.g. Wine Culture, Human Resources, Journalism and Publishing Studies), offering employers a swift route to pre-trained employees who can be useful from the day they are recruited. Universities today regularly have to demonstrate that they are boosting employability and relationships with industry and such courses are a good source of relevant examples and statistics. Work experience has become much more significant on the CV than was formerly the case and staff are needed to help support students in finding and managing such opportunities.

This offers important background on the climate into which your marketing materials are being sent, and the trends that will become increasingly important. Here are some practical hints on how to manage the process of promoting publishers' products to academics on a day-to-day basis.

Promoting textbooks to the academic market

Textbooks are promoted to academics teaching at universities and colleges in the hope that they will be adopted. Adoption means that they will appear under the heading 'essential' at the top of the reading list that accompanies each course, and consequently be purchased in large numbers by both the students taking the course and the libraries serving them.

Promotions of textbooks (by email and in print) are generally geared to getting a sample (or 'inspection') copy of the new book into the academic's hand. Each new academic year the local bookshops that serve college populations ask academics for details of what they will be recommending to students and the numbers likely to be taking the courses. They then stock copies according to their experience of what will sell: what the libraries will take, how many students will share a copy, and how many will have the motivation or cash to buy a copy of their own. These are stocked ready for the start of term.

There will, however, be pressure to retain the existing resource and before trying to persuade academics to change the one that is already in place, it's worth thinking about why they might *not* want to change their main resource:

- **Lack of time** (always the biggest factor).
- **They have been pre-equipped** with lecture notes/slides/handouts by colleagues who taught the module last year, based on the previous title, and thus changing the textbook requires a huge readjustment.
- **Team teaching.** Many universities are moving to larger modules, often with several members of staff involved in course delivery. It follows that changing the core textbook will require extensive consultation. Easier not to change.
- **Familiarity.** Lecturers generally teach the same subject only once a year. Familiarity with the format of the relevant chapters is an obvious attraction.
- **A vibrant market for second-hand titles.** If you change the book, will any students have already bought the old one? Will this mean an academic starts the year feeling unpopular?

Factors that might prompt a change of textbook:

- **A book with a more engaged and student-friendly style,** which means it is more likely to be used.

- **The offer of a free lecture** from a publishing representative on how to use the book and why to buy one.
- **New resources** that go with the book, e.g. lecture slides.
- **Really interesting new case studies** in the book – featuring big brands, particularly ones they use themselves, excite the students.
- **An attractive price** that students are likely to be able to afford (small price differentials can make a big difference to how expensive a resource feels).
- **Lecturer-only website** that offers additional teaching materials (such as sample exam questions and worked examples). They are often little used but can be a key differentiator in this market.
- **A prize that students can be entered for** – this is popular with the students, and the university's marketing department is always keen to cover prize-winners in its publications, website and social media usage.
- **A really attractive cover** that will motivate students to want the book, and encourage them to think the lecturer up to date for choosing it.

There are also a range of softer issues that can be raised: lecturer motivation and an enhanced feeling of professionalism that come from investing in your teaching material and feeling on top of your subject. This might be tackled through guilt ('When did you last update your textbook?'), envy ('How up to date do you think your resources are?') or by questioning your dedication ('What does your choice of textbook say about your commitment to your classes?').

In short, when writing to academics, think about their needs and priorities, and not just about your publishing house and why you are pleased with your new title. Promotional copy that begins 'x publishers are proud to present' is perhaps not the best opening.

The best time to tell academics about new resources

Contacting the academic market is less time-specific now that different institutions organise their time in different ways. For example, there are traditional three-term years, three-term/two-semester years and two-semester years. Send advance information on forthcoming titles with guidance on how to get an inspection copy as soon as you have it, but always back this up with a realistic idea of when the title will be published. Academics will find it extremely frustrating if they change the key course book only to be told it is not available until halfway through the first teaching term. If this has been their experience of your house, they will be wary of adopting your titles in future. Margaret French again:

> Their students will complain too if the core reading is not in the LRC or available as an ebook at the very start of the course. If a book is placed on a reading list, students expect to see it on the library catalogue. A lack of core book stock can result in negative course feedback and affect the reputation of the library.

Distribution of free copies

It is usually worth distributing a number of copies of a new textbook free to key academics without requiring them to recommend it or show how many copies have been bought as a result. Likely recipients include heads of department where particularly large numbers of students may buy the book, or key respected academics within the book's subject area who may respond with a favourable quotation that you can use in your publicity material.

Most large academic publishing houses employ reps who visit universities on a regular basis, to find out who is teaching what, which resources are being used, spread information on their new titles – and pick up ideas for new products (courses that have large and growing student numbers but are inadequately resourced). Their visits are the ideal opportunity to hand out free copies of existing resources. In return you should ask for feedback which may help with subsequent copywriting as well as providing endorsements likely to influence the market.

Academics tend to be well aware of their key role in the profitability of textbook publishing, and regard free copies as their right. If you look after a stand at an exhibition or conference you may have several soliciting free copies on the basis of the large student numbers to whom they have it in their power to recommend. To provide every university department with a free copy in the hope of securing sales could erode a book's basic profit margin, so be careful with your largesse. Never give away free copies of non-textbook titles. Profit on these titles is achieved with all the marginal sales – the odd ones here and there. If you have given these away, there will be no profit at all. An effective strategy may be to offer a discount to the market for pre-orders.

Summary books and study aids

Sales of these titles have become particularly strong in recent years, to the detriment of the standard (and it has to be said generally longer) course texts and background reading. Some are available as printed texts, others as websites or downloads.

These summaries are a guide to passing exams, listing all the key information candidates must be able to deliver in order to optimise their chances of passing. With students under severe time-pressure, and academics keen to maintain student numbers to keep the course running and themselves in a job, such products have a widening market.

Also in this category are business encyclopaedias and general reference titles aimed at the professional community, which feature summaries, lists, double-page spreads and a glossary of terms. These may have higher prices, but their professional format and 'grown-up' appearance may make them attractive purchases for students and their parents. Lecturers may find such resources equally useful for setting exam papers (each one needs a guide to marking, and lists of key areas to be covered are very useful). If you are promoting a title to a professional market, and feel it may have a wider audience in universities, it may be worth offering a student discount – or a bulk purchase to libraries.

Research monographs

The scholarly monographs promoted to academics are often the result of a PhD or other long-term research project. Markets for these titles are necessarily small, and most of the sales will be single copy, to interested individuals or libraries. Print runs and promotion budgets therefore tend to be small too.

Although these titles may also end up on reading lists, they will usually be listed as 'further reading'. As multiple sales are unlikely, inspection copies are not offered; rather, they are generally available 'on approval'. After a period for examination they must either be returned in good condition or paid for.

Although marketing budgets are small, markets are highly specific and easy to target; extensive and costly campaigns are not required. It also pays to capitalise on all additional paths to the potential market. Much use can be made of penetrating the viral networks through which academics involved in particular subject areas communicate. With a print run of 500, sales of 200–300 can recover the costs; selling a further 50–100 gets a good margin, and profits on sales above that can be very substantial.

Professional resources

In some areas of the academic curriculum, particularly within profession-orientated disciplines, publishers preparing relevant resources will be keen to get students using them – on the grounds that habits acquired as students may last a lifetime.

Finally don't forget the part the author can play in getting academic titles better known (see Chapter 11). Most universities now have PR and publicity departments and they like to show their staff as rounded individuals and hence feature a range of their wider activities and publications – and not just academic ones.

Selling to academic libraries

There has been a revolution in how academic libraries work and how information is delivered within universities. Today librarians are part of the selection process, and may even decide to deliver resources in another way. Decisions about the purchase of new material are made on the basis of knowledge about the entire collection, including electronic resources. Many institutions, perhaps the majority, now spend more on e-resources than print.

Many have now changed their organisational name – university library, learning resource centre (or LRC) and learning centre are the most common names – and this reflects a change in their role, now often with a considerable expansion of the range of services under their management. This is partly due to student preference – students demonstrably prefer accessing information online – and partly due to logistics, where it is more appropriate to locate relevant services. With a reduction in educational intimacy through the teaching experience (increased class sizes and the wider use of group assignments rather than individual essays), access to supporting information through their local resource centre is becoming an important part of the student experience. Surveys have found that many students visit the library or information resource centre every day, the vast majority at least once a week. Many institutions now offer 24-hour opening, at least for part of the teaching terms, and of course all can access information 24/7 through their computers.

This centrality to the student experience is further strengthened as the range of services available through information resource centres expands. Whereas there was experimentation within some universities with the incorporation of computer services within information provision, in the process making libraries responsible for all computer services from lecture delivery mechanisms offering handouts to discussion forums that support them, there is a move away from the complete amalgamation of library and computer services. The current trend is to use libraries as a base for delivery of student support. Through the information resource centre, students can now routinely access learning support agencies (offering advice on how to research and present academic assignments), careers information, help with finance and housing as well as with special educational needs such as dyslexia. Information professionals and librarians are also increasingly involved with the educational objectives of what is being taught, as well as with planning and content of both course structure and assessment strategy. There are two main drivers of this trend.

First, employers increasingly demand graduates who are self-starters, who can investigate and explore issues themselves, and thus challenge and innovate in the workplace rather than simply replicate what has been done before. Their experience as students is fundamental to this personal development and the supported learning environment that libraries and learning resource centres play a vital part.

The second driver is economic. With larger class sizes, and a wider geographical network of students (because of financial pressures many students now opt to live at home, travelling long distances to reach their local university), the resource centre becomes increasingly important to their student experience. Many information centres are also moving to a delivery model that suits the students and their working patterns, which are often intense and last minute. While online delivery mechanisms have long been accessible around the clock, the centres are now increasingly physically open longer and are becoming a haven where students can come to meet each other, research, write and keep warm.

Another common view among publishers is that academic librarians work on percentages, dividing up the budgetary pot into amounts for journals, books and other resources such as printers and photocopiers. Rather, information resource managers are increasingly involved from the beginning of course development. It is common practice for each curriculum area to have an associated 'information specialist' who not only reviews the resourcing, but examines whether these resources provide a suitable basis for possible curriculum extensions.

It's worth a quick digression to understand the value structure of the librarianship profession – which is often difficult for essentially entrepreneurial publishers to grasp. Publishers may spend just one or two years in each job, particularly at the beginning of their careers. Job hierarchies within libraries or the information profession tend to move much more slowly, associated staff feeling a deep sense of loyalty to the organisation they work for. Information professions similarly have a deep commitment to their user base – but they see themselves as *conduits*, providing access to what is available, rather than committed to housing any particular type of resource. They are increasingly unsentimental about books and the printed format. They want value for money for their institutional budgets and to hold resources that enhance the relevance and prestige of their collection and its usefulness to their clientèle.

What academic librarians buy

When deciding in which resources to invest, librarians look for a dynamic mixture that will best suit the academic needs. This may be part books, part purchase of licences, part printed journals – but the mixture chosen will match the learning needs, not any specific or pre-planned portions of a budget. The use of all resources is closely monitored, documented and discussed. Librarians will know which authors and titles receive the most use by students and will purchase additional copies and new editions to meet demand. They are pragmatic and well informed – and above all do not want to tie up funds in resources that will not get used.

Librarians with subject responsibilities will purchase titles for specific curriculum areas in the library. This is because academics are not always very good at recommending books beyond their reading list requirements. It is often left to the librarian to keep an eye on what is being published and purchased by other libraries (COPAC[20] is a good way of checking this) in their subject area. This ensures that the resources budget is used up and spent on stock that is current, relevant and enriching. They are also keen to ensure that students are able to study as effectively as possible. Margaret French comments:

> The expectation of students as independent learners means that many libraries actively promote study skills books and have designated study skills collections. University librarians are often on the lookout for this type of resource and will purchase independently, i.e., without recommendations from academics.

The other point to bear in mind is that resource managers are dealing, on a daily basis, with consumers who are highly technologically adept. Students today have grown up with screen access, and understand how to cut, paste, download – and fast. They are intolerant of system difficulties. There is fast-growing understanding within the student market that information as a commodity belongs to all and must be accessed quickly. At hearings for cases of 'academic misconduct' there is often a real confusion about the role of the author (whether of textbook or student essay) in creating ideas; the student view tends to be that what exists should be accessible to all. And while information managers have a clear grasp of copyright, and are meticulous about adhering to procedures that capture and reward ownership, it can be argued that the student desire for free access to what is available has more in common with the information resource manager's determination to provide access for the market than the publishers' hegemonistic view of their own material as superior to their competitors, and their brand as meaning something.

Increasingly, if information managers can't get what they want from publishers, they will go elsewhere, sometimes turning publisher and distributor themselves. There is a growing trend to assemble resource packs to support student learning, taking material (by agreement) from a variety of different sources to provide students with the best possible learning support. Sometimes what they use is individual chapters from a variety of textbooks, sometimes a direct commission for new material from relevant scholars – remember that information specialists' knowledge of the curriculum is very strong. This saves the students' time, ensures they are relying on high-quality information, offers a wider viewpoint than just one textbook, and gives academics who are teaching the reassurance that students have at least some additional material to broaden understanding. It can be incorporated in the course price, and enhances student appreciation (particularly if well packaged). And because resource managers are motivated by access rather than profit, provision in this way can work out substantially cheaper for the universities than the purchase of textbooks. This is a process of re-intermediarisation; it changes the traditional intermediaries (publishers, wholesalers, retailers) on whom the system of information dissemination has up to now relied while still (or arguably better) meeting student needs. In the process, information managers become competitors to publishers rather than merely absorbers of what publishers choose to produce.

If academic librarians are moving from being resource locators to becoming publishers, taking a broad view of the best format for resources and a direct role in their management and delivery, how is the role of the subject specialist librarian likely to develop? One commented:

> My feeling is that the days of the subject librarian may be numbered in all but very specialist and elite libraries. A model that already exists in some universities is that a small, often centralised, team covers all subjects. This can represent a significant cost saving because subject librarians (with Master's degrees and often teaching qualifications) are expensive in comparison to other library staff. The growth areas in the profession are in technology (obviously) and also in customer services, managing and developing the library space and generalist customer-facing elements of the role. In future, staff are perhaps less likely to be taken from library schools and more likely to come from the graduate schemes of major retailers! To lose the intimate knowledge and association between librarians and their collections and librarians and their students is perhaps not progress. But in order to survive the academic library has had to move away from the storehouse approach to collections with librarians as gatekeepers, enabling relevant access to resources users would not otherwise find.

However this plays out, the role of the academic librarian making qualitative decisions about the value of different publisher resources, and then associated purchasing plans, should not be underestimated.

How to approach academic librarians

If targeting university information resource managers with product or service details is part of your job, here is an important checklist of considerations:

- **Get the words right.** Find out what the institutions and managers you are contacting are called, both their job titles and job functions, and target information appropriately. Ensure your in-house database or the organisation you are renting mailing lists from is up to date too. Information managers are precise people, and getting the most basic information wrong is not a good start.
- **See them as an integral part of your marketing campaign, not an add-on.** While there is probably little point (and insufficient marketing budget) for the preparation of separate marketing information for academics and information providers, you should bear in mind both their overlapping and different priorities, and send relevant additional information in an accompanying email or letter.
- **Specify accurately the courses and areas of curriculum development to which your materials are relevant.** If resources are relevant to a variety of different curriculum areas, it may be possible for information specialists to purchase by pulling money from several associated budgets. They are hence very interested in cross-curricular, multidisciplinary products.
- **They want to know the pedigree of what you are producing.** Author information is crucial, supported by proof of effective information delivery. A whole new hierarchy of effectiveness in academia is emerging (e.g., employability and industry-relevance). Obtain quotes and endorsements and use them on your marketing information.
- **Specify how what you are offering benefits the collection they represent.** Librarians care passionately about the reputation of their library, and so resources that enhance its overall collection or increase its prestige are likely to be well received. For the same reason, offering resources with a high price may offer a bold stocking policy that uses up any unspent budget.
- **Opportunities for the purchase of high-purchase products, or the bundling together of several resources likely to appeal with an associated offer, may prove popular.** If the marketing case is well made, this can present the opportunity to spend a large proportion of the budget in one go (less time-consuming than eking it out over a series of smaller purchases). You may also find that your proposals arrive when there is unspent budget to use up within a short period of time.
- **Treat them with respect.** Information managers are increasingly aware of the important role they play in publishers' sales, so treat them as qualified professionals. Emphasise the shared commitment to your joint market – which they probably understand better than you do, and with which they certainly have more day-to-day access.

Selling to educational markets

Educational publishers produce materials for sale to schools: courses and textbooks; assessment and diagnostic materials; resources on educational theory, practice and implementation strategy for teachers; computer software and other digital resources; and much more.

Teachers continue to see publisher materials as the main agents of the school curriculum and for the publisher who can produce materials that meet the needs of teachers and candidates for a subject that is popular at public examination level, and secure widespread adoption, the rewards can be substantial. But getting a title widely adopted in schools can take a long time. Teachers need to evaluate sample copies of new material and see how they relate to the syllabus and set texts; try them out in the classroom and discuss the results with their colleagues (and in particular the staff member with responsibility for that area of the curriculum), the head teacher or principal and/or local educational advisers.

There are also substantial associated investment costs. Developing new materials in response to government-inspired curriculum changes is expensive, requiring long-term investment, and with no guarantee of adoption, the stakes are high. The major players tend to be specialist publishing divisions within larger companies that can provide the necessary funding. Smaller companies tend to specialise in specific market areas, and recently have done particularly well in revision aids for examinations, where there is both school and parent pressure to improve results.

Competition is fierce: from other educational publishers; other interested parties who see schools materials as an extension of their brand within the youth market (which is both impressionable and increasingly monied in its own right) and those selling other products of interest to the educational market – security systems, furniture, training and development opportunities for teachers. With the advent of digital technology, to support both the development of material and its sharing within teaching networks, it's notable that a growing number of teachers also believe they can develop their own resources.

The response of individual teachers to enforced use of computers in the classroom and digital material is various. School administrators are generally keen but the perception of an educational publisher was that a lot of teachers are being forced harder in this direction than they would wish, with implementation faster in primary than secondary schools. The decision to use digital materials is often based on finance – supported by the need to be seen to be using the latest trend. But educational studies have shown that using print media results in deeper learning. Having a digital edition for use at home does, however, facilitate home study and supported work outside the school.

Recent changes in the educational market

Don't assume the schools market is the same as when you were in full-time education. In recent years there have been huge changes in the priorities and responsibilities of government education policy and much consequent restructuring. In general, these have involved a move towards national standardisation, so that the same areas are being taught in all schools, and the approach is increasingly cross-curricular. Children learn the same topics from different viewpoints, so the child's general understanding of life is enhanced (e.g., reading skills are used in

Maths lessons to teach children how to read a timetable or make price comparisons in the marketing information from holiday firms). All this is supported by rigorous programmes of inspection and monitoring, and the resulting league tables of school performance.

Parameters of learning are set out for teachers and parents, making teachers more accountable to their pupils and giving parents a clearer idea of how their child is getting on. Children are fully monitored by their teachers, and there is a comprehensive formal testing system to gauge pupils' progress. All schools are subject to review, and teachers have regular assessments of their performance. These changes have had a knock-on effect on parental attitudes to education and teachers. Seeing league tables makes them more conscious of their position as both funders of the system (through taxes or fees they pay) and consumers (their children experience the system) – and hence more aware of, and inclined to lobby for, their rights. Teachers have seen a corresponding big increase in parental demands, of varying degrees of reasonableness.

Three important factors influencing educational publishing today are:

1   Large investment in the digital delivery of teaching materials

While educational publishers still find that the majority of their income comes from the sale of print – primarily textbooks and related resources – the major part of their investment is going into the development of digital delivery mechanisms, for which demand is growing all the time. Every printed title must have an accompanying ebook. Some of these additional resources are paid for by schools, others are 'brand-building' (and therefore free). In some areas of the curriculum, it's the books that are becoming incidental. Clare Freda, a fifth grade teacher at Lowes Island Elementary School in Sterling, Virginia commented:

> We are seeing a trend to switch from traditional textbooks to hands-on 'kits' with supplemental textbooks. In some areas, especially science, we are turning away from traditional, formalized testing, to a more hands-on (performance-based) assessment. For example, to teach a unit about time we would encourage the children (my class consisted of those aged 9–10) to learn about pendulums and water clocks and then for assessment give them materials and have them apply the information they have learned to create either time piece discussed, with numerous variables. Two years ago, when I left my last role in New Jersey as a 5th grade special needs teacher, our district was involved in a 'technology boost', ordering 'LCD projectors' and 'smart boards' for all classrooms and funded by the school's annual parent teacher organization benefit.
>
> In my new school we use 'Promethean Boards' rather than smart boards but the concept is the same. There is encouragement to use the 'ProBoards' all day and teachers use PowerPoint-type presentations rather than textbooks to present information to students. These presentations can be shared between teachers through the school-wide/district-wide share drive. We incorporate video conferences and webinars into the curriculum, for example we recently

had a video conference with NASA, and even our state-wide standardized assessment is taken on the computer.

However, educational publishers are finding that switching to electronic delivery has not brought the economies of scale, and hence increased profits, that have been observed from related developments in scientific and academic publishing, and this has resulted in several large publishing conglomerations reconsidering their long-term commitment to their educational divisions.

2   An increasing closeness between the organisations that offer public examinations and educational publishers

There are obviously huge benefits for the educational publisher that can publish what the examiners consider to be the best resource for pupils taking their examination. And while interested bystanders may wonder what controls are in place to ensure best educational practice and avoid vested interests, this is becoming an important factor in what gets published, adopted and widely sold.

3   The increasing sophistication of educational marketing

Twenty years ago most educational publishers sent out their marketing materials via low-cost shared mailings to schools. While this is still an option, there has been huge investment in the acquisition and maintenance of information about the educational market.

Some publishers have built databases themselves, others rely on the investment of educational marketing companies. The resulting information banks (which must be fully data protection registered) record not only the named heads of department as well as senior school staff, but also which texts they have adopted, and even the results of recent school inspections. The availability of this information (obviously at a much increased cost) means that both calls by educational reps and educational marketing materials sent can be targeted, precise and personal – and can be expected to yield the best possible results.

How schools spend their budget

How much individual schools spend on publisher resources is entirely up to them, and it can be variously allocated. Staff training and chairs may compete with publisher resources. One of the biggest costs for schools is the entry of pupils in public examinations, for which the fees are heavy (to cover setting and marking of papers).

When it comes to teaching resources, teachers are for the most part very diligent in determining which published materials will be best for their school, trialling their hunches in the classroom before major capital expenditure is made. Head teachers and department heads may talk to the local advisory staff and their colleagues in other schools. In most schools or departments, areas of priority for spending are outlined, perhaps at the end of a school year. Publishers' websites and catalogues are rigorously checked for price comparisons of both installing new materials and the renewable costs of replacing items that can only be used once, such as workbooks. Discussions – and lobbying – over what to buy take place in staff meetings. There is an increased concern with getting value for money, and teachers respond to the possibility of saving money on what they need as they would to any consumer offer – with interest.

For publishers, the process tends to be win or lose; once schools have made their selection and materials have been adopted, they cannot afford to change their minds. If parents have to buy school books, as happens in many markets – and hence there is a resale market for second-hand copies – the pressure *not* to change a core text can be particularly strong.

How publishers keep in touch with the educational market

Educational publishing tends to be a national market (English language teaching or ELT/ESL will be considered separately), and effective educational publishers need to keep up to date with many different trends in what is happening to education wherever they are based: government educational initiatives, predictions of future demographic developments, and new practices and fashions in teaching. They frequently employ editorial and subject advisers to scout developments and spot good teacher-produced materials being used in schools (the genesis of many a good textbook). They read the educational press (general and subject-specific), talk to local education advisers, school inspectors, examiners and lecturers in teacher training colleges, and attend exhibitions and meetings. They also keep in touch with their sales managers, and visit schools with the reps to hear first-hand how their materials are being received. They know exactly what their competition is producing, and can estimate market share.

Most schools order their materials either directly from publishers or from school suppliers. Digital content aggregation is becoming a common school need and in some territories this is being addressed by booksellers who are hence developing their service to schools far beyond their former wholesaler role. Publishers are also working on their relationships with schools, finding that direct supply brings not only increased profit margins, but also useful information about ordering patterns and time frames (e.g., the best time to send out information on new titles).

Preparing your marketing approach to schools

When targeting information you have to bear in mind the different needs and priorities of those within schools who will benefit from your materials, and who may or may not be involved in the decision to purchase. The difficulty you face is that one set of information has to meet all these needs. For example, the financial responsibility may be with the head teacher/principal or head of department/ grade level leader, but it is the classroom teachers who have to make the material work. A new Maths course available to primary schools could offer the principal the benefits of cost-effectiveness, efficiency, longevity, satisfied teachers and classes. The class teacher, meanwhile, may appreciate the practical benefits of your material working well with mixed-ability classes, so that all children can be occupied on the same material at the same time, leaving the teacher free to concentrate on individual needs and problems. School administrators, who usually place the order, may be more interested in your ordering mechanisms and how efficient your firm is to deal with; they tend to have long memories for past problems.

What are teachers interested in? From my research, several major factors emerged:

- **Relevance to the curriculum or examination syllabus.** Appropriate and attractive material, developed by teachers and examiners for real teaching needs, will always attract attention. Fiona Little, a highly experienced English teacher, commented:

  It's a good idea to target new specifications and syllabus changes; these occur regularly. New strategies mean lots of new texts – and many of the old ones becoming redundant. Teachers feel quite insecure when something new is implemented and look for materials to support their teaching at these times.

- **Digital delivery.** (whether in whole/part or through additional resources such as an effective website). Whatever the preferences of the teachers, children often prefer learning this way, and schools are starting to experiment with individual laptops for each child. Teaching resources that are delivered through a combination of online and traditional methods tend to attract positive attention.
- **Value for money.** Schools are perennially short of money, and there are long discussions at staff meetings over what to buy. Concentration is improved by the knowledge that whatever is selected prevents further spending in that subject area for a number of years. Special offers and money-saving gambits on quality materials undoubtedly attract attention. It follows that you should highlight all the special offers and promotions that you are making available to schools: library packs that incorporate a discount; starter packs for courses; an inspection copy system that can provide teachers with free copies of books. Similarly, lay out complete information on pricing and availability in a clear and consistent way. If you are promoting a scheme and the cost of installing yours is less than that of your competitors, provide installation and running costs. (Your reps may appreciate an expanded version of this with item by item comparisons for use when they are discussing prices in schools.)
- **Teacher support materials.** Whereas many governments lay down what should be taught, in general they do not specify how. Back-up materials for teachers who spend increasing amounts of their time recording and assessing, and therefore have less time for actual lesson preparation, are thus increasingly important.
- **What's new.** Teachers are interested in new materials for new needs. If they have been in teaching for a while and worked in several schools they probably know your backlist already; stress what *won't* be familiar.
- **The relevant level.** Indicate the level at which the material is aimed clearly and consistently. On web pages or in catalogues you can offer a series of 'running

heads' along the top or perhaps down the side of the page or screen so that the teacher can see at any one time the subject and age range of the material being looked at. Repeat the information, with any additional relevant details, under the individual title entry (e.g., header: 14–16; resources for which courses).

- **Series of titles.** Teachers are in general more interested in complete series that can cater for pupils over a number of years than one-off books that require a hunt for new materials once the final chapter has been reached. Even if the series you are promoting is new and you have only two or three proposed covers of the first few stages available, draw a diagram indicating where the different stages will fit in; show planned materials by outlining covers. This will show your intentions and attract attention to a major new series.

- **Illustrations.** Use covers, illustrations from the books and specimen pages. Make the specimen pages large enough to read.

- **Marketing information that they can access quickly.** On websites and in catalogues ensure your searching capabilities are good and the structure logical. Ensure the cross-referencing and website links work and that printed materials have an effective index. On the contents page, list new titles and provide page references. Some publishers produce new book supplements that appear in the centrefold of the catalogue; extra copies of these can be usefully run-on for use at exhibitions or insertion in mailings.

- **A friendly approach.** Have a professional and yet chatty introduction on your home page, or include a letter with your catalogue. Some publishers put a signed letter from the subject editor (and occasionally a photograph) on the inside front cover of the catalogue, and research shows it gets read. This can be a very useful place to remind teachers that you are interested in their suggestions for publication, which bonds your interests.

- **Practical effectiveness of the materials on offer.** Show that your materials work. Include information on how particular schemes are working, include quotations from other teachers on the benefits of your products, details on the progress of new materials under development. Lay out the scope and sequence of new materials in an easy-to-read manner, to help teachers quickly assess whether or not it will be easy to plot their lessons in between the hectic schedule of a school day that includes assemblies, field trips, presentations, birthday celebrations, meetings, etc. You are selling to a very specific market; write about what interests them.

- **Information that is easy to respond to.** Print telephone numbers and website addresses large enough for them to be found in a hurry. Allow teachers to register for inspection copies via your website, and include freepost inspection copy request cards in your catalogues. Put them on a separate sheet or an extension of the back cover of the catalogue rather than the back cover itself: teachers are reluctant to destroy books, even promotional ones. Perforate where the tear has to be made to detach them. Include a stock list or order form in case schools have difficulty in ordering and a card asking for a representative to visit the school.

How to reach the market

There are a number of well-established methods for promoting to educational markets:

- mailings to schools;
- emails to teachers;
- representation within schools;
- mounting displays at exhibitions and conferences;
- an effective website;
- telemarketing;
- despatch of inspection, approval and free copies;
- getting involved in support mechanisms for teachers;
- educational press for reviews and space advertising;
- free publicity.

Mailings to schools

Printed brochures and catalogues are still the most common form of promotion to schools. This is because so many people tend to be involved in educational buying decisions. Teachers are natural collaborators; they have to discuss the materials they are considering buying, and printed marketing pieces are not only easier to discuss, they also give a flavour of the quality of the final product. So while email alerts to individual teachers can work well to announce new materials, or tell them about materials they may buy for themselves, there is still a strong demand for printed information.

When to mail? Schools receive their annual budgets at the start of the new financial year, and educational publishers therefore tend to send their main information (usually their catalogues) a few months before this, when teachers are considering how to spend the next year's budget. This can be followed up with mailings at other times of the year, usually just before the budget arrives and at the start of the new school year. It's often a good time to email or mail a reminder about 6 weeks before the end of the financial year, as there may be money still in the pot that cannot be carried over to the next year.

What to send

Publishers producing materials for the youngest children usually produce an annual catalogue in full colour, and follow this up with specific emails, leaflets on major courses and other information sheets during the course of the year. Most publishers for secondary-age pupils produce a series of individual subject catalogues, one for each curricular area in which they publish and a complete catalogue listing everything. Again, these are followed up with specific promotions on major works. Extra stock of everything produced should be sent to the reps visiting schools for them to hand out as required (and additional information should be up on the website before the mailing goes out, for those who seek more details).

Bear in mind, however, that teachers are as susceptible to feeling that they are reaching information overload as any other profession, but are perhaps more inclined to respond with an ethical objection. Repeated mailings of printed material look wasteful. As schools tend to file the catalogues when received, only one physical mailing a year followed up with emails referring to the website or the catalogue is probably enough.

Whom to send to

Specialist marketing organisations have built databases from which to contact this market (and some publishers have built their own). The costs of building and maintaining lists should never be underestimated, but as schools tend not to move, this may be a good investment.

Most educational marketing organisations offer a two-tier system. Publishers can pay a one-off fee to send out information to all schools of a particular type (e.g., secondary, primary, private). To receive a higher level of service, and for an annual subscription, publishers can gain access to a highly sophisticated programme recording each school's specific text adoptions, staff responsibilities and contact details, budget, feedback from the most recent school inspection – and much more. Of course such information is expensive to research and maintain, but it may well be worth it. For example, access to such a detailed profile before a rep's arrival in a school can make a considerable difference to the relevance of their presentation, and the key people within the school whom they try to meet during the visit. Primary school publishers can note large schools that adopted a rival publisher's materials several years ago and may be considering a change – and hence might be receptive to the idea of a formal presentation to staff, after school hours.

When considering mass mail-outs, primary publishers usually send their material to the head teacher, principal or head of subject. Mail addressed to the head is routinely opened by the school administrator and passed on. After a quick look through by the head – and perhaps a short note to the subject coordinator involved if something looks particularly interesting – the catalogue tends to be stored, along with material from other publishers, in the staff room or the head's office until the time comes for deciding how much to spend and on what.

In secondary schools the overall budget is divided between the various departments, and it is the department heads who have responsibility for spending. Specific mailings can be addressed directly to them (again names are available from list rental companies), but for the general despatch of catalogues, publishers often send a package consisting of separately marked items for different department heads to the school administrator, together with a letter asking for the contents to be divided up as appropriate. This is obviously considerably cheaper.

In some (not all) markets you have the choice whether to send your material yourself (bearing all the costs of postage and despatch) or to join with others in a shared mailing, which costs less. Schools tend to say they don't care how the promotional material arrives, but if a catalogue reaches the school on its own it is perhaps more likely that a teacher will sit down and browse through straight away.

Most people would be daunted by the simultaneous arrival of four – or more – catalogues, and perhaps put off looking through them until later. On the other hand, the fact that all publishers tend to send their material at the same times of year could adversely affect this theory.

If you do decide on a shared mailing:

- **Try to find out who else is to be included in the pack.** There are bound to be certain major competitors with whom you do not wish to join hands as your materials arrive in schools.
- **Do specify a position within the pack.** If the mailing house is using plastic envelopes, find out whether your catalogue can go on the outer edge.

Don't forget other potentially interested parties, for example, teacher training colleges, subject advisers, teachers' centres, school suppliers who may stock and promote your titles.

Emails to teachers

The attitude to email within schools varies. Some schools see teachers receiving information this way as a benefit – in that it reduces the amount of post entering the school and the time taken to open up shared mailings, divide the contents – as well as deal with all the personally addressed items.

Others see it as a managerial issue, and would rather their staff were planning lessons, teaching or consulting with colleagues than reading emails. A significant indicator is how individual schools encourage parents to correspond with teachers. Some see it as a quick and easy way of getting and giving feedback, others feel they must protect their staff, and that encouraging parents to get in touch through the school office, or the regular opportunities to meet at parent–teacher events, cuts down time away from the classroom.

Educational marketing companies are now routinely collecting institutional email addresses from teachers where they are provided, and other teachers pass on their home email addresses when they attend exhibitions. Coverage is not yet uniform or entirely reliable, but will surely only increase. One teacher commented, 'Email is definitely the way to go! I rarely use the telephone during school hours because I do not have a telephone in my classroom, and the few phones accessible to me are in a noisy faculty room.'

For teachers who do like to receive information this way, email alerts are useful, directing those who are interested to a website where they can request a sample copy. Email alerts also work well for titles they may consider purchasing for their own use, and paying for themselves.

Representation within schools

In the struggle to get your materials adopted in schools, the reps who visit them are immensely valuable. The feedback in terms of sales figures and emails, that results from mailings is statistical but largely impersonal – you do not know *why* your material was chosen or not chosen. It is the reps who get the eyeball-to-eyeball reactions to your pricing, subject coverage, durability of format and so on.

Your house may have its own sales team, or you may employ the services of an external agency. Typically separate teams concentrate on secondary and primary schools. Reps (who are often ex-teachers) are usually briefed by the editors and the marketing team at regular sales conferences, held twice or three times a year in preparation for the major selling seasons ahead. (For more specific advice on presenting at sales conferences, see Chapter 12.)

Visits to schools are usually made after appointments have been set up; display materials and sample copies are carried in for presentation during morning and lunchtime breaks, preferably in the faculty or staff room. What the reps carry has become more complex in recent years. They travel in estate cars loaded with display boards, posters and boxes full of inspection copies, and write reports on every visit they make.

The sales manager organising reps' activities won't want to set up a separate and time-consuming chain of command, whereby a host of additional people receive reports, but do make the most of your contact with them. You may get the chance to talk to them at sales conferences, but if you can, arrange to go out visiting schools for a day with them. You will cramp their style as most reps value their independence. Make the most of the opportunity and learn from their swift delivery of sales benefits; there is not time to pass on all the background information you may consider relevant. It's a very useful lesson in copywriting, particularly for those who up to now have spent a lot of time thinking up bullet points on product benefits rather than understanding the practicalities of funding materials in schools.

Many publishing houses have used the difficult market as the justification for upping their sales effort, requiring reps to demonstrate products at faculty or staff meetings rather than just represent them. The stakes between winning and losing adoptions in schools are so high that detailed explanations of products by the reps after hours are increasingly common. Teachers can be asked from a variety of different schools in an area, perhaps with an editor in attendance to explain the background to the new scheme. Similarly, when schools are involved in the development and piloting of new materials, the publishers not only demonstrate their commitment to practical and workable products but build up long-term loyalty.

Mounting displays at exhibitions and conferences

Professional conferences for teachers tend to occur outside term time, for regular exhibitions and conventions sometimes staff are given time off to attend. Returning to Clare Freda: 'In New Jersey, a teachers' convention is held annually in Atlantic City. All teachers in the state are given a four-day weekend in order for them to go to attend workshops, presentations, and to receive free material and samples.'

Attending such events is a useful extension of the rep's activities. Some firms have mobile exhibition teams that mount large stands; others require the rep to do this as well. If you can, do go along to important meetings in your subject area.

Not only do they provide a very useful opportunity for both editorial and marketing staff to meet school contacts made by the rep, and to explore current teaching trends, they also allow you to view the competition.

An effective website

An educational publisher needs an efficient website, giving both basic and additional information whenever the teacher needs it – and providing a feedback mechanism for individual queries. The teaching day is heavily prescribed; there are only specific times at which teachers are free to find information, and so accessing it via a website makes the best possible use of their time. A query can be sent and the answer received whenever the teacher is next free to pick it up – when there is not the time for a phone call. It should be easy to read, interesting, kept constantly up to date and monitored so that feedback is dealt with efficiently. See Chapter 9 for more details.

Telemarketing

In-bound

The publisher's website can deal with many basic questions ('frequently asked questions' [FAQ] sections are particularly useful), but in addition, most publishers offer a telephone helpline for information and direct orders. Most schools have an organisational credit card for ordering items people need in a hurry.

Out-bound

Bearing in mind the very limited times of the day that reps can talk to teachers, telemarketing can be an effective means of making direct contact with specific subject teachers. The telephone numbers of schools (and often email addresses of teachers) are offered as an additional service by firms offering mailings to schools. There are some departments (e.g., music, art and any form of technology) that tend to have their own staffroom and kettle, and so tracking staff down to these locations, at the right times, can be a very good way of securing their attention.

Dispatch of inspection, approval and free copies

Teachers need time to look at material they are considering for adoption in their schools, so most educational publishers offer a system of supplying books 'on inspection'. Orders can be placed via the web, freepost reply cards are included in mailings for teachers to request the titles they would like to see, and reps are encouraged either to hand out inspection copies or order them for the staff members they talk to.

The rules for getting them vary slightly from company to company, but the principle is the same. A teacher may keep a book requested on inspection if multiple copies (usually 12–15) of the title are ordered for use in the school. In general, a book available on inspection must be one capable of being adopted for class use. Other books tend to be available 'on approval'; after the inspection period has elapsed they must be returned to the publisher in good condition or purchased. There is a grey area in between for some teaching practice-type titles, which could be sold in multiple copies through colleges of education to student teachers. In such cases the lecturer recommending the book may qualify for a free inspection copy.

In general, publishers spend too long describing the mechanics by which copies are available, and insufficient time encouraging teachers to really get to know the materials they request and discuss them with colleagues. Most books sent out for review will end up being pulped on return anyway, as they are 'un-saleable' (or it's just too expensive to put them back into stock). Teachers will be more likely to get to know a resource they are encouraged to look at than one they are frightened of damaging.

When you do despatch samples, send out a form with each one asking for the recipient's comments. Those that get returned will be an invaluable source of promotional quotations later on; first-hand feedback from practising teachers will be very convincing to the market.

Getting involved in support mechanisms for teachers

There are other methods of getting information to teachers. Teacher training facilities, usually (but not always) within universities, offer a chance to impress trainee teachers with your materials when they are impressionable and idealistic, and often long-term loyalties are formed in the process.

Some local education authorities have a teachers' centre where staff can meet one another, attend training sessions, use the library and much more. There are also school advisers variously available, from being suddenly parachuted in to support short-term crises, to offering support and advice on a long-term basis. All are qualified and experienced teacher/managers. The extent to which they are used or listened to depends on the views of the principal or head of department (some regard them as spies, others as offering extremely valuable fresh viewpoints) and the disposition of the advisers themselves. Contact lists are available by the subject or age of children on whom they advise. Keep them in touch with your publishing programme.

There are organisations that offer teacher training and development days in schools. All these are valuable marketing conduits for information on publishers' products.

Educational press for reviews and space advertising

Education has a supporting professional press, and educational publishers regularly send materials to education correspondents in the hope of a positive review that is likely to influence teachers. For similar reasons, other key people may be targeted – government ministers (in the hope of gaining influence rather than specific recommendations that they would not be allowed to give), well-known former teachers and some parents.

Whether you should advertise in the professional press is more complicated. The relationship between paying for advertising space and hence supporting an educational publication, and expecting coverage in return, is a complicated one. Advertising pays for editorial yet advertisers are not rewarded with automatic coverage. You do however have the right to have your materials at least considered for review.

Chapter 5 offers advice on the organisation of space for advertising and promotions, increasingly linked areas of marketing activity today.

Free publicity

Chapter 10 deals with securing free publicity.

Selling educational material to international markets

English language publishers used to export educational texts to their connected overseas territories virtually unchanged. As curricula were altered to reflect growing local nationalism and priorities, many such publishers set up subsidiary houses in these locations, e.g., in English-speaking Africa and the Caribbean. They used their expertise to train local staff to edit and handle the production of texts specifically for the immediate market.

While some English language publishers still produce textbooks for export, in particular in science and mathematics (some funded by aid agencies), such export sales have in general declined. But for the publishing industry as a whole, the decline has been more than offset by the dramatic rise in sales of English language teaching materials. In contrast with home educational markets, where stable populations have ever-less money to spend, the expanding markets for English language teaching materials, both at home and for export, offer such publishers dramatic potential for growth.

The group term for all the materials is ELT (English Language Teaching) and this can be further subdivided into EFL (English as a Foreign Language, e.g., teaching English to French nationals) and ESL (English as a Second Language, e.g., teaching English to those who have moved to English-speaking countries). The English that is taught may be British English, usually called TEFL (Teaching English as a Foreign Language), or American English called TESL (Teaching English as a Second Language). TOEFL is the qualification in English language to get into an American university or professional institution.

In addition to selling to those teaching or learning English in their home market, UK and US publishers compete to sell their wares overseas and their success is influenced by geographic location, political trends and hostilities, and the job and course aspirations of students. For example, in Latin America TESL is mainly learned, in Europe and the Gulf mainly TEFL, and both sectors compete for Japan.

The main markets for ELT materials are Europe, the Middle East, North Africa, the Far East and Southeast Asia, the Pacific Basin and Latin America. The opening up of Eastern Europe and the expansion of the European Union both offered important opportunities for the sale of materials. The private study market also offers big potential for sales to 'adult learners' (note the vocabulary, which distinguishes them from younger sounding 'students'). Language school courses, usually taking place during the summer, also offer considerable potential for sales and are often where new ideas on how to teach language are developed.

The main ELT publishers are a few large companies that can provide major courses supported by reference and dictionary material. Smaller publishers moving into this area need substantial backing.

Marketing responsibilities for those looking after ELT materials are varied; similar to those used for other educational texts but even more time-specific – the selection and delivery of materials in time for teaching is crucial. Most houses produce catalogues and leaflets (print and digital) which are circulated to colleges and teachers. They also rely on teams of representatives who make visits and they keep their community of users connected through social media communications (see the Cambridge University Press case study in Chapter 9).

Some UK publishers have formed co-publishing deals with European publishers to gain better access to overseas sales, others produce special editions for particular markets through deals with regional authorities or ministries of education. The industry has spawned its own press, both specific to certain examinations and in general, and in markets where ELT publishers are active there are often lively subsections of the main professional organisations for publishers and authors.

Marketing to doctors and other healthcare professionals

The healthcare market is an important one for publishers and is served by a range of different organisations, from large international groups to small associations who manage a few society journals.

While editors and those commissioning titles will generally have sector experience, it's not uncommon for marketing colleagues to work in this area without the benefit of previous academic or professional experience, so some general guidance may be helpful.

The first important thing to convey is that far from being a joined-up profession, medicine is a whole series of different careers, with specialisation the likely outcome of them all. Governments tend to talk about 'doctors' as a group, but in reality generalisations are difficult and even what would seem to the external observer to be clear subject areas are a series of sub-professions. Some common ground may, however, be identified among doctors:

- **They were successful at school,** were accepted to study a subject that was highly competitive, a source of considerable prestige for their educational establishment and their family, and which offered a direct route to an employable future. They have been in formal education for longer than most of the rest of the population.
- **They are robust.** As part of their training, all doctors get to examine, and often dissect, a complete cadaver (usually that of someone who has given their

body to medical science). Week by week, in dissection practicals, they reduced it to bits (or did this virtually). They tend to be self-assured and, perhaps fuelled by their experiences, often seem to display a dark sense of humour. There is a significant number of comedians and performers who are doctors or ex-doctors; at arts festivals medic 'revues' are plentiful.

- **They feel time-poor,** and perhaps as a consequence are entirely used to accessing information, extracting and digesting what they need to know and making quick decisions. A glance at databases offering drug information, available to all prescribing doctors, is useful background information on how to format information for this market. It presents a no-frills approach with which doctors are comfortable.

- **Constant observers of the accidents and unkindnesses of daily life, and in general themselves well remunerated, they are consumers of lots of things besides materials from medical publishers.** At a recent focus group I asked a group of doctors which advertising campaign had caught their attention in recent weeks. Of the six present, one said a political party, another a brand of drink, a third pet insurance, a fourth clothes and a fifth holidays. The only marketing aimed specifically at doctors to be mentioned was a campaign from a drug company that they had found incomprehensible. One later commented:

> Medics are no different from the general population. Perhaps with a more healthy understanding of how little we really know. Perhaps with a more realistic understanding of how much can be done.

How to communicate effectively with doctors

Doctors like you to be specific

Medicine is a vast profession. Whereas the specific structure varies, in most systems the process of becoming a doctor begins with a degree at medical school that includes clinical training. After graduation there is now a 2-year foundation period, rotating through a range of specialities, extending the duration and breadth of the old house jobs. Then most will head in one direction or another to specialise further, with general practitioners opting to specialise in the delivery of medicine within the community.

Medicine is a very hierarchical profession, and certain specialities attract more prestige than others. The more specialised the branch of medicine in which doctors are working, the more specific the information sent to them should be. It's also important to appreciate the divide between them and the various medical, technical and administrative support they receive, e.g., nursing colleagues and those offering support for patients within the community. Such groups may constitute an additional market for the same product range, but perhaps need separate targeting.

This is also a profession in which personnel move fast, and keeping track of such changes can be difficult. In the early stages of a hospital career, job moves may be particularly swift; certain branches of medicine receive more funding, and clinical developments may be faster in some than others (e.g., knowledge and developments tend to move faster in oncology than psychiatry). Maintaining contact lists of trainees is very difficult and it's hard to keep lists up to date. For example, in the UK the address supplied by all practitioners to the General Medical Council may not be helpful as this is probably their parents' address. On the other hand, GP principals and partners and hospital consultants may be stable for years. For this reason, investment in the management of market data will have to be a priority, whether it is managed in-house or your publishing house relies on a third-party organisation to provide contact lists. An effective alternative is to rely at least in part on the professional organisations all doctors belong to for direct delivery of marketing materials, often through flyers placed in their journals.

Should you communicate with doctors by leaflet or online?

One common complaint from doctors is that they receive too much marketing information. Although they seem to be generally aware of what they are sent, there is simply not time to read everything in detail. Preferences emerged:

> (I prefer) mobile, straightforward electronic access.

> I now prefer to receive things by email probably because it is easier to handle. If it fails to capture my attention I can easily delete.

> Email gives me the opportunity should the need arise to easily find cross-references and other relevant research.

> I have to say now that emails just get deleted. A flyer might get a few seconds of my time.

Although there was some generational bias, with younger doctors generally preferring online access, much more commonly commented on than the format of the marketing material they received was its relevance to them, and this they could assess very quickly after receipt. Also significant was the helpful overlap of different marketing materials often leading to an order, for example the email that reinforces the leaflet in a journal they subscribe to, followed by the opportunity to see the title at a conference they were attending:

> I personally feel that there is too much email traffic and email flyers are a turnoff. I prefer to read off paper. I find the flyers I get in journals for new publications are most useful at catching my attention. I have the time at conferences to peruse the trade stands and regularly review new books on my areas of interest there.

Other factors are significant too, such as topicality:

> I get both print and online. More online. Slightly more likely to pay attention to online marketing but really don't pay much attention to either unless it is something I have been thinking about at the moment I get the material.

And ease of access:

> Emails usually have links to the sites, which are easier to access. What irritates me is if I get an email, click on the link and it asks me to sign in. I never get beyond that.

It follows that mechanisms for finding out more – and ordering – should be easy to use. Ensure telephone ordering lines are established before you make them publicly available and that online facilities are fully navigable. Doctors are under strong pressure and dislike wasting time.

Some doctors respond to the vast amount of post by giving their home address for the delivery of mail rather than their work address. A large and (growing) percentage of general practitioners work part-time, and some of these seem to receive their professional post at home. The medical marketing materials sent thus have to compete for attention with the domestic mail. The scale of the post received in this way is enormous. One recently retired UK GP commented: 'When I retired, I wrote to the Medical Mailing Company to delete me from their lists. Two months on the amount of mail we receive at home has dropped by two-thirds. I knew I received a lot of information, but had not registered quite how much it was.'

What is sent is not all direct competition in the form of other marketing leaflets. The post includes a wide range of free and paid-for magazines and journals, and samples. There is also the chance to receive medical and related books free from pharmaceutical companies, who purchase such titles from publishers and then give them away as promotional incentives, to encourage them to take an appointment from a representative or attend a presentation.

Another common strategy used by doctors to limit the amount of information they receive is to concentrate on what they have requested – so anything from their professional association will get opened, and they may use its organisational intranet to search for further relevant information.

It follows that marketing materials to send to medics need to be:

* Adequate for the job

Remember that this is a market used to receiving lavish promotional materials from pharmaceutical companies, supported by presentations from well-qualified and trained representatives. While you should not waste money or produce over-costly materials, if you want to get noticed you must offer something that at least holds its own.

* Clearly identified as coming from a specialist publisher

Medical marketing materials should have authority. Make it clear early on (in the subject line of an email or on the envelope) that you are a publisher (not a pharmaceutical company). Present your information clearly for what it is, rather than using bland promises of career enhancement or humour (an oblique approach often used by drugs companies). For example, 'New titles from Bloggs Medical Publishers' or 'Look inside for substantial savings on Bloggs Medical Titles' are more likely to be effective than 'Getting to the top can be tough. Bloggs' new book makes it easier.'

> I tend to bin junk-mail by default. This covers anything I do not expect or comes from a sender I do not recognise. I tend to look at mail sent with RCR[21] (and other professional bodies) documents closely though. Glitzy marketing materials are not what gets my attention but rather evidence. So statements, facts are what I notice. While I accept that you have to do something to attract the attention of your prospective buyers, some of the marketing materials I receive do not look any different from materials used to sell shampoo, which is why I do not take notice of some materials.

- Correctly addressed

Think carefully about how you address this market; although regional variations in title will occur, in general they prefer to hear themselves referred to as 'doctors' rather than 'medics':

> *Medics* to me is a term originating from university days used to differentiate medical students as a group from other university students. It carries with it images of 'Medics' Rugby Team', 'Medics' Ball', 'Medics' Revue' – all very social, non-professional and implying familiarity.
>
> We may use *medics* as a term about ourselves, especially when at med school, but most doctors in the profession will prefer to be written to as *doctor* or as *medical.* The term *clinical* is increasingly applied in a more generic manner to other healthcare professionals, therefore is not specific enough.

- Logical

Your text should be laid out in a concise and predictable order, with photographs of covers next to blurbs, information precise and free from adjectives and overwriting. Doctors can cut through the blurb and need to know quickly what is in it for them.

Several doctors commented that any product worth buying has to make its case. There has to be enough information to enable the doctor to make a buying decision. One said: 'Too often, marketing information promotes a brand, and the accompanying brand image, but spends insufficient time early on in explaining the significance of the product. I don't want to have to hunt for this information, I want them to tell me.'

With a lot of information to wade through, ensure that your text is in a large enough type size to be read, and that design features enhance your message rather than compete with it. In many areas the quality of the reproductions included will be particularly significant, so your marketing materials will need to convey an accurate impression.

Remember too that the medical community is international and doctors take up exchange programmes and courses worldwide. So never assume that the recipient of your information is necessarily a native English speaker.

- Correct

Be sure to include and emphasise key terms and acronyms within the profession. If you are unsure, get them double-checked by someone who does know. Getting them wrong is worse than not trying to be up to date.

The following information is essential:

- Who has written this and where they are based. Medicine is practised differently in the US, UK and continental Europe.
- Subject matter and level.
- Contents list.
- Publication format.
- Price. If the title or resource you are promoting has a high price, make it look appropriately weighty – have your designer 'airbrush in' the spine and pages – to show value for money or show how many print books an online resource replaces. Many doctors reported that it was actually seeing a book at a medical conference that made them buy a title they had only previously heard of.
- Testimonials are helpful; from people who are known in the field rather than the names of the publications in which their comments appeared. Peer opinion is very important and authors can be asked to approach the right people.

  I am more likely to look at something seriously when referred to it by a colleague than if it just drops through the letter box.

- Sample pages, perhaps with captions highlighting particularly significant points. The reproduction quality of photographs should convey the standard of the title's publication.
- Avoidable, if they so desire. Tell them how to unsubscribe.

It's not widely understood that in order to delete a name from a mailing list the original sender needs to know from which list that name was taken (usually identified by the code at the top of the letter or address label). Ensure all your envelopes carry a return address in case they are undeliverable. Why not add a mini-questionnaire asking for additional information on whether the right person is being mailed at the same time?

Make it clear that if the envelope is returned without opening, you do not need a stamp to return it. Alternatively, instruct recipients to put the contents in a new envelope and return it to a freepost address. Otherwise they simply won't bother and you will not be aware that you are wasting money on mailing those who are not interested in your products, or should not be on the mailing list at all – and at the same time promoting an impression that you are out of touch and environmentally unsound (all those needlessly wasted trees). In the process you may also be alienating future authors.

- Cost-effective

Doctors are as susceptible to special offers as the rest of the population, so do remember to make some. Medical texts are very expensive, so added value to encourage them to buy more and save at the same time is good. Interestingly, whereas the corporate and business markets can respond very well to offers to take up a 'multiple buy' (coordinate an order for something that all your colleagues need and receive a special discount for doing so), this idea is generally resisted by doctors. They are too busy and this feels too commercial.

When is the best time to promote to doctors?

There is a year-round demand for medical services and services are provided year-round to match. Academic holidays can be a good time to reach academics (with no teaching and the students away on electives, they have more time to read what you send). General practitioners tend to find that the workload is lighter in the summer and given that doctors in a practice are never all away at the same time, they have more time to read your material.

Conferences

Professional and association conferences are a good place to sell to doctors according to their specific professional interests. Many view these as a short holiday, away from their day-to-day duties. They have time to read in the evenings and meet their colleagues.

> Books to browse at conferences are very tempting and a great way to see them. Most medical libraries have limited funds for new books now, especially in my field, so the opportunity to see what is available is appreciated.

If your organisation decides to attend a medical conference, circulate information through delegates' packs, course administration and associated exhibition space. Sales may be particularly good at conferences where participants don't know each other very well – delegates can wander round the stands at coffee time rather than make it obvious that they don't have anyone to talk to. Ask your authors which conferences they would recommend you attend or send information to.

Case study

A British consultant in Accident and Emergency Medicine commented on the materials she receives from publishers

Personally I tend to delete or bin almost all medical marketing. If I do give anything a second glance it is a very quick scan of title, author, contents and price. If it comes as a mailshot, I never read an accompanying mailshot letter; I expect the marketing to give me all the info I need to know and I want that info to be contained on one piece of paper. The decision to keep or bin is usually made within about 10 seconds.

In general I look up the answer to a question as it arises. Toxbase[22] and eMedicine[23] are good sources of information, although to be honest I would much rather pull a book off the shelf and look it up as it is usually easier and quicker. The books I find most useful have a no-frills approach and are divided into sections that are easy to skip through to find the relevant part, but then do offer further info if required.

I would rather be written to at work than at home as I want to read other books/escape work at home. The time I spend on-call alone ensures that my home life is invaded enough by work and I resent being reminded even more of work when I'm at home.

I do, however, get irritated by the vast amounts of marketing info we receive for junior doctors who have long since stopped working for us – I like the idea of having a tick box area on the front of the envelope 'no longer at this address, do not send further mail' with obvious free return. We never forward marketing mail.

Conferences are a good marketing location – I have bought books from them before, browsing through them first definitely makes me more likely to buy. I do like the feel of a book and the ability to become familiar with the location of the contents. I was once told that 'it is impossible to know everything in medicine. The skill is in knowing what you don't know but knowing where to look it up.' This is the essential service that publishers provide for us.

Other opportunities for publishers in this area

- Doctors as consumers, not just consumers of medical products

Doctors are regular purchasers of all kinds of products (not just medical titles) and as regular consumers they are on the receiving end of lots of marketing materials, which they expect to be suitably professional. One responder to my research questionnaire commented that the experience of the wider marketing industry should be deployed by publishers and summarised this as the ability to:

Sell the product on its benefits; give logical and emotional reasons to buy in a ratio of 2:1; write advertising copy which overcomes dominant reasons not to buy (based on a survey of the potential market); offer time-limited discounts with strong calls to action and bonuses for frequent purchase and have a proper website with functioning PayPal links.

In other words, marketing material from publishers should be presented in the same professional way as all the other approaches they receive: to them as consumers rather than as doctors.

The purchasing patterns that affect their professional reading needs spill over into their private reading habits:

> I even buy novels from iBooks now. I bought myself a paperback as a treat for my Easter holiday.

> I got dragged along to an antique book sale once, probably only time in the last few years I would have bought a book if could have afforded it!

> I now treat print books as a treat. They tend to be coffee table books on climbing, wildlife, cooking, etc.

- The popularity of audiobooks

Audiobooks emerged as an underused but popular medium. They have many of the same accessibility benefits of ebooks but perhaps permit information to be absorbed more empathetically:

> I prefer ebooks. Really though I prefer audiobooks. I am an avid listener of audiobooks. I would love to have medical texts read to me. I'm not sure this has been tried.

> The only hard books I would purchase are reference books. I am now more into ebooks than before. One of the advantages I find is portability. I am in fact now getting into audiobooks.

- Opportunities for material within continuing professional development (CPD)

Continuing professional development is the requirement for all professionals to keep up to date in their field. It is recognised as important across all areas of professional activity but monitored with various meticulousness. Within medicine it is particularly important.

For CPD, both reading materials and monitored tests are needed, and this throws up new opportunities for the marketing and sale of related products:

> Perhaps publishers could try a new angle – register their books for CPD and then have short online quizzes based on the book or book chapters with CPD points attached. I learn much better from a book than from a computer screen, but online learning that produces a certificate seems to be the only way that is accepted nowadays. My children have an 'accelerated reader scheme' at school that works in a similar way – this would be a great marketing strategy as the time reading the book would actually be recognised and count for revalidation and CPD purposes.

> I download journals for work and research. I have bought very few medical ebooks. The last ones were exam question books for FRCR.

Case study

CPD – continuing publishing development? An interview with Dr Stephen Hancocks

Stephen Hancocks Limited started life as a publisher of dental books and journals, based on my previous experience working for other publishers and as a clinical dentist. One of the exciting, and scary, aspects of running a small business is that one never quite knows in which direction it might develop. Quite often thoughtfully conceived, carefully planned and diligently executed schemes fail to catch customers' imaginations and turn out to disappoint whereas following up a chance remark, answering a question or getting an unexpected approach can change everything one does.

In terms of CPD, we began with a postal programme in one of our journals that the society who owned it then asked if we could put online. At that time, some ten years ago, our website (www.shancocksltd.com) was purely a bookshop but we asked the IT folk and they created a program that permitted this to happen. No sooner had we launched this than another customer for whom we publish and mail a CPD journal, which has a circulation of up to 80,000 copies depending on time of year and target market, wanted the same service. It went live while we were on holiday in Greece and a few days into the first week my email inbox was full with more than 1,000 registrations on the site. That chance request has now led to our having more than 40,000 dental care professionals registered on our site who regularly follow our journals, CPD and new products.

Having realised the potential for online CPD opportunities but discovered that dental users in particular still very much liked print publications, we pondered how we could utilise this in the more mainstream CPD market place. The General Dental Council (GDC) – the equivalent of the doctors' GMC – made CPD mandatory for dentists in 2002 and for other dental care professionals (DCPs) such as hygienists, therapists, nurses and technicians in 2008. Included in the requirements were a set number of hours' study of 'core' subjects: radiology/radiography, medical emergencies, cross-infection control and ethics/handling complaints. Anecdotally we heard that dentists were finding courses on these subjects either difficult to find at all, or quickly filled as soon as they were advertised but expensive to go on (there was the significant cost of the course plus expenses but additionally a lost half-day or day's income) as the overwhelming majority of dentists are self-employed.

So, we hit on the idea of supplying a package of four books covering each of these core subjects and writing CPD programmes for each of them amounting to the equivalent of the five-year requirement for the number of hours. The only exception was medical emergencies where we offered less than the required number as we, and the authors, felt that dentists should also have 'hands on' experience of this aspect of care and that theory alone was not sufficient. The package of 4 books and 15 hours (subsequently 18 hours when the GDC requirements were raised slightly) was launched to huge demand and our local post office at the time couldn't believe the car boot full of parcels that we regularly drove up to their door. And actually neither could we!

Each book came with one set of questions but it was only days before we had a phone call from a husband and wife team asking if they both needed to buy the books and questions or could they buy one set of books but two sets of questions? In retrospect it seemed such an obvious service to offer that we couldn't believe that we hadn't thought of it. Needless to say we immediately made modifications to offer the purchase of additional sets of questions.

We also began adding CPD programmes to all the books that we published as well as setting up agreements with other publishers. The advantage here is that the publishers benefit from additional sales, and a percentage of the CPD programme income, without the additional work created by the administration and marking of the responses. In modern parlance this is a real win-win situation.

The continuing changes in the technology of the delivery of electronic media and the developing nature of CPD, GDC requirements and expectations mean continual assessment and updating. While dental professionals still like the duality of print and electronic availability, we have to make estimates of how this might shift in the future and try to anticipate how we can continue to best serve our customers. To date they have indicated that they like the quality and efficiency of our services as well as the 'comfort' of real books and the convenience of completing CPD at their own convenience and, if they chose, in their own time allowing great savings from not having to take time out of the practice with lost income.

Much pressure is being placed on CPD as 'proving' that professionals are keeping up to date whereas all it can do realistically is provide the resources and content for them to implement as they choose. However, rightly, there is increasing need for quality control and prevention of cutting corners that, for example, we have responded to by imposing a 'voluntary' 50 per cent pass mark for all our CPD which I am pleased to report that the overwhelming majority of our users easily gain, indeed our audits show that over 85 per cent of users gain more than 75 per cent of correct answers.

In the same way that we are excited by opportunities we also have to be mindful of competition and of changing requirements, habits and expectations. Publishing might seem like a genteel business but it is a tough economic environment so we still look forward to the next chance remark or left-of-field approach that sets us off with another idea in another direction.

In conclusion to this section, and looking ahead, the future for the delivery of medical content is firmly online. Doctors want access to accurate information wherever they are:

> Things are developing so fast that I feel that printed books are almost out-of-date by the time they are printed. I read mostly online journals. I download journals for work and research.
>
> My reading: medically targeted queries because I need to for a clinical case – start with online search, library request if no access or have to pay for article. From CPD and a personal reading point, when I get the chance (usually on train, etc.) I use a tablet or mobile device – if I can't download it or access it directly I may as well forget it.

But things may not be moving as fast as we assume, and many doctors retain a vestigial attraction to the look and feel of a book:

> Medicine is continually moving forward and it is said that a book is out-of-date before it's even in print, further disadvantages of books include the space to store in busy work environments, and they are difficult to disinfect. But there are advantages – it's easy to save a page or mark a relevant area, avoids multiple printing off of the same page, and is easier on the eye to read.
>
> I could look online, but it's often easier just to reach behind me and pull a title off the shelf.
>
> My perception of publishers is that prices are largely inflated for information that is otherwise available online, albeit with a little more effort on my part. Increased accessibility of content at reasonable cost may be another way forward, e.g., subscription rather than one-off costs for books, journals and other materials may be the future.

Publishers need to think about the value they are adding to information that is routinely available, and their expertise in storing, cross-referencing and commenting. The traditional skills of the publisher in the effective management of information may turn out to be the most crucial.

The role of medical librarians

If doctors complain about getting too much information within their particular specialisation, then medical librarians are besieged by information on every specialism offered by the institution in question. Librarians have to juggle the different demands of various departments and specialities in an environment where budgets never match requirements. They can be an excellent source of information for publishers seeking to approach medical markets. For more information on contacting this market see the section within this chapter on marketing to academic librarians.

Interestingly, many medical libraries are collections culled from various different sites. For example, the library at our local hospital has three names (based on who originally gave the funding), but they all are the same place. Cross-check the lists you are using to ensure you are not sending more copies of your information than needed.

Selling to professional and industrial markets

For those planning a long-term career in publishing, a role in supplying information and related tools to fast-developing professional markets is a pragmatic move.

Professional people such as accountants, lawyers and financial services advisers need information on which they can rely, and on which they can base services to their own customers. Given time, they could themselves compile and update the detail they and their staff need, but instead often choose to rely on publishers, who are after all experts in the management and delivery of information, to handle the process for them. Using published material also gives professionals access to a wider range of expertise than they may have within their own organisation.

The larger firms have substantial budgets to spend on the information resources they need, and the more bespoke or value-added publishers can make their service, the more valuable it becomes – and the more they can charge for it. And because the profits can be high, and because marketing staff responsible for promotion tend to use measurable marketing techniques and can thus track and prove how effective their efforts have been, there is a tendency for them to be better paid than their colleagues in other areas of publishing.

Important information for approaching professional markets

- **Business and professional markets often buy supplier brand, rather than individual contributor.** They are buying from publishers core and ongoing values such as consistency, confidence and competence, often to a greater extent than the temporary brilliance (even if amazingly far-sighted) of an individual and perhaps maverick brain. Given that they will be relying on the service provider to access, store, update and anticipate the information on which both their professional service and their professional requirements of compliance are based, they want to be assured that they are buying from an organisation that prizes quality and accuracy, cares about the responsibility that accompanies provision, and that they can trust. *Their* reputation will be based on the reliability of what *you* provide.
- **They are very time-conscious.** Post-university, few professionals are reading a textbook from start to finish. They are consulting resources to find answers to questions and problems, so the searching/filtering functions, to help them find the relevant content, are the key features of the service on offer.
- **Publishing relationships through official professional associations or representative bodies can work particularly well in this market**, as they reinforce that closeness to the profession. For example, the publisher might become a publishing partner of one of the leading professional bodies or associations in sectors such as accountancy, finance, tax or law. The more niche the

professional area concerned, the more professionals are drawn to publications produced by relevant professional bodies.

- **When working with this market, you are a supplier as well as a publisher.** These markets demand good service from their suppliers, fully aware of how much they are paying. They want to access competence quickly, in whatever format they find most useful. They want the systems to be easy to use; compatible with internal systems and work when they need them (they are very intolerant of mistakes); the functionality to be smooth and easy to operate; indices that allow swift access to content; cross-referencing that is efficient and imaginative. If they lose or destroy what you provided, they still want you to sort it out – and quickly. What is more, this deliverability of the supplier's promise will colour whatever information you send to them in future. Thus if they have an ongoing issue with your organisation about a separate service that they are dissatisfied with, it will influence how they both view and talk about you to their colleagues and competitors in the much longer term. They will not be impressed if they seek to tell you of a difficulty and you lay the blame (even if correctly) at the feet of another department. To them you are one supplier or maybe even one part of an international corporation, and every aspect of delivery is your responsibility.

- **Provision by the publisher of professional detail is a given, something they take for granted – it is what they can do with it that interests them.** Insight into the interpretation or application of the information in professional practice is highly valued. Thus they will appreciate an information source if it serves as a tool for effective strategic planning, or an imaginative use of cross-referencing and linkage that enables them to demonstrate and bill for an additional competence to their clients. The publisher's immediate absorption of, and commentary on, the latest legislative or tax changes enables them to offer a more complete service to those they work for or advise, to show that they understand the implications of changed provisions within nanoseconds of their being announced. Access to information that is kept up to date is critical and has been a major reason for a shift from printed to online materials in this market.

> Information publishing is of limited value if it simply serves to inform but does not form part of a profit and growth strategy for the customer. We need to understand our customers' relationships with their customers and help them achieve their objectives. Motives of fear, greed, self-esteem and social standing are powerful drivers in encouraging sales.
>
> Robert McKay, director, Dunedin Academic Press and
> regular writer on professional publishing matters

Publishers can charge a lot of money for the additionally managed availability of the service they provide. Consider email or telephone advice and information lines, staffed by real experts, after standard office hours, or advice sections featuring frequently asked questions, all provided in a format that makes it clear the information is tailored to the individual or organisation subscriber, rather than to the profession or client base.

- **This market expects you to know them; their workflow; worries and priorities.** They identify you as being part of their market – rather than a distant supplier – and expect a high level of involvement in return for the high level of investment they provide. You need to know who they are, to be at their get-togethers, and have a sufficient grasp of their subject matter to be able to keep an intelligent conversation going. Editors and those managing content will most probably have a specialist subject knowledge of the relevant area; marketing staff may not, but it may not occur to your market to ask whether or not you are similarly qualified (they may just assume that you are). So if you are viewing being a professional publisher as a step on the route to working in another area of publishing, keep it to yourself. They will not expect you to talk up your long-term ambition to work on thrillers by Stephen King rather than taxation resources.

- **They want the information delivered in the format that best suits their needs,** irrespective of how you may prefer to deliver it, or what your other professional customers require. This may be as subscription products, online resources, books and magazines, blogs, conferences and training. They may prefer delivery through their professional organisation (see above) rather than directly from a publisher. Some providers of information sell their product rather like television subscriptions – you can have a basic service and then add on niche products such as PLC Tax and PLC Restructuring in return for paying a bigger subscription.

- **This is an area of publishing where only extremely serious players tend to do well.** The major publishers in this area are few in number but enormous in size, and highly concentrated in their specialisations. All have access to the same basic information; it is the format, functionality or back-up services that distinguishes one supplier from another. As one business lawyer commented:

> In the UK legal market PLC and Westlaw are market leaders. As a user of information it's the quality of PLC content which it continuously updates that makes it probably the top choice of business lawyers. In the UK you can access all legislation on the government's own website but Westlaw have managed to sell their legislation service because they provide a function that allows you to look at a section of an act and then scroll through previous versions of the section in force on different dates, which cannot be done on the government site.

In a field of maybe no more than four competing services, these publishers want to be first or second, not third. Whereas much of the publishing industry is grounded in friendly competition, with staff sharing information about markets, and joining in related camaraderie, this area is highly competitive and less collaborative. Focus on the external competitors is total.

- **This is a market driven by change.** Professions are constantly affected by change, through precedent, government intervention or the news agenda, and the information resources publishers develop and maintain must match. This means that updating must be constantly ongoing – and of course as a chargeable service to consumers. Publishers are judged by the speed of access they offer to updated material. They also need to be able to innovate, as the market can become intolerant of long-familiar but inefficient services. Don't forget that professionals being targeted see technological innovation in other aspects of their lives, from how they order food in restaurants to how their children download music for pleasure. Publishers need to be up to date on all delivery mechanisms and standards of customer service, not just those that have applied in their own industry up to now.

The professions may have other, and self-supporting, ways of managing their need for information, which do not rely on publisher services. For example, blogs (in legal circles 'blawgs') are increasingly important and widely used for sharing ideas on practice and both commenting on, and lobbying for, potential developments. Associated articles emphasise how they have become a key component of the totality of learned and practical information content and how the traditional publishers are being challenged by them. Publishers too are using blogs as a way of connecting with their market, and are often using LinkedIn, Facebook and Twitter prolifically, but such contributions work best if they demonstrate expertise and situation analysis of value rather than just offering services for sale.

Events since the financial crash of 2008 have raised compliance, risk and governance as areas of core concern for many businesses not traditionally involved in this market, providing opportunities for publishers to market products to a wider range of organisations than just mainstream professional practice. For example, organisations involved in financial services need information on risk management and governance functions.

Format of published and marketing material

There is a drive to provide all published products for the business and professional communities online; print copies are expensive to produce, store and distribute. But whereas some markets have fully embraced technological access to information, not all are equally comfortable. For example, lawyers often seem to prefer print – perhaps this relates to the need for evidence-based documentation that is unlikely to change in translation, such as the original text of cases or legislation, as well as to their financial models for charging out their services. Often they favour PDF files over HTML documents, as they can be sure that a document sent as a PDF cannot be altered by the recipient. For markets such as these, a model has emerged of an annual printed book, supported by an online and integrated information service that is updated all the time, so an individual can look in the latest edition, establish the principles of the subject, then go online to find out what has happened since it was passed for press.

Nowadays, as enhanced technology makes reading onscreen easier, and new generations joining the professions are more comfortable with online than print, more and more resources are available in this way. This continuing move to online resources has enormous implications for the relationship between publisher and customer, as once a company has adopted a particular publisher's system, rolled it out via its intranet to fee-earners and employees and encouraged them to add organisational specific references for local use by colleagues, moving to another delivery mechanism with another publisher can be very problematic. Convenience is a substantial factor, and works in the existing supplier's favour simply because it may be too much effort to change.

For this reason, another useful marketing approach is to invest time and effort in getting products installed within universities and organisations offering professional training. If students get used to using particular resources while they are learning about their future profession, reliance can become a lifelong habit. Making products available at heavily discounted prices to the university market can thus be a very good investment.

You might assume that online delivery of a service would mean that marketing information about why and how to subscribe to it is best delivered online too. Not necessarily. Publishers in these areas tend to rely on a range of marketing methods that offer direct communication with the market: direct marketing; face-to-face representation; social and business media; blogs on relevant websites; demonstrations of technical support at exhibitions or arranged within the supplier's or prospect's offices; sponsorship – all as part of the marketing mix, and tracked to find out how effective each has been. The marketer's task is to combine these marketing methods into an integrated communication pattern rather than rely on any single one. As Robert McKay has written:

> Take direct mail, once the basic form of product communication. One senior executive told me recently, though I don't necessarily believe him, that no marketing person below the age of forty would even think of wasting money in that way. Maybe it makes sense, though. Response rates, even in chasing existing customers for renewal purchases and business in general are pitiful and ever-declining, making expenditure in that direction often not cost-effective. Even lower response rates are achieved by email campaigns but at least the minimal cost of mailing large numbers of addresses and coping with flawed data continues to make this an area of activity. Of course, there must be a problem that, with, say a 0.25% response rate, and a need to sell 1,000 items or subscriptions, 400,000 names need to be mailed. Then the question must arise as to where in a discrete market is anyone going to find so many prospects. They simply don't exist.[24]

If a decision to install a particular supplier's system needs to be discussed with colleagues, then printed marketing materials will most likely be needed. People expect a service that has a high price tag to be presented professionally and, even if it is delivered entirely online, a high-quality marketing brochure explaining the benefits may be required, simply to convince customers that it is being offered by a professional service provider that considers all their needs.

In professional markets a direct response to an initial sales approach is unlikely to be immediately successful; rather, a series of customer contacts is likely to be required, including demonstrations and technical support, and each of these stages must be supported by appropriate marketing materials. A trial period of access to online materials may be needed by potential customers for them to fully appreciate the potential of the product. You should also consider how the competitors are promoting their service, and decide whether to match them – or be different. Your most basic guide for what materials to produce should be common sense supported by an understanding of the market and the emotion likely to be involved in purchase. A key question you should be asking yourself, at all times, is 'Would I buy from me?'

You will need to develop a specific writing style for this market, one that recognises the concept of understanding your client and your client's client. You need to speak to the professional adviser but help them communicate with their clients. The words you use need careful attention – and it's helpful if you can recruit members of the market to comment on your marketing approach and vocabulary. You should consider presenting your company as 'providers', 'researchers', 'integrators' and 'compilers' rather than simply as 'publishers', and it may be helpful to adopt the vocabulary of the library for those that manage information, hence as 'professional support service' or 'knowledge management service'. Similarly, high-priced products and services are best described as 'in-depth resources', combinations of 'workflow tools' and 'professional information services', 'compendiums of information and guidance' or 'dossiers of the latest research and guidance' rather than 'databases', 'manuals' or 'books'. Remember that there are legal risks in suggesting that publishers provide 'advice'. They don't and are normally not qualified to do so. That's the work of the professional advisers themselves, who are suitably qualified and insured.

It is similarly vital that the impression you provide affirms the overall organisational brand, from well-put-together sales information to personal contacts who are highly informed and professional in appearance. This market wants precision, so spelling mistakes, casual uses of English, poor grammar and an inappropriately 'matey' style will all undermine the image your organisation seeks to create.

These are complex products, and no sales representative could be expected to answer all the questions a potential customer has. So your marketing information should answer likely questions; anticipate and reassure by offering information on issues they had not thought to enquire about, but still need to know. Investment in a business's information provision is very expensive, and those making the purchasing decisions need to show that they have gained good value for money for their organisation and, more importantly, will profit from the investment through client billing. Images should reaffirm the value and potential for profit increase on offer. If your resource provides access to a range of advisory services, can these be represented by showing how many words/volumes/years of professional experience and related research – or people – are involved?

Ultimately it is vital for those marketing products to this market to remember that their market has a choice, and because of the huge financial consequences of changing supplier, a decision to exercise that choice is very damaging for the rejected publisher. Sometimes quite small instances of annoyance or inefficiency – perhaps the product of an 'unreasonable' attitude on the part of the customer or thoughtlessness on the part of a very junior member of the publisher team – can become long-held grudges that influence buying decisions years into the future. The more embedded supplier and customer can be, at all levels of their business relationship, the longer-lasting their professional relationship is likely to be.

Notes

1 Variously ascribed: Confucius, the Bible, Abraham Lincoln, Mark Twain.
2 Romaniuk, J., Nguyen, C. and East, R. (2011) 'The accuracy of self-reported probabilities of giving recommendations', *International Journal of Market Research*, 53(4): 507–22.
3 www.societyofauthors.org.
4 www.brandguild.co.uk.
5 Academic.mintel.com/Sinatra/academic/my_reports/display/id.
6 www.nosycrow.com.
7 www.thebookpeople.co.uk.
8 www.booktrust.org.uk, now running for 80 years.
9 www.worldbookday.com.
10 www.readingagency.org.uk/children/quick-guides/summer-reading-challenge.
11 www.literacytrust.org.uk.
12 www.rif.org.
13 www.roehampton.ac.uk/Research-Centres/National-Centre-for-Research-in-Child ren-s-Literature/
14 Broadly this means extending readers' experience, encouraging them to try new authors, genres and types of format.
15 The Orkney Islands are off the north coast of Scotland.
16 A basic shelter, usually left unlocked and available for anyone to use.
17 Published 1859; author George Eliot.
18 The 'arms race' for supplementary materials is discussed in Masikunas, G. and Baverstock, A. (2011) 'How well do UK publishers of marketing textbooks investigate and understand the market to which they are selling?' *International Journal of the Book*, 8(4): 93–102.
19 Library and Learning Services, Nightingale Centre, Kingston University.
20 National Academic and Specialist Library Catalogue, www.copac.ac.uk. A means of accessing rare and unique research material by bringing together the catalogues of around 90 major UK and Irish libraries (and growing).
21 The Royal College of Radiologists.
22 The primary clinical toxicology database of the National Poisons Information Service, www.toxbase.org.
23 A quick reference online research tool for doctors, www.emedicine.medscape.com.
24 www.slaw.ca/2011/12/20/reaching-and-retaining-customers.

Glossary

Above and below the line: The traditional distinction between different sorts of advertising. 'Above the line' is paid for (e.g., space advertisements taken in newspapers). 'Below the line' marketing involves no invoice; it is normally negotiated in a mutually beneficial arrangement between two or more organisations (e.g., books presented on cereal packs). The usual result is an augmented offer to the consumer (more than just the product being sold), often with a time limit. The distinction between 'above' and 'below the line' is blurring as techniques are used in combination; many marketing agencies are now offering 'through the line' services.

Advance notice (or advance information sheet; AI): A single sheet giving brief advance details of a forthcoming publication. Usually circulated six to nine months before publication, it is sent to anyone who needs the information: bookstores, reps, etc.

Advertorial: Advertising copy that masquerades as an editorial item.

Affinity marketing: Marketing based on choices made by consumers that indicate they are likely to be attracted to related products and services. Penguin's promotion of fiction titles on the back of Galaxy chocolate bars is an example of affinity marketing in that both products (a good read and a bar of chocolate) are assumed to appeal to the same person. The proposal becomes particularly effective if the two products can be enjoyed together (read while you eat chocolate).

Answers: Shorthand used on a publisher's or distributor's invoice to show the status of particular titles ordered by a bookseller and not immediately available. These are less significant today as so many titles can be kept in print through 'print on demand' technology. The most common abbreviations are:

nyp – not yet published
nk – not known
oo – on order
op – out of print; no plans to reprint
os – out of stock (reprint under consideration)
rp Jan – reprinting, will be available again in January

App: An app is an abbreviation of the term 'application software'. An app is a computer program that is designed to operate on smartphones, tablets and other mobile devices, usually available (some are free, others must be paid for) through the same distribution platforms associated with mobile devices. Apps are available for a range of leisure and professional uses from games and enhanced content delivery (e.g., a recording of a musical performance with additional text and related versions to enable the listener to compare) to processes for checking prices or transport connections. Apps are now considered a more popular activity on mobile platforms than internet access.

Approval staircase: The series of stages/departments/individuals a consideration must go to or through before a decision can be reached.

Arrears: See *dues*.

Artwork: Typesetting and illustrations were conventionally pasted on to board to form artwork that could then be photographed to make printing plates. Today most artwork is produced on computer and despatched online.

Author: The person whose name appears on the front of the product and who will be most closely identified with its creation; usually (but not always) the person who wrote it. Authors have often struggled for years to get a publishing deal, to craft their manuscript and then see it reach a final format, and hence care passionately about how their work is presented. Publishers, who have more than one author or title to look after, can find such single-mindedness a little daunting. All authors tend to underestimate the role played by the publishing house in seeing a book prepared for publication, and to lose sight of the fact that publishing is a business, in which the publishing house is investing its money, not a social service, however ultimately life-enhancing or culturally enriching the product. Authors complain that publishers frequently underestimate the amount of effort required to write a book. The relationship between authors and publishers, which is utterly symbiotic, works best if both parties understand and manage the expectations of the other. For example what kind of product is being produced, what level of marketing budget is it awarded and at what kind of long-term sales/life is it aimed? Both authors and publishers tend to be creative people, and arguments and misunderstandings can brew quickly. Effective explanation should produce cooperation, more effective publishing and a longer-lasting relationship.

Auto-response: In email marketing, auto-response(s) are prearranged and automatic emails triggered by the actions of the customer. Commonly an auto-response is sent when a customer subscribes to a mailing list and they then may receive additional messages at regular intervals and also at particular points in their customer journey (e.g., after ordering/once goods have been despatched or when no order has been received for a while).

B2B: Business-to-business, short term for business transactions between businesses, for example, a publisher's business relationships with production companies, wholesalers or retailers.

B2C: Business-to-consumer.

B2G: Business-to-government.

Backlist: Older titles on a publisher's list that are still available.

Barcode: A machine-readable unique product code. The barcode usually appears on the back cover of a book, and is used for stock control and sales.

Benefits: In a marketing context, benefits are the advantages that come to the user/purchaser from a product or service's features. Publishing copy is often feature- rather than benefit-orientated; by contrast, readers are far more interested in what the product will do for them than in how the publisher has set up its specifications. For example, product features of a guidebook might be lavish illustrations or high paper quality. The benefits to the reader, however, might be that it provides a lasting souvenir of the holiday, really gives a flavour of the place to be visited before they get there or stands up well to use throughout the trip because it is well made. Similarly a picture book for very young children may offer attractive illustrations by a well-known artist, but be appreciated by grandparents because it makes a welcome present that they can enjoy reading together.

Blad: Originally this meant a section of a book printed early to help in the promotion, and be shown as a sample. Today blads can consist of marketing information about, a random assortment of pages from, or a synopsis of a forthcoming publication, and do not necessarily constitute a distinct section.

Blawg: Blog written for legal circles.

Bleed: Printed matter that extends over the trimmed edge of the paper; it 'bleeds' off the edge. To obtain a bleed in a magazine ad, you have to book a full-page space.

Blog: A user-generated website where entries are made in journal style and displayed in reverse chronological order. The term 'blog' is derived from 'web log', but it is also used as a verb, meaning to run, maintain or add content to a blog. Blogs can include photographs, be tagged with keywords and allow readers to comment – they can thus play a valuable role in promoting two-way communication and driving traffic to a website.

Blogosphere: A term that originally referred to all blogs and the connections between them, but is now often used generally to refer to online communication in which people can publish their opinions.

Blurb: A short sales message, generally about product content, for use in leaflets or on jackets.

Body copy: The bulk of the advertising text, which usually follows the headline.

Bottom line: Financial slang referring to the figure at the foot of a balance sheet indicating net profit or loss. Has come to mean the overall profitability, for example: 'How does that affect the bottom line?'

Bounce rate: A term used in connection with traffic analysis on the internet. It refers to the percentage of website visitors who end their visit on the first page they see, i.e., they do not extend their exploration by looking at other pages of the website.

Brand: A product (or service) with a set of distinct characteristics that makes it different from other products on the market.

Break-even: The point at which you start making money. In a publishing context, reaching break-even means that sufficient copies of a publication have been sold to recover the origination costs. The break-even point in a mailing is reached when enough copies have been sold to recoup the costs of the promotion.

Bromide: A type of photographic paper. Producing a bromide is a one-stage photographic process on to sensitised paper or film which is then developed. *PMTs* are routinely produced on bromide paper but alternatives now include acetate or self-adhesive paper.

Budget: A plan of activities expressed in monetary terms.

Bullet point: A heavy dot or other eye-catching feature to attract attention to a short sales point. A series of bullet points is often used in advertisement copy both to vary pace and to engage the reader's attention. They:

- are good for attracting attention
- help create uneven sentences and surrounding spaces that draw in the reader
- allow you to restate the main selling points without appearing over-repetitious.

Buyer: The job title within a retail or wholesaling firm responsible for selecting/ordering stock. Large shops will have a different buyer for each department.

b/w: Abbreviation for black and white.

Call to action: A firm suggestion to the recipient of a piece of marketing communication telling them what to do next. Options include placing an order, signing up for a newsletter, visiting your blog, etc.

Camera-ready copy: Frequently abbreviated to 'crc'. Artwork that is ready for photography, reproduction and printing without further alteration.

Card deck (also called business reply card mailing or cardex mailing): A collection of business reply cards each offering a separate sales message to which the recipient can respond by returning the card concerned. Handily recipients often tend to pass on individual cards to others they know may be interested. Often used for selling technical, business and professional titles.

Cased edition: A book with a hard cover, as opposed to *limp* or paperback.

CD ROM: Short for compact disc, read-only memory. A high-density storage device that can be accessed but not altered by those consulting it. Very popular in the late 1990s some still circulating.

Centred type: A line or lines of type individually centred on the width of the text below. Type on a blank title page can also be centred on the page width.

Character: An individual letter, space, symbol or punctuation mark.

Cheshire labels: Old-fashioned format for labels. Cheshire labels are presented as a continuous roll of paper that is cut up and pasted on to envelopes by a Cheshire machine. Still sometimes used for the despatch of items bought on subscription, i.e., where customer loyalty is established.

Closed market: Created when local selling rights are sold to a particular agent. Retailers in an area that is part of a closed market must obtain stock of titles from the local agent rather than directly from the original publisher. This arrangement is under threat from the internet, which knows no geographical boundaries.

Coated paper: Paper that has received a coating on one or both sides, e.g., art paper.

Colour separations: The process of separating the colours of a full-colour picture into four printing colours (cyan, magenta, yellow and black) done with either a camera or an electronic scanning machine. The separated film may then be used to make printing plates.

Competitive advantage: A characteristic or attribute that enables an organisation or individual to perform better than its competitors. See the work of M.E. Porter in the Bibliography.

Competitive differentials: What a company is good or bad at; the things that set it apart from its competitors.

Controlled circulation: A publication circulated free or mainly free to individuals within a particular industry; advertising sales paying for circulation and production costs. Much used in medicine and business.

Cookie: A cookie is a small piece of data that comes from a website and is stored in a user's web browser for as long as they browse that website. It enables the website being accessed to record users' browsing habits and histories.

Cooperative (or shared) mailing: A mailing to a specialised market containing material from several advertisers that share the costs between them.

Copy: Words that make up the message, often used of material prepared for advertising or newspaper features.

Creative Commons: A method of sharing content online, as an alternative to copyright. The attachment of a Creative Commons licence can specify that content can be used provided an attribution is given, www.creative commons.org.

Cromalin proofs: See *digital proofs.*

Crowd-sourcing: Securing support (time/money/help in kind) for the agreed goals of a third party. For example, seeking resources to support the production and sharing of books that would not otherwise be commissioned.

Customer lifetime value: The net (predicted) profit from a particular customer during their relationship with you/your organisation. The length referred to is this relationship, not their natural life.

Cut-out: An irregularly shaped illustration that will require handwork at the repro stage of printing.

Dashboard: The control panel for activity, which is not visible to the consumer, who sees only the resulting outputs. For example, the central coordination of your website or blog that controls what appears and when.

Database marketing: Building up increasingly complex information about customers in order to serve their needs more precisely and sell more to them in the future. The long-term aim of *direct marketing*.

Database publishing: Publishing from information stored on a database. Can be a fast method of producing complex material or material that will date very quickly.

Desktop publishing: Now a slightly archaic term. It originally referred to producing *camera-ready copy* and artwork on computer screen (rather than the previous old method of pasting down on to board). This allows easy experimentation with different layouts and formats. This is now the norm, but you still may hear the term used.

Die-cutting: A specialised cutting process used whenever the requirement for a cut is other than a straight line or right angle (i.e., when a guillotine cannot be used). A metal knife held in wood is punched down on to the item to be cut. Many old letterpress machines have been adapted to form die-cutting equipment. Used on book covers to allow material beneath to show through.

Digital proofs: Digital proofs are of two broad sorts: high-res (short for resolution) or low-res. High-res proofs are made from the final printing files, normally PDFs. There are a number of quality levels. At one extreme, they may be little more than the sort of colour prints you would get from an office LaserJet printer and, although they may look fine, they won't necessarily represent the printed product very faithfully because they are produced in a fundamentally different way. To get closer to this ideal, most printers use special laser printers which are calibrated to the plate-setter (the device that exposes the printing plate) in a very direct manner. Digital cromalins are these sort of proof: high-res, calibrated proofs that can be used to check for colour before the item is printed. Low-res proofs, by contrast, are for position and content only, and are made using standard office equipment.

Direct costs: Costs attributable to a specific project, as opposed to general overheads or indirect costs. For example, the printing bill for producing a particular title is a direct cost; the photocopier used to copy proofs that are circulated is an indirect one.

Direct marketing: The selling of services directly to the end consumer – various methods exist including email, direct mail, telemarketing and house-to-house calling. See Chapter 8.

Direct response advertising: Advertising designed to produce a measurable response, through email, mail, telemarketing, space advertisements, etc. This compares with direct promotion, whereby material is sent directly to the market, which may, or may not, produce a direct response back.

Disintermediarisation: An interruption in the former process of doing things. For example, authors who offer their content directly to users, by self-publishing or publishing through their websites, are changing the usual sequence of intermediaries (publishers, distributors and booksellers).

Display type: Large type for headlines, usually 14 point or more.

Dues (also called *arrears*): Orders for a new (or reprinting) publication before it is released. Publishers record the dues and fulfil orders as soon as stock is available. Checking the dues of forthcoming titles is a good way of finding out how well the reps are subscribing particular titles in bookshops and hence estimating levels of interest and predicting eventual sales.

Dump-bin: Container to hold, display and stock in retail outlets; usually supplied by the manufacturer to encourage the retailer to take more stock than might otherwise be the case. Most are made from cardboard, to be assembled in the shop. Supplied free but on condition that a stock order to fill it is received too.

Duotone: A half-tone shot printed in two colours. This is a more expensive way of printing a photograph than simply using a single printing colour, but can add depth and quality to the image presented. It is usually printed in black plus a chosen second colour. An alternative effect can be produced by using a tint of the second colour behind a black and white half-tone.

EDI: Electronic Data Exchange.

EFL: English as a Foreign Language, e.g., teaching English to French nationals.

ELT: English Language Teaching (see Chapter 15 on the education market).

Embargo: A date before which information may not be released, often used on press releases to ensure that no one paper scoops the rest. Sometimes ignored by the media to secure just such a competitive advantage.

EPOS: Electronic point of sale. Machine-readable code that can be read by a terminal at a shop checkout to establish price, register any appropriate discounts and reorder stock.

ESL: English as a Second Language, e.g., teaching English to those who have moved to English-speaking countries.

Extent: Length of text. For example, for a book, extent: 192pp (192 pages); for a leaflet, extent: 4ppA4 (four sides of A4 paper).

FE: Further education: education that is beyond school but not within university (those still at school under the age of 19 receive secondary education). FE can be academic (e.g., GCSEs and A-levels) or vocational (e.g., GNVQs), carried out in the student's own time or supported by an employer.

Features: The specifics of a product or service that distinguish it from other products and services produced (e.g., extent, illustrations, level of content). See also *benefits*.

Firm sale: The orders placed by a retailer from which the publishers expect no returns. In practice most publishers have to be flexible and allow at least a credit for unsold titles, to ensure goodwill and the stocking of their titles in the future.

Flush left (or **justified left**): Type set so that the left-hand margin is vertically aligned, the right-hand margin finishing raggedly wherever the last word ends.

Flush right (or **justified right**): Type set so that only the right-hand margin is aligned vertically.

Flyer: A cheaply produced leaflet, normally a single sheet for use as a handout.

Font: The range of characters for one size and style of type.

Format: The size of a book or page. In the United Kingdom this is usually expressed as height x width, in the United States and most of Europe as width x height.

Freemium: A pricing strategy/business model whereby you give away the core product or service to a wide group of users but sell a premium version to smaller numbers of potential users who require a bespoke or personalised version of the same thing. Thus you might make a short story by an author available free through a website but offer a personal appearance to read it at a special occasion for a significant fee. The word originates from a combination of 'free' and 'premium'.

Friends: In the context of social media 'friends' are people who request a link to you online and whom you then accept; called 'friends' on Facebook, 'followers' on Twitter and 'contacts' on LinkedIn. On some social media sites you have to accept a friend request before a connection is established.

gsm (or **g/m^2**): The measure by which paper is sold: short for grams per square metre.

Half-life: The point at which the eventual outcome of an experiment can be predicted.

Half-tone: An illustration that reproduces the continuous tone of a photograph. This is achieved by screening the image to break it up into dots. Light areas of the resulting illustration have smaller dots and more surrounding white space to simulate the effect of the original. A squared-up half-tone is an image in the form of a box (any shape), as opposed to a cut-out image.

Hand-selling: A term used in retailing for face-to-face selling; promoting through personal recommendation rather than through official marketing materials received from the publisher or agent.

Hardback book: A book in which the pages are generally sewn (rather than stuck) and that is then bound with a protective, rigid cover. Hardback is the UK term, in the US this format is known as hardcover.

Hard copy: Copy on printed paper as opposed to copy on a computer or other retrieval system (which is soft copy).

Hashtags: Keywords or phrases without spaces with the prefix # that can be clicked to see a group of recent posts including the same #link on the same platform. Messages on blogging sites and social networking sites (e.g., Twitter, Facebook, Google+ or Instagram) may be tagged in this way but the links do not work between different platforms.

HE: Higher education. Study at university level and above.

Headline: The eye-catching message at the top of an advertisement or leaflet, usually followed by the body copy.

House ad: An advertisement that appears in one of the advertiser's own publications or promotions.

House style: The typographic and linguistic standards of a particular publishing house. For example, there may be a standard way of laying out advertisements, standard typefaces that are always used and standard rules for spelling and the use of capital letters. Most publishing houses provide their authors with a sheet of instructions on the house style.

Hype: Short for hyperbole, it literally means exaggerated copy not to be taken seriously. It has come to mean overpraising, and is part of the generation of interest in titles that appeal to the mass media.

Impression: All copies of a publication printed at one time without changing the printing plates. Several impressions may go into the making of a single edition. The first impression is the one most valued by collectors.

Imprint: The name of the publisher or the advertiser that appears on the title page of a book, or at the foot of an advertisement. One publishing house may have several imprints, e.g., Grafton is an imprint of HarperCollins, Puffin of Penguin.

Indent: 1. To leave space at the beginning of a line or paragraph; often used for subheadings and quotations. 2. To order on account; to 'indent for'.

In-house and out-of-house work: Jobs that are carried out using either the staff and resources within the firm or those of external companies or freelances.

In print: Currently available. Enquirers will often ask whether a particular title is still 'in print', although today this is much harder to establish as *print on demand* means titles can remain available while recording a very low rate of annual sale. This situation is being monitored for its fairness to authors (who might like their rights returned so they can self-publish).

Insert or loose insert: Paper or card inserted loose in a book, journal or brochure, not secured in any way.

Inspection copy: Copy of a particular title (usually a school text or other educational book) supplied for full examination by a teacher in the hope that a class set will be bought or the title will be recommended as essential on the course reading list. If the title is adopted and a certain number purchased, the recipient may usually keep the inspection copy. Books for which a multiple sale is unlikely are generally available 'on approval': after inspection they must be either returned or paid for.

ISBN: International standard book number: a system of providing each edition of a book with an individual identifying number. The appropriate ISBN should appear on any piece of information to do with the book: it is essential for bookshop and library ordering, stock control, despatch and more.

ISDN: International standard data number, use of a telephone line for the exchange of data between computers.

ISSN: International standard serial number, a similar system to ISBN for identifying serial publications. The number allocated refers to the serial in question for as long as it remains in publication. It should appear on the cover of any periodical and in any promotion material. Libraries catalogue and order titles by ISSN.

Jacket: A detachable dust-jacket on a book, usually made of paper, wrapped around the actual book cover. Generally used in the presentation of hardback books as both an added sophistication and to carry title information (blurb, author information, etc.).

Jacket rough: A design for a book jacket prepared for the approval of author, editor and marketing department.

Justified type: Type set so that both left- and right-hand margins are aligned vertically.

Lamination: A thin film available in matt or gloss applied to a printed surface, often used for book jackets, glossy brochures or the covers of catalogues which can expect a lot of use. Varnishing has a similar effect and is becoming less expensive; it adds less to the bulk than lamination, but is not as durable.

Landscape: A horizontal oblong format, i.e., wider than it is deep (as opposed to *portrait*).

Letterpress: A printing process whereby ink is transferred from raised metal type or plates directly on to paper. All newspapers used to be printed by this method.

Lift letter: In a direct marketing campaign, a lift letter is a (usually additional) letter designed to convince the market, often a testimonial from a satisfied user or someone whose opinion would impress the intended audience, e.g., senior management or a media personality.

Limp (or **C format**): A format midway between hardback and perfect bound paperback; the spine is usually sewn but encased in card covers rather than boards.

Line work: Illustrations such as drawings that consist of lines only rather than the graduated tones of photographs. The cheapest kind of illustration to reproduce.

List: All the publications a particular publisher has for sale. Also used for a group of new publications, e.g., Spring List.

Literary fiction: High end fiction; a variety of other interpretations from 'challenging to read' to 'not widely understood'.

Litho: Short for lithographic. A printing process that works on the principle of greasy ink sticking only to those parts of the wet plate that are to be printed. Most usually ink is transferred (offset) from a printing plate on to an intermediary surface ('blanket') and then on to the paper. How most marketing materials are printed.

Logo: Short for logotype. An identifying symbol or trademark.

Mark up: 1. To prepare a manuscript for the typesetter by adding the instructions needed such as type specification, width of setting, indentations, space between paragraphs and so on. 2. To increase the price of a particular title above that shown in the list price. Examples of use include when individual copies rather than class sets of school books are ordered (this is also called double pricing) or when selling expenses are likely to be high, perhaps with an export order.

Market share: The demand for a product as a percentage of the total demand of the market.

Maven (sometimes **mavin**): Someone with expertise in a specific field who is both trusted and keen to pass on their knowledge to others.

Measure: The width of text setting, usually measured in pica 'ems' (the m is chosen because it is the widest letter for setting).

Merchandise: Branded goods.

Merchandising: In a publishing context, this means persuading retail outlets and those who supply them to stock branded goods related to a key title, for example a stationery range that relates to a key children's title. Merchandising is a key function of the reps in bookshops, now that so much buying is done centrally.

Metadata: In a publishing context, the metadata consists of the specifics of a product or service, so for example the title, author(s), extent, formats, brief description, etc. These will be loaded on to industry and organisational databases to ensure the associated product can be found.

Monograph: A single-subject study by an author or group of authors, usually of a scholarly nature.

Negative option: A practice often used by book clubs whereby, unless a member responds to say a particular title is not required, it will be sent – e.g., the 'book of the month' is often a negative option. The process will have been part of the terms and conditions of membership.

Net: The final total. In the case of a price or sum to be paid, the net price means that no further discount or allowances are to be made; net profit is the surplus remaining after all costs, direct and indirect, have been deducted, as opposed to gross profit which is the total receipts, only allowing for the deduction of direct costs. For a mailer, asking for a list of net names means that several lists are run against each other to eliminate duplicates so the final mailing list, while containing names from several sources, will only include each individual once.

Net Book Agreement (NBA): In the UK, the NBA guaranteed resale price maintenance, so books could not be sold at less than the retail price set by the publishers. The legislation still exists, but was no longer defended by publishers after 1995.

Nix(ies): Addresses on a mailing list that are undeliverable by the carrier. If these amount to more than a certain percentage of the total list supplied, a reputable list owner or broker will provide a refund or credit.

Online: Connected to a telecommunications system. More and more publishers' products are available this way, with customers gaining access through a telecommunications link to the continuously updated publishing information database.

Open access (OA): Unrestricted access online to scholarly research that has been peer reviewed; originally for academic articles but increasingly book chapters and academic monographs too. There are two ways in which scholars can provide open access to their work: first by archiving their work in an open access repository (green OA) and, second, by publishing in an open access journal (gold OA). There is a third option of hybrid OA journals available on subscription but that provide gold OA to articles for which an OA publishing fee has been paid (either by the author, their institution or the organisation funding the research). Demand for OA has been fuelled by an appreciation of the lower dissemination costs of material made available via open access. Who funds the associated publishing costs of preparing material for dissemination (management of material received, peer review, checking, managing revisions, editorial preparation), costs that are often not evident to the reader unless absent, is a topic of extensive discussion among academics, librarians, university administrators, funding agencies, governments and publishers.

Open-ended questions: Those that don't encourage the responder to say 'yes' or 'no' but invite a more engaged answer.

Over-run: 1. Type matter that does not fit the design and must either be cut or the letter and word spacing reduced in size until it fits. 2. Extra copies printed, over and above the quantity ordered from the printer (see *overs*).

Overs: Short for over-run. The practice of printing a slightly larger quantity than ordered to make up for copies spoilt during either printing or binding. It is commercially acceptable for the printer to allow 5 per cent over or under the quantity ordered unless otherwise specified. You will be charged for the overs.

Ozalid: A contact paper proof made from the film and usually used as a last-minute check on positioning on more complex jobs. A final check before printing, unless a printed proof is requested.

Perfect binding: The most common binding for paperbacks. The different sections of the book are trimmed flush and the pages glued to the inside of the cover. This is more expensive than *saddle stitching* but cheaper than sewing.

PMT: Short for photo mechanical transfer. The production of a PMT is a two-stage process: the creation of a photosensitive negative that is then developed with a chemically sensitive carrier. The line image produced provides artwork.

Podcast: A series of electronic media files, such as audio or video, that is distributed over the internet by means of a web feed, for playback on portable media players and personal computers, at a time that suits the audience. Used to mean either the content or the method by which it is made available (although this is also referred to as podcasting).

Point of sale: Eye-catching promotional material to be displayed with the product where purchases are made. For example, publishers produce showcards, posters, bookmarks, balloons, single copy holders, dump-bins and counter packs for display by the till point.

Point system: A typographic standard measure based on the pica, e.g., 12 pt.

Portrait: An upright oblong format, i.e., taller than it is wide (see also *landscape*).

Pos: Abbreviation for positive – e.g., pos film – or point of sale.

Positioning: A marketing term for how you want your designated customer to feel about the product or service you are offering; the emotional relationship you want them to have with it.

Post: A contribution to a blog, most usually text but also possibly images or a podcast. A post generally invites response, whether mediated or non-mediated.

Print on demand: As printing technology becomes cheaper and specialist publishers increasingly target highly niche markets, it may be cost-effective to print only the number of copies you have actual orders for. This can work particularly well for a high-price product relevant to a very small market, for example, a market research report. Don't forget, however, that before any printing on demand can begin, the origination costs must be covered. It follows that this is not as cheap an alternative to conventional production as is often imagined. Unit costs for print on demand in general are higher than for litho printing – if you are producing at least 2,000 copies it's generally cheaper to select litho printing.

Print run: The number of copies ordered from a printer (see also *overs*).

Profile: How you describe yourself when signing up for a social networking site. The options are generally a photograph, basic information about yourself (usually subject to a tight word limit) and the URL of your website or blog. Information and photograph supply are optional but think carefully about how to present yourself in order to promote authenticity and trust.

Pro forma invoice: One that must be settled before goods are despatched, often used for export orders or where no account exists.

Progressive proofs: A set of printed proofs showing each colour individually and then in combination.

Promotions: This originally referred to mutually beneficial arrangements between non-competing organisations approaching the same target market (now often referred to as affinity marketing); today the term is used more generally, to refer to general pushing or promoting of titles to a wider prominence.

Proofreading: Reading typeset copy for errors. There is a standard series of proofreaders' marks that should be made both by the mistake and in the margin. When copy was keyed manually, typesetter mistakes were habitually noted in red, and the author's and publisher's in black or blue. Now that most typesetters work with author's electronic files, publishers usually request that the proofreader use one colour (red or blue) consistently.

Publication date: The date before which stock may not be sold, to ensure no one seller saturates the market before all have the same opportunity. Sometimes ignored to secure a competitive advantage (see also *release date*).

Reading copies: Copies of a forthcoming title distributed before publication date to key people in the trade (notably booksellers and wholesalers) to create enthusiasm and promote word-of-mouth. Done on the grounds that those who sell books are more likely to enthuse to customers about titles they have themselves read and enjoyed.

Recto: The right-hand page of a double-page spread (with an odd page number). The opposite of *verso*.

Register: Trim marks that appear on the artwork supplied to a printer should reappear on the plates made, and need to be matched up when printing to ensure the whole job will be in focus or register. If the plates have not been aligned according to the register marks or the marks were placed incorrectly the job is said to be 'out of register'.

Release date: Date on which stock is released from the publisher's warehouse for delivery to booksellers in anticipation of the *publication date*. Some booksellers complain release dates are far too early and they end up warehousing the books instead of the publisher. This can fuel the temptation to sell early.

Remainder: To sell off unsold stock at a cheaper price, often to 'remainder shops' such as discount bookstores.

Repro: Short for reproduction; the conversion of typeset copy and photographs into final film and printing plates.

Resale price maintenance: A process through which a manufacturer sets the product price and distributors agree not to sell above (a price floor) or below (a price ceiling) this price. This is the principle behind legislation that used to exist widely, but is no longer universally maintained, which encourages retailers to stock a wide range of merchandise on the grounds that they cannot be undercut on price. The retreat from observing resale price maintenance in some markets saw the widespread rise of discounting of books.

Response device: How the order or response comes back to the mailer, for example a link to the website to place an order, reply card or envelope.

Retouching: Adapting artwork or film to make corrections or alter tonal values.

Return on investment (ROI): The eventual profit received by a publisher on a project; based on a calculation of how much the publisher invested in the first place, and how much it subsequently got back, after the deduction of associated costs. The period over which ROI is calculated, and eventually deemed acceptable or unacceptable, will depend on the nature of the publishing project, its long-term significance to the house and the specific market being targeted.

Returns: Unsold stock of particular titles that may be returned to the publisher by the bookseller with prior agreement. Reps often use the authorisation of returns as a bargaining point in persuading booksellers to take new titles.

Retweet: A tweet that is passed on.

Reverse out: To produce text as white or a pale colour 'reversed out' of a darker background colour, as opposed to the more usual practice of printing in dark ink on a pale background. This technique can be very effective in small doses, but for lengthy passages of text it can be very hard to read. Never reverse text out of a photograph or illustration – it's impossible to read.

Review copy: You will hear this term used widely to mean 'free copy', and probably receive many calls and emails requesting one. In precise terms, a review copy is a title sent to a potential reviewer (or review editor) in the hope of their featuring it in the media. Early copies released this way end up for sale in second-hand bookshops and through online bookselling mechanisms, often before publication, and this practice is an ongoing source of tension between publishers and the media.

Review slip: The enclosure in a book when it is sent out for review by a publisher. It should include details of title, author, ISBN, price and publication date, as well as a request for a copy of any review that appears.

Rights: The legal entitlement to publish a particular work. Permission is given by the copyright holder (usually the author or editor) to reproduce the work in one particular format. Subsidiary rights for other formats e.g., paperback, online, film, merchandising deals and so on, are then sold by either the firm's rights manager or the author's agent. The major occasion for selling rights is the annual Frankfurt Book Fair, but much is also now done online.

Roman: Upright type (not bold), as opposed to italic.

Royalty: The percentage of list price or net receipt paid on each copy sold to the copyright holder, usually the author. There are national variations in the period over which royalties must be paid. In the United Kingdom, royalties are paid to the author's estate for 70 years after his or her death; the manuscript is then deemed to be out of copyright and may be reproduced by anyone without paying royalties.

RRP: Short for recommended retail price. Usually set by the manufacturer, this is the basis for calculating the discount given to the retailer. The actual selling price is decided by the retailer, who may choose to lower prices and take a reduced profit margin in the hope of selling a greater quantity.

Run of paper: Refers to the position of an advertisement that will appear in a particular journal or paper wherever there is room, at the editor's or designer's discretion. This is usually cheaper than specifying a particular (or preferred) position.

Run-on costs: In the context of getting material printed, the run-on costs are the costs of producing additional materials while a press is producing a particular job. They are often much less per thousand than the set-up costs might imply. Ask about run-on costs for an additional thousand or two when requesting a basic printing price.

Saddle stitching: A method of binding pamphlets or small books (48–64 pages is probably the limit for saddle stitching successfully). Wire staples or thread are used to stitch along the line of the fold. Also called wire-stitching.

Sale or return: Retailers or wholesalers take titles 'on sale or return' on the understanding that if they have not been sold after a specified period (usually six to twelve the months after ordering), and provided the titles are still in print, they may be returned for a credit. This leaves the long-term financial risk with the publisher but the process was established in order to promote wide stocking. The opposite of *firm sale*.

School supplier (also called **educational contractor**): A firm that seeks to supply both schools and local education authorities with books and other educational products.

Screen: 1. The process used to convert continuous tone photographs into patterns of dots, in order to reproduce the effect of the original when printed (see also *half-tone*). A coarse screen is used in the preparation of illustrations for newsprint and other less demanding jobs. 2. Short for silk-screen printing.

Search engine marketing (SEM): An attempt to raise the profile of your website online by using *search engine optimisation*, paid-for word placements and accepting links from other sites. In the process it is possible to improve your position on search engine results pages (SERPS).

Search engine optimisation (SEO): The process of trying to affect the visibility of a website or web page through editing its content and HTML coding to increase its relevance to specific keywords. This promotes more effective indexing by search engines and hence a higher ranking.

See safe: Bookstores or wholesalers usually take books on a 'see safe' basis. They are invoiced immediately for the total taken; those they do not sell may be returned for a credit or exchange. While the immediate financial outlay is thus with the shop, they are protected by the practice of *sale or return*.

Self-mailer: A direct mail piece without an envelope or outer wrapping. Often used to refer to all-in-one leaflets, which combine sales message and response device. Space for copy is limited so this format works best when the recipient already knows of the product being advertised.

Serif, sans serif: A serif typeface has 'handles' on the letters, like the typeface used in this book; a sans serif face does not.

Show-rooming: The practice of looking in local shops and then buying online. Reverse show-rooming is the opposite, looking online and then buying in person.

Showthrough: How much ink on one side of a printed sheet of paper can be seen through on the other side.

Social bookmarking: Saving a website address or material on a social net-working site. If #links are added, you allow other people to see what you have bookmarked as well.

Social media: Permission-based communication online that allows people to build, share and exchange information with each other. There are a variety of different media for getting involved including blogs, social networks and podcasts.

Social media marketing: Using social media networks to create or support business relationships.

Social networking: Involvement on sites where people can present a profile and network with others, e.g., Twitter, Facebook and LinkedIn.

Spam: Unsolicited or unwanted electronic advertising messages sent in bulk and received by individuals as emails.

Specs: 1. Short for type specifications. Designers may refer to 'doing the spec' by which they mean laying down the parameters of text design, choosing a typeface and size. 2. The specifications for printing a job are all the production details (format, extent, illustrations, print run, etc.) sent to printers for a quote.

Split infinitive: 'Splitting the infinitive' means dividing the two words that make up the infinitive in English (e.g., to love). So you would always write 'to love passionately' not 'to passionately love' – which splits the infinitive. The principle is based on the nineteenth-century British educationalists' obsession with Greek and Latin. So, because in those languages, and incidentally in all modern European languages, the infinitive is never separated, because it is one word (*amare, aimer, lieben* mean 'to love' in Latin, French and German), we should never do this in English either. It's pedantic and nonsense, but still something of an obsession for the English. The Americans seem to care less – one of the most famous split infinitives is the opening of *Star Trek*, which announces the mission of the *Starship Enterprise* 'to boldly go'.

STM: Scientific, Technical and Medical.

Subscribe: To secure orders from bookshops and wholesalers before publication date, either by phone or through a rep visiting. The results are recorded by the publishing house as *dues*.

Tag line (or **strap line**): A line of copy that sums up the product or the general philosophy of the company. Often displayed on the front cover of books. Examples from films work well – e.g., 'In space no one can hear you scream.'

Telemarketing, teleselling: Using the telephone to sell. While it is often thought of as the making of calls to promote products, effective telemarketing means considering the way incoming calls are handled as well as the way outgoing calls are made.

Terms: The discount and credit conditions on which a publisher supplies stock to a bookseller or wholesaler. Terms will vary according to the amount of stock taken, the status under which it is accepted, what the competition are doing and how much customers want the book (see also *see safe, firm sale* and *sale or return*).

TESL: Teaching English as a Second Language (US term).

Tint: A pattern of dots that when printed reproduces as a tone. Using tints is a good way to get value from your printing inks. For example, even if you have only one printing colour, try putting the text in solid, and using a 10 per cent tint of the same colour to fill in and highlight certain boxes around copy. Further variations can be achieved if you are using more printed colours.

TOEFL: The qualification in English language to get into an American university or professional institution.

Trade discount: The discount given by publishers to booksellers and wholesalers on the price at which they will subsequently sell. The amount of discount given usually varies according to the amount of stock taken or the amount of promotion promised. 'Short discounts' are low-scale discounts on products that are either very expensive (often those that are extensively promoted by the publisher directly to the end user) or those that are sold in sets (e.g., school textbooks).

Trim: Short for 'trimmed size' of a printed piece of paper, i.e., its final or guillotined size.

Trolling: Harassing online, generally by posting unpleasant, provoking and unsigned messages (or signed by a pseudonym) described as 'pure vandalism' by Dennis Coday, editor of the *National Catholic Register*, and the activity of 'psychologically disturbed people' (Robert Fisk). Irish columnist Breda O'Brien commented that, while she had to adhere to strict guidelines in her work as a print journalist, it was 'bizarre' that 'people can comment on my articles with impunity and say anything they like about me or about others. The sheer level of nastiness is difficult to describe.'[1]

Turnover: The total of invoice value over a specified period for a particular organisation's sales.

Type area: The area of the final page size that will be occupied by type and illustrations, allowing for the blank border that will normally surround text.

Typeface: The style of type, e.g., Garamond, Helvetica.

Typescript: The hard copy (usually a printout) of the manuscript or copy to be reproduced and printed.

Typo: Short for typographical error.

Unjustified type: Lines of type set so that the right-hand margin does not align vertically and thus appears ragged. This can also be described as 'ranged left' or 'ragged right'.

Upper and lower case: Upper case characters are CAPITALS, as opposed to lower case.

URL: Unique resource locator, the precise term for a web address.

User-generated content: Material that is contributed to a website by those using it, e.g., Wikipedia. The term is also used for content added to organisational resources by those using them, e.g., examples of how the processes used have worked within the organisation in question for the benefit of colleagues. User-generated content is most often text but can also be pictures or podcasts.

Verso: The left-hand side of a double-page spread (even page numbers). The opposite of *recto.*

Viral marketing, viral advertising: Marketing techniques that use social networks that already exist to produce an increase in awareness. Because they use pre-existing (and usually online) social networks, and encourage the spread of word-of-mouth as a personal communication, they can be a very useful and effective means of reaching a large number of people quickly.

Visual: A mock-up or rough layout. A layout of planned printed work showing the position of all the key elements: headlines, illustrations, bullet points, body copy and so on. Blank 'dummy' books are often created before finished copies are available for promotional photographs.

Website: A collection of related web pages, videos and other digital assets hosted on a particular domain or subdomain on the world wide web. See Chapter 9.

Weight of paper: Paper is sold in varying weights defined in gsm or g/m^2: grams per square metre. Printers can offer you samples of various papers in different weights.

WhatsApp: A mobile-messaging app, available on a variety of networks, which lets you send and receive messages without having to pay for SMS.

Wholesaler: An organisation that purchases resources in bulk (and usually stores them) in order to supply retail outlets quickly and efficiently, often securing higher than usual discounts in return for the large quantities taken. The national bookshop chains, and outlets with large designated markets (e.g., library suppliers and school suppliers) will similarly demand substantial discounts from the publisher for large quantities of stock taken.

Wiki: A website that can be added to, e.g., Wikipedia.

Note

1 www.independent.co.uk/voices/comment/robert-fisk-our-addiction-to-the-internet-is-as-harmful-as-any-drug–and-what-passes-for-comment-these-days-is-often-simply-foul-abuse-9433535.html.

Appendix

2 Park Square
Milton Park
Abingdon
Oxon
OX14 4RN

**MARKETING QUESTIONNAIRE
FOR AUTHORS AND EDITORS**

This questionnaire provides essential information for people in our editorial, marketing, production, sales and foreign rights departments in the UK and the US. Please take the time to complete it as comprehensively and accurately as possible and remember that the marketing process for a book begins before the manuscript is delivered.

We realise this questionnaire is long, however it is crucial. You are our primary source of information about market and readership. In formation in this questionnaire is used to:

- Provide basic marketing information for promotional material including back cover blurb, catalogues, leaflets and flyers.
- Update our marketing database which feeds directly to our website, other web-based booksellers and the main bibliographic services that provide information to the book trade.
- Brief sales representatives who in turn will present your book to booksellers.
- Brief our colleagues in the US office who will market your book in North America.

PLEASE COMPLETE, SIGN AND RETURN THIS QUESTIONNAIRE AS SOON AS POSSIBLE.
WHERE POSSIBLE PLEASE COMPLETE AND SUBMIT THE FORM ELECTRONICALLY.

THE BOOK

Title (as it should appear on the book)

Subtitle

Author/Editor Name(s) (as you would like it to appear on the book).

Series (if applicable)

Series editor(s)

Contributors
If applicable, please attach a list of contributors including name, title of chapter, address, telephone number and email address.

Signed: Date:

Please attach the following:
   Academic CV
   Contents list for your book.

Indicate if you have attached any of the following additional material:
   Contributor List
   Book reviews/print media articles/interviews (see question 11)
   Cover artwork suggestions

PERSONAL (NB if there is more than one author/editor please copy this page and fill out one copy each)

1. **Full Name** (please include your title e.g. Professor, Dr, Mr, Ms)

2. **Nationality**

3. **Date of birth** (day/month/year)

4. **Contact details**

> **Work address**
> Tel.
> Fax
> Email
> Homepage

> **Private address** (if we may contact you at home)
> Tel.
> Fax
> Email

5. **Absence**
Will you be away from your usual address for any length of time between now and the eventual publication of the book (approx. 8 months after delivery)?

6. **Biography**
Please write a brief biographical note (max. 45 words) including current affiliation, research interests and your most important or relevant publications. We will adapt this for the back cover blurb.

7. **Career**
Please attach a copy of an up-to-date academic CV.

8. **Previous Publications**
On your CV please asterisk those books which are most relevant to the new book and indicate price, publisher and binding (paperback or hardback).

9. **Special information**
Please detail any special qualifications, awards, expertise not already mentioned on your CV.

10. **Foreign editions**
Please list the title, date and publisher of any foreign-language editions of your previous publications.

11. **Media**
Please list relevant interviews, reports or articles that have appeared in print and/or broadcast media.

THE BOOK

12.   **List of Contents**

Please attach your latest list of contents and indicate if it is final. (Even if it is not final it is useful to have an idea.)

13.   **Key sentence**

Please explain your book in one, short sentence.

14.   **Description**

Please describe your book in 200 words, explaining the main theoretical, methodological and/or practical contents of the work. We will write the back cover blurb using this description so:

- try to avoid jargon
- remember non-specialist readers (i.e. a bookseller or librarian)
- think about the geographical and temporal range of the work
- highlight any well-known or topical case studies
- emphasise any groundbreaking content.

15.   **Copyright Permission**

Permission needs to be sought for any text or illustrative material which has been published before. **We cannot proceed with production until all permission have been sought and granted.** Please list below any part or parts of your book that have been published before. (This includes any extracts of prose more than 400 words long, as well as poetry and illustrations.) Read Chapter 6 of your *Instructions for Authors* booklet if you need help with this and if in doubt please speak to your editor.

16.   **Cover**

If your book is a paperback, please give details of any images or ideas you would like the designer to consider for its cover. While we cannot promise to use these ideas, it is extremely useful to know about them. Please attach any images you would like us to consider.

17.   **Index**

Please tick your preferred option:

a) You will prepare the index

b) Routledge will commission a professional indexer and the cost will be offset against your future royalty earnings.

c) Other arrangements have been made in agreement with the editor. Please give details.

MARKETING AND SALES

This section is vitally important in ensuring our marketing is accurate and reaches the right audience. Please take your time to complete it to the best of your knowledge.

17.   **Sales points**
Please list four or five key features of your book which you would like us to stress in our promotion. Remember that some of these points need to be non-specialist. Points to bear in mind.
- Avoid jargon and expressions e.g. unique, groundbreaking, stellar, accessible, cutting edge
- Include information which isn't obvious from the book description
- Mention if a book is especially topical or is likely to appeal in particular geographical areas.
- Remember that artwork and contributors could be important selling points.

i)
ii)
iii)
iv)
v)

18.   **Subject areas**
In which three subject areas would you expect a bookshop or library to categorise your book (most relevant first)?

i)
ii)
iii)

Are there any related subject areas we should be aware of?

19.   **Level** (N.B. It is important to be realistic)

a) Please underline **one** description which most reflects how your book will be used on a course.

Essential stundent purchase
        Is it a textbook?(e.g. includes study and teaching aids, glossary, study skills, chapter summaries)
Recommended/supplementary reading
Research monograph
Professional handbook
Other (please specify)

b) Please underline all academic levels at which your book would be used

A-level/ age 16-18
Undergraduate/First Degree
Postgraduate/Second Degree
Postdoctoral research/Further research

c) If your book is an essential purchase please indicate what courses/modules it is likely to be used on, including details of areas or countries where these are taught (e.g. UK, US, Australia, Scandinavia)

d) If your book is a professional handbook, which professionals is it aimed at?

20. **Overseas**
List any areas of the world outside the UK and US where your book has particular relevance.

What foreign editions would be particularly successful and why?

21. **Competing Titles**
Please give full bibliographic details of three or four books that compete with your own. For each book write two or three points about its strengths and weaknesses and how it differs from your new book. If there are none that compete directly, please still give an indication of books that compete in part.

Title:	
Author:	Publisher
Date	Price

Comments:

Title:	
Author:	Publisher
Date	Price

Comments:

Title:	
Author:	Publisher
Date	Price

Comments:

Title:	
Author:	Publisher
Date	Price

Comments:

22.   **Reviews**
Please give full contact details for any journals that are likely to review your book. It is helpful if you split these up into the following geographical areas - UK, US/Canada and elsewhere. If you have a particular contact, please give their name and job title. **N.B. We have a limited number of review copies to send out. Please provide the full postal address for each journal and asterisk essential journals.**

UK

US/Canada

Elsewhere

23.   **Desk copies**
If your book is in paperback we will send copies of your book to lecturers, academics etc in case they would like to recommend it to students and colleagues or review it Please list names, affiliations and full addresses for anyone you think would be interested in order of preference. **Again we have a limited number of books (<u>max 10 copies</u>) to send out.**

UK

US/Canada

Elsewhere

24.   **Associations**
Do you belong to any relevant associations or societies? Please provide address and website details.

25.   **Conferences** (NB Routledge has its books represented at all relevant major conferences.)
Please provide full details of any smaller conferences at which it would be important to represent your book and asterisk any you will be attending. It is not possible for a Routledge representative to be present at every conference but we may be able to send fliers and/or a copy of the book.

26.   **Publicity**
Does your book have media or news value? If so, what, and how do you think it could be exploited?

27.   **E-marketing**
Please list any websites, listservs or e-mail groups we could use in virtual aspects of marketing

Many of our subject areas now have on-line Resource Centres (visit www.Routledge.com) which advertise our books in that area and provide links to useful websites. Have you, or your department, got a site with which we could establish a two-way link? If so, please let us know the URL and a contact in your department.

Bibliography

A&C Black (ongoing annual) *The Writers' & Artists' Yearbook*, London: Bloomsbury.

Anderson, C. (2009) *The Long Tail*, London: Random House Business.

——(2010) *Free: How Today's Smartest Businesses Profit by Giving Something for Nothing*, London: Random House.

——(2012) *Makers: The New Industrial Revolution*, London: Random House.

Athill, D. (2011) *Stet*, 2nd edition, London: Granta.

Baines, P. (2005) *Penguin by Design: A Cover Story*, London: Allen Lane.

Baverstock, A. (1993) *Are Books Different?* London: Kogan Page.

——(2006) *Is There a Book in You?* London: Bloomsbury.

——(2012) *The Naked Author*, London: Bloomsbury.

Baverstock, A., Bowen, S. and Carey, S. (2009) *How to Get a Job in Publishing*, London: A&C Black.

Bhaskar, M. (2013) *The Content Machine: Towards a Theory of Publishing from the Printing Press to the Digital Network*, London: Anthem.

Birkerts, S. (2006) *The Gutenberg Elegies: The Fate of Reading in an Electronic Age*, London: Faber.

Blake, C. (2007) *From Pitch to Publication*, 2nd edition, London: Macmillan.

Bolton, G. (2010) *Reflective Practice: Writing and Professional Development*, London: Sage.

Bullock, A. (2012) *Book Production*, London: Routledge.

Butcher, J. (1992) *Copy-editing: The Cambridge Handbook for Editors, Authors and Publishers*, Cambridge: Cambridge University Press.

Clark, G. and Phillips, A. (2014) *Inside Book Publishing*, 5th edition, London: Routledge.

Coker, M. (2011) *Smashwords Book Marketing Guide: How to Market Any Book for Free*, Los Gatos, California: Smashwords Guides.

Collins, J. (2010) *Bring on the Books for Everybody: How Literary Culture Became Popular Culture*, Durham, NC: Duke University Press.

Cottrell, S. (2011) *Critical Thinking Skills: Developing Effective Analysis and Argument*, 2nd edition, Basingstoke: Palgrave Macmillan.

Crompton, A. (1987) *The Craft of Copywriting*, 2nd edition, London: Random House Business Books.

Darnton, R. (2009) *The Case for Books: Past, Present and Future*, London: Public Affairs.

Davies, G. (2004) *Book Commissioning and Acquisition*, 2nd edition, London: Routledge.

Davies, G. and Balkwill, R. (2011) *The Professionals' Guide to Publishing: A Practical Introduction to Working in the Publishing Industry*, London: Kogan Page.

Elliot, S. and Rose, J. (2009) *A Companion to the History of the Book*, Oxford: Wiley-Blackwell.

Ellis, M. (2011) *Managing and Growing a Cultural Heritage Web Presence: A Strategic Guide*, London: Facet Publishing.

Falla, J. (2011) *The Craft of Fiction*, Abergele: Aber.

Fanthome, C. (2005) *Work Placements: A Survival Guide for Students*, London: Palgrave Macmillan.

Feather, J. (2005) *A Short History of British Publishing*, 2nd edition, London: Routledge.

Fisk, P. (2006) *Marketing Genius*, London: Capstone Publishing.

Forsyth, P. (1997) *Marketing in Publishing*, London: Routledge.

Fried, J. and Heinemeier Hansson, D. (2010) *Rework: Change the Way You Work Forever*, London: Vermilion.

Garfield, S. (2010) *Just My Type: A Book About Typefaces*, London: Profile Books.

Gladwell, M. (2009) *Outliers: The Story of Success*, London: Penguin.

Godin, S. (2008) *Tribes*, London: Piatkus.

——(2011) *Poke the Box*, Amazon: Create Space.

Gombrich, E. (1995) *The Story of Art*, London: Phaidon Press.

Gomez, J. (2007) *Print is Dead: Books in Our Digital Age*, London: Macmillan.

Guthrie, R. (2011) *Publishing: Principles and Practice*, London: Sage.

Hall, F. (2013) *The Business of Digital Publishing*, London: Routledge.

Hill, A. (1988) *In Pursuit of Publishing*, London: Heinemann.

Howard, C.R. (2014) *Self-printed*, 3rd edition, Amazon: Create Space.

Jack, B. (2012) *The Woman Reader*, London: Yale.

Jenkins, H. (2008) *Convergence Culture: Where Old and New Media Collide*, New York: New York University Press.

Jones, H. and Benson, C. (2014) *Publishing Law*, 4th edition, London: Routledge.

Kawasaki, G. (2011) *The Art of the Start*, London: Viking.

——(2011) *Enchantment: The Art of Changing Hearts, Minds and Actions. How to Woo, Influence and Persuade*, London: Viking.

Kent, P. (2008) *Search Engine Optimization for Dummies*, 3rd edition, London: Wiley.

King, S. (2000) *On Writing*, London: Hodder & Stoughton.

Klanten, R. (2008) *Fully Booked: Cover Art and Design for Books*, Berlin: Gestalten.

Klein, N. (2000) *No Logo*, London: Fourth Estate.

Kotler, P., Armstrong, G., Harris, L. and Piercy, N.F. (2013) *The Principles of Marketing*, London: Pearson.

Leadbetter, C. (2008) *We – Think: Mass Innovation, Not Mass Production*, London: Profile Books.

Lewis, J. (2006) *Penguin Special: The Life and Times of Allen Lane*, London: Penguin.

Longson, S. (1999) *Making Work Experience Count: How to Get the Right Work Experience and Improve Your Career Prospects*, London: How to Books Ltd.

Lovell, N. (2013) *The Curve: From Freeloaders into Superfans: The Future of Business*, London: Penguin.

Lyons, M. (2011) *Books: A Living History*, London: Thames & Hudson.

Maher, T. (1994) *Against My Better Judgement*, London: Sinclair-Stevenson.

Malhotra, N.K. and Birks, D.F. (2007a) *Marketing Research*, 3rd edition, London: Routledge.

——(2007b) *Marketing Research: An Applied Approach*. London: Prentice Hall/Financial Times

Mantel, H. (2009) *Wolf Hall*, London: Fourth Estate.

Matthews, N. (2007) *Judging a Book by its Cover: Fans, Publishers, Designers and the Marketing of Fiction*, Aldershot: Ashgate.

McLuhon, M. (1964) *Understanding Media: The Extensions of Man.* Toronto: McGraw Hill Book Company Inc.

Meerman Scott, D. (2011) *The New Rules of Marketing and PR*, 3rd edition, London: Wiley.

Moor, L. (2007) *The Rise of Brands*, London: Berg.

Morgan, N. (2011) *Write to be Published*, London: Snowbooks.

Naughton, J. (2012) *From Gutenberg to Zuckerberg: What You Really Need to Know about the Internet*, London: Quercus.

New Hart's Rules: The Handbook of Style for Writers and Editors (2005) Oxford: Oxford University Press.

Ogilvy, D. (1983) *Ogilvy on Advertising*, London: Pan Books Ltd.

Osterwalder, A. and Pigneur, Y. (2010) *Business Model Generation*, New Jersey: Wiley.

Owen, L. (2010) *Selling Rights*, 6th edition, London: Routledge.

——(2013) *Clark's Publishing Agreements*, 9th edition, London: Butterworths.

Penn, J. (2013) *How to Market a Book*, Amazon: Create Space.

Phillips, A. (2014) *Turning the Page*. London: Routledge.

Porter, M.E. (1998) *The Competitive Advantage of Nations*, 2nd edition, New York: Palgrave Macmillan.

Reed, J. (2013) *Get Up to Speed with Online Marketing*, 2nd edition, London: Prentice Hall.

Ries, E. (2011) *The Lean Start-up: How Constant Innovation Creates Radically Successful Businesses*, London: Penguin.

Ritter, R.M., Stevenson, A. and Brown, L. (eds) (2005) *The New Oxford Guide for Writers and Editors*, Oxford: Oxford University Press.

Rose, F. (2011) *The Art of Immersion: How the Digital Generation is Remaking Hollywood, Madison Avenue, and the Way We Tell Stories. Entertainment in a Connected World*, New York: Norton.

Shirky, C. (2008) *Cognitive Surplus: Creativity and Generosity in a Connected Age*, London: Penguin.

——(2009) *Here Comes Everybody: How Change Happens When People Come Together*, London: Penguin.

Smith, J. (2008) *Get into Bed with Google: Top Ranking Search Optimization Techniques*, Oxford: Infinite Ideas.

Solomon, M.R., Bamossy, G., Askegaard, S. and Hogg, M.K. (2013) *Consumer Behaviour: A European Perspective*, Harlow: Pearson.

Squires, C. (2007) *Marketing Literature: The Making of Contemporary Writing in Britain*, London: Palgrave.

Stevenson, I. (2010) *Book Makers: British Publishing in the Twentieth Century*, London: British Library.

Stewart, D. and Simmons, M. (2010) *The Business Playground: Where Creativity and Commerce Collide*, Harlow: Prentice Hall.

Stokes D. and Lomax, W. (2008) *Marketing: A Brief Introduction*, London: Thompson.

Striphas, E. (2011) *The Late Age of Print: Everyday Book Culture from Consumerism to Control*, Columbia: Columbia University Press.

Stutely, R. (2006) *The Definitive Business Plan*, 2nd edition, Harlow: Prentice Hall.

Thompson, J.B. (2012) *Merchants of Culture: The Publishing Business in the Twenty-first Century*, Cambridge: Polity Press.

Vaynerchuck, G. (2009) *Crush it! Why Now is the Time to Cash in on Your Passion*, London: Harper Business.

Weinberger, D. (2007) *Everything is Miscellaneous: The Power of the New Digital Disorder*, New York: Henry Holt and Company Inc.

Woll, T. (2010) *Publishing for Profit: Successful Bottom-line Management for Book Publishers*, 4th edition, Chicago: Chicago Review Press.

Young, D. (2012) *Sell Your Books!* Bristol: Silverwood.

Index

Note: tables are indicated by locators in bold and figures are indicated by locators in italics.

Able, Vanessa 281
academic librarians 392–6
academic titles 65, 72, 340; promotion of 389–91; publishing costs **70**
academics: inspection copies 389, 390, 391; promotion of textbooks to 385–9; research 388, 392; role of 388; textbooks, change of 389–90
accountants 422
acronyms 320–4
advance information sheets (AIs) 19, 81, 96–8, 429
advance notices (ANs) 96–9, 125, 429
advance title information (ATI) 125
advertising 4, 109, 111–12, 125; above/below the line 429; classified 111; colours 354; direct response 353, 435; discount 77; educational press 408–9; 'free advertising' 257; internet 109; magazines/newspapers 344, 353; radio 112; semi-display ads 111; space/layout 353; 'spot colour' 354; television/cinema 112; typeface 353; *see also* advertorials; events; exhibitions; free publicity; marketing materials; promotional parties
advertorials 111, 429
affinity marketing 429
AID(C)A (attract, interest, desire, conviction, action) 320–1
airport bookshops 6, 122, 248
Amazon 70, 71, 156; Goodreads and 250–1
Anderson, Chris 84
answers 429

antiquarian books 164–5
Apple: App Store 86, 244; iPad 85, 87; marketing principles 5
approval staircase 174, 205n3, 430
apps 25, 244, 430; children's 85, 370–1; *see also* Touch Press; WhatsApp
Arnold, Sue 83
arrears (dues) 435
artwork 430
Ashman, Peter 32–4
audiobooks 26–7, 81–4, 418
authors 430; academic 43, 95; bookshops and 153; branding 17, 30; case studies 250–3, 289–92; children's books 373–4; earnings 287; ego 284–5; feedback 288; fees 269, 282n8, 289, 290; free publicity 77; information about 40, 102, 274–5, 337; interviews 250–3, 269, 273–6; launching 67; literary festivals 309–11; market research and 45, 46, 68; marketing 4, 30, 38, 40–1, 117, 168, 283, 288; marketing department and 284; media coverage 257–8; meeting 373–4; online involvement 248–9; pseudonyms 291; public lending right 383–4; publicity/publicity forms 76, 95, 116, 287; publishers and 283–4, 293–4; royalties 70, 90n2, 444; self-publishing 45, 68, 71, 283–4, 288; signing sessions 68, 310–11; social isolation 285; social media 250–1; tours 258, 305, 377; websites 288; working with 287–8
Ayrton, Pete 56

B2B (business-to-business) 181, 259, 430

B2C (business-to-consumer) 220, 221, 431

B2G (business-to-government) 431

backlist 104, 122, 132, 158, 431; children's books 372, 374; Grub Street 166, 168; promotions 64, 73, 173; self-publishing 71

Baker, Michael J. xix–xxi

barcode 431

Bartle, Bogle and Hegarty 323

Bartlett, Michael 81–4

benefits 120, 321–2, 329, 431

Berry, Kit 289–92

Betty's Reading Room, Orkney 384–5

binding 66, 441; saddle stitching 444

Bitly 212, 232, 243

blad 431

Blake, Alison 174, 177, 184

Blake, John *266*

blawgs 425, 431

bleed 431

bloggers 20, 167–8, 226–8

blogosphere 377, 431

blogs 249, 250, 253, 431; blawgs 425, 431; *Game of Thrones* and 246, 247; online marketing 224–6; professional market 425; templates 224, 225; writing 225, 248

Bloomsbury: Book Club 314; Institute 313–15; Publishing 313–15, 362

blurb 39, 40, 96, 101, 102, 431; disentangling long/difficult 337–40

BMJ 32–4

Boden 335

body copy 265, 324, 343, 353, 431

book clubs 32, 123; Bloomsbury 314; discounts 70; editions for 28; negative option 440; Richard and Judy 260, 281n3; school 372

book fairs 26, 116, 156, 158, 159, 315; international 378, 444; school 372, 374

book launches *see* promotional parties

Book People, The 371

book publishing courses: Kingston University 43, *226*; textbooks xx 134; *see also Inside Book Publishing* (Clark and Phillips); Ooligan Press

BookMachine 128, *217*, 220–1

books 23–4; antiquarian 164–5; book club editions 28; 'crossover titles' 370; English language titles 6;

facsimile 164–5; hardback 24–5; limited editions 24; own-brand editions 28, 371; paperback 25; print-on-demand 6; remainder sales 28–9; reviews 257; self-published 6–7; special sales 28; 'universal format' 23–4; *see also* academic titles; children's books; ebooks; format; inspection copies

Bookseller, The 267–8

bookshops 7–8, 45; academic textbooks 389; airport 6, 122, 248; children's books 372; closures 372; independent 90n2, 153; seasonal promotions 72; selling to 153; visiting 11

Boorman, Elaine 198–202

Borders 222

Borough Press 255

bottom line 431

bounce rate 432

Bowker 7, 125

Brandguild 367–8

brands 16–17, 432; branded items 109, 372; licensing 370; management 209, 291; organisational 365–9; partnerships 371; public perception 45; publishers as 29–30; rebranding 366–9; social media and 209, 212, 221

break-even 432

Brewster, Beth 261, 262, 263

British Medical Association (BMA) 32

British Medical Journal, The 32, 33

bromide 432

budget 432; *see also* marketing budget

bullet point 432

bundling 66, 71, 396

business markets 65; information resources 65, 66; *see also* professional markets

buyer 432

call to action 216, 218, 240, 241, 432

Calliope Gifts 222–4

Cambridge Dictionaries Online 245

Cambridge English Teacher 244

Cambridge University Press 243–5

camera-ready copy (crc) 432, 434

card deck 432

cased edition 432

catalogues 39, 42, 75, 103–6, 125; academic 106, *107*; covers 105; illustrations 106; last minute entries 106; layout 105; major titles 104;

ordering mechanisms 104–5; schools and 403–5
CD ROM 432
Central Books 19
centred type 433
Chang, Jung 309
character 433
character licensing 370, 373
Châtel (France): book set 89–90; sales proposition, creating 89–90
Cheshire labels 433
Chesterton, G.K. 327
children: apps for 85, 370–1; education 397–8; library usage 379; literacy 31; market research and 57; meeting authors 373–4; social media and 376–7; *see also* children's books; Reading Force; schools
children's books: backlist promotion 374; book fairs 378; branded items 371, 372; co-edition deals 378; digital products 369, 370; educational 373; exporting 378; free publicity 376–8; long tail backlist 374; marketing 369, 376–8; marketing difficulties 374–6; new formats 370–1; nostalgia market 334, 372, 374; packaging 372; price-sensitivity 375; publishing opportunities 370–4; school books 372; selling locations 371–2; vocabulary 374–5; websites and 373, 376
Children's Education Advisory Service (CEAS) *203*
Christmas market 72, 83, 152, 223, 300, 373, 375
Clark, Giles and Phillips, Angus 132–42
Cleave, Chris 250–3
closed market 433
coated paper 433
Coday, Dennis 447
Coker, Mark 86
Collins, Suzanne 370
colour separations 433
commissioning meeting 95
competitive advantage 433
competitive differentials 433
CompletelyNovel 239–41
conferences 378, 406–7; medical 416, 417; press 305; *see also* sales conferences
content media *see* blogs; email; websites
controlled circulation 433
cookies 219, 433

cooperative mailing 433
COPAC 394, 428n19
COPE (coherence, objectives, planning, execution) 214–15
Cope, Wendy 103
copy 128–9, 316–17, 343–4, 433; acronyms 320–4; basic principles 318–20; benefits/selling points 329; blurbs, disentangling 337–40; direct marketing and 177–83; editing 328–9; endorsements 331–2; grammar 319; guarantees 335; headlines 335–7; humour 333; ideas 334–5; illustrations 330; language 324–7, 333–4; learning about 320; negative, using/avoiding 332–3; patronising the reader 332; personalising 328; presenting/defending 340–1; quotations 330; repetition 333; rules 317–18; sentence length 324, 327; space/visual variety 329–30; storytelling 327–8; testimonials 330–1; titles, not understanding 337; writing techniques 316–41
copyright 64, 82, 123, 394; *see also* licences; rights
Costa Book Awards 102, 250
CPD (continuing professional development) 29, 418, 419–20
Creative Commons 433
Crimson Cats 81–4
cromalin proofs *see* digital proofs
Crompton, Alastair 336
'crossover titles' 370
Crow, Justine 325–6
crowd-sourcing 80, 214, 434
Curtis-Kogakovic, Susan 18–20
customer lifetime value 62, 190, 434
customer relationship management (CRM) 18, 171
customer services 115, 130, 132, 244, 294, 295, 355; online forms and 185
customers 7–8, 9; building relationships with 148–50; buying behaviour 146–8; feedback 45, 85–6, 87, 104, 193, 207, 218, 295; product price 10–11; professional buyers 146; *see also* Nielsen Book Services; specific interest markets; students; teachers
cut-out 102, 159, 186, 434

Daly, Claire 314
dashboard 434

database marketing 174, 181, 185, 434;
  see also Reading Force
database publishing 434
databases 125
Daunt Books 19
Davies, John 165
de Botton, Alain 276
dentists/dental care professionals
  419–20
design 342–3; good design 343;
  promotional text 343–4; *see also*
  designers; jackets; marketing materials
designers 344–6; amendments 349–50;
  appreciation of 351; briefing 346–7;
  budget 348; completion date 349;
  correction bills 351; house style 348;
  illustrations 349; information needed
  by 347–9; job progression 350–1;
  managing without 352–4;
  proofreading 350–1; viewpoint
  349–50; working with 347–9
desktop publishing 434
Devani, Eela 314
die-cutting 434
digital marketing 41, 42, 68, 84; case
  study 245–8
digital printing 354–5
digital proofs 434
direct costs 434–5
direct mail 171, 178, 179, 333, 426;
  response rates 172, 426; *see also*
  Reading Force
direct marketing 42, 43, 170–1, 435;
  addressee 181; audience 174–5;
  brochure 182–3; business-to-business
  181; campaign essentials 172–3; case
  study 196–205; checklist 195; copy
  platform 177–83; design services 188;
  despatch system 188–9; direct mail
  171, 172, 178, 179; direct promotion
  173; direct response 173; freepost
  184, 186, 189; fulfilment services
  191–3; inclusions 187–8; information
  gathering 185; L-shaped cards 184;
  loyalty cards 171; mailing costs
  188–9, 190–1; media and 175–6;
  monitoring methods 189–91; offers
  175; plans 173–4; postage and
  packing 192–3; principles 171; print
  172–3; response devices 183–8;
  response tips 185–7; returns 193;
  telemarketing 193–5; testing 189–90;
  timing 176–7

Direct Marketing Association (DMA)
  172, 184
direct response advertising 320, 353,
  435
direct selling 36, 144–5
disintermediarisation 29, 435
display type 435
distributors 19, 20
Doctorow, Cory 71
doctors 417–18; case study 416–17;
  communicating with 411–16;
  conferences 416, 417; CPD materials
  418, 421; emails to 412–13; leaflets
  and 412; mailing lists 412, 413;
  marketing materials 413–16;
  marketing to 410–11; online materials
  421; timing of promotion 416
Dolamore, Anne 165–9
Dollin, Nigel 355
Downer, Philip 222–4
Drabble, Margaret 284
dues (arrears) 435
dump-bins 109, 153, 435
duotone 435

ebooks 6, 25, 32, 56, 418; access costs
  387; discounts 70; free downloads 86;
  publishing costs 65–6, **69**; textbooks
  398
e-content licensing 387
editors: advance notice writing 97; blurb
  writing 96, 100, 337–8;
  commissioning 37, 95, 284, 410;
  editorial/marketing relationship
  37–43, 160, 406, 407; literary 271–3;
  review 269–70
education: funding models 385–6;
  model of delivery 386–7; online
  learning 387; textbook model 387
educational market 65, 66, 147–8;
  changes in 397–9; children's
  publishers 373; digital delivery 398–9;
  digital materials 397; how to reach
  403–9; inspection copies and 273;
  marketing approach preparation
  400–2; public examinations 399;
  publishers' contact with 400; school
  budgets 399–400; selling to 396–409;
  textbooks and 389–91; university
  academics 385–9
educational press 408–9
EFL (English as a Foreign Language)
  409, 435

ELT (English Language Teaching) 243–5, 409–10, 435
email: advantages of 229; case study 232–4; doctors 412–13; ESP services 230, 231; how to write 231–2; journalists 277–8; mass mailing systems 233, 234; online marketing 221, 229–32; response rates 426; school mailing lists 404; shared mailings 404–5; subject lines 335; teachers 405; Toddle template 233
embargo 435
English Grammar in Use 244
EPOS (electronic point of sale) 435
ESL (English as a Second Language) 409, 435
ESP (Emotional Selling Proposition) 323
EU Culture Fund 18
events 29, 377; audience 297, 298; author tours 305; case study 313–15; context 297; feedback 299; organisational meetings 300; preparing for 297–300; press conferences 305; promotional parties 302–5; sales conferences 300–2; slides, use of 299; time available 298; timing 315; title launches 302–5; venues for 312–13; what to wear 299–300; *see also* BookMachine; exhibitions; literary festivals; promotional parties
exhibitions 311, 378, 406–7
export market 155–7; case study 157–61; children's books 378; *see also* international markets
extent 436

FAB (features, advantages, benefits) 321–2
Faber & Faber 17, 29
Facebook 4, 124, 177, 208, 236, 253–4; author's views on 250; brands and 221; Cambridge University Press 244–5; children and 376; CompletelyNovel 239–41; online marketing and 211, 212, 220; Ooligan Press case study 236–8; self-publishing and 210
Fachbuchhandlung für Faksimiles 164–5
facsimile books 164–5
Farmer, Sue 151–2
Farmiloe, Tim 126

FE (further education) 436
features 436
festivals: temporary 154; *see also* literary festivals
financial services 422, 425
finishing 355; *see also* binding
firm sale 67, 145, 436
Fisk, Robert 447
flush (justified) left 436
flush (justified) right 436
Focal Press 38
font 436
Food Illustrated 166
format 25, 27, 28, 436; A format paperback 6; bundling 66; limp (C format) 66, 439; reformatting 66
Frankfurt Book Fair 444
Franklin, Andrew 310
Freda, Clare 398–9, 406
free publicity 77, 257–8; author interviews 273–6; book trade events 377; children's books 376–7; events sponsorship 377; inspection copies 273; journalists and 260–3, 276–81; literary editors 271–3; literary prizes 377; local initiatives 377; media, dealing with 258–60; press releases 263–9; promotional links 377; review lists 269–71; social media 376–7; *see also* advertising; advertorials
'free advertising' 257
freelance staff 295–6; designers 342, 344–6; relationship with 296
freemium 80–1, 436
French, Margaret 387, 390, 394
friends (social media) 436

Game of Thrones 245–8
Ganley, Anna 368
general reader 363–6
gifts: free 186, 272, 298, 377; gift appeal 55, 56; gifting market 24–5, 28, 56, 371, 372, 373; *see also* Calliope Gifts
Gombrich, Ernst 343
Goodreads 237, 251–2
Google 7, 219, 245, 254; Analytics 221
Google+ 212, 237, 255
Gordon, Hattie 196–7, 202
Green, Toby 97, 98
Greene and Heaton 240
Grub Street 165–9
Guardian 83, 102, 167, 281, 318

Hachette Children's Publishing *110*
half-life 436
half-tone 436–7
Halls, Meryl 372
Hancocks, Stephen 419–20
hand-selling 161, 207, 437
hard copy 437
HarperCollins 17, 83, 245–8, 255, 437
Harry Potter series 271, 370, 375, 376
hashtags 214, 229, 241, 242, 243, 246,
    437; campaigns 255
HE (higher education) 388, 437;
    funding 386; internationalisation 387;
    'massification' 385
headline 437
healthcare market 410–11; *see also*
    dentists/dental care professionals;
    doctors
Heaney, Seamus 85
Hegarty, John 323
Henningsgaard, Per 236–8
heritage organisations 154
Herrmann International *149*, 150
Hertfordshire libraries 379
Hodder, Clare 32
Hopkins, Claude 333
Horne, Alastair 243–5
house ad 437
house style 348, 437
Hunt, Matthew 213
Hybert Design 343
Hybert, Kate 343
hype 437

Impress Print Services Ltd 357
impression 437
imprint 437
in print 438
in-house/out-of house work 437
indent 437
independent publishers 17, 18–20, 75,
    165–9
information managers 387, 394–5, 396
initial situation analysis: macro-
    environment 121; marketing plan and
    120–3; micro-environment 121;
    PESTLE 121, 122–3; SWOT 121,
    122
insert/loose insert 438
Inside Book Publishing (Clark and
    Phillips) 132–42
insight hypothesis 46–7
inspection copies 41, 42, 43, 104, 106,
    273, 438; academics and 389; 'on

approval' 183, 392, 408, 438;
    teachers 273, 407–8
Instagram 210, 212, 254
integrated marketing communications
    (IMC) 17–18, 41
international markets 409–10
International Publisher of the Year
    (2000) 165
internet: access 123; advertising 109;
    mobile access 254; *see also* email;
    online marketing; social media;
    websites
Isaacson, Walter 44
ISBN 6–7, 53, 438
ISDN 438
ISSN 438
Istros Books 18–20

jacket rough 438
jackets 438; author information 102;
    back cover blurb 101; book title
    100; cover brief 39; layout of text
    102–3; librarians and 381, 383; online
    marketing 39; product promotion and
    125; shout/strap line 100–1
James, Clive 248–9
Jobs, Steve 44
Joel, Jennifer 253
John Dollin Printing Services Ltd 355
Johnson, Paula 271
Jones, Paul 357
Jones, Sue 379
Journal of Marketing Management xx
journalists 260–3; emails to 277–8;
    literary editors 271–3; phone calls to
    278–80; press liaison 30; promotional
    parties 302, 303, 304–5; PRs and
    261, 262; selling ideas to 276–81; *see
    also* press conferences; press coverage;
    press releases; review lists; reviews
Juckes, Sarah 239–41
junk mail 172, 229, 414
Junor, John 262
justified type 438

Kennedy, Jo 350
Kennedy, Niall 37–43
Killick, Ruth 259, 261, 276, 281
Kingsley, Mary 97–8
Kingston University: blog *226*;
    Publishing MA 43
Kipling, Rudyard 97
KISS (Keep It Simple Stupid) 324
Klein, Naomi 386

Kogan Page xiv, xviii, 135
Kotler, P. et al. 5, 146, 152

lamination 438
landscape 438
lawyers 422, 424, 425
learning resource centre (LRC) 392–3
Lee, Jeremy 307
Leech, Helen 381–3
leisure outlets 155
Leonardo da Vinci 208
Lessig, Lawrence 31
letterpress 439
Leverhulme, William Lever, 1st Viscount 211
librarians: academic 392–6; medical 421–2; public 378–81; publishing information and 380–1
libraries 154; academic 392–6; case study 381–3; public 378–83; publishers and 381–3
licences: character 370, 373; collective 27, 32; e-content 387; short-term reprint 27; *see also* copyright; rights
lift letter 439
limp (C format) 439
line work 439
LinkedIn 42, 176, 239–40, 425; marketing 210, 211, 238–9
list 439
literacy 31, 377; organisations 377
literary agents 4, 85, 113, 161, 240, 291
literary editors 271–3
literary festivals 30, 258, 305–8; authors and 29, 284, 309–11, 373; publisher collaboration with 306–8; *Times* Cheltenham Literature Festival 308–9
literary fiction 439
literary prizes 102, 311–12, 377
litho (lithographic) 354, 355, 356, 439
Little, Brown Book Group 157–61
Little, Fiona 401
logo 83, 291–2, 348, 369, 439
long tail 374
Lovell, Nick 88
Lyall, Gavin 102

Macaro, Antonia 332
McArt, Simon 157–61
McCartney, Linda 24
McCartney, Sir Paul 24
McCrum, Jo 70
McKay, Robert 423, 426
MailChimp 234

mailing lists 128, 190, 223, 230; analysis 118; authors 291; auto-response 430; deleting names 415; doctors 412, 413; mass-mailing 233, 234; nixies 440
mailshots 106, 124, 127, 173, 178–83; analysis/records 231; costs 191; fundraising 71; medical case study 416–17; the PS 180, 329; reading 180, 329, 344, 417; returns 415, 417
Mansfield, Katherine 84
Mantel, Hilary 208
mark up 439
market analysis organisations 49
market insight 46–7, 59
market intelligence 47, 59
market research 47–8; budget 68; case studies 59–60, 362–3; commissioning 52; 'desk' research 48–9; freelance staff 296; marketing plan 118–19; online questionnaires 52; primary research 50–2; publishers 44–5; qualitative 50; quantitative 50–1; questions to ask 118–19; secondary research 48–50; self-publishing 45; syndicated 53–7; uses 45–6, 57–8
Market Research Society 47
market segmentation *see* segmentation
market share 439
marketing 3–8; checklists 8–12; customers' needs 9; editorial relationship 37–43; meaning of 5; personnel 36–7; place 12; price 10–11; principles 5, 362; product 10, 22–3; promotion 11–12, 13; strategy 11–12; timing 12; *see also* direct marketing; online marketing; specific interest markets; telemarketing
marketing budget: allocation 129–30; cash flow management 78–9; categories of expenditure 62–4; contingency amount 64; core costs 63; costings 68, **69–70**, 70–1; development costs 65–6; discount negotiation 77; drawing up 62–4; financial support 79–81; free publicity 77; freemium 80–1; funding models 80–1; individual titles 63; making it go further 74–7; market research 68; monitoring 71, 73–4; product prices 68; profit margins 65; publishing lifecycle process 66–7; retaining 81; return on investment 61–2; 'smaller' titles 64; sponsorship 79–80; timing

of expenditure 72–3, 75; variable factors 65–8

marketing information 95–112; advance information 96–9; advance notices 96–9; announcement 95–6; catalogues 103–6; commissioning meeting 95; dump-bins 109; jacket/cover copy 100–2; leaflets/flyers 106–8; point-of-sale items 109; posters 108–9; radio/TV/cinema 112; space advertising 109, 111; website entry 99

marketing initiatives 29

marketing materials 153; advertisements 353; brochures 71, 76, 108, 124, 182–3; children's titles 376; clarity 352–3; cost of 74, 76; design 76, 188, 342–3; design job progression 350–1; designers 344–51; dump-bins 109; flyers 106, 108, 436; impact/impression 129–30, 352–4; layout/dissemination of 342–8; leaflets 106, 108; managing without a designer 352–4; medical 413–16; online presentation of 145; posters 109; printers/printing 354–8; promotional text 343–4; proofreading 351–2; reading promotional text 343–4; schools 403–5; visual variety 353; *see also* catalogues

marketing mix 12

marketing plan 4, 41–2, 113–42; budget allocation 129–30; case study 132–42; checklist 132; communicating 130–1; evaluating results 131–2; formulating 124; implementation 131; in-house communication 130–1; individual titles 126–9; initial situation analysis 120–3; market research 118–20; marketing basics 124–6; monitoring of 131; objectives 123; product research 115–18; product/service benefits 120; promotional mix 13, 41–2; SMART objectives 123; strategy 124

marketing strategy 124

Markkula, Mike 5

Martin, George R.R. 245

Maslow's hierarchy of needs 7

maven 439

measure 439

media coverage 257; authors and 257–8; contacts and 259–60; journalists and 260–2; media agencies and 260, 269; news agencies and 260; timing 258–9

media planning 127–8, 175–6

merchandise 439

merchandising 439–40; character licensing 373; cross-merchandising 373; rights 30–1, 291; trademarks 291–2

metadata 440

metrics: email campaigns 42, 231; website usability 103

Meyer, Stephenie 370

Midas PR *266*, 272, 274

Millington, Roger 181, 328

Minecraft 370

Mintel 49, 370

Miradorus 148–50, 151

Mixpanel 221

Mollison, Craig 384–5

monograph 440

Mulliken, Tony 272, 274

National Centre for Research in Children's Literature 379

National Children's Book Week 377

National Literacy Trust 377

negative option 440

net 440

Net Book Agreement (NBA) 71, 169n1, 440

news agencies 260

newsletters 75, 125, 199, 213, 223, 230, 291; case study 233–4, *235*; libraries 379, 382, 383; sign-up forms 230

niche markets 36, 66, 152–3, 422–3, 424; print on demand 442

niche publishers 24, 165–9

Nielsen Book Services 6, 53–4, *54–5*, 125

nix(ies) 440

non-retail outlets 371–2

nostalgia market 334, 370, 372, 374

Nosy Crow 85, 370–1

O'Brien, Breda 447

off-site staff 294–5, 296; *see also* freelance staff

O'Flynn, Catherine 102

Ogilvy, David 111, 321, 324, 330–1, 343

Onatade, Ayo 226–7, 228

ONIX for books 39

online 440; directories 223; gaming 365, 370

online marketing 75, 206–55; advantages 207–8; author case study 250–3; author involvement 248–9; bloggers/blogging 224–8; case studies 220–4; core principles 208–13; email 221, 229–35; future of 253–5; key elements 213–14; offline selling and 222–4; push to pull shift 207–8; social media 210, 211, 212, 213, 220, 238–8; strategy 209–11; websites 215–19

Ooligan Press 236–8

open access 34, 388, 440–1

open-ended questions 440

ordering 47, 74, 78–9, 153; coding an order form 187, 192; direct marketing 170–1, 173, 183–8; direct orders 78; forms 76, 108, 187, 192; mechanisms 104–5; online 36, 54, 145; payment facilities 215, 339, 417; pre-orders 72, 86, 209, 214, 391; 'top-up' orders 47

organisational meetings 300

Orion 291

Orkney reading room 384–5

over-run 441

overs 441

own-brand editions 28, 371

Oxford International Centre for Publishing Studies 135

Oxford University Press (OUP) 135, *334*

ozalid 441

Page, Stephen 31

Palgrave Macmillan 32

Palmer, Dee 82, 84

Palmer, Jessica 232–4, *235*

Pareto's Law 213, 256n7

Parker, Cornelia 338

Paul, Korky *334*

Paxman, Jeremy 260

Penguin Books 29, 254, 366, 429

perfect binding 441

Perkins, Samantha 132–42

PESTLE analysis 121, 122–3

Pfeiler, Anton 164–5

Phalippou, Jérôme 89

Phillips, Angus 132, 134, 135, 136, 137

Pike, Eleanor 37, 38, 40–3

Pinterest 177, 210, 212, 220, 254, 255

PMT (photo mechanical transfer) 432, 441

podcasts 6, 441

point of sale 109, *110*, 153, 441

point system 441

portrait 441

positioning 13–14, 119, 120, 347, 441

post 442

Powell, Jenny 151

presenters 108

press conferences 305

press coverage 49, 79; food press 166–7; literary prizes 312; planning 259

press liaison 30

press releases 260, 263–9, 333; exclusive 268–9; headlines 265, *266*, 267; images, tips for 267–8; literary editors and 271–3; role of 263–4; sample *266*; structure 265, *266*; supporting quotes 267; trade press and 267–8; writing 264–5, 274–5

Prictor, Betty 384–5

print on demand (POD) 6, 84, 153, 442

print run 27, 442; academic texts 65; costings **69–70**; marketing materials 355; research monographs 392

printers/printing 354–8; CMYK print work 357; commissioning 354; costs 355; delivery methods 355; digital printing 354–5; estimates 355–7; information required by 355–6; litho 354, 355, 356; methods 354; order confirmation 355; problems after delivery 358; proofs, types of 357–8; run-on (r/o) price 356; screen printing 354

Prior, Joanna 261

pro forma invoice 442

product: definition 22–3; price 10–11, 68

production costs 65, 68, **69–70**, 191; bundling of formats 66; ebook publishing 65–6; publisher overheads 65; reformatting 66

professional markets 422–5; blogs/blawgs 425; formats 424, 425–8; information resources 65, 66; market leaders 424; marketing materials 426–7; requirements 424–5; retailers 171; subscription 26; writing style 427

profile 442

progressive proofs 442

promotional mix 13

promotional parties 302–5, 313; follow up 304–5; invitations 303; journalists

302, 303, 304–5; media coverage 302; photographs 303, 305; refreshments 304; speeches 304; timing 303

promotional text *see* copy; marketing materials

promotions 13, 73, 442; competitions 111; free gifts 186, 272, 298, 377; offers 175; price 186, 244; seasonal 72, 83, 152, 223, 300, 373, 375; *see also* promotional parties

proofreading 351–2, 442

proofs 357–8

pseudonyms 17, 291

public lending right 383–4

publication date 442

publicity *see* free publicity

publishers: authors and 283–7, 293–4; freelance staff 295–6; libraries and 381–3; literary festivals and 306–8; market research and 44–5; marketing of 29–30; off-site staff 294–5; overheads 65; service providers 292–3; temporary staff 296; working with colleagues 293–5; *see also* independent publishers; self-publishing

publishing: advice on 31; branding 16–17; competition 6–8; costs **69–70**; financial structure 70–1; integrated marketing communications 17–18; market research 44–5; marketing and 3–20; marketing checklists 8–12; relationship marketing 18–20; sales and promotion 13; segmenting/targeting/positioning 13–16

Publishing Talk **139**, 253

Publishing Training Centre *133*, **138**, **141**

publishing-ese 326

Puffin 99, 369

Pullman, Philip 370

radio 26–7, 30, 258; advertising 99, 111, 112, 260, 264, 265; interviews 273, 275

Random House 17; Century 83

Reading Agency 377, 378, 379, 383

reading copies 366, 442

Reading Force 196–205; database 198, 199; email 199; SMART objectives 201–2; telemarketing 202–5

Reading is Fundamental 377

reading room 384–5

ReadySteadyBook 213

recommended retail price (RRP) 444

recto 443

Redmayne, Charlie xvi

Reed, Jon 109, 206, 253–5

reference titles 65, 103, 391

reformatting 66

register 443

re-intermediarisation 395

relationship marketing 18–20

release date 443

remainder 28–9, 443

Rennoldson, James 314

repro 355, 443

resale price maintenance 443

response devices 183–8, 443

retail price maintenance 67, 123, 144; *see also* Net Book Agreement (NBA)

retailers 154–5, 379; children's books 371–2; discount 67, 70, 71; non-retail outlets 371–2; online 154, 167; selling prices 67–8; *see also* bookshops; supermarkets; superstores

retouching 443

return on investment (ROI) 61–2, 443

returns 47, 78, 116, 191, 335, 443

retweet 443

reverse out 354, 443–4

review copy 270, 271, 444

review lists 269–71

review slip 270, 444

reviews 257; audiobooks 83; children's books 376; educational press 408

Richard and Judy Book Club 260, 281n3

rights 444; merchandising 30–1, 291; sales 23, 26–7, 161–3; translation 26, 168; *see also* copyright; licences

Robuchon, Joel 165

Roeschel, Dieter 164–5

Roman 444

Routledge 37–8, 43, **107**, **133**, 134–5, 137

Rowling, J.K. 370

Royal National Institute for the Blind 378

royalties 70: 82, 90n2, 369, 444; *see also* public lending right

Rubin, Nicolas 89

run of paper 444

run-on costs 76, 356, 444

Rushmoor Borough Council 192, 196

saddle stitching 444

Sadler, Katie 245–8

sale or return 67, 445
sales conferences 41, 103, 300–2, 406;
  export sales 156, 158; guidelines
  301–2
sales development consultants 148–50
sales proposition, creating 89–90
sales representatives 77, 366, 405–6
sales/selling 144–69, 152–7; antiquarian
  books 164–5; bulk sales 28, 79, 105;
  buyer behaviour 146–8; case studies
  157–61, 165–9; communication tips
  150–2; customer relationships
  148–50; direct selling 144–5, 163–5;
  export market 155–7; facsimile books
  164–5; home market 153–5;
  individuals and 148–50; rights sales 23,
  26–7, 161–2; schools 147–8; seasonal
  72, 83, 152, 223, 300, 373, 375
schools: book fairs 372, 374; budgets
  399–400, 403; digital delivery 398,
  401; mailings to 403–5; marketing to
  400–2; materials to send 403–4;
  purchasing patterns 147–8; sales reps
  and 405–6; supplier 445; teacher
  support materials 401; *see also* teachers
Scott, David Meerman 211
screen printing 354, 445
search engine marketing (SEM) 445
search engine optimisation (SEO) 94–5,
  445
see safe 445
segmentation 13–15, 41, 119;
  differentiated marketing 16; factors to
  consider 15–16; undifferentiated
  marketing 16; yearbook case history
  14–15
self-mailer 445
self-publishing 6–7, 45, 71, 136, 283–4,
  288; marketing and 289–90; social
  media and 210, 239–41, 290–1
serif, sans serif 445
Services Children in State Schools
  (SCISS) 198, *203*
Seuss, Dr (Theodor Seuss Geisel) 324
Shaw, George Bernard 367
Shields, Carol 249
Shots (website) 226
show-rooming 223, 445
showthrough 348, 445
Shriver, Lionel 30, 56
Signature Book Representation (UK) 19
'silent salespeople' 126
Simenon, Georges 324
Simpkin, Claire 318

Sleight, Cathryn 17
SMART objectives 123, 201–2
Smashwords 86
Smith, Zadie 249
Smyth, Sarah 308–9
social bookmarking 254, 445; *see also*
  Pinterest
social media 124, 126, 208, 445–6;
  blogs and 225; Cambridge University
  Press and 243–5; disengaging from
  249; email marketing and 230; free
  publicity 376–7; images, use of 177;
  marketing 210, 211, 212, 213, 220,
  253–5, 446; optimal times 212;
  professional market 425; self-
  publishing and 210, 239–41, 290–1;
  students and 386; writing and
  249–53; *see also* Facebook; LinkedIn;
  Twitter
social networking 446
Society of Authors, The 66, 70, 310,
  366–9
Solomon, Michael 148
Solomon, Nicola 366–7, 368–9
Sony Walkman 45
space advertising *see* advertising
spam 78, 172, 218, 232, 446
special sales 28, 79
specific interest markets 361–428;
  academic libraries 392–6; academic
  market 389–91; case study 362–3;
  children's books 369–78; current
  trends 364–5; dentists/dental care
  professionals 419–20; doctors
  410–18, 421; educational markets
  397–409; general principles 362;
  general reader, finding 363–6;
  healthcare professionals 410–21;
  international educational markets
  409–10; medical librarians 421–2;
  organisational brand and 365–9;
  professional markets 422–8;
  professional resources 392; public
  lending right 383–5; public libraries
  378–83; research monographs 392;
  summary books/study aids 391;
  university academics 385–9
specs 446
Spiers, Jane 384–5
split infinitive 319, 446
Steinitz, Dominic 177
Stephen Hancocks Limited 419–20
stock lists 63, 103, 105; seasonal 39,
  125, 300; *see also* catalogues

Stokes, D. and Lomax, W. 5, 23, 93, 113, *120, 121*
Stonewylde series 289–92
Stotter, Mike 226
Strathclyde University xix
Straus, Peter 253
students: attitudes to education 386; book-buying resources 385, 390; degree, reduction in value of 388–9; education delivery model 386–7; international 387, 388; LRCs and 392–3; numbers 385; social media 386; summary books/study aids 391; textbooks, availability of 390
subscribe 446
subscription 26, 33, **34**, *35*; promoting new journals 66–7; services 49, 53
Sullivan, Andrew 320
summary books 391
Summers, Laura 128, 220–1
supermarkets 28, 155, 161, 166, 371; direct marketing 171; discounts and 67, 70, 90n2; own-brand books 371
superstores 371, 373, 375
Surrey County Library Services 381–3
Sweller, John 299
SWOT analysis 121, *122*
syndicated market research 53–7

tag line (strap line) 100, 446
targeting 13, 119
Taschen 24
teachers 397, 398; catalogues 404–5; digital materials 397, 398–9; emails to 405; inspection copies 273, 407–8; league tables 398; marketing approach to 400–2; series of titles 402; support materials 401; support mechanisms 408; telemarketing 407; trainee 408
TEFL (Teaching English as a Foreign Language) 409
telemarketing 193–5, 403, 407, 446; AID(C)A 320–1; call structure 178; case study 202–5
terms 67, 145, 446
TESL (Teaching English as a Second Language) 409, 447
Thema 95–6
Thomas, Valerie *334*
Thwaite, Mark 213–15
Times Cheltenham Literature Festival 308–9
tint 447

titles; choosing 100; classification 95–6; copy information 337; launch parties 302–5; marketing individual titles 126–9; proposal stage 38
TOEFL 409, 447
Touch Press 84–8
trade discount 67, 70, 71, 90n2, 271, 447
trademarks 291–2
translation: literature in 18–20; rights 26, 168
trim 447
trolling 213, 447
Tumblr 225, 237
Turner, Lynnette 97, 98
turnover 447
Twitter 124, 177, 229; business use 242–3; case studies 239, 243–8, 251; children and 376; marketing 211, 212, 220, 221, 242–8; self-publishing 210; *see also* hashtags
Twyman, Michael 23–4
type area 447
typeface 447
typescript 447
typo 447

Unilever 17
universities: collective licensing 27; distance learning 59–60; publishing house *see* Ooligan Press; sales teams' visits 41, 43; *see also* academic librarians; academic titles; academics; book publishing courses; HE (higher education); students
unjustified type 447
Unwin, Sir Stanley 3
upper/lower case 447
user-generated content 448
USP (Unique Selling Proposition) 322–4

VAT (value added tax) 68
verso 448
video 31, 254, 398–9
viral marketing 75, 161, 448
visual 448

Walker Books 369, 371
Walker, Sebastian 369
Walliams, David 370
Walters, Gary 307
Waterstones 137, **141**, 222
Watt, Jane 248

Webb, Kaye 369
websites 99–8, 125, 215–19, 448;
    analytics 219, 221; authors and 288;
    case study 220–1; catalogues 103;
    children's books 373, 376; design/
    designers 221, 344; educational
    publishers 407; search engine
    optimisation 94–5, 219; URL 447
weight of paper 448
Weir, Caroline and Robin 165
Weldon, Fay 340
WH Smith 222, 223, 281n3
WhatsApp 246, 448
wholesalers 70, 448
WIIFM? (What's In It For Me?) 324
wiki 448

Wikipedia 23, 448
Wilkinson, Carl 305, 307
Williams, Tom 84–8
Wilson, Bee 166
Wilson, Jacqueline 331, 373
Wilson, Kate 370–1
work experience 296, 389
World Book Day 377
Writers' and Artists' Yearbook, The 313,
    314, 362–3
Wurmser, Yory 172

yearbooks 14–15, 72
young adult (YA) market 29, 289,
    370
YouTube 4, 42, 86, 175, 237, 254